Yale Law School and the Sixties

STUDIES IN LEGAL HISTORY

Published by the University of North Carolina Press
in association with the American Society for Legal History
Thomas A. Green, Hendrik Hartog, and Daniel Ernst, editors

Yale Law School and the Sixties

Revolt and Reverberations

LAURA KALMAN

The University of North Carolina Press
Chapel Hill

Manufactured in the United States of America
Set in Minion
by Tseng Information Systems, Inc.

This book was published with the assistance of the Thornton H. Brooks
Fund of the University of North Carolina Press.

The paper in this book meets the guidelines for permanence
and durability of the Committee on Production Guidelines
for Book Longevity of the Council on Library Resources.

Library of Congress Cataloging-in-Publication Data
Kalman, Laura, 1955–
Yale Law School and the sixties : revolt and reverberations / Laura Kalman.
p. cm. — (Studies in legal history)
Includes bibliographical references and index.
ISBN 0-8078-2966-8 (cloth : alk. paper)
1. Yale Law School—History—20th century. 2. Law—Study and teaching—
United States—History—20th century. I. Title. II. Series.
KF292.Y314A55 2005
340′.071′17468—dc22 2005010247

09 08 07 06 05   5 4 3 2 1

For W. Randall Garr

Contents

Illustrations

Acknowledgments

In one way or another, each book I have written has revolved around Yale Law School. None did so more directly than my first, *Legal Realism at Yale, 1927–1960*. It explored a period when Yale sought to provide an alternative to the traditional legal education against which I had chafed as a law student during the mid-1970s. So far, so good: because most history is in some way autobiographical, each generation must write its own. At no time, however, did I imagine writing a sequel.

Everything changed when Dean Anthony Kronman invited me to teach legal history at Yale Law School in 2001, asked me to give a public lecture about Yale's recent past at semester's end, and offered me the archival access necessary to tell the story. During my visit, I noticed that the school seemed transformed since my last sustained sojourn there in the late 1970s and early 1980s. When I left New Haven in 1982 to teach at the University of California, Santa Barbara, the law school was literally crumbling, as I could attest—having spent days fending off cockroaches and silverfish as I worked my way through the dean's papers then in the library's basement. Faculty and students alike broadcast their dissatisfaction with the school's policies and penury.

That saddened me. *Legal Realism at Yale* ended in 1960, when the law school seemed poised for greatness. So I imagined anyway: the files of its deans and presidents were then closed. But by the early 1980s, the law school's problems seemed legion.

Yet here I was in New Haven twenty years later, and Yale had become the nation's premier law school, boasting largely pleased students and teachers alike. And the law school of the millennium was obviously, especially to someone housed in a history department, flush. How else to explain the fact that it could bring the grandchildren of the German woodworkers who had installed the chestnut panels in its hallways in 1931 back from Germany to restore them?[1]

What had happened to change the law school's fortunes? I went back to where I had left off as a graduate student and worked my way forward. This book is the result.

My explanation for the turmoil in the 1960s and of Yale's subsequent trajectory is just that. Though I could not have written this book without the cooperation of Yale's deans, archivists, librarians, faculty, students, and staff, and my narrative sometimes possesses triumphal overtones, mine is not an official account. Nor is my story comprehensive. While occasionally, for example, I have alluded to events of public record at the law school after Guido Calabresi's deanship ended in 1994, my narrative makes little mention of his successor, Anthony Kronman. I cut the story off in the mid-1990s because by then the shape of the contemporary school was evident, and because Kronman had ensured that I would receive such access and support that the notion of writing at length about the school during his tenure made me squeamish.

The story, as I have told it, also displays an instinctive sympathy for the "student revolution" in the university. I was fifteen when Nixon announced the Cambodian "incursion." I did little to demonstrate my opposition to the war or my support for racial equality, and I showed no interest in reforming my high school. The book's wistfulness and hopefulness doubtless reflects, at least in part, my own regret at missing out on the sixties. And in following my tale to its logical conclusion in the 1980s and 1990s, a period in which I began teaching, I have come to understand my own academic politics better and to realize the extent to which, as a professor, I am a child of the sixties. Here, too, history is autobiography.

*   *   *

It is a pleasure to acknowledge the many people who have made this book possible. I thank Melissa Murray, Jen Baker, Lucas Cupps, Derek Dorn, Dixie Rogers, and Matt Sneddon for outstanding research assistance. As they have since I was a graduate student, Nancy Lyon and the staff of Manuscripts and Archives at Sterling Memorial Library provided invaluable help. Karen Alderman, Marge Camera, Janet Conroy, Toni Davis, Nancy Moore, Elizabeth Stauderman, Carroll Stevens, and Kelly Waldron quickly and effectively responded to all my pleas, and without Georganne Rogers, I probably would have given up. The staff of Yale Law Library is justifiably legendary, and Gene Coakley, Bonnie Collier, Harvey Hull, and Blair Kaufmann were especially so. Librarians at Columbia, Georgetown, Harvard, Howard, New York University, Rutgers, Stanford, and the Universities of California, Berkeley, Michigan, Pennsylvania, Washington, and Wisconsin Law Schools graciously tracked down old law school newspapers and other information. Ann Hill, Richard Hughes, Geoffrey Kabaservice, and Walt Wagoner kindly shared materials from their own collections. I am also grateful to my fellow historians of Yale:

John Langbein, Gaddis Smith, Jeremy Weinberg, and Jodi Wilgoren, and especially Robert Gordon, Geoffrey Kabaservice, Anne Standley, John Schlegel, and Robert Stevens.

I thank the many people who took the time to talk with me about their Yale Law School. The decency of Lou Pollak and humanity of Guido Calabresi inspired me, and I will always be grateful to Tony Kronman for the many forms of generosity he showed me.

The list of people who read as I wrote stretches from A to Z. I am indebted to Richard Abel, Bruce Ackerman, Christine Adams, Lee Albert, Jack Balkin, Stuart Banner, John Blum, Elliot Brownlee, Guido Calabresi, Paul Carrington, Peter Carstensen, Otis Cochran, Jan Deutsch, William L. F. Felstiner, Catherine Fisk, Owen Fiss, Justin Florence, Robert Gordon, Sarah Barringer Gordon, Tom Grey, John Griffiths, Ariela Gross, John Harrison, Tom Hilbink, Ann Hill, Morton Horwitz, N. E. H. Hull, Geoffrey Kabaservice, Newton Kalman, Amy Kesselman, Mark Klugheit, Pnina Lahav, George Lefcoe, Sanford Levinson, Stephen Munzer, William E. Nelson, Louis Pollak, David Rabban, Charles Reich, John Schlegel, Eran Shalev, Larry Simon, Avi Soifer, Clyde Spillenger, Robert Stevens, Eleanor Swift, David Trubek, Mark Tushnet, Walt Wagoner, Harry Wellington, G. Edward White, Adam Winkler, and Rosemarie Zagarri for reading versions of this book, often more than once. I thank the faculties of Harvard, Rutgers-Camden, UCLA, the University of Virginia, and Yale Law Schools for the opportunity to present parts of the manuscript and for the many helpful comments I received when I did so.

As he has done with every project I have undertaken over the past quarter-century, John Blum watched over this one with a critical and loving eye. And I feel extraordinarily fortunate to have three friends and colleagues who understand, and generously discuss, constantly, every aspect of my personal and professional lives: Elliot Brownlee, Sarah Barringer Gordon, and Pnina Lahav.

I would have followed Chuck Grench anywhere, but it was a special pleasure to trail him to the University of North Carolina Press and the Series in Legal History, the home of my first book about Yale. My editors, Tom Green and Dirk Hartog, forced me to devote far more time to this project than I would have wished. I am extremely grateful to them. Among other things, they chose two remarkable readers whom I also thank, Dan Ernst and Edward Purcell. At the University of North Carolina Press, I am much indebted to Amanda McMillan and Paula Wald. I am also very thankful for the astuteness with which Eric Schramm edited my manuscript and to Jeanette Nakada and Kay Banning.

After our visit at Yale, W. Randall Garr and I traveled further east for the 2001–2 academic year, he to accept a fellowship at the Institute for Advanced

Studies in Jerusalem and I to be Fulbright Research Professor at Tel Aviv University Law School. To have lived in Jerusalem during this period is an experience I will long remember. I thank the Fulbright Foundation for its generous support; the Institute for Advanced Studies for providing us with a beautiful place to live; and my dean, David Marshall, for making our travels feasible. At TAU Law School and in Jerusalem, I am grateful for the kindness of Daphne Barak-Erez, Leora Bilsky, Osnat Cohen, Michal Gordon-Keret, Robert Johnston, Menachem Mautner, Ariel Porat, Reuven Tabibi, Avihu Zakai, Zehava Zimmer, and especially Ron Harris and Assaf Likhovski. Steve and Celia Fassberg made it possible for us to be in Israel, and I especially want to celebrate the memory of Miriam Fassberg. Eran Shalev took such good care of me that I joked the Israeli government must have assigned him to be my guardian.

Gardeners in three parts of the world heartened me: those at the greenhouse at Kibbutz Ma'ale Hachamisha in Abu Ghosh, Pamela Blum in New Haven, and Penn Borden, Jesus Gil, and Daniel Richman in Santa Barbara. For two memorable vacations from this book in Paris, I thank Amèle Chehida; Alex, Charlie, and Nat Dennett; Wendy Fisher; Rhoda McGraw; Andy Reinhardt; and Connie and John Schweizer. For a third, in Tuscany, and for so much else, I thank Judy Shanks, and, as ever, Jamie, Mira, and Talia Gracer. In Southern California, I am grateful to Mary Brownlee, Jane De Hart, Lupe Diaz, Hope Firestone, Rena Fraden, Guy Garr, Cyndi Griffin, Richard Hecht, Leslie Jacobs, Eva and Ruthie King, Alice and Tremper Longman III, Eva Madoyan-Ktoyan, David and Daniel Marshall, Kate Metropolis, Thasana Nivatpumin, Aiko Noda, Jeff Richman, Kate Saltzman-Li, Meg Taradash, and Candace Waid. Pat Bagley, Celeste Garr, and Lee and Newton Kalman provided constant support.

And finally, above all, there is W. Randall Garr. This book is for him.

Yale Law School and the Sixties

Prologue

New Haven, Saturday, April 26, 1969. Alumni Weekend. As Yale law students and graduates crowded into the law school auditorium to hear about "Concerns of the Yale Law Student Today," the faculty surely fretted. The previous year, law students had walked out of a session entitled "Law and the Urban Crisis" on Alumni Weekend, designed to underscore the faculty's liberal good intentions. They complained the event featured white law school deans and staged their own counterpanel entitled "Law Is the Urban Crisis." This year, the school was turning the podium over to student speakers. What would they say and do?

Plenty. Student Negotiating Committee members made the first presentation. Their proposal for "joint student-faculty rule" had caused consternation among professors all semester: they wanted to replace the faculty as governing body with a council comprised of elected student representatives and professors. Now, committee members inveighed against their teachers' "inertia and self-satisfaction." Yale, they complained, was far from the "very progressive institution on the very frontiers of legal education" they expected, and their professors refused to make it "a real community."[1]

Then Judith Areen, later to become the first woman dean of Georgetown Law Center, took her turn. The popular professor Friedrich Kessler had called on her during virtually every class her first term—because she was a woman and focusing on her "was a way of capturing the class's attention." She focused on "the serious underrepresentation of women in the Law School and in the profession."[2]

Black Law Students Union chair J. Otis Cochran and seven BLSU members followed. The previous December, they had forced the faculty to increase minority enrollments in a tense stand-off that some had feared would turn violent. Nevertheless, Cochran lamented that "the great liberal faculty of this great liberal institution could find no way to make black enrollment at Yale Law School more than a token." On the same day that African American militants stood in front of Cornell's student union brandishing guns and wearing

"Students Provide Welcome for Alumni." (Yale Advocate, *May 1, 1969.*
Courtesy Yale Law School.)

ammunition belts, another BLSU member to.d alumni that "you can go on for
only so long and there's going to be a fire."[3]

Meanwhile, other law students celebrated Alumni Weekend by showcasing
a photograph of one of their number, complete with gun and cartridge belt,
lounging under a poster advising "Hands Off the Vietnamese Revolution!" in
a school newspaper article entitled "Students Provide Welcome for Alumni
Weekend." Student Negotiating Committee supporters had pretended to organize S.H.I.T.F.A.C.E., "Students to Help Increase the Faculty's Authority and
Control over Everything," and the halls were decked with posters declaring
S.H.I.T.F.A.C.E. support for the most controversial faculty policies. Activists topped everything off by building a gallows in the law school courtyard,
where, Robert Bork recalled, they hung Alexander Bickel in effigy. Staring at
the noose, one drunken alumnus repeatedly asked what the students "really"
sought. "We want a Law School that graduates nobody like you ever again,"
came the reply.[4]

This book is about an institution in the grip of the sixties. What were the
sixties? As Edward Purcell has said, during the 1940s and 1950s, the focus
on "consensus, balance, and progress" created an "ideology of national success" that played down persistent racism and inequality, while playing up the
American duty to win the Cold War. In contrast, the common thread through
the events and documents we associate with the sixties was one of "communitarian subjectivism"—be it in King's "I Have A Dream," Friedan's "Problem That Has No Name," or Savio's "There is a Time"; Dylan's "Ballad of a
Thin Man," Sly's "Everyday People," or The Who's "My Generation"; Mar-

cuse's *One-Dimensional Man*, Neill's *Summerhill*, Roth's *Portnoy's Complaint*, Brautigan's *Trout Fishing in America*, or Vonnegut's *Slaughterhouse Five*; the Port Huron Statement, Freedom Summer, the Free Speech Movement, Stop the Draft Week, or Stonewall; yippies' nomination of a pig for president or feminists' "No More Miss Americas"; the cry for Black, Brown, or Yellow Power; and the reminder that "the whole world is watching," to "make love, not war," or that "the personal is political." Communitarian subjectivism fused disapproval of authority; distrust of the Establishment; alienation from the system; attack on the hegemony of the power elite; skepticism about neutrality and objectivity; enthusiasm for egalitarianism, individual creativity, and passion; a focus on the emancipatory power of both "doing one's own thing" and cooperation; with a sense that "mind" could remake the "reality" believed to exist largely in the mind's eye. The Students for a Democratic Society's Port Huron Statement summed up the ethos, with its ideals of replacing "power rooted in possession, privilege, or circumstance by power and uniqueness rooted in love, reflectiveness, reason, and creativity" and attaining "the establishment of a democracy of individual participation." Communitarian subjectivism showcased the importance of the vertical pronoun, participation and democracy as signposts on the path to liberation of self and society. And the interplay between politics, society, and culture — the mingling of demands for political and social change with new lifestyles and ideas — transformed the sixties into an era in which the old language no longer worked and gave the period a spirit that could prove at once exhilarating and excruciating.[5]

Communitarian subjectivism hit older liberals, particularly those in the university, hard. They had long placed their own liberalism — "an understanding that the federal government had the responsibility, power, and ability to reduce inequality, protect historically oppressed minorities, champion American interests and values around the world, and balance the private sector's singular focus on making money with a broad concern for the nation's long-term good" — at the left edge of pragmatic social criticism. Now, as their students turned on them, they talked uneasily about the possibility of revolution and anarchy in the university, as well as the larger society. "You know the worst thing you can do with a New Left radical is to tell them how you sat at restaurants with Whitney Young and how you helped start the Peace Corps and how you were against the war in Vietnam — but you weren't for revolution," one dean reflected later. "You were a despised liberal." The tension between liberalism and communitarian subjectivism pervaded the sixties, and liberalism went on the defensive.[6]

But when were "the sixties"? The usual narrative of the period portrays students prodded awake by John F. Kennedy's inaugural challenge to "ask not what your country can do for you"; turning left when events abroad showed up the president as just another Cold Warrior, and when early attempts to organize the poor did not win the support of conventional liberals; returning home to go "part of the way with LBJ" in 1964, beckoned by Lyndon Johnson's vision of a liberal Great Society, linked to a liberal Supreme Court; turning left again as Democrats' fear of a backlash, the Great Society's limitations, the fruition of Black Power, and the Vietnam War caused liberalism's unraveling; then sometimes clasping hands with older liberals for a brief moment of hope during Eugene McCarthy and Robert Kennedy's presidential campaigns, until the summer of 1968, when society seemed to come apart at the Democratic convention in Chicago. After that apocalyptic moment, the story goes, the left broke apart and declined, taking liberalism along with it. The sixties subsided, despite aftershocks such as feminism and the environmental movement, and at the national level, conservatism triumphed.[7]

Recently, as historians have belatedly turned their attention to that conservatism, they have begun to chip away at the conventional tale of a liberalism torn asunder by assaults from the left during the 1960s. Among other things, they have questioned whether a liberal consensus on race prevailed during this period. They have also demonstrated the existence and endurance of conservative activists in the university, at the grass roots, and at the national level. Still, so far as elite universities are concerned, the focus remains on the development of conflict between liberals and the left. We may now gesture to the new scholarship by mentioning in passing that some universities possessed Young Americans for Freedom chapters, or that some college students, such as George W. Bush, actually seemed apolitical. But the conventional narrative of a liberalism ascendant until the left queried it remains largely intact.[8]

This book reinforces that narrative. Perhaps future scholars will portray Yale Law School as a fount of contemporary conservatism. After all, Robert Bork was a Yale law professor. The first national chairman Young Americans for Freedom elected in 1960, Robert Schuchman, was a Yale Law School student. Michael Horowitz, a 1964 graduate, proved a key player at the Hudson Institute. Stephen Hadley, national security adviser in the second George W. Bush administration, was a member of the class of 1970. Ben Stein and Michael Medved, later to become celebrated conservative critics, graduated from the school in the 1970s. Clarence Thomas became an alumnus in 1974. The first student division of the Federalist Society was organized at Yale. But few, if any, law students at Yale during the 1960s identified with conservatism or would have said so if they had. Those on the left possessed the voice, and the left-liberal conflict took center stage. Thus I have focused on how Yale fashioned a liberal image for itself, the repercussions that had for professors' relationship with students who challenged liberalism from the left, and how the faculty subsequently reaffirmed its liberalism.

*   *   *

While my story applies aspects of the conventional narrative to Yale Law School, it begins the sixties late in the decade. I argue that the first part of Yale's sixties took place between 1967 and 1970. What marked this period in the university at large, one historian has recently pointed out, was "the fracturing of the relationship between conventional liberals and left-liberal to radical protest movements," a pattern evident when students to his left challenged Dean Louis Pollak, a liberal stalwart.[9]

In retrospect, we can indeed see the breadth of the student movement and realize how many of its members were not radical or left, but what we would call today "left-liberal." And yet, although generally Yale law students were, at most, moving from liberalism to left-liberalism, liberalism and the left were so at odds during the late 1960s that characterizing young activists as left-liberal seems anachronistic. From liberals' perspective, a chasm separated them from radicals on the left, relating to the issue of incremental reform. If one believed the system salvageable, as liberals did, reform would render it more just. Consequently, reform would ultimately strengthen the status quo, the very reason to shun incremental change if one were radical and to press instead for changes liberals dismissed as utopian. Though Yale law students during the sixties often spoke the language of communitarian subjectivism, most of them were reformers, rather than revolutionaries — radical only in the eyes of their professors. Like true sixties radicals, however, many Yale law students became fed up with their teachers' liberalism, particularly when it showed up as support for the institutional status quo. Raised to place their faith in the United States, the young came to blame racism, poverty, and imperialism on the very liberals who had pledged to eradicate them. While Yale law professors shared some of the disillusionment, they also took students' articulation of it personally and understood that the young thought them part of the problem. Consequently, some faculty members considered law students' challenge of their own liberalism a threatening move toward the left and radicalism, although, in absolute terms, most students did not move all that far.[10]

The period of 1967–70, the first phase of Yale Law's sixties, thus brought tension as students who would later become professors, lawyers, and public servants, including Hillary Rodham Clinton, faced the faculty. During the years following that acrimonious time, when the conflict shifted into a new phase, the student body included Bill Clinton, future law professors such as Lani Guinier, and Clarence Thomas. The students' presence and experience at Yale helps to explain contemporary legal education and scholarship, the affirmative action debate, and their school's current celebrity.

Inspired by the social unrest around them, a vision of democracy and citizenship, and a sense of their school's historic importance as innovator in legal education, Yale students of the late sixties branded law professors hierarchical, accused them of racism and sexism, and disrupted law school life. The young worked feverishly to win a voice in the school, with an eye toward making their legal education more humane, egalitarian, and relevant, and toward supplanting the corporate attorney with the public interest lawyer. They were a part of a social movement calling for student power. The issues on which law students focused reflected their dissatisfaction with society and with their competitive and hierarchical education. They forced the faculty to make the grading system more egalitarian, to tolerate some student participation in the school's governance, and to increase admissions of underrepresented groups.[11]

Yale students were at once unique and typical. They worked to unlock a democratic vision of law and social change that they associated with legal realism, a progressive jurisprudence and approach to legal education long associated with Yale. Realism stressed the interrelationship of law and society, the inevitability of idiosyncrasy in the judicial process, and the importance of interdisciplinarity. Students appealed frequently to the sense of the school's special history that they shared with the faculty and charged their professors with trading on the school's glory days.

But the young were also creatures of their time. Their disaffection with their schooling and with the profession was hardly unique to Yale. Their disdain for the corporate bar illuminated the role of education in shaping professional identity and, ironically, may have helped reduce elite lawyers' concern with the public interest. And even after the members of Yale's sixties generation had themselves become hired guns, opting for more traditional careers in the very law firms they had once condemned as the "worst piece of shit I ever saw,"[12] their youthful attitudes left an imprint on the school.

The very issues that led to the unraveling of whatever postwar American liberal consensus existed and the emergence of identity politics also loomed large at Yale. The young battled with their professors over the issues dividing liberals from the New Left as they called for participatory democracy, community, equality, black power, a women's movement, and a counterculture. There was irony here too, for students' and teachers' objectives overlapped.

Most, for example, opposed the war in Vietnam and dreamed of dumping Lyndon Johnson. Even so, what separated them overwhelmed what might have brought them together. The rhetoric of generational warfare thus reflected the young's particular disillusionment with Yale, while pointing up a more general unhappiness with legal education, the profession, and society. It mirrored the tension between students and faculty at other elite law schools during the 1960s, as well as that between undergraduates and their teachers.

Of course, this book is as much about faculty as students. Activists challenged their professors during a charged moment in the history of the United States and the law school, and the resulting clash pitted young against older in a very human story. Caught in a web of their own aspirations for their craft and their sympathy and antipathy for the young, Yale professors struggled. In what was not that much of an overstatement, one recalled later that "[e]very issue from student disciplinary procedures to the grading system or the food served in the lunch room became a matter of principle and threatened to fracture the faculty and the students." As some professors perceived it, left-wing students were destroying the law school and meritocracy in a Kulturkampf that sought to bring the faculty to its knees. One future dean would refer to the period of 1967–70 as "the Dark Ages." In his view, Yale's student Visigoths had sacked legal Rome.[13]

In the fifteen years after 1970, the second phase of Yale's "sixties," some of its well-known professors embraced liberal scholarship and politics anew. While liberalism disintegrated in the standard narrative, it regained its strength in New Haven. During the early 1970s, professors insisted on scholarly and, perhaps, ideological standards once students turned their attention elsewhere. Junior faculty members who had recently witnessed their seniors wringing their hands over student demands were deemed inferior scholars and denied promotions. And as it rebuilt, the faculty proved unwelcoming toward two left-of-center jurisprudential movements rooted in both Yale's legal realism and the sixties: Law and Society and Critical Legal Studies. Those who attended Yale Law School during 1967–70 played a key role in the formation of the latter. But Yale, which had embraced forward-looking legal realism in the 1930s, rejected realism's descendant, Critical Legal Studies, at the same time that Harvard Law School, which had once turned its back on realism, made a home for realism's child and for scholarship that represented one logical extension of sixties activism. In part, that may have reflected local events: having suffered through one bruising battle with what they perceived as the left, Yale law professors may have been fearful of becoming embroiled in another. They were also responding to the broader political changes outside law school walls associated with the sixties, such as the end of the Warren Court, and the realignments that were taking place.

In addition to seeing the sixties as a period, then, I also view it as a complex of events that together suggest Yale professors' rejection of progressive legal thought to their left. During the second phase of its sixties, Yale embraced a culture of timidity, along with an interdisciplinary liberalism, forged out of a sanitized realism. I suggest that memories of the late 1960s at Yale and in the nation may help to explain professors' actions and that Yale's promotion decisions of the early 1970s, like its faculty scholarship of the late 1970s and early 1980s, may have represented, in part, a reaction against the earlier student agitation. The contours of the modern law school that began to appear in the late 1970s may have reflected a desire to avoid the kind of conflict that had earlier beset the institution; they certainly indicated a desire to rebuild sixties-style liberalism after its local and national vicissitudes. After the crisis of 1967–70 and the promotion controversies of the early 1970s, the developments between the mid-1970s and mid-1980s gave Yale Law School its contemporary shape.

When Guido Calabresi became dean in 1985, the school's fortunes improved dramatically. As I suggest in Chapter 10, Yale flourished for some reasons that had little to do with its past, such as the winning of financial independence from the central university administration. Yet the school also succeeded because the new dean tamed sixties-style protesters as he confronted multiculturalism and other forces to which the sixties had given rise. My two themes — the problems of legal academia during the sixties, as told through the history of Yale, and the birth of the contemporary Yale Law School — are thus interrelated and interdependent.

*   *   *

So are Yale's intellectual and institutional histories. Of professors' publications, my account makes mention. But it pays more attention to them during some periods than others because scholarship ebbed and flowed in its importance to life at the school. If, as one faculty member said, no students "seemed to give a damn about what we were teaching" during the late sixties, then certainly no students gave a damn about what professors were writing. American politics and student demands proved more pressing.[14]

I do not maintain that ideas are ever irrelevant to understanding Yale. The school's intellectual history accounted for its faculty's political liberalism, sense of uniqueness, and reactions to student movements during the 1960s. It enabled Yale to present itself as breeding ground for those who would use law to transform society, spawning high expectations that students then deemed unfulfilled. Along with political concerns and dissatisfaction with legal education, a remembrance of Yale Law School in times past animated its students. Yet ideas per se proved less important in explaining what happened than did the gulf between students and teachers, reflected in their different status, attitudes, values, goals, and institutional roles.

By the late 1970s, on the other hand, the school bred law professors, and scholarship had become more important to institutional life. Students of the sixties had linked the whiteness and maleness of the faculty to a lack of intellectual diversity, but students of the eighties did so even more pointedly. Some professors during the 1970s and 1980s also grappled with, and tried to reshape, the meaning of the sixties in their work. Consequently, intellectual currents receive more attention.

As intellectual product seems more important during some periods than others, so sources are richer for some than others. For 1967–70, I found a cache of materials in manuscript collections, full faculty minutes, and a vibrant newspaper, which I occasionally supplemented with oral history. I have told the story chronologically, so the reader may see how the tension between faculty and students intensified each year. I have focused on the nitty-gritty of relationships negotiated in close quarters, personalities and interests, and general intellectual and political perspectives, while making dips outside Yale to contextualize events within. The multifaceted story thus becomes complex. I have made the narrative messier still by trying to present enough evidence so that a reader could "write the same book differently" from it, while understanding why I have come to my conclusions. That has entailed telling my story, insofar as possible, in the words of the actors, while recognizing that another individual, confronted with the same evidence, might have shaped every quotation and placed every ellipsis differently. And it has meant that this book is incomplete. Like most archival collections, Yale's is not ideal. No historian can be sure why some materials make their way into the record and others do not. Perhaps those that have survived represent the significant, and/or the significant materials have been destroyed. I have largely assumed the former for 1967–70, which may be problematic. In focusing on the voices of the professors, student officials, and dissidents I have found in the archives, I may exaggerate their representativeness. I have still less confidence in the fullness of the record for the later period. The minutes of faculty meetings, for example, rich in detail for 1967–70, become frustratingly discreet in the years that follow and, indeed, not all have survived, making speculation about motivation more difficult.[15]

Focus on the institutional shines a spotlight on hierarchy and grandiosity—

the very reasons I submit that yet another book about Yale is not one too many. During the late sixties, Yale was both typical and special. Many students at other elite schools shared the politics of their Yale counterparts, if not the rhetoric about Yale's celebrated history. During the thirty years after 1965, Yale became ever more dominant in legal education. It became more atypical as it assumed a position of unusual importance in training the nation's leading political figures and professors. In addition to providing a case study of institutional development, examination of the school's past illuminates the historical importance of hierarchy within the legal academy. Exploration of Yale's history thus provides a prism on both the past and prospect of all legal education.[16]

Chapter One

Setting the Stage:
Law Schools and the Sixties

Every year, new books about the undergraduate revolt during the sixties appear. And we know that while medical students remained less activist than undergraduates, some combined white coat with clenched fist, protesting racism and the Vietnam War, urging their schools to provide better community health care, and working for changes in admissions, grading, governance, and faculty recruitment. Yet although many characterized law students as "the future leaders of the nation," law schools and students during this period have received short shrift. That is ironic, since both undergraduates and medical students proved more satisfied with their education than their counterparts in law schools.[1]

Law students during the 1960s found plenty to be concerned about besides racism and the war — the method of instruction, the tenseness and tedium of the classroom, a system of education that gave them little sense of how well they were doing at the same time it made grades all important, the impact of school upon their personal and professional lives, and the inattentiveness of legal education to the poor's problems. It all made for turmoil in elite law schools across the nation as students' unease with school and society led them to lodge a variety of grievances. Who pressed for change, what complaints and demands were articulated, and what conflicts resulted?

A PORTRAIT OF THE ACTIVIST AS A YOUNG MAN

Thanks to the work of Richard Flacks, Kenneth Keniston, and others, we possess a portrait of the wave of American undergraduate activists from the early sixties to the end of 1968 — at least, of the young white men who dominated the protesters. They were bright individuals from relatively affluent backgrounds who attended elite institutions and disproportionately studied social sciences and the humanities. They echoed their parents in identifying with liberalism or the left and in feeling a sense of social responsibility. Though a disproportionate number of activists were Jewish, they also followed their parents in defining themselves as nonreligious or nontraditional practitioners of their religion. Despite disagreement about the students' motivation, it seems more likely that they reflected rather than rebelled against many parental values. They had much in common with their professors too. Seymour Lipset repeatedly pointed out between 1964 and 1970 that most professors and students were closer to each other, politically, than either group was "to the rest of the American body politic."[2]

No matter. Bring such youths into the undemocratic, competitive, impersonal, authoritarian multiversity, or even elite private colleges, where they could not escape paternalism's lash or a sense of powerlessness, "and poof!" Whatever had started the protesters down the road to revolution—be it the war, their institution's links to the military-industrial complex, racial inequality, curricular irrelevance, a dislike of deferring to teachers and administrators, the repressiveness of parietal rules and definitions of permissible speech, and/or the university's encouragement of competitiveness and its failure to allow for self-determination—many students could join forces to demand student power. They sought to transform institutional structure and to help change the way they learned. As Gerald Farber famously put it in a much-cited essay, activists shared a sense of "the student as nigger." Theirs was a mood aimed at democracy and citizenship, more than an ideology.[3]

In contrast, there are few empirical studies of law student activists during this period. As Robert Stevens once observed, legal scholars who write about education become polemical, refusing to "soil arguments with data." Stevens's work on students at Boston College, USC, Yale, and the Universities of Connecticut, Iowa, and Pennsylvania Law Schools remains the only large-scale and comparative empirical study of law students during the late 1960s.[4]

At all schools, "students were becoming openly hostile to legal education, especially to the case and Socratic methods." At the same time, over the decade between 1960 and 1970, entrants "became increasingly liberal or radical," and their interest in public interest law increased dramatically. That should have put them in line with their professors, for like undergraduate teachers, most academic lawyers identified themselves as liberals. But it was Yale, Harvard, and the other prestigious law schools, Stevens stressed, that "had become part of the student revolution," just as elite undergraduate institutions proved its center.[5]

The profile of Yale students, the most "radical" of those in Stevens's study, bears some resemblance to that of undergraduate activists. Most undergraduate activists were male, as were most Yale students. More than 90 percent of the members of the class of 1970 and 80 percent of the class of 1972 were male, and almost all were white. Most of the men hailed from relatively privileged, well-educated families. Almost 30 percent were Jewish. Virtually all had graduated at the top of their college classes, where nearly three-quarters of them majored in the social sciences, and a quarter in the arts and humanities. Fifteen percent of the members of Yale's class of 1970 and 32 percent of the class of 1972 described themselves upon entry as "far left" as compared to "liberal" (62 and 45 percent, respectively; of course, in the context of the 1960s, loaded words such as "liberal" and "far left" possessed many meanings). Well over a third of the students in the class of 1970 and nearly 60 percent of those in the class of 1972, a significantly higher percentage than at the other schools in the study, characterized their desire to restructure society as "great." So, too, more Yale students declared their "great" desire to serve the underprivileged — more than a quarter of those in the class of 1970, and nearly half in the class of 1972. Indeed some entered with experience in the civil rights movement, the New Left, and the antiwar movement. Stevens included no data about parental politics. Further, by 1969, Yale's relatively few women and minorities proved more likely to identify with the left than men, a pattern that may have held true elsewhere in universities by the post-1968 period. Otherwise, beginning law students at Yale and elsewhere (if Stevens correctly used Yale to generalize about elite law schools) apparently fit the model of undergraduate activists.[6]

Many Yale law students, however, found professional training particularly dissatisfying. While over 60 percent of first-year students in the class of 1970 at Boston College, Connecticut, Iowa, and USC found law school more intellectually stimulating than college, at Yale, only one-third did. For students at similar institutions in particular, attending law school during the late sixties "was like having to go to summer school while your friends were all out playing ball." And with the war in Vietnam raging on, many students at elite law schools faced boot camp should they leave school. It only seemed that they had entered it already.[7]

THE UNCHANGING NATURE OF ELITE LEGAL EDUCATION:
"BOOT CAMP" CIRCA 1967

Students in the class of 1970 faced a system of legal education changed only slightly since Christopher Columbus Langdell revolutionized it when he became Harvard's dean in 1870. Acknowledging how little difference a century made, the Harvard catalogue boasted that "[i]n the first year of law school, the predominant method of instruction is the case method, first developed as a technique for law teaching by Dean Langdell in 1870, and since extensively employed in virtually all American law schools." Transport a first-year student out of a 1967 Contracts class back into Langdell's, and it would have felt familiar. Langdell would have paid more heed to English law, but the basic diet would have remained the same — "casebooks, large classes, Socratic dialogue, and single written examinations." Transport the student of 1967 into a Contracts class at another prestigious law school, and he would have felt the same way. Elite legal education was remarkably static and uniform, its structure, style, and content set by Harvard, just as it had been in 1870.[8]

Recent scholarship suggests that no figure in the history of American legal thought and education has been more unfairly maligned than Langdell. Yet the changes he wrought, with the support of Harvard University president Charles Eliot, secured the law school a place in the modern university at a time when other disciplines were riding similar intellectual currents toward concentrating on thinking about, as opposed to memorizing, texts. Even so, Langdell became the favorite whipping boy for every woe in legal education. In part, it is because of the life he breathed into the case and Socratic methods; in part, because the professionalization of legal education in the late nineteenth century shaped the contours of modern law practice.[9]

There were professional law teachers before him. Yet the site of legal education B.C. (Before Christopher) was mainly the office, with most students learning as apprentices. Wherever they studied, they likely memorized and recited Blackstone and Kent, among others. If law students were in offices, they also did clerical work and ran errands; if in school, their classes were often taught by part-time practitioners, many of whom lectured. Wherever they learned, many likely hoped to become lawyer-statesmen and leave their footprints on law and public affairs.[10]

Langdell centered legal education in the university and shifted its explicit focus away from statecraft. He had the prestige of Harvard and Eliot behind him, and the two men understood that if they made university law study "hard and long," prospective students would line up "to prove they could do it, and so acquire status within the profession." Thus the new dean tightened admissions requirements, lengthened the course of study, introduced grades, and insisted on instruction by full-time teachers.[11]

These changes formed the backdrop for Langdell's popularization of the case method. Because "the number of fundamental legal doctrines is much less than is commonly supposed," he explained in the introduction to his collection of appellate contracts cases, "it seemed to me, therefore, to be possible to take such a branch of the law as Contracts, for example, and without exceeding comparatively moderate limits to select, classify, and arrange [in a casebook] all the cases which had contributed to any important degree to the growth, development, or establishment of any of its essential doctrines" for "all who desire to study that branch of law systematically." This large claim would be whittled down in time. Where Langdell touted studying appellate opinions as a way of acquiring substantive knowledge and mastering legal reasoning, his successors celebrated the case method principally because it taught legal reasoning.[12]

That was no small thing. Recognizing the potential of classroom case study, Langdell had turned students toward close reading of the appellate opinions rendered in disputes, forcing them to hone in on the legal questions at issue and focus on rendering legal rules "consistent and coherent with each other, so that like cases are treated alike." He had introduced them to doctrinal analysis.[13]

But Langdell did not stop there. He paired appellate cases with the Socratic method. He and his colleagues embraced the cold call, engaging individual students, apparently selected at random, in a series of questions about a case without ever identifying the correct answer, a process designed to elicit the kernel from the nut and communicate the lawyer's craft. The law school could justify its large-class instruction because teaching by "hazing" guaranteed attentiveness. The danger they might be called upon next and the unacceptability of pleading lack of preparedness induced students watching the teacher-controlled "dialogue" to read assigned cases beforehand and "to participate vicariously—to silently pretend that they must answer the question."[14]

Ideally, the case and Socratic methods inculcated students into the distinct language of the law. They launched neophytes on a voyage of discovery designed to teach them the difference between arguing from law and from other disciplines or from policy or morality. Langdell and his colleagues were hardly unaware of law's relationship to social science, but there was little room for it in their curriculum. That was for college. Nor, despite the growth of the regulatory state, was there space at first for administrative law, legislation, constitutional law, antitrust, or jurisprudence. Tyros learned how to distill facts; derive legal rules and principles from cases; determine their precedential status; apply precedent, principles, and rules to different fact-situations; engage in case analysis, "the art of generating broad holdings for cases, so they will apply beyond their intuitive scope, and narrow holdings for cases, so that they won't apply where it at first seemed they would"; and articulate the grounds, such as the need for certainty and flexibility, that "lawyers use in arguing that a given rule should apply to a situation, in spite of a gap, conflict, or ambiguity, or that a given case should be extended or narrowed."[15]

But to enthusiasts, the combination of case and Socratic methods taught something more — clear thinking, judgment, and toughness. In their own way, they prepared law students for public service or anything else. At Harvard, Edward "Bull" Warren became a legendary instructor in the early twentieth century. In his memoir, appropriately entitled *Spartan Education*, Warren warned young law teachers that "too much lecturing is bad" for students — "very bad." It had produced the "large proportion" of the young, who, "on coming to law school fresh from the *dolce far niente* college years, would rather walk two miles than think for three minutes." The law professor's task was to train students "to become *accurate*, *clear*, and *terse* in their statement of facts and issues, and *sensible* in their exercise of judgment." That required the teacher to be "a full man," a master of his topic, and "a ready man," good on his feet. His students must learn to manipulate law with quickness and confidence. One Harvard Law graduate of this period, Dean Acheson, confronted Franklin Roosevelt; another, Joseph Welch, Joe McCarthy. "If you could stand up to The Bull, you could stand up to FDR or Joe McCarthy."[16]

The gendered nature of Warren's language was appropriate. Even after Harvard began to accept women in the mid-twentieth century, the school remained "a totally aggressively male institution." Each year, at the annual dinner Dean Erwin Griswold and his wife hosted for the few women students, the dean famously would ask his guests, after the stewed chicken and lima beans, "Why are you at Harvard Law School, taking the place of a man?" When one replied that she had come to Harvard because Yale had rejected her, Griswold, in the recollection of future congresswoman Pat Schroeder, went "crazy, flaming crazy, saying, 'That's not true, Yale always lets more women in than we do,' and so forth, the implication being that Yale had much lower standards than Harvard." Like most other elite law schools, Harvard enrolled few usurpers. Of the practicing lawyers in the United States in 1960, just over 7,500 were women compared to more than 205,000 men. (Both women and men, of course, were disproportionately white.) Further, professors and courses universally stressed skills then associated with men—rationality, the ability to draw distinctions, razor-sharp incisiveness.[17]

Thus students learned to "think like lawyers" as they began to understand how to state the significant facts and issues of a case and apply principle, rule, and precedent mined in a multiplicity of scenarios spun out in classroom hypotheticals. In a case in which a person held in a nursing home claimed false arrest, for example, the professor's questions first guided the students through the dispute and opinion to the legal principle that the litigant must prove "direct restraint." Then the "what ifs" began: What if the plaintiff were in a locked room on the first floor, but the windows had removable bars? What if it were a locked room with open windows and a broad ledge on the fourth floor, near a fire escape? What if the room were unlocked, but employees had forced the plaintiff to strip to his underwear?[18]

Despite its nod to policy questions and the importance of achieving "outcomes that could efficiently serve social policies somehow inhering in the legal system," the process generally left little time for such considerations. How should one weigh the nursing home's interest in the detainee's security against his right to the maximum possible freedom? "In the law school classroom, where the professor decides the limits of debate, the ideological basis or social impact of judicial decisions and accepted legal principles is barely considered," one student said. "When a serious problem of conflicting social interests emerges, it is brushed aside as beyond the scope of appropriate inquiry or dismissed as a matter involving the resolution of balancing interests, which can be done without wasting much class time." To spend time would turn the classroom into a "bull session." Pedagogy drained law of its ideological and political content, encouraging students to believe law was separate from morality and preference.[19]

That was often intentional. The case method and Socratic teaching stressed analytical ability by permitting students to imagine how they would employ legal doctrine, depending on whom they represented as lawyers or whether they acted as judges. Thus would students realize that reasonable people could differ and that good attorneys could comfortably craft a strategy for representing corporate titans or civil libertarians. Lawyers should dedicate themselves to their clients, selling their "services but not their souls," leaving it to the legal system to determine results.[20]

After resisting them at first, by 1910 professors nearly everywhere had embraced the case and Socratic methods. Langdellianism had the prestige of the nation's largest and most powerful university and law school behind it. It rendered a standardized product who had received "a legal education that stressed science—the leading intellectual as well as industrial theme of the time," and who fit into the specialized, rationalized, and hierarchical law firms then emerging. Because Langdell's system permitted large-class instruction on the cheap and made the law school a cash cow for the university, administrators appreciated it. Simply by lengthening law school to three years, holding classes by day, and requiring a college degree, Langdell also made entrance to elite schools impossible for most women and minorities and more difficult for white immigrants. That provided affluent white Protestant men one more way of preserving their hegemony. The case method also gave the new professional law teacher, then replacing part-time attorneys and judges, something to do. Since one need not practice law to parse cases expertly, the professor need not dirty his hands by working in a law firm before he walked to the podium. Often, the aspiring academic left Harvard after graduation to spread the gospel of the case method through "colonial service" at a less prestigious school in the hinterland.[21]

*   *   *

Legal realism remains the most concerted attempt ever to challenge Harvard's control over legal education. When judicial decision makers and those who studied them reached out to social sciences from economics to psychology, organized data according to fact-patterns in addition to legal doctrine, and acknowledged the role of human idiosyncrasy along with precedent in accounting for outcomes, the mantra went, law would be understood as a tool of policy. Jurisprudentially, there was little special about realism. The rebellion against what was variously called "formalism," "classical legal thought," "classical legal science," "conceptualism," "Langdell's orthodoxy," or "Langdellianism"—rarely with any agreement about its definition—long preceded the realists. Holmes had announced that the life of the law was not logic but experience and that judges made law in accordance with the "felt necessities of the time" sixty years before realism received its name. The sentiment was not unique then, either.[22]

So, too, well before the realists, Roscoe Pound urged the profession to shift attention from law in books, or legal doctrine per se, to law in action, or the social context and operational effects of legal rules and judicial decisions, in his famous—and again, not entirely original—call for sociological jurisprudence. Well before the realists, Pound had exhorted judges and lawyers to seek guidance from the social sciences in self-consciously making social policy. Law professors must lead the way: "[T]he modern teacher of law should be a student of sociology, economics, and politics," he preached. But in an inexplicable and perhaps the most "remarkable volte-face" in the history of American legal thought, Pound fought change and realism as dean of Harvard Law School between 1916 and 1936. Though more public law courses entered the curriculum, inside the Harvard classroom, sociological jurisprudence remained bare of the social sciences. Where Pound as sociological jurisprudent dreamed of changing legal thought, the realists sought to apply sociological jurisprudence to legal education and produce an alternative to the Harvard style.[23]

The realist project first took root at Columbia, with the hiring of the proto-contemporary law professor, Robert Lee Hale. He studied economics as an undergraduate, law at Harvard, and then entered Columbia's doctoral program, determined to unite law and economics. That he did as a teacher, organizing his subject according to social problems, such as the emptiness of current conceptions of property rights; illustrating his points with nonlegal as well as legal materials; and challenging the case method. The effort gathered momentum when Hale's colleague, Herman Oliphant, produced a celebrated report recommending reorganization of the curriculum along "functional lines" instead of by legal categories. It charged traditional legal education with obscuring the social policy behind legal rules, creating a barrier between law and the social sciences, classifying human relations in legal categories "too broad to give intimacy of view and too old adequately to disclose contemporary problems," and exaggerating the difference between substantive law and procedure. But when Columbia's president passed over Oliphant to name a traditionalist as dean in 1928, realism lost its grip there.[24]

That left Yale leading the charge against Harvard and Langdell. Its faculty and affiliates in the 1930s included a marquee of public figures identified with realism—William O. Douglas, Thurman Arnold, Jerome Frank, Abe Fortas, Walton Hamilton, Underhill Moore, and Eugene Rostow. Frank proved the most flamboyant. After writing one of the classic realist texts attacking the craving for certainty in law, and while serving in the New Deal, Frank turned his attention to skewering Harvard-style legal education because of its concentration on the appellate opinions. He blamed Langdell for creating "the myth that upper courts are the heart of court-house government." Characterizing Langdell as a "brilliant neurotic" who had "seduced" American legal education by introducing the case method, Frank maintained that "[t]o study those eviscerated judicial expositions as the principal bases of forecasts of future judicial action is to delude oneself." He likened students trained by the case method to "prospective dog breeders who never see anything but stuffed dogs." And he called for the replacement of the case method by a "clinical lawyer-school" that would embrace clinical legal education, place the law office at the core of the curriculum, and include academics who had practiced law for awhile before they began teaching. The Yale faculty treated him as a brilliant flake, doing nothing to implement his costly program.[25]

Other Yale professors shared an important portion of Frank's program. In labeling appellate opinions "eviscerated judicial expositions," he was pointing to how much they left out and the importance of indeterminacy and idiosyncrasy in decisions. The realists saw and taught that for each legal rule or principle that pointed toward one result, at least one more pointed to another. Legal rules and principles were in "the habit of hunting in pairs."[26]

Like Langdell's Harvard successors, the Yale realists thus placed doctrine at the center of legal scholarship. Where the Harvard traditionalist, "with the consummate skill of a master analyst," revealed that all cases were "consistent" in an area, a realist would employ "an equally analytical technique" to prove them inconsistent and law neither easily predictable nor determinate. Where their Cambridge counterparts penned synthetic treatises intended to reconcile conflicting cases, the New Haven realists wrote treatises demonstrating the incoherence of legal doctrine — and their competitors' product.[27]

Law was not distinct from politics and autonomous from society, the realists repeatedly said. The "T-square rule" of decision making that Justice Owen Roberts had articulated in striking down New Deal legislation did not describe how judges reached decisions: "When an act of Congress is appropriately challenged in the courts as not conforming to the constitutional mandate, the judicial branch of the Government has only one duty, — to lay the article of the Constitution which is invoked beside the statute which is challenged and to decide whether the latter squares with the former." At Harvard, Felix Frankfurter, Thomas Reed Powell, or James Landis would have told students the same thing: there was nothing new about the insight that, to some extent, public law was policy, politics, and preference. But the realists spent more time teaching it during the 1930s, a period when constitutional and administrative law were constantly debated in the public sphere, and they expanded its application beyond public law. According to the realists, social, political, and economic forces all shaped and were themselves shaped by private and public law.[28]

In contending that their Cambridge colleagues imbued the rule of law with a false internal integrity, the realists debunked in order to reform. In questioning the predictive force of age-old rules, for example, the realists maintained that they laid the groundwork for the production of better ones. The realists contended that traditionalists were not adequately doing their job as scholars or teaching students adequately to forecast the course of law for future clients. Their counterparts at Harvard, realists contended, actually reduced the legal predictability and certainty lawyers sought by, for example, herding disparate fact-situations into abstract, legal categories such as "intent." [29]

Thus significantly, the realists preached functionalism, the classification of doctrines, rules, principles, and concepts by factual as well as legal context. In contractual disputes, for example, whether the activity at issue involved building a house or providing services routinely affected the judge's determination of whether substantial performance had occurred: why not acknowledge that? Thurman Arnold compared the traditional formation of legal concepts, rules, and principles to classification according to the possession of trunks. Observing that the word "trunk" had originally been used in conjunction with trees, he pointed out that a cataloguer might subsequently place elephants, trees, and tourists under the heading "trunks," on the grounds that all possessed them. "The answer to the objection that the trunks are of different kinds can easily be met by saying that to a nicely balanced analytical mind, they all have one inherent similarity, *i.e.*, they all are used to carry things. The elephant's trunk carries hay to the elephant's mouth, the tree trunk carries sap to the leaves and the tourist trunk carries clothing." Theoretically sound as "new abstraction was," it created "verbal confusion and the necessity for a great many fine distinctions." [30]

In attending to factual context, along with legal concept, the realists questioned the boundaries between fields of law and talked in terms of creating new geography. Why should a first-year law student be instructed on the legal remedies for breach of contract in Contracts and only learn he had the choice between legal and equitable remedies the following year in Equity? The realists understood, to quote Arnold again, that "[t]he queer country of scholarship has been mapped out in little irregular patches of domain, staked out and appropriated by different groups with names derived from Latin and Greek sources." [31]

Challenging the boundaries between public and private was one aspect of the realists' remapping. For once the realists saw that the notion of "unimpeded voluntary action, of the free economic agent situated in a realm of pure choice and motivated by competitive Darwinist instinct" was fantasy, confronting the myth of laissez-faire and realizing that private law was really public law were the logical next steps. Growing as it did out of their concern with marketplace operations, as opposed to the theory of the marketplace and abstractions such as an invisible hand, the realists' assault on the boundary between public and private was part and parcel of their functionalism. The realists wrote and spoke more about private law than prior jurisprudential rebels, such as Frankfurter and Pound. But in pointing out that coercion lay at the heart of all bargains, be they public or private, realists also debunked "the notion of a freestanding, self-regulating market, by showing that the market was ineluctably constituted by the legal regime in which it operated." They made private and public inextricable.[32]

The use of institutional economics by scholars such as Hale and Walton Hamilton to shatter the public/private distinction pointed to another goal of the realists, "integrating" law with the social sciences. It always remained unclear exactly what such individuals hoped the social sciences, which had undergone dramatic changes when social scientists became captivated by the method of natural scientists after World War I, would do for law. The realists' master strokes were few. So were their rewards. At Yale, as almost everywhere, save perhaps Wisconsin and Chicago, law professors' overtures to outside scholars were spurned. Social scientists treated them as amateurs: the lawyers' courtship was premature.[33]

The realists' success in "using" the social sciences in the classroom was slighter still. On the one hand, the realists and almost everyone afterward changed the titles of their casebooks "from 'Cases on X' to 'Cases and Materials on Y.'" On the other, there was widespread agreement that with but few exceptions, realist casebooks made ineffective use of the social sciences and did not significantly depart from their precursors. In general, the realists focused on the dissection of the appellate opinion and did less with other disciplines than they suggested. They put interdisciplinary legal research and education front and square on the agenda—at the same time that they ensured that social science would be "kept at its proper Japanese-wife distance: law and," with the "and" functioning to marginalize social science.[34]

Thus the Yale realists dressed up law study. Their handiwork was unpopular in Cambridge, as was the realists' delight in mocking Harvard's stodginess in prose and verse. Frankfurter condemned Yale professors for "overjazzing" legal education, displaying too much cynicism about law in the classroom, and demonstrating a "smartaleck, wisecracking attitude" that he considered a function of their inferiority complex about Harvard. When it came time to discuss the weight the upstarts placed on the desirability of incorporating nonlegal materials in teaching, the Harvard faculty had fun playing gotcha: "Consequently, one would expect realist casebooks prepared by these teachers to contain a considerable amount of such materials. However, while some materials are presented in some recent volumes; they are not very extensive; and there seems to be little difference between the recently published casebooks of the 'functionalists' and those of the 'traditionalists' in this regard."[35]

That was only one reason realism's heyday was short. Some also faulted the realists for demonstrating that the emperor of law lacked certainty and objectivity. Particularly after "the Germans reduced their courts to tools of the Nazi Party," the autonomy of law from society came to seem more important.[36]

In the end, realism changed the lives of teachers more than students. It made many elite law professors wonder whether they should move closer to the university. But that created a sense of unease. Thomas Bergin would famously characterize the post-realist law professor between the 1940s and 1970s as "a man divided against himself." Torn between the campus and the profession, he was a victim of "intellectual schizophrenia," which had him "devoutly believing that he can be, at one and the same time, an authentic academic and a trainer of Hessians," or practitioners. When feeling "a raw lusting for academic respectability," the law professor found himself "deploring the case method, establishing research centers, loving the social sciences, teaching the far-out seminars, aching to reform the law, and secretly wishing to be named to a modest federal post such as Secretary of State." He then offered one of the many "law and" electives in the law school catalogues, such as Law and Psychology or Law and Religion, that popped up virtually everywhere to break the monotony in realism's wake and that Bergin believed academic lawyers, who might not have studied psychology or religion since college, were incompetent to teach. When his "Hessian trainer side" appeared, and he put students' "feet to the fire of the cases," however, the professor did "not want all the courses to be required — only the grim ones" and identified himself as a "lawyer."[37]

And even on his "academic" days, the law teacher must continue training potential lawyers to pick apart cases. That meant, Bergin said, that just as writing distracted him from educating practitioners, so teaching prevented him from doing writing worthy of someone housed in a university. Since a good lawyer was supposed to be a jack-of-all trades, a good law teacher must fill whatever hole in the core curriculum arose, no matter how much time preparation consumed. Most law professors published little beyond casebooks, treatises, or the occasional doctrinal article, if that much.[38]

So in the post-realist classroom, professors might applaud themselves for introducing legal and equitable remedies in Contracts, saying a word about business practices in Commercial Transactions; demonstrating that legal doctrine took a more tortured path than Langdell had maintained; and even making policy arguments in the close case. Further, many felt compelled to sound a cautionary note at the beginning of each "grim" course. A case might well have turned out one way during one period and another thirty years later because the personnel and times had changed. But students must learn to take the language of the law seriously. Wherever they were, law professors might begin a course by reminding students that "we" were "all realists now," then minimize the realists' insight lest they be fated to spend class after class presenting the opinion as smoke screen for preference. And they still raised their young on a diet of appellate opinions and the Socratic method. Ironically, the realists enshrined the autonomy of law by introducing just enough realism about it so that the citadel could remain standing.[39]

The case method was itself "functional," it turned out — not as the realists had meant, but in terms of getting law students educated cheaply. That allowed the law school to become the university cash cow, or, in the case of the quasi-autonomous Harvard, rich. Had Harvard introduced something as revolutionary for the twentieth century as the case method was for the nineteenth, change might have followed. (Leave aside the fact that no one could specify the contours of that revolution, though there was a vague consensus it would entail greater hands-on training and would prove pricey.) If Harvard, with its large student body and its reputation as the most prestigious law school, had overthrown Langdell, its competitors might have felt obliged to follow suit. Ironically, perhaps only Harvard was capable of toppling Langdell. But it did not. Why fix what was unbroken? And no one else, including those at Yale, did either.

*   *   *

Consequently, twentieth-century American students often seemed to spend as much time complaining about legal education as they did studying. The gripes generally began with the Socratic method. Many of their teachers had nothing in common with Socrates other than that they "both asked questions." Too many professors drilled students about the content of assigned cases, peppering them with questions both unfocused and tedious. Despite professors' protestations of loyalty to the Socratic method, many actually used "an inefficient and time-wasteful lecture system," devoting forty minutes of an hour class "to a groping expression of views by a relatively few students." Then the teacher summed up. "A fifty minute period has become a ten minute lecture, for the preceding discussion has failed to serve as a dueling of intellects." The masters of the Socratic method never summed up. They prided themselves on "hiding the ball," asking endless questions without ever indicating the answer. They relished "leading students out on a limb and then lopping it off." That way, the young would come "to realize that whatever it was that they thought they had just grasped was going to slip through their fingers by the end of each class hour," an epiphany that would reinforce professors' majesty and authority.[40]

Whether or not their professors would have won the approval of Socrates, many students disliked teaching by questioning. They maintained that it wasted class time, since lectures covered more ground more quickly; intimidated, traumatized, dehumanized, and sometimes humiliated students; bred uncertainty, confusion, and competition; gave their classmates, rather than the expert, an opportunity to blather; and forced them to respond in terms of what was legal or illegal, rather than right or wrong. Though many shared their dissatisfaction, the discontented would not necessarily have known that. They seemed confident that their professors "probably are rotten to their families," their "fellow students . . . here to make a buck." They worried that law school taught students to "*feel*" like lawyers—as if it were "right" to act "controlling, cool, dispassionate, unfeeling, arrogant."[41]

After all, that was the way the prototypical drill sergeant-law professor behaved in creating the "law-school-as-boot-camp" atmosphere. He was memorialized in *The Paper Chase*, whose protagonist, Professor Kingsfield, might have been modeled on The Bull. The book presented the first year at Harvard as "an exercise in intimidation—apparently serving the same purpose as the rule that novices scrub the floor of the monastery chapel."[42]

The "depersonalization" and lack of opportunity for teachers and classmates to know one another as individuals made the gap between what first-year law students had expected and what they encountered all the more alarming. Most started school believing law a set of rules and principles to memorize. The instruction the beginner encountered in the generally required first-year courses of Contracts, Torts, Property, Criminal Law, and Civil Procedure exploded that misconception and, by focusing on the art of prospecting from cases, introduced them to doctrine and analytical method. That professors assigned no papers and gave only a final examination—generally consisting of long, hypothetical fact-situations, with the instructions to spot the legal issues, specify the relevant legal rules, and apply them—only increased anxiety and disorientation. All that students could read from their professors on how to succeed in examinations was the sarcastic advice that faculty occasionally published to blow off steam (write illegibly, spell poorly, be repetitious, etc.); they rarely had a chance to receive feedback on practice tests. Consequently, students remained unsure whether they were mastering the material during the semester, and their course grade depended almost entirely on their performance on one day. They received little feedback afterward that might enable them to improve, either. At mid-century, students apparently could not even review their graded examinations "as a matter of right" at most law schools. Thus they conceived of their professors "as experts with unchallengeable authority who possess the priestly power of dispensing . . . mysterious symbols."[43]

Of course, students might have impressed the faculty during the semester through their classroom performance, but that made little difference. Professors generally read Blue Books blind, "covers turned back, so as to eliminate identification while grading." Some teachers then took students' contributions to the class into account. But at best, consistently good classroom performance could only marginally improve an individual's grade.[44]

Grades had long been considered arbitrary. In 1924, the first study of law school grades had revealed "large differences" in the standards used by different professors at the same institution in their grading and in the standards "used by the *same* professors at different times." The charge did not go away, though the risk of failure lessened. By the 1960s, at Harvard, for example, the notorious predictions of bygone days to entering students—"look to the right of you, look to the left of you, one of you will not be here next year"—no longer held true. Thanks to the introduction of more rigorous admission standards, almost all survived.[45]

But some things stayed the same. "I have never seen more manifest anxieties in a group of persons under 'normal' circumstances than is visible in first year law students," one psychiatrist said. First-year grades remained crucial. They sorted out the students who had been admitted through the more competitive process, determining eligibility for another innovation of the Langdell years, the student-edited law reviews that published faculty scholarship. Law review membership was a prerequisite for judicial clerkships and the elite positions after graduation. Harvard law professors spoke for legal elites everywhere when they said, "We can hardly deny the omnipresence of the question, 'Was he on review?'" Nor did most teachers want to: although arguably they were the ones least in need of individual instruction, students who "made" law review received the most attention from the faculty.[46]

To most students, it therefore seemed as if their first year would set the contours of their entire professional career—as indeed it probably did, if they accepted the definitions of prestige advanced by the law schools and legal profession and wanted to enter the great corporate firms or join the academy. Law school grades, many complained, were inexplicable and unexplained, did not measure achievement, and failed to motivate students while creating unconscionable pressure and competition. Further, grades "trapped" the student "in a game not of his own choosing." The first year of law school, a partner at one powerful firm explained, constituted "The Race. To do well in the first year is to win The Race and to secure your success in law firm practice forever." One also needed to win The Race to become an academic. "Our faculties tend to reproduce themselves; and in the process may by the continual inbreeding be producing even narrower law students than they were themselves," Erwin Griswold acknowledged. And while one might get lucky and win elective office and some judgeships without an excellent academic record, good grades generally helped with securing the "best" government jobs straight out of law school.[47]

Oddly, though the first year determined one's opportunities, the second and third were more of the same, leavened by an occasional "interdisciplinary" seminar, and even more boring. The first year might bring the excitement of learning how to read an appellate opinion, but even after the skill had been acquired, the opinions continued coming. As one professor acknowledged, the case method was "not exacting in its demands on any but the morbidly conscientious student" after the first year. Since the bell of first-year performance could rarely be unrung, and law review membership had already been set, a cloud of sullenness hung over the second and third years: "To pursue the same method of study through three long years requires the persistence of a saint and the patience of Job."[48]

Not all students experienced law school as tedium, but those who did might have found it more worthwhile had it prepared them for lives in law. The case method did teach students to analyze appellate opinions, a skill worth acquiring for the briefs they would write as lawyers, though critics claimed it could be learned in a year. But by the 1960s, few attorneys spent as much time writing briefs in preparation for litigation as they did avoiding court altogether. Far more devoted themselves to counseling clients, negotiating on their behalf, drafting agreements, working to settle disputes without trial, and interpreting statutes and regulations—skills that received little attention in the classroom.[49]

Insofar as the cases students read provided preparation for practice, they focused on the problems of the rich. The cozy relationship between the law school and elites had long been apparent. Perhaps Langdell "did not consciously plan a law school with a view toward the growth of law firms and their corporate clients." But it seemed clear to many that the case method facilitated their expansion. So did the advanced curriculum, historically top-heavy in courses on corporations, taxation, and commercial transactions.[50]

Assignments focusing on the poor as clients might have made up for the curriculum's corporate focus by enabling students to assist some of the less affluent *and* develop some of the drafting, counseling, and negotiating skills they would require as lawyers. Many schools possessed legal aid programs, in which students could volunteer, generally without receiving credit, or moot court, in which they could develop their advocacy skills by playing lawyer. But clinical education barely existed in 1967; few could even agree on its definition. And although some said the law school would agree "to operate a 'skunk farm' if there were any money in it," there was not yet money in the clinic. That did not come until 1968, when the Ford Foundation formed the Council on Legal Education for Professional Responsibility and began to pour cash into proposals to establish clinical programs submitted by elite law schools filled with bored students demanding greater relevance. Even then, clinical education remained a "stranger in an elitist club." The law student of 1967 who wanted to help the less fortunate or learn practical skills had few means of doing so.[51]

THE STUDENT REVOLT

And indeed the expressions of unhappiness, always present since 1870, seemed more frequent, intense, and broad-ranging in the late 1960s as students came to see legal education not just as demoralizing and boring, but as symptomatic of a sick society as well. When a first-year Harvard student actually committed suicide just before final examinations, the event inspired an eight-hour dialogue between students that was reported in the *Journal of Legal Education*. For all the disagreement, one conclusion was clear: law students were really unhappy. Disappointed by law school and "confused about the role of a lawyer in society," they were also anxious about how the socialization process was affecting them personally.[52]

As they came to identify law school with "the Establishment," the young imposed their social and political concerns on their educational experience. Rutgers' Arthur Kinoy observed "a deep and profound crisis" that had "suddenly . . . manifested itself," with its "symptoms of deep malaise, boredom, frustration, and dissatisfaction . . . erupting in every major law school." Ralph Nader took to the pages of the *New Republic* to denounce law schools for training attorneys who labored "for polluters, not antipolluters, for sellers, not consumers, for corporations, not citizens, for labor leaders, not rank and file, for, not against, rate increases or weak standards before government agencies, for highway builders, not displaced residents, for, not against judicial and administrative delay, for preferential business access to government and against equal citizen access to the same government, for agricultural subsidies to the rich, not food stamps for the poor, for tax and quota privileges, not for equity and free trade."[53]

At a time of "huge demand for law grads," corporate law firms expanded pro bono programs and raised salaries to attract the best and brightest. But law students saw the firms' behavior as "a display of recruiting weakness." The *American Bar Association Journal* carried articles about law students entitled "Will They Enter Private Practice?" and reported that none of the *Harvard Law Review* editors planned to do so. When, at the dedication of the Georgetown Law Center, Chief Justice Warren Burger delivered a keynote address that warned against looking to courts as vehicles of social change, three hundred students gathered at a "counter-dedication" to listen to radical lawyers exhort them to do exactly that.[54]

Oddly, despite recognition of the young's dissatisfaction with law practice, there was some sense that law schools remained in stable, if sulky, condition. "Teaching civil rights to law students who are still treated as disenfranchised minority living in an academic Lowndes County . . . is like celebrating life in a mortuary," one professor said. He maintained that "the student revolts that have rocked campuses across the country have left the law schools relatively untouched."[55]

"Relatively untouched"? Compared to what? To liberal arts colleges and graduate programs in the humanities and social sciences, perhaps; but not, on the basis of what we know, to other professional schools. In 1968, after the faculty voted to convene classes during the undergraduate occupation of the campus, Columbia law students mounted an effective strike. The following year, a law student from Berkeley's Boalt Hall was tried for inciting a riot because he had urged students to destroy the fence around People's Park. When Harvard students struck in 1969 in support of the undergraduates who had been "busted" for occupying University Hall in protest against Harvard's failure to expel ROTC from campus and treat the neighboring poor more equitably, among other things, an all-night vigil took place at the law library. There, according to the *Harvard Law Record*, "a suggestion that the study-in discuss the eight demands of the Harvard College strikers was hooted down" in favor of something even more pressing—"a free-flowing give-and-take session on grading, evaluation and alienation at Harvard Law." Thirty African American law students forced major concessions from the Columbia administration when they occupied the law library and held a "study-in" to protest the "intransigence of the law school on certain matters respecting an institutional commitment to black and other minority students." The Association of Black Law Students at Rutgers-Newark circulated an "indictment of the Rutgers Law School Community" that scorned the curricular focus on "the private interests of white society" and demanded that the school offer courses relevant to African American students, taught by professors they had selected. Howard law students seized their school, chained its doors, and locked the faculty out, calling for, among other things, student participation in faculty committees and meetings and pass-fail grading. In the spring of 1970, someone placed a Molotov cocktail on a shelf in the Columbia International Law Library, lit it, and disappeared. It did little damage; a suspicious fire that broke out late at night in the Yale Law Library two months later caused more.[56]

*   *   *

What lay behind the burst of law student agitation? Did the "Paper Chase" atmosphere mobilize students? Did they fear that by its very structure, law school gave professors the power to determine their futures? Did they view their institution as a microcosm of the very establishment that both attracted and repelled them, a love-hate syndrome that Duncan Kennedy, then a Yale law student, and later a Harvard professor, aptly labeled "Hip Law Student Neurosis"? The answer was "all of the above." Kennedy correctly observed that "students at just about every 'national' law school in the country" were trying to change legal education.[57]

Open the newspapers published at elite law schools during the period, and you will find common themes beneath the dust. United in their condemnation of their education as sterile, dissatisfying, and needlessly competitive, law student agitators sought to end hierarchy and alienation. They agitated for community, citizenship, democracy, and relevance. They fretted about American, as well as academic, politics. They worried constantly about the draft, they grappled with racial injustice, they confronted sexual inequality (though it chiefly concerned women), they saw their professors as symbols of the system and society, and they wondered how they could serve the larger world. The issues on which law student activists concentrated were similar too. They involved grade reform and often, as a corollary, law review participation; student participation in law school governance; increased enrollments of, and an end to discrimination against, students of color, chiefly African Americans, and women.

If one commonality marked the process through which elite law school transitions took place, it was the intense discussion that they generated. At one Harvard Law School student-faculty mass meeting, "[t]housands of words were spoken; speeches for and against proposals, seconding, voting, counting, confusion and decision-making took place." When black students struck at the University of Wisconsin in 1969, law students and faculty helped by doing what they did best—talking. They established a "Rumor Center" to confirm, deny, and explain the gossip circulating around the campus. Whether apathetic or engaged, the University of Michigan Law School's student paper observed, Michigan law students agreed with their professors that "there are two sides to every issue" — and that they had to be rehearsed endlessly. Meetings "took flight." Both the babble and posturing were extraordinary.[58]

*   *   *

Just as acrimony, chatter, and posturing also characterized the sixties at Yale Law School, so did the search for community, citizenship, democracy, and relevance. From 1967 to 1970, the issues of competition, hierarchy, paternalism, and alienation crucial at elite law schools everywhere inaugurated a law student revolt in New Haven. As it progressed, Yale students — white and black, men and women — broadened their focus to encompass larger social issues. Their efforts and achievements were among the earliest and most considerable of the law student power movement. That was at least in part because Yale's smallness contributed to engagement. More of its students entered public interest law upon graduation than those from other elite law schools, and were, at least temporarily, committed to the vision of the left it represented. All Yale students were undistracted by one burning issue elsewhere, whether their law school should award the Juris Doctor degree instead of the Bachelor of Laws. Unlike activists at other elite law schools, the young at Yale were urged on, rather than reined in, by the student press. And where students at other elite schools did not always produce lasting reforms — with most law schools, for example, reverting to multi-tier grading systems by the mid-1970s — the changes won by Yale students proved more likely to endure. Their actions thus profoundly troubled their professors.[59]

Many Yale students perceived the school as a symbol of society. That often led them to treat professors who shared their political aspirations as enemies. It was elite law schools' "most brilliant graduates and professors," who, as policymakers, directed "the prosecution of the war, the urban displacement of the poor, the repression of war dissenters," as one New Haven malcontent observed. Whatever one decides about the value of student efforts, one conclusion seems incontrovertible: Yale's particular intellectual history made students already stirred up by the the sixties more eager than ever for change.[60]

Chapter Two

The Yale Law School
on the Eve of the Sixties

Spring 1967. Imagine a college senior just accepted at Yale. Most such students were male, and many had attended an Ivy League college, where student unrest was only just beginning. At the time, San Francisco expected thousands for the summer of love, but the typical future Yale law student had his sights on different spires. What would his vision of the school be when he entered in the fall?

If Yale had its way, he would focus on its storied association with legal realism and liberal judicial activism. "[I]f you wanted to get rid of realism at Yale," Professor Ronald Dworkin told the *New York Times* in the 1960s, "you'd have to flush out the place for three years and fumigate the halls." Even then, eradication would have been difficult, for the law school gloried in its association with legal realism. In explaining why, person for person, Yale Law's graduates possibly occupied "more seats of political power than the alumni of almost any other institution" and proved "even more influential" in the academic world than in political life, a 1963 issue of *Newsweek* credited the school's realist roots: "During the '20s and '30s, the legal realists on the Yale faculty preached and practiced the doctrine that law is not a self-contained set of unchanging rules, but a vital tool for structuring and restructuring society." Realism transformed Yale, giving the school its identity as the anti-Harvard and laying the groundwork for its association with a liberal judiciary linked to the civil rights movement, even as it did not transform the classroom experience inside or outside Yale. The vision of its history that Yale promoted was designed to attract a certain kind of student during the late 1960s. At the same time, it helped to create a faculty certain of its own righteousness and liberalism—just as the attack on liberalism was gaining strength.[1]

MYTH AND MYSTIQUE

Despite the limited achievements of realism, the myth that it was unique and revolutionary created Yale's mystique. Proto-realist Arthur Corbin had created the modern Yale Law School in the early twentieth century by persuading his colleagues to insist students possess a college education, hire full-time teacher/scholars, and adopt the case method. Taking the helm at the age of twenty-seven in 1927, Dean Robert Maynard Hutchins launched the realist experiment with a charm offensive. Having ingratiated himself with Yale's president, he hired a psychologist, a political scientist, and an economist without law degrees. It was not the first time Yale Law School had tried to find salvation in interdisciplinarity, but it was the first time Yale's claim to have become the "premier center of advanced interdisciplinary legal studies" amounted to anything other than "sheer chutzpah."[2]

Hutchins also introduced selective admissions. As always, Harvard provided the impetus: announcement of the law school's endowment drive spurred action. Enlisting his colleague Charles E. Clark, the dean drafted a plan for Yale to become "the first honors or research school in America." It would restrict its enrollment to 300, increase its endowment, require student research, and "discover the actual operation of the law," coordinating it with the social sciences and advancing "beyond the classical case study of the Harvard type." This was, simply, a way of advertising Yale's distinctness from Harvard, which required the minimum in credentials and counted on first-year examinations to weed out the first-year class. And in one sense, the dean's declaration represented no change in direction for Yale, which historically had small enrollments.[3]

Still, it proved a pivotal moment in the school's history. As Thurman Arnold said, "it was a bold announcement to the world and particularly to Yale's competitor, the Harvard Law School, that Yale intended to remain a small school not because few students applied, but because it had voluntarily resolved to remain small." It was also an announcement that Yale would not open the gates wide. Reviewing catalogues, Clark found only four other schools that did not accept "all candidates with the required preliminary education and character." Between two and three students applied for each of Yale's one hundred seats, and the process was onerous. When the Admissions Committee made its decisions, it did so on the basis of a file that contained the formal application, undergraduate transcript, at least two recommendations, a report on the required interview, and the results of a legal aptitude test especially designed for prospective Yale law students.[4]

Charles E. Clark. (Portrait by Franklin Chenault Watkins, 1959.
Courtesy Yale Law School.)

Thus the social sciences justified the school's smallness and selectiveness. Indeed, the point of discriminating admissions was to establish what Clark called "an intellectual aristocracy."[5] Yale had found its niche. It would advertise itself as the boutique law school for intellectuals.

It would also acquire its home. The new Sterling Law Buildings consumed an entire block in the heart of the campus. The paean to College Gothic was

Sterling Law Buildings under construction. (Manuscripts and Archives, Yale University Library.)

magnificently imposing, if claustrophobic, transforming the law school into "almost a self-contained unit, like a little city." Classrooms, library, professors' offices, student cafeteria, and faculty dining room took up three sides of the block. A large courtyard lay in the center; dormitories squared the complex. By the time the edifice had taken shape in 1929, Hutchins had departed to become president of the University of Chicago.[6]

During the next decade, thanks to Dean Clark's stubborn determination, Yale developed its identity. The law school became a player when its professors and affiliates attacked Harvard and became involved in New Deal statecraft. Realism enabled Yale to edge out Columbia for second place. Further, it imbued Yale with its allure "as the only law school that wasn't like a law school" and "where it was possible to do something more than study law." The song of legal education stayed the same in New Haven, while the tune changed. Though Harvard set the words, students and faculty shared the music "in the halls" that law was a tool of reforming public policy.[7]

*   *   *

Sterling Law Buildings today. (Photograph by Michael Marsland.
Courtesy Michael Marsland, Yale University.)

The excitement of Roosevelt's election "swept through the Yale Law School faculty like a cyclone," "strengthening the opinion of conservatives that the Yale Law School was to the New Deal what West Point was to the Army." Here, Yale realists could join forces with those few, important Harvard professors, such as Felix Frankfurter, who might consider New Haveners' attempt to distinguish their pedagogy silly, but who shared their commitment to making lawyers the pillars of the administrative state. Dean Roscoe Pound was no ally. He flirted with the Nazis, accepting an honorary degree from the University of Berlin. Where Frankfurter placed his protégés, "the Happy Hot Dogs," in New Deal agencies after they had graduated at the head of their classes, Pound insisted that the goal of the law school was to turn out "well-trained competent practitioners."[8]

Dean Clark, on the other hand, gloried in his school's association with the New Deal. Unlike most law school deans, he supported Roosevelt's court-packing plan, just one of many acts that earned his school a reputation for "radicalism." In 1939, one newspaper even featured a cartoon of a Yale law professor hoisting the hammer and sickle of the Soviet Union up the school's flagpole.[9]

Clark recognized that the Depression created the chance for Yale to market itself as the place for policy wonks as well as intellectuals. The Depression

*Joseph Parrish,
"Another Color on
the Campus."
(Chicago Tribune,
January 21, 1939.
Copyright Tribune
Media Services.)*

proved that "the corporation lawyer of the past decade must give way to the public counsel of the next," and rightly moved Yale professors to challenge "the subservience" of "the brilliant minds in the profession" to big business. It would be "disquieting" were faculty members not invited to serve the government. The pattern was for the law professors to go to Washington themselves for a time, either commuting between New Haven and the capital or taking a leave of absence, and bringing their best students, the "Young Hot Dogs," with them. In fact, Clark's sometime colleague Jerome Frank contended that legal realism made the New Deal possible. He maintained that Roosevelt's objectives would stymie the law's "Mr. Absolute," the traditionalist unaccustomed to viewing law as a tool of policy. But "Mr. Try-It," the legal realist who shared the New Deal's experimentalism, would expeditiously devise a program for making them legal. And as Frank always added, the "Langdellian fog" was "less choking and blinding" at Yale than it was anywhere else. When he was writing a brief in *Nebbia* v. *New York*, one of the early challenges to New Deal–type legislation and the case that toppled the old barrier between public and private, "the School seemed to know of nothing but the Nebbia case—Charlie [Clark] writing in his office, Thurman [Arnold] bellowing wherever he happened to be, seminars writing briefs and papers." The equation of Yale with realism and the New Deal contributed to the esprit and sense of the school's uniqueness.[10]

New Deal liberalism thus underscored the ideal of intellectual excellence in public service and in the universities with which it developed such close connections. The word "meritocracy" would not become popular until the 1950s, but the concept of an aristocracy of intellect underlay selective admissions at Yale, and the New Deal. Of course, as long as a school like Yale represented the eye of the needle, few but white men would pass through it. Still, after matriculation, performance on examinations proved all-important. Though parentage and golfing skill might prove as significant as grades in determining the graduate's success in private practice, meritocrats and New Dealers envisioned a world in which academic performance accounted for placement in the university and government.[11]

Consequently, New Dealers and meritocrats believed that the best faculty and government positions belonged to those with the strongest records. And gradually, beginning in the 1930s, and then, with the spread of standardized testing and the increased emphasis on credentials in admissions and hiring during the postwar era, the university, like government, did open up, at least for Jewish men. At Yale, as at other elite institutions, the process was evident in the law schools before the college and other departments. By the 1950s, the Yale law faculty included many Jews, while the Yale College faculty, where the old boys congregated, still possessed few. Religion became less of a barrier to faculty hiring—so much so that for many of the law professors who would teach the students of the sixties, meritocracy became a new religion. The emergence of the "best and brightest" as a distinct class linked elite law professors to modern American liberalism.[12]

These developments in the 1930s deepened the animosity between academics and the profession at the same time that they sharpened the image of the Yale law professor as left of center. If it was "hard to exaggerate the sense of professional jubilation" with which leading corporate attorneys greeted the Supreme Court's decision invalidating the centerpiece of the early New Deal, it was equally difficult to overstate such lawyers' contempt for professors. Despite Clark's dogged defense of his faculty, the university's president wearily concluded that "law faculties tend to harbor relatively more men of leftward-looking political tendencies than are found in academic groups generally," a pattern "at variance, I should say, with the prevailing trend in bar and bench."[13]

The coincidence of the emergence of the Yale law professor as realist-reformer troubleshooter/policymaker with the call for the alliance between law and social science also contributed to the arrogance Yale law students would decry during the 1960s. What Mark Tushnet called "the 'lawyer as astrophysicist' assumption" gripped law professors: "We are people who have a generalized intelligence, and can absorb and utilize the products of any other discipline in which we happen to become interested." In practical terms, that meant any of them could "read a physics book over the weekend and send a rocket to the moon on Monday." Even modest souls who doubted their command of astrophysics came to believe they understood its implications for public policy better than anyone else.[14]

Again and again, in the years after the New Deal, the realists, policy, and social science served as Yale's public touchstone. The charge that realism was totalitarian had little impact on Yale as an institution, and some of its inhabitants had an answer anyway. Myres McDougal and Harold Lasswell opened their famous 1943 article, "Legal Education and Public Policy: Professional Training in the Public Interest," by proclaiming that the policy science they promoted incorporated the lessons of realism while preparing law students to become policymakers in the regulatory state. Law, they maintained, embodied the democratic values of shared knowledge, power, and respect, verifiable by the social sciences, and legal education could serve those values only by becoming "conscious, efficient and systematic training for policy-making." In international law, McDougal and Lasswell's policy science predictably became a stalking horse for Cold War liberalism, imbued as it was with "a mission not merely to promote democratic ideals but to save the free world." But policy science had little impact at Yale outside of international law beyond contributing to the notion, already popularized by legal realism, that lawyers should be trained to make public policy.[15]

And so Yale hitched its wagon to legal realism's star. The refrain remained the same in the decades that followed. "We take it to be self-evident," the Yale Law School Curriculum Committee declared in its first report after World War II and again in 1955, "that law is one of the social studies, and that the study of law will be most fruitful and critical when the skills and perspectives of history, economics, statistics, psychology, political science, sociology and psychiatry are fully and effectively used in the work for the law schools." The need for "a combined approach in the study of social problems" was "nowhere more urgent than law." Eugene Rostow, who became the school's dean in 1955, boasted that realism had long "represented the prevailing approach to legal studies at the Yale Law School to a greater extent than has been the case in any other law faculty of the world." When Victor Navasky, Yale Law School '59, summed up the clichés about Harvard and Yale a decade later, each one signaled the extent to which legal realism was bound up with Yale's identity and image: "Yale trains judges, Harvard trains lawyers; Yale doesn't teach you any law, Harvard teaches you nothing but; Yale turns out socially conscious policy-makers, Harvard turns out narrow legal technicians; Yale thinks that judges invent the law, Harvard thinks that judges discover the law; Yale is preoccupied with social values, Harvard is preoccupied with abstract concepts; Yale is interested in personalities, Harvard is interested in cases; Yale thinks most legal doctrine is ritual mumbo-jumbo, Harvard thinks it comprises a self-contained logical system; Yale cares about results, Harvard cares about precedents; Yale thinks the law is what the judge had for breakfast, Harvard thinks it is a brooding omnipresence in the sky."[16]

There was more, the constant insistence that the realism entailed aiding outsiders. Yale also defined itself as the anti-Harvard in its progressiveness. Wags said the fact "Debtors' Estates" at Yale was named "Creditors' Rights" at Harvard symbolized "an ideological difference between the two schools." Yet where New Dealers had placed their hopes in public control of business and redistribution of wealth, Cold War liberals proved more concerned with civil liberties and rights. As they perceived it, conservative control of the executive branch and Congress placed business largely off limits. Further, many had come to appreciate the role of large corporations, along with countercyclical spending and mass consumption, in making possible a rights-conscious liberalism that preached the power of abundance to soften differences of race and class. The federal judiciary, more reformist than either the president or Congress in the 1950s must protect individuals and disenfranchised groups from the abuses of government. Yale's Thomas "Tommy the Commie" Emerson defended communists in the courts during McCarthy's heyday. His colleagues attacked the government's loyalty program, worked with the National Association for the Advancement of Colored People, and urged the abolition of the House Un-American Activities Committee. For students applying to law school in the 1960s, Yale was as synonymous with Cold War liberalism's quest for civil liberties and civil rights as it had been with New Deal liberalism.[17]

THE PREVALENCE OF PROCESS

During the postwar years, Yale's identity therefore became bound up with a new point of difference from Harvard. Yale came to represent legal liberalism, the trust in the potential of courts, particularly the Supreme Court, to bring about "those specific social reforms that affect large groups of people such as blacks, or workers, or women, or partisans of a particular persuasion; in other words, policy change with nationwide impact." It was that mission the Court had signaled it would accept in the 1938 decision of *United States* v. *Carolene Products*, when Justice Stone suggested that his colleagues would uphold all reasonable economic regulation, while subjecting to stricter scrutiny legislation that abridged the Bill of Rights, restricted operation of the political process, or targeted religious, national, or racial minorities. Stone created a new agenda for academic lawyers by claiming that the defects of the majoritarian process necessitated judicial review to protect those harmed by legislative failure and to serve democracy. Historically, judicial review had been derogated at times for interfering with the will of the people. Yet sometime criticism of courts was different from the larger "intellectual problem of justifying judicial review" that now "gripped the academy nonstop."[18]

In fact, members of the legal process school, associated with Harvard, became obsessed with whether judicial review was undemocratic, an issue that proved urgent for liberals in the 1950s when the Court started to go their way and the executive branch came to seem more conservative. For Henry Hart, Albert Sacks, Herbert Wechsler, Learned Hand, and Justice Felix Frankfurter, the lesson of conservative Supreme Court justices' activism during the progressive era and the 1930s was that the Court should respect the people's democratically elected representatives. They had lived through a period when the public turned on the Court, and much as they appreciated a judiciary that protected their values, "they were sure such an institution inevitably would run afoul of popular opinion" and become a target. They wondered how lawyers could justify the Court's power if law and justice did not appear determinate. Despite realism's interrelationship with the legal process school, most process theorists regarded their own work as a response to realism's failure to provide objective foundations of justice. In their vision, conceiving of law as a form of "social ordering" would not redivide the pie more equitably, but increase its size and leave "all interests . . . better off than they were before," while draining law of the ideological content that created intense conflict.[19]

Process theorists insisted, as Frankfurter said, that the Court they had condemned as a "superlegislature" when conservatives used the despised doctrines of substantive due process and freedom of contract to strike down progressive legislation should not become a "'superlegislature' for 'our crowd.'" They feared that the use of liberal federal courts to circumvent elected conservatives undercut institutional integrity and led to unprincipled opinions.

And they placed more emphasis than legal realism on institutional competence and when judges appropriately should defer to the other institutions also empowered to settle disputes — institutions, process theorists thought, that might demonstrate greater responsiveness to popular will.[20]

This was not to say they would deny judges discretion. The two most celebrated process theorists, Hart and Sacks, for example, insisted judges confronted with the task of interpreting a common law precedent must determine what purpose it served, just as the judge wrestling with a statute should not search for the intent of its legislators but determine its purpose and interpret the statute so as to achieve it. "Purposivism is an attractive alternative to intentionalism because it allows a statute to evolve to meet new problems while ensuring legitimacy by tying interpretation to original legislative expectations." But Hart and Sacks carefully asked their Harvard students, "Is there a danger that a judge who lets himself think this way will tend to arrogate to himself the functions of the legislature? Or, on the contrary, does the successful discharge by the legislature of its own functions depend upon its enactments being interpreted in this spirit?" Though they believed the latter, they worried about the former. That was one reason they so stressed the need for "reasoned elaboration" by judges in opinions. Hart and Sacks hoped that craft techniques and the exercise of creative reason, along with deference to elected branches of government, would promote judicial objectivity at the same time that they recognized its impossibility. Although they never divorced the normative from the positive or advocated an entirely procedural theory of justice, they were obsessed with institutional legitimacy. Therein, they believed, lay society's survival: "[C]itizens have a duty to follow 'duly arrived at' decisions by the state."[21]

Many constitutional theorists at Yale responded, on the other hand, to *Carolene Products* by suggesting that the old Court had simply engaged in the wrong kind of activism. Instead of protecting property rights, the Supreme Court should now safeguard the individual rights that loomed large on the liberal postwar agenda. In a loose way, legal realism became proxy for legal liberalism. Writing on the Supreme Court in a 1947 issue of *Fortune*, Arthur Schlesinger Jr. associated Frankfurter's calls for the Court's restraint and craft with Harvard, labeling the section of his article on the activism of Justice William O. Douglas and others, "Yale on how to be a judge." As Yale's Abe Goldstein said: "Whatever the underlying truth of his characterization, many of us at Yale felt ourselves to be specially charged to use the law to make things righter than they had ever been before." His colleague Fred Rodell launched a perfect salvo of articles in the popular press condemning Frankfurter and his "sycophants" for their preoccupation with "legalism" and saluting Douglas of Yale for his liberalism and intellectual integrity in embracing judicial activism.[22]

Though Rodell frequently embarrassed his more genteel colleagues, many shared his anti-Harvard bias. That did not mean Yale, citing the legacy of realism, taught its students that judges always did more good than elected politicians or that poorly reasoned opinions were acceptable. Indeed, like many elsewhere, Yale professors were working to transform the legal realism of the 1930s and 1940s into a scholarly perspective that melded realism with more conventional conceptions of professionalism to produce a jurisprudence for an age that had endured totalitarianism. But in this Harvard-Yale debate, Yale came across as more court-centered and less craft-concerned than Harvard and more focused on justice. As one Yale professor put it, Justice Stone's theory of judicial review in *Carolene Products* was no more objective than anyone else's, but at least Stone had made "an open declaration of personal beliefs," and judicial candor was "the next best thing" to objectivity, which the realists had shown was impossible anyway.[23]

The Harvard-Yale debate over activism and craft flared anew when the Warren Court relied on social sciences and instrumental reasoning about the importance of education to democracy in outlawing school segregation. *Brown* v. *Board of Education* tested process theorists, who approved of its political liberalism while disapproving of its legal liberalism. In 1958, Learned Hand gave the prestigious Holmes Lectures at Harvard. He approached the lectern at a time when for the first time since the Civil War, Congress was threatening to reduce the Court's appellate jurisdiction because it was at once too activist and too liberal. Nevertheless, Hand criticized *Brown* as judicial legislation, queried the legitimacy of judicial review, and rejected judicial activism on behalf of all but First Amendment rights.[24]

The following year, Herbert Wechsler used the Holmes Lectures podium to defend *Brown* — after a fashion. It was not "a principled decision," he said, "one that rests on reasons with respect to all the issues in the case, reasons that in their generality and neutrality transcend any immediate result that is involved." The result was right, the justification unpersuasive. The Court had simply subordinated one constitutional value, freedom of association for whites resisting integration, to another, freedom of association of African Americans suffering segregation. Though Wechsler described *Brown* as one of the decisions with "the best chance of making an enduring contribution to the quality of society of any that I know in recent years" and spoke up for judicial review, too, he sounded troubled. To him, the case demonstrated the near-impossibility of writing an opinion that justified the choice between two values through reason.[25]

Like Wechsler, Henry Hart cast his lot with *Brown*, but his constant emphasis on craft and institutional competence sometimes led Harvard students to question his politics. When the Court sought to aid minorities by venturing into the vexed political territory of state legislature reapportionment in *Baker* v. *Carr*, a decision that provoked Frankfurter's anguished dissent, Hart's students worried that their critical professor did not notice "the air of jubilation" in his classroom. The editors of the *Harvard Law Review* publicly complained that "[t]he compelling logic of the Frankfurter-Hart school has often appeared to impose a deadening hand; one has felt impelled to choose between rejecting progressive judicial positions for lack of coherent, principled rationales and abandoning the commitment to principle in frank or disguised result-orientedness." They tweaked the faculty by dedicating one issue of the *Review* to Warren. As one member of the *Review* later recalled of the Warren years, "it was understood that Harvard did not speak . . . for the young, who looked to the Court as an inspiration, the very reason to enter the profession." [26]

*   *   *

But Yale did — or, at least, most there told the young it did. To be sure, Yale's resident process theorists, Alexander Bickel and Harry Wellington, added an especially biting dimension to process jurisprudence with their 1957 charge that Warren and Company's sloppy craftsmanship, "opinions that do not opine," subjectivity, and activism threatened the Court's future. Theirs was the indictment Hart cited when he thundered that the Court was functioning "as essentially a voice of authority, settling by virtue of its own ipse dixit the questions that duly come before it." Yet Thurman Arnold contributed to the sense that the disagreement over the Warren Court reflected a debate between Harvard process theorists and Yale realists when he published a feisty rejoinder to Hart.[27]

Paradoxically, as Yale students came to see during the 1960s, despite their school's reputation as the center of realism, process theory mattered enormously in New Haven, far more than the policy science sometimes assumed to be Yale dogma. Indeed, it was Bickel who ensured that process theory would thrive by transforming "neutral principles" into a viable — and realist — theory of judicial review: prudentialism. On the one hand, he famously declared that the "root difficulty" with judicial review was that it was "a counter-majoritarian force in our system" in his 1962 book, *The Least Dangerous Branch*. He downplayed the suggestion of Yale's Robert Dahl that the judiciary generally advanced the interest of the governing coalition; like most law professors, then and now, Bickel had little use for political science. Judicial review seemed to make him, as it did many of his other liberal contemporaries, uneasy. According to Bickel, "when the Supreme Court declares unconstitutional a legislative act or the action of an elected executive, it thwarts the will of representatives of the actual people of the here and now; it exercises control, not in behalf of the prevailing majority, but against it." For that reason, and despite the effort of the Constitution's Framers to blur matters by presenting the judiciary as the agent of the people and a tool of popular sovereignty in *Federalist* 78, "the charge can be made that judicial review is undemocratic."[28]

Yet within pages of introducing his classic epigram, "the counter-majoritarian difficulty," Bickel came round to a more positive view of judicial review. On some occasions, such as *Brown*, Bickel maintained, the Court must inject itself "decisively into the political process." Such instances were "relatively few," and the Court must bank its prestige for them because they were so important. Indeed, the Court should follow Justice Brandeis's footsteps, rediscovering the "passive virtues" and using doctrines such as standing, ripeness, mootness, political question, and nullification of a statute by desuetude to duck cases that might undermine its credibility and ability to fulfill its "grand function as proclaimer and protector" of "principled goals" in rare instances. "No good society can be unprincipled; and no viable society can be principle-ridden," he answered Wechsler. Where the biggest social problems were concerned, there was room for "guiding principle" *and* "expedient compromise." As Gerald Gunther said, Bickel stood for "100% insistence on principle, 20% of the time."[29]

As a Harvard graduate, Bickel originally viewed New Haven as exile. In the late 1950s, he complained that the Yale faculty comprised "the shoddy, the thoughtless, the stupid, the ill-intentioned." His colleagues mooned after "wooly-headed social scientists," he complained. "Just a core of us opposed . . . and we seem like such small-minded unimaginative bastards." But by the time he wrote *The Least Dangerous Branch*, a book he predicted the "'neutralists'" at Harvard would criticize, he had come to acknowledge his debt to legal realism. Yale and realism gave Bickel his intellectual independence. And he used it to protect *Brown*, whose specter haunted *The Least Dangerous Branch*.[30]

Where the Bickel of the early 1960s defended *Brown*, many more at Yale applauded it and the entire Warren Court oeuvre. The school's alumni and faculty members, Charles Black and Louis Pollak, had helped to draft the NAACP's briefs in *Brown*, and Thurgood Marshall "knighted" Black a Negro for his efforts. Black contended that the Fourteenth Amendment forbade "inequality" and "the disadvantaging of the Negro race by law" and that its drafters had certainly "anticipated that the following of this directive would entail some disagreeableness for some white southerners." The task was to use "every governmental power to its fullest extent" to eliminate racism, rather than to worry about which "branch or organ of government is most nicely suited to dealing" with it. In a reply to Wechsler, Pollak insisted that "judicial neutrality" did "not preclude the disciplined exercise by a Supreme Court Justice of that Justice's individual and strongly held philosophy." According to Yale's enthusiastic Dean Rostow, the Court's reliance on social sciences in *Brown* signaled "the triumph of legal realism." [31]

As one of Rostow's future colleagues said, for law professors and other liberals, *Brown* became the "paradigmatic event," representing "*the* turning point in terms of people's conception of what the law could do." *Brown* represented a high point in the era of legal liberalism that Black, Pollak, and Rostow personified. Thomas Emerson did too, when he persuaded Justice William O. Douglas and his colleagues to adopt a right to privacy in *Griswold* v. *Connecticut* that would prove the cornerstone of the right to abortion. [32]

Let Harvard-trained slaves to process thought during the 1950s and 1960s worry that Warren and Company were legislating from the bench and ignoring craft, or charge that *Griswold* was a substantive due process case disingenuously wrapped up in right-to-privacy clothing. In the view of the Yale publicity machine, legal liberalism was the salubrious outgrowth of realism's emphasis on law as one of the social sciences and as a tool of social policy. So successfully did Yale academics align themselves with the view that courts rightly brought wide-ranging social change that students chose to study law in New Haven in part because of its unique connection to the civil rights movement.

Yale's graduates testified to that relationship in both word and deed. Leon Higginbotham left Yale as *Brown* was beginning to work its way up to the Court. He credited its former dean with writing him a letter of recommendation boasting of Higginbotham's prowess in oral advocacy and giving him money to buy a new suit for interviews. According to one study, more than half the members of the Yale Law School class of 1960, quadruple the percentage at any other law school surveyed, believed their professors had emphasized the importance of developing the "ability to use legal techniques to achieve policy goals." The civil rights wing of John Kennedy's Justice Department was full of Yale alumni, from Nicholas Katzenbach and Burke Marshall on down. Eleanor Catherine Holmes, who would become Congresswoman Eleanor Holmes Norton, received her Yale law degree in 1963 and went to Mississippi to work with the Student Nonviolent Coordinating Committee. Told she needed to secure

Fannie Lou Hamer's release from prison, Holmes enlisted the help of a local police chief to keep her out of harm's way, telling him that "I'm from Yale Law School and I've called everybody up there, and I know a lot of folks." Marian Wright left Yale the following year and became the first African American woman to be admitted to the Mississippi bar. The Yale legend was crafted and burnished to appeal to such activists. In contrast, although Harvard law professors' participation in the Kennedy administration lent the school prestige, the placement office showed "little understanding of or support for Harvard Law School graduates going into the social justice world."[33]

"GENE'S BOYS"

In 1965, Dean Eugene Rostow himself symbolized Yale's arrogance, faith in meritocracy, liberalism, and "dress British; think Yiddish" mentality. The polished, well-groomed, and deliberately jocular Rostow took pains with himself and could be overly cute about it. The child of Russian Jewish immigrants, he had been named after Eugene V. Debs, but Rostow and his brother, named for Walt Whitman, were no radicals. Rather, they were the Jewish answer to the Bundy brothers. Walt Rostow was about to replace McGeorge Bundy as Lyndon Johnson's national security adviser, while Eugene Rostow was about to leave Yale to join William Bundy in Johnson's State Department. Eugene Rostow's appointment as Johnson's undersecretary of state for political affairs capped his climb from the lower middle class to Yale College; to Cambridge; to editor-in-chief of the *Yale Law Journal*; to the Yale law faculty, where he had proven a "shovel-carrying Legal Realist"; to its helm, where Rostow had been the only Yale Law School dean to get along with the central university administration since Robert Maynard Hutchins. Meanwhile, stints with the foreign policy establishment, as well as the name he had made for himself when he raised his voice against the internment of Japanese Americans, urged the breakup of big oil companies, and defended *Brown* and the Warren Court, had all burnished his credentials as a Cold War liberal. He believed that the same skills that had enabled him to rebuild Yale would enable him to fix the war in Vietnam.[34]

And "Gene the Dean" had done so much for Yale that some would credit him with creating the modern Yale Law School. Inheriting an institution that had lost a third of its faculty between 1954 and 1956 because of deaths, tenure denials, and voluntary departures, he had organized what he called a "great talent hunt" between 1955 and 1959. Because of his pedagogical innovations,

*Eugene V. Rostow. (Yale Law Reporter, 1970, published by the Yale Law Student
Association. Courtesy Yale Law School.)*

Rostow needed to rebuild and expand quickly. He introduced the tradition
of one seminar-style course for each first-termer, guaranteeing beginners a
"small group" experience in one of the school's only mandatory courses: Contracts, Constitutional Law, Procedure, and Torts. (Students had to take Criminal Law sometime before graduation. Yale was virtually the only law school
not to require Property, which may have contributed to its left-of-center reputation.) Small-group instruction during the first semester, like the lack of requirements afterward, made the school more distinctive. Rostow also ushered
in the divisional program, requiring each student to choose a specialty for serious scholarship. Time-consuming for professors, it was abandoned within a
decade—after the dean had used it, with small groups, to justify doubling the
size of his faculty and promoting many of his professors. Here was another
pivotal moment for Yale. The dean's coup made its student-to-faculty ratio
of 1:17 enviable, particularly in comparison to competitors Harvard and Columbia.[35]

As Rostow said, using a phrase that would later seem irksome, "several hundred men, and several women" were seriously considered for professorships. To the distinguished cadre of senior scholars that remained — Boris Bittker, Thomas Emerson, Grant Gilmore, Friedrich Kessler, Fleming James, Myres McDougal, James William Moore — he added "Gene's boys and girl." Among Rostow's recruits were people who would have a lasting impact on the school in the 1960s and afterward: Alexander Bickel, Charles Black, Robert Bork, Guido Calabresi, Ronald Dworkin, Abraham Goldstein, Joseph Goldstein, Leon Lipson, Ellen Peters, Charles Reich, and Harry Wellington. Rostow hired and/or promoted the school's next four deans. The faculty he left behind, the *National Law Journal* later said, "was as brilliant, diverse and eclectic a group of legal scholars as has ever been gathered at one law school in the country."[36]

It was indeed a remarkable group. Rostow had taken advantage of its senior member's unhappiness at Columbia to prevail upon Charles Black to accept a chair at Yale. Simply to say that Black was a Texan who left graduate study in Classics at Harvard to chase a Russian ballerina, learned Old and Middle English in Yale's PhD program, graduated at the top of his class from Yale Law School while dodging service on its law journal, and had worked with the NAACP Legal Defense Fund did not convey a sense of his uniqueness. Black was also a painter, serious poet, and jazz aficionado, as well as a player of the trumpet, harmonica, and cornet. Ellen Peters was equally special. Having escaped Germany as a child in the 1930s, she graduated first in her law school class at Yale and became only the seventh woman to obtain a tenure-track position at an Association of American Law Schools–approved school, the first tenured woman at Yale, Harvard, or Columbia, and the first woman to serve as chief justice of the Connecticut Supreme Court.[37]

But despite such exceptions, in some ways, the group was not so diverse, as its members' reaction to the student upheavals of the late 1960s would confirm. Rostow's additions largely constituted an age-bounded cohort of individuals who had come to maturity during World War II and begun their teaching careers at Yale. Like Peters, some had fled Europe to escape the "good war" in which many of them had fought. Some had excelled at elite colleges, others at that melting pot, City College of New York. Whether they had attended Yale Law School, as most had, or Harvard, all had compiled superb records and generally served on the editorial board of their school's law journal and had often held prestigious clerkships too. Many had gotten to know each other in college, law school, or while they lived in Washington afterward. Disproportionately Jewish, often of Eastern European descent and from humble households (though some, such as Pollak, a German Jew, came from more privileged backgrounds), many were emphatically assimilationist, wont to joke that sex was a subject for the dinner table, religion for the streets. Like Rostow, most of those who joined the faculty during his deanship were anticommunist liberals until the escalation of the Vietnam War moved most of them, though never Rostow, to question the American mission abroad.[38]

Though Yale Law had never been the radical institution myth made it, the school's professors had stuck their necks out when they served in the New Deal and challenged the House Un-American Activities Committee. The Rostow hires detested McCarthyism, carefully challenged it on occasion, and supported civil rights. Still, the Cold War left its mark. Shortly before Rostow became dean, Yale had refused to promote law professors Vern Countryman and David Haber, citing concerns with their scholarship. Some thought that the decision really reflected dissatisfaction with Countryman's attack on the committee that explored "un-American" activities at the University of Washington and his courtroom defense of Communists. They wondered whether Haber's politics hurt him too. Together, the two actions may have created a local motivation for caution. Obviously, the larger political climate also discouraged dissent.[39]

Charles Reich, who had become acquainted with many of the other Rostow additions in Washington during the McCarthy era, found them and himself to be relentlessly ambitious and politically timid. Like him, they were fearful of taking risks, "extremely averse to any form of activism," and they "ran away" from anything that sounded left. It was vital that nothing suggest "the slightest left-wing or activist thing on your record." It was acceptable to be an Adlai Stevenson supporter who wished the Illinois governor were stronger on civil rights, but one must never sound like Henry Wallace.[40]

Reich also remembered certain affectedness about many who Rostow brought to Yale. Because of the presumed need to lure them away from practice, law professors had long received salaries social scientists and humanists considered princely, particularly since academic lawyers could supplement their income by consulting and producing the treatises and casebooks on which practitioners and students depended. Still, first-generation realists lived relatively simply and were plainspoken. Reich recalled James William Moore—a short, plump, former amateur boxer who wrote the leading treatises on bankruptcy and federal practice—coming by his office at five o'clock each afternoon to ask Reich why he was not leaving: "Haven't you made your dime yet?" As Rostow's recruits moved to large old houses on Saint Ronan Street or New Haven surrounds, entertaining elegantly and sending their children to private schools, they seemed to value wealth and savoir faire. At dinner parties, some spoke a precious legalese, asking partners to "waive your rights to the salt," though they might use Yiddish expressions with other insiders. Urbanity and style mattered to them. Anglophiles, they taught in expensive suits. Long before many Americans had become intrigued with wine, Rostow had made Ronald Dworkin the school sommelier, and the assistant professor regularly ordered the wine for faculty dinners and parties.[41]

For Dworkin, a Harvard law alumnus, Yale was "a place full of stars." He joined the constellation when Stanford and Boalt decided to woo him away from Wall Street. Harry Wellington had been enlisted as a Stanford detractor, and when Wellington mentioned his mission, Guido Calabresi suggested that if Stanford and Berkeley wanted Dworkin, Yale should look at him. In those days, prospective professors did not give a paper. Rather, they answered questions from the faculty at lunch. There, Myres McDougal, who announced beforehand that Yale had hired enough Harvard graduates, charged repeatedly, and Dworkin parried gracefully. Then came the smaller interviews. "So you're Harvard," Dworkin was told repeatedly during the day, as if he had something to live down. Still, all was straightforward until the day's last scheduled meeting, when Bayless Manning and Leon Lipson steered the conversation toward the later Wittgenstein, "though they didn't know much about the later Wittgenstein." When Calabresi came for Dworkin, he sensed it had not gone well. Lipson was "orating in one direction," Manning in another. And sure enough, after others endorsed Dworkin at a subsequent faculty meeting, Manning and Lipson began raising doubts. At this point, Calabresi recalled, McDougal spoke up: "I said I wouldn't vote for another Harvard person, and I'm true to my word so I'm not voting for him, but if any of you vote against him, I'm never speaking to you again."[42]

Though "the rhetoric was against Harvard Law School," Dworkin settled in easily. His forty-odd colleagues were "clever people who spoke well," he remembered. "People emphasized a certain kind of presentation of self and diction," as academics did generally during that period of the history of the American university. Yale law professors spoke in paragraphs and made speeches at faculty meetings. To a later generation, such individuals would seem pompous and pretentious. But Dworkin found the law school a "hothouse" with a rich intellectual life. He remembered wandering down the long "Gothic kitsch" corridors that reminded him of Kings College Chapel and being pulled into colleagues' offices for discussion. "Lunch was just a question of collecting people." He recalled one lunch during the darkest days of the Cuban Missile Crisis, when all opined that "the world would be destroyed very soon." No one predicted that Khrushchev would back down. "We were wrong about everything," he laughed later, but there was a "camaraderie of intellect. It was sort of Athenian." For the right person, Yale Law School was a wonderful club.[43]

*   *   *

To some extent, Bickel, who became one of the group's leading intellectual and political presences, epitomized Yale Law School. The son of scholars, Alexander Mordecai Bickel fled Romania as a fourteen-year-old with his family in 1938 and served as a machine gunner in World War II before enrolling in City College of New York. At Harvard Law School, he was treasurer of the *Harvard Law Review* and he remembered being "a trouble maker" and "a real bad guy." At student-faculty parties, "I'd be the drunk that lurched around and assaulted some faculty member in a drunk way," he said later. "I think my frame of mind was screw you guys, if I'm going to get anywhere here it's going to be in spite of what you think I am and it's going to be because you just can't help it." Perhaps it was his clerkship with Frankfurter that somewhat tamed him. In New Haven Professor Bickel projected a different image. He lived on Saint Ronan and appeared in class in beautifully tailored suits, "Phi Beta Kappa key displayed prominently," hair slicked back. Status mattered to him. With superiors, such as Frankfurter, he was sometimes almost smarmy, and he disliked student challenges to his authority. He wrote with elegance and could talk that way too, though intimates also found him witty, acerbic, and, at times, undiplomatic. A disastrous, brief marriage to a woman apparently on the rebound from another relationship, who left Bickel to resume it, "devastated him." The incident may have intensified an inner insecurity and a fragile ego. "If I had to do it all over again, I'd be more confident," a friend remembered hearing the dying Bickel say. Certainly, Bickel had always taken affronts to his status seriously. Reich remembered how he shook with fury after attending a Yale Commons meal for a visiting British scholar who handed Bickel his coat and tray: Bickel thought he had been "treated like a flunkie, and that drove him up the wall." But whatever his private feelings, Bickel worked to maintain a self-assured exterior. Neither his first nor second wife was Jewish.[44]

Traditionally an anticommunist Democrat, Bickel joined a growing number of Cold War liberals who had begun to speak out against the war in Vietnam by mid-1967. As he put it, "We are the most powerful nation on earth, and are savagely fighting one of the smallest and poorest, and ruining it," and neither the survival of the United States nor its key allies was at stake. Predictably, Bickel jumped Lyndon Johnson's ship at the beginning of 1968. "I know that it is very risky to abandon an otherwise liberal, sitting democratic President,

*Alexander M. Bickel.
(Yale Law Reporter,
1970, published by
the Yale Law Student
Association. Courtesy
Yale Law School.)*

and I am proud to this day of never having been tempted to desert Truman in 1948, but I am sick at heart with the Vietnam War and with all it has done to the country," he said. At first, he supported Eugene McCarthy. When Robert Kennedy entered the race, Bickel did an about-face. By the spring of 1968, Bickel was characterizing Kennedy as "our best hope" and comparing him to Brandeis. Bickel gave himself to the contender "heart and mind" with a dedication that outstripped "any prior political commitment," believing, he wrote in the *New Republic*, that Kennedy "above all other public men would . . . stop war and heal suffering because he had the trust of those whose trust we so desperately need."[45]

That did not mean Bickel had much patience for students to the left of him, some of whom also gave themselves to McCarthy and Kennedy heart and mind. Without a doubt, Bickel felt real sympathy for those who shared his revulsion for the war. Beyond that, his sense of himself as a true political liberal on the national scene may have freed him to display skepticism. Bickel viewed left students as "'phonies,' and he couldn't stand phonies," a friend said. To him, the rebels who wanted to share power with their professors were spoiled brats.[46]

Jurisprudentially, Bickel proved more conservative than many of his students, radical or not. Indeed, his courses, like Wellington's, reminded students that though Yale had ridden the realist bandwagon to fame, process theory coursed deep there. Having coined the phrase "counter-majoritarian difficulty," Bickel occupied a special place in the pantheon of process theorists.

One mid-sixties student, Tom Grey, recalled Bickel denouncing Tenth Circuit judge Skelly Wright for going to Georgetown Hospital, "robes flapping," to order a blood transfusion doctors had determined essential to save the life of a Jehovah's Witness, who had refused to consent to it. The decision, Bickel maintained, represented activism run amok. "[T]his was seen as drawing the battle lines," Grey said. As one of the few southern circuit judges hastening the march of racial equality, "Skelly Wright was the students' hero." Bickel took pleasure in warning those who took his courses that they placed too much faith in federal courts as forces for social change. He liked to needle students that "federal judges were not inevitably 'little Earl Warrens in black robes'"—to which they responded that he could not make them into "little Alexander Bickels in blue jeans." Yet this difference in view, like their teacher's stature as public intellectual, made for a memorable course as Bickel queried students about constitutional law.[47]

To them, he seemed smug. Bickel worshiped in the temple of meritocracy. Law journal editors were treated to cognac and conversation at his house.[48] A double dactyl in the school's newspaper suggested how most saw him in the classroom:

Higgledy Piggeldy
Mordecai Bickelby
Nattily dressed in a
Three-piece with fob.

Barbs he dispenses so
Self-Satisfiedly—
Why doesn't he get a
Toastmaster's job?[49]

Intellectually, as politically, at this stage Bickel was less traditional. His interest, as *The Least Dangerous Branch* revealed, was in history and political science. For all their talk of social science, the first generation of realists often devoted much of their professional lives to untangling—and tangling—vast fields of legal doctrine. They were lawyers who saw the social sciences as tools that could make law more just *and* predictable, thereby increasing its efficiency. However traditionally they might teach, the individuals Rostow hired who did produce scholarship tended to produce relatively interdisciplinary work.[50]

For another example, Joseph Goldstein's interest lay in psychoanalysis. Indeed, his work with his wife, Sonja, herself a Yale law alumna, and with Anna

Freud and others, transformed the field of law, psychiatry, and psychoanalysis and significantly affected criminal law, family law, and mental health. That meant the young viewed him with some skepticism, despite his role in founding New Haven Legal Assistance and his support for clinical education. Goldstein acknowledged great "student resistance" to psychoanalysis. When he spoke of using it to determine the child's best interest in family law disputes, his critics balked, perhaps fearing that "approving the widespread use of psychoanalytic guides will somehow in other contexts empower the state to mold whatever kind of adult the state may want at any given time—button pushers for the new machines, astronauts, or what you will."[51]

Where Bickel could be snide in responding to criticism, Goldstein was simply blunt. His was a froglike voice of unusual candor and rigidity, so much so that one colleague who witnessed Goldstein's frequent "skewering[s]" of others in faculty meetings thought him "slightly mad to speak so simply" and directly about matters that demanded "circumvention" and "tactful deception." He was a person whose "feelings showed in the set of his mouth, the expression of his eyes." While he could seem "loving," he could also display a tough "impatience with human weakness." Asked in an interview by his daughter how his own class and background affected his understanding of child placement in custody disputes, he reproached her for posing a question suited to *People* magazine and "curbstone psychoanalys[is]."[52]

Goldstein resembled Bickel in his liberalism, as well as in his interdisciplinarity. He respected the distinction between public and private, supporting decriminalization of sodomy, minimization of state intrusion into family life in the best interest of the child, as well as the separation of law from politics. Thus at faculty meetings, Goldstein generally sided with Bickel. Indeed, their colleague Guido Calabresi believed that Joe Goldstein and Bickel were the two members of the faculty "most scared and most burned by what was going on in the 1960s." Students on the left challenged them most, perceiving them as liberalism personified, and attacked each in his "weakness, Alex for his dandiness and Frankfurterian pomp, and Joe for the fact that he was so psychoanalytic." Like Bickel, Goldstein obviously felt "threatened."[53]

"Brilliance" mattered most to Bickel, Goldstein, and their colleagues as they evaluated others. The stress on brilliance, measured partly in terms of how nimbly colleagues thought one talked, suggested the Yale law faculty's snobbishness. Indeed, Bickel and some of "Gene's boys" at times disdained the older generation as pluggers or second-rate intellects. They could seem patronizing toward women and others without their credentials, and toward those with them they deemed simply solid.[54] To some extent, Rostow had replicated himself, and those he hired were most interested in searching for more of the same.

SEEDS OF DISSENT

That is not to derogate Rostow's accomplishments as dean. He put the bloom back on Clark's rose. His creative financing enabled the law school to thrive by bleeding the central administration. Many of those he hired were as extraordinary as they thought. Rostow also gave the school intellectual shape. To the irritation of old realists, such as Clark and Arnold, he broadened the school's horizons by self-consciously reaching out to Harvard and Frankfurter-trained process theorists, such as Bickel and Wellington.[55]

Yet despite these accomplishments, the school was experiencing problems in 1965. Rostow's second term proved less successful than his first. When the dean responded to Cornell offers for one of the self-described faculty "barons," Myres McDougal, and his research team by working to promote two of McDougal's protégés, Rostow's attempt "came within inches of breaking us up as a faculty." Though McDougal stayed, Rostow's campaign to take care of the team "left considerable scars," most notably the departure of Grant Gilmore for Chicago in a pique. Prospective junior and senior professors declined offers to join Yale's faculty. And Rostow himself now turned his attention outward, as he mulled the possibility of becoming a judge or joining the Johnson administration. At the same time, the dean irritated his colleagues by signaling his interest in serving a third term.[56]

Rostow had preserved for Yale the place in the hierarchy to which Clark had projected it. This was no small achievement, but as during Clark's deanship, Yale still played junior partner to Harvard. So clearly established was the school's standing as second best that on the first day Rostow's successor entered the dean's office, he found a welcome sign bearing the slogan Avis Rental Cars popularized in its chase after Hertz, "We Try Harder."[57]

The joke was not wholly appropriate. In 1967, Yale was the first choice of some students, who considered it the country's most intellectual law school and appreciated its small size, its favorable student-faculty ratio, and its emphasis on "the interdisciplinary and social policy approach" that some thought would prepare them to become better lawyers, better public servants, or better law professors. But as Rostow himself had lamented a decade earlier, when he asked his colleagues whether Yale was "still known as a country-club" in the nation's colleges, "if the LSAT Ranks have even prima facie meaning, and they do . . . they show that Harvard probably has a better class than we do—a much better class." And as an internal memorandum five years later declared, Harvard was still ahead. Further, most Yale law graduates were headed for law firms. "Myths to the contrary notwithstanding, upwards of 75% of Yale LL.B. recipients go into private practice," the dean's office privately acknowledged. "Perhaps 15% go into government, at all levels; and the small balance are widely scattered—on the bench; in teaching; and a few out of the profession." Even administrators wondered about the extent of the school's commitment to other disciplines: some realized that "our students and faculty have much to gain from the books and people looming on the shores dimly seen across Wall and High Streets, and vice versa." In 1965, Rostow left an institution still overshadowed by Harvard and one less distinctive than its administrators liked to insist.[58]

*   *   *

Dean Rostow's successor, Louis Pollak, was a model of civility, who believed that if Yale Law School "stands for anything, it stands for our shared ability to disagree in friendship." The tall and balding constitutional law professor had no arrogance himself and was a genuinely nice person, at once gentle and wry. Like his father, the distinguished civil libertarian Walter Pollak, who had been one of the first two Jewish lawyers at Sullivan & Cromwell (the other was Walter Pollak's brother), Lou Pollak possessed outstanding civil rights credentials. (His academic credentials were excellent too. Like Rostow, he had been editor-in-chief of the *Yale Law Journal*.) Having attended law school during the postwar period, when Yale "had begun to preen itself on being an extraordinary place, maybe as good as Harvard, and maybe even better because it was rightly based on sound liberal principles, where Harvard was a reactionary tool of the stodgy elements of the profession," he had a firm grasp on what he called the Yale "mythology." He had assisted the NAACP's legal team in *Brown*, helped write the brief in *Cooper* v. *Aaron*, acted as attorney for Yale Chaplain William Sloane Coffin and other Freedom Riders, and served as observer at the 1963 confrontation between Martin Luther King and the Birmingham sheriff's office. A member of the board of the NAACP Legal Defense Fund, he was the professor to see if a student wanted to work with the civil rights group. Pollak had stood with King in Montgomery at the end of the march from Selma. But just as the Selma-to-Montgomery march represented the last gasp of liberal interracialism, so the deanship of the "eminently decent, somewhat paternalistic, and cautiously benevolent" Pollak suggested to stu-

Louis Pollak. (Portrait by Joseph Hirsh, 1973. Courtesy Yale Law School.)

dent and faculty detractors later that liberalism was ill-equipped to deal with the "radical" challenge.[59]

Yale University's new president, Kingman Brewster, probably did not anticipate the tensions between students and professors when he engineered Pollak's selection in early 1965. Brewster was already famous, having made the cover of *Newsweek* in 1964, as he would of *Time* three years later. Descended from Elder Brewster of Mayflower fame, the forty-six-year-old Brewster's "handsome patrician features, his sonorous New England accent, his tailored English suits, and his closetful of sailing trophies from summers on Martha's Vineyard" seemed to make him, as his biographer observed, "born

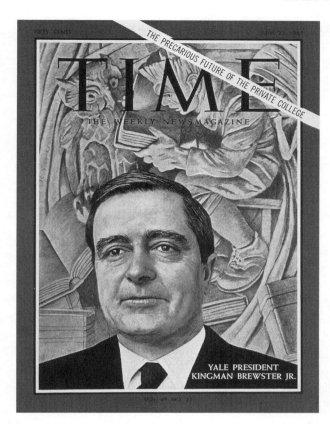

THE PRECARIOUS FUTURE OF THE PRIVATE COLLEGE

TIME

THE WEEKLY NEWSMAGAZINE

YALE PRESIDENT
KINGMAN BREWSTER JR.

Kingman Brewster.
(Time, *June 23, 1967.*
Time-Life
Pictures/*Getty
Images.)*

to leadership." He had Franklin Roosevelt's presidential mien and sense of noblesse oblige. As Brewster said, "privilege always carries its burden of guilt." He resembled Roosevelt, too, in believing reform necessary to avoid revolution. Further, like FDR, he considered "the moral center" he sought "a product of the opposites that press on it from all sides," believing it best formed "by the debates that rage along its edges." Witty, genial, magisterial, elegant, and urbane, Brewster also possessed Roosevelt's "confident gusto" in which Brewster had delighted even when he disagreed with the president. That happened frequently. Brewster's involvement as a Yale College student in America First, the infamous isolationist organization formed on the eve of Pearl Harbor to oppose American intervention in World War II, may have helped to explain the sympathy and shrewdness with which he treated student antiwar activists and Black Panthers during the 1960s: he knew what it was like to rebel against both a war and the consensus. Influential, too, Brewster surely would have stressed, was the civility that had marked the debate between interventionists and isolationists at Yale, "in contrast to the hysteria and acrimony" of their quarrel on the national scene. That was a quality Brewster had also drawn from drinking at the well of process theory as a Harvard law student and professor. Yale's president remembered Henry Hart saying that Fats Waller had summed up the legal process message: "T'aint Whatcha Do (It's the Way Whatcha Do It)." He repeatedly described himself as a "due process radical," maintaining that "if you put some faith in the process, everything would work its way out."[60]

Brewster's own emphasis on civility would mark Yale College more than the law school during the sixties, and make his university "one of the few American institutions of any description that was strengthened rather than damaged" by the turmoil of the times. He steered a middle way between more hardline university presidents, such as Harvard's Nathan Pusey and Columbia's Grayson Kirk, who committed administrative suicide by bringing in the police to punish protesters, and conciliators, such as Cornell's James Perkins, who did so by refusing to call in police when armed students occupied the university. Brewster displayed empathy for the sixties young, who in turn used their yearbook to trumpet that as a student, their King had also turned down the quintessential stamp of approval from the Yale elite, membership in Skull and Bones. Imbued with the reticence of a certain kind of WASP male, Brewster kept his dissenters peaceful by maintaining his temper, listening to their demands, and often making them his own. He showed faith—at times, some thought, too much—in "the decency" of students, professors, and policymaker friends, such as McGeorge and William Bundy, who led the United States deeper into Vietnam. Yale's president belonged to the breed of gentlemanly liberal Republicans that would disappear as the GOP attacked some of the very changes during the sixties over which he and his circle presided.[61]

To date, the law school had been the least of Brewster's worries. His attention had centered on the still-provincial Yale College, where, in his opinion, too many students had been admitted because a relative was "Blue" and too many professors hired because they were. During his tenure, Brewster would build on initiatives launched during the administration of A. Whitney Griswold, whose provost he had been, to reshape Yale to stress "merit rather than background" and redefine "leadership to include individuals from nonprivileged circumstances, minorities, and women." Brewster's plan, in short, was to bring Yale College closer to the way the law school saw itself. (The presence of professors with Yale law degrees did not bother him, for unlike a Yale PhD, a Yale law degree was considered evidence of a discerning mind. Whereas an Old Blue like Brewster had proven his intelligence by proceeding from Yale College to Harvard Law School and excelling there, the ideal Yale law professor did so by acing his courses at Harvard College—which had begun placing more emphasis on an applicant's academic record than his relatives in the 1930s— or at CCNY, before choosing to attend Yale Law School because of its liberal reputation.)[62]

After the faculty refused to approve a third term for Dean Rostow, Brewster formed an advisory committee of Yale law professors. When Brewster also invited faculty members to consult with him personally, some began to suspect that the president intended to meddle in the selection process. As a former law professor at Harvard, he had a long acquaintance with Yale Law School's cast of characters. Nevertheless, the Yale law faculty had grumbled at giving him tenure when he joined Yale's administration, with some characterizing him as "a straight-shooting mediocrity."[63]

Most faculty members would have tolerated Brewster's interference so long as he made Boris Bittker dean, since Bittker was everyone's first choice. But Bittker took himself out of the running. So did Abe Goldstein, who was the second choice of some, though strenuously opposed by others.[64]

*   *   *

The strain of realism so embedded in Yale's halls might have mutated differently had Bittker or Goldstein led the school during the late 1960s. For each advocated a different approach to the student unrest that no Yale law professor had anticipated in 1965. In 1969, when the world had changed, Nelson Polsby wrote Bickel, "Of the things that do not vary significantly from campus to campus, the most striking is the deportment of the faculty." According to Polsby, a political scientist focused on the decline of faculty sovereignty and governance, professors split into several camps. The "faculty-club revolutionaries," who mistrusted the universities, either professed "Rousseau-like ideals" or were "simply Oedipal about any structure of authority." Their models, Polsby said, were "Herbert Marcuse and Stalin." Then came what Polsby called "the Permissives," worshipers at the shrine of Dr. Benjamin Spock, expert in the art of raising children and prominent in the antiwar movement. "Permissives" made statements such as "When our students yell at us 'fuck you,' they are trying to *tell* us something." To Polsby, such remarks captured "the Permissive mind— vaguely guilty, anxious to forgive, utterly defenseless before any demand, any accusation." Then "we have the barricades itself," the metaphorical wall dividing "Revolutionaries" and "Permissives" from people like himself and Bickel. On the other side were "the Liberals." "This term is, of course, one of opprobrium and is sometimes contemptuously applied by Radicals to Permissives."

By "Liberal," Polsby referred to individuals who were strong Democrats in national politics, often members of the Americans for Democratic Action, "but in the university setting [were] reformers, basically believers in the system." As such, they were "institutional conservatives." They found allies in the two rightmost groups, the "Student Haters" and "deep-dyed conservatives who resist reform."[65]

Polsby's characterizations were inaccurate, incomplete, and uncharitable. Radicals did not revere Stalin, and Permissives were not spineless. And as John Griffiths, then an assistant law professor at Yale, observed later, Polsby had said nothing about the "paranoiacs" "who saw brown-shirts marching behind every obstreperous student" or the "frustrated authoritarian fathers" who took out their dissatisfaction with the impact of the sixties upon their children on their students — and, some would say, their junior colleagues.[66]

Still, Bickel thought that his friend was onto something. Responding, he said that at Yale Law School, he could classify "all of my colleagues in one or another of your five groups," but that "time and again," those he respected fell in the "liberal" camp. What Bickel did not recognize was how many of his colleagues qualified as "liberals."[67]

By Robert Bork's recollection, the faculty included only two Republicans — himself and one other, probably antitrust and patent expert Ward Bowman. Bork, Bowman, and, later, their fellow conservative Ralph Winter did not play much of a role in faculty politics during this period. Nor did the students bother such individuals: unlike the "liberals," conservatives had not created the high expectations that enticed the young. Bork recalled that "nothing good was expected" of him and that he was largely left alone. Politically, most professors embraced liberalism, some more enthusiastically than others. With but a few exceptions, such as Rostow, everyone opposed the Vietnam War by early 1968.[68]

Though students tended to see the faculty as a monolith, a clash of cultures was brewing there too. The middle-age faculty members Rostow catapulted into control did feel some pressure from colleagues to their left. But none of the challengers qualified as revolutionary.

Thomas Emerson, "the representative of the Old Left at the Yale Law School," was wary of the New Left, believing it intolerant of dissent.[69] Nor was he an institutional radical. He was simply somewhat more permissive than liberals.

Charles Reich was no radical either. Then in his late thirties, he had already dazzled legal scholars by arguing for the expansion of property rights to include entitlements to benefits distributed by the welfare state. One of his articles would win the most citations in the history of the *Yale Law Journal* and provide ammunition for the Court's procedural due process revolution. As Rostow prepared to leave office, Reich had begun to worry aloud that law schools were "in trouble" for disappointing "idealistic students." He was "known around the school for his liberal views" and for having condemned traditional law school teaching methods as "stifling," and his 1968 course on "Property: Social and Intellectual Perspectives" would draw over a third of the student body. Law students considered him permissive. He was certainly no revolutionary, either institutionally or otherwise.[70]

By the time Polsby wrote Bickel, Reich had begun withdrawing from the law school and turning toward Yale College. By decade's end, he had emphatically distanced himself from his colleagues by publishing his bestseller, *The Greening of America*, dedicated to "the students at Yale, who made this book possible, and . . . their generation." *Greening* celebrated the turn from the meritocratic culture of the Yale Law School faculty, "Consciousness II," to the communitarianism of Yale College students, "Consciousness III." And it exhorted readers to break "the power of the Corporate State" and transform society by recovering themselves and changing the way they lived *now*. "The plan, the program, the grand strategy is this: resist the State, when you must; avoid it, when you can; but listen to the music, dance, seek out nature, laugh, be happy, be beautiful, help others whenever you can, work for them as best you can, take them in, the old and the bitter as well as the young, live fully in each moment, love, and cherish each other, love and cherish yourselves, stay together." As a scholar, Reich's head lay with legal liberalism; *Greening* revealed that his heart lay with the counterculture attack on liberal lifestyles, not with the New Left challenge to liberal politics. The younger professors of the late 1960s were not radicals, either. Two of them, John Griffiths and Richard Abel, were obviously sympathetic to some of the changes students demanded. But neither was anywhere near the forefront of the revolution.[71]

Nor was Pollak as permissive as Bickel and others later believed he had become. The dean took some steps to conciliate students at times. But he remained a liberal.

Bittker, on the other hand, was more permissive than Pollak. The master of the Internal Revenue Code was much like Pollak—genial, wry, and witty. Early on, Bittker had shown sympathy for unusual remedies to end racial injustice. Perhaps because he had been involved with the Old Left as a student in the 1930s, though, Bittker considered himself "one of the relatively few people on the faculty who had much sympathy with the students, at first with the primarily white students who were protesting and then later with black ones. I disliked their tactics very much, but I thought some of the things they wanted were justifiable." He and student agitators respected each other. One "radical" student who worked as research assistant on Bittker's pioneering book, *The Case for Black Reparations*, lauded his professor as "the utopian technician." Because of Bittker's support on the faculty, because he might have been able to mobilize professors who were inclined toward permissiveness, and because he might have appealed more to students, Bittker might have had a better chance for success as dean than Pollak.[72]

In contrast, Abe Goldstein was Bickel and Joe Goldstein's liberal comrade at the barricades, though, unlike Bickel, he made a point of not being "fancy." The son of an immigrant pushcart peddler, Goldstein had grown up on New York's Lower East Side and in Brooklyn. "It never occurred to me that I would ever get here," he reflected later, private institutions such as Yale being "the stuff of dreams and storybooks." But World War II intervened after his graduation from City College of New York. After serving in the army as a demolitions man, a military policeman, and military counter-intelligence agent, Goldstein enrolled in Yale Law School and found "what seemed to me a new meritocracy which was emerging as a result of the GI Bill." He was articles editor of the *Yale Law Journal* and first clerk to David Bazelon, "who had a reputation as a radical judge of that period," and who played a pivotal role in reshaping the insanity defense. Then, as a Washington lawyer during the McCarthy era, Goldstein had established his liberal credentials when he mounted an important challenge to the government's loyalty program. A distinguished scholar of criminal law and procedure who had recently declined a professorship at Harvard because "the existing ties of loyalty and friendship are too strong to be set aside," Goldstein described himself as "a specimen Yale" in integrating law with the social sciences. His 1967 book, *The Insanity Defense*, displayed an encyclopedic knowledge of the literature on insanity in psychiatry and sociology, and a realist's sensitivity to the importance of context. He had thought hard about the curriculum. As an opponent of the Vietnam War and an expert in criminal defense, Goldstein would prove a pillar of support when William Sloane Coffin, who advocated resisting the war through civil disobedience and who assisted students who turned in their draft cards, was indicted and tried for conspiring to counsel, aid, and abet resistance to the draft.[73]

But in Goldstein's case, especially, neither political liberalism, nor enthusiasm for educational experimentation, nor scholarship in law and social science implied a willingness to share power with students. "Compared to Lou, Abe was a much tougher man, sort of a policeman," Dworkin said. Other professors described Goldstein as "judicious," "thoughtful," "powerful," "deter-

Abraham Goldstein.
*(*Yale Law Reporter,
1970, published by
the Yale Law Student
Association.
Courtesy Yale Law
School.)

mined," even "stubborn," while radical students considered him "reactionary." Had Abe Goldstein been dean during the sixties instead of Pollak, one of his colleagues later observed, "the law school would have gone up in flames."[74]

*   *   *

Just as Goldstein had formidable antagonists in 1965, so did every candidate for the deanship who possessed any support except Bittker. Consequently, Brewster decided he had a free hand. The president developed a short list of eight candidates for the law school deanship and took an advisory vote. On that basis, Brewster narrowed the pool further to three internal candidates. One was Bickel, who lacked the personality for the job, as most of his colleagues apparently realized. The second was process theorist Harry Wellington, whom Brewster thought had "more maturing to do." The third was Charles Clark's son, Elias (happily, given his and his family's devotion to Yale, nicknamed Eli), an old friend of Brewster's from Yale College days. The external candidate on the list was an alumnus of Yale College and Law School, Burke Marshall.[75]

After another round of votes, Brewster offered the deanship to Marshall. It was, in many ways, an extraordinary act. Marshall's appointment would have meant going outside, something Yale Law School had not done since 1916. And Marshall was known as a lawyer, not a scholar.[76]

If these were the negatives, there were also positives. At Harvard, Dean Erwin Griswold concentrated on turning out corporate lawyers. Brewster was signaling his desire for a different product, just as he had during his first commencement ceremonies as Yale's president in 1964, when he exhorted graduates to eschew "moral neutrality" and embrace "the intellectual revolution of your time," then awarded an honorary doctorate to Martin Luther King. That had begun his problems with conservative Yale College alumni, who alleged that "Yale was violating institutional neutrality by 'upholding a petty criminal as an example to American youth.'" As assistant attorney general for civil rights during the Kennedy and Johnson administrations, Marshall had become a link between the national government and the civil rights movement. "In times of great struggle and conflict in the South—during the Freedom Rides of 1961, when young people were beaten by angry mobs in Montgomery and when fire hoses and dogs were being turned on people in Birmingham—people always said 'Call Burke,'" John L. Lewis reflected.[77]

To be sure, Marshall also symbolized the federalism of Kennedy, Felix Frankfurter, and the legal process school in his reluctance to sanction federal intervention to protect civil rights workers, lest Washington "start down the path that would lead inevitably to the creation of a national police force." As Marshall himself acknowledged, "the greatest single source of frustration with and misunderstanding of the federal government, particularly among young people . . . [was] federal inaction in the face of what they consider, often quite correctly, as official wholesale local interference with the exercise of federal constitutional rights." Where he maintained that schools and universities had apparently "not taught them much about the working of the federal system," Yale law students insisted that it was Marshall who did not understand federalism. Even so, to many activists, Marshall symbolized the role law could play in achieving equality.[78]

Yet as Brewster, the faculty, and others had predicted, Marshall turned Yale down. And the unease about the commonly mentioned internal candidates remained great. Fearing "bloodshed," Pollak advised Brewster to beg Bittker to take the job. The fear of "bloodshed" surely related to acrimony among faculty members; no law professor yet worried much about student opinion.[79]

Yale's president had a different idea. Convening the faculty, he resurrected Pollak's name from the original list and asked for "a written expression of preference for the deanship" among Bickel, Clark, Wellington—and Pollak. The president then called the law professors together again. Vaguely, and without revealing the preferences, he observed that the "men under consideration were divided only by feathers in the faculty's opinion. He interpreted the vote as one indicating faculty support for any one of the men as Dean; the faculty, that is to say, in effect gave him a choice among possible nominees, as was customary and proper." He then announced he had selected Pollak. "[H]e didn't even allege that Lou was the faculty's first choice," one professor remembered. "And indeed, from the talk around the faculty, although that was quite unreliable, I had the feeling that what was involved was that Lou was practically everybody's second choice."[80]

Guido Calabresi went to Pollak and warned him that because the selection process had revealed the weakness of his backing, he could not succeed as dean. Others were apparently anxious too. Though Wellington thought Pollak a wonderful person, he later recalled that "there was quite a bit of opposition by a number of people" when his appointment was announced, and that "I wasn't very happy about Lou. It seemed to me that he was too interested in making everybody happy." But Pollak took the job anyway, at first delighting some who would later complain he had capitulated to activists. Perhaps because the new dean could not draw on a deep well of internal support, however, some soon found him overreliant on the Brewster administration. That was unfortunate, since Rostow had left the school with a large deficit. Still, at the time of Pollak's appointment, Brewster could justifiably have thought he had appointed the candidate who, because of his identification with the civil rights revolution, was most likely to please the young.[81]

Yet Yale's close connection with legal realism and with legal liberalism, its stress on meritocracy, the collective impression created by "Gene's boys," and the law school's sense of itself as an intellectual treasure chest in which carefully chosen elites interacted in close quarters almost guaranteed that the sixties would hit the school especially hard. The school's emphasis on its realist legacy ensured that it attracted activist students and that they entered with high hopes. And its association with legal liberalism made it an obvious site for one of the intergenerational clashes between "liberals" and "the left" that occurred throughout higher education.

Chapter Three

The Sixties Come to Yale

"[L]iberal as it was, Yale was unprepared for the shock when student radicals first appeared in our midst," Robert Bork remembered. "The change at the law school began abruptly with the class that entered in 1967." To professors, it seemed that "[t]urmoil" had become "the order of the day" as insurgents condemned their failure to display Yale's legendary innovativeness. The sixties came to the law school, brought there by the Vietnam War and dissatisfaction with the classroom. In challenging the status quo, students hoped to become citizens of the school and transform it into a locus of democracy and community, pierce the smugness and elitism of its faculty, and redeem the lost promise of Yale in the 1930s.[1]

"HOW THE YALE LAW SCHOOL FAILS"

Consider 160 first-semester Yale law students, more than 90 percent of them male. During their first semester in 1967, they went from Contracts to Torts to Civil Procedure to Constitutional Law almost daily. Compared to students at other law schools, they were fortunate in some ways. At other institutions, the entire first-year curriculum was mandatory. At Yale, though three of the required first-term courses were taught to classes of between seventy-five and ninety, they studied the fourth in a "small group" of fifteen to eighteen students.[2]

Nevertheless, and despite the law school's preservation of a clubby atmosphere by providing waiters who served the students meals, Yale could also seem extraordinarily competitive. At other law schools, the first set of exams usually came at the end of the first year; at Yale, at the end of the first semester. Elsewhere, one's entire career depended on how one performed the first year, for that determined law journal membership and clerkships. At Yale, "the first semester settled everything forever" and was, as Charles Reich said, "indelible." As a result, the atmosphere inside classrooms was tense. When James William Moore called upon an individual in Civil Procedure, he or she stood. Each classroom was an autocracy in which the professor "determined the parameters of the discussion, called on people to respond and ruled on the relevancy of any student comment."[3]

Where once a student would have tolerated, in the parlance of a later generation, a professor "in his face," such treatment now seemed wrong. In a 1950s book that became required reading for the restless, Paul Goodman had stressed "how it is desperately hard these days for an average child to grow up to be a man, for our present organized system of society does not want men": men thought for themselves. Society and its schools, he contended in *Growing Up Absurd*, transformed "bright lively children with the potentiality for knowledge, noble ideals, honest effort, and some kind of worth-while achievement . . . into useless and cynical bipeds, or decent young men trapped or early resigned, whether in or out of the organized system." By the mid-1960s, Goodman was describing middle-class students as the country's "exploited class," and Students for Democratic Society was turning its attention to radicalization of students, characterizing them as "the new working class." Toward decade's end, A. S. Neill's *Summerhill School: A New View of Childhood* became must reading for intellectually curious students too. At Summerhill, the children's school Neill founded, lessons were optional, teachers need not "refuse to be people of flesh and blood," and students and teachers made the rules governing the school together. Experimental colleges with similar ideals, such as UC Santa Cruz, which shunned letter grades and emphasized the importance of fostering learning through close relationships between student and teacher, were flooded with applicants.[4]

More generally, talk of democracy and citizenship had been in the air in many college and universities since Berkeley's 1964 Free Speech Movement, which had stressed both. As at Berkeley, students were demanding to know whether they possessed the rights of citizens on campus. Their rebellion against administrators' insistence that they acted in loco parentis and against the imposition of parietal rules was underway too. "On almost every campus, students are either attacking *in loco parentis*—the notion that a college can govern their drinking, sleeping, and partying—or happily celebrating its death," *Time* declared. The times and its own progressive reputation made Yale law professors vulnerable to demands the faculty should reconsider its relationship to students.[5]

*Duncan Kennedy. (*Yale Law Reporter, *1970, published by the Yale Law Student Association. Courtesy Yale Law School and Duncan Kennedy.)*

*   *   *

Duncan Kennedy's much-circulated critique of legal education, "How the Yale Law School Fails — A Polemic," represented the first extended attempt to articulate student dissatisfaction. The child of Stevenson Democrats and a graduate of Andover and Harvard College, Kennedy had worked in an anticommunist CIA-front organization before entering Yale Law in 1967. He had, he cheerfully admitted, nearly impeccable "ruling class" credentials. Kingman Brewster was the brother of Kennedy's stepmother, and Kennedy presented the screed he wrote about his first year at law school to his step-uncle at a family gathering as a "taunting joke."[6]

The polemic possessed the energy and intensity of a piece written quickly. Kennedy's theme was alienation from his professors, and his reliance on the vertical pronoun symbolized a break from their studied rationalism. At times, he characterized the relationship between teacher and student as one of priest and acolyte; at others, as one of lovers locked in a destructive relationship; at still others, as one of fathers and sons. And because everyone considered Kennedy brilliant, the polemic had to be taken seriously.

Kennedy decried the "truly extraordinary narcissistic phenomenon" of the Yale law professor, who "preen[ed]" before his classes. While acknowledging that "most teachers at the Law School love their students, and in a way which is admirable," he contended that there was "something deeply corrupting about the daily exercise of a license to inflict pain." In addition to breeding an atmosphere of "collective terror" in the classroom, professors thrived on terrorizing the individual, as anyone could attest, who had suffered the various "elements of fear: (a) the teacher will ridicule you; (b) the teacher will disapprove of you; (c) fellow students will ridicule you; (d) fellow students will disapprove; (e) the teacher will not deal with material in a comprehensible way; (f) the teacher will demonstrate to you that you didn't understand the material when you studied it; (g) the teacher will raise issues that will frighten you because you haven't dealt with them before; (h) the teacher will discover you have not studied the material assigned." Those forms of fright rendered the law student "defenseless before a person who has a demonstrated desire to hurt him."[7]

Though less eloquent, the empirical data bore out Kennedy's observations. In studying first-year Yale students, the school's own Robert Stevens found that "the most frequent complaint" about "the case class and Socratic method" related to "its perceived tendency to demean and degrade students." Eighty percent also reported that "law school teaching methods created classroom anxiety for themselves or others." According to Stevens, they characterized the professor "as a 'fearful trial court judge,' 'an inquisitor,' or a 'pounding . . . adversary.'"[8]

The problem was not that law, by nature, was "cold[er]" than other disciplines, Kennedy said, but what professors did with it. "If English literature were taught as law is, and by professors with the same complex of emotions toward their students and their work, I do not doubt for a minute that it too would be seen by students as 'inhuman.'" Some professors managed to maintain an atmosphere of good humor, as did one of Kennedy's heroes, Friedrich Kessler, a master of both the Socratic method and contract law. Kessler, who believed that "a great teacher needs to be a moral being first and foremost," routinely and "benignly" told the errant student: "That's beautiful, beautiful, Mr. Smith; fancy footwork—but you couldn't be wronger." Other teachers were simply snotty.[9]

Kennedy wrote more sympathetically about his fellow students, but they came in for their share of the blame. "Students in first year classes at the Law School are rapt as no other students I have ever seen." They proved "as cruel if not crueler than the teachers," howling gleefully as their classmates were "dismembered." They were a mass of contradictions. According to Kennedy, they proved "so emotionally enthralled by the process going around them" that they lost their cool and became befuddled, displaying "an astonishing humility" to their teachers. Yet most repeatedly asked themselves one question about their professors through their first year: "Why am I taking this shit from them?" And Kennedy seemed certain each of his fellow students wondered whether it was "acceptable, after years spent dealing with the complicated emotions inevitably involved in the relations of aggressive and intelligent young men with their fathers, to plunge oneself into an essentially paternalistic community where the route to success is to establish yourself firmly in the affections of powerful older men."[10]

The experience not only created classes Robert Stevens acknowledged most Yale first-years found "more stifling than liberating," but scarred students as well. Kennedy deplored the withdrawal of the lower half from "the hostile pressure . . . into almost comatose passivity . . . before even the most outrageous, or fascinating statement made in class" or into a "quiet contempt tinged with cynicism for the whole business." Stamped with a sense of "academic inadequacy," these students shied away from their professors, considering themselves undeserving. As one first-year told Stevens, "[y]ou go from that [college] atmosphere where you are encouraged to do a lot of writing, you do a lot of independent work, making a continual effort . . . and bang, you are thrown into a big class where you sort of stick your neck out when you say something." (Only someone educated at an elite institution, perhaps, would have lodged the first part of this complaint.) This one maintained that most learned not to "open their mouths because they see they are going to get their heads chopped off" in law school. And students at the top were bruised too, Kennedy said. Prefiguring his later attack on the possibility of separating the public from private, he proved equally critical of the successful and engaged, who sought to create a refuge from school by building "a 'private self' as a counter-model to the 'public self,' . . . as though it were really possible to turn selves on and off like faucets." Such an attempt at compartmentalization could only cause perversions of both selves.[11]

The "boring and dead" classes also meant that "the Yale Law School fails miserably to live up to its academic and intellectual pretensions." Kennedy complained that the school lacked "the feeling of intellectual tension which comes of the confrontation of ideas in the process of growth," a quality Yale "notoriously had" in the 1930s. He condemned its professors as "bizarrely parochial." Despite the "more 'sexy' aspects of the Law School's reputation," the Yale law student who read the Harvard catalogue might have "the feeling that Harvard is Yale and Yale Harvard." [12]

Except for the self-described "radicals," however, whom Kennedy identified with the New Left, he believed few students wanted to transform the school. Still, though there were not all that many "radicals" in the school, he characterized their impact as "great." As one of his classmates observed, the "straighter students" generally "lionized" them. And, Kennedy maintained, they frightened the faculty. While professors "constantly" questioned left students' "'representativeness,'" implying they were "a mere handful . . . intoxicated with utopian concepts who probably should not have been here in the first place," faculty members also made "frequent embarrassed jokes about the likelihood of confrontations, an end to 'rational discourse,' mobs, demagoguery." Kennedy considered the "constant jokes about revolution" a tip-off that professors sensed their classes were not dead simply because students were bored stiff. And he thought the left deserved more credit: "The radicals are highly representative in the sense that their active protest expresses feelings which almost all students share in one complicated variant or another" and pointed up "the underlying problem of *being* at the Law School." [13]

Radicals denounced "competition," "selling out," and irrelevance in the curriculum and preached institutional transformation. Those were hardly novel complaints, Kennedy noted. "What makes the radicals important," he said, "is that they have an explanation—albeit a simplistic one—and are committed to action to bring about change." They blamed Yale's problems on "the structure of the institution and especially the distribution of power in it," and they were working to increase "participation" in the school and to construct a "counter-community" within it. [14]

Then a self-described "liberal," young Kennedy did not subscribe to the "radical" solution. He did not consider structural change a substitute for "an attack on the underlying forms of human relations which give the structure its meaning." (By the time he published the polemic, he had denounced liberalism, decided resistance must begin at the local level, and decreed transformation of institutional structure worthwhile.) The focus should be on making professors "less hostile" and students "less passive," even if, as a result, "the Yale Law School might turn out a marginally smaller number of Under-

Secretaries of State." The real breakthrough, he believed, would come when the "psychic territory" was changed and "students and faculty treat each other decently."[15]

*   *   *

The efforts of students to achieve Kennedy's modest goal, and the real trouble, began when Kennedy's colleagues in the class of 1970 entered Yale. Doubtless, some made the decision for law school to obtain a graduate school deferment that would exempt them from going to Vietnam. Some may also have thought a law degree would come in handy. More than a quarter of the members of the class of 1970 told Robert Stevens that they had not intended to practice law when they entered, twice the number at any other school and twice the percentage of Yale students in 1960. Many had been politically active before starting law study. In some cases, that involvement had moved them to apply to law school. One first-year had been jailed in Mississippi when he went South to work in the civil rights movement. "It's not the worst place in the world, there's a bed to lie on and there's food and everything, but you can't open the door and go out when you feel like it," he recalled of prison. "And I remember thinking, the people who know how to open that door are the lawyers."[16]

The doors he pushed open at Yale Law School stood just a few blocks from the ghetto. Thanks to the work of its Democratic mayor, who knew how to make Washington pay for urban and "human" renewal, the Great Society liberals surrounding Lyndon Johnson had once hailed New Haven as "the greatest success story in the history of the world." But racial violence had swept the city for four days in August 1967, and tension between the black community and the police and the mayor's office had climbed in its wake. Although it did not yet possess a chapter of the Black Panthers, the city did house the Hill Parents Association, which rightly considered itself more "militant" than other local civil rights organizations. Under the leadership of Fred Harris, the Hill Parents Association had effectively called attention to the poor conditions of local public schools and housing, as well as police harassment of African Americans, and had staged demonstrations to demand changes in the welfare system. As some law students who became involved in the association noticed, Yale liberals who had "rush[ed] all over the South some years ago in the sit-in demonstrations" had "not lifted a hand" to improve conditions for their African American neighbors.[17]

Whatever students' politics, by the fall of 1967, the war surrounded everything for almost all of them. Vietnam permeated every aspect of law school life. A spring 1966 poll of Yale University students had shown strong support for the Johnson administration's Vietnam policy. But everything had changed. By 1967, "a dark cloud had moved in," and hatred of the war fogged the old objectives of academic and social success. Though most professors clearly shared their feelings, Brewster's remained a question mark. "We know the country is in trouble," he told students at the beginning of the fall term. The president's objections to the war at this point, however, remained quiet, in part because so many of his friends directed it. But the students cut him some slack, perhaps because he was a Rockefeller Republican rather than a liberal Democrat.[18]

Meanwhile, Yale law alumnus Allard Lowenstein had launched the movement to deny Lyndon Johnson renomination. Despite Lowenstein's "deep and transparent devotion to Robert Kennedy," his candidate was Eugene McCarthy because Lowenstein could not then persuade Kennedy to enter the race. By fall 1967, the idea of dumping Johnson had caught fire: Lowenstein had accurately sensed the despair the left wing of liberal Democrats felt about the war. His focus on winning mainstream support for the antiwar cause set him apart from radicals, with their more broad-ranged critique of American institutions. Lowenstein's idea of a good protest involved clean-shaven young men singing "The Star-Spangled-Banner" and claiming the mantle of patriotism.[19]

Others elsewhere on campus advocated a more oppositional approach. Doug Rosenberg and Rick Bogel, two Yale graduate students active in the northeastern antiwar group known as the Resistance, would soon announce that in October, antiwar activists all over the country would turn in their draft cards. Rosenberg and Bogel viewed this act of civil disobedience, which would likely lead to arrest, as a more vigorous way of protesting the war than marching against it. But because turning in a draft card was also less provocative than burning it, the protest possessed the potential to mobilize middle-class students made passive by deferments. In 1967, Resistance methods were radical for Yale. As University Chaplain William Sloane Coffin said, when Rosenberg and Bogel disclosed their plans, "you could feel stomachs contracting all over the Law School auditorium." The director of Selective Service, General Lewis Hershey, would soon announce that any individual who "abandoned or mutilated" his draft card would be drafted at once, while those who obstructed recruitment or interfered with the operation of their draft boards would be immediately prosecuted. While Brewster, a member of the National Advisory Commission on Selective Service, did not favor civil disobedience to resist the war, he successfully protested Hershey's decree on behalf of Ivy League presidents, insisting that "fundamental values of due process of law will remain in serious jeopardy unless you make it clear the draft is not to be used as punishment and that draft boards are not to become extralegal judges of the legality of acts of protest."[20]

But the price of defiance still remained high. Whatever the government's stated policy, some draft boards viewed protest less sympathetically than others. Further, those who turned in their draft cards were subject to FBI investigation. And to most, it seemed evident that no law student who turned in his draft card "had more than a prayer of ever being licensed as a lawyer," just as no graduate student in physics who did so would be able to win a government clearance. Though Coffin presided over numerous events at which individuals turned in their draft cards, he warned one Yale law student who wanted to surrender his against being "a fool."[21]

The larger issue of guilt lay behind that of draft resistance, and guilt permeated higher education. Brewster publicly lamented that the burden of the draft was born disproportionately by "those who cannot hide in the endless catacombs of formal education." That did the university no good; better to lessen its "corruption" by choosing those who must go to Vietnam by lot, as Richard Nixon would begin doing near Christmas of 1969, and make broad provision for conscientious objectors. As one SDS leader said of Yale, "I was there because otherwise there was this guy named Lyndon Johnson trying to kill me, and college was the best place to hide," but by providing students with a hiding place, the university "made us hate it. That was another side of its hypocrisy."[22]

The Johnson administration soon began to address the problem. It announced an end to automatic deferments for graduate students who were not enrolled in medical, dental, or divinity school. Any other graduate student who had not completed two years of school would be eligible for the draft. That meant that as a group, law students in the class of 1970 were the first to face the end of graduate student deferments and the threat of going to Vietnam. Turn in their draft cards, and they would surely come to the attention of their draft boards, which might well turn their cases over to the FBI for investigation, send them off to Vietnam, and risk their professional futures.[23]

Thus the war helped ignite the sixties for Yale law students in the class of 1970. They were not alone in their fear. The editors of the *Columbia Law School News* highlighted the uncertainty that confronted almost all male law students when they expressed the hope that "the pulchritudinous 23 member female contingent of the first year class" would enjoy its legal education. "We would extend the same welcome to the rest of the class but for the seeming futility" because of the "announcement that at the end of this year their deferments will not be renewed and they will go to other places." By spring 1968, the Yale admissions dean would be predicting that half of the first-year class would be drafted. He overestimated, but ultimately the class of 1970 would lose more than 20 percent of its members to the war over the summer.[24]

First-year students had long experienced legal education as surreal. But anxiety about their futures increased their sense of having stepped through the looking glass. And Kennedy's polemic indicated other reasons for tension, such as the rise of "radicalism." First-years felt as if professors were "on another planet."[25]

"PANIC"

Their teachers sensed that. The faculty had ensured that college graduates with a social conscience would hail Yale Law School as a haven. But by the late 1960s, some of the "radicals" of whom Kennedy spoke were coming to think that law did not necessarily make society better, which made their school seem even more absurd. In the early 1960s, "to be trained in the law, for those with a social conscience, was to be trained to create change," one member of the class of 1970 said. "In 1964 we elected a liberal President, pledged to a Great Society and to a peace in the Vietnam War." But since that election, "[t]he best of a whole generation of Americans have been gassed in the streets." (Like their teachers, Yale law students had high opinions of themselves.) And since they took constitutional law in their first semester, Yale students saw the Warren Court, their school's beacon of social justice, reacting in questionable ways to that "gassing" from the beginning.[26]

As some came to recognize, sometimes the Court legitimated the status quo in the very act of upsetting it. Nowhere was that more evident than in an area both the Warren Court and Yale claimed as their special domain, civil rights. Charles Black understood why the Court's civil rights decisions bred skepticism among his students about whether law was "apt for doing any useful work at all." Since *Brown*, "law by its only known means—judicial decisions, statutes, administrative rulings—washed out of its fabric every trace of racism—or as nearly as that is possible in human political action." Nevertheless, Black acknowledged, African American discontent had only increased because ending segregation in law did not finish it in fact, and "surely there is a great deal in the assertion that law, having made so fair a start, has simply failed to solve the problem of a racism fatally linked by history with a poverty with which law knows not how to deal."[27]

Black readily admitted, then, that law had not solved all the problems he and other legal liberals had hoped it would. He did not concede a deeper rea-

The Yale law faculty in the late 1960s. Standing, left to right: *John Simon, David Trubeck, Arthur Leff, Daniel Freed, Lung-chu Chen, Robert Bork, Henry Poor, Ralph Winter, Arthur Charpentier, Christian Determann, John Hart Ely, Lee Albert, Ward Bowman, Gordon Spivak, Larry Simon, Robert Stevens.* Seated, left to right: *Quentin Johnstone, Elias Clark, Harry Wellington, Alexander Bickel, James William Moore, Ellen Peters, Fleming James, Myres McDougal, Eugene Rostow, Louis Pollak, Abraham Goldstein, Friedrich Kessler, Ralph Brown, Thomas Emerson, Joseph Goldstein, Leon Lipson, Joseph Bishop, Boris Bittker. Among those absent are Richard Abel, Charles Black, Marvin Chirelstein, Jan Deutsch, Ronald Dworkin, Steven Duke, William Felstiner, John Griffiths, Robert Hudec, Jay Katz, Harold Lasswell, George Lefcoe, Charles Reich, Fred Rodell, and Clyde Summers. (Manuscripts and Archives, Yale University Library.)*

son for skepticism about legal liberalism and the Warren Court — that law had not "made so fair a start." The charge that liberals worked to avert revolution by introducing changes aimed at satisfying the have-nots with "half a loaf" was a staple of the left critique of American reform during the 1960s. By this analysis, the Warren Court handed a victory to the disenfranchised by lifting the lid off the pot and awarding constitutional rights in *Brown.* The left could point out that the consciousness of new rights helped reconcile minorities to their exploitation and allowed them to believe they were participating in a narrative of progress and vindication. Further, the Warren Court then delayed implementing those rights until the kettle had boiled over.

And sometimes, particularly where the war was concerned, the Court intentionally upheld the status quo. In Thomas Emerson's course, students of the
late 1960s would read Warren Court decisions upholding statutes prohibiting
flag desecration and the burning of draft cards. Emerson, the first to stress the
distinction between "expression" and "action" for First Amendment purposes,
implicitly condemned the opinions. According to him, when communication
involved both expression and action, as flag desecration and draft card burning
did, it deserved First Amendment protection if "the element of expression was
the essential feature in [the] conduct and the element at which punishment was
directed." Yet Emerson rued the claim of Herbert Marcuse and the New Left
that "the system of freedom of expression is a meaningless sop, designed to
siphon off protest and delude the populace into believing it has a participating
voice." Though contentions that democracy veiled and perpetuated tyranny
possessed "some factual foundation," they provided no justification for "the
position that the system should be ignored, opposed, or discarded," Emerson
argued.[28]

Some would have considered his assessment the ultimate lawyer's trick, con-
fession and avoidance. "For students who have experienced the . . . countless
number of demonstrations, protests and draft resistance movements that have
struck almost every campus in the country[,] the refusal of the law to accord
the same degree of constitutional protection to symbolic conduct that it has
conferred upon conventional speech is an insistence that lawful speech be lifeless speech," one *Yale Law Journal* article said. Thus when the Warren Court
failed to give First Amendment protection to symbolic expression, it tamped
down "a new politics, however neutral the legal rhetoric in which the policy of
repression is wrapped may appear."[29]

Yet strikingly, Yale law students often let members of the Warren Court off
the hook. When Kathy Boudin wrote her *Bust Book* to counsel protesters on
how to behave after arrest in the late 1960s, she attacked rights. "To rely on
'legal rights' is to ignore entirely the fundamental reality of a class society, that
when those 'rights' have been granted by a ruling elite, those same 'rights' can
and will be ignored when their use threatens the power of those who granted
them," she said. But Yale Law School had refused to admit Boudin, and "true"
radicals rarely went to law school during this period.[30]

Thus the Warren Court helped provide the glue that would hold the school
together in the late 1960s. Dissatisfaction with the Court there sometimes was.
Where students of the mid-1960s defended the Court from Bickel, some came
to challenge it later. Nevertheless, the Warren Court never came in for the opprobrium heaped upon its partner in liberalism, the Johnson White House. For

all the Court's imperfections, those studying law at Yale and elsewhere saw it and, more generally, the federal courts as symbols of hope.[31]

They displaced some of their frustration with legal institutions onto the faculty. Although their professors saw themselves as part of an "interlocking directorate" with the Supreme Court justices whose work their scholarship bolstered, students viewed teachers more critically. Familiarity bred suspicion. And professors who had applauded student activism aimed at opponents of civil rights disliked becoming its target.[32]

Like others, Charles Black came to sense the young's mistrust. And from a legal liberal's perspective, his answer was eminently sensible: law professors should stand ready to help those who aimed at "the jugular of social injustice" to sharpen their knives, as long as the young believed that "the best possible training in thought" was "the right whetstone." But students who sought more immediate action and relevance did not belong behind the desks. While Black possessed some sympathy for those who would "change our law schools into agencies of social action," he labeled their aim unsound. Its implementation would unsettle institutions, "where, to the highest degree possible in our culture, men think carefully, write and teach about the rational governance of our polity." The distinguished law schools of the United States were a "supremely precious . . . national asset," which must be maintained.[33]

To a man, the Yale law faculty in 1967 was convinced that the asset it safeguarded and embodied was "supremely precious." Traditionally, their students had agreed. But as the attitudes of the young changed, beginning in 1967–68, the words professors spoke to students, like those uttered by students to professors, often seemed shrill and strange.

Black confessed publicly that as he and many of his colleagues confronted student activists they felt not just "discontent," but "panic." They discerned an "anti-intellectualism" among those entering law school. Black openly criticized students' "mystique of 'involvement,'" their emphasis on the relevant, their dedication to "action," which made "thought . . . ancillary." As another Yale law professor said, "No one seemed to give a damn about what we were teaching." From the faculty's point of view, what little interest the students did show was devoted to criticism, and the young demonstrated little in scholarship, either. A later generation of students, for example, would find Black's advocacy of structural interpretation in constitutional law in the 1960s inspirational. But at the time, one student reviewer in the school newspaper dismissed his book introducing structural interpretation as a padded, "readable ten-page article" that contained "too many comfortable words and nice thoughts and not enough disquieting words and unpleasant ideas." So, too, one

Yale Law Journal editor scorned Goldstein's *Insanity Defense* for devoting "too much attention to patching up the status quo and too little to considering the need for and possibility of an approach qualitatively different from the present regime."[34]

"ONE MUST CHANGE FIRST WHAT ONE KNOWS BEST"

The new newspaper underscored the gulf between professors and students. The first issue of the *Yale Advocate* was the work of first-year Richard Hughes. Raised in "a very conventional Southern family, not particularly well-off," Hughes had considered himself "quite the liberal growing up." His parents had refused to allow him to accept a full scholarship to Yale College, believing it "a hotbed of rad-lib sentiment." When Hughes arrived in New Haven for law school in 1967, after graduating from the University of Virginia, where he edited the newspaper, the contrast between New Haven and Charlottesville seemed "pretty stark" and the ferment at Yale Law School "dizzying." Hughes became "quickly involved in the activist wing at the law school," an experience he later described as an "intellectual revelation." Soon after fall term began, he saw an announcement of a meeting for those interested in starting a law school newspaper. Though only three people attended, "we decided that we could get this thing started."[35]

In both 1967–68 and 1968–69, Hughes would serve as one of the *Advocate*'s two editors. The first issue, which appeared on December 11, 1967, announced that tuition was higher at Yale than at any other law school. It mocked the school's claims to be "[v]ery progressive, realistic, policy-oriented — a DYNAMIC institution." It reported on steps by members of the Yale Chapter of the Law Students Civil Rights Research Council to investigate police behavior during "the August riot in New Haven." It called attention to the critics of the draft law and condemned the abstruseness of the Warren Court's privacy decisions. It endorsed the candidacy of Eugene McCarthy, maintaining that the senator "provides the only focus for dissent [against the war] within the established political framework of the nation." At Yale, as elsewhere, control of a newspaper would prove crucial to the student movement. And the array of topics raised in the first issue reflected an ongoing discussion among students about the ideal focus and means of achieving social change.[36]

Should Yale law students concentrate on the "Yale Citizens for McCarthy Committee" formed at the law school, sue General Hershey, and launch a voter registration campaign? After all, few were ready to turn in their draft cards.

The Yale Advocate

Vol. I, No. 1   YALE LAW SCHOOL, NEW HAVEN, CONNECTICUT   December 11, 1967

Tuition At YLS Highest In U. S., Pollak Believes

Law School Dean Louis H. Pollak has announced "with regret" an increase in the tuition of Yale Law School, from $1900 per academic year to $2150. Mr. Pollak says this makes Yale "The most expensive law school in the country," as far as he knows.

Those now receiving financial aid will most likely receive additional aid to meet the extra expense, Mr. Pollak suggested.

May It Please The Court . . .

MOOT COURT — The Thurman Arnold Prize Argument, capstone of the fall moot court competition, was held December 2. Winner was David Rigney, '69L, counsel for petitioner. Kent Morrison, '69L (shown above), won honorable mention. The Prize Bench which heard the case, Jones v. Mayer, included, l. to r., federal district court judge Caleb M. Wright; New York Court of Appeals judge Kenneth Keating; federal courts of appeals judges J. Skelly Wright (partially hidden) and Wilfred Feinberg; and Harvard professor Archibald Cox.

Group Forms Here To Back McCarthy

Last Tuesday night a "Yale Citizens for McCarthy" committee was formed at Yale Law School. The committee, composed largely of law students, is intent on getting support for McCarthy's candidacy from faculty and students through the Yale Community. It will expand its board to include representatives from each of the 12 colleges at Yale, from each of the graduate schools, and from the faculty.

"There are many reasons to support McCarthy at this point," says Eugene Moen, one of the board members, "the most obvious of which is that he is the only candidate to actively oppose Johnson's policies in Vietnam."

Committee members believe that McCarthy's candidacy, as a respected political figure, is bound to have a good effect. A successful showing in the primaries in Massachusetts, New Hampshire, or Wisconsin may:

1. open up the Democratic convention as far as its platform on the war and on candidacy,
2. influence the Republican nomination, possibly encouraging the candidacy of Rockefeller or Percy,
3. influence Johnson's policies in Vietnam.

Chairman of the committee, Jim (Cont. On Page 3)

"It's essentially a matter of 226.N.W.2d costing more than 225 N.W.2d," explained the Dean. The new rate will apply for the 1968-69 academic year.

"But the need arises not just from the additional expense of buying books," continued Mr. Pollak. "Salaries must be raised across the board to meet the levels of the other law schools."

At present, he said, Yale Law School faculty salaries are slightly below those of a few other major law schools. The increased revenue from tuition is expected to help meet salary raises.

Moreover, more funds are needed to expand the size of the faculty as well as insure its quality. As the Dean explained, "In our case the increase in expenses are compounded because we are trying to enlarge the size of the faculty while keeping enrollment at its present size."

Historically, law schools have been among the cheapest graduate schools to run since they tolerate higher teacher-student ratios than the others and require little more than that expenditure other than for books. But in this regard Yale Law School is not like the other schools.

Says Dean Pollak, "We have always had the cost of keeping the teacher-student ratio at Yale particularly low." This makes an enormous difference in the cost per student of running the school.

Harvard Ratios

Harvard Law School for example, where the teacher-student ratio is about 1:25, can operate much more cheaply, in terms of cost per student, than Yale Law School, where the ratio is about 1:18. And Yale Law School's goal is a ratio of 1:12 or 1:13, Mr. Pollak added.

Efforts at raising funds continue at all levels. "Just because we're increasing tuition doesn't mean we aren't actively soliciting funds from other sources," emphasized the Dean. "The recent Russell Sage Foundation grant is an example of that. And so is the very gratifying increase in the rate of alumni giving over the last few years. Two years ago gifts from alumni totalled about $125,000; last year they were $150,000; and this year they are expected to reach $175,000." Mr. Pollak suggested, however, that the average gift per alumnus of Yale Law School is substantially (Cont. On Page 3)

First-Year Students Will Face New Legal Aid, Forensic Plan

Having cleared an initial hurdle of student antagonism, a new program of legal service and forensic activities for second-term students appears ready to be put into operation, at least for what those who have any idea as to how it will work call a "trial run."

The program provides the former requirement that all second-term students take part in moot court for one semester of credit with a requirement of two semesters of ungraded credit which may be fulfilled by participation in moot court, Barristers' Union or legal aid.

The faculty decision to initiate the program came on top of two years of study and discussion of the shortcomings of the old system and the needs which is left unfilled. According to Ralph K. Winter, associate professor of law and chairman of a faculty committee appointed to oversee the development and execution of the program, it was felt that the single semester moot court program, which was unusually crowded into the first two months of the spring term, was too loosely administered to be of value to the students.

Mr. Winter has scheduled a meeting with the first-year students to explain the new program to them and answer their questions. The meeting will be early this week, possibly Monday. The students will have until this coming January, before they must decide in which of the three activities they wish to enroll for credit.

The new program, whose general outlines grew in part out of talks with the student organizations involved, is designed to accomplish two purposes: the broadening and overall improvement of the legal activities aspect of the law school curriculum; and the upgrading of the activities of the three organization, affected by the program.

The two-term scheme will consist of one term of "pre-participation" and one term of actual participation, in the area chosen by the student. In the case of legal services, a full year of actual participation will be required, rather than just one term.

Each organization is preparing its own pre-participation outline but generally each will consist of (Cont. on Page 4)

Four New Courses Set; Seminars On Draft Law, Welfare Featured

Several new courses and seminars will be offered during the spring term. Summaries of these new courses offerings follow.

SELECTIVE SERVICE RESEARCH SEMINAR:

Assistant Professor John Griffiths will be offering a 2-4 unit research seminar on draft law. "It is inconceivable," says Griffiths, "that the kind of outrage which are tolerated in the draft law would be tolerated in any other area of the law. I regard this seminar as being related to a desire to do everything possible against the Vietnam War and the draft system connected with it."

The seminar will require each member to produce one or more memoranda on current problems in the Selective Service law. The memoranda can be designed for inclusion in a "Selective Service Reporter," a planned looseleaf service which will contain: reports of cases and decisions; up-to-date statutory, regulatory, and other materials; and memoranda in depth on specific problems. Credit for the seminar can vary with the amount of writing each member commits himself to do.

(Cont. On Page 3)

Grads Want Phi Gam House

Center Seen As Sub-University

Graduate and professional students at Yale are treated by the University like "second-class citizens," according to Bill Davis, last year's chairman of the Academic Committee and one of the leaders of the recent movement to convert the facilities of Phi Gamma Alpha, now-defunct undergraduate fraternity, into a Graduate-Professional Center.

In an interview, Davis made it clear he was not directly criticizing that part of graduate-professional life that is contained within the classroom. Nor, however, was he speaking only to the admittedly inadequate social facilities provided for the postgraduate student body.

The improved social life for graduate and professional students that would result from University acceptance of the Graduate-Professional Center proposal is to Davis basically little more than a means to an end: realization of the goals of inter-disciplinary communication to which so much lip service is paid by various members of the faculty and Administration at the University.

Davis believes the proposed Center would lead to continuing contact graduate and professional students in all departments and schools. By providing a place conveniently located (for every (Cont. On Page 4)

Law students and faculty protest the war. (Yale Advocate, *March 3, 1969. Courtesy Yale Law School.*)

Doug Rosenberg, who went to Yale Law School much later and became a lawyer, despite having turned in his, recalled that in the late 1960s, members of the Resistance "felt sort of superior" to law students who had decided they would prove "more effective inside the system" at the time. But that did not mean all law students could admit they had decided on "the system."[37]

If they did, they knew their professors shared many of their concerns. One of them, John Griffiths, was deeply involved in the antiwar movement. "It is inconceivable," Griffiths was quoted as saying in the *Advocate*'s first issue, "that the kind of outrages which are tolerated in the draft law would be tolerated in any other area of the law." Perhaps Yale law students might best oppose the war by studying the rights of prospective inductees with him. "I regard this seminar as being related to a desire to do everything possible against the Vietnam war and the draft system connected with it," Griffiths said. Many of his colleagues signed a letter warning those who had turned in their draft cards against talking with FBI agents who questioned them without first obtaining information about their rights. "Somebody at Yale is obviously concerned about the personal welfare of the students," the *Columbia Law School News* approvingly noted.[38]

Or should law students launch a critique of prevailing conceptions of professionalism? Here, their professors proved sympathetic, but insistently traditional. Paul Gewirtz remembered that his writing assignment for Griffiths as a first-year involved a tort action against the CIA for illegal spying and invasion of privacy. When he was assigned the CIA as his client, Gewirtz objected, complaining that he had not gone to law school to be a "hired gun." Griffiths replied he must learn to be a professional.[39]

Or were "radical" law students at Yale right to insist that transformative change must begin at the local level? At bottom, the "social turmoil of the sixties was really a battle over power," with the left claiming it "should flow from the bottom up rather than from the top down." Thus the SDS preached, "People have to be organized around the issues that affect their lives." Though there was no SDS chapter in the law school, and most of Yale's SDS members were undergraduates, left Yale law students shared the SDS conviction that all politics are local. Thus they contended that "one must change first what one knows best." While those in the liberal mainstream argued that challenging the grading system "would take precious energy away from such activities as war resistance and pressing for needed social change within the cities," those to their left saw grade reform as a means of transforming Yale into "a cooperative rather than competitive community . . . in which the study of law is more intellectually rewarding and in which the educational process itself is more immediately involved in the mechanism of social change." And so, amidst all the angst over the war and the first year, an issue of concern to elite law students everywhere either presented itself or was found, one sure to increase their professors' discomfort: grades.[40]

"DYNAMITE TO A BOMBER"

In New Haven, the grade issue was not new. Insisting that they intended no "Berkeley-style protest," Yale law students had first politely raised the issue in the spring of 1967. It took on urgency that fall because one member of the class of 1970, Richard Balzer, saw its potential as an issue.[41]

Balzer had been the administration's "house radical" at Cornell, where he had been active in the antiwar and civil rights movements and the New Left. Passed a note from President Perkins, an excellent speaker, after he had held forth at a rally, Balzer opened the envelope anticipating congratulations on his oratory. Instead, Perkins included a five-dollar bill and a note saying Balzer needed his hair cut. It was the first step in a campaign to tame Balzer, whom Perkins kept close. Arriving in New Haven in the fall of 1967 after a postgraduate stint working with teenage gangs, Balzer found Yale Law School less radical than Cornell and was surprised that students "so talented could be cowed by an institution." Nevertheless, he at first focused his attention on working with the Hill Parents Association, not organizing the law school. Having received no letter grades during his last two years of college, however, Balzer saw no reason to begin getting them now. When he explained his situation to his professors,

Richard Balzer. (Yale Law Reporter, *1970, published by the Yale Law Student Association. Courtesy Yale Law School and Richard Balzer.*)

one told him to take it up with the authorities. The official in the dean's office reacted negatively even after Balzer said he had secured his teachers' approval. If Balzer were permitted to opt out of receiving grades, the administrator explained, everyone must be.[42]

The remark handed "dynamite to a bomber," Balzer laughed later. He shifted his focus to the law school, seeing grades as an issue that could mobilize and radicalize his classmates. Balzer called for a pass-fail system, which according to the *Advocate*, "would mean, in effect, no grades at all," since it was widely believed that no one flunked out of Yale. A poster declaring that the school's eight-tier grading system ranging from A to F made no sense launched the campaign. One hundred and thirty first-years, almost 80 percent of the class, also signed a petition that proposed immediately inaugurating pass-fail grades for all three years on the grounds that "the present grading system [is] antithetical to the learning process and a negative barrier in the pursuit of an imaginative legal education."[43]

Grades were only one "symptom" of "the basic problem which afflicts the system," the *Advocate* editorialized. "That problem is the *means* by which grades — whether they are letters or words like 'competent' — are arrived at and the *purpose* they are to play." To the editors, means seemed even more distasteful than purpose. "Ability" could not be, and should not be, measured so "narrowly," they contended. At bottom, "the system of examinations" that yielded grades just might be flawed.[44]

Grades' defenders focused on purpose. At Yale, as elsewhere, myriad justifications for grades were advanced. Grades gave students reason to do well and teachers a way to evaluate work. They were indispensable for sorting students and sending the best to the most prestigious jobs. Grades underlay meritocracy, encouraging law firms to consider criteria other than a person's "background" and "compatibility." Even at an elite institution, students could and did point to practitioners' warnings that if only one law school ceased providing grades, prestigious law firms would prove less likely to hire students from it. Eliminating grades would not end the informal ranking by which professors determined who received high-status positions, Guido Calabresi warned. Because grades' disappearance would make students "equal to each other," faculty recommendations would become still more important. "Students would fight like mad to get into a certain course with a teacher whom a certain Supreme Court justice relies on for clerks." A system of favoritism at once "degrading and disgusting" would result, turning the law school into "a pig-sty."[45]

But did the sort of students who had secured acceptance to Yale really require incentives? Grades' attackers maintained that motivation for such individuals "comes from the inside" and that grades "actually divert energy from the learning process and hamper it." Could grades take the place of teacher-student feedback as a "meaningful estimate of work"? Were they even uniform? Was not one law professor's B another's C? Were law firms even Yale's concern? Balzer told students that "the educational goals of Yale Law School and the professional goals of the law firms cannot both be met: they are antithetical." Although the "nearly exclusive reliance" on grades had been "cited as perhaps the greatest democratizing influences on the hiring practices of law firms," grades had existed long "before discrimination began to dissipate." And would the end of letter grades really increase favoritism?[46]

Such discussions took place at many law schools in the late 1960s and early 1970s, often most intensely among those who had just entered. First-years "before they get their first grades are always the best recruits for abolishing grades," one professor said wryly. The editors of NYU Law School's newspaper claimed that by 1971, a majority of the school's students understood that "grades are an incentive . . . to submit to an *unwilling but fearful worship* of the man behind the podium." Grades prevented one from questioning what their teachers said at the same time that they informed "prospective employers how much silliness the applicant will tolerate." The debate occurred at the undergraduate level too. As Nathan Glazer observed, "where there are number grades, it is argued they should be replaced with letter grades; where there are letter grades, it is argued they should be replaced with pass-fail grades, and the most radical argue there should be no system of judgment at all." Because Glazer thought "grading, or something like it" crucial to sorting students on the basis of merit, as opposed to status, he predicted that the meritocrats would "turn back . . . the attacks of reformers and radicals."[47]

That was apparently the intention of some Yale law professors. As the discussions began, Abe Goldstein worried that "students may think they ought not to study as much for their examinations because of the holding out to them of some possibility that we might do something on the pass-fail proposal." He urged Pollak to declare that "it would be a mistake for students not to study for the examinations and that they ought to approach the matter as though they were going to be graded."[48]

*   *   *

Instead, the dean appointed a faculty committee chaired by Ellen Peters. It proposed a four-tier grading system of Excellent (roughly 10 percent of students), Passable (about 75 percent), Competent (about 15 percent, less the rare failures), and Fail in large classes; written comments in smaller courses and seminars; abolition of class ranking; and establishment of a faculty committee that would select law journal members once rankings had disappeared. Almost two hundred law students jammed an open meeting to protest.[49]

It was not the four-tier grading system that irritated them so much as the prospect of "insidious" written comments in seminars. *That*, they alleged, would increase favoritism and provide professors with too much power over their futures. "You'd encourage students to 'play up' to their professors, and just create new artificial distinctions," one student leader complained. First-year students elected an eight-member committee, including Duncan Kennedy, to represent them. It contended that teachers should employ the four-tier grading system in all classes, regardless of size.[50]

Silence from the faculty ensued until the *Advocate* announced in March 1968 that Peters had informed reporters of "a firm proposal" to professors, while declining to provide its details "or to speculate on when the faculty might reach a final decision." Meanwhile, although it had released upper-class grades, the school was withholding the fall term marks of first-year students, pending the faculty's arrival at a solution. Then Pollak announced that the faculty had rejected the four-tier grading system of the Peters Committee, but that the school would become less ranking-conscious. Henceforth, it would simply report to prospective employers and other schools whether a particular student stood in the upper fifth of his or her class.[51]

Students balked. While professors worried about locating the three or four outstanding students at the top, rankings only accentuated the problem with grades for everyone else, creating "meaningless distinctions" between the large percentage bunched together at the mean. In addition to ensuring that potential employers would continue to judge students on the basis of a grading system considered unfair, the Yale faculty's action gave a bonus to those just above the 20 percent line at the expense of those just below it. Equally important, students thought that professors had acted undemocratically. They charged that the "secrecy with which the faculty deliberations were obscured" revealed "a failure to take seriously the views of concerned students." They disliked their professors' refusal to justify their action: one student compared Pollak's announcement to "the Supreme Court's saying, simply, 'yes or no.'" The class of 1970 adopted a statement condemning their teachers' "total failure to communicate with the students" and accusing them of "a failure to offer a reasoned explanation for the rejection by the faculty of the student proposal and, likewise, a justification for the change initiated."[52]

The faculty's reaction was an "organizer's dream," Balzer said. Professors played the role of "the bad employer." Obsessed with "retaining power," they struck him as terrified and outraged by students' "smallest sniff" for it. And the teachers' unwillingness to "buy off" students with reform "radicalized," at least temporarily, many once cowed into subservience.[53]

*   *   *

Amidst all the meetings, one faculty member who stopped to consider the significance of the students' agitation was gloomy. Colleagues agreed that Jan Deutsch had been one of the most brilliant students in Yale Law School's recent history. By the time he was twenty-seven, he had received his PhD in political science and LLB from Yale, and he had won tenure at the law school in only two years. Though his own work appealed to students on the left by stressing the political and indeterminate nature of law, their institutional politics did not appeal to him.[54]

In a memorandum to his colleagues, Deutsch portrayed the unrest as a function of the presence of "a considerable number of students who would not be attending at all but for the Vietnam war, and who have no interest whatsoever in the law as such." It also reflected, he believed, young peoples' "new view of their own importance and power as a force for change," gained from their work for the civil rights and antiwar causes, *and* their frustration over the limited effectiveness of both movements. Deutsch said that the grading issue was simply "a manifestation of what students regarded as unsatisfactory about the Law School as an institution." They equated grades with "the society they reject. In particular, they see law — at least as it is taught here — as lacking in relevance to the problems that concern them; they see the competitive nature of the academic experience as projecting an image of a competitive society which they believe can lie at the roots of many of the ills which they decide to ameliorate; they see what they perceive as a lack of interest on our part in qualities other than those measured by our examinations as reflecting a kind of institutional impersonality which they find it easy to analogize to the attitudes of Department of Defense planners toward Vietnam." And it would do no good to respond that "conceivable alternatives are at best Utopian." Since students believed that "our society's paramount objective ought to be to humanize all institutions," they *were* "Utopians."[55]

For the faculty, the risks loomed large, Deutsch warned. They did not just entail the possibility of incidents that would escalate into confrontations from which there was no exit. At bottom, Yale was a professional institution, dedicated to impersonal instruction in, and evaluation of, law. It was attractive to most of its faculty "basically because this is in the last analysis a thoroughly anarchic institution," which enabled professors to control their teaching and research. The student demands cut "deeply against the nature of the Law School as an institution, both as it necessarily must exist if it is to continue to be a law school and as the faculty individually desire[s] it to be."[56]

If professors wanted to be left alone, what exactly did the students at Yale, who called for greater "communication" with them, *really* want? Technically, communication was extraordinarily effective at Yale Law, a small place where word traveled more quickly than it did in most high schools. Like law students elsewhere, the agitators at Yale sought community, an environment at once less competitive and more meaningful, in which "real" learning could take place. The students aimed, as Kennedy said, at achieving "the communication which is really desired — that of student and teacher in a setting undistorted by the fear and anger of the law school classroom." But at Yale, as elsewhere, few would "think of consulting a teacher in his office, and some teachers would disdain a student seeking such private help as one seeking an unfair advantage over his competitors." Yale law students did not want to spend as much time individually with their teachers as those working toward PhDs, but they disliked feeling that their professors "considered their non-classroom hours as private time," one said. Though Yale's A students had access to professors who viewed them as "promising junior versions of faculty members," the majority left the classroom convinced "that any relationship with a faculty member is hopeless."[57]

Thus, as Kennedy pointed out at the time, the system possessed its own beautiful efficiency. Yale's law professors could maintain an "open door policy," and treat those who crossed the thresholds of their offices with "dizzying warmth," for they could be confident that none but the "best" would dare cross. Both the student and the teacher-student hierarchies were solidified. "Elite students . . . become even more elite," and when they entered, they did so as disciples. In the mid-1960s, *Yale Law Journal* editors published little, if anything, that their faculty masters had not first approved. In this setting, and one in which so many of the young were not recognized as the "best" for the first time in their lives, "one of the most important, although least expressed reasons for demanding the elimination of letter grades was that they symbolized the denial of time to the mass of students," Kennedy said. "In short, grades symbolized the absolutely minimal extent of the involvement which the faculty was willing to suffer for the average student, and at the same time the faculty's determination to select a group of favorites on whom involvement would be lavished."[58]

And the situation was only deteriorating. Some students thought that while "the beloved older professors" at Yale, such as Friedrich Kessler, were "dedicated to teaching," Rostow's hires were "intellectual picaros, seeking greater fame and fortune," who considered teaching "strictly secondary." Yale student activists may have perceived that their professors' identities were changing as, increasingly, they presented themselves as scholars, not teachers. Whether or not they published much—and Kennedy, at least, seemed skeptical—the research took time. The attentiveness to research could have proven intriguing, had professors brought their work into the classroom, but there is little evidence that they did. As Kennedy recognized, the contemporary emphasis on consumerism, like that on alienation and egalitarianism, made matters ripe for change.[59]

*   *   *

Consequently, tempers ran sufficiently high that when the dean announced the faculty had done nothing more than rethink rankings, Kennedy's fellow first-years voted in favor of a one-day boycott of all classes. Pollak averted a walkout by turning the matter over to yet another faculty committee, this one chaired by Alexander Bickel. It pledged greater consultation with students, including the Class of 1970's newly elected "First Year Demand Committee," and consideration of a broad range of curricular issues, in addition to grading.[60]

By designating Bickel chair, Pollak probably meant to signal to students that the faculty considered student concerns crucial. Widely respected for his intellectual honesty, Bickel was then involved in Robert Kennedy's last campaign and the most prominent public intellectual on the faculty. Still, the choice of Bickel to head the new committee was unfortunate. In the context of the debate over grades, surely students found it more significant that he exemplified the "intellectual picaro" who had more time to expound upon student unrest in the *New Republic* than he did for the large segment of Yale students whose grades did not render them worthy of attention.

At Bickel's first meeting with students about grades, one complained, the professor accused the young of treating their elders as bulls "cowering in a 'bullring,' surrounded by the hisses and cheers of the attendant multitudes." Further, Bickel took a dim view of grade reform. Grades, he said, had "enabled the academic legal profession to raise standards of law schools, law firms and judiciary . . . [and were] the only real measure of the caliber of the students' intellectual performance."[61]

The First Year Demand Committee was unimpressed. "We are not a radical class," its members contended, "but dissatisfaction is widespread with the role we are asked to play in the design of our graduate education here." The remedy was simple: listen to the students. The reward would prove substantial. The school would deserve the reputation on which it traded. "If Yale has lost some of the magic of the thirties," the committee patronizingly informed the faculty, "perhaps we can help it to construct a greater relevance for the 60's and 70's." The 1967–68 academic year ended with the grading situation unresolved.[62]

"A DIFFERENT SYSTEM"

In the fall of 1968, as Kennedy, now entering his second year, was putting the finishing touches on his polemic, the new first-years raised the grading issue again. This time, their leader was Ann Hill. Like Balzer the year before, she was moved by personal experience. Upon graduation from Wellesley, "where you almost felt you were wearing an armband distinguishing you from the rest of the student body as a scholarship student," she had won a Fulbright to the Free University of Berlin. She studied at the Otto Tsur Institute, where she participated in the student takeover that resulted in power being divided equally

Ann Hill. (Yale Law Reporter, *1970, published by the Yale Law Student Association. Courtesy Yale Law School and Ann Hill.*)

between students, workers, and faculty, and grades being abolished. She then applied to Yale and Duke, avoiding Harvard, which she had disliked when she sat in on a friend's classes there. She planned to go to the school that gave her more financial aid, and she knew nothing of Yale's intellectual reputation. She chose it because she had heard Yale was small and she had thought twice about Duke because Richard Nixon had gone there. She assumed that she and her fellow activists could transform Yale into the Tsur Institute. She soon realized, however, that the faculty did not want to share power with students and staff or end grades. "We've seen your kind at Yale before," she remembered Guido Calabresi telling her. "In twenty years, you'll probably be writing contracts for General Motors." He meant to warn her that intolerant leftists in youth might become intolerant members of the right with age; she heard him saying that she should not be taken seriously because she would sell out to corporate America.[63]

Nevertheless, she and other Yale students now had statistics on their side as they agitated for changing the grading system. Even a new faculty study branded the current system of letter grading as arbitrary. Each professor had his or her own definition of the meaning of each grade. This time, too, students possessed some faculty support. Pollak had wisely turned the grading issue over to the Curriculum Committee, which welcomed student representation and was chaired by Thomas Emerson, one of the professors relatively friendly to the students. Some students were distressed, however, when they learned that the Curriculum Committee was proceeding on the premise that students wanted the Distinction-Competent-Pass-Fail system they had earlier seemed to recommend to the Peters Committee, and that the faculty was preparing to decide the issue without first meeting with the students.[64]

And so the cycle began anew. A new student committee circulated a protest against professors' "false notions of privacy," complaining that "comments behind closed doors do not produce an atmosphere of trust and cooperation in the law school community." Contending that "grade reform is a student issue — to be discussed and decided with the students," the "Committee for Open Meetings" maintained the faculty should meet with students about grades.[65]

First-years also organized a referendum in which over 90 percent of their number took part. A resounding 93 percent of those voting did not support the current grading system. Pass-Fail was far and away the most popular grading system among students for first-year courses. For the second- and third-year courses, Distinction-Competent-Fail just barely edged out Pass-Fail as first preference. Just 15 percent supported the Distinction-Pass–Low Pass–Fail system the Curriculum Committee was considering. The news made Emerson uneasy. "It seems pretty clear to me that we'll just have to start over again," he told a reporter.[66]

But the faculty did not want to start over. With final examinations scheduled for January, it met three days into Christmas vacation to resolve the grading problem. In a rare gesture, professors invited two witnesses to articulate student desires. The students argued for either Pass-Fail or Distinction-Pass-Fail for all three years. Though his committee had not reached consensus, Emerson, the students, and some other committee members liked the idea of taking a step toward better faculty-student communication by shifting to Pass-Fail for first-years as an experiment.[67]

Bickel was appalled. "Pass-Fail is not an experiment," the faculty minutes recorded him saying to his colleagues. "[I]t's adopting a different system. That new system (of personal evaluation, conferences, etc.) is one he wants no part of: it's not what he understands as the function of a law professor."[68]

Nevertheless, the following morning, the Yale law faculty adopted the grading system it still uses today. The minutes record relatively little discussion: perhaps everyone was talked out. Students in first-semester courses would be given grades of Credit or Fail. Thereafter, with the exception of a limited number of advanced courses that instructors could offer on a credit-fail basis, courses would be graded Honors, Pass, Low Pass, and Fail. Prominently high-lighting the comment of one Yale student that "I didn't study less—but I wor-ried less," the *Harvard Law Record* and Michigan's *Res Gestae* reported the fac-ulty vote as a triumph for the students.[69]

Compared to what would happen elsewhere, it was. The grade revolt move-ment would spread to other elite law schools during the late 1960s and early 1970s, as grades came to symbolize the hierarchy and competitiveness that stu-dents hated. A student who reviewed other law school newspapers labeled the complaints about grades "fairly obvious, fairly uniform, and fairly widespread: grades tend to accentuate competition, they are not an accurate reflection of legal talents, they tend to hamper creative thought, they are not valuable feed-back tools for the student." So, too, were faculty responses outside New Haven predictable, uniform, and widespread: "first, grades are needed to provide in-centive, and second, they help employers to make accurate hiring decisions."[70]

As at Yale, the passion for grading reform had been building at Harvard since 1967, when a *Record* survey had demonstrated that "the present examina-tion system is about half as popular with Harvard Law Students as Barry Gold-water was with the American people in 1964." Just weeks before the 1969 "bust" at Harvard College, 150 Harvard 1 Ls called for pass-fail grades in the first year. "Grades create a status hierarchy with very few winners but many losers," they claimed. Soon after the bust, the Harvard law faculty acted, permitting first-years to opt for pass-fail grades. Some of Harvard's most politically liberal fac-ulty members treated the change as proof that Armageddon, in the form of surrender to the students, had arrived. One reportedly informed the members of the class of 1970 that they were "the last to earn their degrees." And the new second-years were outraged when prospective employers broke the rules of the faculty resolution and questioned students about whether they had chosen the pass-fail option the previous year. Their first-year successors would unsuccess-fully agitate for the mandatory credit-fail system that now existed in the first semester at Yale.[71]

Other schools also refused to give much. At Stanford, the faculty decided that students could receive either a number grade or grades of Credit–Restricted Credit–No Credit in their courses. As at Harvard, those who chose the latter risked queries from prospective employers about whether they could take the heat. At Columbia, where students traced their efforts to transform law school culture back to the 1968 revolt against the university, grading practices changed so rapidly that many graduated from the school in 1971 with traces from three different systems on their transcripts—letter, credit–no credit, and a five-tier approach ranging from Honors to Fail. At NYU, the faculty rejected a proposal hammered out by a student-teacher committee for Honors-Pass-Fail grading, opting for Honors–High Pass–Pass-Fail grades instead. Students branded their professors' action "a symptom of the actual malady at N.Y.U. Law School, that is, a total absence of any real student participation in the final decision making process." At Michigan, where almost half the students polled believed that students should possess a pass-fail grading option in all their courses, law professors tried to cope with demands for change by announcing that some students in the second and third year could take one course on a pass-fail basis.[72]

But at the time, Yale students did not see their new grading system as a victory. True, it gave them time to adapt to law school. True, it avoided the essentially A-B-C-F grading some other schools adopted, in which there were three clearly delineated grades above Fail: Honors, High Pass, and Pass. True, the rest was similar to the portion of the Peters Committee recommendation the students had liked—with the new Honors grade analogous to the Peters Committee's grade of Excellent, Pass equivalent to its Passable for work in the B+ to C range, and Low Pass parallel to its Competent. True, too, had Yale professors announced the change after the Peters Committee's deliberations, students might have claimed victory. But since the school had adopted a regime that after the first semester contained more gradations than Pass-Fail or Distinction-Pass-Fail, they did not. "We thought it [the school] did have grades" despite the changes, Hill stressed, and "we never thought we succeeded there." "Stand together, not on top of each other!" her classmates would joke in their graduation yearbook. "Abolish Grades! Remember—Richard Nixon was third in his class at Duke Law School!" When the *Advocate* resumed publication after winter 1968 exams ended, it did not even mention the faculty's action.[73]

Further, Yale students were soon complaining that their teachers still neither turned in grades on time nor provided feedback, in the form of comments on examinations, about individual performance. They were further dismayed when the faculty subsequently voted that if an individual received 30 percent or more Low Passes in advanced courses, with Credit marks in advanced credit-fail courses counting as Low Pass for this purpose, he or she would be expelled. At the time, an occasional Low Pass still sullied transcripts, and two Fails meant one was out. Though that fate befell few, the threat hung over all. Worse, the faculty proceeded to expel several students who had received too many Low Pass or Credit grades the following summer—an action retracted only after student protest. "All students accomplished," one grumbled, "was to trade off excess competition in exchange for a greater risk of failure."[74]

"The Inner Logic of Grades."
(*Yale Law Reporter, 1970, published by the Yale Law Student Association. Courtesy Yale Law School.*)

In retrospect, the faculty had taken another important step in the history of the school, contributing to the distinctiveness of the student experience there. Most law schools would soon abandon the 1960s experiment with grade reform and return to letter or numerical grades or a five-tier system in which the possibility of Honors or High Pass stood as a silent remonstrance for the student who received the lowly Pass. The shift back occurred in part because of student pressure. Once jobs for lawyers became scarcer during the 1970s, many students wanted a clearer signal about where they stood, and many of their teachers did not object to the return to the old standards. Yet Yale stayed the course. And in later years, few professors would give grades of Low Pass or Fail, opting instead for a system that, except in rare cases, was one of either Honors or Pass.[75] In 1968, however, Yale students would have thought that after being pushed to the wall, their professors had done the bare minimum.

Still, at the time, students largely accepted the new grading system. Grade reform had illuminated deeper problems within Yale Law School. The young now had bigger fish to fry.

Chapter Four

Student Power

As the *Advocate* recognized, by the start of the 1968–69 academic year, the pressing issue had become the larger one of "student power." Teachers could reason that whatever students had said about making the classroom less competitive and more collegial during 1967–68, they had sought grade reform as a way of gaining greater control over their own futures. The quest may even have strengthened some professors' smugness by reinforcing their image of students as spoiled children too soft for legal education. Further, even when students had organized a "First Year Demand Committee" to deal with grade reform, the young had been more likely to beseech than bully. But by 1968–69, they were agitating to become equal partners in running the school. Like the New Left, which had given way to a mass "student movement," the young at Yale talked of participatory democracy. While African Americans sought to increase the diversity of the student body, white students wanted to share power over the school's governance with their professors. Here were real and frightening threats to the faculty's maintenance of its power. Professors reacted to the demands of black and white students very differently.[1]

MYTH'S "PIONEERING INSTITUTION"

Campus activism frequently followed a logical sequence. Agitators at first focused on substantive problems, such as grades and minority recruitment. When they experienced difficulty getting what they wanted, however, their goals changed. Then the young often demanded "an end to the faculty dictatorship which exists in our school."[2]

That was the pattern at Yale. In 1967–68, the issue of shared governance took a backseat to grades. At the first faculty meeting in fall 1968, Alexander Bickel condemned "communications" with students the previous year as "inadequate" and expressed the hope that "we can do better this year." No one seemed to be listening; the professor who spoke next complained about the lack of mail delivery on Saturdays. But Boris Bittker had been looking into student-faculty communications, and his proposal to permit students to participate in faculty committees was on the next meeting's agenda. Professors decided to ask student representatives to participate in some of the faculty committees that considered nonconfidential matters on an experimental, undefined, nonvoting basis.[3]

Inviting students to sit on some committees was not radical. As Bittker told his colleagues, "American law schools not only allow students to run the law reviews that are basic to our educational programs and to our professional reputations, but take pride in this phenomenon." (Bittker acknowledged that if student control of the *Yale Law Journal* were proposed now "on a clean slate, it would no doubt seem to be a risky and unprincipled erosion of our responsibility for the program and professional reputation of the school.") Other institutions were allowing student representatives on committees, though confidentiality considerations barred students who took part in discussion of general policy matters, such as admissions, from access to materials involving individual cases at this point. Nor was hiring at issue: "Strong sentiment" among faculty members ensured that there would be no student representation on the Appointments Committee.[4]

Predictably, professors' invitation to participate on some committees, "excluding those dealing with confidential, disciplinary, faculty or important matters," did not sit well with students. The *Advocate* decried teachers' proposal "begrudgingly to tolerate some student representation on some of *their* committees" as one more example of the "faculty paternalism" that prevented the school from becoming "a community." A fall 1968 editorial declared:

A malaise pervades Yale Law School like the smell of formaldehyde masking decay in a morgue. Everyone senses it at first, then soon becomes accustomed to it. It exists because Yale Law School is not the pioneering institution which its myth would have one believe. It exists because of the almost grade-school-like relationship between most faculty and students. It exists because students cannot meet as equals with faculty, to explore the relationship of law to change, of the law school to society, of intellectual stimulation to classroom instruction. It exists because for most people education here is merely floating a gutterlike stream of courses until their momentum turns them into lawyers and empties them into the sewer of Wall Street.[5]

As students accused the faculty of resting on its laurels *and* perpetuating hierarchy, the generation gap became more pronounced. It was not just at Yale. Most yearbooks told the same story: students in the 1968–69 academic year were less likely to ape their teachers. To Thomas Emerson, who had returned to Yale from sabbatical, "it seemed that the school had changed radically." It was not just that "[o]utward appearances" were "drastically" different, with students wearing blue jeans to class (when they did not have job interviews), smoking pot, and listening to rock music in the law school courtyard. There had also been a change, Emerson said, in "inward appearances."[6]

Like elite law students elsewhere, Yale's young wanted to transform academic politics and culture; they sought political and personal liberation. Theirs was a culture of theatricality. One member of the class of 1970, future Nixon speechwriter and game show host Ben Stein, remembered going to class "high as a kite on Demerol" and threatening to take off all his clothes in Antitrust unless the professor "did not stop with his Socratic games."[7] Others shared his penchant for the outrageous.

"BRINGING THE SYSTEM DOWN"

While the issue of greater representation on the faculty committees hung fire, that of diversity, another matter involving participation in the decision-making process, brought students closer to the barricades. Doubting the predictive value of the LSAT and college grades for all "whose childhood and family background are remote from the experiences and aspirations of (primarily white) middle class America . . . long before such skepticism was fashionable," the faculty had given "less weight to the LSAT and the rest of the standard academic white apparatus in assessing black applicants" for some time. Beginning in 1948, Yale law professors had admitted any African American who, "in our judgment, was qualified in the sense that he or she could successfully complete the three years required to obtain a degree. All other applicants competed on a best-qualified basis—with the exception that, as a 'national' law school, we guarded against overrepresentation of particular regions of the country." The statement was not quite accurate. As one internal memorandum admitted, "[W]e should be fooling ourselves if we refused to acknowledge" that "Yale connections" did not give children of law school alumni and those strongly supported by faculty members an edge in the admissions process too. The Yale Admissions Committee did not keep the African American track of its special admissions program secret, but did not publicize it.[8]

Yale supplemented its special admissions program with outreach. It recruited African Americans by sending its admissions officer out to speak about the school and awarding financial aid to those accepted, when possible. The approach was sufficiently effective that in 1965, Howard Law School charged Yale with cherry-picking, "'grabbing' the cream of Negro undergraduates interested in studying law."[9]

Even so, Yale's affirmative action program had traditionally yielded no more than six black students annually, some of whom—Harvard College honors undergraduate Haywood Burns, for one—would undoubtedly have been admitted anyway. Small as that number was, it was substantial at a time when minorities were underrepresented in law school student bodies and the profession, and it contributed to Yale's image as the law school concerned about social justice. In the mid-1960s, African Americans made up about 12 percent of the nation's population and 1 percent of its lawyers. In 1964–65, about 1.3 percent of all law students were black, and over a third of them were enrolled in predominantly black law schools. All of twenty black students were enrolled at Case Western, Emory, Illinois, Maryland, Mississippi, NYU, Pennsylvania, and UCLA in 1965–66. Because of the insistence on credentials, there were perhaps a dozen African American law professors outside predominantly black law schools in 1968. "Law teaching probably is still the least open segment of the profession today," one professor admitted.[10]

The Yale faculty largely supported admitting minorities, while dividing over the wisdom of affirmative action. Though Ronald Dworkin became less active at the law school after he became master of one of Yale's residential colleges in 1966, he remained sufficiently involved with his colleagues to have one overriding memory of the period: "continuing and sometimes heated discussion about affirmative action." To those such as Bickel, "reverse discrimination" in favor of minorities rewarded the intellectually inferior and brought in students who could not keep up with the majority. It also awakened memories of the quotas Ivy League schools had used to restrict the number of Jewish students admitted with superior academic credentials.[11]

While Dworkin restricted admission to his seminar to better students, he remembered strongly supporting affirmative action. As he articulated it later, individuals did not *deserve* a place in law schools because they were bright: "[L]egal education is not so vital that everyone has an equal right to it." What counted was whether applicants' admission would "serve a useful social policy." A liberal like Bickel, committed to equality of opportunity, viewed the issue in terms of meritocracy versus privilege, with the meritocratic classes sweeping aside those who had once claimed admission to the university as a matter of right. To Dworkin, however, another kind of liberal, the question was one of meritocracy versus fairness, with society possessing an interest in making the scarce resource of higher education available to those historically denied it. Further, Dworkin maintained that the concept of "merit" obscured more than it clarified. What did the statement that law school applicants "should be judged on merit, and merit alone" mean? If that stricture implied that Admissions Committees should consider only "scores on some particular intelligence test, then it is arbitrary," and in any event, law schools had never done that. Sometimes they preferred those who worked hard to those they judged bright and lazy. If that stricture meant that schools should accept those it predicted would become the "most useful" lawyers, then different kinds of lawyers proved "useful" at different kinds of jobs. "There is no combination of abilities and skills and traits that constitutes 'merit' in the abstract." If the Admissions Committee believed that "a black skin, as a matter of regrettable fact," enabled lawyers better to serve the black community, color constituted merit. "That argument may strike some as dangerous; but only because they confuse its conclusion—that black skin may be a socially useful trait in particular circumstances—with the very different and despicable idea that one race may be inherently more worthy than another." [12]

Pollak, too, stood for affirmative action. Years later, the dean recalled a discussion in which Leon Higginbotham pointed out that the percentage of blacks in the profession in the mid-1960s was just what it had been in 1900. The dean attributed his belief in affirmative action to a "strong sense that this was a profession that had, one way or another, managed to freeze blacks out, and that now was the time when that profession, perhaps more than any other slice of responsible American life, had to help bring about a real restructuring of where blacks stood in the society." [13]

Doubtless, discussions about affirmative action first occurred in the abstract over lunch. The special admissions program operated *sub silentio*. As long as it remained small, there is no record that Bickel or anyone else did anything but approve it.

Thus Yale apparently possessed the first affirmative action program of any kind at an elite, predominantly white American law school. Its counterparts do not seem to have established similar programs until the 1960s. Some law school administrators may then have come to share the sense with some at Yale that the LSAT was culturally biased, even though the assumption could not be tested—because "data collected to date indicated that there were not sufficient numbers of Negro students in any one law school to produce meaningful results." Further, since many law schools had long provided at least an informal preference for alumni children, there was a precedent for affirmative action. And at a time when the surge in applications had not yet occurred and grade inflation was only beginning to take flight, admitting an individual "qualified in the sense that he or she could successfully complete the three years required to obtain a degree" would not have seemed extraordinary. Boalt Hall, for example, automatically admitted any college graduate with a B average until 1961, as well as many applicants with inferior grades who had performed well on the LSAT. When the school inaugurated its special admissions program for students of color, it initially admitted all who qualified, just as it had done earlier for virtually all applicants, regardless of race,.[14]

By that time, Boalt's program, like Yale's, was just one among many. The winds of change began to blow in the late 1960s when elite law schools joined the "parade" of minority recruitment. In the fall of 1969, the Association of American Law Schools could report that minority enrollments were double what they had been two years earlier. Law school administrators agreed that a fair proportion of those students "would probably not have been admitted had they not been members of a minority group."[15]

Other efforts at outreach for minority law students "who are not admissible by traditional criteria" were appearing. In 1966, NYU established a summer orientation program for minority admittees, and Harvard, Yale, and Columbia cooperated on a similar venture. In 1968, Stanford inaugurated a "stretch-out" program that gave disadvantaged students four years in which to complete law school. By this point, the Association of American Law Schools, the Law School Admissions Test Council, and others had formed the Council on Legal Educational Opportunity. CLEO funded summer institutes for students of color without high grades and LSAT scores, designed to interest them in going to law school and to increase their success there by acclimatizing them to the rigors of the first year. But CLEO possessed limited funds, most minority students did not come to law school through that channel, and most required financial aid.[16]

Of course, white administrators were not the only ones concerned with minority enrollments. The *New York Times* reported two youth revolutions proceeding largely in isolation from each other at campuses from Columbia to Berkeley: unlike "white left radicals," who sought "to bring the university down," black students "do not want to destroy the university but to make it relevant to them [and] . . . do not want to bring down the Establishment but to become part of it." The *Times'* account paid no attention to activism by women and other minorities, and its picture of both white and black student protest was questionable. Increasingly, for example, African American students sought economic power without cultural assimilation. But the notion of two separate campus movements—one white, the other black—was widespread at the time, particularly in eastern schools, where the black-white paradigm reigned. According to one eminent African American political scientist, whites focused on "abstract and symbolic goals," while African Americans concentrated on more "realistic" ones. Thus while white law students talked of community, African Americans worked to expand their numbers. At NYU Law School, A. J. Cooper, former mayor of a small Alabama town, formed the Black American Law Students Association in 1968, declaring that "if the System is allowed to continue unchanged," he and other African Americans who received advanced degrees would "still [be] considered niggers."[17]

As competition from other institutions increased, Yale experienced greater difficulty attracting the students of color it wanted most. Though the number of African Americans enrolled in both college and law school was increasing, Yale Law's African American enrollments were declining. And students inside the school were proving less willing to trust their professors' good intentions. Once Yale Law had been a central site for an interracial civil rights movement committed to nonviolence and the achievement of social change through law. But when the Watts uprising occurred five days after LBJ signed the Voting Rights Act of 1965 and inner cities burst into flames, many African Americans' trust in law and interracial nonviolence flagged. Black nationalism, with its emphasis on black political, economic, and cultural mobilization and self-determination, grew. In the words of one enthusiast, "blacks were taking care of business" in the ghetto and on the campuses.[18]

That was evident in New Haven by 1968. "Cultural nationalism started hitting a lot of the northern cities," New Haven included, the Hill Parents Association's Fred Harris recalled. "People started wearing dashikis and other stuff and more and more of our membership was coming to be all black."[19]

The growth of black nationalism was also apparent at privileged universities, such as Yale, located in inner cities. Organized black students were insisting that campus administrators should admit more African Americans, hire more black professors, make the curriculum more relevant, and give African Americans their "own space." They were also warning that university administrators' unwillingness to honor those demands could lead to demonstrations, occupation of buildings, and even violence. As so many contemporary accounts made clear, whites on the left, while sympathetic to the goals of black nationalism, were still largely intrigued by it from a distance. Their romance with it would not come until 1969–70. But white Establishment liberals already felt anxious about black nationalism. *Pace* the *New York Times*, some Yale law professors would come to think that it was the black students who wanted to "bring the university down."[20]

*   *   *

The tension had become obvious in the spring of 1968 when, in the aftermath of Martin Luther King's assassination, students learned that the incoming first-year class at Yale would include few African Americans. New Haven had remained largely peaceful after King's murder. Some two thousand individuals, most of them black, had gathered, and Kingman Brewster and William Sloane Coffin led a large march of students in King's memory. The university shut down for a day, and Brewster pledged that Yale would answer the "urgent and welcome call for the university to commit itself to more about discrimination, poverty, poor education, poor housing, all of which deprive many of New Haven's citizens of the opportunities which America is supposed to stand for." To back up his promise, he created the Yale Council on Community Affairs, providing $40,000 in start-up money and involving members of the black community in its work. At the same time, as Brewster recognized, the fact that the university had been working to develop an African American studies program even before King's murder lent credibility to the administration's gestures and made Yale College students more willing to ascribe good intentions to their president.[21]

Law professors were not as lucky. Several black law students had already helped develop a Hill Parents Association offshoot, Operation Breakthrough, which sought to provide jobs for inner city youths. Criticizing Yale Law's failure "to respond creatively and vigorously to the urban racial crisis" after King's death, Operation Breakthrough's president, JeRoyd Greene, a Yale law student who played a major role in the uprising at Howard Law School, joined with Don Howie, Richard Thornell, and another African American student to ask the school to reopen admissions to increase the number of African Americans in the class of 1971. "We cannot stand by idly while our numbers diminish here — as they have from 17, four years ago, to 12 at present," they said. They offered to assist in recruitment. The Admissions Committee reacted cautiously, with the acting dean of admissions declaring he was "perfectly glad to sit down and talk" to Greene and his colleagues about the matter, while warning that the school might face "some trouble" if it tried to reopen the admissions issue.[22]

Meanwhile the *Advocate*'s editors also had the poor taste—or so professors believed—to publish an editorial about the "appalling" absence of African American students in the same issue in which the late associate dean in charge of admissions was eulogized. "Not only are Negroes conspicuous by their absence from the Law School, so too are southerners, midwesterners, north westerners, and westerners," the editorial maintained. The "bias" was not simply geographical, either; more than three hundred of those at Yale Law, 50–60 percent of the average student body, had done their undergraduate work at Ivy League schools. Yale, "for a variety of reasons, which probably includes some conscious discrimination, has not attracted students from the diverse reaches of the nation." Despite its reputation as a national institution, its "parochial admission policy" meant that it was simply a regional school full of "Easterners, non-Negroes and Ivy Leaguers." Calling for "more honesty," the *Advocate* exhorted the new Bickel Committee, which was studying grades, to "discuss thoroughly whether this should be a national law school or a regional one."[23]

That was not a charge Bickel wanted to accept. When students came before his committee to talk about the absence of African Americans and to offer help with recruitment, he told them that the school was already making "the most vigorous efforts to find Negro applicants who met our qualifications, rather generously construed in their favor." If the task was becoming harder, that was simply an indication that other law schools were now competing with Yale. Given his private views, Bickel probably thought he was tactful. "I don't think it well advised to admit more Negroes who are at best very marginally qualified into the regular, three-year LL.B. program, and I don't see the point of relying for help in recruiting them on the least responsible and least cooperative element in our present group of Negro students," he wrote Pollak. And Bickel considered a proposal from Richard Balzer to introduce a stretch-out program varying the course load or periods of study for minority students pursuant to a special admissions program "high-risk." Nevertheless, despite the "[m]any misgivings" voiced, committee members believed Balzer's proposal deserved study. A majority, Bickel disapprovingly added, even favored a commitment "to the essential objective of the proposal, that is to say, to the objective of bringing LL.B. candidates to Yale who are unqualified under our present standards, and giving them remedial training here in conjunction with an extended LL.B. program, in the hope of ultimately being able to award the LL.B. to at least a substantial proportion of them."[24]

Once again, Bickel raised the meritocratic standard when students faulted the faculty because "it lacked a Negro member." He and his colleagues had "firmly" told the students, he assured Pollak, that "it would be disastrous for a faculty to start recruiting on a racial basis." There the line must be drawn. For "it was one thing to conceive an obligation on our part, while maintaining our standards, to train Negro lawyers, but something else again, and no service to any worthwhile objective, including the training of Negro lawyers, for us to tamper in any way with the criteria for faculty appointments. The presence of a Negro on our faculty would clearly be a stroke of good luck, but it would be absolutely disastrous to hire a Negro whom we would not have taken if he had been white." Nor was he moved by the demand for courses more focused on the legal problems of the poor, insisting that he and his fellow committee members did not understand the young's demand for "telling it like it is" *and* condemning students as insufficiently intellectual. His reaction was impolitic. Student appeals for courses about poverty, urban, and civil rights law were growing.[25]

That became clear when Greene, Howie, and other African American students walked out of an Alumni Weekend panel that took place just days after King's death on "Law and the Urban Crisis" because it featured white law school deans, not students and/or African Americans. With a dashiki-clad Fred Harris and other Hill Parents Association members, the students created a "counter-panel" entitled "Law Is the Urban Crisis." It was a public relations nightmare. The "Law and the Urban Crisis" panel, obviously meant to highlight Yale's reputation for racial justice in the aftermath of King's murder, had been scheduled shortly before a luncheon featuring Chief Justice Earl Warren and Justice Potter Stewart, an alumnus. The counter-panel must have given some alumni nightmares if Paul Gewirtz rightly remembered the rage in Howie's speech there. As Gewirtz recalled it, Howie began: "I have a dream. Let me tell you about my dream. There's a big meeting of Yale Law School alumni, and black men with machetes come in and chop the heads off of everyone, and chop, and chop, and chop, and the heads fall." The *Advocate*'s editors, however, considered it a salutary development that "these people, many of whom pride themselves on being alumni of 'socially conscious' Yale, had the meaning of social consciousness brought home to them, in a way that might, hopefully, cause them to lose some sleep."[26]

To students, the decanal panel also revealed "the substantial disparity between what we want to say Yale Law School is like, and what it really is." Why should the administration's selection of panel members surprise? "As long as the Law School pretends that its present curriculum and institutional structure are suited for preparing students to find ways to make the law serve the urgent

Scenes from Alumni Weekend, 1968. At left is the "counterpanel": Richard Thornell at far left, Fred Harris at far right. At right is the Alumni Luncheon. Left to right: *Cyrus Vance, President Kingman Brewster, Justice Potter Stewart, Dean Louis Pollak, and Chief Justice Earl Warren. (*Yale Advocate, *May 3, 1968. Courtesy Yale Law School.)*

needs of society, it will likewise be satisfied to have the law school deans expound on the crisis of the cities." And, students complained, the Bickel Committee displayed no interest in addressing the problem. In an open letter discussing its distress over the small number of African Americans accepted, the First Year Demand Committee characterized the "fiasco" of the "Law and Urban Crisis" panel as "a convenient symbol for our dilemma. . . . When left to their own devices, the Deans will meditate among themselves about events and trends that they are simply not equipped to understand by themselves." The students likewise charged that the meetings of "the so-called Bickel committee" were "characterized by indiscriminate topical promiscuity, fuzzy thinking and general lack of purpose. Nothing has been sought and nothing attained."[27]

Actually, something was about to be achieved. But it was not in response to any specific student threats, and there is no evidence that the faculty felt it acted under coercion. Instead of reopening admissions, the faculty decided in May 1968 to admit an additional thirteen students, "presumably to be Blacks," some of whom were already on the waiting list. The discussion apparently proved short. Boris Bittker supported the motion, Joe Goldstein objected to it, and Ralph Winter added he "doesn't want present Negro students recruiting: warns of dangers." Clearly, Winter feared that the students would search out others with their political proclivities—as indeed Greene already had. The motion passed 19–5. The outcome probably reflected liberal guilt over King's death, hopefulness as Robert Kennedy's presidential campaign gathered steam, and a desire not to lose bragging rights to other law schools about minority enrollments. As when they changed the grading system, professors received slight credit. The faculty's decision, coming at academic year's end, received little publicity.[28]

*   *   *

It did, however, alter the composition of the student body. The new first-year class entering in fall 1968 possessed the usual complement of Establishment figures' children. But thanks to the recruitment efforts of black students and the Admissions Committee, it also included the largest number of African Americans yet.[29] There were twelve black students in the class of 1971.

J. Otis Cochran was one of them. On a recruitment trip with the assistant dean of admissions the previous spring, Greene and another African American student had focused their energies on Cochran, a political science major at Morehouse. He had grown up in Atlanta, the oldest of three children. His parents were divorced, and money was tight. Cochran's father was a shipping clerk; his mother, a domestic who had once been a teacher in a one-room schoolhouse. As a Baptist, Cochran was experienced at giving testimony. Knowledgeable and charismatic, he was once described as a combination of "Chaucer and chitlins." Having held elected leadership positions since grade school, he possessed a great store of political shrewdness. Active in the civil rights movement since he was a high school student, he was also a skilled and savvy organizer. He had become interested in studying law when he was arrested at a demonstration and given poor counsel. When the telegram announcing admission to Yale came, his mother reassured her son that she would borrow the money to enable him to go; Cochran would also earn money by teaching at New Haven and Yale Colleges. Before he left for New Haven in 1968, Cochran had been out of the South just once.[30]

Arriving at Yale with a Harris tweed jacket given him by two relatives who had waited tables to buy it, Cochran had planned to become an "Ivy League boy" and focus on studying. He immediately "fell in love with the courtliness and civility" of many he met at Yale, especially Thomas Emerson, he recalled later. Any number of other professors, including Bittker and Pollak, also treated him with kindness, inviting him to their homes or out to lunch.[31]

Even so, the transition proved a shock. Cochran found some northern whites at Yale more patronizing and racist in their way than southerners. Like some on the faculty, he saw the students on the left as poseurs. When he would raise his hand in class, he could feel his colleagues looking at their feet, worrying that he would embarrass himself. Then, when he did not say something stupid, he remembered, his classmates wanted "to cheer you to the rafters." Despite the fact that Cochran's predecessor from Morehouse-Spelman was the

J. Otis Cochran.
(Yale Law Reporter,
1970, published by
the Yale Law Student
Association.
Courtesy Yale Law
School and J. Otis
Cochran.)

distinguished civil rights activist Marian Wright Edelman, Yale had created a sense of "marginality" for graduates of colleges from which it did not traditionally draw. White liberals often grated, as when one informed a friend of Cochran who said "nigro," as southerners did, that the correct pronunciation was "kneegro," or told Cochran how "horrible" the South was. Some teachers annoyed him too. They achieved "professional status on the basis of their frequent and often esoteric publications in law journals — publications which too often have little or no impact on the immediate legal problems of society," and they judged activist students of color by traditional criteria, instead of "by standards that measure our commitment and contribution to the alleviation of poverty, inequality, and the injustices of this society." Cochran also had a memorable encounter with Averell Harriman. "Young man, I have a grandson I can't get in here," he recalled the statesman saying. The implication was that black students were ungrateful, their concerns inappropriate. "I quickly started to get angry," he remembered. He would refuse to become a "jurispru-dential Stepin Fetchit."[32]

Cochran organized the Black Law Students Union, Yale's BALSA chapter, and became its first chair. He held out the prospect that "soon we'll be at the point where black students will not have to spend an awful lot of time making this Law School not merely a place that arms the country with Supreme Court clerks, Undersecretaries of State and corporation heads, but what it pretends to be: a community armed with the highest intellectual, political and social awareness." In the meantime, as the *Advocate* said, he turned the BLSU into the "most active group at the Law School today." As at Columbia and Harvard Law Schools, black awareness became more manifest in the fall of 1968.[33]

As Cochran broke down the needs Greene and others had begun to articu-late the previous spring, he decided he must address the priorities of all his constituents. Some BLSU members felt isolated socially, and whenever they tried to sit down together, "here come white people asking us to analyze our-selves for them." They hoped for a place of their own. Others craved more rele-vant coursework. Others hated the frequent identification checks by campus police seeking to make sure they were Yale students, rather than members of New Haven's black underclass. All wanted larger black enrollments and more financial aid.[34]

*   *   *

On December 10, 1968, the BLSU delivered the result to the faculty. For pro-fessors in the dumps about Richard Nixon's victory in the presidential election and student dissatisfaction with letter grades, here was more bad news. The BLSU's "presentments" included demands for an increase in the number of African Americans in the student body to 10 percent (up from 4 percent) and the enlistment of "presently enrolled Black students to serve as advance men" to help the school achieve the goal. Financially, the organization requested the funding of a permanent chair for a black faculty member, an increase in aid for black students, and Yale sponsorship of a Council for Legal Educational Op-portunities Institute during the summer to prepare black students for the first year. The BLSU also wanted a room of its own in the law school and a separate table for black students in the dining hall. It had curricular aspirations, too— courses focusing on poverty, discrimination, and other topics that would help lawyers who served the black community. Finally, the BLSU called for a halt to harassment of black students by campus police.[35]

A week later, Pollak sent his reply. Dodging the recruitment issue, the dean said that he and his colleagues shared the students' interest in attracting "more qualified black students and qualified black professors." But Pollak objected in principle to a target percentage because "that would smack of a quota." Professors also wanted to increase coursework related to poverty and discrimination, he said. He denied the demand for a separate dining table. (One took root anyway.) But the dean provided an office and made vague but encouraging "we'll have to study this but we're all people of good will here" noises about everything else.[36]

"We were astonished" at the faculty's reaction, Cochran recalled. To the BLSU, it seemed that professors had again assumed the role of bad employer. By this time, Cochran had become friendly with a senior member of the powerful Yale Corporation that governed the university. Edwin Foster Blair made a point of seeking out "the most radical of students," and he and Cochran struck up a relationship when the Yale College and Law School alumnus invited the BLSU chair to a series of luncheons at Mory's, Yale's all-male eating club. A successful attorney, Blair purchased a television for the BLSU and persuaded IBM to donate a typewriter to the organization. As this suggested, the faculty might have met many BLSU demands with little trouble.[37]

But professors seemed frightened. "They weren't scared of me," Cochran said later. "They were scared of my message." He remembered hearing that Bork had likened BLSU members to the Gestapo. "How can twelve scared-ass students be compared to the Gestapo?" Cochran asked. And he recalled hearing a classmate say that the faculty reacted to the BLSU presentments as if they came from a grand jury.[38]

Seeing it had struck a nerve, the BLSU turned up the heat. "The general insensitivity and unwillingness of the Dean of the Law School to respond to our previously stated demands clearly demonstrates his ineffectiveness in responding to the needs of the black students," the BLSU said in its reply to Pollak. It insisted on an immediate meeting with professors and observed that though it was making "every effort to approach this grave situation with fairness and restraint, we cannot allow our unanswered demands to wallow in committees and discussion. We must have positive answers by the time we return from the Christmas break, or we must seek avenues other than discussion and debate."[39]

The BLSU had thrown down the gauntlet. At its gathering to decide on grades, the faculty permitted the BLSU to appear. "These are demands—not for discussion," Cochran said. One by one, the more than ten BLSU members accompanying him set out their requirements. A black faculty member was vital. The law school must have a 10 percent black population by the following fall, use African American students as recruiters, and write "heads of Afro-American societies throughout the country soliciting Black applicants."

The school "was doing little with New Haven's plight," and law students should receive academic credit for community work unsupervised by the faculty. Courses must focus more on minority problems: "Yale College changed its curriculum, why not YLS?" Black students needed better financial aid; the BLSU, money and space. Yale must force the campus police "to respect the rights of Black students." Pollak temporized. When the dean replied that the faculty found the airing of student views useful, more conversation was necessary, and he was establishing a committee to discuss these matters further, Cochran answered that the BLSU required results. There were "[n]o grounds for compromise. Significant progress must be visible by [the] end of holidays. Otherwise *drastic action* will be taken to prevent School's operating." The students then departed. "Let's not buy peace at a price that may haunt us," Charles Black and Alexander Bickel urged.[40]

Bickel's response was less surprising than Black's. Bickel had shown his uneasiness about affirmative action when he had responded to the students who had appeared before his committee: No one would have expected him to support the BLSU's demands. Black, though, maintained that "we've always had affirmative action, whether for alumni children or football players," and observed that affirmative action's fairness was challenged only when it involved African Americans. It was not the substance of BLSU's demands that bothered Black so much, apparently, as the fact that the organization claimed a voice in governance. As the battle lines between students and faculty hardened, Black agreed with Bickel that the faculty must retain unilateral control over affirmative action and every other policy it had traditionally set.[41]

Given the attitudes on both sides, the dean was understandably anxious when he reported in to the president and provost. "[T]here is a very substantial likelihood that . . . the Faculty will not, at least as of now, be disposed to go any substantial distance beyond most of the positions outlined in my letter . . . of December 16, and that . . . the BLSU will not enter into real discussions of these issues with [the] committee," Pollak said. "With matters in this posture, the BLSU rhetoric of post-Christmas threat may be a very serious matter."[42]

That was enough for the central university administration, housed in Woodbridge Hall. Provost Charles Taylor appeared at a special luncheon faculty meeting. By now, professors had drafted a reply to the BLSU vaguely affirming their commitment to change. "Specific questions in Black demands are not plainly answered," the provost complained. "What about [demand for] 10% [representation in student body]?" According to Taylor, the law school might be "right in rejecting a quota," but it must "increase the intake of Blacks." (Actually, university administrators had recently welcomed a report that said the proportion of African Americans at Yale College should match that of African Americans in the general population.) Taylor also warned faculty members that they must "increase the intake of Blacks" and consequently should "decide how far we're willing to go . . . before a confrontation so as not to appear to be yielding under pressure." On Christmas Eve, Brewster was brought in. By this time, professors assumed the BLSU "may be unwilling to discuss differences and want to do something active." With finals approaching, they worried that the BLSU would picket or bar entry to exam rooms.[43]

And the faculty, dean, and university administration were divided about how to respond to the threat of occupation. Everyone agreed on the need to deescalate the conflict "and in particular, to prevent the extremist black students from gaining adherents among the other students, and to dissuade the students as a whole from engaging in disruptive action." But they differed over means to that end. While most law professors seemed to think that "the faculty should offer a firm and immediate response to any student transgression of certain rigid rules," some argued that professors "should make certain tactical concessions in order to avoid a confrontation." Pollak was among those willing to compromise on disruptions; Brewster took a harder line. The dean and president had been at odds over tactics the previous spring as Yale tried to plan for possible "Columbia-type" student takeovers. Brewster believed "intimidation cannot be accepted as a means of effecting change in an academic institution and disruption, it must be made clear, will be met with dismissal." The dean, however, whose "misgivings re University Policy have been growing as likelihood of trouble has increased," worried about "overkill" and thought universities should focus on sending in campus police to secure critical files when students occupied administration buildings. When Pollak said that "student occupation of a professor's office, or of a classroom, should be punished — but doubts that occupation of the Dean's office should be treated as seriously leading to disciplinary action," the faculty heard him threatening to quit. Guido Calabresi told the dean that this was "the worst possible time for a resignation — it would be the 'one best thing' for the Black students."[44]

After affirming his faith in the dean, Brewster turned to the faculty's draft response to BLSU presentments. Here, the president was more inclined to make concessions than Pollak seemed to be publicly. Stressing "Yale's responsibility to adopt a posture that's meaningful in other universities," Brewster urged the professors to say that they could not "drop standards, for sake of Blacks — students or faculty." The president always insisted that Yale College, where the black enrollments were rising, and where, oddly, Brewster compared African Americans to "foreign students" whose presence broadened whites, "did not maintain an affirmative action program as such," while stressing "that the admission of nontraditional students was an especially subjective process calling for 'some gambling, some risk-taking,' and flexibility in interpreting SAT scores in light of background." (His stance outraged many alumni. "You will laugh," William F. Buckley reportedly said, "but it is true that a Mexican-American from El Paso High with identical scores on the achievement test, and identically ardent recommendations from the headmaster, has a better chance of being admitted to Yale than Jonathan Edwards the Sixteenth from Saint Paul's School.") Thus probably Brewster wanted the law faculty to adopt the students' demands *and* reiterate its commitment to "standards," lest African Americans be stigmatized.[45]

But the faculty was not buying. Those most closely connected to process theory proved particularly vocal. "We're using a double-standard now," Bickel said. Harry Wellington added: "Last spring we took Blacks we shouldn't have taken. We're taking people who are not only not qualified but whose interest is in bringing the system down. We must come to grips with this dilemma."[46]

To the relief of Woodbridge Hall, the faculty came to grips by accepting most of the black students' demands. By New Year's Eve, professors had confirmed that the law school's admissions policy would "*continue*" to give "substantial weight to past educational disadvantage and cultural difference." Significantly, while refusing to admit "a given percentage or a given number of black law students or, for that matter, any other group of law students," on the grounds that it could not predict how many applications it would receive, the faculty extended the application deadline for African Americans. It also announced a program to expand recruitment, which would make use of both black students and graduates, led by Leon Higginbotham. Most important, it promised to reserve an extra ten to fifteen places for "black and other minority or disadvantaged students who meet the admissions criteria. Any students thus selected will be in addition to the roster of students who apply and are admitted during the normal period—a roster which should itself include a number of black students." In effect, the school agreed to commit 10 percent of its positions in each first-year class to minority groups.[47]

Professors made a number of other promises to the BLSU. They would increase financial aid for African Americans. Yale would also participate in the Council on Legal Education Opportunity Institute. Harvard Law dean Derek Bok had passed along the information that introduction of the "CLEO program took much heat off" his school. Ultimately, Cochran, a member of the CLEO Council, and other students of color at Yale administered a month-long orientation course during the summer of 1969 for all admitted under affirmative action. Further, professors discussed additions to the curriculum that would permit students to receive credit for faculty-supervised work in the community. They promised to inquire into campus police mistreatment of black students and pledged a financial contribution to the BLSU. They explained how the Appointments Committee was working to recruit black faculty members, without promising to hire any. And they renewed their commitment to faculty-student cooperation.[48]

*   *   *

Here was an example of black student power. Though the faculty had used face-saving rhetoric and had not accepted all BLSU demands, it had agreed to a good number of them. Pollak could not have been displeased at the outcome. Despite his public condemnation of anything that would "smack of a quota," he was one of the more vigorous proponents of affirmative action. The dean signaled his support when he defended his professors' action in an exchange of private letters with Judge Macklin Fleming, soon published in the *Public Interest*.[49]

A member of the school's executive committee, Fleming had queried Yale Law's "abandonment of an objective system of admission based on intellectual aptitude (painstakingly evolved over a period of decades)" to the committee and the Yale Corporation. "The faculty can talk around the clock about disadvantaged background, and it can excuse inferior performance because of poverty, environment, inadequate cultural tradition, lack of educational opportunity, etc.," Fleming said. But the use of "benign" quotas to aid the disadvantaged, as opposed to the "malignant" ones once used to keep Jews from dominating professional schools, favored the group over the individual, violating the "American creed" that Yale had long "proudly" espoused. Nor was he swayed by the argument that the "mission" of Yale Law School "to train national leaders . . . for all segments of the population" justified its decision to work harder to enroll African Americans. The bottom line was that, though well intentioned, the goal of training more minority lawyers would not "be furthered by putting unqualified or poorly qualified black students in competition with students at Yale Law School who average in the 97th percentage of intellectual achievement." African Americans would be stigmatized as a result. Let the minorities go to good local or regional or local law schools instead. Whatever the flaws in aptitude tests, Fleming insisted that they predicted performance well and reported that he had heard that "academic difficulties are being experienced by the underqualified black students in the first year class at Yale."[50]

Emphasizing that the faculty had long doubted the predictive value of grades and the aptitude of minorities and/or the poor, Pollak's reply reiterated that the Admissions Committee had also long accepted "numerous black students (and indeed, occasional white applicants whose histories seemed culturally atypical)" who did not meet its academic standards. Few had failed, and "[a] few" had received high grades, even achieving membership on the *Yale Law Journal.* "Not surprisingly," though, "given their lesser academic preparation[,] most of these students have not achieved academic distinction at the Law School." What counted, however, the dean stressed, was that "so many black alumni have, entering upon the profession, speedily demonstrated professional accomplishments of a high order."[51]

The Admissions Committee was only changing its admissions practice now by seeking a higher number of students of color, and—Pollak emphasized—disadvantaged whites. Thus "the real question is whether the School was warranted in enlarging its numerical commitment to this objective." Pollak was certain it was, because the country must train more African Americans for leadership positions, and lawyers were leaders. There was no down side, he contended. According to Pollak, the faculty believed that "if the number of students with prior educational deficiencies is a minor fraction of the total student body," the learning environment would not suffer. Further, it seemed "reasonable to expect that the number of black applicants who are well prepared academically will increase markedly within the next few years, as a corollary of the increasing number of blacks matriculating at first-rate colleges," and that if Yale raised more money for financial aid, it could attract many of them.[52]

The Yale faculty's action struck many as enlightened. One might have expected Pollak's admission that few law students had done well academically to elicit charges of paternalism. But reporters at the University of Michigan Law School's newspaper singled Yale's dean out for praise: "It is time to understand that one comes to law school not to get good grades or make law review, but to become an accomplished lawyer."[53]

Certainly, Fleming's confidence that regional and local law schools would accommodate minority demand if Yale did not step up to the plate seemed odd. When a new assistant dean arrived at Stanford in the summer of 1968 to take charge of minority recruitment, "the Law School had graduated only one black as far as anyone could remember—and that was in 1968." Students alleged that King Hall, UC Davis's Law school named after Martin Luther King, did not deserve its name, having graduated three African Americans between its opening in 1968 and 1971.[54]

In a world where "lesser" law schools aped the most prestigious, it was significant that Yale publicized its expansion of its earlier quiet program at a crucial period in the history of affirmative action. "Happily, law schools throughout the country—including Harvard, Columbia, and other major schools—are recognizing the depth and urgency of the training obligation which our profession must assume," Pollak told Fleming. "In this setting, if Yale Law School can play a larger role than it has before in meeting this important national need, it ought to try to do so." Owen Fiss, then a young law professor at the University of Chicago, recalled that academic lawyers everywhere followed Yale's experiment. When Yale stuck its toe in the water, schools with activist student bodies of their own proved more likely to follow with their feet: in 1971, the Boalt faculty adopted a policy essentially reserving one-quarter to one-fifth of the seats in the first-year class for students of color.[55]

Though black students at Yale criticized their professors' unwillingness to go further, they seemed largely acceptant: Pollak declared himself "encouraged by the relatively temperate conversation" he had with Cochran after the BLSU received the faculty's letter. African Americans threw themselves into their role as "advance men" to sway more of their number to apply and to enroll. In an open letter to the faculty and student body, Cochran even praised the faculty for its "forthright and gratifying" response to some BLSU issues.[56]

To be sure, tension between black students and the faculty had not disappeared. Students were annoyed that the administration had not committed itself to a 10 percent figure for the entire student body and was focusing instead on the first-year class, as the law school insisted it was bound to do, since it did not accept third-year transfers and possessed only a limited number of spots in the second year. The draft call had been lighter than anticipated, and the 207 first-years enrolled in 1968 already represented a 30 percent increase over the school's target number of 165. Likewise, the BLSU declared itself "disappointed" that the faculty had not spoken "more forcefully to the question of hiring black faculty members."[57]

And there was another flare-up between the administration and BLSU when the faculty formally set out the criteria for a two-track admissions program administered by one committee in the spring. The law school typically measured "academic competence" in part by use of the "Combined Prediction," a score it determined by combining a grade point average (weighted, so as to give a higher score to transcripts from Ivy League institutions) and LSATs. While admitting "the limitations" of the CP and insisting that each applicant's entire record must be reviewed, the faculty stressed that most whites and students of color admitted through the general admissions program must possess minimum CPs of at least 3.2. It declared its expectation that minorities accepted through the special admissions program would possess a CP of at least 2.0, and preferably 2.5. And the faculty said that the "closer it came toward obtaining its target goal of disadvantaged students from minority groups," the less it would tolerate lower CP scores.[58]

The BLSU objected to the "colonial benevolence" of the intimation that "high-risk" black students were compromising academic quality: "We assume that Yale's admissions policy with respect to black students is not a 'benign' double standard at all, but a hard-headed and correct assessment of the loss the Law School will suffer if it allows a culturally biased test and similar 'objective' standards to deprive it of the valuable potential of able black students." The faculty's announcement that it would make fewer allowances for cultural bias as the school achieved greater success in recruiting African Americans also annoyed. When the BLSU had demanded a minimum number of admissions the previous December, professors had declared quotas anathema. Now, black students charged, the faculty was in effect establishing a ceiling on special admissions, "a negative quota, a limitation on the number of [black] students in the first-year class."[59]

But beyond lodging a letter of protest with the faculty, the BLSU did little. Its letter made no mention of resolving the differences by means other than discussion. It did not demand another audience with professors.

Doubtless that was because the process was yielding better results than anyone had expected. "[W]e got through last year rather well," Associate Dean Ralph Brown acknowledged after admissions season had ended in 1969. "The first interest of our black students was, I think, that their numbers be increased. In this we have been very successful, in that perhaps 15% of the entering class are from racial minority groups." A more effective affirmative action program had taken root at Yale.[60]

*   *   *

To the discomfort of many professors, relevance in coursework also took root alongside the stronger affirmative action program. Brown joked that the law school catalogue should be rewritten to say: "Because of its colonial, capitalist, white racist inheritance, most of the faculty and curriculum of the school are irrelevant to the central issues of our time." Bickel charged that students clamored for "a radical and disastrous shift in objectives, a return to vocational training." He blamed the faculty, which no longer knew "what we are about as a collegium," and was descending into "collective incoherence." From his perspective, there was reason for irritation, for, as students sardonically acknowledged, Yale *had* added "a sprinkling of urban and poverty law courses" to the curriculum. That was a shrewd move. The *Yale Daily News* had recently charged the law school with misusing its Ford Foundation grant to develop the urban curriculum, and administrators had made matters worse by admitting that "much of the courses served under the rubric of Urban Law could be offered anyway even if the Ford grant never existed."[61]

The grant did enable the school to hire high-profile visitors, such as Edward Sparer, founder of the Center for Social Welfare Policy and Law, to teach poverty law. That helped make up for the fact, perhaps, that Columbia Law School had the Center itself. Apparently, there was no thought of keeping Sparer on permanently: the Brooklyn Law School graduate and former member of the Communist Party would not have fit in with "Gene's boys." Still, Yale's enlistment of one of the nation's most distinguished welfare litigators to teach poverty law impressed students. Sparer's seminar on public welfare law had to become a full-fledged course when more than eighty students signed up. The school's reestablishment of the intensive semester, a World War II experiment that now enabled students to receive credit for a semester's work or study outside the law school, also satisfied the hunger for relevance.[62]

Even more important, BLSU unrest, like that of white activists, lay the groundwork for a real expansion of clinical education. Yale's student-run legal services program, dating back to the 1920s, supervised those who wanted to do legal aid work and assist local public defenders on an extracurricular basis. Jerome Frank had breathed vitality into the clinical movement, and students had established an office of the New Haven Legal Aid Bureau in the school in 1948. After Frank's death and the creation of the New Haven Legal Assistance Association, the student program became the Jerome N. Frank Legal Services Organization. But it had too few openings for the many wanting exposure to urban and poverty law during the late 1960s. Now, clinical education became "one battle in a war against the academic law school as an institution."[63]

Law students of the sixties at Yale, like those elsewhere, sought more clinical opportunities. First-year student Avi Soifer was typical. As a Yale College student, he had pressed the administration to approve coeducation, helping to organize Coed Week, which brought hundreds from women's colleges to live and learn at Yale for a week. (Characteristically, Brewster stole the march by announcing Yale would admit women at the beginning of the first Coed Week. But when he called for the segregation of freshmen women students in one residential college, Soifer charged that the university president was reacting so nervously because "you're afraid of too much fucking going on.") Arriving at Yale Law School, Soifer and his classmates established a clinic for Connecticut Valley Hospital, a "snakepit" of a mental institution with "no law at all." Students working with legal aid attorneys represented individual patients in civil commitment hearings. "My first victory was getting someone out," Soifer recalled wryly. "Within a month, he died in a rooming house fire." With another classmate, Soifer also filed an unsuccessful suit in federal court challenging the constitutionality of Connecticut's civil commitment proceedings. "'Relevancy' was a cry of the age," Soifer said later, and "for those who were 'not on the barricades' or who had not dropped out," legal services work reflected the sense of litigation as an effective tool of social reform.[64]

Anxious about whether clinical education was sufficiently "academic," the faculty nevertheless applied for Ford money to develop a program in 1969. The application successful, the school hired Daniel Fried to develop the clinical program, and the Danbury Project, in which students provided legal services to inmates at Danbury Prison, was launched. Professors asked Soifer and other LSO Board members to help them find attorneys to operate the new in-house clinic, and the students threw themselves into the search, though they understood that its successful conclusion would mean they no longer supervised themselves. By their lights, it turned out to be yet another attempt to co-opt them. After pretending to consult the students, the school hired "two white guys with Establishment credentials": Dennis Curtis, who had been a lawyer for the Navy, and Stephen Wizner, from Mobilization for Youth. The partnership between students and lawyers was off to a "rocky start." But the students came to like and respect both men, and the clinic "continued to be a subversive oasis where you could be a wiseass about Yale and its pretensions."[65]

The Yale faculty was apparently trying to gain greater control of the clinic *and* buy off the sixties generation. As clinical professors, Wizner and Curtis did not receive tenure, and the faculty cited the establishment of the Intensive Semester and the "proposed Legal Services Clinic (a storefront center)" as evidence of its good faith in negotiations with the BLSU. Perhaps academics expected that the clinical program could absorb the demand for relevance, enabling them to be left alone. Perhaps they also hoped that clinicians would so enjoy teaching Yale's bright young that they would add some of the cordiality that students said their professors withheld. But clinical education still made "regular" professors nervous and suspicious, with one warning that "clinical programs may themselves be escapism for some people, escape into what is sometimes called 'real life.'" Another reportedly, but famously, told students: "You have to understand you're wasting your time in the clinic because you have to understand you're mandarins." At first, students could receive only "forensic," not "academic," credit for clinical work. "We are probably a little more obsessed than we should be with a fear of such programs," Abe Goldstein admitted.[66]

Power at Yale remained with the professors. As at other institutions, there was a tension between the academic and clinical faculty, reflecting the former's anxiety that clinical education was insufficiently theoretical and overly expensive. Clinical instructors were "unapologetically treated as second-class citizens by most of the academic faculty, who were determined to keep clinical work out of the core curriculum."[67] Yale professors preserved their prerogatives through reform.

So it was with affirmative action. As one student said, in 1968–69, "the faculty agreed to admit more minority group members, but refused to permit students to review applications." Even so, some of Pollak's colleagues who thought he should have taken a harder line surely nodded their heads when the *Advocate* editorialized that in the blowup with the BLSU, Pollak had played the role of "The Amazing and Silent Collapsible Dean."[68]

*   *   *

To professors, the student body seemed as monolithic as students' perception of the faculty. Thus many assumed that white and black students alike had united behind the BLSU. At the critical faculty meeting, Harry Wellington had told his colleagues that it was "most important that [the] Law School's answer be such as to keep [the] White law students." The implication was clear: lose the whites by alienating African Americans and the school would surely be shut down.[69]

In fact, the situation among the students was more complex. The relationship between whites and blacks had grown strained in the fall of 1968. BLSU members wanted a place of their own, for example, in part because white students had sometimes taken over the law school television. After the December crisis between the BLSU and the faculty peaked, the *Yale Daily News* reported that Yale Law School Association president John McDonough and several others had pointed to the "serious racial tension and hostility" in the school, and appealed to the faculty to address the BLSU's demands in December. Yet they were apparently among the few white law students who had any idea what was happening. Most could not understand the school's strained atmosphere. "If only Dean Pollak, or the faculty, or the blacks, or someone had explained it all," the *Advocate* mourned in January.[70]

At a meeting that month which drew more than a hundred students, the tension between white and blacks was evident. The BLSU, with its twenty-odd members, requested nearly one-sixth of the Law School Association's funds to enable it to bring in speakers, produce a newsletter, and work in the inner city. President McDonough expressed support. An "overwhelming majority" of those in attendance favored the motion to allocate $1,200 of the $7,500 budget to the BLSU. So far, all was going to plan. But some whites wanted to know if BLSU members favored segregation. Just before the votes were counted, one asked about the purpose of the BLSU and its criteria for determining membership eligibility. "McDonough, are you going to let any bodies fall in front of your train before you railroad this thing through?" another shouted. "Are you going to vote for a group that is radically restrictive?"

After McDonough acknowledged he had engaged in some "steamrolling," the rules of procedure were suspended to permit further discussion. The issue of whether the BLSU was "restrictive" would not go away. The *Advocate* reported that one student articulated "the frustration of many in the room" when she said, "We can play parliamentary games all you want, but communication has completely broken down in the Law School. I can't talk to blacks, blacks can't talk to whites."

At this point, Otis Cochran departed from the script to address student comments, "something," he stated, "that all of the BLSU members had previously agreed *not* to do." Declaring his surprise at finding so much "political immaturity and insensitivity to this moment in [the] history of the country" at the nation's "most liberal law school," he affirmed that the BLSU shared the goal of a single community. Adding that "as we try to approach this community, we need to support ourselves in some ways," he asked his white listeners to imagine themselves members of a small isolated group among six hundred. It was not just a matter of race, but class, too, he stressed. According to Cochran, at mixers and other school functions, black students just met "Protestant white girls from Vassar." He alleged harassment of the BLSU, saying that "since September BLSU signs have been marred or torn down" and reporting that he had received "phone calls at 2:00 A.M. saying 'Nigger, when you come down those steps from your room, we're going to blow your head off.'" He wanted to think his caller was unaffiliated with the law school, Cochran told his audience, but he feared otherwise.

African Americans' alienation helped to create their demands upon the faculty. "I have yet to hear anybody discuss with me our sense of urgency in getting more black students to come to the Law School," Cochran lamented. His white counterparts only wanted to know, he said, where the BLSU had gotten its new television. Cochran expressed dismay at whites' complaints at being left in the dark as the BLSU negotiated with professors. "What hurt us all very much is that we tried to move in the Law School in a manner showing respect for this institution, and this was misunderstood," he said. "We dealt at first directly with the faculty because we saw how in working for grade reform you dealt directly with them." The BLSU had not publicized its discussions with the professors out of respect for their privacy. The *Advocate* reported Cochran's peroration and its consequences: "Addressing the whites directly, Cochran concluded: 'We don't want your sympathies, we don't need your praying lips. Helping hands are a whole lot better.' At that moment clapping hands was the only thing the whites could give—but it was a beginning. Following Cochran's talk, the Student Association voted unanimously to appropriate $1,200 to the BLSU for its proposed projects."[71]

It was hard to believe that white students had inspired the BLSU. Nevertheless, Cochran's virtuoso performance flattered whites for achieving grading reform, displayed black pride, and tapped into left-of-center whites' guilt and their desire for social change. Like black students elsewhere, he had told the white "radicals" whom he actually considered quite conservative, "'We'll Do Our Thing, You Do Yours.'" And he had done it so as to guarantee support. Condemning the Student Association for miring "the meeting in a welter of points of order," the *Advocate* nevertheless applauded Cochran's "lucid and specific exposition of the aims and situation of black students."[72]

Perhaps something good might come out of the BLSU-faculty showdown, the editors speculated. The "unhappy experience of the past few weeks" demonstrated anew that there was "no substitute for open, unambiguous communication." That required "common knowledge of facts" and "common knowledge of viewpoint, orientation, working assumptions, main concerns and motivations." At present, there was a "chasm in our midst."[73]

Students' recent proposal to share in law school governance promised "to bridge" it, the *Advocate* added. But negotiators would achieve success, the newspaper warned, only if student and faculty negotiators "shed the notion that they represent mutually antagonistic interests." That would prove a notion tough to shed.[74]

"S.H.I.T.F.A.C.E."

Thus as the BLSU crisis subsided, the issue of student participation in governance, from which black law students had remained isolated, returned to the school's front burner. It was already simmering elsewhere at Yale. "The buzzword on campus from 1968 to 1970 was 'governance,'" one historian of Brewster's presidency has observed. The administration staved off demands for student voting representation at Yale College faculty meetings, even summoning police to keep undergraduates out on two occasions. The process remained peaceful, and Woodbridge Hall stalled by creating a study commission on governance. It also agreed to place students, and a considerable number of them, on the Executive and Disciplinary Committees, as well as on search committees for college masters and deans. It was preferable "to err on the side of generosity, rather than on the side of stinginess," the administration decided.[75]

That, of course, was Brewster's philosophy. The developments reflected his genius for co-optation, his genuine respect for students, and his devotion to process. What mattered most was that all who cared know those in charge of making policy had taken their feelings into account, Yale's president publicly maintained. "Once decision has been made, for better or for worse, common purpose and common loyalty usually succeed in moving beyond disagreement to renewed support of the common enterprise."[76]

Thus it was not that Yale College students received so much on governance as much as that, for the most part, the administration intelligently gave what it believed it could. But few administrators anywhere possessed Brewster's political skill. Further, because of the careers they had chosen and because they were older and even more sensitive to being treated like children, law students proved even more interested in governance than undergraduates. That made fireworks over the issue more likely at the law school than the college.

After three months of internal deliberations, the law school's elected Student Negotiating Committee of nine white men and one white woman unveiled its plan for change in February 1969, "joint student-faculty rule." The committee envisioned governance by a Law School council that would replace the faculty. Elected student representatives and professors would possess equal voting power. In addition, all committee meetings would be open, and students and professors would possess equal voting power there. The student utopia was itself hierarchical: the proposal gave no power to staff.[77]

The student press liked it anyway. The *Advocate*, one of whose editors, Richard Hughes, was a Student Negotiating Committee member, applauded the SNC for trying to bring faculty and students together and characterized the plan as "ideal." Superficially, the committee's proposal seemed "as radical as any in the nation's most troubled universities," the *Yale Daily News* reported. "But given the friendly spirit of the 'revolutionaries,' the smallness and cohesiveness of the Law School, and its recent history of controversial issues, 'radical' hardly seems a fitting description." The *News* celebrated the "peaceful revolution" at hand.[78]

THE YALE ADVOCATE

Vol. 2, No. 6   YALE LAW SCHOOL, NEW HAVEN, CONNECTICUT   February 6, 1969

Otis Cochran

Blacks Get $1,200 For Projects After Procedural Wrangling

By Ann Hill '71L

Before the Law School Student Association met on January 28th, its budget for 1968-69 ($6500 of which are dimes, nickels and quarters from the vending machines) allotted $2,930 of a total $7,568 to beer and cheque, wives and Muzak (fall cocktail party and banquet, $700; social committee, $1,600; spring cocktail party, $500; Law Wives, $390). One hundred dollars went to a nonexistent organization (World Community Association), $600 to a once-yearly publication (Yearbook) and its well-paid editor, $500 to the bi-weekly Advocate, $300 to keep the Coke Lounge clean (what price beth), $400 for administrative expenses (drawing up the contract with the Coke Lounge cleaner?), $578 for a TV and insurance, $1,500 for guest speakers and a student $600 to LSCRRC, appearing for the first time on the budget this year.

These allocations had been made at a full meeting which attracted little attention and only a few serious observers.

In contrast, the January 28 meeting, chaired by John McDonough, President of the LSSA, drew to a Faculty Lounge crowd exceeding 100 members of the Law School community. Purpose of the meeting: to decide upon a request by the Black Law Students Union for $1,200 to finance an ambitious program which includes a series of black speakers, a newsletter and a recruitment catalog, and working in the black community in New Haven.

In the discussion following a motion to approve the budget as submitted, McDonough disclosed that many of the expenses and allotments in the original budget had been overestimated, that in fact a projected $1,225 could be culled from the earlier appropriations, $700 of which came from Forum Committee funds. In absence of the BLSU request this money would have gone presumably to reducing the $1,789 deficit plaguing the LSSA.

question of where the money coming from once settled,

John Thomas '69L asked the members of the BLSU who were present to explain the nature of their organization, its membership qualifications and its objectives. McDonough pointed out that these questions were irrelevant to a discussion of the BLSU's detailed budget and that traditionally the Student Association did not question the validity of an organization that had been formally recognized by the Administration. Other members of SA supported McDonough and Stu Beck '71L moved that the budget be voted on.

The vote — an overwhelming majority in favor — was taken, but not counted, when the first voice from the floor — that of Robert Webb '69L — boomed forth "McDonough, are you going to let any bodies fall in front of your train before you railroad this thing through? Are you going to vote for a group that is radically restrictive? That is what I want to know." In reply, McDonough admitted to a bit of "steamrolling" on his part, and the members of the Student Association voted to suspend the rules of parliamentary procedure for ten minutes to allow further discussion. Several students continued weaving Webb's string of questions, addressing themselves to the BLSU representatives at the meeting and asking for an answer as to whether the group was racially restrictive. Speaking for the BLSU, Joseph

(Continued on Page 3)

BLOW YOUR MIND

It happens on February 14 — "the first day of the rest of your life" — and the law school may never be the same again.

In conjunction with the social committee of the Law School Student Association, Cosmic Laboratories (a group of law students interested in environmental experimentation) is sponsoring the Cosmic Mixer, which, in the words of Jon Krown '70L, head of Cosmic Labs, can only be described

as "an experience for the whole law school community."

Music will be provided by possibly five different bands, including the Group Image from New York, the Grateful Dead from San Francisco, and a classical ensemble, among others.

The Hog Farm Commune, a 50-member group from Los Angeles, will spend three days at the law school prior to the mixer, setting up sound and light effects by the

dining hall.

The Pageant Players, a New York acting troupe similar to the Living Theatre, will perform during the evening, and Krown promises that there will be "things for everyone to do."

The entire production is being put on at no expense, and there will be no admission charge. Krown mentioned the possibility that the event will be covered by national news media.

Negotiating Committee Asks Joint Student-Faculty Rule

PREAMBLE

The present governmental structure at the Yale Law School does not allow sufficient broad-based participation in decision-making. It does not meet the substantive needs of the members of this academic community. Our relationships with one another are marred by failures of communication and periodic bitterness between student and student and between student and faculty.

The past year has witnessed dramatic evidence of our shared dilemma. It has also witnessed some promise of solution. The gradual opening of some committee work to full community participation, and presence at some faculty meetings of some students, though for severely limited purposes, and the increase of communication generally in less formal situations confidence maintained by the faculty alone, even a year ago.

What little we have seen so far of a decision-making process shared by faculty and a mature student body, acting out of mutual respect and equally responsible to the larger community, shows promise for the future. The uneven quality of this process, to date, and the almost total failure of the school to cope with some of the severe problems we share—in any manner which resembles a common undertaking—make it imperative that our institutional structure be reformed to accommodate our mutual needs and insure continued progress.

The Student Negotiating Committee thus proposes a series of reforms which draw on our experience to date. The goal is continued and increased student-faculty cooperation. These proposals are clearly departures from well-established custom in the law school. But they reflect a conviction that some basic changes in structure are necessary, and that the law school must seek to become a true community promoting human values rather than the sterile acquisition of technique. More glamorous and elaborate forms of supplication will not serve that end. It is the shared task of governing the affairs of the community, and the shared burden of responsibility, that is the key to the successful and realistic readjustment of the law school society. To accomplish this readjustment, the following changes are proposed:

A. LAW SCHOOL COUNCIL

1. The Law School shall be governed by a Law School Council composed of all voting members of the faculty and elected student representatives; is shall retain the powers of the present faculty meetings.

2. Students shall be given substantial representation on the Law School Council, and this shall be accomplished by means of the selection of a

(Continued on Page 3)

A set of eight proposals for the restructuring of the administration of the law school — including a provision for equal student and faculty representation in a Law School Council which would replace present faculty meetings as the governing organ of the school — was released today by the Student Negotiating Committee. (See adjacent box.)

The proposals and the "preamble" which accompanies them will be the working document in negotiations between the ten-member committee and its faculty counterpart, which will begin on February 17. On Wednesday, February 12 at 4 p.m., the committee will hold an open meeting to explain and discuss the proposals with interested students.

Negotiating Committee member Bob Spearman '70L characterized the proposals as building upon "the experience we've had so far this year in working jointly with the faculty" on various matters. "This is an attempt to extend that principle of cooperation, and to institutionalize it.

Spearman explained that the proposals reflect the belief of the committee "that the law school is not just a collection of competing interest groups, but it—and ought to be—a real community."

Bill Taylor '69L noted that the committee had two principal concerns in mind in formulating the proposals: the substantive content of future decisions concerning law

(Continued on Page 3)

LSO Takes All

By Robert Borosage '71L

On January 31, the Board of Directors of the Legal Services Organization announced that the eighty-two first-year students registered for legal services would be enrolled in the program. Reacting to student criticism, the Board thus reversed its intention of limiting enrollment to thirty students.

The impetus for the change in policy came from a proposal by Bill Drayton '70L combined with the efforts of an ad hoc organization of first-year students.

The Drayton proposal suggested that the legal services program could be expanded by shifting the focus of LSO from the clinical model of legal aid work to the "models of a Populist Attorney General's Office and of a Ralph Nader."

Specifically, the proposal suggested that interested students should organize to investigate consumer fraud, search out violations of housing standards, and investigate the possibilities of legislative

(Continued on Page 2)

"Negotiating Committee Asks Joint Student-Faculty Rule."
(Yale Advocate, February 6, 1969. Courtesy Yale Law School.)

Wishful thinking. Now, at the beginning of 1969, the Student Negotiating Committee faced a series of meetings with its counterpart of faculty heavyweights. The first was inauspicious. Professors maintained that the university's bylaws required the faculty to serve as the Law School's governing body. (Students subsequently heard that Black, Bickel, and Wellington had circulated a memorandum damning their proposal as unconstitutional.)[79]

Of course, the bylaws could be changed, faculty negotiators acknowledged, but the dean insisted that "the Bylaws are right." The professors expressed sympathy with the students' ideal of greater "community." Nevertheless, according to the notes of student negotiator Hughes, Abe Goldstein insisted that the faculty was "not prepared to give up the vote—but assuming that, cannot community still be achieved?—& the burden is on the students to show where communication, etc., has broken down."[80]

But as the student negotiators saw it, the real heavy was Rostow, "the self-appointed father image," who while derogating faculty meetings, presumably as wastes of time, maintained that the young lacked the expertise to understand the issues under discussion, much less to vote on them. Recently returned from Lyndon Johnson's State Department and living in a guest suite in the law school, Rostow faced students who wanted to talk with him night and day about the war and who held "The Rostow Brothers Film Festival," featuring movies critical of U.S. policy in Vietnam and coverage of atrocities committed there. As Rostow raised the lawyer's "parade of horribles" with Student Negotiating Committee members and contended that concessions might lead to a revolution at Yale comparable to the one that gave students control of Latin American universities, Hughes, doubtless dressed more casually, was struck by the former dean's appearance: "& lo and behold—he wears garters!" Rostow's insistence also surprised Hughes: "[H]e draws the line rather harshly—the faculty will maintain its authority over policy 'against all comers'—& he has the audacity to speak of striving toward community." But Hughes seemed grateful to the State Department's former number three man because "it appears that, oaf though Rostow may be, he is the most candid of all of them—he says what they are probably all *really* thinking."[81]

Not all of them. Declaring that in his thirty years on the faculty, "everything that has ever come up has been too radical for this group," James Moore supported the student franchise. So did Clyde Summers, a labor law professor by his own experience inclined to support antiwar activists and democracy. A pacifist who had claimed conscientious objector status during World War II, Summers had appealed his own subsequent exclusion from the Illinois bar to the U.S. Supreme Court—and lost. Later, he had become an academic who seemed to feel marginalized on the Yale faculty, excluded from the corridors of power. Where Wellington taught labor law from the more conservative legal process prospective, Summers was a lifetime agitator for union democracy. He had helped write the Landrum-Griffin Act that clarified the rights of union members to participate in their own governance and was sometimes credited with its enactment. His work was "marked by a passion for justice and concern with the rights of rank-and-file union members," and he exemplified the idealistic and pragmatic "activist scholar." Tellingly, Summers now compared the faculty-student negotiations to conversations that must have occurred when Walter Reuther demanded codetermination for workers at Ford Motor Company. Here, too, Summers said, the faculty employed "the arguments of generous and benign management who could not understand why those on the other side, who were treated so well, should be making such demands—a management with such a sense of institutional responsibility that they felt it would violate the underlying principles of the institution to render any measure of management prerogatives." He understood the importance of participatory democracy to students, a key issue about which liberals and the New Left disagreed.[82]

Like the (mainly) white men in the Students for Democratic Society (SDS) who wrote the Port Huron Statement, the young at Yale who spoke through the Student Negotiating Committee believed that political involvement could reduce isolation, produce community, and improve individual lives. According to Summers, Yale's law students saw meaningful participation as "a basic right with all of the emotional fr[e]ight and feeling which that terminology implies." He warned his colleagues it would come, either through integration of students in the faculty processes of decision-making, or through the adoption of a collective bargaining model in which students and faculty faced off. But Summers and Moore were in the decided minority.[83]

Consequently, negotiations went downhill after the first meeting. Though they had secured no concessions from the faculty toward joint rule, student negotiators now advanced a new proposal designed to meet professors' concerns. The Law School Council could include two professors for every student, they offered. Were the faculty to disagree with a council vote, professors could reverse it by majority vote in "an Extraordinary Session of the faculty" that student representatives could attend, but at which they could not vote. Though they would retain ultimate authority under this proposal, the professors still were not buying. "[I]f this means that the faculty can't call itself into being on its own, for any reason, then it's just as objectionable as last week's proposal," Abe Goldstein advised students. At bottom, professors were unprepared "to give the *decision-making* role over to a body in which students have a vote." Meanwhile, sounding "just like he's at a goddamn diplomatic mtg" and using "all the fucking meaningless words in the book," Rostow lectured students about the "historical & traditional role of faculty."[84]

"Why not vote?" Bickel asked the SNC representatives on another occasion. "I'll tell you why not. We're professionals and as Mr. Rostow says, we have professional responsibilities. You wouldn't vote on a surgeon's techniques." While the faculty saw matters in a professional context, the students were just future graduates, or as Bickel termed them, "premature alumni." No current student concern could match that of the faculty, who possessed a "lifetime interest" in Yale Law School. Bickel cited a conversation with a recent alumnus who had announced that "a whole generation gap" divided him from the school's current students. "This generation gap is moving too fast today," Bickel continued. "You'll end up making one decision this year and two years later, the students will come along and say it has to be reversed."[85]

For Bickel, academic freedom was also at stake. Students argued that they deserved a vote because it resembled "a body politic." Bickel countered that given their eagerness to transform the university into a more positive force for social change, "the balance between the inner-directedness of the university as the haven of independent scholarship, on the one hand, and on the other, the university as the long-term servant of the society, responsive to its faculty needs . . . would be destroyed, to the great detriment of scholarship and ultimately of society, if students were given a decisive voice in setting the curriculum or otherwise directing lines of intellectual inquiry."[86]

Here was a classic clash of the 1960s. Students and faculty alike shared a commitment to institutional improvement. Yet, unlike their teachers, students saw the university as a microcosm of society. Consequently, the young worked to make the university more democratic, and they insisted that reform required awarding them a voice in the university's operations. When professors resisted, citing academic freedom and the authority their training gave them, students pushed back, attacking "the faculty's claim to authority based on expertise" and asserting "authority based on their own experience—they knew the kind of education that would meet their needs. In this manner, they claimed for students a right that conflicted with the faculty's understanding of their own academic freedom." Most professors thus found student demands for a role in the formulation of educational policy and curriculum design more threatening than calls for grade reform. Democratization of governance would affect faculty lives more. At most, academics generally believed "students enjoyed First Amendment rights on campus grounds but not in the classroom," the professors' domain. "Freedom within the classroom was limited to those people who had earned the right to speak with intellectual authority—those faculty who had been trained in the rigors of an academic discipline and were acknowledged by their colleagues as experts in their field."[87]

So Yale law professors delayed, and with spring recess approaching, students suspected them of trying to run down the clock. In March 1969, just after the break, the faculty finally acted. It approved a resolution Pollak had written seeking a middle ground between faculty opponents of "student power" and the few supporters. In it, professors formally rejected the Law School Council on the grounds that faculty decision-making powers should not be "diluted, or delegated (whether in whole or in part) to another body." There could be no compromise on one principle. Pollak contended that the power to govern the school legally and rightfully belonged to the faculty. The resolution reflected the dean's conviction that it would be "insulting to ourselves" and to the students to give them the "appearance" of sharing in authority.[88]

Still, Pollak tried to dress up the faculty's action as a victory for students. In their resolution, professors insisted that they were "impressed" by the need for student representatives to participate in some faculty meetings. The resolution credited students with making a convincing case that on occasions when professors considered matters students had helped shape as committee members, there should be "student participation in discussion (although not decision) at the level of the Faculty itself." Thus the faculty hoped "to explore with the Student Negotiating Committee arrangements which look in this direction (provided, of course, that such arrangements would guarantee the Faculty's right to meet by itself on any issue at any time)." Professors thus gave students a pat on the back for persuasiveness and signaled their willingness to contemplate continued student membership on selected committees and limited participation in some faculty meetings, at the same time that they announced their refusal to give students a vote at faculty meetings or a regular place at the faculty table.[89]

Following the example of the BLSU, the Student Negotiating Committee rejected the faculty resolution. A week after SNC members had resigned from all committees in protest and walked out of a meeting with professors, they published an open letter to the faculty. In attempting to codify the "inadequate procedures created this year," it alleged, professors proposed a model "of co-optation and supplication" that institutionalized "the subordination of student views and interests." The end product was a "disheartening statement about the courage and intellectual integrity of those faculty members who require the cloak of secrecy to shield their views from others in this community."[90]

As they so often did, students flung history and expectations at their professors. The episode "explode[d] the myth of the 'progressive,' adventuresome Yale Law School that you purport to embody." The failure of this "effort at liberal reform" pointed up "the conservative, establishment character of this faculty and the Yale Law School of 1969—whatever it may once have been." Refusing "to continue to be treated as children," Student Negotiating Committee members grandiosely announced that they were releasing all the information about "this fiasco" to the media and darkly warned of "collective action by students to bring about a reversal of this decision." The faculty's action "fatally undermines those of us who would seek to move forward by means of rational discourse among men of mutual trust and good will," they said. It demonstrated that radical students, who had predicted SNC failure from the beginning, warning that the "Christians had a better chance against the lions," had been right all along. Urging their professors "to consider the entire context of current American higher education before they proceed further down this shortsighted perilous course," student negotiators alluded pointedly to "the message of Berkeley and Columbia and Howard Law School. These were painful, disruptive events precisely because administrations and faculties isolated themselves from students, and refused to heed students seeking reform through appropriate channels and moderate discussion."[91]

The editors of the *Advocate* piled on, inveighing against a faculty "[c]linging blindly to the privileges and power of professorial status" that had obviously resolved to "meet the students head-on in combat." Professors were on a fool's errand. "The faculty may be patting itself on the back for its smooth disposition of the grading issue and black students' demands," but professors had seen "nothing yet." With "increasingly concerned and aware students" entering the school, the paternalism at its core would be challenged and, perhaps, subjected "to violent shaking. Yet the faculty has blocked the one avenue open to it by which it could very likely meet and overcome those and other challenges which the school must face." Students would not go to "the barricades" over "the issue of participation itself," the newspaper predicted. "But when the proper issue arises—and it will—the breakdown of orderly processes at the law school will be directly traceable to the faculty resolution."[92]

For an instant, it looked as if the "breakdown" might indeed occur over the faculty resolution. As police poured into Harvard's University Hall to arrest student protesters who had occupied it in April 1969, more than three hundred Yale law students were responding to signs around the school, along the lines of "Tired of being —— by the Faculty?" inviting them to an open meeting to protest the Yale faculty's action.[93]

Student negotiators had hoped that the professors participating in the open meeting would increase their classmates' resentment, and the faculty played into SNC's hands by choosing Rostow and Pollak as its representatives. "The idea that law students here will trust to the good faith of a hawkish Johnson adviser is too much to swallow," one student reporter wrote. But Pollak, who had been "noticeably nervous and angry," fared no better: he seemed like "a prep school headmaster reading the Riot Act." After the dean warned that "if you pursue as the only issue before you the question of voting on the faculty, I don't suppose that you will succeed," the floor was opened. "I thought it was a dumb idea in the fall," Duncan Kennedy said of the move to increase student participation in faculty governance, because he was sure that the faculty would "figure out a real cooptative, chummy scheme. I was wrong." Because so few professors "had a brain in their head on this," there was "a real opportunity" to make the most of student dissatisfaction. "The impasse was precipitated by a system of administration that is based on anti-human relationships," Kennedy concluded. "Shut this school down — or burn it down," black activist Don Howie exhorted. Someone else urged students to form a group called S.H.I.T.F.A.C.E., "Students to Help Increase the Faculty's Authority and Control over Everything." It could hold an organizational meeting "as soon as it gets the faculty permission."[94]

Ultimately, students and faculty drew away from the abyss. When both groups went back to the table and student negotiators proposed regular rather than limited nonvoting student representation at all faculty meetings, save those in executive session, they were astonished. "Yoicks!" Hughes noted. "Goldstein comes out in favor of our point — says let's try it — things couldn't be worse than they are now." The faculty would allow the Law Student Association to hold elections for ten representatives each fall. The elected representatives and "a number" of appointed student representatives would serve on standing faculty committees, save appointments and promotions. The Admissions Committee would include student representatives, but they would not initially participate in the disposition of individual cases. The extent to which students would participate in disciplinary proceedings was left unresolved. Nor would any students take part in meetings of the Governing Board, the tenured faculty gatherings to determine appointments and promotions. Still, elected representatives would serve as nonvoting participants in all faculty meetings, except when the dean or three other professors decided the faculty was meeting in "executive session."[95]

But what constituted justifiable grounds for an "executive session"? Therein lay the new "blockbuster." Hughes reported that "Rostow suggested this one:

SDS decides to burn down the Law School, & their leader is a student rep. (typical)." In the end, professors agreed to make explicit the understanding that most faculty meetings would not occur in executive session. And although the spirit of the negotiations suggested that they would notify students of meetings in executive session before they took place, the agreement that went to the professors to vote upon proved ambiguous on that point.[96]

Pollak was hopeful the faculty would accept it. He told Woodbridge Hall that "some faculty, though not a majority felt that the resolution he supported could be taken by students as a sign of weakness." To dispel that possibility, Rostow successfully moved that professors recast the "Proposed Declaration of Principles Regarding Student Participation" as a "Faculty Minute on Principles Regarding Student Participation." That way, there would be no suggestion that a "bargaining process between the faculty and students" had taken place and professors' control would remain intact. Even so, Black, Ralph Winter, Bickel, and "Bickel's understudy," Ward Bowman, rejected the resolution. Though Goldstein would not vote with them, he was unhappy that the young had transformed "a simple matter" into "issues of participatory and parliamentary democracy, consumerism, the nature of power and authority." "I wish the students would get off the structure bag (all this talk about the vote) and get into substantive matters," he told the *Advocate*. "[T]hey got so involved in Constitution-making." Pollak also sensed that "a few faculty would be willing to go further than the resolution and that some might want to give students a few votes." Nevertheless, the dean told Woodbridge Hall, correctly, that "this resolution will carry and that he can live with it in terms of his own commitments on the issue since it maintains the incontestable limits of no voting on the part of students and the right of the faculty to meet in private." And he predicted that the Student Negotiation Committee would agree to it.[97]

Yet although all agreed that the approach of summer left no time to renegotiate the plan, none of its student negotiators liked it. Even the most supportive advised the larger student body that "we are disappointed in the outcome of the negotiations" and that "a majority of the faculty still clings to its prerogatives with persistence." But they accepted the compromise, and in yet another referendum held during the spring of 1969, the student body did too. "It puts the students in the body of ultimate authority," the *Advocate* said approvingly of the new arrangement, "and, but for the vote (which, probably, in most cases will be unimportant) it will allow for the development of the sense of common endeavor so badly lacking in student-faculty relations until now." The agreement would not solve all the school's problems: "[T]he question of 'executive sessions' may plague the plan for some time, and there may arise issues soluble only through dramatic confrontations no matter how effective our community institutions." Nonetheless, the bargain would "allow for the development of the sense of common endeavor so badly lacking in student faculty relations until now" and begin to break down "the barriers which surround the faculty."[98]

*   *   *

Few professors who have sat through faculty and committee meetings will read this tale of student demands for participation or the *Advocate*'s hopeful forecast without a sense of poignancy. Why were the young surprised to find that their professors wanted to institutionalize "the subordination of student views and interests" or sought to shroud their decisions in a "cloak of secrecy"? Whatever the result of joint faculty-student rule might have been, students were naive to think that their teachers would have agreed to it. And perseverance for anything less than joint faculty-student rule, especially some seats on the less important committees and nonvoting participation in faculty meetings not in "executive session," was pathetic. Pollak himself later characterized the outcome as a "Rube Goldberg arrangement."[99]

Unless they were prepared to go to "the barricades," the young had picked the wrong battle. Yale College's SDS could have told law students that. Unimpressed by Woodbridge Hall's move to involve the young in some decision making, SDS insisted that "[b]y implicating students in the implementation of its objectively anti-working class policy," the push for student power just helped "the ruling class, . . . for it will become more difficult for students to fight back against such a policy when they themselves have been deluded into participating in its application." As one academic who tried to bridge the divide between liberals and the left by calling for radical liberalism would have said, law students had allowed "participatory democracy to trump political effectiveness." To be sure, the crisis at the law school had ended by placing ten students in a position to embarrass their teachers by reporting on what they said at most faculty meetings—a prospect one Yale law professor engagingly said "most of us are scared to death of"—and this most likely would but create more choreographed and less frank exchanges between faculty members. Yet why would students have imagined that this outcome would produce a "sense of common endeavor"?[100]

In a *Yale Law Journal* article excoriating traditional legal education, a dissident professor underscored the students' innocence: "Of course, there are student representatives on many of our committees, but nobody really expects them to tell us what to teach or how to teach it, and even if they try, we outnumber them, so we can either bludgeon them into submission or simply outvote them." And no matter how many positions they held on the curriculum committee, students had no voice on appointments, promotions, or the budget. Yet "they are so eternally grateful to us for our magnanimous tokenism."[101]

PARENTS AND CHILDREN?

Why had white Yale law students even begun this hopeless quest for shared governance? Writing of student activists through the ages, one sociologist hypothesized that the young involved themselves in "the generational revolt" as a way of rebelling against the old and killing their fathers. "Emotions issuing from the students' unconscious, and deriving from the conflict of generations, impose or attach themselves to the underlying political . . . movement, and deflect it in irrational directions," he claimed. "Student movements are thus what one would least expect — among the most irrationalist in history."[102]

Irrationalist? Surely who governed mattered. That was why their professors resisted the students so fiercely. Yale students learned how who governed mattered in their law school classes. Others elsewhere had absorbed the lesson too. Like those on other campuses, Yale law student activists wanted a prize rarely won: government with the consent of the governed.[103]

Were the young at Yale also engaged in surrogate patricide? To use Kenneth Keniston's phrase, Yale law students were "protest-prone." Recall that as a group, they were academically talented, economically privileged, disproportionately Jewish, and disproportionately self-identified as liberal or "left" when they entered law school. Their protest-proneness was a function of the political orientation of those Yale Law School attracted and students' perception of their treatment by faculty. Robert Stevens's research demonstrated that at most institutions, more students felt that they possessed more "warm, free and informal relationships" with their professors in 1970 than they had in 1960. "The major exception to general improvement is Yale. In 1960, it had the closest student-faculty ties of the schools studied; in 1970 the most distant." Yale students' activism reflected the "polarization."[104]

The Yale drama did possess some Oedipal dynamics. Clashes between generations frequently do. But it was a long way from Oedipus's killing of Laius on the road to Delphi. The elders' hostility was at least as striking. And, as some pointed out, though Oedipus had unwittingly slain his father, there were alternate stories in which father destroyed son. Most famous was the Persian myth of Rustum and Sohrab: Rustum, a warrior, killed Sohrab in combat and then, to his grief, learned that Sohrab was his son as his victim lay dying. As one scholar said, "the interpretation of the student movement of the 1960s as an Oedipal revolt may tell us more about the fathers than it does about the sons, or more accurately, the children."[105]

At Yale, the imagery of parents and children seemed to matter more to professors than students. "When we entered the lists of controversy," Abe Goldstein said, "we did it with all the intensity of an overly involved family." When Boris Bittker's alumni contemporaries asked him how he could tolerate the younger generation, he often reminded his friends that the students are "my children and yours" and that "many of the things that the students wanted were things they had learned to prize at home." Bittker believed that the students' agitation for change reflected their absorption of their parents' lessons. John Hersey, master of one of Yale's residential colleges, may have had it right when he said that in "five years of living closely with students I encountered very few who disliked their parents" and "numerous members of the faculty, especially senior ones," whose feelings about their students ranged "from mild distaste to loathing."[106]

Like the average family, Yale students and teachers did share close quarters. During the 1960s, many blamed student activism on the impersonality of the large postwar university, the poor quality of education, and the lack of student-faculty contact there. Upon closer examination, sociologists found that explanation unpersuasive. Significantly, Harvard, the "multiversity" of law schools, remained quieter than Yale Law. Surely Yale Law's smallness was one reason for its disruption. Yet Yale University as a whole remained calmer than the larger Harvard and Columbia campuses. That was partly because of Brewster's obvious fondness for, accessibility to, and effectiveness at dealing with students; his luck; and the willingness of African Americans students, faculty, and community members to negotiate with the administration. Clearly, size alone was no determinant: just as smallness promoted tension in the law school, it fostered relative tranquility in Yale College. "One of Yale's foremost strengths" in avoiding the turmoil that beset Harvard and Columbia, Hersey observed, was its "residential college system—far more alive recently than Harvard's similar house system, the decline of which was noted by the Harvard Corporation as one of the reasons for Harvard's blow-up in the spring of 1969." Another college master told a reporter that while he had "some radical types here who'd take terrific risks charging up the [New Haven] Green," they also possessed "a strange affection for their college." But no law school during the 1960s was planned to breed affection.[107]

Indeed, Yale law students also acted as they did because they were unhappier with the quality of their education than undergraduates. Recall the large number of Yale law students in the class of 1970 who said that they found college more stimulating. As the faculty sensed, many Yale law students during the 1960s proved relatively disinterested in their classes.

Law students elsewhere may have shared the frustration of Yale students. But they had not entered with the same high expectations that Yale encouraged. Building on an image it had cultivated since the 1930s, Yale advertised itself as the most progressive law school in the country. Is it any wonder that students already fired up by the sixties clamored to participate in reshaping the school when they realized it was not "the adventuresome Yale Law School" that its faculty "purport[ed] to embody"? As Keniston said of the young radicals he studied, "the *relative* deprivation of student expectations" helped to account for activism. Yale students were victims of both the "*credibility gap*" that Keniston considered "likely to open between the generations . . . in a time of rapid social change" and of the coincidental breakdown of "*the institutionalization of hypocrisy*." They could "see the Emperor in all his nakedness."[108]

Yet when they demanded change, law students received half a loaf on grades and even less on governance. Their elders might have "sacrificed the secrecy of the closed faculty meeting, a matter of deep concern to conservative law professors." But Yale professors had averted student voting there "and avoided any 'dilution' of their decision-making power." As Alexander Bickel privately told Robert Bork, "Not without a measure of cravenness . . . we at the law school have kept our students at bay without handing over control."[109]

The story turned out the same elsewhere. At Harvard, an Ad Hoc Committee on Student Participation was urging professors to permit student representatives to attend faculty meetings just as Yale student negotiators staged their walkout, and Dean Bok formed a Committee on Governance to address the issue of student participation in the aftermath of the bust. Yet despite the argument of students on the left that "participatory democracy would be a great improvement over the present system by which the Law School is governed," the Harvard Law School Committee on Governance bogged down in deliberations for two years before it even issued a report. "Student power" brought "fear into the hearts of some," the *Harvard Law Record* concluded. Columbia had begun allowing students to participate as voting members of every committee except appointments just before Yale. But when student members of Columbia's "Soapbox Conspiracy" later demanded the creation of "a fifty-fifty Faculty-Student Senate to decide all issues affecting the law school," the faculty resisted. Professors opposed the proposal on the grounds that it would prevent them from candidly exchanging their views. That left the editors of the *Columbia Law School News* incredulous: "Bullshit. Our professors seldom seem at a loss for words when they talk to students either in class or out. Why should faculty meetings be any different?"[110]

After one professor surveyed more than seventy law school deans, he reported that "[s]tudent power reaches its summit at only one law school where two students participate as full voting members in all faculty meetings and are entitled to put anything on the agenda." Some summit. Law professors were more willing to give in on grades, a measure of their power, than power itself.[111]

*   *   *

On both grades and governance, Yale professors had fought white activists' demands for change. In fact, they had resisted the demands of white students far more forcefully than the demands of the more confrontational African American students. What motivated Yale teachers, and why did they treat white and black students so differently? The questions call for a psychoanalyst, not a historian. Perhaps some identified white students with their own younger selves, even their own children, and felt more betrayed by them than African Americans. Perhaps some reasoned that since they themselves had possessed no power when they attended "boot camp," these privileged young should receive a lesson in patience.

Surely, black activists who called them "racists" scared professors more than whites. The inner cities were in turmoil. Duncan Kennedy later speculated that Bickel "was distressed by the emerging, sometimes-threatening rudeness of student activists, particularly that of the first generation of black students in the law school." Yet teachers may also have viewed African Americans as "the other," deserving relative conciliation. Obviously, faculty members felt guiltier about the situation of students of color than they did about that of white students. And almost certainly, many Yale professors considered black students' demands more legitimate. In a revealing aside, Pollak remarked that he felt more comfortable with Otis Cochran, whom he considered "a real person," than with white "radicals," most (though not all of whom) struck him as "phony." (Brewster agreed, adding that African Americans students "were much more rational about the issues" than "radical" whites.) Further, the president and provost had given the law faculty less leeway with respect to affirmative action than they had on governance.[112]

So, too, at other law schools, campus administrators acquiesced more to the demands of black than of white activists. At law schools, the concessions did not induce gratitude. The national BALSA branded law professors "contemptible . . . people who mourned for Medgar Evers but who said Malcolm X got what was coming to him, as though the rights of one man were any less precious than those of another." Other law students were bitterly sarcastic: "Pity those white liberal faculty whose consciences tell them that Martin Luther King Jr. had something to say, but whose guts just can't take all the unsettling changes in their (very own) school!" What had such professors envisioned when they opened the gates? "The same anxious-to-please students with glib tongues, witty repartee and monstrous egos" with faces of a different color?[113]

Whatever their expectations, the Yale faculty had more clearly maintained the upper hand in its fight with white activists than it had in its struggle with African Americans. Students had won greater representation, but not the franchise. As they said, professors still ran the school and remained "the distinct, controlling caste."[114]

Chapter Five

Alumni Weekend, 1969

The faculty's insistence on control encouraged fragmentation. The conflicts between white faculty members and black activists and between liberal professors and white students to their left were not the only culture clashes. The 1968–69 academic year also witnessed the rise of a counterculture and women's movement at the law school. Instead of a "community," the law school was becoming the site of interrelated communities—white activists; black activists; counterculturalists, or political hippies; and feminists.[1] The splintering between students, and especially between students and faculty, dominated Alumni Weekend.

FARMERS AND FEMINISTS

Thanks to members of the class of 1970, the counterculture came to the law school. As a Columbia undergraduate, Jonathan Krown had helped create the Warmth Committee, a group that received national publicity for distributing free ice cream in Manhattan and collecting clothes for the poor in brightly colored barrels strategically placed around Manhattan. "I had also been exposed to the mystique of the Beat Generation leaders who had hung around Columbia, like Allen Ginsberg," he said. After Krown was admitted to Yale (despite the fact that he was late for the interview because he had lost his pet monkey), he and other law students who would "rather be William Burroughs than Earl Warren" created a group called Cosmic Laboratories "to explore bringing these types of activities to Yale on a large scale." When Krown learned that the Hog Farm Commune, a group affiliated with Ken Kesey's Merry Pranksters, was coming to New York, he was delighted; Cosmic Lab members saw themselves as "the Merry Pranksters of the East Coast, but in button-down shirts."

Jonathan Krown.
(Wavy Gravy, The
Hog Farm and
Friends: As Told to
Hugh Romney and
Vice Versa *[1974].)*

Thus it was that the Hog Farmers received an invitation to come to Yale to do a sound and light show at a "Cosmic Mixer."[2]

"It all sounds so nifty I am a little suspicious," the Hog Farmers' most famous member, "Wavy Gravy," said. But it turned out law students had indeed "spun into the Prankster mystique" through Tom Wolfe's *Electric Kool-Aid Acid Test* "and without the acid. Just into turning people on." Though the Hog Farmers believed mixers a relic of the past, between sixty of them made the first of what turned out to be trips to the law school in early 1969, where they found their "very together" hosts "on top of permits and crash pads and electrical hoo-haws" and forged "our deepest of college connections." The Hog Farmers provided music and introduced Yale students and their dates to "trust exercises" in which Wavy and others were passed round. Among other things, the Hog Farmers would hold "trust" exercises at Connecticut Valley Hospital for patients, the Yale law students who represented them, and staff. The Hog Farmers arrived for the first visit in their psychedelic bus.[3]

After they left, Cosmic Labs, a group of some thirty-odd law students, used huge inflatable plastic portable structures to house happenings at Yale. A tube

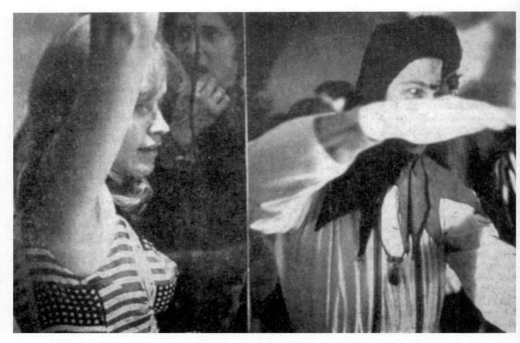

Hog Farmers at Yale. (Yale Advocate, February 20, 1969. Courtesy Yale Law School.)

to the fan in Thomas Emerson's office kept the inflatables inflated when Cosmic Labs held events in the law school courtyard. Designed by architecture students, inflatables could hold hundreds. The largest resembled a whale. Inside, sound and light shows and collective exercises created an alternative reality. Cosmic Labs members wore jumpsuits on which they sported a symbol particularly appropriate for 1960s law students, the scales of justice held up by a lightening bolt.[4]

They sought to blend politics and culture. "[L]egal Yippies," not hippies, they drew their inspiration from Yippie founders Abbie Hoffman and Jerry Rubin. They supported white activists. The S.H.I.T.F.A.C.E. proposition to create a group entitled "Students to Help Increase the Faculty's Authority and Control Over Everything," for example, combined left politics with new forms of protest.[5]

Like the Hog Farmers, women thought that the law school should adopt more enlightened attitudes. Judith Areen was one of them. A member of the class of 1969, she had come to the law school from Cornell only to encounter a large number of graduates from men's colleges who "clearly didn't know how to talk to a woman during the week" and who seemed uncomfortable in her

Hog Farmers' bus. (Yale Law Reporter, 1970, published by the Yale Law Student Association. Courtesy Yale Law School.)

presence. They assumed she was "there to find a husband," and the war made matters worse. As she said, "given Vietnam, there was certainly a sense, and it was articulated some of the time, that it was bad enough that we were in law school, but . . . we were taking the place of a man who therefore had to go to Vietnam; that was a very heavy pressure that all of us felt." When she participated in the compulsory moot court exercise, fellow students arranged for her to have a student judge who was "infamous" for his grim appearance, scheduled her session in the law school auditorium, and announced that she had been "too forceful" in her presentation. Then there were the first-year classes, where Friedrich Kessler called on her constantly, and the popular upper-class courses of Fred Rodell's that she could not take because he taught them at Mory's, Yale's all-male eating club. Rodell had been one of the most insistent defenders of the Warren Court; by intimating that only men made legitimate law students, he underscored how poorly conventional sixties liberalism had kept up with the times. Then there were the summer job searches. A *Law Journal* member, Areen interviewed for summer employment on Wall Street. All seemed to be going well until lunchtime, when her hosts began ticking off the usual haunts they would have to forgo because she was with them. (Areen nevertheless received an offer, but turned it down to become one of the first

Nader's Raiders.) When she began reading about the women's movement, she connected her own experiences at Yale to gender issues.[6]

So did other women students. By approving coed dorms in 1968, the faculty had pleased them (and probably campus police, who, the records sometimes seem to suggest, had spent most of the sixties investigating parietal violations). Women who wished to live in dorms were no longer confined to one of Yale's most dreadful buildings, Helen Hadley Hall, a long walk from the law school. And they were saved from worse — poor New Haven housing for those Hadley could not accommodate.[7]

Yale law women, many of them active in both left and feminist movements, wanted more than decent living space. The class of 1970 was typical in that it included only seven women. Like other law schools, Yale "limited its recruiting and advertising efforts to men's schools from which most of its students came." Largely because of pressure from women, or so women believed, and perhaps because of the draft, the next year witnessed a jump in numbers. In the fall of 1968, one year before Yale College became coeducational, twenty-five women started law school.[8]

Now that women approached a critical mass, they placed liberal feminist issues, aimed at eliminating barriers for women's advancement in the workplace, front and center. They charged that law firm members discriminated by holding recruitment events at Mory's, and openly telling women that "they were better situated in fields other than that of law." As at other law schools, such charges were not new. Betsy Levin, the first woman to become a dean of a major law school, and civil rights activist Haywood Burns had charged law firms discriminated against women and minorities in hiring during the Rostow years. The Yale law women who followed, one student explained, understood the problem as one of enforcement. The law school circulated a pamphlet to all employers who used its facilities prohibiting any form of discrimination in hiring based on race, sex, or religion. But there were no specific guidelines about what that meant or what sanctions were involved. To make matters worse, the dean's designee who investigated complaints was also charged with alumni relations and development and apparently received little instruction about handling violations. To the women, it did not seem that he and others involved with recruitment cared about discrimination. Women students believed progress depended on their readiness "to apply the pressure."[9]

At least Yale women received lip service from the placement office, which warned firms against interviewing at Mory's and did not permit those that "actively discriminate in their hiring practices" to use school facilities for interviews. Pollak, too, was good: Areen recalled him saying the school would not

Dedication page, "Women Lawyers' Centennial, 1869–1969, No Progress."
(Yale Law Reporter, 1970, published by the Yale Law Student Association.
Courtesy Yale Law School.)

allow a firm that discriminated against women to interview. "It was forceful; it was very encouraging too." Women at the University of Chicago, on the other hand, who alleged that its placement office permitted firms that did not hire women to use its services, received so little satisfaction from administrators that they brought a Title VII action against the school. "Our school never even pretended," one Chicago woman said at the first national gathering of women law students that NYU and Yale women organized. The University of Chicago Law School "never wrote any of the little blurbs saying firms shouldn't discriminate." As an institution full of legal liberals, Yale Law School was quick to avow support for feminism in the public sphere.[10]

"WHEN GENERATIONS COLLIDE"

The different currents of student discontent surfaced and converged in April 1969. The law school's Alumni Weekend came at a tense moment for the Ivy League. In April, as Cornell held its Parents' Weekend, African American students occupied its student union; President James Perkins would soon be forced out of office because of his "surrender to intimidation." The same month, Harvard students occupied University Hall. Harvard president Nathan Pusey's summoning of the police two days later and the student arrests, "Harvard's Vietnam," prompted a university-wide strike and the Harvard College fellows' request for his resignation.[11]

Like their predecessors who had walked out of the deans' panel on the urban crisis the previous spring and students elsewhere, Yale's young realized the opportunity Alumni Weekend provided for theater. Students' actions probably reflected, at least in part, their continued anger over Vietnam. The frustration was evident at Yale College, where a debate over whether to expel the ROTC raged that spring. Stephen Cohen, a first-year law student and Allard Lowenstein protégé, who had spent months working on Eugene McCarthy's campaign, thought concentration on ROTC "silly and self-indulgent," simply a proxy for the war, which was better addressed directly. Yet like everyone else, Cohen went to the mass meeting at Ingalls Rink and stood in line to use one of the microphones to address the thousands in attendance, including Brewster and the members of the Yale Corporation. "There is something more important happening here tonight than the issue of whether ROTC is permitted to stay at Yale," he remembered saying. "Up on the stage tonight are Cyrus Vance, Deputy Secretary of Defense under Robert McNamara, and William Bundy, former Under Secretary of State for Far Eastern Affairs." Pointing out that both had participated in the escalation and still defended the war, Cohen pointed to the importance of "convey[ing] to them our sense that the war is wrong" and that it was destroying both Vietnam and the United States. He recalled concluding: "We need to hear how they respond to our criticism. We have to speak out about this, because as [Miguel de] Unamuno said, 'To be silent is to lie.'" The sensational reaction showed that Cohen had laid out "the common ground for most of the people in the rink." But Brewster successfully co-opted the ROTC problem, and law students showed no great interest in the specific issue of ROTC anyway.[12]

Instead, they worked at laying out their grievances about the school for the alumni, which had asked students to speak directly to them. The Alumni Association planned a panel entitled "Concerns of the Yale Law Student today" at its annual weekend and decided to mail a transcript of the session to every alumnus as a special issue of the *Yale Law Report*. Moderated by Leon Higginbotham, the Alumni Weekend panel would include presentations by the Student Negotiating Committee, the Black Law Student Union, and a representative of the women's movement, as well as comments from faculty members.[13]

The Student Negotiating Committee began the Saturday morning panel by showing a movie depicting events at the school during 1968–69. After the screening, volunteers came through the aisles soliciting collections to defray the film's cost. (In a bizarre note, students would subsequently interrupt their complaints about the school to announce that they would pass the money they had collected back, "and those who didn't contribute and who feel they would like some are welcome to take the money out of the box and keep it." The transcript does not indicate whether anyone laughed.)[14]

Then the litany began. The grievances centered, first, of course, on how far Yale fell short of student expectations. "[W]e had visions of a very progressive educational institution on the very frontiers of legal education . . . visions of interdisciplinary work, urban law, a terrific student-faculty ratio, and a real community," which the actual law school experience had dispelled. Their professors had proven a disappointment. "The things that disturbed us most were the inertia and self-satisfaction" of their professors, who were "just satisfied to stay two steps in front of Harvard, maybe three steps in front of Columbia" and who "were pretty satisfied with American society— surprisingly so," given the students' view of "American society as very sick." The faculty's "secrecy" was upsetting, as was its "elitism." In deciding tenure, according to students, their professors required the candidate to approach "the Dworkinian threshold of excellence," that is, possess the intelligence of Ronald Dworkin. And when students had presented "rational arguments for change," the faculty had not listened. That had convinced them they needed "to organize politically, issue by issue," to bring issues to the fore, such as grade reform and governance. "We were animated by the belief that students have a right to participate in the decisions that affect their lives," one said, as well as by the inadequacy of the student-faculty relationship, a dislike of professors' refusal to treat them "as adults," and a dream "of a law school community, a community of scholars in which both faculty and students would participate as equals." But their efforts had been for naught. As they witnessed the "total lack of communication and responsiveness" of their professors, students had realized that the faculty resembled "an English club" and operated by consensus, a goal that made it unwilling to listen to reason. Thus the faculty had responded by "compromise, just enough to satisfy students for awhile but not enough to change the educational institution in a major way." And the slowness with which even compromise occurred would make future students reluctant even to negotiate with the faculty. "And that's why I think there's a real ominous note to the whole proceedings," one self-described moderate concluded.[15]

Faculty negotiator and corporate tax expert Marvin Chirelstein responded for his colleagues. He sardonically observed that the movie "very neatly brought out the brutal regimentation of student life at Yale" and might lead some viewers to "conclude that students spend all their time here painting signs, attending meetings, and drinking beer." But then he acknowledged that "the generation gap tends to encourage one to try out a little empathy, at least in the privacy of one's office, by fantasy if nothing else, and as I roll that around in my mind I guess I can see how a student might come to feel irritated by the feeling that decisions were being made behind his back, in secrecy, through a process into which there was no window whatsoever." That meant students should be permitted to observe faculty meetings, but voting and democracy were altogether different. "[T]he job I have is to train the kids," Chirelstein said. "Presumably we know and they don't. We know something and they don't." It was "illogical" to give power to those who did not. In an odd twist, Chirelstein then reassured his alumni listeners that professors did not operate by consensus, and, in fact, argued a great deal. Certainly they had disagreed heatedly over what to give on governance, he said. And the process had not taken too long, either. "My own career life is to some extent at stake in the decisions that are reached, and I'm not anxious to see those decisions reached without an elaborate and extensive debate." Paradoxically, Chirelstein closed by assuring his listeners that "the future for student participation at this Law School is a bright one" and that "we can get along."[16]

Even two professors from Columbia and Harvard, invited to join the panel for the comparative dimension, proved unsympathetic to Chirelstein's stance. They seemed convinced that "the challenge to us really is one of dropping the complacency . . . and of moving as fast as we can on the merits of the issues." If it was appropriate for students to participate in committees, one said, it made no sense to deny them the vote.[17]

Areen briefly addressed women's issues, declaring that she was "more than a little apprehensive" because of her "strange feeling that speaking somewhere between the discussions of student power by the Negotiating Committee and the concerns of the BLSU, my mention of a slightly different issue would be viewed by all of you as some sort of light interlude or perhaps comic relief." She pointed to how few women students the school admitted. While she acknowledged the unusually large number of women in the first-year class, she speculated that the increase reflected "the draft situation more than any change in recruitment policy." Hers was a strategy of politeness. Areen was certain, she told alumni, that most of them had worked "with some of the outstanding women in the profession" and understood that women made as able lawyers as men. Thus she asked them to work to eliminate discrimination in hiring.[18]

In contrast, the anger of the Black Law Students Union was apparent. Otis Cochran told alumni that law professors had begun to confront the fact that Yale was "a segregated school only when they were pressured to do so by the black students." *Brown* v. *Board of Education* had not spurred them to do so, though in 1954 "professors here rose to new heights of eloquence, praising the courts for outlawing segregation for other schools in other states." Nor had events between 1963 and 1965 led to change, "when crocodile tears over the plight of the Negro flowed in great torrents from the great hearted liberals at Yale." The faculty had only begun to move recently, "and then only with great reluctance and great timidity." Even now, less than 4 percent of the school's student body was black. The BLSU had acted with, to use "Matthew Arnold's felicitous phrase, sweet reasonableness," Cochran continued, but the faculty had dragged its feet. "Cicero's words probably say it very well—How long, oh Catiline, will you go on abusing our patience?" he asked. "Maybe we were too gullible and too trusting this year," he stressed. "Next year we will not be. I want to repeat that. Next year we will not be."[19]

There was still hope. "If the members of the Black Law Student Union thought as many people do think, as many of our brothers in the community think, that the law is simply an instrument of oppression, we wouldn't be here," BLSU member Harold McDougall told alumni. "We're just hoping that you'll be able to prove us right." But the signs thus far were hardly encouraging. Professors behaved as if black students compromised the quality of education at the school. Nevertheless, the BLSU had a concrete proposal: alumni should establish a special scholarship fund for black students and enact "a resolution urging the faculty to bring the black student population at the School up to the national average of 10%" by September 1969.[20]

But when the Executive Committee of the Alumni Association met after the panel and luncheon, Pollak warned that no "substantial increase" in the second- and third-year classes would occur unless "the School were very fortunate" and that efforts must, for the present, focus on the first-year class, where "the faculty's . . . efforts had resulted in a far larger number of qualified black and other disadvantaged applicants than in the past." And the Executive Committee itself was unsure of "the propriety and legality of basing admissions and aid policy on race or color." So the committee partially punted, resolving that it "strongly supports the efforts of the Yale Law School community to *increase the number of qualified students coming from disadvantaged backgrounds, with the objective of achieving a genuinely representative student body as soon as sufficient qualified applicants can be found.*" But the committee agreed to move ahead with the special fund, resolving that alumni must take "appro-

*S.H.I.T.F.A.C.E. posters. (*Yale Law Reporter, *1970, published by the Yale Law Student Association. Courtesy Yale Law School.)*

priate steps to assist the Law School administration in the recruitment process and the provision of the required additional financial aid." Though it would not raise money specifically for black students, it would launch a special campaign to raise $150,000 for "disadvantaged" students.[21]

Even when the meeting ended and alumni could gather for drinks in the courtyard, the reminders of student discontent remained everywhere. There was that *Advocate* photo of an armed Dennis Black, class of 1970, underneath the poster advising "Hands Off the Vietnamese Revolution!" There were the S.H.I.T.F.A.C.E. posters in the halls: those supporting a greater voice in student governance had decided to make the professors' position "appear ridiculous not only to students but to the more sympathetic, liberal members of the faculty, until they are forced to break with conservatives" and had indeed pretended to form a group called S.H.I.T.F.A.C.E. The architects of S.H.I.T.-F.A.C.E. fantasized that their second-year classmate, Jonathan "Toasty" Goodson, who stabled his horse in New Haven, would ride it into the law school courtyard during one of the student-faculty croquet matches, fall off, and pretend to hurt himself, an event that could give rise to a lawsuit "of 'Goodson v. S.H.I.T.F.A.C.E.' and further embarrass the traditional faculty." Alumni could see everywhere, too, the partially playful signs the student negotiators had circulated at the time of their walkout: "Create Two, Three . . . Many Yale Law Struggles"; "Support Class Struggle at Yale Law School"; "All Peoples Support Heroic Struggle of Yale Law Students." There was the gallows students built in the courtyard as their elders watched Saturday afternoon. Some hoped it would

*"Create Two, Three . . .
Many Yale Law Struggles."*
(Yale Law Reporter, *1970,
published by the Yale Law
Student Association.
Courtesy Yale Law School.)*

"symbolize the reality of the effect of the legal system on people (such as minorities) as opposed to the niceties of the law school environment"; others, that
it would just "freak the alumni." Either way, "The alumni were presented with
a cacophonous display of law students hammering on their fingers, shouting
obscenities, stumbling off platforms, wearing see-through pants and drinking
beer." What did members of the younger and older generations have in common beyond the fact that both got high?[22]

An *Advocate* article, "When Generations Collide," captured the atmosphere.
There was the tipsy young alumnus seemingly only five years out who kept asking what "you kids" wanted; the edgy middle-aged one who wanted to know
when "you kids" were going "to burn" someone up there and he would see

some real "action"; the professor who sought to make rules for a life he had not lived, pedantically informing the gallows' builders that they did not know the first thing about construction: "It was Kids' Day in the courtyard — a chance for the 'talented children,' the 'premature alumni,' the nonvoting members of the Law School Com-Munity to . . . To what? To confront some fat cats from Wall Street (and some not-so-lean ones from City Hall and Washington)? Or to *communicate* with our predecessors, to form common areas of understanding? Or to 'do our thing', and let the alums do theirs? Whatever [the] approach, the assumption was that there were two sides: THEM and US."[23]

To "them," the effect was menacing. There was a world of difference between the impertinent friskiness of S.H.I.T.F.A.C.E. and a scaffold with a noose. And when Cochran delivered his warning, one alumnus complained to Pollak, he was "surrounded by eight colleagues on the platform who did not speak but merely sat with folded arms." There was reason for that. After two spells with bleeding ulcers, the BLSU chair wanted his allies near him if he became dizzy. Because he was nearsighted and wanted to maintain eye contact with his audience, he did not wear glasses when he spoke, and he needed friends who could whisper the names of those who made comments or asked questions nearby, he said later. But, as he acknowledged, "I was not opposed to being thought of as a fairly fierce warrior." And that is the way he and his colleagues seemed.[24]

Publicly, the alumni association tried to put on a good face. Urging all alumni to read the account of Yale law students' concerns, it maintained that students' demand for participation in governance and for the recruitment of more minorities reflected their perceptions "of the urgent responsibilities imposed on the Law School by the national concern for the deprived of our society." To the students, that concern required more "relevant" courses and rethinking "the techniques of legal education. And perhaps most important it involves the difficult job of reconciling the right to freedom of protest — even when that protest takes unusual and, to many, bizarre forms — with the preservation of a peaceful and orderly society." Professors had responded "affirmatively and creatively," the association said, though the changes they instituted "were, of course, too limited and too slow to satisfy some of the students" and might "well have been too rapid and too far-reaching for some of the faculty and for many alumni. But the dialogue — *or the confrontation* — continues, and in the long run, the School, faculty, students and alumni alike, should be the stronger for it."[25]

Privately, the distinguished group of lawyers and alumni who constituted the Committee on the Law School sounded even less upbeat when they reported to the Yale University Council around the time of Alumni Weekend.

"This year student dissatisfaction and student demands have become the major issues dominating the Law School scene," they announced, reflecting the increasing "awareness" of students everywhere of their "ability" to change whatever they did not like "by direct political action." The committee commended the faculty for combining "a commendable mixture of firmness on issues of principle and flexibility on details," while condemning "activist students" who appeared "incapable of realizing that they are committing McCarthyism (the 1950 variety) in reverse."[26]

What was to be done? Rehearsing the history of Yale Law School, the committee told the familiar story of how it had become a center for training the best lawyers, law professors, public servants, and politicians. That proud mission was in jeopardy. "Most members of the Committee agree with the faculty decision to apply a special standard to black applicants, as a commendable effort to redress the injustices so long inflicted on those Americans," the committee said, but everyone was anxious. It was not just that the GPAs and LSAT scores of most minority students were so much lower than those of "most of the students" and that the "highest ranking minority student" accepted for 1969 who had sent in the crucial deposit that indicated intent to matriculate stood "in an 8-way tie for 98th out of 128 depositors." The committee no longer understood Yale Law School's goal. Was it training "only the best applicants available" or had it now "become equally important to train a student body as varied and pluralistic" as all American society? And if the latter, why focus on African Americans "and the Spanish-speaking minorities," and not "whites from the Deep South, Appalachians from Kentucky and Tennessee, Poles and Hungarians from Chicago and Cleveland, Italians and Irish from New York and Boston" as well? The school should reconsider its purpose, and, in the committee's view, aim for a diverse student body of *all* Americans, "especially those who feel most threatened by the growing social and economic mobility of black people," even if that required using "some of the special criteria now applied to black applicants" for other groups Yale had historically ignored. But could "present academic standards survive disparate criteria for admission and wider participation for students in the making of educational policy"? The committee seemed unsure.[27]

And how should the law school respond if, as seemed a real danger, "obstructive student conduct is threatened or occurs"? What if the students overcame their differences and joined together — against their professors? The law school had not even set out a definition of "obstructive conduct or the range of sanctions" it carried. Its disciplinary procedures were too sketchy. "Should the Law School decide to invoke a disciplinary remedy for obstructive student conduct, its lack of specific written procedures could conceivably open it to charges of depriving students of some of the basic elements of due process," the committee warned. "In the view of most Committee members, a great law school should not leave itself open to a charge of arbitrariness in adjudicating such basic issues as whether a student has in fact violated a valid law or regulation, upon which his right to remain in school and to receive federal financial assistance may depend." The faculty should forthwith, "after appropriate student consultation (but without accepting a degree of student participation that would paralyze the process) prepare and issue a set of procedures for exercising its disciplinary functions." Otherwise, and perhaps anyway, the school would remain at risk for "a serious wound."[28]

In retrospect, the professors would have done well to take the committee's advice. Compared to what had happened at other elite universities, they had gotten off relatively easy so far. Compared to other elite law schools, though, the Yale faculty had been having a tough time. Yet after the turmoil of 1968–69, the idea of a discussion about the "appropriate student consultation" that should accompany a statement of disciplinary procedures, much less the nature of such disciplinary procedures, doubtless seemed daunting. The committee's report, written by outsiders, did not adequately take into account how much energy the insiders had already expended.

But the report did expose the gulf between students and faculty. In some ways, it was not that large. As McDougall had said, if students believed law an instrument of oppression, they would not have gone to Yale. Yet there, as at other privileged places, the sixties caused strain between older liberals and the young they identified with the left — groups far less monolithic than the rhetoric of the period suggested — as tensions flared over the war, racism, feminism, grades, curricular relevance, community, and the counterculture. What if law students attracted in part by Yale's realist past had arrived in New Haven during the 1960s and had encountered a faculty that crackled with the intellectual excitement and ties to Washington professors had possessed during the 1930s? The connections would have to have been the right ones: Eugene Rostow, after all, had them in spades. Had the young found a faculty knee-deep in the War on Poverty, however, or involved in challenging the constitutionality of the Vietnam War in the courts or organizing abortion rights test cases, might the situation have seemed different? Could the confrontation have been avoided?

Probably not. Alumni Weekend laid bare the psychic dimension of the conflict and the disappointment and anger of both students and faculty. Whether they resented their professors' intimation of intellectual inferiority, as black students did, or disliked the faculty's tone of "we know and they don't," as student negotiators did, many young people found their teachers patronizing and unresponsive. For their part, professors also seemed unsure academic standards could "survive disparate criteria for admission and wider participation for students in the making of educational policy." The faculty seemed mystified, annoyed, and shell-shocked by the drumbeat of constant demands. Where would they end? Thus although their shared hatred of the war and desire for greater justice suggested that faculty liberals and the students on the left "need not have been in absolute or deadlocked conflict," the common cause was lost as they baited each other.[29]

Looking back at his years in New Haven, Duncan Kennedy remembered "the disappointment of my expectation as an apprentice." As one who aspired to "the progressive part of the ruling class" when he entered Yale, Kennedy had initially "identified, easily, quickly, with the leading scholar/activist professors who were liberals." But everything had changed, and he had been "radicalized" by his experiences at Yale, "by my interaction with my teachers." Bickel, for example, "seemed terrifyingly different from how I had imagined him," and he obviously thought that "we, his students, in a sense his followers, were terrifyingly different, too." At first there was a cool exchange, and then a moment in which faculty members "just flipped," Kennedy maintained later. Unlike Brewster, who was "totally machiavellian" and deliberately played "Mr. Tough Cop and Mr. Softie at the same time," Yale law professors were revolted, scared, ashamed "that we were jamming from the left," Kennedy believed. They seemed unaccountably angry, given that "our demands seemed just the extension of what they had taught us, demands [centering] around the war in Vietnam, race, gender, demands for more student power in administering the school." (Like many white male veterans of the left, Kennedy recalled "our demands" relating to race and gender, though no contemporary evidence indicated those were his issues.) "The upshot was that they withdrew from us and we from them, a withdrawal that was hurtful but never complete, because we were bound to them willy-nilly, even when we were angriest at them," Kennedy said. "It sometimes seemed the meanest ones — or maybe just the ones whose meanness hurt the most — were those who had the most unselfconscious confidence that they *were* enlightened American progressivism." Those were the people who would remind the young they were not "'Bolivian peasants,'" but students at Yale Law School. "It was tricky, the feeling of being shamed for one's privilege by a person who was unbelievably more privileged, a person saying to you, 'Because you are privileged you have to do everything I say.'"[30]

As Alumni Weekend suggested, the law school's smallness softened and sharpened the strain. "Most of the time . . . we relied on the fact that the law school was a small community of people who knew each other," Dennis Black recalled. For example, he had developed an informal understanding with the women who worked in the registrar's office. He had learned how to fix their copy machine so that when it broke, they need not wait for a repairperson to come out, and they allowed him to make copies of posters publicizing Cosmic Labs' activities. After posing with gun under the "Hands Off the Vietnamese Revolution" sign, he worried he had crossed "some invisible line, and that there would be consequences." Soon after the issue of the *Advocate* featuring the photograph appeared, he had to use the copy machine. "It was with some degree of trepidation that I walked into the front office, not knowing what to expect from these conservative members of the New Haven community who had become my friends," he recalled. "I walked in and silence greeted me. Then somebody said, 'Well if it isn't the well-known radical revolutionary, Dennis Black,' and all the women started laughing." Yet, just as Abe Goldstein suggested, the smallness of the school made its members "overly involved" with each other. The physical proximity of its members made escape difficult too.[31]

*　*　*

Quite understandably, by the spring of 1969, Pollak was "tired." One of his colleagues reported that "for the whole of the past academic year, we were in no small degree engaged in a struggle for survival" and said he feared the "threats" of black and white activists departing for the summer "that they would see us in the fall." The dean may have felt the same way.[32]

Pollak had assumed a stance different from Kingman Brewster's. Yale's president had kept students' eyes focused on the larger world outside the institution by encouraging change within. Pollak had not exactly promoted change, but he had not repressed it and had made Herculean efforts to accommodate it. Too often at the time, though, critics believed his was a pattern of resistance, denunciation, and compromise — too late to pacify students, who saw it as a sign of weakness. His strategy had created strains on the faculty. Clyde Summers recalled a sense among some colleagues that Pollak "was too soft, that he was not tough, that he should stand up to the students, both black and white." And though the lid of the law school kettle had not blown off, the pot continued to boil.[33]

The dean told Yale's president in March he did not want another term. Brewster may have been relieved. "I think probably he felt that Lou was bending too much and being too indulgent," Associate Dean Ralph Brown recalled, though he never had "any sense of coolness between them." Had he sought a second term, Pollak believed Brewster would have acquiesced, notwithstanding that the president might have become "impatient" with him. But the deanship was a thankless job, so Brewster and Pollak agreed the school would install a new dean come summer 1970. That still left Pollak with the burden of the 1969–70 academic year, which would prove the worst one yet.[34]

Chapter Six

Trials and Tribulations

In the fall of 1969, Yale law students' rebelliousness peaked. To this point, they had focused on the faculty—identifying its shortcomings with respect to grades, admissions, and governance. And students kept up the criticism, challenging their teachers' lifestyles while lambasting them for insufficient dedication to the antiwar movement. Now, though, police harassment of African Americans rose to the fore with potentially explosive consequences for the school. Naturally, some concluded their professors were taking insufficient steps to address the problem, leading to a confrontation and strike. In the process, the concerns of the Student Negotiating Committee and the BLSU, which had previously proceeded on separate tracks, began to converge. Race and governance matters brought white and black activists together, polarizing them and the faculty and revealing the inadequacy of the arrangements reached between Student Negotiating Committee members and professors the previous spring. The resulting crisis deepened the tension between Pollak and his hardliners.

OF "COUNTER-COMMUNITY" AND "INSTITUTIONAL NEUTRALITY"

To the faculty, each entering class during the late 1960s seemed more radical than the last. The trend reflected the times. The class of 1972 possessed a large number of those who identified themselves as "far left." Some had the credentials to back it up too. Ed Baker, for example, had participated in the nine-day occupation of Stanford's Applied Electronics Institute to protest its war research just the previous spring. At the same time, the first-year class also included a significant percentage who looked forward to school: entering students listed the supposed quality of education and its reputed social science orientation as their most important reasons for choosing Yale. "Many thought that Yale had some special perspective in its teaching of law, that it would be 'non-technical,' and 'socially concerned,'" Robert Stevens said, after speaking with fifty members of the class of 1972 once they had spent some time at Yale. "Many of the interviewees stated that these expectations were disappointed."[1]

The agreement reached between the Student Negotiating Committee and faculty about participation the previous spring disappointed some first-years too, who claimed that they deserved to weigh in on whether to implement it. "More cautious (and tired) voices urge that the students accept their gains and move on to areas where their time can be spent more productively," the *Advocate* reported. Students who had been at Yale longer maintained that reopening the issue would be perceived "as a breach of the 'good faith' which students have been demanding from the faculty and will bear out all the horrible forecasts of student irresponsibility which Mr. Bickel and shitface set forth so eloquently last year."[2]

As that suggested, the young continued at first to focus their attention on internal affairs. In its first fall issue, the *Advocate* observed that its articles retained "that same imperfect balance between news, self-indulgence and preaching that readers have come to know and love to varying degrees." They concentrated, directly or indirectly, on "law school functions or malfunctions," including the search for a new dean and students' desire for an outsider; criticism of the school's administration; coverage of student attempts to make the law school more democratic; an excoriation of corporate practice by a Wall Street summer associate; and a lament that *Law Journal* membership continued to serve law firms, instead of law, by remaining "a pedestal for the competitive," instead of "a haven for the scholar." The editors recalled that the staff of a previous issue had once included an editorial on the war, only to be reminded that everyone had already endured endless discussions of the United States' wrong-headed presence in Vietnam. "Should we herald the day when *The Advocate* is silent on grading, law school curriculum and avaricious lawyers as a sign that 'everyone knows they're immoral, wrong and a bore'?" they asked. "Or should we start writing editorials on THE WAR again, lest those inside think we have forsaken the outside for the inside, while trying to bring the inside closer to the outside?" Somewhat wistfully, they concluded: "If we only knew which way walls fall when they begin to crumble — inward or outward — we would know where to stand and watch."[3]

It was an acknowledgment, albeit tentative, that progress was occurring in the student effort to improve the school. The walls were beginning to disinte-

Walt Wagoner. (Yale Law
Reporter, 1970, *published by the
Yale Law Student Association.
Courtesy Yale Law School and
Walter Wagoner.)*

grate. But the *Advocate*'s role as battering ram was coming to a close. Richard
Hughes, the moving force behind the paper, had withdrawn from participation while he struggled with his draft board. The paper would appear twice in
October. Renamed the *Yale Law Advocate*, it was revived in December with a
call for more ideologically diverse members — including writers willing to do
"some shitwork" — and the announcement that it had "abandoned the policy
of including editorial comments representing the views of a staff consensus."
The paper came out once in January and then appeared in a new format, modeled after *The Whole Earth Catalogue*, for three issues beginning in February,
with a new section, "the SHITLIST," featuring tidbits of faculty misconduct,
and was defunct by the following academic year.[4]

The decline of the *Advocate* made the Yale Law Student Association more
important. And "for the first time in recent history, the Student Association's
most important task was of a political nature," holding elections for the ten
student representatives the faculty had agreed upon after a "year's hard labor
and tedious rhetoric." The group's newly elected president, Walt Wagoner, was
a Yale College alumnus slated to graduate from law school in 1970. To faculty
and students alike, he seemed decidedly left. Though Wagoner made no move
to reopen the governance agreement between students and faculty, he did sig-

nal that he intended to provide strong leadership. "This organization was well on its way to oblivion by the end of last year," he said of the Student Association. "It is now a question of either reviving it or helping to see that something better takes its place."[5]

He had helpers. African Americans in the class of 1972 were more likely to identify themselves as "far left of center" than whites. Historically, whites had controlled the Student Association, but at the start of the 1969–70 academic year, four African Americans announced that the group "should be a forum for the views of black students as it has been for white students." Declaring that they were "anxious to see a quick end to the nonsense that has pervaded Yale Law School life," they ran successfully for election to the Board of Directors of the Student Association. "We were trying to institutionalize the participation of Blacks [in the] mainstream as a second step," Otis Cochran recalled.[6]

Black students' move beyond the BLSU reflected their growing presence at the law school. Thanks to the BLSU's success in persuading the faculty to admit more African Americans, as well as to BLSU recruiting efforts, the class of 1972 included some thirty students of color, many of whom had participated in the summer CLEO institute the BLSU had won for them. They hailed from a diverse array of institutions, many of them elite schools in the northeast and the west.[7]

Now a second-year student, Cochran himself had gone on to bigger things. In 1969, he had persuaded Associate Dean William Felstiner to send him, first-year Eric Clay, and second-year Harold McDougall to BALSA's national meeting. The school would provide the money, Cochran remembered Felstiner saying, "but you'd better bring home the bacon." Of course Cochran became a player at the convention, urging BALSA, for example, to testify against Richard Nixon's nomination of the allegedly segregationist Clement Haynsworth to the Supreme Court. Cochran was also elected National BALSA Chair, a position he ultimately held for two years. "Is that enough bacon?" he remembered teasing Felstiner. Yale administrators viewed his prominence as fortuitous confirmation of their own progressiveness, he believed. Reluctantly, because he had typically not been "a leader in the political sense," and although he was also on law journal (where he would soon publish a note making "the case for black juries"), McDougall took Cochran's place as Yale's BLSU Chair. During the fall of 1969, a period of transition, Cochran would play the leading role.[8]

Women of different races made up another growing community. The thirty-five first-year women constituted 17 percent of the class of 1972, "a breakthrough at the time . . . [that] meant that women would no longer be token students at Yale." Hillary Rodham was to become the most famous of them.

At the time, she was decidedly left of center. Her Torts professor remembered her arguing that *Rylands* v. *Fletcher* should have been decided on different grounds. In that case, a mill owner who had hired a contractor to build a reservoir was sued by a nearby mine owner when the water escaped and flooded the mine. The mill owner had argued that he had acted reasonably and without negligence. Deeming that defense irrelevant, the court established the principle of strict liability for anything unnatural brought on one's land that left it. Rodham contended that the court should indeed have found for the plaintiff — but because the mine owner employed many workers, while his neighbor did not. Her women classmates shared her political engagement. Like African Americans, they were more likely to describe themselves as left of center — "liberal" or "far left" — than white men.[9]

*   *   *

Inclined as a group toward political activism, the first-years encountered a very visible counterculture at Yale. Returning to the law school that fall, even Wavy Gravy was impressed by the "[i]ncredible evolvement since the Hog hit the Ivy" the first time. As the 1969–70 school year opened, Cosmic Lab veterans of Woodstock and other law students established a "tent city," a commune in the courtyard. Cosmic Labs took to the road, bringing "the spirit of the revolution," happenings, and inflatables to other schools, including Harvard Law. "Yale Bubbles Up," the front page of the *Harvard Law Record* proclaimed. According to the *Record*, the "incredulous bystanders" who inquired into Cosmic Labs' purpose were told it was "'to pose an alternative to impersonal institutions'; 'to symbolize our rejection of a competitive, anti-human society'; 'to show law students the beauty of real personal relationships and uninhibited communication'; and even 'to give us an excuse to get out of New Haven.'" Their experience in Cambridge showed Cosmic Lab members their situation was hardly unique. "We notice that a lot of people here are really uptight," the Yale students reported.[10]

In New Haven, they slept in twenty-odd tents in the courtyard. Cosmic Lab enthusiasts camped out part of the fall "both to establish a sanctuary in which students could escape the law school atmosphere, and to demonstrate to other members of the law school a counter-community with new values." Addressing himself to those in the Yale Law community who questioned "the rationale," Cosmic Labs' Jonathan Krown described the camp-in as "a reaction against rationale." It reflected the spirit of Woodstock and "an attempt to build trust in an atmosphere in which trust and easy-going smiles are alien." Unlike Woodstock, Yale's tent city discouraged drug use. Though marijuana was as much a staple of law school as college life and Wavy fretted that local police "blamed me for all acid consumed in New Haven," participants avoided using drugs in the courtyard, lest they be busted. Each night, law students would sing songs and declare the courtyard a "people's park."[11]

Charles Reich sometimes joined them. He had spent the Summer of Love in San Francisco and Berkeley grooving to the sounds of Big Brother and the Holding Company and the Grateful Dead. As much as he enjoyed the "great sights & sounds" of "psychedelic" culture and the "idealism" of its participants, however, he was not enraptured. He told his friend Alexander Bickel that the experience had "helped me appreciate your description of Yale as the House of Intellect" and criticized the students he met in California as "profoundly anti-intellectual" and "harshly impatient with doubters and questioners." He himself was "much too conventional" to think in terms of camping in the courtyard, Reich stressed later, saying that he was just curious enough to visit. Still, he apparently viewed the development as such a hopeful sign that a new consciousness had "begun to transform and humanize the landscape" that he alluded to it in the conclusion of *The Greening of America*: "When, in the fall of 1969, the courtyard of the Yale Law School, that Gothic citadel of the elite, became for a few weeks the site of a commune, with tents, sleeping bags, and outdoor cooking, who could any longer doubt that the clearing wind was coming?" Reich's occasional presence, the students believed, kept the tent city in existence, since no one in power at Yale "wanted the embarrassment of a faculty member being arrested." As the students carried on outside, many professors looked on in horror.[12]

The dean was not among them. Years later, he did not even remember the tent city "camp-in." Pollak provided eloquent testimony to the difficulty of deaning when he remarked, "Probably at the time, it seemed like a minor irritant."[13]

*   *   *

The Vietnam War seemed major. Though draft calls had shrunk to a tenth of their size during the Johnson administration, and Nixon was about to change the selective service system from an oldest-first to youngest-first order of call and inaugurate a lottery, Yale law students continued to challenge American policy. When Allard Lowenstein's friends announced the national moratorium against the war on October 15, 1969, two Yale law student veterans of his "Dump Johnson" campaign became organizers of the New Haven mora-

Charles Reich. (Yale Review of Law and Social Action, *vol. 1, 1970. Courtesy Yale Law School.*)

torium. They were Stephen Cohen, now a second-year, and first-year Gregory Craig. As befit Lowenstein, the strategy behind the moratorium was to demonstrate the breadth of the opposition. Avoiding radical rhetoric, Cohen, Craig, and first-year Michael Medved circulated posters and sold buttons with but a single word: "Enough." As Cohen said, "That got the center because it kept lifestyle issues out" and focused on the war. But would Yale Law School honor the self-consciously mainstream moratorium?[14]

Not exactly. In an early faculty meeting, Pollak welcomed "symbolic" student participation of Student Association Board officers because the ten student representatives who would attend faculty meetings had not yet been "formally elected." Reporting that the Student Association Board had "voted unanimously for a stand," the officers then asked the faculty to suspend all classes on October 15 "to symbolize our protest at the continuation of the Viet-Nam War and to allow students, faculty, and staff to participate in the activities planned for that day." Brewster opposed that position on the grounds that "Yale should not forfeit its institutional neutrality for a political cause, no matter how widely backed." The university "must by the nature of its purpose permit its members and faculty alike, to espouse the ideas and causes of their choice," he said. "But Yale as an institution cannot let itself be 'mobilized' for any cause, no matter how noble." Institutional neutrality was higher education's coin of the realm—the prerequisite for individual faculty members' exercise of their academic freedom, operation of the university as "a place for thought, not political battles," and prevention of interference in its affairs. Pollak also spoke against closure, while nevertheless saying "he agrees strongly with student hostility toward the Vietnam War." Junior faculty members Richard Abel and John Griffiths argued that the gravity of the war outweighed the importance of "academic neutrality." The students agreed: becoming "infuriated" with their professors' "blindness," they contended that "we should take an institutional position," with one maintaining that the university and law school "should take a stand on a racist war."[15]

To the unhappiness of Abel, Griffiths, and the students, the faculty proceeded to defeat the student resolution by a vote of 14–2. It did, however, adopt a resolution drafted by Associate Dean Ralph Brown, an academic freedom expert and American Association of University Professors stalwart, acknowledging "the crisis of confidence and conscience that the continuation of the war in Vietnam has created for members of the Law School community, as it has for most Americans." While disclaiming "any institutional position on issues that combine political, legal, and moral judgments which transcend its central academic responsibilities," the resolution declared that "each faculty member, each student, and each member of the staff of the School should feel entirely free to participate in — or refrain from participating in — the lawful events planned for that day to express opposition to the war."[16]

To Yale law students, this result was only barely more satisfactory than that reached by the Harvard faculty. Law professors in Cambridge refused to pass any resolution whatsoever about the moratorium because that would amount to "a political position." At NYU, on the other hand, most classes were canceled or rescheduled, and student-faculty teams canvassed Wall Street law firms on Moratorium Day. Yale's students used what they had witnessed, now that they could attend faculty meetings, as new ammunition against their professors.[17]

As always, "Alex ('The Resigner') Bickel, . . . best known for his character roles as the witty, urbane Man of Reason" and for "invariably stopping the show with his threat of leaving the stage in mid-production," particularly irritated them. (Bickel's myriad offers elsewhere may have annoyed his colleagues too, albeit for a different reason: they were probably jealous. He had recently received an invitation to go to Harvard, which he had declined "because I think conditions at Harvard are no better than here," Bickel confided to a friend. "But the truth is that I cannot bring myself to accept what has been done here over the past two years, and more particularly, the way it has been done, and I can neither abide participating any further in the governance of this place, nor figure out how effectively to withdraw.") The fact that Bickel and most of his colleagues began their performances at the meeting with "a personal, cathartic, denunciation of the war" did not impress the young.[18]

As the students saw it, the only faculty members who got it were the relatively young Griffiths and Abel, who voted against the resolution, and Charles Reich, who did not attend the meeting. Other faculty members did not perceive the conflict between the principles of institutional neutrality and "opposition to government atrocities in an immoral war." For the young, the latter was more important, and their professors' obsession with the former showed their "blindness" about, and antagonism toward, the rise of a more democratic culture that enabled dissidents to express themselves.[19]

The students' rejection of "institutional neutrality" was echoed elsewhere. During the 1960s, the young frequently pointed out that "institutional neutrality" was itself a political position, with political consequences. They focused on the impossibility of achieving it. In a society in which large institutions played such an important role in decision making, how could the "university," any more than "the corporation," remain neutral? Too often, they claimed, their professors seemed guilty of "intellectual schizophrenia, . . . accepting, but defining as nonpolitical, those academic enterprises which support the interests of the government." And why had "neutrality" suddenly become so important? Yale itself had longstanding ties to the intelligence community. Further, "[w]ho decried the politicization of American institutions of higher learning when they made total accommodation in mobilizing for the Second World War?"[20]

The faculty's concept of "institutional neutrality" also seemed strange. Bickel, for example, had suggested that Brewster announce that Yale would not close on October 15 because it was "not the function of a university to take stands on one or another side of issues of public policy," but to preserve academic freedom and promote diversity of opinion. Yet Bickel wanted to have it both ways. He also suggested that the president say explicitly, "[I]t is impossible to ignore the fact that the Vietnam War is for many people an issue of conscience, not an ordinary matter of policy, and it is impossible not to respect the depth and sincerity of moral conviction that underlies opposition to the war." Thus Bickel thought Brewster should emphasize that "Yale understands and respects the reasons that may cause many in its community to undertake one day's postponement of classes and to substitute other orderly activities on October 15." This was hardly a neutral compromise, for Bickel's suggested statement did not seem to recognize that the war's supporters would have considered their cause righteous too.[21]

On October 15, 1969, fifty thousand gathered at the New Haven Green for one of the two largest antiwar demonstrations in the United States. Though the SDS wanted no part of the event, it proved a great day for others who sought to show the breadth of antiwar opposition. Mayor Richard Lee denounced the war, as did Lowenstein, the head of the local AFL-CIO, and prominent Democrats and Republicans. Kingman Brewster made his first public statement against the war. A surprise occurred when the moderator of the Black Students Alliance at Yale, Glenn deChabert, interrupted the proceeding. (It was no shock to Brewster. He and deChabert had planned the incident in advance to increase deChabert's credibility with BSAY members.) DeChabert condemned police brutality against African Americans by New Haven and Yale law enforcement and criticized Brewster and the mayor for permitting it to continue. The same day, the Yale Law School Student Association delivered a statement to Brewster declaring itself "highly disturbed by the administration's evasion of its direct responsibility to Yale students and of its moral obligation to the New Haven community at large, by its failure to take any action to eliminate the unjustified harassment and abuse to which Black people are subjected daily by New Haven police."[22]

"STOP THE COPS!"

Few at Yale openly backed the war; deChabert had raised a more divisive issue. As the law students put up their tents in the courtyard, the Chicago Conspiracy Trial was beginning. The Nixon administration had carefully chosen the eight indicted for disrupting the 1968 Democratic Convention to represent the spectrum of the left. The attention of the Yale community was focused on the eighth defendant, Black Panther Party chairman Bobby Seale. Of course, those who labeled Seale's inclusion unfair, since he had done little in Chicago, would become even more outraged when Judge Julius Hoffman silenced Seale by ordering him bound and gagged just after the moratorium and before Halloween.[23]

But as the school year began, many at Yale worried about what would happen to Seale after Chicago, when he was tried in New Haven the following year. The Panthers had set up shop in New Haven in the spring of 1969, establishing a free breakfast program for poor schoolchildren and a health clinic. It was part of Seale's effort to return the party to its roots as a community service organization after a series of gun battles between the Panthers and the police. Yet the confrontations between the Panthers and the state did not end, in part because J. Edgar Hoover had directed FBI agents to destroy them, and the Panthers had been infiltrated by FBI and police informants, who helped provoke violence. Persecution and prosecution of the Panthers continued. In August 1969, Seale was charged with six counts of murder, conspiracy to murder, and kidnapping in connection with the death of Alex Rackley, another Panther whose body had been found soon after Seale had given a speech at Yale. According to the indictment, the victim had been tortured and murdered at Seale's behest by fellow Panthers (at least one of whom, it later became clear, was an agent provocateur for the FBI), who suspected Rackley of having acted as a police informer.[24]

Many assumed that Seale would be denied a fair trial in New Haven, as well as Chicago. Of Rackley's torture and murder by fellow Panthers there was little doubt. Yet New Haven Police Chief James Ahern, who launched his own illegal investigation of the Panthers in 1969, subsequently acknowledged that Seale's indictment had "astonished" him. Although the New Haven Police Department possessed evidence that Seale had gone to the apartment serving as the local Panther headquarters while Rackley was held there, "we had no solid evidence to link him to Rackley's death or torture," he recalled. But at the same time, the police chief was "personally convinced of Seale's guilt."[25]

Given anxiety about the trial, attention naturally turned to the impact of law on African Americans. The concern was in sync with national trends:

dressed in a uniform of black trousers, leather jackets, and sunglasses, some-times armed in self-defense, Black Panthers had already changed the collo-quial meaning of "pig" from politician to policeman. Now, they were building an alliance with a white left allegedly gripped by "Panthermania" and "radi-cal chic." Some of those white radicals may have seized upon Seale's New Haven trial because of its potential to provoke Brewster into an overreaction, others because of guilt. The concern about Seale also reflected local politics. Yale's relationship with the neighboring community remained tense; a front-page *Advocate* article on the topic was entitled "How Yale Screws." Further, African American students were frequently stopped for questioning by cam-pus police, who suspected they were outsiders up to no good. Relations be-tween the black community on and off campus and the New Haven police were strained too, particularly after deChabert was arrested on disorderly conduct charges.[26]

As African Americans challenged their "degrading, humiliating and arbi-trary treatment" by police, they looked to the Yale Corporation, Brewster, and other university eminences for support. Pollak himself believed that "the prob-lems of police and community relations in New Haven . . . are grave and im-portant and demand our urgent consideration." The campus police practice of stopping African American law students to question whether they were stu-dents frustrated the dean, but his office's proposal that they wear badges iden-tifying them as law students angered Black Law Students Union members. As Harold McDougall acknowledged, "Many of us dressed like Panthers." Still, Cochran remembered telling the dean that the idea of badges offended him, and it should offend Pollak too. Here they were in "an oasis of privilege," Cochran said later, and black students "were being jerked around as if they were in the Delta." And their experience with New Haven police was proving no better.[27]

On Tuesday, October 14, 1969, a black student in Visiting Associate Profes-sor George Lefcoe's property course asked Lefcoe to discuss police harassment. Lefcoe replied that it was not germane. As distressed students discussed the exchange after class, BLSU member Eric Clay, who was not in the course, hap-pened along. After hearing what had happened, Clay later testified, "I said to Mr. Lefcoe that if he didn't stop messing over black people in his classes, he might get his ass kicked." Taken aback, Lefcoe asked Clay for his name. Clay refused to identify himself and warned the professor to remember what he had said. Lefcoe reported the matter to Associate Dean Felstiner. The memories of Lefcoe and Clay about what was said diverged: according to the professor, the student had threatened "to beat the shit out of" him.[28]

As the question in Lefcoe's class had shown, students remained concerned about police harassment. They were dissatisfied, too, by Brewster's proposal for a grievance board to investigate specific allegations of harassment lodged against New Haven and campus police.[29] The following Monday morning, October 20, African Americans acted.

Their target was Sterling Law Building. Fearing there was insufficient support for a demonstration among black law students, Cochran had tried to keep it out of the school. But in absolute terms, there were fewer African American students among Yale Law School than Yale College students, which some believed made the law school a more obvious place for protesting prejudice. Of course, a law school was a logical site for a demonstration against police misbehavior too. Approximately eighty individuals, some of them law students, marched into the school. They divided into several groups and entered three large classrooms. Chanting "Stop the cops!" they marched around each for five minutes. For Harold McDougall, the demonstration was a moment in which he experienced "a great feeling of power, pride and self-actualization as the white [law] students and black undergraduate black students supported us. It was very well-planned and executed." And as a white law student active in both the New Left and women's movements, Ann Hill saw the class disruption as a legitimate act of civil disobedience.[30]

Not everyone proved so positive. Faculty members were upset. "Do you want to stop the class or stop the cops?" Professor Joseph Bishop asked the demonstrators. "I don't think that whatever complaints they have about cops are best expressed by breaking up a torts class," he grumbled to the *Yale Daily News*. And the support of at least some white students was probably soft. "I suppose that I, like some of my fellow students, feared to lose my liberal credentials, or worse, to be labeled a racist," one told Pollak, explaining why she had not spoken out against the demonstration. In fact, she confided, she had been frightened. "The door of the classroom was thrust open. There marched into the room fifteen or twenty young Black men and women, the vast majority of them strangers to the Law School." As the students "marched around the room, chanting, 'Stop the cops!'" they seemed "oblivious to the professor and their fellow students," she said. "The chant was loud, militaristic,—and it was not only I, as a woman, who found it intimidating."[31]

The African American students then proceeded across the street to the plaza in front of Woodbridge Hall. Intercepting them, Pollak climbed atop a car and warned that the law school would not "tolerate further interruption of classes. Any students will be subject to discipline." As the dean tried to speak, the cry of "Stop the Cops!" continued. When the demonstrators refused to listen, the *Yale Daily News* reported, Pollak jumped on the Claes Oldenburg sculpture in the plaza "and shouted: 'Does anybody in this group have enough real interest in this problem to listen to me?'"[32]

Here was another difference between the law school and Woodbridge Hall. Though Brewster had proposed treating those who occupied administrators' offices more harshly than Dean Pollak the previous Christmas, he used this protest to institute a number of changes designed to eliminate police interference with the student body. The law school administration, on the other hand, prepared to crack down on law student demonstrators. At a special faculty meeting called at the request of the Student Association Board, professors did agree to establish a faculty-student committee to explore means of improving police-community relations. By that time, though, Pollak had posted a warning: "Yale students who interfered with the equal rights of other students, instructors, or members of the staff, to engage in their regular academic pursuits," through "demonstrative activity," interrupting classes, or "other aspects of the work of this school," would be "subject to academic discipline." And at the meeting, Bickel had informed the Student Association Board officers that the faculty supported and stood behind the dean's warning. That seemed to portend punishment for law students involved in disrupting class, in addition to those active in future protests. And sure enough, Associate Dean Felstiner soon informed three law student participants in the demonstration that they might face charges. Felstiner also referred Clay's case to the Disciplinary Committee, which sent it to an ad hoc disciplinary panel.[33]

By the weekend, the entire law school community was in an uproar over the three protesters and Clay. Students considered it arbitrary to single out three of the law student protesters for discipline. Felstiner maintained they were the only ones he could identify. To make matters worse, as the Committee on the Law School had warned the previous spring, the disciplinary code was sketchy. There was no provision, for example, to involve student representatives in disciplinary matters. As the student negotiators had informed law students the previous spring, there had been "a substantial disagreement between the Student Negotiating Committee and the Discipline Committee over the role students should play in that committee's adjudicatory work." Consequently, the matter of student representation remained unresolved, though the SNC had inferred that a majority of the faculty would agree to student participation in disciplinary proceedings when the new school year began.[34]

Worse still, from the professors' point of view, the Black Law Students Union was making menacing noises. It sent faculty members a telegram summoning them to a meeting with the BLSU on Monday. Upon receipt, several professors immediately demanded a faculty meeting in executive session.[35]

Pollak thought a secret meeting impolitic. It was legal. Arguably, the agreement reached with student negotiators did not actually become effective until the law students formally elected their representatives (recall, however, that the dean had already welcomed those "symbolic" student representatives at regular faculty meetings). Even then, the faculty could decide to meet in executive session.[36]

But was the meeting legitimate? The agreement with the Student Negotiating Committee had provided that professors would meet without students only under extraordinary circumstances. And as Pollak understood it, the reason for a meeting in executive session should be spelled out beforehand. The purpose of this one was unclear. Was it called to respond to the BLSU's demand for a face-off or to discuss disciplinary proceedings against Clay and the three law school agitators? The dean also perceived the call for a meeting as a challenge to his leadership. As Pollak saw it, however, once three faculty members had demanded the meeting he was powerless to block it.[37]

Therefore, the dean scheduled a faculty meeting in executive session at his house on Sunday, October 26. Brewster went, which Pollak appreciated: "[I]f we had to have this goddamned meeting, which we shouldn't have had, having the President there was something." Richard Abel went twice. Since he had forgotten that it was the last Sunday in October and Daylight Savings had ended, he arrived an hour early. "I drove home and then turned around and drove back a second time so I could formally refuse to attend." At its outset, Abel and Charles Reich moved its adjournment because they did not want to meet in executive session on an issue involving "the whole law school community." Though Reich had little desire to become involved in the controversy, he thought that "the idea of having a faculty meeting in secret at the dean's house on a Sunday was a rotten, stupid move, no matter whose side you were on. Faculty meetings were held in the building during the week."[38]

Less than a third of the thirty professors present sided with Abel and Reich, however. A wrangle then ensued as to whether Pollak should notify Student Association president Wagoner of the executive session. Bickel maintained that he should not, citing the business before his colleagues as "a classic example of why we as a faculty felt it necessary to reserve right to meet without students." Pollak had wanted to tell Wagoner of the meeting before it started, he apologetically explained later. But some of his colleagues "urged . . . that (a) notice of an executive session was not necessary, since the Faculty Resolution . . . will not become operational until ten student representatives are elected and (b) post-meeting notice would in any event be fully responsive to the felt need to report on the holding of the executive session."[39]

The students, however, had heard of the faculty meeting on Sunday morning. Cochran knew about it because of his wide intelligence network: a cafeteria worker who had learned of it from a law professor's maid had tipped him off. But this was a Student Association, rather than a BLSU, issue. The *New York Times* reported that the students had also received "a telephone tip from a sympathetic faculty member." As students understood it, they had a right to advance notice of a meeting in executive session. In fact, Wagoner had already telephoned the dean's house while the faculty was arguing about procedure "specifically in order to give Pollak an opportunity to inform him of the secret executive session."[40]

When Mrs. Pollak relayed a message that the dean would telephone Wagoner "later," the Student Association president and his fellow students concluded that the faculty had violated its agreement with them. Further, they subsequently said, they "believed strongly that the subject for which the faculty had been called together — a response to the BLSU demand for a meeting, and the issue of disciplinary action against certain law school black students — was *not* an appropriate issue of exclusion of the students." If the faculty could prohibit student participation, then the agreement about a student presence at faculty meetings was "meaningless and hollow." And finally, students were certain that "the procedures employed by Dean Pollak in calling the meeting — the secrecy and the lack of honesty when Wagoner called the Pollak home, in particular — would have severely damaging consequences on the atmosphere within the Law School, and would contribute to the growing sense of alienation among students which precludes any kind of spirit of community from developing."[41]

So Wagoner and five Student Association board members went to Pollak's house. "That's just what we invited, and to what end?" Pollak commented later. When the dean heard they were on his porch, he went outside to say that he had been in the process of telephoning Wagoner to say that the faculty was meeting in executive session. Returning, he told his colleagues that "the students are outside this house and are very upset and Wagoner wants to speak to this meeting." Pollak moved that Wagoner be allowed to address it for five minutes. Abe Goldstein demurred. "Why should we now invite students having just decided not to?" he asked. But Pollak's motion carried.[42]

The dean went outside again to tell the students Wagoner could speak briefly and "solely to the question of what the faculty's response should be to the BLSU demand for a Monday afternoon meeting." Since Pollak said nothing about Wagoner's five companions, they assumed they could listen and filed into the living room. "Suddenly," the Yale Law School Student Association account continues, "Professor Abraham Goldstein interrupted: 'Hey wait a minute. What are these others doing here?' (waving his hand). 'We said only Wagoner—and only for five minutes.'" As Ralph Brown recalled, "Abe Goldstein, who was then beginning to be thought of as 'deanable,' really lost his cool. He just blew up." Joe Goldstein spoke up too, as did others, stressing that the professors had only agreed to Wagoner's appearance. Pollak seemed about to protest, but instead "asked all students leave so that the faculty could again discuss the matter. (Wagoner had already gotten up in disgust and left the room.)"[43]

Another argument followed. This time, Emerson moved to invite the students, but to permit only Wagoner to speak. When that motion was defeated, the dean returned to the porch to say that just the Student Association president could enter. Wagoner and his companions left in protest.[44]

The charged incident could have led to reflection on the different meanings of democracy. From the perspective of some on the faculty, the meeting was essential because democracy was in danger. To the Goldsteins, it would have seemed that students had displayed their lack of commitment to democracy by their implicit threats to upset the meeting when they followed Wagoner into it, just as black students had disrupted the classroom. The mob was at the gates, and the citizens must rise up in its defense. Yet Pollak found the assembly undemocratic because it violated, at least in spirit, the agreement negotiated with the students the previous spring. The compromise reached had been intended to make the faculty decisional process more transparent unless the students received explicit notice beforehand that the faculty had good reason to act in private. The mechanisms ensuring that decision making reflected the will of citizens and served that their interest had been flouted. And to the Student Association, exclusion pointed up the underlying problem of professors' insistence on retaining their prerogatives and their continued refusal to treat students as citizens. To students, the faculty had displayed its true authoritarianism and unwillingness to share power. As one of those who had accompanied Wagoner, Ann Hill recalled feelings of "humiliation," "anger," and "total frustration" at her professors' response. Doubtless, those unsympathetic to the students would say that Wagoner knew his was a futile errand and wanted to provoke a confrontation. Perhaps, but as Pollak recognized, Wagoner had every reason to expect at least advance notification of the meeting, and to want a hearing in any case.[45]

Now that the students had gone, the meeting could move forward. The professors were at last ready to address the substantive issue: what did the BLSU want from them, and how should they respond? Everyone believed that the black students' grievance related to the charges brought against those who had disrupted the classes.

Pollak was caught between university administrators and his hardliners. Brewster reported that Cochran, with whom he dealt as one politician to another, had come to him to say that he "objected to our singling out individuals." Yale's president urged the law faculty to pass the buck back to the BLSU and entrust it with finding a better way to identify the "miscreants." He believed that Cochran was worried about both an "intra-University struggle for power among Blacks" and his "national position as BLSU leader." African Americans were "unsure of themselves," Brewster said, "and whether their ranks will hold." But he thought that Cochran was generally trying to be "helpful" and had no intention of staging a "major confrontation." Thus the president urged the faculty to meet with the BLSU.[46]

But Abe Goldstein advocated standing up to the students. Arguing that it would be inappropriate for the faculty corporately to attend the meeting with the BLSU or for too many of his colleagues to go in their individual capacities, he moved for the appointment of a small delegation to represent the faculty instead. Yet while Harry Wellington and Joe Goldstein supported him, the motion did not carry. After Brewster departed and after they had held yet another vote, the professors decided each should make his own decision about attending.[47]

There are several accounts of the two-hour meeting with the BLSU the next day, attended by just over half the professors. According to Robert Bork, BLSU leaders shouted curses at the "very frightened" professors and berated them "in violently obscene" language while two "large" black students blocked the exit from the faculty lounge. But Bork himself did not attend the gathering. Boris Bittker reported that while professors were not made to feel as if they were hostages, they were given the sense that they were in prison. But that reaction in itself was notable. Bittker had opposed Goldstein's suggestion of a delegation and had been the African American students' ally, teaching a seminar on "The Role of the Black Lawyer." Another sometime student sympathizer, Charles Reich, was also upset. He felt sadness that Pollak, "such a kind, gentlemanly person," should have to function as dean in an atmosphere so unpleasant and tense. "I thought it was a low point for the institution." Reich was scared too. "There were two big black students standing at the door looking for all the world like they were guards." Years later, he recalled a whispered question from Alexander Bickel: "How am I going to get out in the hall to pee? He certainly wasn't joking. He was intimidated and spoke to me as a person who would understand how he felt." Bickel, Joe Goldstein, and Leon Lipson later told BLSU officers that speakers had displayed "little readiness to discuss or to reason. Instead we were subjected to a series of tirades, no less abusive for all their earnestness; and when the Dean tried to speak to the issues that had been set out as the basis for the Union's invitation, he was brusquely shut off."[48]

For Pollak, the occasion was a disaster. He well knew that some of his colleagues believed him too "accommodationist," too willing to give the students whatever they wanted. But now, he thought, Bickel and the Goldsteins saw him as a "wimp." Harry Wellington maintained that Pollak was "too much a total liberal. And he was ineffective at the time." The dean was too fearful of appearing "authoritarian," so eager to show he could tolerate dissent, that he allowed students to push him around. Pollak himself later said he had been too "submissive" at the meeting.[49]

Within the university, as within the larger society, "liberals" could do no right. (Brewster was an exception, but he was hardly the conventional sixties liberal.) As Pollak's junior colleague David Trubek observed, for activists, the school's "so-called 'reforms' . . . give too little to be worthwhile; for defenders of the status quo, the changes are a serious erosion."[50] If students and a few on the faculty perceived Pollak as too "hard," many professors thought him too "soft."

Thus the BLSU found the dean and his faculty neither "submissive" nor understanding. "We tried to convey, as honestly and sincerely as we could, the disaffection of black students with the current situation in the Law School," Otis Cochran said to the *Yale Daily News*. But, he complained, professors "sat on the other side of the room and took notes, then tried to feed us legalistic generalities which are completely inadequate when our presence in this University is threatened."[51]

Neither Cochran nor Harold McDougall credited faculty complaints. According to Cochran, no black students barricaded the doors. He knew that some on the faculty considered Pollak too conciliatory to the students. From Cochran's perspective, it would have seemed that the dean's critics had exaggerated the friction at the meeting to demonstrate the need for toughness. While black students' tactics, such as entering in single file, might have seemed "quasi-military," they were borrowed from the sit-ins of the early civil rights movement, in which the faculty gloried. During an explosive period in American history, Cochran believed, the faculty projected national tensions onto Yale and read more into BLSU actions than its members intended. He did not remember anyone threatening the professors, adding that at this point, Yale law professors found any "bearded black men over 5′ 10″ tall" menacing by definition. McDougall agreed that no students had obstructed the exit: "Most of us were shocked that the faculty would be so high-handed; we had relationships with many of them." He thought that the gathering might have been the occasion on which one African American became "very emotional and may have said we would 'fuck them up.'" But it was "clear" to McDougall that the individual was "a very gentle person and highly unlikely to hurt anyone." Further, he "was crying when he said it. He certainly expressed all our disappointments that this place we had come to with such high hopes had shown itself to be powered by the same kind of ultimate political self-protectionism and stonewalling that for me characterized the rest of society."[52]

The Student Association proved equally dissatisfied. Wagoner had wasted no time after he walked out of Pollak's house on Sunday afternoon. He had immediately issued a statement denouncing the secret meeting and calling for all law students to gather on Monday morning. The group had also prepared a position paper characterizing African Americans' disruption of classes as legitimate civil disobedience that did not warrant disciplinary action. Refusing to accept the jurisdiction of any disciplinary panel that did not include student representatives, a supportive committee of 100 law students declared that the secret meeting "symbolizes the bad faith and condescension characteristic of faculty actions toward students."[53]

Pollak's insistence on Monday that the agreement to notify students of faculty meetings had not yet become effective and his acknowledgment that he and his colleagues continued to contemplate action against the four students pushed activists over the edge. All BLSU members signed a statement declaring their "joint involvement" in the disruption, and accusing the faculty of choosing "to single out and try a few of us by [a] procedure which is at least a denial of due process." If the school opted for a trial of those it had identified, "let it be understood that you try us all and that their punishment will be ours." Clearly, they had absorbed the legal lesson that process issues possessed radical and disruptive potential.[54]

And students resolved to strike the following day. That suited one self-proclaimed radical, who confided his hope to the *Yale Daily News* that a strike would bring "a majority of the School behind us." It would "get students together" and force them to "decide whose side they're really on."[55]

By now, the struggle within the law school had hit the *New York Times*. It reported that Tuesday's strike featured "a picket line of placards depicting the scales of justice severed in two by a lightning bolt." According to the *Times*:

"The Yale Law School, a renowned institution with a reputation for rational discourse that would try the patience of a Socrates, got a whiff of the student revolution today."[56]

Of course Yale Law School, along with the School of Art and Architecture — whose administration, one law student reported, was "possibly worse than ours (anything is possible)" — had been at the epicenter of whatever "student revolution" was taking place in New Haven for some time. Because of Brewster, Yale College had remained unusually calm. No student strikes had taken place. The relatively conservative *Yale Daily News* even advised "[t]hose who wonder what Yale might be like without an academic politician as president . . . to examine the current flaps at the Law School."[57]

The *News* seemed uncertain the strike could succeed. Presenting the confrontation between faculty and students as one of head against heart, it hypothesized that at the core of the strike lay what law school activists characterized as "insults to our humanity." The problem was the rationalism and authority of their teachers. As the *News* explained it, those who began law school accustomed "to their status as respected students in their undergraduate majors, . . . tend[ed] to resent their semi-ignorance and sometimes helplessness in classes about the law." Faculty and administrators seemed "singularly unaware of this often subvocal humiliation their students feel" and responded to complaints "in concise inexorably logical legal terms," compounding the students' vague but deep sense of helplessness. But could students who agreed with Duncan Kennedy about "how the Yale Law School fails" coalesce around the strike? "If today's strike deteriorates," the *News* concluded, "it may be because law students used to dealing in specifics will not identify with a strike called on thirty hours' notice on a list of demands and causes an arm's length long."[58]

But the October 1969 strike did not deteriorate. Perhaps its leaders exaggerated when they told the media that 60 percent of the school's 600 students refused to cross the picket lines on Tuesday. Still, according to the *Times*, even "neutral observers" estimated that between one-third and one-half the student body had boycotted classes.[59]

And Pollak backed down. On Wednesday, he issued a memorandum announcing that he had dropped charges against the three African Americans who had disrupted classes because he had received the statement from the additional thirty-five "courageously" admitting they had been "jointly involved." The dean insisted that the "legal proposition" that class disruption represented civil disobedience was "wholly untenable." He proved even less tolerant of the "wholly unpersuasive" claim that the disciplinary panel lacked "legitimacy" because only professors sat on it. Nevertheless, the young's reaction to the faculty's plan to discipline the demonstrators "heightens my doubts that, *as of that date*, the generality of our students fully appreciated, what henceforth no student anywhere in Yale University can doubt for a single instant: that deliberate interference with the academic or other pursuits of any other student, faculty member, or member of the staff, is regarded by Yale as an offense of very serious dimensions warranting the imposition of very serious sanctions."[60]

Yet the dean's tone was, for the most part, lawyerly and conciliatory. He closed his memorandum by calling attention to the new student-faculty committee established on the very day of the class disruptions to address "the manifold problems of police-community relations" and by appealing to professionalism and legal liberalism. Exhorting members of the law school community to "show ourselves worthy of our calling," Pollak urged them to focus on "these and kindred issues of common concern and compelling urgency."[61]

"STREET TALK"

Though the picket lines and the charges against the three protesters disappeared, the Disciplinary Committee action against Eric Clay for "threatening a member of the faculty with violence" still hung fire. Indeed, the Clay case had become more important. The law school had abandoned the idea of disciplining the students who had interrupted classes by shouting "Stop the Cops," behavior most professors and many students surely found more intimidating than Clay's comment, whatever it was. Instead it would concentrate on Clay's statement after he heard that Lefcoe had refused to devote class time to police harassment. It would make Lefcoe's complaint against Clay a proxy for deciding how to discipline disruptive students.

Lefcoe was no stranger to racism. As an Orthodox Jew growing up in the segregated school systems of South Florida, he had regularly engaged in fistfights with the "rednecks" with whom he debated integration in schoolyards. As a high school student, he had given talks in local black churches and visited the separate, unequal black high schools. After graduating from Dartmouth, where he had served on the Disciplinary Committee, he went on to Yale, where he was Note and Comment Editor of the *Yale Law Journal*. When he graduated in 1962, he received various teaching offers, eventually choosing USC because he wanted to be in a city with a vibrant real estate market. Arriving in Los Angeles, he rented a townhouse in the middle-class black neighborhood of Baldwin Hills and set about joining other young Turks who would ultimately transform USC from a local to a national law school. From the time he began teaching, he recalled regularly including discussion of civil rights issues in his property course, including claims of trespass lodged against civil rights demonstrators. After five years at USC, Yale offered him a three-year contract, presumably a "lookover" to determine whether it would invite him there permanently.[62]

In the view of some, the stint had not gone well. One professor remembered that at Yale, Lefcoe had a reputation for nastiness to students. Some African Americans branded him "insensitive" and later complained that he had been "demoralizing black students in that class in a number of ways" even before the exchange with Clay.[63]

To Lefcoe, of course, the situation seemed entirely different. As a professor, he had always believed that "teachers owe their students the moral obligation to secure the integrity of the classroom." Years later, he still remembered a World War II film about the Japanese in the Philippines that highlighted "the heroic efforts of schoolteachers to resist the use of their classrooms for Japanese propaganda even in the face of certain death" for their defiance. When Clay warned him to stop bothering African Americans in his class, Lefcoe feared for academic freedom. Still, he acted cautiously, consulting a number of colleagues before lodging a formal complaint with Associate Dean Felstiner. He was, after all, a visitor, which meant that he had not attended the gathering at Pollak's house. And Lefcoe felt in no physical danger: had he considered his personal safety at issue, he would have contacted either the campus or New Haven police. "The only reason I considered filing a complaint with the law school was because this threat was uttered in an attempt to coerce me to open my classroom to an intimidating diatribe by a few black students about the New Haven police." And "[t]o a man," those he consulted urged Lefcoe to lodge the complaint. "Slightly veiled threats" had become "a way of doing business, and a rough style of bargaining, which we did not deal with very effectively, involving a good deal of confrontation, became standard negotiating procedure," one Yale professor remembered. "The regular defense of faculty and administration was to treat outrageous events as if nothing had happened, showing the vandals that 'they are not getting to us.'" The line must be drawn here, Lefcoe felt.[64]

The law school's disciplinary proceedings were ill-suited to his objectives, however. To take but one example, since the disciplinary panel included no students, Clay would be denied a jury of his peers. Perhaps a civil model, involving monetary damages, would have been more appropriate too. The use of a quasi-criminal model, common at the time in most universities, meant that the threat of suspension or expulsion hung in the air. And that made it more likely a circus would follow.[65]

The faculty apparently hoped to avoid one by resolving the issue quietly. So, at first, did Otis Cochran. Because of his fear about the firmness of BLSU support, Cochran wanted "to lowkey" the statement by Clay and the disruption of classes. But when Pollak threatened to take action against the three students and Lefcoe's formal complaint resulted in the filing of charges against Clay, Cochran thought the dean was trying to demonstrate toughness to his critical colleagues. And that meant, Cochran believed, that the BLSU needed to take a strong position too.[66]

With the ingredients for fire present, the kindling was soon ignited. Clay selected an African American third-year, Mel Watt, as his student attorney. Perhaps Clay and Watt knew each other before Yale: both had attended the University of North Carolina. Perhaps the fact that Watt was a member of the *Yale Law Journal* also impressed Clay. In addition, Watt was an active BLSU member: at the December 1968 showdown with the faculty about BLSU concerns, he had spoken of the modifications in the curriculum necessary to "make it more meaningful to Blacks."[67]

Clay and Watt urged a "trial" to show students "the arbitrary and illegitimate faculty-instituted disciplinary process in operation" and unveil "the problems of black people within the law school," as well as "the inherent racism which black people must face every day of their lives." They maintained that the hearing would "in fact determine whether black students are to be allowed to exist as black people within Yale Law School." The decision was probably an easy one. Ironically, student representation on the ad hoc disciplinary panel would have worked to professors' interests by providing an excuse for insisting on a closed courtroom. But there were no student representatives on the panel who could protect the interests of Clay and Watt or safeguard those of the faculty by reporting back to the student body that due process had been provided. And since the Chicago Seven trial was under way, political trials were in the air. The law school administration's prosecution of Clay seemed politically motivated to some, designed to score an ideological victory for the center and right by silencing the left. In that situation, the defense naturally wanted to make its case to a larger audience than the judges.[68]

But disciplinary panel chair Joe Goldstein refused to open the show to the public. Watt thought he might have come down that way because to do otherwise would mean panel members would have "to treat Clay, a student, as an equal." Joe Goldstein did, however, agree to allow access to the law school community. Held in the school's largest classroom, the trial "attracted an overflow audience which spilled into the aisles and onto the windowsills." Several rows were cleared of chairs. For some reason—perhaps a strained attempt to convey an atmosphere of informality, reject "the posture of a judge," replicate the office in which the dean met students, or to comply with some notion of due process by recreating the office in which hearings normally took place—the disciplinary panel considered it important that its members, Clay, and Watt sit on the couches and overstuffed chairs brought in for the occasion. The atmosphere was tense. Though the audience was "well-behaved" and treated Lefcoe well enough, it was clearly skeptical of the disciplinarians. "This was not a crowd prepared to kowtow to the faculty," Lefcoe said.[69]

Watt and Clay had crafted a neat defense. Clay's language to Lefcoe had to be taken in context. The Supreme Court had recently affirmed the validity of doing just that. It had vacated the conviction of antiwar protester Robert Watts, who had been found guilty of violating a statute that prohibited anyone from physically threatening the president of the United States. "I am not going," Watts told a crowd at a rally. "If they ever make me carry a rifle the first man I want to get in my sights is LBJ. They are not going to make me kill my black brothers." At trial, his lawyer had moved to dismiss. The statement, he said, was made during a political debate, conditioned upon induction, which Watts had said would not occur, and Watts and the crowd had laughed after he made his declaration. According to the lawyer, "Now actually what happened here in all this was a kind of very crude offensive method of stating a political opposition to the President." The Court agreed that the trial judge had erred in denying the motion. Watts's only offense had been to exercise his First Amendment right to state his objection to Lyndon Johnson. "Taken in context, and regarding the explicitly conditional nature of the statement, and the reaction of the listeners, we do not see how it could be interpreted otherwise."[70]

Here the context was Clay's background. Where Clay had grown up in North Carolina, "get your ass kicked" constituted a prediction, not a threat, and not necessarily a prediction to worry about, either. It was just "the hyperbole of street talk," Watt maintained, whose meaning depended on the circumstances that surrounded its utterance. Watt contended that Clay was engaged in "theoretical expression" and intended no violence. Perhaps that was correct. Ed Baker recalled that everyone understood Clay's remark as an expression of "contempt for the teaching that was going on, a contempt that was widely shared," not a threat of violence. And when Otis Cochran was called, he contended that Clay had been "restrained."[71]

Yet "street talk" was hardly Clay's only argot. Lefcoe remembered hearing that Clay had grown up in an inner city housing project, and Clay was the first person in his family to attend college. Still, at the University of North Carolina, Clay and Watt had both graduated Phi Beta Kappa, and Clay had been chairman of the Carolina Political Union and president of the Dialectic and Philanthropic Societies. Lefcoe had no difficulty understanding Clay or any other students at Yale, for that matter; "they were splendidly articulate and clearly comprehensible to one and all."[72]

By suggesting there was a misunderstanding, however, the defense shifted the spotlight from the accused, Clay, to the complaining witness, or accuser, Lefcoe. A prosecutor might have protected Lefcoe. Yet there was no prosecutor. When Joe Goldstein, as panel chair, interrogated Clay, students complained that the panelists engaged "in a mixture of prosecutorial and judicial functions which in itself makes a fair hearing difficult." Today, university counsel might defend Lefcoe's interests. But in the 1960s, university attorneys typically stayed out of such proceedings. A colleague skilled in litigation or administrative hearings could have volunteered to stand by during the hearing to make sure the victim escaped blame. But no one did. As Lefcoe saw it, the law school administration and his colleagues, including some of the very individuals who had advised him to file a complaint, hung him out to dry. Most professors just "ducked for cover." Except for Myres McDougal, Lefcoe's mentor on the faculty, and Bickel, they "kept their distance and offered no legal advice or moral support."[73]

It seemed to Lefcoe that he, rather than Clay, had been put on trial. The disciplinary action, which might have been entitled *Yale Law School* v. *Eric Clay*, became *Eric Clay* v. *George Lefcoe*. Because of the nature of the proceeding, no one examined Lefcoe. Watt, however, cross-examined him at length about his prior experiences with African Americans in an apparent attempt to demonstrate Lefcoe had little and had not comprehended Clay's words. Watt assumed Lefcoe's contact had been limited to interchanges with servants, a supposition Lefcoe found amusing in light of his childhood and status as a younger faculty member. "The notion that somehow I had misunderstood Mr. Clay's meaning, though a clever assertion, was one that I am sure Mr. Clay and Mr. Watt knew to be without merit," Lefcoe said later. Yet Clay and Watt "were just students at the time and I could appreciate how they played their hand."[74]

Elaborating on the point of cultural difference, Watt asked Clay to "tell the panel what the words 'get your ass kicked' means where you come from." Clay responded, "It could mean a number of things, from 'Now you die,' to 'Good morning,' or 'Good afternoon.' " He had "intended for the statement to mean that unless Mr. Lefcoe reformed his behavior, he would in fact suffer consequences," Clay explained.[75]

With this, however,[76] Clay seemed to undercut the argument. The line of questioning had created the chance for him to claim that he had not really threatened Lefcoe with violence. Watt now asked him about the myriad meanings of the remark, "If you continue, you are going to get your ass kicked," in the context of his exchange with Lefcoe:

> Q[Watt]: Did that include a threat that you personally were going to kick Mr. Lefcoe's ass?
>
> A[Clay]: I don't know that the consequences would necessarily follow, be dependent on whatever action I would take. The statement was intended to mean that such occurrence—and I still do think—that such occurrence will come to pass if Mr. Lefcoe does not alter his behavior. Whether I would do it or someone else would do it, I don't know.
>
> CHAIRMAN GOLDSTEIN: Could you tell us what consequences you have in mind?
>
> THE WITNESS: No.
>
> CHAIRMAN GOLDSTEIN: You are refusing to, or you don't have any idea in mind? I didn't understand the answer.
>
> THE WITNESS: I am refusing to.[77]

The defense had nearly accomplished the impossible. It had demonstrated the chasm between the culture of Yale Law School and that of the inner city while creating the chance for Clay to back down without apologizing. Years later, Harold McDougall still recalled the "bravura performance by Mel Watt," dressed in an Edwardian suit, "the fashion of the time, when you weren't wearing a bush jacket. He cut quite the dashing figure, and was the center of attention. He seemed to be making the statement that we were lawyers and had these tools at our disposal, as well as demonstrations."[78]

While Watt and Clay had shown that their legal education had served them well, they had convinced few faculty members in attendance that Lefcoe had misunderstood Clay's intent. Clay's comment to Lefcoe was "clearly a case for discipline," Charles Reich emphasized later. "It's not just street talk. It's unacceptable."[79]

Had Clay seized the opening his counsel had created for him, the incident might nevertheless have been dismissed as a misunderstanding in the interest of moving forward. But Clay had underlined the political nature of the trial in his reply to Goldstein, with his insistence that his conduct was right. In a dramatic moment, he had *appeared* to depart from the script after the stage had been set.[80] His action made his words seem more menacing than ever.

HARD CHOICES

Consequently, the Disciplinary Committee proved ill disposed to be gracious. It unanimously agreed that "[no] explanation or interpretation of Mr. Clay's language could render it anything less than a threat of violence." It considered all the language variations, ranging from "beat the shit" to "suffer the consequences," threatening and "intended to have coercive force." Nor did the committee find at all persuasive any of the arguments offered as defense or in mitigation, including the contentions that Lefcoe had not appeared frightened; that the episode reflected the need for increased white sensitivity to black culture; or that assuming, arguendo, Clay *had* made a threatening remark to Lefcoe, "it was a very deserved statement."[81]

But the panel divided over the punishment. Joe Goldstein and Ward Bowman recommended Clay's immediate suspension. Under their plan, Clay could reenroll the following fall as long as he provided "satisfactory evidence (preferably in written form) to the Dean and faculty that he understands that what he said—whatever his intent at the time—conveyed a threat of violence, that he disclaims the use of or the threatened use of violence and that he will abide by these requisites."[82]

That did not sit well. Some thought Goldstein had acted more like prosecutor than judge. One student representative to the Disciplinary Policy Committee that was just starting to hammer out a code of rights and duties of members of the Yale Law community contended that the trial was "fraught with personalities. Most noticeably there was a clash between Mr. Clay and Mr. Goldstein, yet Mr. Goldstein would not disqualify himself." She and others on the committee maintained, in fact, that "the issues involved in the Clay case became so smothered in personalities and fears that emotional detachment was impossible by the tribunal."[83]

The other three faculty members of the panel—Robert Bork, Jay Katz, and Robert Hudec—argued that Clay should be given twenty-four hours to provide "satisfactory evidence" of his understanding that he had threatened violence and of his willingness to abstain from it now. If he did not issue the appropriate statement, his suspension should automatically follow. They speculated that Clay "may have had the impression that this School was not prepared to respond firmly" to his "unacceptable behavior." At Yale Law School, as elsewhere in the academy, "the rhetoric of personal abuse bordering on threats of violence *has been permitted to escalate so far without clear response* that the principle of the intolerability of threats of violence has itself been placed in jeopardy." The school must stress anew that punishment would follow violent threats, they declared. If Clay were allowed to issue a statement straightaway, he and others could "focus on the principle in question rather than on the issue of whether our position has been made clear in the past."[84]

In other words, the majority wanted to reprimand its administrators along with Clay and seized upon due process to do so. If the defense hoped to lay the incident on a failure to understand black culture, Bork, Katz, and Hudec wanted to blame it on a failure of white authority figures, such as Pollak and Brewster, to be tough enough. The three in the majority obviously considered Yale's administrators part of the problem. They wanted to underscore the un-acceptability of accommodation and pledge the school to future sternness.

But to the dean, who had the authority under the bylaws to reduce the com-mittee's sentence, though the majority's solution seemed "generous," it was unworkable. Publicly, Pollak said that after consulting with Clay, Watt, and others, he was certain no assurances would be forthcoming. Clay would view rendering them "to be degrading," the dean reported to the entire school after Thanksgiving. "The fact that the majority's proposal was not perceived by the majority, or by me, in the symbolic terms in which Mr. Clay perceives it, is un-availing." The majority's solution thus represented no "real option" for Clay and would simply guarantee his suspension. And since Pollak agreed with the majority that at the time Clay spoke to Lefcoe, Clay had no reason to believe his threat would result in suspension, the dean did not believe suspension was appropriate now.[85]

Kathy Pollak said that the night before he handed down his verdict in the Clay case was the only time her husband had ever had trouble sleeping. His solution doubtless gave others sleepless nights. The dean decided simulta-neously to suspend Clay and to suspend the suspension. He placed the student on probation. The dean also warned that if Clay engaged in comparable mis-conduct in the future, expulsion would follow.[86]

Few professors were satisfied. Pollak said that his decision "came closer to dividing the faculty than any other issue." Lefcoe, for one, objected to the pro-cess. "Edicts are OK, but only from people driving the bus," he said.[87]

Yet what else could Pollak do? Building a consensus would have involved making compromises that might have enabled his faculty critics to tolerate the outcome. But no concessions could have satisfied the hardliners without setting off the students. For example, in the aftermath of the Clay incident, professors and students were drafting "The Rights and Duties of Members of the Yale Law School," as the Committee on the Law School had earlier rec-ommended. The document, which was ultimately adopted, made it clear that "[t]hreatening the use of physical force or violence to harass, abuse, intimidate, coerce or injure any member of or visitor to the Law School or University in circumstances which, in the judgment of the trier of the facts, create a reasonable fear that force might be used" constituted grounds for probation, suspension, or expulsion. The "Rights and Duties" provided for two student members on the five-person hearing panels. It said that the hearing panel would reach its findings by majority vote, and, in the event of suspension for more than a year or expulsion, by a vote of at least 4-1. Joe Goldstein objected that allowing students to participate in the vote to exclude one of their numbers was tantamount to permitting them to vote in faculty meetings, and Bickel strongly agreed that "it is a radical, and to me wholly inadmissible, abdication of our responsibility." So perhaps Pollak might have won support from Joe Goldstein's faction for his decision in the Clay case by promising to take a strong stand against student representation on future panels.[88]

But that outcome, coming on the heels of the Clay trial, could itself have provoked student demonstrations, perhaps ones tinged with overtones of violence. To students working with Rostow's Disciplinary Policy Committee on drafting the statement on rights and duties of law school members and rules for disciplinary hearings, the Clay case demonstrated "that an objective decision may be impossible under the present situation, particularly in cases where the victim of an alleged offense is a faculty member. Mr. Clay was denied a hearing by his 'peers,' no matter how that term may be defined." Even without "the explosive emotional atmosphere now pervading this school, . . . it is quite evident that rational deliberation is almost impossible under the present disciplinary procedure." Goldstein's recommendations for a punishment "so manifestly disproportionate to the alleged offense" proved that. Although the students "emphatically" supported Pollak's resolution of the Clay case, at least at first, they were sure that "one man should not have the burden of mitigating a faculty panel's suggested sentence."[89]

That was indeed a "burden." Pollak simply did not possess the faculty support to govern by consensus. The situation had degenerated too much. Thus the dean had to impose an outcome on the Clay case, as a president might unilaterally grant a pardon.

And a suspended sentence was the only feasible solution. For one thing, the absence of an explicit definition of obstructive conduct in the disciplinary code, the near non-existent nature of regulations governing pre-disciplinary and disciplinary hearing procedures, and the failure to specify the range of sanctions for particular offenses rendered a more punitive decision imprudent. Anything more stringent than probation would have opened "a great law school . . . to a charge of arbitrariness in adjudicating such basic issues as whether a student has in fact violated a valid law or regulation," just as the Committee on the Law School had warned the previous spring. For another, after the "Stop the Cops" demonstration at the law school, Yale members of Students for Democratic Society occupied the university's personnel office in Wright Hall to protest the firing of Colia Williams, an African American dining hall worker. It was the first Yale building that had been taken over, and, as it turned out, the only one that would be. One goal was to goad Brewster into a misstep. Alleging that the dismissal symbolized Yale's racism, students remained there for hours. "As the students voluntarily filed out of the basement offices tonight, deans [of Yale's residential colleges] stood nearby, trying to recognize as many as possible, so that disciplinary action against them could proceed tomorrow," the New York Times reported.[90]

The day after the "takeover," the university suspended forty-four of the protesters. So far, all had proceeded in accordance with the "faculty-approved 'scenario,'" which Brewster had contemplated in his Christmas 1968 meeting with the law school faculty. He had developed and formally laid it out for Dean John Perry Miller the previous spring with the same attentiveness to choreography Lyndon Johnson used in setting out the Gulf of Tonkin Resolution, and his office had distributed the warning to the entire Yale community. In the eyes of "liberal moderates," such as Drama School dean Robert Brustein, the "scenario" was enlightened. By threatening students who disrupted campus operations with academic sanctions, such as suspension, Brewster avoided outside police and criminal prosecution, which he affirmed he would use if all else in the scenario failed. It was classic Brewster. The scenario "attracted wide publicity because it was a strong statement against disruption but also affirmed 'the encouragement of controversy, no matter how fundamental' and 'the protection of dissent, no matter how extreme.'"[91]

But to the surprise of Brustein, and perhaps Brewster, just as Clay's trial was about to begin, the twenty-two-member Executive Committee, a body that included six students, suspended the suspensions of the Yale undergraduates. It ordered the students to withdraw for the year, but provided for their immediate reinstatement and placed them on "disciplinary probation" for the rest of the year. To Bickel's anger, the Yale faculty approved the Executive Committee's decision. The Executive Committee did not require the SDS protesters to recant and promise to behave properly. For Pollak to have risked Clay's suspension by requiring him to do so, when he knew Clay would not, and at a time when the law school administration was already perceived as more authoritarian than Yale College's, would have precipitated another crisis.[92]

Further, BLSU members had privately warned Pollak that all African American students would quit school if he implemented either disciplinary panel recommendation in the Clay case. Cochran had also turned up the heat by suggesting that possibility to Brewster and the Yale Corporation's Ted Blair. "I was bluffing," Cochran subsequently admitted. Although a walkout might have occurred, "not everyone would have stayed home." And Cochran wanted to avoid this divisive step. Had black students left two months into the first year with a large black enrollment, the BLSU's work in 1968 and 1969 would have been in vain.[93]

White activists were up in arms too. As a student representative to Rostow's Disciplinary Policy Committee told the *Advocate*: "Both the Goldstein-Bowman minority and the Hudec-Bork-Katz majority reports are too harsh in that they recommend suspension and unreal in that they require written acknowledgment that the threat occurred and assurance that it will not recur, while Mr. Clay denies that such a threat was ever made." And, she said, well he should, since "Mr. Clay's words were intended as a warning or a prediction, not as a threat," similar to "my telling the Dean, 'If you don't get this school together, you'll suffer the consequences.'" Activists had made it clear to Pollak, he remembered later, that unless he modified the panel's recommendations, they would be "mighty unhappy" and might even leave too.[94]

To date, the Yale Law School, like Yale College, had not been radicalized. By 1969, probably few on "the left" had thought the law school could be. Had its administration proven completely unyielding on grades or affirmative action, the school might have reached the boiling point sooner. But it had bent. The *Advocate* had suggested that the issue of governance would not radicalize students the previous year, but in the context of a disciplinary proceeding, it was dynamite. Upholding Clay's suspension by a panel of professors, amid an atmosphere of concern about police harassment, racial injustice, and free speech, might well have brought students to the barricades and created the impression that, even more than Yale College, the law school treated its students as children. Pollak shrewdly decided against making Clay a martyr, particularly since he had not violated any explicit school strictures.

Even so, the dean could have damaged Clay's career, or, at least, caused trouble for him with a state bar committee later. Instead, while Mel Watt was becoming one of the two African Americans elected to Congress from North Carolina in the twentieth century, Clay was making his own way. He clerked for District Judge Damon Keith after graduation, then helped establish one of the nation's first large minority law firms. At the same time, he became active in community groups such as 100 Black Men, an organization Clay credited with rescuing "dozens" of youngsters from "a life at risk" in the inner city. When Bill Clinton appointed Clay to the Sixth Circuit in 1997, Judge Keith administered the oath to Clay in front of an audience that included Clay's Yale friends Clarence Thomas and Lani Guinier. Keith proudly maintained that his protégé "is full of courage, yet articulates his point of view without being offensive."[95]

Among other things, Judge Clay wrote an opinion striking down a program that awarded school vouchers to low-income Cleveland children for use at private schools as a violation of the constitutional prohibition against church and state. He revealed himself to be a stickler for protecting defendants' rights in death penalty litigation. And he voted to uphold the constitutionality of race-based admissions at the University of Michigan, using oral argument to ask the lawyer representing rejected white applicants why he opposed the university's practice of awarding extra points toward admission to students of color, but did not object to Michigan's practice of giving points to children of alumni. Clay bridled at the proposition that the university's program would permit it to "give diversity preference to a 'conventionally liberal' black student" who was the child of Grosse Pointe lawyers. "It is insulting to African Americans, or to any race or ethnicity that has known oppression and discrimination the likes of which slavery embodies, to think that a generation enjoying the end product of a life of affluence has forgotten or cannot relate to the enormous personal sacrifice made by their family members and ancestors not all that long ago in order to make the end possible," he replied. And it was "naïve" to think that an affluent African American had "not known or been the victim of discrimination such that he or she cannot relate [to] the same life experiences as the impoverished black person." Rich and poor African Americans, for example, might experience police harassment. While some, of course, might condemn Clay's opinions as "subjective" and "bad," Lefcoe had no doubt that in retrospect, Clay's "lifetime of achievement should not be diminished by a youthful indiscretion." Whatever his skepticism about the way the decision had been reached in the Clay case, Lefcoe believed that the dean had done the right thing.[96]

At the time, it was harder for some to take the long view. The process, along with the solution Pollak selected, poisoned the atmosphere further by angering those who wanted him to show more firmness. As the dean recognized, Joe Goldstein considered his action so "grossly improvident" that Pollak could only comfort Goldstein by reminding him that he would not remain dean much longer. It was a gracious gesture that may also have been spurred by rumors that Goldstein, Bickel, and others were talking about decamping from Yale to establish their own research institute. Bickel, Guido Calabresi, Friedrich

Kessler, and Ralph Winter circulated a memorandum insisting that the school's disciplinary standards had always been clear and that the dean's decision on Clay jeopardized academic freedom:

> Quite apart from President Brewster's letter to Dean Miller in April—which clearly declared coercion an unacceptable tactic in an academic community—and similar statements by the Dean himself, there has not been the slightest breath of a prior hint that the adequacy of the notice of our standards was at issue. The student himself has simply and forthrightly maintained, and continues to maintain, that he has an absolute right to adhere to his personal code of conduct, no matter how it impinges on the School's educational mission or how it violates the established qualifications for membership in this academic community.
>
> The freedom to teach and to write according to the dictates of one's conscience is the cornerstone of any academic institution worthy of the name. A threat to use physical force to change the manner in which a faculty member conducts his classes, much less to compel discussion of a non-related matter, should offend all—students and faculty alike—who value the academic commitment. It is an affront to free scholars everywhere. And the assertion that this has not always been well understood within the Yale Law School community is unacceptable.[97]

While Pollak had gone too far for his disgruntled colleagues, he had not gone far enough for many students. Clay had "won," but only because the dean had stayed a sentence handed down by a body many students considered unjustly constituted. The sound and fury of the clash between the Student Negotiating Committee and the faculty the previous year had signified nothing. The Yale College Executive Committee included a significant number of students, but the disciplinary panel that heard the Clay case did not. The episode had strengthened law students' conviction that their school employed a caste system. Though Clay had gotten off and future disciplinary panels would include student representatives, these were hollow victories. Watt recalled feeling "empty" after the trial and certain that graduation could not come quickly enough.[98]

The "Stop the Cops" protest and the Clay trial had united white and black student activists. That was something. But discord still prevailed. When Robert Stevens interviewed fifty Yale first-years at the end of fall 1969, he asked them to identify how, if at all, law school had changed their political outlooks. Five said they had swung away from radicalism, five toward it; three, that they were now more liberal; six, that they had become more conservative. "In all, we found the remarkable fact that nearly half the first year class reported some political change in a two-month period." Overall, there had been a "slight" net switch "toward more conservative politics, whether the individual was initially liberal, conservative or radical. Most of those adopting a more conservative position appeared to have been influenced by the student radicals who led the law school strike."[99]

The responses pointed up the volatility of the times and environment. The strike and the Clay trial had taken their toll. They had driven students farther apart from the faculty and from each other.

Chapter Seven

Bringing Us Together Again

The promise to "bring us together again" was Richard Nixon's. But as at other law schools, 1969–70 proved "a year of movement for Black and women students" at Yale. The echoes of discontent sounded as loud as ever as feminists called for the school's transformation and BLSU members cried betrayal. And the world outside intruded more. Indeed, Bobby Seale's trial raised so many questions about Yale's treatment of African Americans and the fairness of the rule of law that some law professors came to fear that both their school and city would go up in flames. Yet they also came to see that their students were not so far from them, after all. Unlike some young radicals, most Yale law students retained their faith in the legal system, as they demonstrated during the trial and Nixon's invasion of Cambodia. Ultimately, the trial and its aftermath restored a semblance of unity and peace to the law school.[1]

WINTER OF DISCONTENT

That prospect seemed especially unlikely during early 1970 after the Clay trial. In New Haven, women law students were supplementing liberal feminism with a more radical version. They had formed the Yale Law Women Association and had invited all staff, students, and faculty and student spouses to participate. On one front, liberal feminists worked to bring women into the mainstream by winning equal rights in the public realm. On another, radical feminists sought to transform male-female relations in both public and private spheres by challenging male supremacy and working toward women's liberation. The movement's diversity gave it strength, and its strands were intertwined at Yale. Strikingly, there, as elsewhere, by late 1969, liberal feminism had absorbed the assumptions of radical feminism. Liberal feminism had not become radical feminism, but it had embraced both its watchword, "the personal is political," and its practice of consciousness-raising.[2]

Slogan and activity were intertwined. Borrowed from the civil rights movement and the New Left, consciousness-raising (c-r) led naturally to the new understanding of the relationship between public and private, which became feminism's most important insight for a larger society. In c-r groups, women could share their most personal and private experiences in a way they never had before, be they rape, illegal abortions, or men's pressure for sex. And when ten women first compared private notes and saw that "others share those same difficulties," one Boalt feminist wrote, the next step was to consider the broader implications. Shared private experiences made many aware that what had once seemed a particular personal problem was common, shaped by the social, political, economic, and cultural institutions that kept women subordinate to men. The solution was political action.[3]

From a feminist perspective, plenty was necessary. Law school culture remained distinctively male. At Stanford, women complained that the darling of the left, Anthony Amsterdam, insisted on addressing his students as "Gentlemen." When a woman who had agreed to teach a course at Georgetown withdrew because of illness, students alleged that the angry associate dean lectured his class about the unreliable "girl law professor." At Berkeley, the law school newspaper had once "proudly" featured a foldout of Playboy Bunny Vikki, "Boalt's Study (?!) Date of the Year," photographed in her Bunny costume and holding a copy of the California Appellate Reports. There, one woman grieved that "[a]lmost no one challenges professors on sexism." Others complained that the same law schools which made efforts to recruit minorities made no attempt to attract women, claiming that they were "disinterested."[4]

Despite the increased presence of women law students at Yale, the situation there was little better. Women complained that the "socialization process" for tyros was designed "to break you apart, to isolate you and make you doubt yourself—then to rebuild you as a Yale Law Man, polished, individualistic and competitive." Like women involved with the Students for Democratic Society, women faced constant reminders that left politics did not always mean right attitudes. When Abe Fortas's 1968 nomination to become chief justice of the Supreme Court was in disarray, in part because of Senate Judiciary Committee concern over the Warren Court's obscenity decisions, the Law School Film Society sponsored a "Justice Fortas Film Festival" on "the first day of 'Co-ed Week,' traditionally male Yale's first experiment in bi-sexual undergraduate education." Screened before more than 1,500 titillated moviegoers were seven pornographic movies the Warren Court had allowed to remain in circulation. "Mixer," one announcement in the *Advocate* had recently winked. "Smith girls and Kentucky Fried Chicken in the Courtyard. Plenty of legs and breasts."[5]

Women established associations to address such concerns at many law schools in the late 1960s and early 1970s. They had seen how African American student organizations moved school administrations to action. At the same time, involvement with civil rights causes and the New Left had taught them that other movements for social change too frequently reflected societal prejudice against women.[6] The women's liberation movement came to law schools at the same time it came to society.

In New Haven, two second-years, Ann Freedman and Gail Falk, organized the Yale Law Women Association in 1969, a group open to students, their spouses, staff, and faculty. Both were Radcliffe graduates active in New Haven Women's Liberation. Neither Ellen Peters nor staff attended the meetings, but a few professors' wives did. Students and students' spouses constituted the bulk of the Law Women Association's membership. A few women belonged in both categories.[7]

The group's name signaled a shift. When Jane Lazarre moved to town with her husband, Doug White, so that he could begin law school in 1968, she received a call from a pleasant-sounding member of the Law Wives Association inviting her to one of its meetings. Swearing "not to be an eastern snob," and trying "to forget that I was a swarthy Jew and my husband an even swarthier Black," Lazarre asked what the Law Wives Association did. She was taken aback to learn that the group comprised various clubs that focused on cooking, sewing, winetasting, and reading. The wives also discussed "law school business," the caller added with a giggle, "because our husbands never tell us anything." Told Lazarre's interests lay with politics, she replied, "We don't get too political."

Despite Lazarre's obvious disinterest, the clubwoman insisted she should attend a meeting, at least to read the Law Wives' flyers. Lazarre marveled at her persistence, speculating that it stemmed from her awareness that the group was in its death throes: "Perhaps she realized somehow that within one year the Law Wives Association, having carried hundreds of young women through an otherwise meaningless, lonely three years of watching their husbands go to school, having given them at least someone to talk to, would be wiped off the law school activity with not so much as a 'pleasant to have met you' and replaced by the Law Women's Association, an offshoot of the growing women's liberation consciousness-raising group which met every Sunday night in the meeting of a local radical organization."

In contrast, when Lazarre attended a meeting of the new Law Women Association, which included not only the wives of law students but female law students as well, she did not feel very "sisterly," and she did not think the other wives, with their "well combed" hair and "perfectly applied" makeup, did either. As she herself did, students assumed that wives' lives were dull. She gazed with envy at the students, "their brown leather briefcases left casually all around the floor, their messy hair which they'd had no time to brush since morning, busy as they were with crucial matters, their comfortable disregard for their incomparably expensive surroundings, a disregard which could only come from years of familiarity." They seemed so secure. By appearance alone, they seemed to shout their fearlessness — or, at least, that any sense of inadequacy "can be hidden, covered, efficiently and effectively, with a list of my academic achievements." And indeed the Law Women Association acknowledged that its efforts to involve staff members and students' spouses had frequently proven "dismal failures, showing us how much elitism the law school fosters even among its less welcomed students."[8]

Still, others who stayed with the group, as Lazarre did not, found it rewarding. Alex Denman, who was married to Ben Stein, agreed that "these incredibly energetic, bright women law students were pretty damned intimidating" and that "the wives couldn't get over their bad hair and plain way of dressing and most of all no makeup!" Even so, "the best thing about it from my point of view was getting to know the law school women" and coming to realize they shared her aspirations and anxieties. Her "only human experience" in law school, student Ann Hill said publicly at the time, occurred at the Law Women Association's weekly meetings, where "people relate to each other as people" in a process that proved "slow," sometimes "painful," and always "real." Participants heard about the husband with the "terrible temper" and the left woman student "having an affair with a married professor, which, of course, was oppressing the professor's wife." The meetings helped Hill transcend what she had been taught at both Wellesley and Yale — that "if we 'acted like men'" and "repressed our 'natural emotional bent,'" a law firm might hire "the *best* of us for jobs that paid *almost* as well as those offered to the mediocre and worst of our male counterparts."[9]

In addition to consciousness-raising, Yale Law Women Association members engaged in organization, education, litigation, and direct action. Freedman and Falk spearheaded a student-taught course on women and the law, nominally presided over by Ellen Peters, then successfully persuaded the dean that Yale needed to bring in a professor to teach it. Yale law women launched a legal challenge against sexism. With their classmate Barbara Brown and their

Women picketing Mory's. (Photograph by Virginia Blaisdell.
Courtesy Virginia Blaisdell.)

teacher Tom Emerson, Freedman and Falk wrote the celebrated *Yale Law Journal* article on the proposed Equal Rights Amendment. In 1969, women law students joined with local New Haven women to file *Abele* v. *Markle*, the suit that overturned Connecticut's statutory prohibition against abortion. Yale law alumna and Black Panther attorney Catherine Roraback, who had been Emerson's co-counsel in *Griswold* v. *Connecticut*, acted as lead counsel for the women; Ann Hill would become another of their lawyers, as well as executive director of the Connecticut Women's Education and Legal Fund, and Yale Law Women Association members were also involved.[10]

Feminists at the law school also protested the exclusionary policies of Mory's, Yale's all-male eating club. Walt Wagoner "took about 20–25 of us into Mory's for lunch and caused quite a ruckus even though we . . . ladies just sat down at various tables as if we were going to eat," Denman recalled of one sit-in. Class of 1970 alumna Kathryn Rosen Emmett would successfully file a petition with the Connecticut Liquor Control Commission to revoke Mory's liquor license on the grounds that the establishment was not, as it claimed, a private club because it did not allow its members to vote on the admission of women members.[11]

Those involved with the Yale Law Women Association also dreamed of an interracial alliance of women of all classes, making "WOMEN OF THE LAW SCHOOL UNITE!" a rallying cry. They organized the clinical program's Women Prison's Project to provide legal services to indigent women held in the state's prison for women. They protested the treatment of Panther women held in prison without bail, particularly those who were pregnant or had just given birth. They used the *Advocate* to expose the treatment of law school secretaries, all of whom were women, and to lament that though "Yale works hard to clear its name of racial discrimination (and why are there so few black secretaries in the Law School?), it continues to follow a policy of blatant economic discrimination toward its women employees." They pointed out that poor pay was not the worst of it. The *Advocate* announced that the registrar behaved like an "authoritarian" grade school teacher to the secretaries, whom it encouraged to strike and unionize.[12]

In short, with the exception of lesbian rights, Yale law women raised just about every issue on the agenda of the women's movement. Betty Friedan came to the school to speak about "Unsexing the Law" in early 1970, followed by a "Women's Week" conference, where Kate Millett and Naomi Weisstein took center stage. An impressed Rita Mae Brown reported that while "Yale reeks of the rich, white man and the law school stinks of the ugliest kind, the man who upholds and defends the establishment or at best tries to reform it through its courts of 'justice,'" this "hotbed of privilege" deep in "the heart of the polite pig structure" had been the site of "one of the most exciting Women's Liberation Conferences to date."[13]

Between the Friedan and Millett visits, the *Advocate* kept up the momentum by devoting an entire issue to the treatment of women. (Its principal reporter, Ann Hill, would provide one of those rare moments of lightness for the community when she married Student Association president Walt Wagoner on the first day of spring. An inflatable dragon filled the whole ceiling space of the reception room of Yale's Dwight Chapel, and Cosmic Lab ushers, clad in their signature jumpsuits, led Dean Pollak, Abe Goldstein, and other guests to seats from which they watched the bride and groom exchange wooden necklaces. Wagoner wore a suit, and his Lawrenceville history teacher played the wedding march as the bride walked down the aisle, "but other than that nothing was traditional," Hill recalled. "It was fun.") Some of the *Advocate*'s charges were predictable, reflecting the extent to which, in many ways, Yale was a typical law school of its time. Ellen Peters was the only woman on the faculty. There were also few women law students, and the administration paid too little attention to increasing their numbers. The admissions office "fatuous[ly]" averred it unimportant to distinguish between men and women. It refused to grant the Yale Law Women Association's request for a woman representative on the Admissions Committee, and student representatives agreed, saying the students had not elected women: "But sirs, who was voting? The vote was by class, and no class has more than 10% women."[14]

Admissions was a tree worth shaking. The Admissions Committee subsequently agreed to begin "affirmative recruitment" of women. That meant, for example, that it distributed information about the school to prelaw advisers at women's colleges. The number of women applicants then doubled, though women still made up only about one-fifth of the applicant pool. Women soon regularly constituted about 16 percent of the first-year class. That percentage could easily have been higher. When Ann Hill won a seat on the Admissions Committee, she remembered the stir created when one professor said he was seeing wonderful applications from women and predicted that they would make up half of the next year's class. When Hill saw his colleagues' look of mortification, she realized he must have intended to sabotage the acceptance of more women.[15]

Other allegations in the *Advocate* proved still more embarrassing. Hill charged James William Moore, whose research assistant she had been and "whom I dearly love," with displaying an "intense interest in women law students." And that, said Hill, who had organized "a sentimental 64th birthday celebration" for Moore just recently, was the least of it. "Professors who are not so open about their 'appreciation' of women must be having *awful* times repressing their desires," she wrote in the *Advocate*. "The Law School is a blatant overstatement of the transfer of sexual desires into the drive for power." But in this dance, most professors did not follow the example of Moore, "perhaps the *healthiest* professor of the Law School." Rather, they made sure women remained wallflowers. They ignored women, either not calling on them at all or calling on them without listening to what they said. Privately, she spoke scathingly of professors on the prowl. "It was like the women in class were being picked off by these guys," she said later. Hill publicly chastised her male classmates too. They had developed strategies for dividing women. At parties, they talked law, which enabled students to participate, but often not wives; or "family affairs," which enabled wives to join in, but often not students. Adopting the "bad habits" of their mentors, male students cried poverty to "our sister secretaries" when they needed typing done. But soon after they graduated, they would receive "astronomical salaries," while the secretaries would remain underpaid and would have to continue typing papers "for the next generation of Yale leaders."[16]

The answer for women, Hill believed, lay in following the example of the BLSU and uniting for the benefit of students and society alike. "The black students are effective in making demands, and getting a racist institution to bend somewhat because they are *together*," she reasoned, even though they did not all share the same philosophy or background. It was fine to think of oneself as an individual, "but the first thing anyone notices about a woman is that she is a woman — especially when so few of them are around." The faculty was running scared, where African Americans and women were concerned. Professors who knew they could co-opt white male activists were more anxious about the women, while African Americans almost seemed to threaten their "manhood."[17]

*   *   *

At the same time that the *Advocate*'s special issue on women appeared, there was another round of charges about affirmative action. It appeared as if some people might flunk out of Yale Law School after all. The BLSU heard that the faculty was debating the number of Fails or Low Passes a student could receive and still graduate, as indeed professors were doing in executive session. While a number of students had done poorly on first-term exams, two entering minority students had each flunked two first-term courses. The faculty was deciding whether to change its two-flunk rule, which made the offending students ineligible to continue, and instead allow them to remain another term on probation. Professors who argued for modification maintained that since "some faculty members are using a double grading standard, the fate of an individual student rests on the instructor of the section the student gets in his first term." Because Yale did not require blind grading, some professors may indeed have employed a double standard: Judith Areen remembered going with a group to make the case to an administrator that grading could not be "objective since it was not anonymous," only to be told that "to change to anonymous grading would disadvantage the minority students." But since no one would admit to using a double standard at the meeting, and some agreed with Emerson that "one term is too short a time for many minority students to adjust," the meetings that ultimately resulted in the faculty's retention of the two-flunk rule were long and acrimonious.[18]

The BLSU also learned that professors contemplated a first-year class with 10 percent minorities, down substantially from the previous year. The law school tried to put a good face on it. It was a positive sign, the public argument went, that there was "a significant narrowing of the gap" between the average Combined Prediction scores for minority students admitted for 1970–71, pursuant to the special admissions track, and the scores for others accepted pursuant to the general admissions program.[19]

But privately, professors spoke of the situation differently. Asked by Brewster's biographer whether he had felt that "the Law School bent its admission standards in the case of blacks," Pollak responded readily: "Yes, sure." Queried how much, he answered, "Substantially, for some—at least measured by the numbers we were used to." Associate Dean Ralph Brown recalled that "we were admitting blacks very indulgently, and a lot of them barely could do the work." When courses required in-class exams, minorities tended to end up "in the bottom," Charles Reich said. "You couldn't disguise that." One could get around it, he added, by having students write papers that, after several drafts, might well deserve a high grade, as he did with Clarence Thomas. But first-semester courses required exams.[20]

Yale's experience demonstrated anew the problems with the meritocratic ideal while underlining why so many threw in their lot with grades and test scores. Professors who attributed their careers to meritocracy remained devoted to it and understandably remained unconscious of its and (their own) blind spots. Writing of the Harvard Law School of the early 1960s, one of the rare women accepted could describe it as "an absolute meritocracy: no amount of money, no pedigree, no social connections, would make a difference in whether you were admitted, how well you did there, or how far you would go after graduation." But clearly they did. Otherwise Harvard would not have had a student body composed almost entirely of white men and would not have admitted only those women who were "smarter and tougher and better organized, and . . . could look after" themselves. Enforcement of traditional criteria ensured an uneven playing field. Further, because some liberals on the Yale faculty remained convinced that equality and meritocracy conflicted, its commitment to meritocracy prevented the school from realizing its ideal of equality: during this period, many there patronized students of color. Recalling her days as a student, Ann Hill stressed the atmosphere of "racism," along with that of "institutionalized sexism." "Every faculty member thought black students admitted were of lower intellectual quality," she said. "Blacks had to have known this."[21]

They did. It affected different individuals differently. Lani Guinier, who would become the first tenured African American woman on the Harvard Law School faculty, and who would join Mel Watt and Eric Clay in arguing for racial justice in the voting booth and academy, simply felt invisible, a member of "the minority within a minority, whose existence, even physical presence, had been swallowed up." But her classmate, Clarence Thomas, became embittered. Though affirmative action enabled him to enroll in the law school and make contacts that helped make his career possible, he always felt "offended" by talk of "how they let me into Yale. . . . All they did was stop stopping us." In fact, he also felt so stigmatized and demoralized by the very program that had brought him to Yale that he would later credit the law school with prejudicing him against affirmative action. "You had to prove yourself every day because the presumption was that you were dumb and didn't deserve to be there on merit," he recalled. "Every time you walked into a law class at Yale, it was like having a monkey jump on your back from the Gothic arches." As a Supreme Court justice, he would even sometimes suggest that affirmative action students did not "deserve to be there on merit" when he scorned elite law schools for tantalizing "unprepared students" with the offer of a degree and its perquisites. "These overmatched students take the bait, only to find they cannot succeed in the cauldron of competition," he would insist in arguing against affirmative action from the bench. "These programs stamp minorities with a badge of inferiority." [22]

Clyde Summers expressed similar sentiments earlier. In 1970, Summers used a symposium on affirmative action to announce that preferential admissions standards were "an unreal solution to a real problem." Implying that all schools had thrown open their doors to students of color, Summers maintained that anyone who had a C average and a 350 LSAT score could get in somewhere. Affirmative action, he argued, simply allowed the student of color who otherwise would have gone to Pittsburgh or North Carolina to go to Pennsylvania or Duke. "In sum, the policy of preferential admission has a pervasive shifting effect, causing large numbers of minority students to attend law schools, whose normal admission standards they do not meet, instead of attending other law schools whose normal standards they do meet. But preferential admission does not add substantially to the total number of minority law students, except to the extent it results in the admission of students who have less than a 'C' average and a 350 test score," who did not belong in law school anyway. And, Summers contended, the preference awarded students of color meant they found themselves in classes with much abler and more articulate white students, creating an atmosphere that "almost ensures a sense of lostness and defeat." Some would fail, he said, but liberal guilt would ensure that most passed. [23]

Allegations that African Americans were poorer students were not unique to Yale. Law journals announced that "one major law school (and probably others) reportedly has quietly applied a double standard of grading with black students being passed on an easier scale." It must have been particularly hurt-ful when Yale faculty members, who had publicly defended affirmative action, began openly to express doubts. Yet Summers remembered receiving no heat from students about the article. Perhaps to many, it simply seemed an admis-sion of what they had come to assume were their teachers' inner thoughts.[24]

African American Yale law students fought the faculty's perception that they were losers. BLSU members who heard that the faculty was reconsider-ing the two-flunk rule believed that their professors were scapegoating blacks for poor exam performance by whites and minorities and were trumpeting the view of affirmative action as "a process by which semi-literate aborigines are allowed to defile this bastion of intellectual excellence." Their professors, they charged, wanted to have it both ways: "While the Faculty took credit for the great strides in black admissions you allowed your 'hard-liners' to work as hard as they willed to cut down black admissions." And according to the students, when "we raise these and other issues we are met with inertia and reactionary 'hard-liners' (*viz.*, the Clay trial), a process which augurs ill for all students in the school."[25]

MAY DAY

Though their concerns did not disappear, and they continued to find fault with the faculty's "sacrosanct elitism" and disregard for "the real world," BLSU members' anxieties, like those of the rest of the Yale community, mushroomed beyond internal matters to the impending trial of Bobby Seale, whose legal de-fense team included two Yale Law alumni, and the Panther Nine. The Panthers had announced a three-day fund-raising event on the New Haven Green, be-ginning May 1, and the Panther Defense Committee was predicting that hun-dreds of thousands would descend to donate money and protest the trial. After all, the Chicago Seven's chief attorney, William Kunstler, told an audience of 1,500 that the object of the Panther trial was "to destroy, inhibit or emasculate a political movement." Meanwhile, famous white radicals such as Jerry Rubin promoted May Day as their opportunity "to 'get Yale'" and throw Brewster off balance.[26]

By spring, the Panther trials consumed everyone in New Haven. On April 14, an officer had told two Panthers observing a courtroom proceeding to stop talking with each other. When they refused, the officer put his hand on one's shoulder. A scuffle ensued, and the writer, Jean Genet, who later said he had also been talking aloud, assisted the Panthers. Genet received a warning; the two Panthers, six months in jail. For many, the incident made "fair trial" an oxymoron. The following day, Abbie Hoffman told a rally that on May Day, "radicals would go to New Haven to burn Yale down; Hoffman's audience then marched on and trashed Harvard square." For Brewster, this was a sign that the trial was being used "to bring together a great 'radical happening,' and Yale was clearly one of the announced targets." For Professor Peter Brooks, one of the liberals more sympathetic to the left, it was a signal that the trial brought to the fore the issue of Yale's relationship—and that of the society it represented—with African Americans within the university and the community, the relationship "between military adventurism in Asia and repression of the internal 'colony.'" The university had a problem, and it could unravel everything: "I had long realized that the only real possibility for disruption at Yale— where the white radicals were weak, divided or coopted by the general progressivism of the institution—would come if the internal Blacks ever linked their situation to that of the New Haven Blacks, who had a number of grievances against Yale."[27]

In this climate, tens of thousands of demonstrators were expected to descend on New Haven for May Day. On April 21, over four thousand members of the Yale community attended a mass meeting at Ingalls Rink. There, Yale College students voted to assist the protesters and agreed that they themselves would engage in a nonviolent "strike."[28]

Two days later, their professors met. The previous week, the faculty had "refused to vote anything at all in connection with the trial, and it was expectable that the banner of 'institutional neutrality' would prevent anything but the mildest statement of concern," Brooks recalled. But the combination of Yale's African American community and Brewster ensured a sea change. "God knows, the tension was high, because it was just the kind of issue on which other institutions like Cornell, Harvard, and so on had split wide open, not only between faculty and administration, but within the faculty," Yale's president said later. His pragmatism and that of the group of African American professors and students, which carefully "played its cards" to bargain for "more tenure slots for black faculty and more money for African American projects," carried the day. While a crowd of undergraduates roared outside, and in an atmosphere that reminded one professor of 1789, the faculty voted overwhelmingly in support of a resolution introduced by the African American faculty to "modify . . . the normal expectations of the University." There would be a temporary change in the regular academic schedule, so as to give "all those concerned and interested a chance to discuss the issues and ramifications of the issues and to plan what direction we should take in this crisis." Classes would still meet, but professors and students were encouraged to discuss Panther trials and related issues.[29]

Conservatives would later claim that Brewster had violated institutional neutrality by supporting the "modification." But as his biographer said, insofar as there was a coherent "conservative position" at the time, "it was to cancel the semester, shut the university down completely, and flee," an idea Brewster rejected "on the grounds that it was worth a great deal of risk to show that Yale was strong and confident enough in its tradition of openness to meet any challenge to its central values, while continuing to maintain its educational mission of teaching and research." Given that conclusion, modification for an indefinite period made sense. It reduced the possibility that professors would create crises by turning down the requests of students like Eric Clay to discuss extracurricular topics. Either the solution then seemed sensible or the conservatives were cowed, for Alexander Bickel and others were "completely silent at the meeting," Peter Brooks remembered. "I think they were scared, even terrified, at dealing with the Black faculty and students."[30]

Further, Brewster announced that Yale would open its campus to all demonstrators, housing and feeding them. It was another "pragmatic" act. Arrival at locked gates might have incited riot. But it was also an idealistic one. Brewster told his friend Cyrus Vance, who came to New Haven to help, that May Day was "a test as to whether we are right" about the students, or whether Richard Nixon's view of student protestors as "bums" was more accurate.[31]

And after defending the principle of institutional neutrality while urging members of the Yale community to speak out about the trial and race matters at the faculty meeting, Brewster also made his famous declaration: "So in spite of my insistence on the limits of my official capacity, I personally want to say that I am appalled and ashamed that things should have come to such a pass that I am skeptical of the ability of black revolutionaries to achieve a fair trial anywhere in the United States." Though the remark was subject to many different interpretations, Francine du Plessix Gray speculated that it was "precisely the boldness of his stand — its dose of moral overkill — which enabled Brewster to bring about an alliance not only between the college's black and white communities, but also between its liberal and radical factions, something no university president had been able to do before." While Otis Cochran told Brewster that "I believe I would have made a more emphatic statement about what is happening to the Panthers," Cochran maintained that "what you said did go far toward restoring my confidence and the confidence of others that every member of the establishment is not insensitive to the problems, the inequities, and the injustices that plague so many Americans, particularly black Ameri-

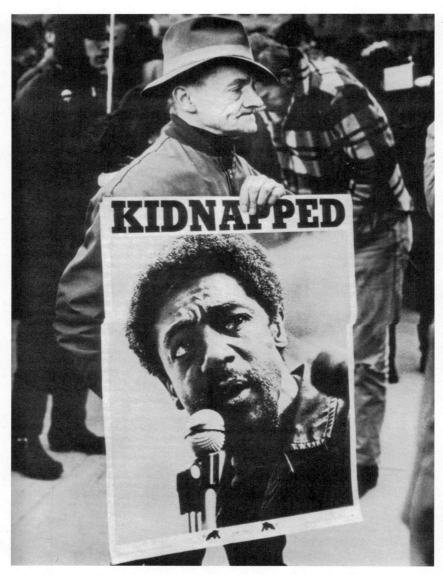

*"Kidnapped": Bobby Seale. (*Yale Review of Law and Social Action, *vol. 1, 1970. Courtesy Yale Law School.)*

Meeting at Yale, ca. 1970. (Photograph by Richard Balzer, from Richard Balzer,
Street Time [1972]. Courtesy Richard Balzer.)

cans." The real criticism came from conservatives, with Spiro Agnew urging
Yale alumni to demand that a "more mature and responsible person" head the
institution.[32]

But notwithstanding such sentiments, preparation for the strike continued
"with deadly seriousness. No American university had any experience with
challenges of this kind, and it was not improbable to imagine buildings burned
out and the university closed down, with all the attendant confusion. It was
even easier and more probable to consider that we might well lose control of
the university for a time." But to whom? "Fear of right-wing violence was as
intense as fear of radical violence, putting almost every group on the defensive."[33]

Since the entire university had pledged to aid students and outsiders, all
understood that no strike against Yale was in progress. "Rather, it is a sort of
joint testimony to Yale's sense of responsibility toward the black community,

a joint response to a feeling of crisis aroused by the Black Panther trial in New Haven," the *Washington Post* editorialized. What distinguished campus unrest at Yale from upheavals elsewhere was that "the university administration, the faculty and most of the student body are firmly united. There is an exhilarating, perhaps unique, solidarity on the Yale campus today." Brewster deserved the credit for transforming "seeming division and discord" into unity and purpose, though to be sure, "he owes an incalculable debt to Vice President Spiro Agnew." The *Post* reported that Brewster had recently said "that he has never been so proud of Yale; it is patent that Yale has never been so proud of a president."[34]

*   *   *

Over at the law school, it was not so patent. Opinion there about the trial ran the gamut. At the first large meeting on the subject, a second-year law student had proposed that one hundred members of the Yale community make a suicide pact. Each day, one of them, chosen by lot, would kill himself until the Panther Nine were freed, enabling participants "[t]o die like a Panther, to die like a man." Claiming that the response to the trial would show the world "whether Yale Law School possessed concerned and active civil-libertarians, or know-nothings who will turn their backs to the use of courts for genocide," BLSU member John Doggett had called on every member of the faculty to work to guarantee the Panthers a fair trial. "If you fail, . . . New Haven and this Law School could easily burn as black people vent their fury on the system you present," he warned. Pollak, who publicly compared Agnew to Joe McCarthy, was on Brewster's side "[b]ecause I was in the civil rights business, and he was my President."[35]

But Bickel, who was coming to regret his vote in support of the strike, was not. As a trial observer, he believed the judge had acted reasonably and that the proceedings could be labeled neither an "instance of repression" nor a "political trial." Nor was Bickel impressed by the Panthers' defense strategy. He thought their lawyer deserved "a Goebbels Memorial award" for the way he had manipulated the media to ensure it downplayed Panther violence in torturing and murdering police informant Rackley. With Joe Bishop, Charles Black, and others inside and outside the law school, Bickel privately asked Yale's president what he had been thinking when he made his declaration about black revolutionaries: "We are aware of no evidence that the responsible legal and judicial officers of the state of Connecticut are unable or unwilling to see to it that the defendants receive a fair trial." Behind the statement was a question: Was this "official welcome" of protesters evidence of the "institutional neutrality" to which Brewster had pledged allegiance?[36]

Only later did Bickel publicly accuse the young of whipping themselves into hysteria over the "trumped-up crisis of the trial." Reviewing his and his colleagues' strike vote, Bickel concluded that he and they had been scared by the violent confrontations at other universities and the "assaultative, vicious speech," the "incitement to violent action," the "bullying," and the "kind of aggression almost physical, in content," which passed for "dissent" on college campuses everywhere. And he had not felt "ashamed" of his vote to modify expectations and support the strike, Bickel confessed in the *New Republic* more than a month after May Day, until he and his colleagues left the faculty meeting and students hailed them.

> [T]here *is* cause to be ashamed. We did not return a rational answer to our students, because we were too alone and it was too late. If we had said what is true, that the trial was no crisis, that it was inconceivable not to let it proceed, and that there is no reason to equate the police [who had battled with rioters at the 1968 Democratic Convention] in Chicago with the courts in New Haven and with the state and federal courts that sit to correct the errors of courts in New Haven; and if we had added that the university would continue to function, its members being held to no more than their normal duties (which do not include constant attendance at class) and no less—if we had said all that, we would have been denounced as rigid, unresponsive, authoritarian; we would have risked riots and destruction, and been saddled with responsibility for possible police overreaction. That is what it has come to. Truth and the function of the university are irrelevant and dangerous. They are pitfalls. I have to be grateful, and I am grateful, that we avoided these pitfalls, and that we had steady and shrewd leadership which saved us whole.[37]

A few were bolder than Bickel. What he said privately as the Yale community waited for thousands to converge on New Haven and publicly afterward in the *New Republic*, Dean-Designate Abe Goldstein was declaring now. As the work week leading up to May Day weekend began, Goldstein, an expert in criminal procedure, announced that he could "see no evidence yet that the New Haven Panthers cannot get a fair trial here."[38]

Meanwhile, and despite the fact that Yale College students had been wondering when their law school counterparts would say something about the strike, law students, like most graduate students, had continued to attend classes. To law student liberals, there was an obvious reason for silence. Some white and black students had done research for the Panthers' defense counsel, while others had joined some professors in educating the nonlawyer public. Recall that the New Haven police later admitted lacking hard evidence linking Seale to Rackley's torture and murder; Seale's trial would ultimately result in a deadlocked jury and mistrial. Nevertheless, some law students had seen evidence suggesting that Seale had been involved in inflicting the excruciating pain Rackley suffered. "On that basis, we couldn't justify joining the strike," Stephen Cohen remembered. At the time, Cohen told reporter and Yale law alumnus Jeff Greenfield that the strike was "all very vague" and that the Panthers were being tried for "murder, and brutal and sadistic torture. What's going to happen if the people of Yale find they've *trusted* this guy and it turns out the whole strike is about brutal, sadistic people. Distasteful as it sounds, you have to make an independent judgment of the evidence — that's what I try to say to the undergraduates."[39]

But Cohen found few Yale College students were listening. Literature professor Peter Brooks realized why when he began to understand the gulf that separated him from undergraduates. "It came through to me — as it had begun to do with the Chicago Conspiracy trial — how much my generation had been determined by the Warren Court, how much we looked to the judicial branch as our guarantee of existential freedom in a country with so many pressures to unfreedom." Though they were not of his generation and some told Greenfield that they felt more warmly toward "revolutionary violence," most Yale law students would have agreed. That was one of the reasons many of them were in law school.[40]

Yet young radicals "had no such image of the courts," Brooks realized. "The gap between the 'real country' and the 'legal country' had grown too great; the latter no longer had any purchase on the former." Yale undergraduates did not believe Seale's guilt was the issue, and they had their own strategy. They wanted to call attention to the government and legal system's violation of dissidents' rights and ensure that Seale was treated fairly. "And the feeling was that the only way to do it, because of media politics, was that you didn't say something like, 'Let us discuss whether or not Bobby Seale can get a fair trial,'" the chair of the Strike Steering Committee recalled. "What you had to say was, 'Free Bobby Seale.'" Thus law students and undergraduates remained at an impasse.[41]

At what price? At 1:04 A.M. on Monday, April 27, 1970, law student Paul Gewirtz telephoned the Yale University Police Department to report that he and others smelled smoke in the basement. Rushing to Sterling Law building, Yale police found a fire "of suspicious origin" in the International Law

Library. Some five hundred books had been destroyed, some structural damage sustained. The police sergeant on the scene reported that law students "did a very commendable job in forming a bucket brigade to salvage as much as they could" and that "some girls also took part."[42]

Pollak sped to the scene. Indeed, the fire reminded students that the dean was someone of "gentleness and wit," who "preserved a sense of community in the law school when confrontation was the prevailing mold." One second-year subsequently recalled the mass meeting that began after the fire had been extinguished and the burned books removed. About 3 A.M., a student proposed that the school obtain a temporary restraining order "to stop an onslaught of what he called 'a bunch of crazies' who were presumably planning to disrupt the law school the next morning." Pollak paused, then responded. "It may be a bit late in the day to tell you this," he said, "but I have absolutely no idea how to get a T.R.O."[43]

Now a fire had occurred, and Cohen and other liberals attributed the fire to the refusal of the law school to participate in the strike. Thus they saw the fire as arson — retaliation, as Cohen remarked wryly, "because those of us who went to class were still going to class." And later that day, the *Yale Daily News* reported, law students defeated a resolution "calling for institutional suspension of classes" for the week by a vote of 150–117. "But the law students went on to overwhelmingly endorse the Yale College Faculty resolution of April 23." Big deal: even their professors had already done so.[44]

What did it all mean? In a front-page article about the fire, the *New York Times* reported that Pollak had told students he was "sure you will find the faculty relatively tolerant in regard to paper deadlines, the adjustment of examination schedules and so forth." But the *News* sung a different tune. "Much student dissatisfaction appears to center around an attempt to pin down Dean Pollak on the issue of academic penalties for missed work and classes," it said. "Most students seemed to feel Pollak's remarks before the vote on whether to strike encouraged extracurricular participation in activities surrounding the trial, while after the crucial vote, he stated that it was 'up to the individual student' how fully he studied for his exams."[45]

To the *News*, only one thing was clear. The overwhelming passage of a "canopy resolution" reflected "what appears to be the most common sentiment" of the assembled: "We the students of the Yale Law School affirm our belief [in] and commit ourselves to insure the right of the New Haven Panther defendants to receive a fair trial. We oppose any attempt to stop the trial of the New Haven Panthers by extralegal or coercive means."[46]

Beyond that, the *News* declared its own uncertainty about the "exact sense of the meeting." It observed that some law students had "attacked the meeting as a reaction to undergraduates' attempts earlier in the day to 'coerce them,' though according to Law School Dean Louis Pollak, the strikers 'operated within the limits of the First Amendment.'" So Pollak must have been referring to catcalls law students received from strikers, not to the fire itself. But when a bomb hit Ingalls Rink during May Day weekend, Brewster, who was anathema to the Nixon administration, "considered it equally likely that the bomb could have been set by a provocateur from the left or right." Did Yale law students also consider the possibility the right had set the fire? Probably not. The *News* quoted one third-year who "called the proceedings a 'visceral reaction to books being burned.'" Did that mean law students viewed the fire as a message that they must capitulate or worse would follow, and thus they endorsed the April 23 Yale College vote? Or did the remark suggest that those who might have otherwise endorsed the strike refused to do so because they felt blackmailed? At the time, the students gave few clues about how to interpret their actions, though Ed Baker later remembered some arguing that law students should go out on strike to conciliate the undergraduates and to avoid the law school being "trashed," and other law students told the *Times* they felt their group "had been intimidated into action." Third-year Lanny Davis explained that law students had decided against shutting down their school because "that was asking us to go beyond what happened on the undergraduate campus." They had endorsed the Yale College faculty's resolution, however, to demonstrate their "full sympathy with the undergraduates."[47]

In any event, the outcome pleased the faculty. Clyde Summers found it "remarkable" that the law students reacted to the fire "as if they had been attacked" and had "immediately set up a twenty-four-hour guard patrol for the law school and the library. It created a whole climate of protecting the Law School." Pollak later characterized the fire as the event that had made his deanship worthwhile. He thought it revealed students' commitment to the institution and the library as its heart. "The one gratifying aspect of all this," he said at the time, "is the marvelous way in which our students sensed the insult to the School and the profession—more than a hundred of them gathered at 2 A.M. to start cleaning up the stacks and maintaining a security guard from then forward." The dean exulted that "our students were as deeply shocked as we elderly Faculty members were at the mere possibility that anybody could be sick enough . . . to burn books."[48]

Abe Goldstein believed that the fire had returned law students to reality. "It was not a major fire, but it was dramatic because there were these burned books, water soaked lying on High Street" outside the school, he recalled.

Surveying books saved from the fire in front of the law school. (Photograph by Alan Waggoner. Courtesy Alan Waggoner.)

"Many of us at the time felt that event more than anything else suddenly tamed the order of the firebrands, tamed the order of our homespun student radicals. They calmed down because it looked like things might be getting out of hand."[49]

Yet although the law school seemed to be coming together, Pollak and Dean-Designate Goldstein decided to cancel the upcoming Alumni Weekend anyway. As the weekend approached, Ralph Winter informed a reporter that "[i]f ten percent of the rumors spreading around here are true, there will be no New Haven on Monday." A number of law professors who lived close to campus and had already been worrying about whether their homeowner's policy covered riot damage rushed to buy fire extinguishers. Bickel, who was still pondering leaving Yale, removed his papers from his office and had them microfilmed. With everyone expecting trouble, her neighbors were "packing up their children to send to grandparents," Jane Lazarre reported. "Now the fear of Blacks was stark, intense, unembarrassed." "We thought this was Armageddon," George Lefcoe recalled.[50]

Against the background of the approaching May Day, then, the law school fire represented unity and chaos. Because it had been detected early, the fire had done relatively little damage. Still, as Pollak said at the time, "the symbolism bulked large and remains." At the very least, along with the 145 pounds of mercury stolen from Yale's chemistry laboratory and the 280 riot guns taken from a truck, it suggested May Day might well prove bloody. The *New York Times* story about the incident included a photo of Robert Bork pondering the hundreds of burned and waterlogged books left outside the law school to dry. "Fire at Yale," the caption read. "Burned books cover the sidewalk outside the Law School Library . . . where an arsonist set fire to the basement, destroying property worth $2,500."[51]

In fact, police had reported the cause of fire "undetermined," and two months later, Pollak still awaited the official verdict on whether the blaze had been deliberately set. Officials subsequently told him it had been accidental, and he believed them. He knew the library basement had been in such disarray that fire easily could have broken out there.[52]

Nevertheless, the fire went down in collective memory as a case of arson. When Hillary Rodham Clinton spoke at Yale's Class Day some thirty years after the event, she joked about "a cottage industry of folks" claiming she had set it. "But actually I joined the bucket brigade of students to save the books and it was an odd feeling to be in one of the greatest institutions in our country saving books from people who were so frustrated and so angry and so outraged that they . . . [followed] the traditions of fascists and others of oppressive political beliefs and burned books." When Bork wrote his memoirs, he portrayed the fire as a pivotal event in his journey toward cultural conservatism. He insisted that arson, implicitly committed by law students, had hit the library, compared students to Nazis and fascists, and deplored the surrender of Yale and other universities to them. Bickel's *New Republic* article described the fire as "obviously set" too.[53]

*   *   *

With Ellen Peters, Guido Calabresi, and Friedrich Kessler, Bickel was one of four refugees from fascism on the faculty. (Though his wife had fled Hitler's Germany, Joe Goldstein was born in the United States.) All except Peters had cosigned Bickel's memorandum charging that Pollak's action in the Clay case threatened academic freedom. Calabresi believed that refugee status did affect worldview. One reason he had signed the complaint about Clay was because "I understood their pain." As he had opposed "the politicization of the universities in Nazi Germany," so Kessler fought it at Yale during the 1960s. Indeed, he would use his retirement dinner to speculate publicly that the law school might be "in a crisis."[54]

Bickel, whose uncle had lost hope for a position at Berlin University when the Nazis came to power, explicitly likened the actions of campus radicals to the deeds of those bewitched by "fascist romance" and exhorted professors to resist intimidation. Students, he maintained, had been right about the war and racism, but they were "wrong about repression." Though flawed and troubled, American society was "free and open." It was the young, with their emphasis on "ideological orthodoxy" and "emotional solidarity," who were often responsible for whatever repression there was. Hence the restoration of "order in speech and action" must begin in universities, a process requiring the rededication of higher education to the principle of "political neutrality." Indeed, Bickel would now tolerate only political activism that advanced the cause of political neutrality, "the sort of political involvement that the German universities in the 1930s failed to undertake." To Bickel, students on the left who pushed the university to take political positions were Nazis in blue jeans.[55]

The *Yale Daily News* observed that this kind of talk was common among a group of professors, many of them émigrés, who believed that Brewster and other campus administrators had acquiesced too much, and who heard "echoes of the past in the slogans 'All Power to the People' and 'Right On.' Without too much imagination, they claim one can see the same crowd shouting 'Sieg Heil!'" And as the *News* said, if the students represented incipient Nazis to such professors, that made the administrators Weimar. Bickel, who had become scornful of "[l]iberals who want no revolution [and who] are forever trying to appease the revolutionaries in order to entice them back up on the raft," may well have agreed.[56]

Yet such professors often compared the situation in American universities to the Europe of 1939 rather than of 1933. The latter analogy would still have enabled professors to liken the students of the late 1960s to the Nazis who had contributed to the collapse of Weimar. Nevertheless, the formative experience of faculty members had often occurred with respect to Nazi, rather than Weimar, Germany—either as refugees from it or combatants against it. And more people had heard of Neville Chamberlain than Gustav Stresemann or Heinrich Bruning. By comparing "soft" administrators to Chamberlain, they could capitalize on his association with "appeasement" and liken students to storm troopers, despite the fact that students were not agents of the state. The 1939 analogy may also have particularly resonated for law professors, who liked to believe that they had dedicated their lives to serving reason in its battles with passion and power and who felt caught between students wearing jackboots and administrators carrying umbrellas. So, just as those who supported escalation in Vietnam misleadingly equated retreat with Munich, some professors stressed the need to stand up to latter-day Nazis.[57]

Of course, one did not need to be a refugee to find the students of the 1960s upsetting. Joseph Bishop, who had stood by as students marched through his class shouting "Stop the Cops!" compared the New Left to McCarthyism, as well as Nazism. To that self-described traditional liberal, "a storm trooper is no less a storm trooper because he decorates his armband with a peace symbol instead of a swastika and drowns out opposition by chanting 'Power to the people' instead of 'Deutschland erwache!'"[58]

*   *   *

To liberals such as Bickel and Bishop, who viewed events at Yale during the late sixties as assaults on their life's project, May 1–3 must have seemed anticlimactic. "The tension was too great; a cataclysmic rendezvous of American society seemed in preparation, and Yale, par excellence the naive liberal institution if one of the most enlightened and communitarian, could not survive such a rendezvous," Peter Brooks wrote of the anxiety beforehand. Fear of a "bloodbath" sparked by left or right reigned. John Hersey would recall the "plywood being nailed over store windows all around Yale; a stenciled sign, FREE THE PANTHERS, on the plyboards, protecting J. Press, arbiter of fashion for generations of well-to-do Yale men." But all went well. The famous Brewster luck, "a force of nature that dictated it would never rain on official events like commencement but would always rain on protest rallies," held. Despite the influx of ten thousand protesters and four thousand National Guardsmen the governor had insisted on sending, the weekend proved relatively tranquil at the law school and on campus. Thankfully, the explosion at Ingalls Rink occurred soon after everyone had left for the night. Working with the New Haven police, who possessed an "extensive wiretap machinery" on the Panthers and other May Day organizers, and using some tricks of their own, Brewster and his administrators kept the peace.[59]

They had lots of help. In the end, as Jeff Greenfield observed, "crisis" brought "community." Everyone, including the Panthers, pleaded for nonviolence; Abbie Hoffman and Kingman Brewster hugged. Law students acted as marshals to ensure crowd control at the New Haven Green. They worked to as-

May Day rally on New Haven Green, just outside the gates of Yale University, 1970. (Photograph by Lee Lockwood. Time-Life Pictures/*Getty Images.)*

sure the availability of legal services, should large-scale arrests occur (as they did not). They quickly put out another suspicious small fire "set, symbolically in the jury box" of the Moot Courtroom and guarded the law school, as they had since the fire in the library. A relieved Bickel remarked that "training still tells a little." More buoyantly, Pollak claimed that he was "enormously proud of the loyalty to our School and our profession displayed by students." In his eyes, the week leading up to May Day weekend had reunited the school.[60]

KENT STATE

There was no time to celebrate. Nixon's April 30 announcement of the U.S. invasion of Cambodia had caught everyone by surprise. On Monday, May 4, just as Yale was celebrating the successful completion of the weekend with "a surfeit of self-congratulation," and announcing the resumption of "normal expectations," the National Guard killed four students — or, Nixon publicly said, "bums" — at Kent State University. As Brewster's biographer said, "The killings were terrible testimony to what could have happened at Yale" during May Day had the National Guardsmen, whose guns held live ammunition, gotten edgy or been allowed closer to the demonstrators. The antiwar movement that had reemerged with the moratorium against the war the previous fall gathered great, renewed force.[61]

Thus began yet another crisis of the sixties at Yale Law School. Graduate and professional students who had largely surrendered May Day to Yale College now moved out front. Law students gathered Monday night, intending to be at the forefront of the effort to launch a nationwide student strike to protest the Cambodian invasion. First-year Hillary Rodham moderated the meeting. She had cried after learning of the Kent State shootings. When she encountered Kessler and "told him I couldn't believe what was happening," the refugee from Nazi Germany "chilled me by saying that, for him, it was all too familiar." By the time the meeting began, she had regained her composure. As Rodham "presided over the crowded and tumultuous room," her "extraordinary poise" impressed Abe Goldstein. "There was a lot of angry rhetoric being exchanged. She somehow managed to keep the discussion calm." It was almost as if Rodham were "a translator," a classmate marveled later. "Somebody would say something in the typical rhetoric of the day. She would say, 'I hear you saying this,' or, 'If you could be in a room with Professor So-and-So, is this what you would say? Hillary did what nowadays would be international summitry—flying back and forth between both sides."[62]

As was so often the case, the tension was between student liberals and the left, and the two groups were not all that far apart. When one student reported that Senator Fulbright "urged student moderation in order to forestall a backlash against Senate doves," those who wanted no part of "student political gurus" assailed him. "No one here knows how the country feels, so let's act according to our own consciences for once," another replied. But the disagreement was over means, not ends. Most students shared Rodham's commitment to "engagement," rather than "'revolution,'" and virtually everyone ultimately supported the motion to strike, which carried overwhelmingly. Only two students voted against the next motion, which urged the faculty to give them credit for their courses without requiring them to sit for final examinations. To Rodham, what stood out in retrospect was "how seriously" all students "took both the law and their responsibilities as citizens." Even in those "difficult and very turbulent times," she would recall, "when we were at Yale Law School, arguing, worrying about what was going on around us, we were not only given many reasons to believe that the system can work, that law can be a tool for positive change and for uplifting the human condition, but we were also given examples of how that could be done." A 1992 headline would announce that "Hillary Rodham Clinton . . . learned to love 'the system' at Yale Law School."[63]

She and her fellow students possessed a grandiose faith in their own influence. Declaring that they would "educate the public and actively support the campaigns of progressive candidates for national office," they seemed certain they would have an impact on public opinion. With most Yale law students sure their action would make newspaper front pages, they told a *New York Times* reporter in attendance to "get the story right."[64]

Just as the *Times* gave the students no coverage, so the faculty paid them little heed. Like liberal students and those on the left, professors and students had much in common. But what divided them mattered more. On the afternoon of May 5, the faculty gathered to consider students' motions about the spring 1970 calendar. The student representative, who himself had been one of the lone voices against the vote for credit without final examinations, had presciently predicted that "many, probably most, faculty members will be opposed. And thus, once again, the Law School 'community' will fall to bickering—bickering between student and teachers about matters which should be secondary to a unified faculty-student effort to turn this country around."[65]

At the beginning of the meeting, Pollak asked student representatives to present their proposals. One informed the professors of the three alternatives: "(1) continue as scheduled; (2) take incomplete and make up later; (3) certify substantial completion of work in course activities and get a Satisfactory." The students, of course, preferred the third possibility, to which Charles Black immediately objected. At this point, Abe Goldstein introduced a motion, on which he and Pollak had clearly collaborated, aimed at mitigating "the effect upon students of the extraordinary confusion and dislocation of events of recent weeks, in New Haven and elsewhere." In courses and seminars where it proved "reasonable" for a professor to give the student a grade or credit on the basis of work completed already, no final examination or paper would be required. To this extent, the faculty would accommodate the students. But what of courses where performance on the final determined one's grade? "In all other offerings, while examination or paper will be required, instructors are urged to be as flexible as reasonably possible in working out delays in examination or paper requirements or modification in examination arrangements in response to individual requests." In any event, students should normally complete alternative arrangements by mid-September.[66]

The reaction varied. While willing to go along, Bickel wanted the unusual nature of the circumstances stressed. Student representative Ben Stein urged the faculty to issue a statement "supporting students." Meanwhile, Tom Emerson maintained that "[w]e're sticking too closely to normal academic procedures." Nixon's Cambodia invasion "[s]hould be treated as a national emergency and [the law school faculty should] be willing to waive the rules." Emerson unsuccessfully moved to amend Goldstein's motion to enable faculty members who agreed with students at least to grade the spring semester work of third-years on a credit-fail basis. With Pollak emphasizing that Goldstein's motion reflected university policy anyway, it then carried.[67]

Actually, university policy allowed greater latitude. Brewster insisted that "students' striking against their own education was irrational and counterproductive, and warned that 'the clenched fist' and the 'shut it down' rhetoric simply help Mr. Agnew and Mr. Nixon to sterilize the political influence of universities, their faculties and students." He did lead a delegation of students, professors, and Yale Corporation members to Washington to consult with Yale alumni in Congress about "how to stop the war and how to counter the White House effort to make scapegoats of the universities and their students," an action he acknowledged came close to violating the principle of institutional neutrality. Beyond that, Yale's president would not go. While the strike forced the closure of hundreds of colleges and universities before term's end, Yale remained open, its graduation ceremonies featuring the usual academic procession to the New Haven Green, complete with marching band. Nevertheless, because of the disruption caused by May Day, the College had already decided against requiring undergraduates to take final examinations. Yale College students could either receive a grade of Pass in their courses or sit for the final examination in the fall and, perhaps, win an Honors or High Pass. Thus university policy would have permitted law students to receive credit for all their courses without completing their papers or examinations.[68]

The law faculty's motivation for refusing to give it was unclear. Possibly, professors worried that they would jeopardize third-years' eligibility for the New York Bar if they agreed to students' credit-without-examination proposal. A week after the faculty meeting, the New York Court of Appeals issued an order declaring that no graduate could take the bar examination "unless he or she had taken and passed an authentic examination in each of his courses of study in accordance with the previous practice of the school." Only when law schools begged the court to reconsider did it soften just a bit and agree to permit take-home examinations, even if the school had not previously administered them.[69]

So, as Goldstein said, unlike many law schools, Yale refused to call off finals. "We were liberal as we often had been in letting people take them at different times, but we never let our students have the experience which some others had, which was to be denied admission to the New York Bar because they had been given passes in courses in which they were not examined," he remarked. "We spared them that travail by standing fast against their pressures." Professors may also have reasoned that since the fire, they had regained the upper hand in their struggle with the students and should not yield now. Whatever moved them, the students read the resolution as a commitment by the faculty to "business as usual." [70]

They caved quickly. By the morning after the faculty meeting, their strike had collapsed. Almost all students had returned to class. Bitterly, graduating Student Association President Walt Wagoner railed against "the hypocrisy" of his fellow students. Their abnegation of "the goals they set for themselves only two short days ago signals a further decline in the prestige of their school and may be symptomatic of the gradual disappearance of the traditionally reformist role of American students in this nation's political system." [71]

Of course, to others, the episode symbolized students' return to the reformist politics of the mid-1960s from the politics at the school in fall 1969 and augured the ascendance of "student political gurus," such as Bill Clinton, who would enter the law school in fall 1970. Yale law students still worked against the war. During the last week of classes in May, some went to Washington to lobby their representatives, on occasion joining forces with Bickel. An impressed Mary McGrory reported, "Among the thousands of students learning to lobby for peace on Capitol Hill, the Yale Law Students Lobby Group has moved out front." Up to forty students at a time took to the halls of power in a "glossy" and "high-powered operation," which, their leader freely admitted, involved "shameless . . . name-dropping." Predictably, "Senators who can't find time for Franklin and Marshall make time for Yale, when they hear that Burke Marshall, Cyrus Vance, Paul Warnke, or Edward Burling, former Republican finance chairman and senior partner of Covington and Burling, will be in the group." They even pored over the Yale law students' brief, "complete with quotations about Congressional powers in foreign policy going back to Thomas Jefferson." [72]

And, the dean informed the alumni, there was more good news to report about the reading and final examination periods. The crisis atmosphere had "substantially diminished." Further, despite the faculty's "flexibility" about deadlines, most students had taken exams and submitted papers on schedule, "and all students appear to understand and appreciate the School's insistence that regular academic standards are to be observed." [73]

Summing up his deanship as it now came to a close, Pollak pointed to the

*Hillary Rodham and Bill Clinton's Prize Trial Competition, 1972. (*Yale Law Report, *Spring 1994. Courtesy Yale Law School.)*

increased enrollment of women and minorities and called attention to the inauguration of student participation in faculty governance. It had sometimes seemed that "disputation between students and faculty was the dominant motif," he acknowledged semi-humorously, and "vast quantities of decibels, petitions, graffiti, statements of quasi-nonnegotiable demands, and elaborately orchestrated moral posturings were expended on a bewildering array of issues: *e.g.,* the grading system; the admissions system; disciplinary procedures; student participation in faculty decision-making; and faculty responsibility for (a) police brutality and (b) the Vietnam War." But once again, he focused on progress by term's end, insisting that by May Day, "the great majority of our law students" had demonstrated "their determination to master the law and use it as an instrument to advance the values of the democratic order."[74]

MYTH-MAKING—AND STRENGTHENING

The "vast quantities of decibels, petitions, graffiti, statements of quasi-nonnegotiable demands, and elaborately orchestrated moral posturings" had done something more. They had strengthened the myth of Yale Law School. Though "house radical" Thomas Emerson characterized the school's reputation for being "far out and liberal" as "undeserved" and its faculty as "pretty middle of the road and quiet," Yale retained its progressive mystique. It did so because Yale boasted (or was embarrassed by, depending on the identity of the speaker) the first law professor in the history of the academy to celebrate the counterculture for millions, as Charles Reich did in 1970 in *The Greening of America*. It did so because, for all their doubts about whether the school deserved it, the students did their best to burnish this image.[75]

There was the push for higher enrollments of women and students of color. There was the assault on the Socratic method and grades. There was the association with realism. "Yale is where law was utterly de-mystified by the legal realist professors in the 20's, 30's and 40's, and we 'radicals' were trying to further that process by applying legal realism to the teaching too," Ben Stein stressed. There was the clinical program, which built on the realist legacy of Jerome Frank. There was the Yale Law School Legislative Services, begun by a member of the class of 1970 to research bills before the Connecticut legislature that had task forces working in fields ranging from abortion law reform to marijuana sentencing. There was the work to end the war.[76]

There was the fascination with public interest law and enthusiasm for alternative careers. Of course, Yale graduates had long been active in public interest law, and in many ways someone such as John Shattuck (class of 1970) followed a traditional path when he moved to the ACLU's national office, becoming its executive director and national staff counsel. But Yale graduates also participated in shaping the "new" public interest law. Consider environmentalism. Aided by Charles Reich and Boris Bittker, several Yale law students received a grant from the Ford Foundation on the condition that they join forces with experienced New York Establishment attorneys fighting to halt the construction of a Con Ed plant on Storm King Mountain. The result was the Natural Resources Defense Council, a forced marriage made in 1970 to secure funding. Unlike the NAACP Legal Defense Fund, which exemplified the traditional public interest law firm and represented a group all considered disadvantaged, or the ACLU, which defended civil liberties on behalf of all Americans, the NRDC was something new. It received funding despite Ford's fear of losing its own charitable tax exemption for financing class actions on behalf of environmentalists who were "not necessarily poor," and despite Ford's anxiety that the Natural Resources Defense Council relied, in large extent, on "five fellows who had just graduated from Yale Law School, who didn't even know where the courthouse was yet," and who planned to file lawsuits that irritated the powerful. The NRDC achieved early and substantial victories when it won passage of the Clean Air Act and "sued the federal government so often" that some nick-named the organization the "shadow" Environmental Protection Agency.[77]

Thus the sense of professional opportunities expanded. When the placement office sent out a questionnaire about the employment plans of the members of the class of 1970 just before graduation, it turned out that forty-six were going to law firms, twenty-six to clerkships, six to government, five to miscellaneous legal jobs, five to miscellaneous nonlegal jobs (including three to Cosmic Labs), five to the military, and four to corporations, with twenty either waiting to hear about government or teaching jobs, planning to travel, or undecided. Ten members of the class were going directly to jobs in which they did legal aid/services work or defended political dissidents. That was a much smaller percentage than Rutgers, which sent at least 20 percent of its graduates into public interest work. Nevertheless, and especially when *New York* magazine broadcast that Cosmic Labs was the "largest single employer of 1970 Yale graduates," the figures reinforced Yale's alternative image among elite schools. And that image stayed strong even after one of the NRDC's co-founders became CEO of "one of Southern California's largest polluters," and graduates of the 1960s who had once planned careers as public interest lawyers ruefully jumped ship for private practice and/or lost faith in "government by elite."[78]

Of course, corporate partners at the time worried that law students at elite schools everywhere seemed to share the commitment to public interest lawyering. Yale was hardly the only place where students came out of job interviews certain that "LAW FIRMS ENGAGE IN ONLY TOKEN EFFORTS AT SOCIAL JUSTICE" that just legitimated "the status quo." The campaign to circulate questionnaires to leading firms about their political and social views and hiring practices, for example, was originated by law students from various schools who had worked with Ralph Nader, though Yale had its own version of the questionnaire, which the *Law Journal* and BLSU circulated.[79]

Still, Yale students continued to cultivate the impression their school was special. That way, they could reproach the faculty and exhort it to improve by returning to its roots. Thus the first issue of the *Yale Journal of Law and Social Action* in 1970 featured Duncan Kennedy's "How the Law School Fails" and classmate Robert Borosage's "Can the Law School Succeed?" alongside articles about the Panther trials.[80]

So, too, the *Yale Law Journal* focused on legal education in 1969–70, emphasizing its relationship to the profession. A debate at the *Journal* about the relevance of relevance had clearly been resolved in favor of the pros. One issue featured an article about the politics of legal education that spelled out everything wrong with it. The May Day number, published soon after the *Journal* opted to decrease competition by opening its ranks to virtually anyone who wanted to join, continued the coverage. It included a pioneering student note on the relationship between legal realism and "a legal education dedicated to such values as the public interest and social justice." The issue also contained comic relief, an essay about the editors of the *Harvard Law Review* that satirized their devotion to "the good old days when men were men and grades were zero to one hundred."[81]

Students also used the *Journal* to needle their professors and alumni about professional norms. Though Yale had long welcomed student enthusiasm for public interest law, it followed other schools in teaching students that lawyers should never surrender control over legal strategy to clients and that the ability to represent all clients, no matter how distasteful their activities, reflected a mark of professionalism. That was how former New Dealers and realist Yale law professors Thurman Arnold and Abe Fortas rationalized their decision to become "hired guns" when they founded their famous Washington law firm. Yet piece after piece in the May issue explored, often empirically, and celebrated the "new public interest lawyers" who engaged in "cause-lawyering" by representing only those clients whose politics they shared and who flouted traditional norms of professionalism by encouraging them to participate in setting strategy. Their authors realized, of course, that corporate lawyers also did pro bono work and that government lawyers sometimes advanced social goals too. But times had changed. Thomas Emerson, who had gone to work for the government soon after he graduated from Yale in the early 1930s, acknowledged, "Your class can't go down to Washington the way we New Dealers did and make an impact. I was just lucky." And although writers applauded the pro bono program of Arnold and Fortas's firm, which enabled one partner to work full time and other lawyers to spend up to 15 percent of their time defending cases and clients for the advancement of social justice, they did so unenthusiastically. Indeed, they queried whether it was possible to combine traditional private practice with representation of the public interest. That was ironic, as the editors suggested, in light of the dedication of the issue to the memory of Thurman Arnold. The articles about the legal profession that appeared amid the memorial tributes, the editors said, "at least implicitly, question his life as a model of the future."[82]

Like so much else about the sixties, this challenge had unintended consequences. Yale students of the period helped to further the growth of a discreet public interest bar that had begun to emerge when NAACP lawyers took to the courts to argue against segregation. But the increased visibility of the public interest bar just gave elite lawyers at Thurman Arnold's firm and others, who had once felt a duty to serve the public from their perch in private practice, one less matter about which to worry. Once they had considered themselves members of a governing class, charged not just with the duty of pursuing client interest and making money, but also with the obligation, at least in theory, "to promote the public good . . . [by] providing free legal services to those who could not afford them." But the young cabined public interest from self-interest, undermining governing class ideology and relegating responsibility for the public interest to "public interest" lawyers. Corporate lawyers might still need to advertise their firms' willingness to do what was increasingly called pro bono work, but they did so to attract young lawyers and to satisfy the 1970 ABA Code of Professional Responsibility, which adjured them to "find time to participate in serving the disadvantaged," as much as out of a sense that they were following in the steps of Brandeis. And as "the predominantly left-of-center public interest bar defined the public good to suit its values," Russell Pearce has pointed out, corporate attorneys had a harder time convincing those who paid their bills that they could serve both clients and the public interest. Though many might well share the politics and causes of public interest lawyers, corporate lawyers had to fear alienating "predominantly right-of-center big business clients." As a result, elite lawyers, who had historically coexisted uneasily with the "hired gun" model, became more likely to embrace it. That probably made it easier to rationalize what they did as professionals and to preserve their own identity as individuals. Would left-of-center causes have fared better in the years that followed if the legal left of the sixties had shown more tolerance for the Arnold model?[83]

Perhaps. Left-of-center causes might likewise have fared better if Yale's students and liberal faculty had realized how much they had in common. In promoting faith in law as a tool of progressive social change, Yale had long encouraged students and professors alike to see themselves as both members of, and rebels against, the Establishment. But the times spurred polarization, just as they moved students to tweak their teachers by accusing them of betraying Yale's past.

Ironically, the accusations, along with students' loyalty to their version of Yale's history, helped to make "the myth of the 'progressive,' adventuresome Yale Law School" a partial reality. In the 1930s, when Arnold joined other New Dealers in the commute between Washington and New Haven, Yale professors had worked hard to identify their school with the advocacy of a different form of legal education and a different law practice. In the 1960s, Yale law students threw up the example of realism to their professors at the same time that they treated realists, such as Arnold, with the skeptical affection some members of the New Left would have accorded grandparents who had once belonged to the Old Left. Their activism breathed new life into Yale's storied reputation as a place where one went to do good and well.[84]

Chapter Eight

After the Fire

The period between 1967 and 1970 had witnessed a clash of cultures at Yale Law School—between students, between professors, and between students and professors. Students remained interested in the school afterward, but shifted more of their attention to national concerns. That suited the new dean, who celebrated the end of the psychodrama of the 1960s and preached a realist renewal. Appointed to restore stability, Abe Goldstein hoped to put the "Dark Ages" behind the school. Yet although an "eerie tranquility" returned to the student body during his deanship, the composition of the faculty changed dramatically. Senior professors retired, resigned, or died and juniors were not asked to remain. While hardly the sole reason for the turnover, the psychodrama of the late 1960s may have played a role in causing it. The sixties did not end at Yale simply because the decade did.

"THE DARK AGES"

The process by which Goldstein was selected as dean in 1970 underscored the continued strain at the school. Professors' missives poured into Woodbridge Hall, though no one entirely trusted Brewster: the fear he would impose his choice on the faculty only heightened anxiety. Letter after letter stressed the "disintegration" of the school; "the gradual erosion of this institution, the loss of élan, the evaporation of its sense of high corporate purpose"; the factionalization of "our difficult faculty"; the fact that the "law school is a terribly unhappy place"; the need for a lift similar to that Rostow had provided when he became dean. As David Trubek summed it up for Brewster, "The word is out that the Yale Law School is in trouble." Some professors wanted Yale's president to appoint their former colleague, Dean Bayless Manning of Stanford; others recommended Harry Wellington.[1]

Many promoted Abe Goldstein. Yet white students branded him a "hard-liner." The BLSU had "not had an especially cordial relationship with him," either. And some professors thought Goldstein had destroyed his chances for the deanship by lobbying so hard against student participation at the secret meeting at Pollak's house in front of Brewster.[2]

Student activists hoped Yale's president would go outside. They sought a dean who could provide that "push from the outside" they believed their professors so desperately needed—someone like clinical education advocate Anthony Amsterdam; William Kunstler's partner, Arthur Kinoy; poverty law pioneers Edgar and Jean Cahn; antiwar and "jurisprudence of insurgency" advocate Michael Tigar; or civil rights lawyer Constance Baker Motley. Issuing the familiar indictment of disappointed expectations, elected student representatives informed the Yale Corporation that "Yale Law School, once the great innovator in legal education, has ceased to experiment," and begged Brewster to appoint a "strong dean, acting with more nearly full student participation." It was difficult "to find any faculty member besides Charles Reich who has developed politically beyond the problems of the 50's, and our youngest professors were educated along with the silent, apathetic masses of the 50's," one group of dissidents told Brewster.[3]

Brewster consulted extensively with students, as he had not done four years earlier, then appointed Goldstein anyway. Calling the faculty together two months before May Day, the president thanked Pollak for his "monumental dignity" during the school's troubles and announced that Goldstein was the choice of the administration and faculty. Fifteen professors had voted for Wellington, twenty for Goldstein.[4]

Why Goldstein? His appointment made sense, since he had been considered for the position in 1964. Further, the Harvard-Yale rivalry with respect to legal education still loomed. Goldstein had attended Yale Law School, and his work was in the realist tradition, but he would appeal to the "Harvards" on the faculty. Finally, Brewster had apparently decided that the students needed a firm hand, and as everyone acknowledged, Goldstein personified toughness. He had not joined "the group that wanted to give the students everything they ask for whenever they ask for it," the incoming dean told the *New York Times*, which announced the appointment of this pushcart peddler's son in a front-page article highlighting the school's recent unrest and the disappointment over Goldstein's selection among "white radicals and blacks." Just as the French students' uprising gave France a right-wing government, so law students' agitation played a role in Goldstein's appointment.[5]

*　　*　　*

At Yale, May Day abruptly brought the period of greatest turmoil to its terminus. There was a limit to how much excitement even students could take, some thought. What Kingman Brewster called an "eerie tranquility" descended. Writing in the fall of 1970, the Committee on the Law School sounded as bemused as Yale's president. "The Law School this Fall, like other parts of the Yale campus, is remarkably free of the tension that plagued it last year," the committee reported. The school's "crisis of confidence, its period of hesitation about basic values, appear to be passing"—just as they began to permeate Boalt and NYU. While Yale students remained skeptical of "national goals and policies," the committee observed, "most of their criticism is oriented outward, rather than toward the University or the Law School."[6]

Chief among the "outward" targets of criticism, of course, was the war. After the Cambodian invasion, Stephen Cohen and Gregory Craig helped organize "Project Purse Strings," which promoted the Cooper-Church and McGovern-Hatfield Amendments, legislation that would have ended American military activity in Cambodia and funding for the war. Some, such as Bill Clinton, enlisted in Joe Duffey's 1970 Connecticut Senate campaign. "Clinton [was] rarely attending class, working day and night on the Duffey campaign for months, [which] was not particularly out of the ordinary at Yale Law," where others also concentrated on causes more than classes. After Nixon bombed Hanoi and Haiphong in 1972, more than a third of Yale law students attended a meeting called on short notice. They voted to hold a one-day moratorium on class attendance to protest the "senseless killing," and they released a statement announcing that they were "appalled by and vehemently opposed to the President's refusal to end American involvement in the War in Southeast Asia, and particularly his recent escalation of American bombing in both North and South Vietnam."[7]

Students did not altogether lose interest in law school conditions. BLSU members still protested low African American enrollments during the 1970s. But the atmosphere did not become heated, and the demand for more African Americans was "undercut by the relative success of the school in black recruitment as compared to other law schools." Women students remained active in feminist causes. The Yale Law Women Association insisted that "[w]omen are second rate citizens at the law school," protested the school's inattentiveness to law firms' discrimination against women, worked for abortion rights and with prisoners, and agitated for the Equal Rights Amendment. Student activists also supported staff. When dining hall and custodial workers in Local 35 struck in 1971, Ann Hill and others joined the union supporters who left trays of food on Brewster's lawn. But no one symbol of faculty power spurred a large number of students to come together in protest, and as the Committee on the Law School had suggested, their energies seemed more focused on conditions outside Yale than within. The young "left the faculty alone more," Hill said.[8]

Indeed, New York magazine reported in 1972 that law students in general, and Yale's in particular, had become more conventional. The secretary of Yale's class of 1970 mentioned the piece in alumni class notes: "A recent article in New York magazine . . . noted that the radical trend (which may be an overstatement) in law schools of a couple of years ago (remember when we were at Yale? the grading dispute? the Student Negotiating Committee walkout? the secret faculty meeting? the strike? . . . the what!?!) has all but vanished, and our beloved alma mater was prominently cited. The article did point out that the largest single employer of the Yale Class of 1970 was Cosmic Labs ('. . . a traveling freak show . . .') with three, but we know, don't we, that Cosmic Labs too, has gone the way of law student idealism." That provided fodder for an observation and a question: "Maybe we're all still traveling; and where is a place of rest?" The answer, it turned out, was largely in private practice. As the secretary of the class of 1971 asked at mid-decade, "who would have thought that the most radicalized Yale Law Class in recent memory would, a mere five years after graduation, have 60 percent of its members in law-firm practice?"[9]

Some even suspected that Yale professors intentionally began to screen out more "radical" students for admission beginning in 1970. While searching for an academic job, class of 1972 graduate Ed Baker went to one Association of American Law Schools meeting where Goldstein addressed the alumni and recalled hearing the dean say "he was committed to not having a class like the one they had just graduated." Charles Reich complained that the admissions office was intentionally trying to increase the "numbers of straight law students." Yet perhaps more applicants were "straight" generally. Certainly, the explosion of applications in the 1970s meant more sought law degrees just when the economy was collapsing, a trend that may have discouraged some from taking chances.[10]

Unlike Reich, many professors appreciated "straight" students. "The Yale Law School is a different place," Harry Wellington exulted. "It is quiet and seems to be committed to teaching and scholarship as in the old days." In one sense, nothing had changed: despite the Committee on the Law School's pleas, 80 percent of all students hailed from relatively privileged families, with 50 percent of the student body coming from the northeast. But the "quiet" was still welcome. After talking with a number of his colleagues, Robert Bork reported to Bickel: "The students are friendly, relaxed and cheerful. The black students, the new ones at least, are not segregating themselves" and "speak very well, indicating that we have attracted a very different group this year." Yet although in general, "the old ease in the classroom has returned, there does not seem to be the same skill in intellectual games that many of the students displayed three or four years ago," before the law school's troubles began. Unlike the "sullen" students of the late sixties, those of the early 1970s were ready "to deal with a hypothetical, but they get their feet tangled in their underwear rather more frequently than one could wish." Yet although the young were "solemn, note-taking, and relatively unaggressive intellectually," Bork's allusion to "the old ease in the classroom" indicated professors had regained control. That made teaching more satisfying than it had been during the late sixties, if not as much fun as it had been before that. So did "the feeling that the place has a core again."[11]

Yale's new dean was happy too. Abe Goldstein reveled in the calm after what he publicly referred to as the "Dark Years" or "Dark Ages" had ended. During the "psychodrama" of the late 1960s, virtually all the controversies that hit American college campuses transformed Yale Law into a "combat zone," and "almost all of them were too well publicized in the *New York Times*," he told alumni. Everyone's nerves had been "rubbed bare":

> When we at the law school discussed grading reform, it seemed to be a contest for the soul of our students. . . . When we discussed the adequacy of the Socratic method, it was put to us in the apocalyptic form—Why has the Law School failed? When we considered questions of student participation in governance, it was not a simple matter of should we let the students know what we are doing or not. We were discussing issues of participatory and parliamentary democracy, consumerism, the nature of power and authority. When we dealt with minority admissions we found ourselves trying to reconcile social and academic obligations in an atmosphere too heavily fraught with guilt and recriminations. When we rejected the notion, as we did again and again, that the Law School should take official positions on issues like the Vietnam war or police misconduct or the Panther trials, we found ourselves considering the nature and function of a university.[12]

Though one of the first commencements over which Goldstein presided took place during the Local 35 strike, and Hill and others disrupted graduation to demonstrate their solidarity with the strikers, the dean remained upbeat. He told the graduating class that students might have learned that liberals had been right all along and the radicals were wrong. It had turned out, Goldstein contended at graduation, that the university was not "a microcosm of the larger society and its problems," and students had misplaced their energy by transferring their hostility toward the Establishment to the university. Bringing the university to heel did not guarantee the remainder of society would fall into line. Reminding students that he and his colleagues shared many of their goals, he asked them to consider "how plain it has been that university people are opposed to the war and want to cut it short; or that faculty and students in overwhelming numbers want more personal freedom, more experimentation in life style and politics, more radical reform of many aspects of our lives; . . . *and* how deeply resistant — politically and emotionally — the larger society had been to those preferences." He believed "even activist students" now possessed "a soberer sense of where the problems are." But during the time it had taken the young to learn this lesson, he told them pointedly, they had alienated many professors. "In the university, more than elsewhere," Goldstein said, "we had the seeming collision of cultures, the suspicions of foot-dragging, the impugning of motives."[13]

Others interpreted history differently. To some students, the sixties proved that the university was indeed a microcosm of society. The problem had been that sixties liberalism could not fix the problems of either society or the university and had not opened the door wide enough to allow in those with better solutions. As one activist later stressed, even when the young did not realize a specific goal, the issue had never been the issue. Their movement did not just aim at achieving individual objectives, such as grade reform, but at sharing power and finding community. Though protest did not always bring as much change as activists hoped, it could transform identity: "[T]he act of demonstrating, the numbers, the chanting and posturing, all released a sense of individual energy and power." That was why Yale law graduates of 1970, 1971, and 1972, who shared 1969–70 in common, continued — ironically, proudly, and nostalgically — to trumpet their association with the "Dark Ages" or "Dark Years" and to characterize themselves as members of Yale's "most radicalized class" long after they had become lions of the corporate bar. The disagreement about whether activists had wasted their time underscored another "truth" too: as with the sixties, the value of the "Dark Ages" would be contested for years to come.[14]

"THE SLAUGHTER OF THE INNOCENTS"

In the early 1970s, Yale's tenured professors who constituted its Governing Board declined to promote or advance six junior faculty members who had arrived at Yale during the Dark Ages. During the last days of Pollak's deanship, the Governing Board voted against making Assistant Professor John Griffiths an associate professor without tenure. It refused to promote Robert Hudec and David Trubek in 1972. It declined to advance Larry Simon in 1973. Soon afterward, the Appointments Committee decided not to bring the case of Associate Professor Richard Abel before the Governing Board for a tenure vote. The last to go was Lee Albert in 1974. The reasons for these decisions, along with their validity, remain in dispute to this day. All that seems fairly clear is that they were not a function of the university's poor financial shape or the central administration's judgment.[15]

Yale's growing deficit affected retentions elsewhere in the university. Revenues had declined as the university grew spectacularly under Brewster's leadership during the 1960s; alumni reduced donations because of anger about his May Day "radicalism"; and federal grant and foundation awards shrank during the straitened seventies. Between 1971 and 1973, most Yale departments had to cut their budgets by almost 20 percent. Finances, perceptions of quality, and, some junior faculty members believed, distaste for their politics and lack of deference, led the political science department to fire five of its ten junior faculty members. Yet although the university's budgetary problems did leave a scar, the law school was not involved in its personnel reduction program. "We have, in fact, 'made out' better than all of Yale," Dean Goldstein acknowledged.[16]

The law school's promotion process also demonstrated its relative autonomy from the rest of the university. As part of his drive to modernize Yale, Brewster had tightened the requirements for tenure. When he arrived in New Haven, Brewster told former Harvard College dean McGeorge Bundy, "I found Yale's 'Harvard Complex' suffocating and stultifying." By the late 1960s, Brewster delighted "in some signs of a developing 'Yale Complex' in Cambridge." Of course, the improved quality of Yale's faculty was attributed to the new insistence on tighter standards. Had political science been able to keep all its assistant professors, it would have subjected them to a review after seven to ten years that did not routinely result in promotion. As at other elite private universities, candidates for tenure in the humanities generally possessed little chance of success unless they had published two books, one of which was a revised dissertation, and received enthusiastic extramural letters from leading scholars in their fields. Teaching was secondary, though not irrelevant at institutions such as Yale that prided themselves on their interest in undergraduates and often asked all students in a class to evaluate a professor. The tenure process was similar in the social sciences and natural sciences, where the quantity bar for scholarship was equally high, with articles often substituting for books. Senior colleagues usually voted on promotions by secret ballot. Department chairs had to justify the result to university committees and administration officials, who might reject them.[17]

Like law schools elsewhere, however, Yale generally awarded tenure after a shorter period — generally five years after the initial appointment as assistant professor. At the law school level, the candidate passed through the eye of the needle at the time of hiring, and assuming all went well in the years that followed, the chance for tenure was good. Because academic lawyers during this period rarely possessed advanced degrees, few had dissertations they could turn into books or articles, and law schools acknowledged that they started the scholarly game at a disadvantage by demanding less in terms of publications. "[L]aw professors trade on a university name, built up by historians, classicists, and theoretical physicists," one Governing Board member acknowledged later. "We put ourselves forward as professors of law at *Yale* University (to pick a name at random). Yet even knowledgeable outsiders do not always recognize that lawyers become professors on the basis of a publication standard that embarrasses their colleagues in the rest of the university." Nor did Yale Law School regularly seek extramural letters on tenure candidates. Like other law schools, at least in theory, Yale also placed greater weight on teaching than did undergraduate institutions. Information on teaching, though, was gathered anecdotally, through interviews with selected students by the dean or his designate. The results might well reflect the interviewer's predispositions and the way he asked questions.[18]

The law school's tenure meeting operated differently from Yale College's too. Like a department chair, the law school dean scheduled the Governing Board meeting that would decide promotion. There was no secret ballot. The dean then contacted those who had been absent to describe the discussion and to ascertain their votes. His summary of the discussion might affect how absentees cast their ballots, as could the fact that Governing Board members had a right to know how absentees voted. At Yale, a law professor had to receive two-thirds of the vote at one meeting or a majority at two separate meetings to win the endorsement for promotion. Unlike departmental decisions, the law school's decision, at Yale or elsewhere, was rarely second-guessed. The latitude the law school possessed meant that when the Governing Board did not advance six individuals within a short period, attention would focus on the dean and the board.

*   *   *

To some, the decisions seemed entirely legitimate. It was not as if all junior faculty members during this period were denied tenure. John Ely, Arthur Leff, and Michael Reisman were promoted from within between the end of 1970 and 1972. Those three cases would have been easy. The faculty greatly valued Ely and Leff, who were promoted simultaneously, and with Goldstein's support. The Leff corpus provided ample evidence of its author's quirky brilliance, and Ely's near book-length tenure article would become one of the *Yale Law Journal*'s most cited. Of "our current non-tenured crop," Robert Bork thought only Ely and Leff strong. Students considered Reisman an excellent teacher. Among other items, his curriculum vitae listed two books in press, and he had written a number of articles on international law with Myres McDougal and others. Though McDougal's influence was waning, international law remained his fiefdom at Yale, and the faculty would have found this protégé far stronger than some whose promotion he had urged earlier.[19]

Those who defended the failure to advance the other six junior faculty members reasoned further that many of "Gene's boys," who decided on tenure, had first arrived at Yale in the 1950s after another failed promotion and advancement—that of Vern Countryman to professor and David Haber to associate professor. Senior professors, the argument goes, would thus not have considered tenure automatic. Tenure had not been assured for them, although, in a highly unusual step that had made Woodbridge Hall anxious, the Governing Board had promoted most of "Gene's boys"—including Bickel, the Goldsteins, and Harry Wellington—in one swoop.[20]

And as long as senior faculty members helped those who were pushed out to find good jobs elsewhere, they believed it appropriate to stick to the same "absolute standard" of scholarly excellence that they maintained had been applied in their own cases. That was what had been done, Goldstein insisted—and, he implied, with kindness. "I felt that it was terribly important at that time, in order for us to have a fair consideration of each of the people we were talking about, that the faculty become persuaded that a denial of tenure or a denial of promotion at Yale Law School did not mean that these individuals would be consigned to outer darkness, or to oblivion," Goldstein said. Consequently, as dean, he remembered devoting himself to "facilitating the movement of people who did not succeed here to other places." Eugene Rostow explained: "Such a practice is far less traumatic for the faculty member and his family, and better for the system as a whole." It freed Yale to be discriminating. The real difference between the Harvard and Yale faculties, according to Rostow, was that at Harvard, tenure was then automatic. Yale promoted only if the candidate's publications provided "serious ground for believing that he has promise of 'scholarly distinction.' This is supposed to be, and I think really is, the sole criterion for appointment to tenured rank at Yale." Interestingly, Rostow seemed to say that teaching was unimportant. During the year before he became dean, he added, "we had a promotion controversy about two associate Professors which stirred the dovecotes from here to there."[21]

Those who disagreed with Rostow and Goldstein about Yale's wisdom in failing to advance the six maintained that the early 1970s witnessed the second "slaughter of the innocents" at Yale. They saw the dismissals as the successor to the first slaughter that had "stirred the dovecotes," which they blamed on Countryman's and Haber's left-leaning politics during the McCarthy era. To such individuals, the faculty's resolution of the six cases between 1970 and 1974 reflected an attempt to change the standards applied in tenure cases.[22]

*   *   *

The decisions were peculiar — for legal education and Yale. "I know of no other sequence of such concentrated firings" at any law school, one scholar wrote later. They also contradicted expectations at Yale. The presumption there was in favor of tenure, even if the candidate had written relatively little. With characteristically self-deprecating wit, Pollak explained that the negative vote against David Haber in the 1950s had apparently rested on the judgment that he had not yet written enough to justify advancement. "But I have been told by one of my most senior and respected colleagues that if Dave had been judged by the standards of productivity which just a few years later were applied to my faculty generation, Dave would unquestionably have been promoted. Thus have we little men come into our own." Ronald Dworkin remembered writing "one thin article" prior to his promotion. "I cannot understand how you ever got tenure," he recalled Robert Brustein, his Saint Ronan Terrace neighbor, telling him. "You write so little."[23]

Of course, like Dworkin, a number of Rostow's recruits had indeed published considerably more than most law professors after receiving tenure, if not before, and had acquired venerable reputations, grounded on an impressive body of scholarship. Abe Goldstein rightly observed that many of them thought they had ushered in "yet another of the Law School's periodic 'golden ages.'"[24] Whether or not they did, junior faculty members who arrived at the school during the late 1960s could have looked to history and seen that all those hired during the Rostow era who were considered for tenure had received it. (As Rostow said, some junior faculty members obviously had taken a hint and departed before the Governing Board had to vote on their promotions.) Without a doubt, beginning academics also noticed that "Gene's boys" included some who produced very little before and after their promotions: some "little men" had indeed come into their own.

That was one reason for an academic to anticipate promotion. Yet another was that his seniors told him to expect it. "If we could not hold out the hope of permanency, we simply could not hope to draw top-flight young lawyers into law teaching," Pollak stressed.[25]

Thus it seemed strange when "the hope of permanency" shrank. "I think we thought we were applying the same standards [as had been applied to us], but I don't think we were," Harry Wellington said nearly thirty years later. As he pointed out, whenever a new cohort comes up for tenure, standards seem to change.[26]

Even in 1975, the Association of American Law Schools' accreditation team seemed dubious about whether Yale's retention decisions reflected change or continuity. It suggested that the law school might have to "clarify its policy in hiring juniors." Traditionally, Yale had followed other law schools in hiring only junior faculty it expected to promote. "That a young man or woman invited to the Yale Faculty would normally get tenure made it possible to have equality in fact and in spirit among all faculty in the common enterprise; it meant that instruction in the heart of the curriculum was effectively by tenured or tenure-worthy faculty; it meant also an essential identity and continuity in the heart of the institution." As the accreditation team recognized, however, recently the school had not offered tenure to "a substantial number of young faculty." Why? "It may be those decisions reflect commendable adherence to the highest standards, the faculty having decided that these individuals had not fulfilled their promise (or that hiring them had been a mistake)." But that just suggested a need to make more careful decisions at the outset. And even then, it might prove necessary "to assure future candidates that Yale has not changed its hiring policy, that all invited are deemed promising of tenure, and that tenure will be forthcoming unless—unexpectedly—that promise fails."[27]

Despite the accreditation team's delicacy, its report pointed to disagreement about whether the faculty changed the standards, and whether it did so with adequate notice. But changing the standards is not necessarily bad, though the process may damage the individuals caught in the transition. Institutions improve themselves by raising them. Senior faculty members had worried about standards in the struggle over grades, fighting against pass-fail.

Perhaps they were now transforming the tenure evaluation system from something like pass-fail, in which virtually everyone who survived until the final test passed, to one in which only honors recipients won tenure. If so, what criteria entered into their decision to award or withhold honors? More important, were such decisions applied uniformly and fairly?

Many people suspected that they were not. Collectively, the Griffiths, Hudec, Trubek, Simon, Abel, and Albert outcomes became known as the "purge." The individuals involved, it is said, "were in one way or another seen as 'left.'" Yet none had radical politics. Goldstein, a political liberal, considered some "unmistakably to the right of me" and volunteered, "I don't think we were acting on political grounds." Nor is there evidence of a conspiracy to fire the six. Even so, the failures to advance them could nevertheless constitute more than mere coincidence. Griffiths maintained that what "happened was a *structural firing* by an *institution* of a whole group of people, not just some isolated instances that happen to add up to a group."[28]

What transformed the six junior faculty into a group, in this view, was its experience at Yale during the Dark Ages. Tenured professors got rid of their younger colleagues because they perceived their juniors as more acceptant of students of the late 1960s. They may even have made their juniors surrogates for the students, the Dark Age barbarians. "They were angry, they were intimidated, they were threatened," Charles Reich said of his Governing Board colleagues in the aftermath of the 1960s. In his view, the experience of warring with the students "skewed their judgment," rendering them unable to make the distinctions between candidates those good lawyers would have made otherwise.[29]

I have struggled with this period in the law school's history, often waking up one morning with the opposite opinion of the one I had the day before. There is no smoking gun, no definitive conclusion. We can observe that it is simplistic to ask whether there was the kind of intentional bloodletting that the word "purge" implies. We can point to the charged meaning of "purge" and disagree over how many "innocents" must be sacrificed to qualify as one. We can remind ourselves that causation and motivation are so multilayered as to make their study nearly futile. We can say that the historian's job is to historicize — to recreate the past as it appeared to those who lived through it — rather than to judge. We can contend that the 1970s are "current events," too recent to constitute history.

Yet although historians are not judges, we do pass judgment, sometimes more obviously than others. So, too, do we grope, however inadequately, with causation and intentionality. And though privacy considerations prevent me from relating all I have been told — or, at times, from attributing comments to specific individuals — the "current events" argument still seems lame.

*   *   *

The cases must be seen as intellectual, as well as institutional, history. They reflect a rising wind in the legal academy. And in one way or another, the intellectual ferment threatened the traditional Yale way of doing business.

As Goldstein became dean, prominent legal scholars had begun to echo students' age-old complaint that law school took too long. In 1971, Paul Carrington's report for the Association of American Law Schools called for the reduction of law school to two years. The following year, in making a similar recommendation, the Carnegie Commission characterized the second and third years as "academic wasteland." The idea of a two-year law school had been gathering momentum for some time, and like the deans of other elite law schools, Goldstein opposed it. It was a creature of the 1960s, he maintained, reflecting an "impressionistic and time-bound sense of student dissatisfaction" during a period "of anger and tension growing out of an unpopular war, searingly confusing race relations, and conflicting life styles." That period had ended, he noted thankfully, and "passions have run their course and education is again perceived as neither a scapegoat nor a panacea for more fundamental problems."[30]

From his perspective, it was time to get back to work. Indeed, at his speech at the *Yale Law Journal* banquet in April 1970, a week before the fire, Goldstein had maintained that at a time when law was more complex than ever, it made no sense to cut law school to two years. He considered the proposal to do so anti-intellectual, shaped by the mistaken view that legal education still taught "the very set of analytic techniques and rhetorical styles which so many regard as entirely inadequate to the solution of social problems." In fact, Goldstein insisted, the task of legal training was to go "beyond the facile use of cases and doctrine and on to an assessment of the jobs which legal institutions can do best," as well as render judgment about which should be left to the church, the family, and the market.

The mission, or at least so the new dean defined it for students and faculty, was to "fulfill the promise of sociological and realist jurisprudence." Yale, he said at the dinner, was "at the brink of an educational precipice." For other law schools, "it is enough to move to where we were twenty and more years ago. They can count themselves successful by making the curriculum largely elective, by developing some seminars and writing experiences and by appointing an economist or a psychiatrist to the faculty." But Yale had done that. What it had not done, the dean said, was to consolidate "the best from the past" and use it as "a base upon which to build for the future." Here was the familiar mix of Yale arrogance, ambition, and insecurity.

Exactly what Goldstein meant by it all was understandably opaque: he was speaking at a banquet. He stressed the need to find the proper balance of "course, clinical and field research experience" for each law student's specific interests, and the clinical program did grow stronger during his deanship. He talked of the end of the day of the lawyer as general practitioner and of the need to introduce "fields of concentration" to train lawyers in specialties, which did not happen in any formal way during his years at the helm. He spoke of the importance of training professionals with renewed faith in their "capacity to develop solutions" for social problems, ones who saw "law as part of the social process" and were not "passive instruments of the institutions they happen to find." Realism was read as the old mandate to integrate law with the social sciences in a reformist fashion. Beyond that, the vision seemed blurry.[31]

As his predecessors had often done since the 1930s, Goldstein seemed to be summoning up the past and promising to do the realists' work right this time. He would hire imaginative legal liberals with tenure, such as Bruce Ackerman and Owen Fiss. He would seek Yale's salvation in its history. That justified, among other things, a three-year law school.

The two-year degree was not the only pressure. Yale administrators during the early 1970s were also confronting new scholars in areas that had come to be known as Law and Economics and Law and Society. They too laid claim to the realist heritage to which Goldstein nodded.

At the University of Chicago, the relationship between law and social science and empirical research had blossomed after World War II. The funding that Chicago's Law and Behavioral Studies Program obtained from the Ford Foundation had made several large-scale empirical projects possible, including the famous Kalven and Zeisel study of the American jury. Law and Economics had also gripped the Chicago law school faculty. The school's romance with economics had begun when Assistant Professor Henry Simons was transferred from Chicago's economics department to its law school because of a fight between his mentor, Frank Knight, the father of Chicago's brand of neoclassical economics, and New Dealer Paul Douglas. Knight's student and Simons's successor, Aaron Director, put modern Law and Economics on the map. As the economic analysis of antitrust evolved in the 1950s and 1960s, it substantiated Director's thesis about the instability of monopolies, moving Chicago toward domination of Law and Economics.[32]

Meanwhile another form of Law and Economics—the application of economics to fields of law "ranging from adoption to zoning" — was also emerging at Chicago. In 1960, Ronald Coase had set its law school afire by moving the spotlight away from regulation, with his theorem that as long as there were no transaction costs to prevent parties to a transaction from bargaining to their mutual benefit, "the legal rules don't matter — or more precisely, the parties will always bargain their way to an economically efficient outcome, regardless of the legal rule." By the end of the decade, Richard Posner was about to hurl Chicago-style Law and Economics "like a bomb on the academic legal world," with its theses that the common law promoted economic efficiency and regulation just gummed things up while hurting the very individuals it was intended to protect — all the while insisting that Chicagoans made no value judgments and possessed no political agenda. A finding that "legislation designed to protect the consumer frequently ends up hurting him" did not constitute an endorsement of the free market and conservative politics, he said. That was hard for some to swallow, particularly once Posner had proclaimed law's purpose, justification, and foundation as the maximization of wealth, which included "no *public* duty to support the indigent." Under this system, when the Nazis decided "to get rid of the Jews . . . it would have had to buy them out," and infants could legally be sold for adoption, along with body parts. There was "no immorality in the idea of a baby market, when morality is derived from economic principle itself."[33]

Most found the roots of Chicago-style Law and Economics in legal realism. Perhaps that was poor intellectual history. Among other things, unlike the realists, who looked to all social sciences, practitioners of Law and Economics treated economics as something more than just one promising avenue for law. As Neil Duxbury put it, they made economics their (and social science's) "queen." Indeed, their resort to it "implied a rejection of more general social-scientific inquiry." Only economics, Chicagoans believed, was "capable of providing analytical models which facilitate the discovery of precise, verifiable answers." Nevertheless, so long as Law and Economics was labeled a realist offshoot, it was natural for Yale to show interest in it.[34]

In fact, Yale professors already possessed links to Chicago-style Law and Economics. Bowman and Bork, both Director students, had maintained that antitrust policy should focus on the achievement of efficiency in the 1960s. But Bork's famous book on antitrust making that argument would come only later, and during the 1950s and 1960s, Chicago and Harvard arguably dominated the antitrust field. In any event, antitrust was "only one aspect of law and economics." The 1968 tenuring of Wellington's protégé, Ralph Winter, would give Yale another toehold in Chicago-style Law and Economics, but Winter had as yet published little more than a coauthored essay, a review essay maintaining that laws forbidding discrimination in employment did not help the African Americans they were intended to benefit and jeopardized individual freedom, and a book on labor law with Wellington. During the "boom" period of Law and Economics, the late 1960s and early 1970s, Chicago dominated.[35]

The work of Guido Calabresi, however, enabled Yale to begin to carve out its own niche in the field. Indeed, it developed a reputation for housing an alternative and progressive vision of Law and Economics, which recognized the state as a more positive force for good than the Chicago rendition did. As Posner recognized, Calabresi's 1961 essay, "Some Thoughts on Risk Distribution and the Law of Torts," deserved a place alongside Coase's as an article that launched the field. There, Calabresi attributed the survival of the doctrine of respondeat superior, which made the employer liable for employee acts conducted in the scope of employment, to something other than society's need to end accidents or resolve disputes by finding fault. Displaying the concern with distributional consequences that would come to mark the Yale brand of lawyer-economists, he demonstrated that the doctrine's persistence reflected its utility in spreading losses even as it ensured that the price of goods and services reflected the total cost of producing them, which would promote safety and foster other social goals. By Calabresi's account, those goals meant that the cheapest cost avoider, the individual or institution most cheaply able to avoid the costs of accidents, must assume them. His 1970 book, *The Cost of Accidents*, took it "as axiomatic that the principal function of accident law is to reduce the sum of the costs of accidents and the costs of avoiding accidents"—and serve justice, which Calabresi was very clear "must ultimately have its due"—by charging them to the cheapest cost avoider. Calabresi's theory that tort law was not about the cause of accidents but controlling their costs and his concern with justice were obviously indebted to legal realism and gave New Haven a distinct place on the Law and Economics map.[36]

But to stay current and demonstrate its dedication to realism, Yale also needed a presence in Law and Society, a scholarly area in which some of its younger faculty members worked. Thanks to substantial foundation money, Wisconsin, Boalt, Denver, and Northwestern had become the headquarters of the Law and Society movement during the 1960s. Dedicated to forging an alliance between law and social science, its enthusiasts planned to do the empirical research of which the realists had only dreamed. Their studies reflected their hope to enlist facts and "objectivist knowledge" in the service of legal liberalism. They revealed the gaps between legal rules and reality, exposing the circumstances under which legal doctrine was "defeated, diverted, or distorted by social forces in need of reform." Among other things, Law and Society research would reveal the surprisingly low costs of ordinary litigation; challenge the notion of Americans as a "litigious people" caught up in a "litigation explosion"; verify that juries function as better fact-finders than judges; suggest that the experience of the legal process is itself the punishment in the lower courts; expose businessmen's indifference to contract law as they executed contracts and developed rights and remedies in their negotiations; and explore lawyers' ways of maintaining autonomy from their clients so that they could promote client interest while still fulfilling their professional obligation to act as officers of the court.[37]

This scholarship reached backward to law's revolt against Langdellianism, as well as out to social scientists. It was most indebted to sociologists, some of whose findings raised questions about the work of the professors Yale presented as its most pioneering. If formal law, for one example, did not influence rights and remedies in welfare law as much as had been supposed, did those engaged in welfare reform best spend their energies on lobbying the Court to build procedural safeguards into the protection of Reich's "new property"?[38]

As a founder of Law and Society, Willard Hurst ensured that historians played a key role in the movement. A legal historian, he credited legal realism with enabling him to outgrow his Harvard Law School education. Yale had tried to woo Hurst away from Madison with a higher salary during realism's heyday in the 1930s, but he had stayed at Wisconsin, making it a center of sociolegal work. As a teacher, he co-edited one of the earliest Law and Society casebooks. As a scholar, he wrote what was called either sociological history or historical sociology, depending on whether one focused on the care and detail he brought to his narrative of how the legal system operated or on the "big" questions and methods behind it. Where the realists tended to write constitutional history, showing how social, economic, intellectual, and idiosyncratic forces affected judicial decision makers, "I didn't want to wind up knowing nothing except all the gossip about the judges," Hurst said. Instead, he turned out pioneering studies of the historical interaction between economic development and law, broadly conceived. His "progeny" dominated the Law and Society Association founded in 1964. Like Hurst, and even more than those in Law and Economics, those in Law and Society viewed themselves as the realists' intellectual heirs.[39]

Yale, which considered itself the fount of legal realism, originally displayed relatively little interest in Law and Society. Bickel sometimes wrote constitutional history, and Robert Stevens taught and wrote legal history and sociology. Other sociologists had not lasted long. Richard Schwartz sat at the head table of the Law and Society Association's first breakfast and became both the first editor of the *Law & Society Review* and the association's third president. With sociologist Jerome Skolnick, Schwartz had been a "kind of a two person team at the Yale Law School" in the late 1950s. Schwartz had enjoyed teaching there. He thought that "the legal Realist approach found a natural home at Yale, and it was alive and well and quite respected when I was there in the '50s." Still, Yale did not offer either a permanent home. By the 1960s, they had both moved on, Schwartz to Northwestern and Skolnick to Berkeley. By decade's end, Yale moved to fill the gap by hiring Trubek, Abel, and Griffiths, three scholars whose work helped to define Law and Society.[40]

The emergence of Law and Society and Law and Economics was just the tip of the iceberg. In the late 1960s and early 1970s, many law professors outside Chicago, Madison, Berkeley, and Denver believed that the love affair the realists had kindled with the social scientists was about to be consummated. The 1969 Association of American Law Schools Program theme was "Contemporary Social Science Research: The Law and the Law Schools." Minnesota's Carl Auerbach was sure, or so he said at the meeting, that "the time will come when no law teacher will be regarded as competent who does not possess some competence in some field of social science." Auerbach urged those who wanted to become academic lawyers to obtain a PhD.[41]

Thus as the Dark Ages ended, the Yale faculty may have felt in danger of eclipse, challenged by both those who sought to make law school less and more intellectual. Perhaps they really did fear, as Goldstein said, that Yale was "at the brink of an educational precipice," but were not so sure as their dean that it was at least twenty years ahead of its competitors. It was not just students of the late 1960s who queried their right to realism and, more generally, the cutting edge, but colleagues elsewhere as well. In this institutional and intellectual setting, the faculty made decisions on six of its junior members.

*   *   *

It seems that the faculty viewed the first victim, John Griffiths, as a walking reminder of the Dark Ages. Griffiths suffered an especially unusual fate when his case was considered during the week leading up to May Day. Pollak had virtually proclaimed that Griffiths was in trouble from the outset with his announcement of the meeting on Griffiths's proposed advancement: "Without meaning to anticipate in detail the thrust of Appointments Committee and Board discussion of John's situation, it is apparent that many people have misgivings about his long-term future here."[42]

Even so, if tenure was not routine, advancement from assistant to associate professor without tenure was. An alumnus of the school and *Yale Law Journal* editor, Griffiths had published two pieces of his own in the *Journal* while still a student, and had one of his final examination essays extracted in the *Journal* by an admiring professor. He had clerked at the Supreme Court for two years—first for Arthur Goldberg, then Abe Fortas—before entering teaching. When Dean Pollak and Guido Calabresi came to Washington to urge him to return to New Haven, Griffiths remembered, "they were quite explicit that Yale only hired people it intended to give tenure to, and in particular that advancement to associate professor after 3 years was automatic." Generally, the candidate needed only to be able to fog a mirror to become an associate law professor at Yale. Now, in 1970, instead of treating promotion to associate professor as guaranteed, the faculty seemed to be changing the rules.[43]

Griffiths probably seemed sympathetic to the students. He had longer hair than his colleagues, and he was married to a member of the class of 1969. Told she was ineligible to take the Connecticut bar examination because she was a Dutch citizen, she took her grievance to the U.S. Supreme Court, which agreed that the prohibition against admission of resident aliens to the state bar violated the Fourteenth Amendment's Equal Protection Clause. Griffiths and his wife were also "rather close to some of the active women students." And during the grading controversy, he had told the entire faculty that "we could fairly be accused, collectively, of hypocrisy, because we invoke basic principle only to ward off proposals coming to us from the outside, of which we happen to disapprove, but almost never does it figure in our own deliberations." Further, he had chided his colleagues for seeming so "hostile to student concerns."[44]

His own concerns went to strategy. As an activist at Berkeley in the early sixties, Griffiths had observed that its administrators "had a genius for getting itself locked into rigid, 'principled' (as they liked to think) positions, which led only to an escalation of protest and ultimately to violence," and he worried that the Yale faculty's strictness and resistance could prove provocative. He supported affirmative action, but as Griffiths remembered it, the younger professors maintained a low profile with respect to internal law school politics. Insofar as they were involved, "we all pretty steadily supported Pollak as Dean. He seemed to me/us the victim of an almost continuous volley of often mean-spirited and even vicious abuse from some members of the senior faculty, most prominently Bickel."[45]

Although the campaigns for shared governance and grade reform did not move Griffiths, Vietnam did: "What took up most of my waking hours when I was not teaching or writing was the war." The Selective Service seminar he established at the law school, possibly the first such course to be taught in any

American law school, created a new field of law. Almost nothing was available to inform those with draft problems about their legal rights. Students in the seminar set out to fill the vacuum by producing articles and creating the body of material that would form the basis for the *Selective Service Law Reporter*. Griffiths also wrote widely distributed pamphlets on the draft law. Because so few people knew anything about the subject, he also did a great deal of advising. He regularly counseled students with draft problems on how to defend themselves and wrote letters for them demanding reconsideration of their status.[46]

Activism paid scholarly dividends. Among the articles Griffiths wrote was an enterprising foray in Law and Society, which he considered the only "source of intellectual excitement" at Yale when he taught there. It grew from the counseling he and seminar members had done prior to the FBI's arrival on campus. At a time when left-of-center Yale students were demonstrating that the Warren Court's decision in *Miranda* — so dear to legal liberals, so repugnant to those certain the Court coddled criminals — had little impact on law enforcement in New Haven, Griffiths and a student coauthor empirically examined whether the intelligent individuals they had urged to say nothing, except on advice of counsel, did so. Warnings, it turned out, did no good. Student suspects routinely waived their right to counsel and spilled their guts.[47]

Griffiths believed that his colleagues, who largely shared his opposition to the war, did not mind his work with students and may even have appreciated it. But he had contended unsuccessfully that the law school should buck "institutional neutrality" to support the moratorium. He also remembered maintaining that former Undersecretary of State Eugene Rostow should be prosecuted as a war criminal, a position that could well have alienated some of his seniors. As a Yale law student himself, Griffiths had admired Dean Rostow for the relaxed manner in which he handled breaches of parietal rules and his dictum that "[o]ne of the most important capacities of a dean is the power of constructive ignorance." And after Rostow returned to Yale from Washington, Griffiths noticed that the former dean "got along well with a lot of the 'revolutionary' students, to whom he could be very gracious, and they admired him in a grudging way (I rather held it against some of my student friends that they had such friendly relations with someone they agreed was a war criminal)." As a faculty member, Griffiths himself had little contact with Rostow, but it was cordial: "His style was that of the gracious great man, treating his inferiors in a slightly jovial, friendly way," and when Griffiths and Rostow differed over the moratorium, he found the former dean "patient and condescending." Inwardly, however, Rostow may have seethed, to the assistant professor's detriment. After the faculty refused Griffiths an advancement, Rostow wrote Goldstein that "I was glad to see John Griffiths has left us. Congratulations." The former dean hoped that Goldstein would prove "able to generate comparable offers" for some of the other "weak" faculty members.[48]

While he proved a successful teacher in seminar, Griffiths was still finding his way in larger classes. Soon after they began teaching, he and John Ely had sent around a memorandum to their fellow professors saying that the Socratic method suited neither their personalities nor subjects. "We know of no suitable alternative, and often feel at a loss as to what we should be trying to offer students, as their teachers." Griffiths did not consider it a declaration of self-doubt, but "simply an expression of reservations about the classic 'Paper Chase' Socratic method" that showed he took teaching seriously. A meeting followed, to which new teachers and experienced experts were invited. "I remember being shocked that only two or three senior people came," said William Felstiner, who wondered whether Yale's tenured professors felt a "conscious or unconscious satisfaction in seeing these junior people flounder about." Whether or not they did, it is difficult to believe that Griffiths was experiencing so much trouble as a teacher to warrant denial of an associate professorship, especially since the record indicates that some students found him excellent in the classroom — and much more sensitive than most of his senior colleagues.[49]

It was easy for Griffiths to mention whatever anxiety he felt about his teaching to Pollak, "a beloved person." The dean asked Griffiths how he was making out at a friendly lunch before his promotion meeting. As Griffiths recalled it, "I made some kind of offhand remark to the effect that I found teaching as I would like to do very hard and had not yet learned how to do it to my own satisfaction. It was a piece of rather open (and as it turned out, naïve) self-criticism." For the closest Griffiths came to learning the reason for his fate was when Pollak subsequently told him that the faculty possessed doubts about his teaching. Griffiths objected that "as far as I knew there were no problems at all with my teaching (meaning of course: problems in the eyes of others than myself)." As he remembered it, the dean responded, "But John you told me yourself you were having difficulties teaching." Griffiths described himself as "dumbfounded." That the dean apparently "saw fit to repeat in a formal proceeding, without any notice to me, something told him in confidence in a private conversation" *and* to engage in "willful misinterpretation" of it seemed to Griffiths "a piece . . . of abject unfairness and disloyalty." And Griffiths was given no opportunity to correct the record. Pollak, a person he had tried to support through tough times, had "unceremoniously dumped me."[50]

Possibly, something else also helped to explain the faculty's decision against Griffiths—its perception of the tone of his scholarship, which professors may have taken personally. The *Yale Law Journal* published two pieces by him in 1970. In one case, the editors bumped the tenure article of a UCLA professor, simply telling him their faculty members had priority. While students at Yale, as elsewhere, routinely gave their professors pride of place in their law reviews, rejecting an already accepted article was surely unusual. Recall, however, that the *Journal* had challenged traditional legal education and professionalism in several issues during 1969–70. Perhaps editors saw the Griffiths pieces as yet another way of "sticking it to" the faculty and/or strengthening his case for advancement.[51]

The critique of Herbert Packer's theory of two models of the criminal process appeared in the January issue. Packer had traced the tension in criminal procedure from arrest to conviction between the "crime control," or inexpensive and efficient "assembly line" model, which privileged the state and public order in the interest of repressing criminal conduct, and the "due process," or "obstacle course" model, which focused on individual rights in the interest of setting limits on state coercion. The goal of Packer, a Stanford law professor, was that of the legal realists—to prove the interrelationship of procedure and substance by demonstrating that the contours of the process reflected underlying value choices, or "the ideology of the criminal law," and had "an important bearing on questions about the wise substantive use of the criminal sanction." Writing in 1964, when the Warren Court's revolution in criminal procedure was underway, Packer had concluded by observing a tension between practice and norm. Though the criminal process "probably" operated according to the Crime Control Model in most cases, he said, the Supreme Court was increasingly demanding the use of the Due Process Model. Given the increasing demands that would impose on the criminal process, Packer recommended legislators respond by limiting the use of the criminal sanction in "consensual offenses in which it is not always easy to say who is being injured by whom," such as drug and alcohol use and gambling. Like other liberals at the time, Packer thought it counterproductive to overcriminalize behavior and try to use law to make people act morally unless a large portion of society actually believed the behavior that the law criminalized was immoral.[52]

According to Griffiths, though, Packer misunderstood both ideology and models. For all "the awesomeness of his claim," the Stanford professor was really just talking about the "Police Perspective" and the "ACLU Perspective." While each of the two perspectives built a different bias into the rules of criminal procedure, "Packer had given us only one 'model'—the Battle Model," which assumed a fundamental "disharmony" between the individual and the state and concentrated on jailing the criminal. Nor was the Warren Court's stress on due process necessarily the solution. Having worked on *In Re Gault*, Fortas's opinion for the Court extending the due process model to juveniles, Griffiths considered it unfortunate, for example, that "when juvenile courts totally failed to live up to their promise," the United States "seemed to have no other answer than to declare them unconstitutional and go back to dealing with kids through an adversarial criminal procedure."[53]

Griffiths recommended an alternative to "The Battle Model." "We can start from an assumption of reconcilable — even mutually supportive interests, a state of love," he contended. He proffered a "Family Model" of the criminal process, based "on our family ideology," that would reconceive "the possible and proper relationship of individual man to the state." It would treat the individual as a member of the social family and reconcile the twin interests of individual and community, much as the nuclear family ideally did. Just as parents punished children to preserve well-being of child and family, so any process involving the state and accused would reflect "the full range of their relationship and the concerns growing out of it." In conclusion, he suggested that "speculation about fundamental change in criminal procedure must begin with the development of ideological self-consciousness and speculation about the possibilities of ideological change." Packer's detached work of scholarship, offering suggestions for reform while keeping the system intact, he implied, only revealed the extent to which the author was a product of the prevailing consciousness.[54]

Professors may have believed that Packer was not the author's only target. To senior faculty members raised on Daniel Bell's definition of ideology as "a freezing of opinion" and "the conversion of ideas into social levers" meant to "tap emotion," the very word "ideology" was dirty. They may have thought that Griffiths had tarnished the legal liberalism that *Gault*, the call to reconsider the punishment of victimless crimes, and their own work embodied. He had identified it as an ideology.[55]

Yet while his "deconstructionist" style would be associated with Critical Legal Studies later, Griffiths was always "uncomfortable" with the intimation that his article represented proto–Critical Legal Studies scholarship. He had no use for Critical Legal Studies, finding it "philosophically trivial [and] politically vapid." He was not "trying to unmask or to 'trash' anyone, nor was it any part of my purpose to expose 'liberal legalism'" in his writing about Packer, he maintained. He simply wanted to explore how scholars thought about criminal procedure and suggest new possibilities for its conceptualization. Indeed, Griffiths thought that Bickel and Bork disliked his support for the Warren Court's judicial activism and held it against him.[56]

But regardless of whether they perceived his article as a critique of legal liberalism, Griffiths had nevertheless attacked a sacred cow. Packer himself admitted that his work was "somewhat old-fashioned," drawing as it did "on law, on philosophy, on economics, and on some of the behavioral sciences." As he acknowledged, "Scholars today are supposed to stick closer to their lasts than what was expected of them in the days when we knew less, but knew about it more." His empiricism was of the armchair variety, borrowing bits and pieces from other disciplines to chip away at existing doctrine. Packer's goal, like that of earlier realists, was to "use" the findings of other disciplines to call for reform in legal rules and the legal system. By the late 1960s, those in Law and Society and Law and Economics were increasingly burrowing into one field of knowledge, borrowing its methodology to view legal rules and institutions as sociological and economic phenomena. Yet the Packer essay was the kind of scholarship Abe Goldstein and Bickel wanted more of—"thought" articles that drew on doctrinal analysis, while going beyond it, and Goldstein would also have appreciated its realist tilt.[57]

Goldstein and Bickel had made that apparent when Packer published it in 1964. Bickel said that "he knew of nothing else that so opens a trail for showing the relevance of procedural matters to the purpose, meaning and function of criminal law." According to Goldstein, while "competition between the two positions has been so persistent and so influential that it demanded explanation in terms transcending particular cases," few had previously been available. The Yale professor speculated that was "probably because of our commitment to a common law tradition" that Goldstein considered "antitheoretical and open-ended, built up case by case." What Packer had done, he said, was to situate criminal law as part of the political process. "This is in sharp variance from conventional writing in criminal law which, even to this day, slavishly depends upon recent cases as the organizing focus of its inquiry." Goldstein considered the article "an essential step in the attempt to treat law as a social science."[58]

But if the Packer piece did indeed represent valued scholarship, it would have seemed that Griffiths's article belonged in that genre as well. It too went beyond both case analysis and critique to recommend that third model, and it too possessed policy implications. Nevertheless, it had attacked a piece of work a majority of the faculty had long considered exemplary in the process. Consequently, faculty reaction to the "Third Model" varied. Charles Reich told Bickel that "John has written an article that is truly great—maybe the most brilliant and original law review article in twenty years." Reich rejoiced in its boldness: "What kind of work will our other young men do if we tell them now not to take chances?" he asked Wellington. As Reich saw it, the Griffiths case involved "the future of the school . . . in the most profound sense." But Griffiths remembered Abe Goldstein saying "with a sort of pained sorrow, 'John, why didn't you show it to me first, before you published it? I could have helped you to improve it.'" Perhaps Goldstein hoped to help a young scholar make his argument even more compelling by suggesting where to temper it. But Griffiths doubted that. He believed he and his senior colleague were "intellectually way too far apart" and dismissed the remark as a telling reflection on Goldstein's insistence on being treated as the senior scholar in the criminal law field. That Griffiths was "not properly subservient," that he preferred talking with Joe Goldstein to Abe Goldstein about criminal law, "was never a subject of explicit complaint, but the latent tension was always there." [59]

Six months after the "Third Model" article appeared, and at the invitation of the *Yale Law Journal*, Griffiths would again take to the pages of the *Journal* to publish a review of Packer's book, *The Limits of the Criminal Sanction*, which included a lightly edited version of "Two Models." The review opened with the charge that Packer had produced a "very disappointing book, . . . very, very bad indeed," "thoroughly defective in logical structure," and sporting an argument that "fails at almost every critical point." Griffiths made his opinion of the author's interdisciplinary pretensions clear too, alleging that "Packer proceeds, in the lawyer's habitual fashion, as if anthropology and sociology, political theory and psychology, even history and philosophy and theology, barely existed." In sum, here was "more lawyerish jurisprudence-as-usual," rather than what was "desperately needed, . . . the sort of radically new conceptualizations and theoretical formulations which can only come by taking basic intellectual risks and from opening the mind to fundamentally new ways of comprehending the phenomena of criminal law." Nor did Griffiths think much of Packer's "timid" proposed reforms and conclusions. As Griffiths himself said later, the essay "begins like a sledge-hammer." Though he still thought the review right, he understood how its introduction might have seemed "'blunt,' 'frontal,' 'undiplomatic,' 'uncourteous,' 'aggressive,' or even 'juvenile.'" He remembered Friedrich Kessler's reaction to the piece— "'John, just remember: fortiter in res, suaviter in modo'"—but thought "I was too young to take it to heart." The remainder of the review more soberly, but vigorously, took apart the portions of Packer's book Griffiths had not already discussed in the prior *Journal* article. [60]

Griffiths made trouble for himself by picking on Packer. Despite the fact that Packer had coauthored the Carnegie Commission report calling for the two-year law school, he was popular on the faculty. Some of Gene's boys had a long relationship with the Stanford professor, a Yale Law School alumnus who was Abe Goldstein's classmate. Indeed, the debate over Packer's appointment in the mid-1960s foreshadowed the fight over the Griffiths case. The Goldsteins and Bickel had enthusiastically favored the candidate, speaking glowingly of "Two Models of the Criminal Process." Emerson and Reich, the only two to vote against him, opposed him and that article, in particular, as "pedestrian" and unimaginative. Emerson was certain "we would do better to hire John Griffiths and give him the opportunity to teach criminal law." Packer had turned the offer down, but he remained in close touch with the "hardliners" at Yale Law School, which he thought became "something of an educational shambles" during the late sixties. As a member of the University Council Committee on the Law School, Packer had advised Brewster "to cram Goldstein down the throats of the dissidents on the faculty, and to accept with equanimity the loss of some few of them."[61]

Did some view Griffiths more negatively because of his critique of Packer? Almost certainly. In 1968, Bickel had said that "John Griffiths is the New Left incarnate but he is very, very bright, and it is practically impossible to hire young men with ability without coming upon the New Left incarnate every so often." That was wrong. Though some obviously associated him with radical students, Griffiths lacked interest in the New Left and characterized himself as an "old-fashioned socialist of the Debs variety." But Bickel's remark did indicate a positive assessment of Griffiths's intelligence, from which he seemed to retreat later. When Packer learned of the review, which must have circulated in manuscript prior to publication, Bickel told his friend that he was not surprised that "my young colleague's piece puzzles you. It is all blast and no content. Of course, he doesn't lay a glove on you; there is no glove."[62]

As that suggested, Packer told Bickel, Abe Goldstein, and others of his unhappiness with the Griffiths corpus. To Packer, the two separate pieces Griffiths had published about his work were one. According to the Stanford professor, Griffiths had devoted "the major portion of his scholarly career to date to a total of about 160 pages (accompanied by almost 400 footnotes) trying to discredit my book," in a tone that was "belligerently bludgeoning and personal although I have never met the man." To make matters still worse for Griffiths, as Stanford's vice provost, Packer had suffered a massive stroke the previous year, which he publicly blamed on student radicals, whom he likened to Nazis,

and which ultimately led to his suicide. Some Yale professors may have believed, Wellington acknowledged, that Griffiths had inflicted unnecessary pain
on someone who had suffered enough already.[63]

The files include few of the letters and memoranda about the case that circulated before the Governing Board meeting about Griffiths. Apparently, the Appointments Committee split, with a majority voting against the advancement.
The cursory board minutes indicate nothing about the discussion at the meeting. Abe Goldstein, who participated in the Appointments Committee's deliberations about Griffiths beforehand and who reported to the committee on his
teaching, said at the time that the committee had focused, at least in part, on
that. A contemporary letter from Pollak to one Griffiths supporter challenging
his "petulant attack" on the Appointments Committee's "conscientiousness"
and "competency" suggests the case was contentious. Clyde Summers recalled
the meeting about the case as "outrageous."[64]

That was the recollection of Charles Reich, who championed Griffiths. Reich
thought the day of the long Governing Board meeting about Griffiths "the
worst single day of my career at Yale Law School." Advancement to associate
professor should have been pro forma, he emphasized. Instead, the candidate's
opponents "turned into a lynch mob. . . . They just couldn't stand this guy."
Reich never again felt the same way about the board's standards, procedures, or
objectivity. "The hostility toward John was palpable in this room," he recalled.
Governing board members "were terribly angry at him for what he had written
about Packer," and Reich remembered that his colleagues reported on gossip
that Griffiths had labeled Rostow a war criminal. To Reich, the atmosphere was
at once "personal" and "profoundly political." His colleagues perceived Packer
"as one of their own, and an attack on Herb was like an attack on them." Nor
did he think Griffiths's teaching weighed significantly in the decision: "Lots
of people weren't good teachers. Did that make him special? No way." Reich
thought his colleagues were sending him a message too. As he understood it:
"There was a little bit of patronage on the part of the Governing Board." Reich
had made it clear he cared about the promotion of Griffiths, "without question
the most brilliant student that I ever encountered in all my years of teaching,"
just as McDougal and Wellington would have made it apparent that their protégés' promotions mattered to them. "This was my turn to be accommodated,"
Reich said, "and one of the lessons I drew from that was that I would not be
accommodated the way the others were accommodated."[65]

Nor was Griffiths. The board voted against advancing Griffiths from assistant to associate professor by a vote of 17–16. He could stay at Yale for the time

being, but only if he accepted the stigma of doing so as an assistant professor who had been passed over for advancement.[66]

Instead, Griffiths went to Ghana for two years on a Fulbright. Returning to the United States, he accepted an offer from NYU instead of going back to Yale. For personal and professional reasons, he then moved to the University of Groningen, where he concentrated on the sociology of law, became head of his department, dean of the faculty, and published a significant body of scholarship in several languages.[67]

Griffiths may have fallen victim to the Yale faculty's association of him with the Dark Ages–New Left style because of his take-no-prisoners tone. Ely maintained that "the only proposition on whose basis I think [the Griffiths decision] even remotely justifiable, [is] that poor teaching should disqualify an otherwise qualified man," particularly, he continued, since he considered the Packer review "excellent even though there is room to disagree over the article." But at the time, Ely and others sounded uncertain that teaching was the basis for the decision. Albert remembered hearing the senior faculty characterize Griffiths as "a bright guy who would not grow up." Reich largely attributed the decision to personal animus and the Packer pieces. As Griffiths saw it, the factors that explained his fate were his "anti-war activities (Rostow, McDougal, etc.), judicial activism (Bickel, Bork, etc.), insufficient deference to one's seniors (A. Goldstein), the 'Packer'-factor (various people), identification with obstreperous students (various people), [and] identification with social science (various people)."[68]

The untenured considered the decision bizarre, joking darkly that they would be safer if they published nothing. They closed ranks for an instant: Abel remembered submitting a petition to the faculty claiming that whatever one thought of the Packer review it should not disqualify Griffiths for advancement. It was an unusual act for them, and the document may have helped to reinforce the senior faculty's view that juniors lacked "standards." The decision about Griffiths set the stage for the housecleaning that was to follow.[69]

*   *   *

What of the other five cases, which involved decisions about tenure? That the minutes of the Governing Board meetings have not survived or are cursory renders reconstruction difficult.[70] What sort of intellectual or ideological "politics," if any, did the cases involve? Had the faculty placed the individuals and their work on a political continuum, the spectrum would have ranged from Hudec (slightly to the right of the faculty's liberal mainstream) to Albert (mainstream) to Simon, Trubek, and Abel (slightly to the left). The two candidates furthest to the left, Trubek and Abel, also produced the least traditional, most antidoctrinal, and most interdisciplinary scholarship.

Hudec was considered the most conservative of the five. He had graduated first in his class at the law school, served as editor-in-chief of the *Law Journal*, and clerked for Justice Potter Stewart. Though he had worked with Tom Emerson to introduce the new grading system, he had sided with Bork in the Clay case. Hudec, whose field was international trade law, had written more than enough—two book reviews, two articles on GATT, and a book on GATT in manuscript. His work did not take the Lasswell-McDougal approach to international law and reflected the rise of Law and Society, stressing the significance of politics, culture, and environment in understanding the way members of the international trade community structured law and policies. His research was also empirical: among other things, he had gathered a comprehensive set of GATT disputes. But some on the faculty believed that a professor elsewhere had preempted Hudec's work on GATT, and some found his scholarship pedestrian. Hudec himself considered his case "a tenure decision and nothing more." He landed at Minnesota, then at the Fletcher School, and wrote six books and nearly forty articles or monographs on international trade. By the time of his death, he had become a legendary figure in international trade law.[71]

After hearing about Hudec, Richard Abel became anxious about his own future and those of other junior faculty members. He persuaded his remaining peers to meet "to talk about our prospects collectively," he remembered. "They were so anxious not to be associated with each other that they left the meeting individually and we never met again. We hung separately, although we would have hung had we stuck together."[72]

That became more apparent when the faculty took up the case of Lee Albert, who had graduated first in his class, written an article with Harry Wellington as a student, been editor-in-chief of the *Journal*, and clerked for Justice White. After his year at the Court, Albert lectured at the London School of Economics and worked as poverty lawyer at Edward Sparer's Center on Social Welfare Policy and Law before returning to New Haven to teach poverty law and other subjects. Not everyone proved positive about his appointment. Though some senior faculty members, such as Wellington, thought Albert "absolutely first-rate," others questioned his imagination as editor-in-chief. Still others may have found him difficult personally. Some poverty lawyers associated with the center had been "put off by his faintly superior manner and the unnerving British accent that the Jersey City–raised Albert acquired during his year in

London." Of course, a British accent probably played well at Yale Law School. Even if it did, though, Albert had difficulties readjusting to New Haven and recalled experiencing "some frightful early years" as a young law professor. Among other things, "I was once severely chastised by Abe [Goldstein] for going to Austria for a month at the end of my first sabbatical. Real scholars do not ski while seeking tenure." The surviving evaluations, for what they are worth, do not suggest that he was one of the more popular teachers.[73]

He began to publish in his third year. Albert's most important work was a doctrinal article on standing to challenge administrative action. With Larry Simon, he also coauthored an article respectfully contending that Bickel got it wrong when he said that the Special Prosecutor lacked the authority to sue President Nixon, and Bickel and Calabresi particularly admired Albert's parts of the piece. Even so, Albert said, "my problem was a reality that could not measure up to exceedingly high expectations." He understood the faculty's attitude toward his case as sorrowful: "We had high hopes for Lee, and they didn't materialize." He recalled, too, being "told by several of Gene's boys . . . that my tenure article was rather well liked, but could not overcome the negativism arising from poor social interactions over the years." The other message was that his teaching "lacked nuances." As Albert heard it, Dean Goldstein proved "decisive in my case."[74]

There may have been a Dark Ages aspect to this decision too. Though Albert had not been active politically, Guido Calabresi maintained that there was good reason for his delay in publishing. In recommending his younger colleague for a position at Buffalo that Albert accepted, Calabresi praised the productivity Albert had shown after he had taught for a few years. "Lee, like most of the others who came into teaching at Yale when he did, was severely scarred by the commotion in universities five years or so ago," he explained. "In some the commotion caused unpleasant behavior of various sorts; in Lee it caused self-doubts which delayed his development as a scholar and teacher." Calabresi just wished "one could wipe out" those years of Albert's and other junior faculty members "from the minds of some of my colleagues."[75]

Simon had greatly impressed his professors during his days as a Yale law student, when he had been Note and Comment Editor to the *Yale Law Journal*. One of his papers on the development of compulsory public education had been deemed publishable. Another won the coveted Peres Prize for the best student work appearing in that year's *Yale Law Journal*. After graduation, Simon had clerked for a distinguished district court judge, Edward Weinfeld, and then Earl Warren.[76]

Arriving back at Yale Law School to teach in 1968, Simon had plunged into matters involving race and education. Though he was not involved in the faculty-student conflict, he had much to do with bolstering the law school's reputation with African American and white student activists and the black community of New Haven. He served on a task force that developed a plan for ensuring community control of the schools. He became director of Yale's Summer High School, an Upward Bound program designed to give underprivileged students of color an intensive summer precollegiate experience. Simon, who had traveled around the country to hand-select its 120-odd students, thought Summer High "probably the best thing I've ever done" and pointed with pride to its roster of distinguished instructors. But like participating in redesigning public education, running Summer High took time. His senior colleagues encouraged him to take on such obligations. "Though my stance on race was pretty strong, I wasn't picketing," he stressed. He was "helping the law school with what I did."[77]

Simon was a popular member of the law school community. He was among the few younger professors to be found in the faculty lounge schmoozing with his colleagues, who had ample chance to see his mind at work and who thought about law much as he did. He spoke well and in the way his seniors prized— "in a lively, indeed refreshing fashion," one of them reported. Calabresi maintained that of the six young faculty members, Simon, one of his particular protégés, possessed one of the two most interestingly quirky minds. Simon was a dedicated and well-liked teacher too. He had developed his own teaching materials for his courses on education law and urban law because no casebooks existed. He had also organized an experimental and egalitarian seminar, in response to student demand, on the topic of teaching legal concepts in secondary schools, and had then supervised those law students who wanted to teach law in area high schools. Thanks to the seminar, he had secured something rare among professors, favorable front-page notice in the *Advocate*.[78]

A perfectionist, Simon tended to put his manuscripts "in the drawer" on completion, instead of publishing them. His tenure piece, focusing on which legally permissible systems of school financing were politically viable, fell squarely within the liberal realist tradition. Many thought it excellent, but along with a smaller companion piece, it did not appear until the eleventh hour. Some also remember that Simon had said he did not intend to publish anything again. Simon himself denied ever having made any such remark. As he said, it would have been strategically "stupid," and he planned to remain an active scholar. In fact, apparently all he had done—at least in writing— was to say he wanted to shift his scholarly focus from school finance to urban law. But whatever his plans, like Albert, Simon had given the faculty relatively little published work, relative to most others in his cohort, and there was doubt about his trajectory.[79]

His case therefore seems as if it should have been among the easiest to turn down. Yet oddly, it turned out to be the hardest for the faculty. Simon almost made it. He was in England on leave when a senior colleague wrote "to say how much I regret that our screwed-up Gov. Board failed (by 1 vote) to assemble the necessary ⅔; to say that you ought to know that you had strong support from a wide section of the faculty; to add that the abstaining members (which unfortunately count as no votes) were heavily, perhaps exclusively concerned, not with the quality of your work, which none disparaged and most (or all?) admired, but with their concern about your predisposition to become a published scholar—a subject on which they say they want somewhat more evidence, or something like that."[80]

Simon was angry too. "I felt they broke the deal," he recalled. As he saw it, everyone knew his *Journal* article was very good, and he worked in the community and Yale College at his colleagues' urging. Surely they understood he had less time to publish. Perhaps they did, for they characterized their action to him as a postponement, rather than a negative decision. After the votes were counted, the Governing Board "decided to take no further action" on Simon's case, leaving "open the question whether the matter might be reconsidered next year," and Goldstein offered him a two-year contract. But given his hesitation about publishing what he had written, Simon wondered whether he could satisfy his colleagues in two years, particularly after Bickel told him that Simon must now produce "big-think" constitutional law work. Here, again, was the emphasis on macroperspective. When he received an excellent offer from USC, Simon took it.[81]

David Trubek had also served as Note and Comment Editor of the *Yale Law Journal*. After graduation, he had clerked for the dean of the realists, Judge Charles E. Clark. The two coauthored one of the early challenges to the legal process school. They maintained that in rejecting the realists' focus on the idiosyncratic nature of judging, Harvard theorists were promoting "a new mythology of the judicial process to replace the myth destroyed by the Realists." They were pursuing "illusive certainty" and providing ammunition for political conservatives' reaction against legal liberalism and legal realism, Trubek and Clark charged. Trubek then worked as attorney advisor in the Office of the General Counsel of the Agency for International Development, legal advisor to the US AID Mission to Brazil, and acting director of the Brazil Mission's Office of Housing and Urban Development. The AID experience, where he facilitated the work of development experts at work on the expansion of Latin

America's infrastructure, inspired his and others' effort to "export American legal culture" and the rule of law. The Brazilian legal system did not stimulate growth. The easy solution, or so it seemed, was "to reeducate Third World lawyers, who — we felt — had failed to understand the mix of pragmatic instrumentalism and liberal idealism that had been the staple of our legal education. By exporting the educational techniques of the American law school — socratic method, social science, and all — we would strengthen legal institutions just as AID agricultural technicians were transforming small yellow eggs into large, white ones." But despite their efforts, the results proved "disappointing": Third World lawyers rejected the education and message that law should become both more "instrumental" and "liberal."[82]

In returning to Yale, Trubek sought to combine research on law and the Third World with a teaching career. The school brought him back to join the faculty in 1967 because it wanted work in housing and the nascent field of law and development. Though untenured, he moved into "a big, fancy house" in New Haven after he inherited money. There was a precedent, since Ronald Dworkin had also bought a large, elegant house in New Haven before he had tenure. Still, some may have considered Trubek's pre-tenure purchase presumptuous. As Pollak said, the house might not have helped him, though he would not have been turned down because of it. His colleagues might also have envied the money Trubek had to dispense professionally. He had control over a large grant from AID, negotiated by Robert Stevens, and Trubek thought some resented the power it gave an assistant professor.[83]

Trubek used the grant to develop a Law and Modernization Program that worked to reconceptualize law so that it would become "amenable to study by the social sciences," train young scholars in the sociology of law, bring well-known senior sociologists to Yale for lengthy visits, and teach students to research law's role in the modernization of developing countries. As Trubek envisioned it, Law and Modernization would unite with the program in Law and Sociology, funded by the Russell Sage Foundation, and administered by his colleague, Stanton Wheeler, to become "a broad center for legal sociology" and create "a genuinely comparative sociology of law." With Wheeler, Trubek made an impressive start toward making Yale an eminent center of Law and Society.[84]

Trubek remembered that his efforts were "initially strongly supported by the faculty, especially Abe." Because Trubek saw his brand of Law and Society scholarship as rooted in legal realism, Yale seemed an excellent place for him. And for awhile, it apparently was. In addition to Trubek and Abel, many of the leading names in Law and Society spent some time in New Haven in the late 1960s and early 1970s—William Felstiner, Richard Lempert, Laura Nader, Boaventura Santos, Barbara Yngvesson. Still, the work was difficult. As Trubek once said, "It was not easy to get people to stop thinking about law as command, rule, or doctrine and start thinking about it as system, symbol and behavior," and it was especially difficult in a law school, even one with Yale's reputation. Even in the 1930s, there had been a certain timidity about the Yale realists that led them to flirt with curricular innovation *and* to draw back from their sharpest insights. Gradually, Trubek decided that "the 'law and society idea' and legal education as then practiced were incompatible."[85]

Having reached this conclusion, he went to Goldstein to tell him of "the need for a truly independent center or department of legal studies" that could concentrate on sociolegal scholarship. "The Dean of Yale Law School, known as a champion of social science in law, rejected this idea out-of-hand," he wrote bitterly years later. That left Trubek with a program that he complained to the Ford Foundation was "constantly fighting marginality." Ford agreed that "in spite of its 'surface' strength the 'Law and Modernization' program is rather diffuse and unfocused, and somewhat marginalized at Yale." As Trubek saw it, "we were both threatening and marginal, and we were marginalized in part because we were threatening." The program may have come to constitute one strike against him. The time he spent administering it gave him less time for scholarship too.[86]

Still, Trubek had produced two big articles about legal theory, one on Weber's theory of the role of law in the rise of capitalism, the other on Law and Development thought. The two were interrelated. Trubek maintained that Weber's work provided the means for helping "contemporary scholars continue the task he himself was engaged in: the analysis of the role of law in the rise of capitalism." It would also encourage them to think in terms of exporting something beside "Western experience" to the Third World. There were two coauthored pieces too—an essay examining income group clustering in residential housing and a book to which Trubek had contributed an important section on law, planning, and the development of the Brazilian capital market.[87]

The work suggested that Trubek was becoming a critic of legal liberalism, or what he and others were already beginning to call "liberal legalism." As AID attorney, director of the Law and Modernization Program, and Law and Development scholar, Trubek had provided American and Third World policymakers alike with the "liberal legalist model of law in development" that treated law as an effective tool of social change. "That this view rested on a rosy picture of the role of law in America and involved misguided notions of the institutions and historical forces operating in Asia, Africa and Latin America there can be no doubt," he contended almost as soon as he left Yale in a *cri de coeur* entitled "Scholars in Self-Estrangement," which sought to redirect Law and Development in a more scholarly and less missionary direction. "Nor is there any question that its hope for liberal change in the Third World was excessively optimistic, and that its belief that U.S. foreign policymakers and Third World leaders were really committed to their rhetoric was naïve." Still, Trubek credited liberal legalists with behaving "honestly and unreflectively: liberal legalism may have been ingenuous, but it was not insincere."[88]

His presence at Yale helped to radicalize others less inclined to view legal liberalism sympathetically. In addition to acting as a midwife to Law and Society, Trubek's program served as incubator for Critical Legal Studies. According to Mark Tushnet, "the outlines of what became Critical Legal Studies were sketched" in a Law and Modernization reading group in which he, Duncan Kennedy, other left students, Abel, and Trubek discovered the radical roots of legal realism, the realists' original attention to the indeterminacy of legal rules, and the New Dealers' cooptation of realism and social science as policy-making aids. And, Tushnet maintained, "even a fairly intellectual association with fairly intellectual student radicals" did Trubek "no good in the eyes of the senior faculty," which had taken "on the air of a beleaguered garrison, defending the ramparts at all costs against the assaults of the barbarians. Those who suggested even in the mildest way that the students might be on to something were politically unreliable." No evaluations of Trubek's teaching have survived, but no one criticized it in interviews, and like Larry Simon's teaching, it won favorable notice from the *Advocate*. Perhaps that was one kiss of death. At the very least, John Schlegel maintained, Trubek's teaching and scholarship would have seemed "anti-establishment."[89]

Certainly Trubek felt the strain of his location between students and faculty. As he said, later, his critique of legal liberalism was evident in his scholarship. "The events at Yale and the behavior of the senior faculty had made me question what liberal legalism was becoming. As the faculty moved to the right, I sought to continue what I thought was the liberal ideal and the tradition of legal realism." Intellectually, that pushed him closer to students like Kennedy and Tushnet. Where grade reform, governance, affirmative action, and the other institutional issues that divided faculty from students were concerned, Trubek also considered himself "caught between" students with whom he often sympathized and the faculty. Though he worked to be an "active but low-key seeker for the middle ground," he recalled, "I found there was no middle ground!"[90]

Trubek never received any indication that he was in trouble before his col-leagues decided against promoting him. Like Griffiths, he had joined the fac-ulty believing "all that was required to get tenure was to write a couple of articles and wait a few years." Abe Goldstein suggested that the external evalua-tions of Trubek's work were not glowing. The fact that professors departed from routine to seek them may have indicated he was in poor shape. Because Law and Society scholarship was new at Yale, the faculty may have held his work to a higher standard, although ironically, the school had long touted its receptiveness to interdisciplinarity. According to some, there was also doubt about whether Trubek "really had the marbles" to be a Yale law professor.[91]

Trubek landed on his feet. He went to Wisconsin and became internation-ally known as one of the founders of Law and Society. A quarter of a century later, the Harvard law faculty voted him a tenured professorship.[92]

He saw himself and other members of his cohort as the victims of a gen-eration gap and their interest in curricular innovation. As he remembered it, though junior faculty members supported the students to varying degrees, most did so more than tenured professors, who proved "incredibly hostile toward the students." In his view, he and his peers were "caught in a tremen-dous culture clash" between old and young. Unable to "fire the students," he theorized, senior faculty members got rid of their juniors.[93]

That was also the view of Richard Abel. He was unique among those let go. During this period, Yale—or Calabresi, who did most of the hiring—largely aped Harvard by hiring the "best" of its own recent graduates, who had served as law journal officers and held prestigious clerkships, while requiring its best and brightest to write more for promotion. Some on the faculty thought that the Appointments Committee's adherence to such unimaginative criteria ex-plained the law school's later disappointment with most of its junior faculty.[94]

Abel, however, had not gone to Yale. As a Columbia law student, he had be-come rapidly "dissatisfied with what seemed an unduly narrow focus on legal doctrine." At the same time, he became interested in anthropologists' analy-sis of traditional African legal systems. As a graduate student, he focused on law and development. His field research explored "the interrelationship of tra-ditional and received legal institutions in the context of a developing nation." Though his work was far outside the doctrinal mainstream, the faculty had known that when it hired him. Pollak had told Woodbridge Hall of "a letter of acceptance from a junior man of whom we expect very good things: he is Richard L. Abel, who graduated from Columbia Law School a couple of years ago at the top of his class. He is getting his doctorate in African Studies at

London, and is headed for Kenya this year, to find out at first hand about customary law." Yale social scientists who worked in related areas outside the law school had "warmly endorsed our invitation."[95]

At Yale, Abel taught traditional and theoretical courses. Like Trubek, he came to believe that "we sorely lacked adequate theories about law in society." Consequently, Abel broadened his research and teaching fields to include comparative legal sociology, as well as African law. At the same time, he developed a case of intellectual schizophrenia. He became frustrated while teaching Torts. "I could not simply divide my scholarly life into a traditional approach to American law, and a non-traditional approach to legal phenomena elsewhere; yet I was unable to devise an approach to Torts that went beyond legal rules," he explained. Though Abel realized he could follow Calabresi, he knew "little economics and could not possibly master that discipline while remaining minimally competent in anthropology, sociology, and African studies as well." Thus he began to consider the impact of tort law on relationships between individuals: with the Panther trials looming in the spring of 1970, for example, his advanced Torts course focused in large part on police-citizen relations. He also decided to teach and write about the family. To prepare, he took a partial leave of absence halfway through his appointment so that he could work with New Haven Legal Assistance. He then turned his attention to the family and the state in his own work and began offering family law courses "with a strong clinical component." A quarter-century later, some recalled Abel was viewed as a poor teacher. But the contemporary record suggests that could not have been the case. At the time, though in a letter recommending him for a job elsewhere, to be sure, Calabresi characterized him as "extremely successful" in small classes, "good" in Torts and Family Law, while suggesting that he was "unresponsive in areas in which he does not see the link with his writing interests. In this he is no different from most of us, though perhaps he is a bit more unbending and unwilling to ham than some of us, on the whole wrongly, are."[96]

At Yale, he produced lots of work. As his vote approached, the Governing Board was warned that since Abel's "writings are quite extensive, an early start in reading is advisable." One big article maintained that the literature on customary law was "so lifeless" because so few of the ethnographic accounts that provided its foundation contained description of cases, and it advanced an alternative approach to fieldwork. Another synthesized the literature of dispute institutions in different societies and set out a new theory of the dispute process. There was also a long review essay of a book by Max Rheinstein, which his colleagues may have viewed as a critique of them. Abel took that distinguished scholar to task for unselfconsciously imposing his values on the project. He alleged that Rheinstein lacked understanding of social science research method. And he concluded that the book was "plagued by the perennial dilemma of interdisciplinary research: in its attempt to satisfy the standards of two disciplines, it fails to satisfy either, and risks being disowned by both."[97]

Abel's critique of traditional legal scholarship was all the more devastating because his authorial voice was not snide. He thought, however, that some might have compared it to the Griffiths review of Packer. According to a senior colleague, "undoubtedly his attack on Rheinstein was what caused a violent reaction against him." Though it was not disrespectful, he was highly critical of an émigré scholar many Yale law professors admired.[98]

Abel challenged his colleagues in other ways too. He consistently and strongly sided with the students during the late 1960s. He voted with Griffiths in favor of the moratorium and against—or so his colleagues would have viewed it—institutional neutrality. He objected to the "secret meeting" at Pollak's house. He dressed more casually than other professors. He lived differently too—in "graduate student crummy" rentals that were a far cry from the elegant houses of senior faculty members. He seemed a loner. As he later acknowledged, he taught his classes and left instead of communing with his colleagues the Yale way—over lunch and in the faculty lounge. In part, it was because he wanted to help his wife with infant care. But in addition, "I felt a profound sense of alienation from the senior faculty: I didn't dress like them (and didn't want to) [and] couldn't entertain like them." His apparent disaffection probably annoyed some. Members of the Governing Board remembered that Goldstein, as one put it, had taken a "scunner," or dislike, to Abel.[99]

Abel's case did not even make it out of committee. No Governing Board vote was ever taken.[100] It seems odd that Simon, with his relatively slim publication record, came within one vote of tenure, but there was not even a faculty vote on Abel.

Junior faculty members were expected to remain on good terms with their seniors, who could help place them, when they did not receive tenure. Abel remembered passing one of them outside the law school and saying nothing. Immediately, he felt a sinister and unfriendly hand on his shoulder. "Don't snub me, I can make or break you," he recalled Abe Goldstein warning him. Abel did leave Yale without challenging the faculty's decision "because he had been told that if he left quietly he could tell prospective employers that he had just decided to leave Yale on his own" prior to a tenure decision. He went to UCLA, where he continued to produce a great deal, became editor of the *Law and Society Review*, and president of the Law and Society Association. He thought the firing of so many in his generation was "calculated to appease the faction of the faculty who felt that 1960s attitudes and styles were threatening the school's quality." [101]

*   *   *

How do we judge the faculty's decisions? If we do so by the individuals' subsequent careers, it would appear at the very least that the failure to promote Griffiths, Abel, Trubek, and perhaps Hudec were mistakes. But such decisions themselves shape people's careers. Some denied promotions may be so scarred they write little; some may produce more and better work out of a desire to prove themselves; some may be unaffected.

In the end, the cases point up the difficulty of determining exactly what Yale law professors' standards for promotion were. Why did the faculty consider Abel's case so hopeless that a vote seemed fruitless? Why did Griffiths fail to receive a routine advancement? Why did Simon come the closest to receiving tenure? Did "Gene's boys" perceive him and his work as being most like them and theirs? Did the cases of Griffiths and Abel, considered with Simon's, suggest that what the faculty wanted most was work that reinforced its own? Did Trubek's case, in conjunction with Simon's, indicate that, no matter what senior professors said, publications were less important than the collective judgment that a candidate had "the marbles"? Are the decisions on Griffiths, Abel, and Trubek best viewed as hangovers of the generational wars of the 1960s? Certainly, the faculty's actions with respect to Griffiths and Abel seem particularly strange.

As Calabresi had said of Albert, in a way, the sixties played a role in all the cases. Calabresi had a stake in that interpretation, since he had played so important a part in hiring the six. As he saw it, the times scarred some "extraordinarily promising" young academics and prevented them from teaching or writing to their fullest potential. "The fact was that it was an extremely hard time for anyone to accomplish anything." As a consequence, the students of the late 1960s could see that Abel and Griffiths, at least, were in trouble. That was just one reason Duncan Kennedy would turn down the Yale position he was offered. Did their elders' involvement with the students leave them unable to mentor junior faculty? Probably not. Neither Griffiths nor Abel wanted advice, and Abel was "sure the seniors would have mentored us if we had asked. We didn't. Was it the times? Or our personalities?" [102]

Nevertheless, as they reaffirmed their own status in the face of student challenges, seniors may have come to seem forbiddingly arrogant to juniors. Larry Simon remembered a joke that the main difference between the permanent faculty at Yale and its less productive Harvard counterpart was that Yale professors assumed themselves, by virtue of their appointments, "the smartest people in the universe" and acted accordingly, while those at Harvard believed the school must have made a mistake in their own cases and behaved accordingly. And the strife of the sixties may have left the senior faculty with little patience for the handholding useful in fighting perfectionism or ending writer's block. Lee Albert, for example, believed that "[t]he unforgivable sin is to say something foolish in writing" and that "the instant pressures on young scholars to produce flawless and scintillating work are so great that they often have an inhibiting effect." Simon agreed that the atmosphere was "intimidating" and "debilitating." More generally, senior professors may have been too busy preserving the school they loved to devote much thought to juniors, other than Griffiths, until it was too late.[103]

Then, too, once calm descended anew, Abe Goldstein hoped to return to what he perceived as the realist agenda. But Griffiths, Trubek, and Abel, at least, wanted to redefine it. They stressed the importance of going beyond empirical speculation, for one example, and paying greater attention to legal consciousness for another. They explicitly questioned the work of scholars with whom the senior faculty members identified. They challenged the work Goldstein wanted done, questioning his intellectual authority, just as the students of the sixties questioned his authority. It may have been easier for Goldstein and his colleagues to conclude juniors' work was unworthy or took realism in an unpromising direction than to accept the challenge. Perhaps, at least partially as a consequence, Law and Economics became part of business as usual at Yale, while more progressive legal scholarship, such as Law and Society, did not.

*   *   *

There were other changes in the faculty roster. Goldstein, who was more obviously managerial than his predecessor, had proven pivotal in all these decisions. Where some, such as Calabresi, would have given members of the group "a pass" because of the period, Goldstein "was less willing than most of us would have been to say if they didn't accomplish that much it wasn't their fault, and they'll do better later," Calabresi believed. "Whether it was their fault or not, he never knew or cared." So, too, Goldstein took the lead in securing two resignations. Charles Reich thought he and Ronald Dworkin were both victims of the dean's firm hand and "no-nonsense approach."[104]

Though Dworkin had maintained a low profile at the law school during the late 1960s, he remained a valued member, offering *Law Journal* editors and other worthies an invitational seminar in his master's lodgings at Trumbull

College. There, he worked out the ideas for what would become his seminal book, *Taking Rights Seriously*. In 1969, he was offered H. L. A. Hart's chair at Oxford. Dworkin accepted the position, returning periodically to New Haven to offer seminars. Within two years, Yale thought he could be lured back and extended him an offer. As Goldstein and the Appointments Committee explained it to the Governing Board, Dworkin's acceptance of it in 1972 indicated a willingness to become a Professor at Yale by the fall of 1974, or earlier; to act as Lecturer in Law for an extended visit annually in the interim; "that he promptly inform Oxford University of his resignation and acceptance of our offer"; and "that he inform us promptly of his resignation so that we may make an immediate public announcement."[105]

And indeed Goldstein publicly announced that Dworkin would "return to the law school by the fall of 1974." But beyond that, all was confusion. "Some thought I had a commitment to come back," Dworkin said. But after her initial reluctance to move to England, his wife discovered that she loved teaching at the London School of Economics. Meanwhile, Dworkin continued to receive offers from other institutions that would enable him to divide his time between the United States and England. Charles Reich thought Dworkin's British accent and his obvious wealth irked Goldstein, but that his continued absence grated even more. "He's not here, he's not on the ground, and not treating us with the respect we need," Reich remembered Goldstein complaining. Other faculty members recalled that when the dean heard that Dworkin had not yet resigned from Oxford, word quickly circulated that Goldstein had sent him a telegram questioning Dworkin's status and plans. The notion was that "he had somehow taken the faculty." After "developments" were reviewed, the Governing Board "voted that the arrangement with Mr. Dworkin should be terminated and that the invitation as a visiting lecturer in the spring of 1974 should be withdrawn."[106]

Reich himself wanted a leave of absence. He had long guarded his own secret: he was gay. "I had promised myself that when *The Greening of America* was finished, I would give full priority to looking after my own life," and in the aftermath of a six-month leave spent in San Francisco, he decided to do just that. Since he knew the process of coming out would take time, he went to Goldstein, told the dean he had personal business he could put off no longer, and asked for a two-year leave of absence. Reich had always appreciated the dean's unpretentiousness, and the two had a good relationship. But he thought that now that *Greening* had made him a celebrity, Goldstein saw him as another "dropout" from the law school, a characterization Reich admitted had "some truth to it." So Goldstein turned Reich down, refusing to bring the matter to the faculty or to take it to Woodbridge Hall. Reich resigned, citing the new plethora of "practical-minded" law students who "do not look to law school for speculative thinking about society and social institutions" as a reason. Nevertheless, he wanted to stay. "He could have made provision for Dworkin and me, had he thought either of us was a person to retain," Reich said of Goldstein. "I would have spent the rest of my life at Yale once I had gone through this process. Instead of that, he was very anxious to get rid of us both." [107]

John Ely went to Harvard. Yale tried to entice him back in 1978, but he declined, saying that although he preferred its law school to Harvard's, he favored Cambridge and Boston over New Haven. Some speculated that the fate of his friends on the junior faculty, or what Ely referred to as Yale's "siege of not promoting anybody for a decade or so," might have also played a role in his decision. [108]

The University of Pennsylvania Law School sensed opportunity. Since everyone in the legal academy knew of Yale's troubles during the sixties, Penn's dean gambled he could successfully raid the faculty. Penn went after Pollak, who thought some part of himself might have felt "rejected" by his colleagues' treatment during his deanship. Pollak accepted its offer. So did Clyde Summers. [109]

The faculty lost its far left and right, such as they were, too. Thomas Emerson retired. Robert Bork went to Washington to become Nixon's Solicitor General.

A wave of retirements and a death increased the gaps. Bickel's demise in 1974, when he was only 49, deprived the faculty of one of its best-known members and a moving force in the "collegium." And between 1970 and 1976, the last six professors with ties to the 1930s realists resigned. [110]

Goldstein began the process of filling the holes. He brought Grant Gilmore back and added Burke Marshall to his faculty lineup. He recruited three heavyweights: Bruce Ackerman, Geoffrey Hazard, and Owen Fiss. The dean increased Yale's depth in Law and Economics by hiring Alvin Klevorick and Robert Clark, two lawyers with PhDs. Further, Yale acquired a greater presence in legal history during Goldstein's deanship with the appointments of Robert Cover and William E. Nelson, another lawyer with a PhD. Goldstein also hired the school's first African American faculty member, John Baker, and its second woman, Barbara Underwood. [111]

The spate of hiring and firing may have wearied Goldstein. Yale's law school deans traditionally served two five-year terms. But just as ten years was too long in the divisive atmosphere of the late 1960s, so it was in the early 1970s. Goldstein informed Brewster in 1973 that he wanted to leave the deanship in June 1974.[112]

Why he ultimately agreed to stay on another year is unclear. Perhaps he did so out of loyalty to Yale. The old problem of the differences between myth and reality had again reared its head. As the AALS accreditation team reported, "Ironically, for some students the law school experience suffers in let-down from expectation: Yale's reputation, the renown of its faculty, the quality and size of its student body, apparently lead some of them to expect an intimate community of scholars engaged jointly in quiet contemplation and exploration of verities." But both the nature of Yale and the demands of lawyer training meant that like their counterparts "at other, larger major law schools," Yale students "are impelled to take the same 'bread and butter' courses (in largish classes), to focus on the eventual bar exam and on subjects they think they might need in the practice of law." Further, the school needed money. Among Goldstein's achievements was launching a fund-raising campaign at the end of his deanship in honor of the law school's sesquicentennial that ultimately raised over $15 million.[113]

Summing up his deanship, Goldstein sounded satisfied. In his view, "we got the Law School moving again." Some credited him with eradicating the sixties. At the farewell dinner celebrating the Goldstein deanship, a guest recalled, one of the speakers credited Goldstein with "saving the law school and used the term 'dark ages.' Pollak was not there and went unmentioned." But perhaps because the dean had tired of the term's notoriety, "the first words out of Goldstein's mouth when he got up to speak were that it was silly to talk about 'the dark ages.'" Nevertheless, as Goldstein wrote in his last dean's report, he had taken office after a period in which "[w]e had come through so much and been so hard on one another as we met one new crisis after another." He had sought to "develop again a sense of stability and intellectual purpose," while trying to make "faculty and students to feel good about being here." Now, Goldstein said, they did. The school, he stressed, was "not troubled by important internal divisions among faculty or students. The mood is collaborative and congenial in the best sense."[114]

*   *   *

Dean's reports, of course, are famously upbeat. In October 1974, the *Yale Daily News* had reported that the law school was "frantically searching" for a new dean. The article's author complained that her editors had misleadingly rewritten it to make the situation sound "urgent or emotionally charged." Frantic

Harry Wellington. (Courtesy Yale Law School Public Affairs Office.)

or not, the hunt was under way. According to the *News*, one front-runner was Guido Calabresi, but some "find Calabresi highly egotistical and question his ability to work on a committee." The other leading candidate, Harry Wellington, the faculty's second choice in 1970, was also an insider.[115]

The selection process provided one indication of student attitudes. Protest had not evaporated at Yale Law School, just as it had not disappeared elsewhere.[116] Students continued to sit on committees and insist on the need for change. The ferment persisted, though at Yale, the activists who followed generally seemed less interested in institutional governance issues than their predecessors.

They were also quieter. Thus the *News* reported that Calabresi had recently entered his classroom to find "the huge message, 'NOT GUIDO!' scrawled across the wall." Though the sign was reminiscent of the 1960s, one administrator remarked that next to the sort of denunciation that would have appeared "a few years back," it was "mild." Further, Calabresi found a new message when he entered the room the next day: "Viva Guido!"[117]

Compared to Otis Cochran, Black Law Students Union Chair Michael Darnall also sounded mild when he warned Brewster that the two most often heard criticisms of the law school were that "Yale is losing its 'big gun' faculty members faster than it can replace them, and, even more disturbing, Yale Law School has lost its sense of 'National Mission.'" To Darnall, it seemed that after the "serious convulsions" of the 1960s, the law school was "seeking solace in the Ostrich hole." He pleaded with Brewster to choose a dean interested in increasing the number of minority faculty members and students. But whereas once the BLSU would have made threats, Darnall used metaphor, stressing that "the Ostrich must come out of its hole and face life again" and begging Brewster to choose a dean "willing to commit the school to constructive *change*."[118]

With the students less aggressive, the deanship selection process could easily follow the recent pattern. Once again, there was no "significant faculty support" for an outsider. Once again, students wanted an outsider, preferably a white woman and/or minority, and definitely someone "capable of and likely to attract new and outstanding faculty to remedy the gradual diminution of quality experienced over the past few years." And once again, Yale's president, while soliciting student opinion, did not treat it as dispositive as he considered Wellington and Calabresi.[119]

Even here, the past left its mark. Since there was the usual faculty unease about Brewster's role in the process, Calabresi tried to smoke him out. He did not want to become dean at the time, Calabresi recalled, but he was unsure how Yale's president felt about Wellington. And given Brewster's role in Pollak's selection, Calabresi worried that if he withdrew his name and the president did not choose Wellington, a crisis might ensue. Should he take his name out of the running so that the faculty could put forward the names of a second individual ready to accept the deanship? In that event, Brewster would have more options *and* be foreclosed from selecting a dean his law professors might not want. When Calabresi asked for a meeting with Brewster to talk the matter over, the president received him at breakfast, clad in "a magnificent dressing gown." Calabresi relayed his concerns and indicated that if Brewster had any doubts about Wellington, he would withdraw early so the faculty could nominate another person, but that he himself was happy with Wellington's candidacy. "He listened and stood up to his full height" and majestically declared, "'Guido you have nothing to worry about,'" recalled Calabresi with a laugh. Brewster, who would soon leave Yale to become ambassador to England, picked Wellington, the faculty's first choice.[120]

Wellington faced a tough challenge. "If there was any determination in the first year of my deanship," he recalled, it was to fight "the perception, not reality—i.e., the public perception that earlier the faculty had declined to promote a number of folks and the uninformed assumption that, therefore, Yale was in decline."[121] As the new dean worked to improve his school's image, sixties ghosts continued to linger.

Chapter Nine

The Most Theoretical and Academically Oriented Law School in America

In 1965, Yale law professors had confidently embraced legal liberalism. It rested on the legal realism that had made their school famous; made room for prudentialism, Bickel's refinement of process theory; allied itself to the political liberalism of Lyndon Johnson's Great Society; and underlay the judicial activism of the Warren Court. Fifteen years later, legal liberalism was in shambles, a casualty of a reaction against the sixties. Rejecting both the Warren Court and events at the law school, Bickel moved toward neoconservatism. Sixties liberals lost the Court as it began turning right, along with former Warren Court fans who turned left to Critical Legal Studies. As Wellington rebuilt the faculty during his deanship, Yale law professors developed a new legal liberalism, forged out of a revived legal process theory and sanitized realism. They also embraced interdisciplinarity, a gesture at once cautious and strategic. The revised legal liberalism represented a response to all the forces that jeopardized the old one. It sought, further, to steer between the "law is politics" emphasis of Critical Legal Studies and the focus on efficiency evident in Chicago-style Law and Economics, while preaching a constriction of the more conservative Supreme Court's power.

RIGHT TURN

Some former sixties liberals at Yale turned right, rejecting the moral zeal they associated with student activists and reasserting the need for rationalism. Eugene Rostow's ideological journey led him to become head of the Arms Control and Disarmament Agency during the Reagan administration. Though he left no public explanation for it, Leon Lipson was convinced that "[t]he

interplay of the attacks on the universities and the attacks on United States foreign policy" during the 1960s "strained Rostow's robust democratism, overcame his robust Democratism, and moved him (on principle and interest?) to
support Republican national tickets." That seems plausible. Rostow's own later
work described Mayday as a scene of "mass hysteria," noting pointedly that
the "contagious fevers" had infected some on the other side of "the generation gap. Otherwise serious scholars wondered whether it is wise or moral to
try men duly charged with murder, and whether possible error on the part of
a judge warranted burning a few buildings." He insisted that "our society—as
a society of consent—should not and indeed cannot acknowledge a right of
civil disobedience; that the moral and philosophical arguments advanced in
support of such a right are in error; and that the analogies invoked in its behalf
are inapplicable."[1]

But it was Bickel whose shift received the most attention at Yale, perhaps because of his prominence in both legal and political liberalism. He would use his
1969 Holmes lectures at Harvard, whose delivery was delayed "because Harvard blew up," to turn his back publicly on the Warren Court and demonstrate
his "rank apostasy" to the legal liberalism that had operated in tandem with
LBJ's liberalism. Reporting on Bickel's disenchantment in the *New York Times*,
Anthony Lewis wrote: "To the evident shock of his audience, he argued that
on the two greatest issues which it dealt with—schools and voting—the Court
misread the American future."[2]

In the published version, Bickel abandoned the nuanced legal liberalism he
had endorsed in *The Least Dangerous Branch*, apparently casting his lot with
those who criticized Warren and the majority for "erratic subjectivity of judgment, for analytical laxness, for what amounts to intellectual incoherence in
many opinions, and for imagining too much history." But Bickel, who had once
celebrated the Court for its development of "principled goals" when society
needed them most, did not just rail against Warren Court opinions as poorly
reasoned, but because "I have come to doubt in many instances the Court's capacity to develop 'durable principles,' and to doubt, therefore, that judicial supremacy can work and is tolerable in broad areas of social policy." Bickel conceded, however, that "the Justices of the Warren Court placed their own bet on
the future, even as their more analytical and scientific progenitors, who were
Mr. [Henry M.] Hart's teachers [i.e., Felix Frankfurter], also did. If the bet pays
off, whatever their analytical failings, the Justices will have won everything—
for the moment, at any rate." Bickel concluded, in fact, "It would be intellectual megalomania not to concede that the Warren Court, like Marshall's, may

for a time have been an institution seized of a great vision, that it may have glimpsed the future and gained it."[3]

On occasion, he still made liberals proud. In 1971, he would acquire his first experience as a litigator by representing the *New York Times* when it defied the Nixon administration by publishing portions of the classified "Pentagon Papers" that provided a history of American involvement in Vietnam. Nixon had already signaled interest in the idea of putting Bickel, "a Frankfurter-type," on the Court, and the professor received a message that taking the case would mean forfeiting his chance for appointment. Nevertheless, he helped win it. "Last year, you were that mean-minded reactionary intellectual, who disliked Negroes and had other traits of bad character; whereas now you have become a yeoman of civil liberties and the banana (if not actually the apple) of every liberal eye," one sardonic friend wrote him. But the 1960s had left a scar. Though he challenged Nixon on the First Amendment, Bickel had largely left liberalism behind.[4]

That became still clearer in his last book, *The Morality of Consent*, which he finished just a week before his death. There, he embraced the Whig tradition and the conservatism of Edmund Burke, which he insisted "belongs to the liberal tradition." Burkean thought, as Bickel interpreted it, was "flexible, pragmatic, slow-moving, highly political," moderate, and relativistic. It viewed life largely in "prudential" as opposed to "moral" terms, valuing continuity more than change. Here was a philosophy that understood consent lay at the basis of a stable government, Bickel stressed. "Use of the enforcement machinery of the legal order denotes the point at which it has broken down; the test of a legal order is its self-executing capacity, its moral authority." Bickel justified some forms of civil disobedience and stressed the Court's duty to guarantee First Amendment rights. But he pointed out that the American press had been freer before he won the Pentagon Papers case than afterward, since "law can never make us as secure as we are when we do not need it. Those freedoms which are neither challenged nor defined are most secure." And that meant that there was little room for absolute moral imperatives in law. More accurately, "the highest morality almost always is the morality of process." For the morality of process ensured a result to which the members of society had consented, and Bickel remained a pluralist.[5]

Among other recent events, the Warren Court's decisions, the student left, and Watergate all showed what could happen when law and morality became intertwined, Bickel maintained. The Court had displayed a tendency "to dictate answers to social and sometimes economic problems" without permitting

American democracy to decide its own course for itself. *Roe* v. *Wade*, in which the Warren Court's successors had undertaken to dispose of the abortion issue by imposing what might be "a wise model statute" with no justification, was only the logical outgrowth of Warren Court opinions. So, he said, was Watergate. During the late 1960s, the Court's "assault" on the legal order from within had been joined by one from without waged by left students. Like the white Southerners who resisted the Warren Court, and the civil rights activists who engaged in civil disobedience, "the white middle-class movement against the Vietnam war" and the "radical Left" stepped over the boundaries of moral authority that the legal order relied on to retain its strength. Watergate replicated "the transgressions." The end result, according to Bickel, was that "[t]he derogators of procedure and of technicalities, . . . the armies of conscience and ideology . . . rode high." And democracy had become an end in itself. His tough words for the Warren Court's decisions expanding the right to vote might have been written about Yale law students: "It became irresistible dogma that no qualification for voting made any sense. It did not matter that you were a transient — and wherever the election catches you, you vote with no questions asked."[6]

Campus unrest, especially, he seemed to say, had demonstrated that the "self-righteousness and ideological fixation" linked to authoritarianism threatened consent. Bickel reported that when Kingman Brewster asked him and others to discuss "What is happening to morality today?" in 1969, he had answered: "It threatens to engulf us." Consciously rejecting the values associated with the sixties, Bickel declared his certainty that students' authoritarian, "assaultative speech that amounts to almost physical aggression" jeopardized the democracy they claimed to celebrate. "If the streets belong to the people, they are going to belong to all the people, not just the radicals." Liberal toleration of a zealous left had constituted another threat to the university. Bickel scorned "guilt-ridden and otherwise disoriented liberals" who had tried "to appease the revolutionaries," taking upon themselves the duty of fulfilling "the function of cardinal legate to the barbarians, going without the walls every so often to negotiate the sack of the city." They had legitimated students' actions: "Where nothing is unspeakable, nothing is undoable." Holmes might have said that the test of an idea was its power to win acceptance in the marketplace, but those who followed knew that sometimes the wrong notions won. As he had in the 1960s, Bickel maintained that "a marketplace without rules of civil discourse is no marketplace of ideas, but a bullring."[7]

The intellectual's task, he concluded, was to preserve the institutional neutrality of the university and to save society from "counter-revolution." In the last chapter, Bickel provided a reprise of his and Yale's behavior during May Day, this time with no defense of Brewster. Throughout the period, "we," Yale's adults, had legitimated "verbal violence" by treating it respectfully. The older generation had been in error, and its other concessions were mistaken too. "However embarrassingly unfashionable it may be to insist on power and privilege, inroads on the autonomy of faculties are inroads on academic freedom; the abandonment of any faculty control over appointments, curriculum, and academic standards is the abandonment of the ends of the university."[8]

So, too, Bickel now said publicly that universities supporting affirmative action had submitted "to pressures simply to relax standards. This political concession is wrong." At the time Bickel was preparing *The Morality of Consent*, he had just put the finishing touches on his brief for the Anti-Defamation League in *De Funis* v. *Odegaard*, the first case involving university affirmative action programs to reach the Supreme Court. He replayed his argument on the basis of De Funis, a magna cum laude white Jewish college graduate denied admission to the University of Washington Law School, who charged that the minority admissions program had allowed other applicants in ahead of him because of their race. "To reject an applicant who meets established, realistic and unchanged qualifications in favor of a less qualified candidate is morally wrong, . . . practically disastrous," and bore a suspicious resemblance to the quotas historically used to keep out Jews, Bickel charged both in the brief and again in *The Morality of Consent*. The criterion for admissions must always be "merit," and not racial or ethnic origin. A generation of Americans had been taught that discrimination was unconstitutional, illegal, immoral, antidemocratic, and just plain wrong. "Now this is to be unlearned and we are told that this is not a matter of fundamental principle but only a matter of whose ox is gored."[9]

Plenty of other intellectuals joined Bickel in rejecting liberalism. Some, many of them Jewish, took a new name for themselves that became synonymous with "former liberal": "neoconservative." Affirmative action proved their particular bête noir. At the invitation of the dean of admissions, and "in a low-keyed and non-provocative style," neoconservative Norman Podhoretz had outlined his stance in the early 1970s for the Harvard College admissions office. "As a liberal I believed in the traditional principle of treating individuals as individuals and not as members of a group; as a Jew, I feared that a quota system designed to overcome discrimination against blacks would almost certainly result in discrimination against Jews — and I could not bring myself to believe that the only way to achieve social justice in the United States was to discriminate against my own children; and as an intellectual, I worried about the lowering and erosion of standards entailed by any system of reverse discrimination," he recalled. His audience was having none of it. When he finished, "the questions were so charged with hatred that I found myself wondering whether even a public reading from *Mein Kampf* could have elicited greater outrage. Almost everyone who took the antiquota position in those days had similar tales to tell." By 1972, Jewish intellectuals had formed the Committee on Academic Nondiscrimination and Integrity in opposition to what Nathan Glazer termed "affirmative discrimination."[10]

Bickel became a charter member of this set. Two other former liberals at Yale Law School, Joseph Bishop and Eugene Rostow, also became key members of CANI. Though Bishop's work was rife with excoriations of the "pall of Morality [that] hangs over the campus like smog over Los Angeles," he did not explain what had led him to oppose affirmative action. Nor, at least explicitly, did Bickel.[11]

Soon after *The Morality of Consent* was finished, however, Robert Bork put an end to the mystery. He described "the university tumult of the 60s," which he characterized as "a miniature French Revolution, a 'chaos of levity and ferocity,' in Burke's phrase," as a "precipitating factor" in explaining Bickel's move right. "Alex was astonished and outraged, not merely with students prepared, in a spasm of mindless self-righteousness, to destroy institutions it had taken generations or even centuries to build, but even more with those faculty members who, at the first obscenity or classroom disruption, instantly abandoned the ideal of rationality," he said.[12]

As Ethan Bronner observed, "Bork was writing also of himself." Bork never became a neoconservative; he had never been a liberal. As a libertarian, however, he had sometimes come to results liberals liked. He had saluted *Griswold* v. *Connecticut* in 1968 and announced "that new basic rights could be derived logically by finding and extrapolating a more general principle of individual autonomy underlying the particular guarantees of the Bill of Rights." Rejecting libertarianism in the aftermath of the sixties, Bork now moved toward a conservativism he too considered Burkean. He pronounced his earlier view wholly mistaken, criticizing *Griswold* as "an unprincipled decision" that "fails every test of neutrality" and was "typical" of the Warren Court. Bork now relegated the judiciary to applying statutes fairly and according constitutional protection only to political speech.[13]

ESTRANGEMENT

Unlike Bickel, Bork, and Rostow, most of their colleagues kept the faith. During the darkest periods of the late 1960s on campus, they still had the Court. For twenty years, legal liberals had remained under its spell, their faith in it at once religious and mystical. But the Warren Court was itself a casualty of the sixties. When Warren retired, Richard Nixon signaled his desire to roll back its work. Still, for some time after Warren left the Court in 1969, some had hoped that legal liberalism would retain its vitality. The early Burger Court reassured legal liberals by handing down *Roe* v. *Wade* and the gender discrimination cases. The ruling that the death penalty, as then administered in the United States, was unconstitutional also came as welcome news.[14]

But academics sighed with relief, not satisfaction. The apex of legal liberalism could not be *Roe* v. *Wade*, which officially revived the despised legal doctrine of substantive due process used by the turn-of-the-century Court to strike down progressive legislation. For after *Roe*, the "classic example of judicial usurpation and fiat without reason," Bickel's counter-majoritarian difficulty cast even more of a shadow on the Warren Court.[15]

Was *Roe* the logical outcome of counter-majoritarianism? Had those process theorists, such as Bickel's mentor, Felix Frankfurter, who had warned that the Court that allegedly acted as a "superlegislature" when conservatives controlled it should not become a " 'superlegislature' for our crowd" and who placed more of a premium on the ideal of judicial objectivity, been right? The reappearance of substantive due process as a tool of judicial authority when liberal legal scholars were defending the Warren Court from the charge it represented realism run amok *and* were trying to stave off conservative judicial activism threatened the Warren Court's legitimacy. To academics at the time, *Roe* made the Court seem anti-democratic, idiosyncratic, and unconstrained.[16]

At least *Roe* turned out all right substantively. After blasting the Court for its opinion, John Hart Ely conceded, with Bickel: "Were I a legislator, I would vote for a statute very much like the one the Court ends up drafting."[17] But would liberals who lived by the sword of judicial activism during the heady days of the Warren Court now die by it? What else did the Nixon appointees plan?

In fact, notwithstanding *Roe*, it was becoming increasingly clear that the Court did not embrace the liberal agenda. When the Supreme Court refused to hold wealth a suspect classification in 1973 and refused to enlist in the fight against white flight by routinely ordering busing between the suburbs and inner city the following year, some liberals began to doubt that the Court shared their politics. For Owen Fiss, the 1976 decisions in *Rizzo* v. *Goode*, setting aside lower court orders directed at ending the Philadelphia police force's harassment of African Americans, and *Washington* v. *Davis*, maintaining that those alleging equal protection clause violations in school segregation cases must prove intent to segregate, were the last straw. For others, it was the Court's invalidation of the congressional attempt to bring state employees within federal wage-and-hour standards the following year. Some liberals, including the dissenting Justice Brennan, viewed the majority's decision in *National League of Cities* v. *Usery* as "a step back to the pre–New Deal era in which the Court routinely found reasons to limit the exercise of Congress' commerce power." The editors of the *Yale Law Journal* thought so too. They dedicated their symposium on *National League of Citizens* to Brennan, saying that "we have entered a new era in the history of the Supreme Court and a new jurisprudence is ascendant."[18]

In the mid-1970s, Owen Fiss remembered later, law professors became estranged from the Court. "Warren Burger is a violent man," his colleague, Robert Cover, said. Legal scholars lost historically their most important audience, the judges they hoped to win. Watergate only deepened the despair. Popular politics turned conservative, making courts potentially more important to liberals as instruments of social justice. But Chief Justice Burger was challenging those "young people who go into the law primarily on the theory that they can change the world by litigation in the courts" *and* blaming the law schools for lawyer incompetence, while Justice Rehnquist was attacking the Warren Court's notion of "a living constitution" as "a formula for an end run around popular government." Once the Court was peopled by individuals who might not necessarily pursue the Warren Court's politics, legal realism made it seem more dangerous to sixties reformers. The new justices might not identify themselves with legal realism and liberalism in the way that William O. Douglas and Abe Fortas had done, but might nevertheless have absorbed its lessons. Realism's stress on the idiosyncratic nature of judging might provide political conservatives with a license to harness law to the free market championed by Chicago lawyer-economists and overturn the Warren Court's decisions. Behind that fear lurked the anxiety that realism's account of the nature of the judicial process made rational and constrained decision making impossible.[19]

Critical Legal Studies popularized the view that realism meant indeterminacy. And while its roots lay in New Haven, Yale demonstrated little enthusiasm for the movement. In addition to viewing CLS as warmed-over legal realism and a threat to legal liberalism, Yale professors may have viewed it as an outgrowth of the Dark Ages.

With Law and Economics, CLS proved one of the two most significant jurisprudential developments of the second half of the 1970s and the early and mid-1980s, just as Law and Economics and Law and Society had been the two most important movements of the early 1970s. Like Law and Economics, CLS rejected process theory.

The sixties had undercut the liberal consensus and the assumption of growth that underlay process theory. As American economic woes made "limits" the new buzz word, the preeminent intellectual biographers of Henry Hart and Albert Sacks explained, "our legal culture came to emphasize scarcity, and the concern with limited resources rendered controversies that involved civil rights and fair resource allocation even more intense." Thus many law professors who followed Hart, Sacks, and "Gene's boys" branded "the optimistic legal process baselines 'out of touch with reality.'" Like process theorists, Chicago-style Law and Economics scholars on the right did start with the "desire of human society to maximize the collective satisfaction of its members" and concentrate on the contribution legal rules might make toward achieving that goal with efficiency. But lawyer-economists "reasoned from assumptions of a 'static pie' and were greatly more skeptical of state regulation." On the left, scholars contended that process theory "rested on the complacent, simplistic assumption that American society consisted of happy, private actors maximizing their valid human wants while sharing their profound belief in institutional competencies." Either way, professors had little use for what John Griffiths, writing in the late 1970s, after his departure from Yale, referred to as the "philosophical Pollyannaism and conservative complacency of the Legal Process School." Sacks had become Harvard's chief administrator, but his intellectual authority had come under attack. "In the more cynical, conflictual world of the 1970s, the halls of Harvard Law School during Sacks's tenure as dean echoed with faculty announcements that 'legal process is dead.'"[20]

Critical Legal Studies could not have happened without Harvard. Its faculty demonstrated little interest in Law and Society, but made a place for Critical Legal Studies in the 1970s, just as Harvard and Yale made a place for Law and Economics. Three key figures of CLS—Duncan Kennedy, Morton Horwitz, and Roberto Unger—were tenured professors at Harvard by 1977; their students, foot soldiers in the movement.

Harvard virtually invited the reaction against process theory from the left. Many of its older great names had made their reputations as teachers and authors of treatises. "One of the problems of a law school dean is to find faculty members who *produce*," Erwin Griswold explained. Even though their legal process materials had transformed legal thought, for example, Hart and Sacks had never published them, though Griswold repeatedly begged them to do so. That was a shame, since the materials, like some treatises, represented exemplary scholarship. Even so, Griswold's successor, Derek Bok, wanted his professors to write more for other academics. "When I was hired," Kennedy recalled, "I was interviewed by then-Dean Derek Bok who told me that he and several of his cronies thought the point of the new hirings was to change the school and make it more oriented to scholarship." [21]

Critical Legal Studies could not have happened without Yale, either. The sixties and New Haven had provided the movement's seed ground. Kennedy characterized Critical Legal scholars as "a rag-tag band of leftover '60s people and young people with nostalgia for the great events" of the 1960s. Many had met at Yale. Consider the composition of the first CLS organizing committee in 1976. Of the nine members—Abel, Trubek, Kennedy, Rand Rosenblatt, Mark Tushnet, Roberto Unger, Thomas Heller, Morton Horwitz, and Stewart Macaulay—seven possessed ties to the Yale of the sixties. Kennedy and Rosenblatt were members of the class of 1970, Tushnet of the class of 1971; Abel and Trubek had taught at Yale; Unger had a connection to Trubek's Law and Modernization Program; and after graduating from Yale in 1968, Heller had been a fellow in the program. Indeed, the presence of the Yale contingent may help to explain why Critical Legal Studies in its early years often sounded so much like the Kennedy of "How the Yale Law School Fails." [22]

Yale figured in the movement's genesis in another way. Even more ostentatiously than Law and Society, CLS advocates deliberately rooted it in what Yale law professors considered the most important recent jurisprudential movement, the legal realism of the late 1920s and 1930s. CLS was "best understood as an extension and development of American legal realism," Kennedy contended. [23]

Like the realists, Critical Legal scholars contended that "law varies according to time and place, and that this historical and social contingency applies to legal reasoning, legal rules, and governmental and social institutions." Even so, they insisted—again, echoing the realists—that law was forever "manipulable and indeterminate — principles as always being balanced by counter principles, policy arguments as meeting counter-policy arguments, and so on." Indeterminacy did not make prediction of legal consequences impossible, though opponents of CLS often acted as if it did. But indeterminacy did foreclose the possibility of "settled" rationalizations for those outcomes.[24]

The realist pedigree in place, Critical Legal scholars turned things on their heads. Where legal realism had long possessed a close interrelationship with legal liberalism, CLS attacked "liberal legalism." Karl Klare provided its classic definition. Liberal legalism underlay capitalist societies and was marked by "the commitment to general 'democratically' promulgated rules, the equal treatment of all citizens before the law, and the radical separation of morals, politics and personality from judicial action." It reached back to Hobbes, Locke, and Hume and derived its "metaphysical underpinnings" from their work — "the notion that values are subjective and derive from personal desire, and that therefore ethical discourse is conducted profitably only in instrumental terms; the view that society is an artificial aggregation of autonomous individuals; the separation in political philosophy between public and private interest, between state and civil society; and a commitment to a formal or procedural rather than a substantive conception of justice."[25]

Here was a categorization with rhetorical power. For starters, liberal legalism enveloped sixties liberals and seventies conservatives alike, drawing in, as it did, everyone from "Helms to Tsongas, Larry Byrd to Lady Bird." It encompassed Law and Economics, process theory, legal liberalism, and the Warren Court, whether the decisions of Warren and Company were seen as hymns to procedural justice that pleased legal process scholars, or paeans to individual rights and liberties that delighted legal realists and legal liberals alike.[26]

In fact, the Warren Court decisions came in for special criticism. As students at Yale during the late 1960s, the young had sometimes grumbled about the Warren Court, but largely joined their teachers in glorifying it. Ever-mindful of status and caste, they had, of course, sought positions there while criticizing the liberal professors who embodied its values. A 1969 Advocate story, headlined "We Get 7 Supreme Court Clerks," revealed that Yale law school alumni had received 35 percent of the Court's clerkships for the upcoming term. A decade later, one scholar had observed in Telos: "Contemporary left-wing critics of American institutions either ignore the Supreme Court, or accept the liberal view of it. That view, particularly as applied to the Court during Warren's Chief Justiceship (1953–1969), is that the Court was benign, that it acted as a counterweight to oppressive measures of the 'political' branches, that it did not participate in 'cold war' policies, that its major decisions had nothing to do with economic developments, and that its influence has been highly 'progressive.'"[27]

Now the reaction came. Historians remember the tension between liberalism and the left during the 1960s, but the left legal scholarship of the 1970s was more profoundly anti-liberal. Critical Legal scholars claimed that Warren Court decisions offered the underclass large promise and little protection. The Warren Court had directed attention from collective action by encouraging individuals to view themselves "as isolated rights-bearers ('I got my rights') rather than as interdependent members of a community." According to CLS: "Rights are indeterminate, rights limit our imaginations, rights inhibit political and social change." The emphasis on individual rights favored procedure over substance, legitimated power arrangements, and served as a pressure valve permitting injustice. The Warren Court's liberalism thus prevented transformative social change by perpetuating the dichotomy between individual and community. That was just one example of the false dualities that plagued what Roberto Unger called the "hocus-pocus" of liberalism. The list was endless: public/private, subjective/objective, order/freedom, reason/will, rules/standards, form/substance, individualism/altruism, individual/community.[28]

And all its components were linked. Just as he was about to receive tenure at Harvard in 1976, Duncan Kennedy showed this in "Form and Substance in Private Law Adjudication." Simply by virtue of its appearance in the *Harvard Law Review*, "Form and Substance" suggested Critical Legal scholars wanted to assault the citadel even as they sought to become part of it. Lest anyone miss that, the text made it clear by explicitly challenging Hart and Sacks in its second paragraph, one of Kennedy's missions since his days as a Yale law student. Kennedy maintained that "the arguments lawyers use are relatively few in number and highly stereotyped." Consequently, law could not be determinate. Since legal arguments were applied to infinite, diverse fact situations, the shoe that fit did not do so "because it was designed for the wearer." Further, as the realists had said, "each pro argument" possessed "a con twin." Kennedy undercut process theorists who worked "to restore the prestige of law by vindicating its claim to autonomy from politics" after the realists. As he said, there was nothing new about his conclusion that law was "policy." What was original was his demonstration of "an orderliness to debates about 'policy'" once the claim to law's neutrality had been abandoned.[29]

In American private law, Kennedy maintained, just "two opposed rhetorical modes for dealing with substantive issues" competed. They were individualism, "the ethic of self-reliance," and communitarian altruism, "that of sacrifice and sharing." So, too, two opposed forms provided legal solutions for the substantive issues, the "formally realizable rule" and the "standard or principle or policy." The individualist gravitated toward applying the rule; the altruist toward the standard, which "requires the judge both to discover the facts of a particular situation and to assess them in terms of the purposes or social values embodied in the standard." But to leave it there, Kennedy said, would miss "a deeper level of contradiction" within both the individualist and the altruist. "At this deeper level, we are divided, among ourselves and also within ourselves, between irreconcilable visions of humanity and society, and between radically different aspirations for our common future."[30]

In the most famous of all CLS passages, Kennedy articulated the existence of an intense and pervasive "fundamental contradiction" between the individual and the community: "[R]elations with others are both necessary to and incompatible with our freedom." To quote Unger, "Thrown back and forth between these two manners of organizing their lives and of viewing their places in society, men are unable to arrive at a coherent definition of self." Enter law, Kennedy and Unger contended. It functioned as a process that hid or disguised the fundamental contradiction between individual and community.[31]

That law thus operated provided further proof it was neither neutral nor objective. All law, private and public, was ideological, "politics, all the way down." Morton Horwitz's sweeping 1977 reexamination of American history, *The Transformation of American Law*, maintained that there had been a "Machiavellian" conspiracy between merchant and entrepreneurial groups and the legal profession to help themselves by actively promoting "a legal redistribution of wealth against the weakest groups in society." That rankled. It had been one thing for realists to indict late-nineteenth-century judges with class-biased rulemaking. It was another to carry "the charge back to the early nineteenth century, the period that common lawyers had previously celebrated as their heroically formative era."[32]

In that sense, *Transformation* read as a cry of rage against Harvard and the legal process tradition it symbolized. Horwitz made judges as anti-democratic as the process theorists feared. But where the process theorists counted on craft and the rule of law to discipline judges, Horwitz made craft and the rule of law a smoke screen for conning the masses. The rule of law, he acknowledged, did create "formal equality—a not inconsiderable virtue." But it also "*promote[d]* substantive inequality by creating a consciousness that radically separate[d] law from politics, means from ends," and procedural from substantive justice. The rule of law thus enabled the rich and "the shrewd" to manipulate its forms to their own advantage.[33]

Most Critical Legal scholars provided a still more insidious and less deterministic explanation of law's role in shoring up power. They pointed out that the capitalists did not always win. If they did, the con would not prove so powerful. And society only molded law to a certain extent; internal forces also determined the development of law. Thus the legal system maintained its credibility and apparent universalism, or "relative autonomy," from economic interests and social class.[34]

Clearly, Critical Legal scholars took their critique of the legal system further than most realists during the 1930s had been willing to take theirs. Equally obvious, Critical Legal Studies, more overtly than Law and Society, built on the realist foundation—something even the popular press recognized. As William Fisher said, Critical Legal scholars "reinforce[d] all the challenges to orthodox legal thought originally generated by Legal Realism—the implicit attack on democratic theory, the delegitimation of the institution of judicial review, and the erosion of the ideal of the rule of law."[35]

Like legal realism, however, Critical Legal Studies was not just a theory of law. It possessed an institutional and political, as well as intellectual, agenda: it also challenged legal education. Kennedy gleefully pricked Harvard's preoccupation with merit by proposing admission of students by lottery and equalization of the salaries of professors and janitors. Critical Legal scholars' stress on the impossibility of value-neutral scholarship and its inevitably political nature jeopardized the ideal of the law professorate as a meritocracy too, reinforcing suspicions that academic lawyers hired people who thought like themselves: "[I]f no one is uncontroversially 'qualified,' it is always possible that one has been certified not for one's brilliance but for one's conventionality, for saying well what we all already know."[36]

Faculty disagreements over appointments intensified. Soon, Harvard, historically "the goal of law professors everywhere," had to replenish its ranks largely with assistant professors. As the press made clear, that was because the faculty could generally not agree on a tenured candidate.[37]

To some, the reason seemed obvious. Harvard was "the only prominent law school where people involved in Critical Legal Studies have acquired a large enough base to be effective in faculty politics." It was "as if, after some years in deep freeze," Berkeley activist Mario Savio, often given credit for kicking off the sixties on the campus, "had returned—except that he is all grown up, and he has tenure, and astonishingly, he seems fond of quoting Roland Barthes and the German phenomenologists." Foremost among these sixties activist-savants was Dark Ages veteran Duncan Kennedy. He wanted to transform Harvard. As Kennedy said: "It's a generational battle; it's a cultural-style battle; it's a battle about scholarly paradigms," and, to some extent, it was a "political battle" in which Critical Legal scholars, a small subset of the faculty, and the majority targeted each other in myriad ways. The clash at Harvard, then, was not just one of ideas; the "Rome" of Critical Legal Studies became "the Beirut" of legal education.[38]

*   *   *

Meanwhile Yale, which celebrated its association with legal realism, became known for its alleged intolerance to Critical Legal Studies. Its faculty talked and talked about Critical Legal scholar Mark Kelman in the 1970s, for example, without ever offering him an invitation to visit. Most thought Yale had no use for the very movement to which both its realists and its Dark Ages helped to give birth. Yale was not alone, of course. Stanford, Kelman's school, was the only elite law school other than Harvard at which Critical Legal scholars established a significant presence. Indeed, perhaps Yale did not hire Critical Legal scholars because it preferred to raid peer or near-peer schools. As one of its faculty members was notoriously said to have remarked, when a candidate from Cardozo was proposed, "How far down the food chain do you think we can go?" Given its history, though, the perception Yale was antagonistic to CLS still caused talk.[39]

That Duncan Kennedy, who was to become the star of CLS, was offered an assistant professorship after his graduation might suggest Yale yearned for a radical presence. But faculty members had to invite Kennedy to join them. Some professors thought him as smart as Calabresi and Deutsch, and to have denied him an offer would have proven Yale cared about politics, in addition to quality of mind. So Kennedy received a bid—though one quarter of the faculty voted against his appointment, and Bickel declared himself "glad Kennedy went to Harvard." As Kennedy remembered it, he decided against New Haven because (like everyone else at Yale) he felt that the influence flowed from Harvard and that if he could create a haven for left legal scholarship in Cambridge, the center of "standpattism" and legal process thought, one could exist anywhere.[40]

Other Critical Legal scholars or allies also received offers from Yale in the 1970s and early 1980s. Early in the 1970s, Roberto Unger turned down an invitation to visit at Yale. Yale Law School alumna Martha Minow was offered an assistant professorship in 1978. Like Kennedy, she turned down the offer to go to Harvard, where she became, in the words of one critical legal scholar, a "CLS fellow-traveler." But at the time of her Yale offer, she would have seemed a conventional liberal, and as one of her teachers said in promoting her as a "superb" potential law school dean, she always occupied a special place in Critical Legal

Studies: "[T]hough associated with the 'left' at Harvard (everybody there has to be associated with one side or the other), [she] has always tried to pull the place together and is very well respected by young people who are associated with the opposite side." William Fisher, a Harvard JD/PhD and another CLS ally, opted to stay where he was. So did Paul Brest, a scholar whose work possessed affinities to CLS. He turned down Yale's offer of a full professorship in 1982 to remain at Stanford. Brest's colleague, Robert Gordon, whom Yale began pursuing in the early 1980s, decided to stay put for the moment also. Mark Kelman did too when he was finally invited to visit. Is it fair to blame Yale for hostility to CLS when so many individuals sympathetic to the movement proved immune to the school's blandishments?[41]

Taken together, the offers do suggest that Yale may have proven somewhat more hospitable to Critical Legal Studies than has been acknowledged. But that is not saying much. One story that circulated had Wellington protesting that none of his faculty had been invited to the first conference on Critical Legal Studies, then retreating in satisfaction when the reply came that his professors had not been excluded because they were not smart enough, but because they were insufficiently progressive.[42]

*   *   *

How do we explain the unfriendliness of Yale to the very movement for which it is partially responsible? Begin with the message of Critical Legal Studies. Like Law and Society, perhaps, it was at once too familiar and too threatening. It absorbed realism while revising its agenda.

At the time Critical Legal Studies made its appearance in the late 1970s, Harvard was vulnerable. As legal realism reflected Yale's attempt at product differentiation during the 1930s, so Harvard's leaders realized their institution required new life. The old consensus behind process thought had disappeared, and Harvard's senior professors replaced it with a wealth of different ideological voices on both left and right — creating conflict they surely had not anticipated. And in Harvard, Critical Legal scholars found the ideal foil: their rebellion against its elitism and allegiance to process theory provided the movement both power and publicity. The CLS themes also proved arresting in Cambridge because Harvard had rejected legal realism during the 1930s and embraced process theory as a way of domesticating realism afterward.[43]

In contrast, when Critical Legal scholars talked about indeterminacy, and declared that "[b]y its own criteria, legal reasoning cannot resolve questions in an 'objective' manner; nor can it explain how the legal system works or how judges decide cases," old Yale realists asked, "So what?" Guido Calabresi over-

stated the case when he said of Arthur Corbin that "CLS would not have surprised or troubled *him* one bit (though he was politically quite conservative)."
In fact, Corbin deplored those realists he considered dangerous reformers. But
Calabresi was on the mark when he told Paul Carrington that there was no
way Critical Legal scholars could prove more nihilistic (if Critical Legal scholars were nihilistic, which seems unlikely) than Grant Gilmore or Arthur Leff.
Some CLS scholarship would have reminded Yale law professors of the work
of their own Gilmore or Wesley Sturges. The idea that Critical Legal scholars
asked new questions about the legal system, Calabresi contended, was "both
wrong and ahistoric." He maintained that "those who disagree with CLS at the
Harvard Law School have rather foolishly let CLS dominate the field of 'questioning fundamental assumptions' and that leads graduates of that marvelous
school to believe that the egg Duncan [Kennedy] and others claim to have discovered had not been discovered many, many times before."[44]

On another occasion, Calabresi was more specific. "I have always thought
that the reason CLS took hold at Harvard and not at Yale was the fact that, unlike Harvard, we all were/are so tied to the Realist tradition in New Haven,"
he said. "An unfortunate, because pejorative, metaphor should be that those
with Cow Pox don't get Small Pox." His tone was good-natured: Why credit the
youngsters with originality, rather than their parents? Why fuss over them? So
Calabresi and other prominent Yale professors defended Critical Legal scholars against those who claimed they were nihilists who should depart the legal
academy—but did not deluge them with invitations to join the faculty.[45]

For the CLS message was also threatening. It was threatening because of its
insistence that law is politics. It was threatening because by going beyond the
realists, as Critical Legal scholars assuredly did, and focusing on the relative
autonomy of law, CLS demonstrated that law veiled the value systems of all
decision makers, rather than of individual judges, the realists' point of focus.
It was threatening because the CLS critique of rights underscored the peril of
the rights-consciousness that the liberals' beloved Warren Court made possible. It was threatening because CLS thrived on "trashing" legal texts: "Take
specific arguments very *seriously* in their own terms; discover they are actually
foolish ([tragic]-*comic*); and then look for some external observer's *order* (*not*
the germ of truth) in the internal contradictory, incoherent chaos we've exposed." It was threatening because some senior professors seemed to feel that
"Crits are infected with the rebellious spirit of the '60s, and that if they hire
them, they won't get the kind of deference and respect they want." And CLS
was threatening because of the sense it meant conflict: there was fear in New
Haven it would cause tensions at Yale, just as it did at Harvard. Stanford was

no war zone, but as always, Harvard mattered. Thus as Yale rebuilt its faculty, Critical Legal Studies represented a road not taken. Once again, in the anxiety about "extremists," we may see the specter of the sixties.[46]

*   *   *

Most fundamentally, though, CLS was threatening because legal realism had become threatening. It was not just because Critical Legal scholars' appropriation of realism made it threatening, either. Yale professors who came to realize they had lost the Court had begun to worry that realism gave judges with repellent politics too much power.

As he surveyed the field in 1974, Yale's Arthur Leff acknowledged the force of legal realism. Indeed, he attributed the popularity of Chicago-style Law and Economics to law professors' search for objective foundations of justice in realism's wake. That, in turn, reflected "an attempt to get over, or at least get by, the complexity thrust upon us by the Realists." To state "the current situation as sharply and nastily as possible; there is today no way of 'proving' that napalming babies is bad except by asserting it (in a louder and louder voice), or by defining it as so, early in one's game, and then slipping it through in a whisper, as a conclusion." No one could "tell (or at least . . . tell about) the difference between right and wrong," but everyone wanted "to go on talking. If we could find a way to slip in our normatives in the form of descriptives, within a discipline offering narrow and apparently usable epistemological categories, we would all be pathetically grateful for such a new and more respectable formalism in legal analysis." Since Law and Economics promised that, many embraced it.[47]

Leff sang the same tune about CLS when he reviewed Roberto Unger's 1975 classic, *Knowledge and Politics*. Having exposed law as false messiah, Unger had ended with the words, "Speak, God," and Leff structured the essay as a memorandum from the Devil to Unger. According to Leff, the problem of how one told the difference between right and wrong lay at the heart of Unger's project. And, according to Leff's Devil, Unger was imprisoned in "a Gödel problem: how to validate the premises of a system from within itself. 'Good,' 'right,' and words like that are evaluations. For evaluations you need an evaluator." Religious faith promised to solve the intellectual dilemma. "No more would ethical imperatives consist merely of human beliefs, intuited in privacy, perhaps validated by wide sharing or whatever, but just mortal opinions nonetheless." It just might be, though, that God did not exist, no one "out there" was evaluating, and "everything is permitted." Or perhaps God existed and "still cares" about humankind. As a practical and epistemological matter, though, that would prove "even more terrifying, because then some things are not permitted, and men have got to find out which are which. Since He has the right and power to evaluate you, but no duty to do so, you are bravely right: you must pray." But that just posed another problem as Unger awaited "His revelation": just consider people's behavior. "Now take this hint from what you have seen: If He exists, Me too."[48]

By the late 1970s, Leff saw a "growing and apparently terrifying realization" gripping his colleagues — "that there cannot be any normative system ultimately based on anything except human will." The hopelessness of finding objective foundations of justice meant "everything is up for grabs":

> Nevertheless:
> Napalming babies is bad.
> Starving the poor is wicked.
> Buying and selling each other is depraved.
> Those who stood up to and died resisting
>   Hitler, Stalin, Amin, and Pol Pot — and General
>   Custer too — have earned salvation.
> Those who acquiesced deserved to be damned.
> There is in the world such a thing as evil.
> [All together now:] Sez who?
> God help us.[49]

That was an answer that avoided both Critical Legal Studies and Chicago-style Law and Economics — to stare into the abyss. But most of Leff's colleagues in public law, the field on which the school had staked its intellectual reputation since Rostow's day, had a different one. The more popular and hopeful solution was to turn back to Bickel's jurisprudence without embracing his later politics. Legal process might seem moribund at Harvard, but it would acquire new life at Yale. Professors would rebuild legal liberalism without the more dangerous aspect of realism and revive an improved and reformist process theory.

THE NEW LEGAL PROCESS

It made sense. With the appointment of Harry Wellington as dean in 1975, the school possessed, for the first time since Harry Shulman, who had served less than a year in 1954 before cancer felled him, a legal process scholar at the helm. As a scholar, Wellington maintained that courts must engage in "a complex and robust dialogue" as they elucidated constitutional principles, one fusing a common law approach to adjudication with a concept of "public morality, the ethical principles, the ideals and aspirations that are widely shared by Americans.... Constitutional decisions must be politically digestible." By this model, "*Roe* v. *Wade*, when decided in 1973, went too far" on "political digestibility" grounds — but should not be overruled, either.[50]

Under Wellington's leadership, Yale would head back to the Bickel of *The Least Dangerous Branch* and closer to the Harvard of the 1950s and 1960s by advocating a richer, politically liberal version of legal process theory. Its focus on continuing the conversation in search of public values, despite its recognition no truths would emerge, suited postmodernity. Yale would embrace the New Legal Process, "an attempt to update the 'old' Legal Process and create a jurisprudential form which can withstand criticism from the left (CLS) and the right (Law and Economics)," while taming legal realism. Its professors were not the only ones to do so. The New Legal Process enjoyed a resurgence at Harvard, Columbia, and other law schools. But at no other institution did such a large percentage of the faculty cast its lot with the New Legal Process, and New Haven was rightly considered its headquarters.[51]

Like the original, it focused on who decides, demonstrated a concern with process, valued dialogue as a means of reaching consensus, and possessed a substantive and normative element (which would now become more explicit). At the same time, the New Legal Process left courts more room to mandate equality and proved more skeptical about whether legislatures reflected majority will. As Calabresi put it, the New Legal Process displayed "far greater sophistication in its view of legislative capacities"; more of a focus on "value-asserting-law making institutions other than courts and legislatures," such as juries, administrative agencies, and the executive; "and most importantly, an open recognition of the need to consider separately the issue of rights and value formation. No longer unselfconsciously autonomous, the New Legal Process examines comparative institutional capacities, given the desire to further certain values or protect certain rights," acknowledging that "all its conclusions must ultimately depend on a defense of the validity of the values and rights asserted." It also displayed more emphasis on efficiency and interdisciplinarity, greater interest in interpretation as a source of judicial constraint, and less certainty about the state's ability to "grow" the pie and improve life. The original legal process theorists might have taken it for granted that in contrast to courts, legislatures reflected popular will and "bureaucratic justice" was impossible, for example. But Yale's Jerry Mashaw drew on public choice theory "without succumbing to the excessively negative . . . vision it so often supports" and a close, empirical study of the Social Security Administration's disability program to explore those assumptions.[52]

Despite the differences between the two, the original process theory shaped the newer version. Like the traditional version, the New Legal Process at Yale reflected an attempt to justify Warren Court decisions while arguing more principled ones would strengthen liberalism. As Robert Burt, another who toiled in Yale's New Legal Process vineyard, might have pointed out, Alexander Bickel's portrait appropriately continued to "dominate" the school's largest classroom. For Yale remained "Bickel's law school" — the Bickel of the 1960s — in death, as in life.[53]

Though they were no longer at Yale, both Ronald Dworkin and John Ely helped shape the development of the New Legal Process there. Like other law professors, Dworkin had become taken with the thought of John Rawls. At a time when Robert Nozick was about to press for the "minimal state" in *Anarchy, State and Utopia*, Rawls promoted a philosophical liberalism agreeable to left-of-center Democrats. In his 1971 book *A Theory of Justice*, the philosopher espoused procedural justice, or "justice as fairness." That would be the theory a hypothetical person trapped behind a "veil of ignorance" without any knowledge of his own circumstances would choose, Rawls maintained. But Rawls preached more than the golden rule. He added the gloss of the "difference principle" to justify social and economic inequality when they resulted in "compensating benefits for everyone," particularly "the least advantaged members of society." Between them, Rawls argued, procedural justice and the difference principle would prove a better bet for the individual behind the veil of ignorance than any substantive vision of the good. Citing the legal process plea for "principled decisions in law," he pledged that his theory would also separate law from politics and revive the rule of law. Since it would coincidentally achieve legal and political liberals' goals of maximizing civil liberties and minimizing social and economic inequality, some wondered whether Rawls's own theory of justice was not just another substantive vision of the good.[54]

Drawing on Rawls, Dworkin integrated constitutional and moral theory to develop a rights-based jurisprudence designed to constrain judicial discretion, rationalize the record of the Warren Court, and privilege equality over liberty by forcing lawyers to face "the issue of what moral rights an individual has against the state." The rights foundationalism Dworkin advocated in *Taking Rights Seriously* was a fuller variant of legal process thought. He harked back to the original by stressing that "constitutional activism must be justified by principles that are something more than policy judgments" at the same time that he promoted legal liberalism and interdisciplinarity. He understood why "lawyers dread contamination with moral philosophy, and particularly with those lawyers who talk about rights, because the spooky overtones of that concept threaten the graveyard of reason," Dworkin said. But the field of moral philosophy had improved, he emphasized, with the publication of *A Theory of Justice*, which he adjured every constitutional lawyer to read. Lawyers "must recognize that law is no more independent from philosophy" than it was from sociology or economics.[55]

Some questioned that. What would be the outcome of the race to Rawls and fundamental values, John Ely famously wondered in *Democracy and Distrust*. Would it be decisions that read "We like Rawls, you like Nozick. We win, 6-3. Statute invalidated"? More than Dworkin, Ely dressed the Warren Court in the clothes of the legal process tradition. In advancing his theory of representation-reinforcing review, he argued that the Warren Court concentrated on the realization of "'participational' goals of broadened access to the process and bounty of representative government." Indeed, that had been its mission, not "old-fashioned value imposition." Answering those who maintained that Bickel's abandonment of the Warren Court in 1969–70 reflected his realization that "judicial conservatism" and political liberalism did not go together, Ely insisted that "one perfectly well *can* be a genuine political liberal and at the same time believe, out of a respect for the democratic process, that the Court should keep its hands off the legislature's value judgments," and he produced a theory that justified most Warren Court decisions. Whether it caused them, as his former colleagues pointed out, was another story.[56]

So, too, a more persuasive legal liberalism with a muted nonrealism that did not emphasize "the danger of exaggerating the legal importance of the idiosyncratic" was Bruce Ackerman's aim. His *Private Property and the Constitution*, dedicated to Bickel, sought to reinvigorate prudentialism. Ackerman saw his subsequent *Social Justice in the Liberal State*, a friendly debate with Rawls, as rooted in his experience as a Yale law student "in the mid-1960s," where he was persuaded by Bickel, Bork, Calabresi, Dworkin, and Reich that "political action was futile without systematic reflection. Without this lesson, I would not have responded to the political turbulence of the late 1960s by taking a teaching job." But that required a clerkship. As a result, "While others were marching in the streets in 1968, I was serving as a law clerk to Justice John Harlan of the U.S. Supreme Court. He was worldly, wise and conservative, and I was a callow-but-committed liberal." Ackerman remembered Harlan telling him Supreme Court justices should not vote. "They shouldn't spend a single minute thinking of themselves as Republicans or Democrats": that would make law political and partisan. Ackerman remained "a committed liberal," but one stamped by his experience with Harlan.[57]

Social Justice in the Liberal State showed that. It confronted the liberal problem, the hopelessness of discovering "a final solution to the conflict between self-fulfillment and social justice," and sought to "transform our moral dilemma into a source of creativity." It turned out there was no need to impose one vision of social justice over another, as Ackerman implicitly criticized the Warren Court and Rawls for doing. Ackerman called for abandoning the "shallow Realism that has outlived its time" that he alleged animated CLS and Chicago-style Law and Economics. He would have his readers embrace "liberal dialogue — or the fundamental rights that citizens bound by dialogue are obligated to recognize." All that was necessary was that the dialogue proceed according to principles of "Neutrality." In Ackerman's jurisprudential world, no one could justify the rights for which he argued by claiming superiority for himself as an individual or for his view of the moral good or "a power advantage" on the basis of "pretensions to moral superiority." Those ground rules in place, philosophical and political liberals could rejoice. For the upshot would be "the conditional affirmation of market freedom — conditional on the effective recognition of each citizen's right to enter the marketplace with a liberal education and a fair share of economic power." And since "none of us can rightfully expect to gain anything through a show of pique," conversation would replace the confrontation of the late 1960s.[58]

Whereas Ackerman originally relied on philosophy, his toolbox expanded to include history in the 1980s. Now he differentiated sharply between two jurisprudential schools. Ackerman maintained that Ely and Bickel's process theory privileged the president and Congress, while treating "every aspect of judicial review as presumptively undemocratic." He contended that Dworkin advocated a rights-foundationalism in which liberals' favorite rights trumped democracy. In the place of both, Ackerman advocated a theory of popular sovereignty, which allegedly had empowered a mobilized "We the People" to engage in creative "higher lawmaking" during charged instances in American history, such as the Founding, Reconstruction, and the New Deal, and which had the practical effect of amending the Constitution. In those "constitutional moments," the judiciary fulfilled the function Alexander Hamilton had envisioned for it in *Federalist* 78 by serving as voice of the people. Whereas traditionally, commentators had strained "to save the Supreme Court from the 'countermajoritarian difficulty' by one or another ingenious argument," Ackerman saw judicial review itself as democratic, so long as the Supreme

Court preserved the integrity of the people's effort by engaging in an "ongoing judicial effort to look backward and interpret the meaning" of constitutional moments that had gone before. "Rather than threatening democracy by frustrating the statutory demands of the political elite in Washington, the courts serve democracy by protecting the hard-won principles of a mobilized citizenry against erosion by political elites who have failed to gain broad and deep support for their innovations."[59]

By this account, *Brown* v. *Board of Education* represented the Court's attempt to reconcile two constitutional moments, Reconstruction and the New Deal, by applying the affirmation of equality that marked Reconstruction to an institution that had come to symbolize the activist role the New Deal envisioned for the state, the public school. Indeed, "the civil rights revolution," which reached its apex in 1964–65 when all branches of government showed the Court's spirit in *Brown*, Ackerman said, represented "the last successful example of constitutional politics." Nor was *Griswold*, and by extension *Roe*, a milestone. Instead, *Griswold* simply read "the Bill of Rights to preserve the Founding concern with personal liberty in a way that endures in a post–New Deal world of economic and social regulation." If citizens did not like the way the Court organized the "conversation between the present and the past about the future," they could mobilize for another constitutional moment. Thus Ackerman's constitutional theory justified both *Brown* and *Roe* and said judges were no substitute for higher lawmaking during constitutional moments by "we the people."[60]

Through his engagement with "the republican revival" and "neo-Federalism," Ackerman helped transform constitutional theory and broaden interest in legal and constitutional history. He had begun writing about what Madison, the Reconstruction Congress, and the New Dealers had wrought even before Attorney General Edwin Meese met Madison, but once the Reagan administration discovered "original intent," Ackerman's work received even more attention. As the years went by, though, and Ackerman became even more insistent that "distinguished professionals" who cabined law from politics be appointed as judges, he came to sound more and more like both Harlan and Bickel, circa 1965.[61]

Yale's future dean, Anthony Kronman, who returned to New Haven during the Wellington years, embraced Bickel even more explicitly. Kronman lamented that prudentialism had become "a marginal force in contemporary American legal scholarship" by the 1980s. Like Ackerman, whose project of reviving it he shared, he flagged the "contempt for prudence" in Law and Economics and Critical Legal Studies and blamed both movements on the legal realism of the 1930s. And like Ackerman, he seemed to have little use for the late sixties. Kronman himself had been a student then, but he absorbed Bickel's words about the importance of institutional neutrality. In one tribute, Kronman celebrated the example of Friedrich Kessler in the 1930s and 1960s. The mission of Kessler and Bickel remained his: Kronman advocated resisting the pressure to be "politically correct" and holding aloft "the ideal of academic neutrality despite the fashionable conviction that every ideal is a form of politics in disguise and that politics is at bottom nothing but power."[62]

Bickel's influence was also apparent in the work of another future dean, Guido Calabresi, who dedicated his Harvard Holmes lectures to Bickel. In the book that followed, *A Common Law for the Age of Statutes*, Calabresi took up the shift from common law to statutes in the twentieth-century United States. He focused on the difficulty judges faced in coping with the "orgy of statute making" that no longer represented popular will but that inertia kept on the books, such as the nineteenth-century Connecticut law prohibiting access to birth control overturned in *Griswold*. How, he asked, might courts revise statutes as necessary?[63]

Judges could do so by declaring them unconstitutional, making use of Bickel's "passive virtues," or engaging in the purposive interpretation of Hart and Sacks, of course. But too frequently, such approaches represented "subterfuges," which were best avoided, Calabresi contended. According to him, "courts have been using a pickax and calling it a case knife," refusing to face "the questions of when judicial action to induce the updating of statutes is desirable and what form and limits should be imposed on that function." He would give courts the power of common law judges — "either to make changes themselves or, by threatening to use the power, to induce legislatures to act" — when statutes became outdated. American democracy delegated to judges the duty of principled decision making on the theory that "the legal fabric, and the principles that form it, are good approximations of one aspect of the popular will, of what a majority in some sense desires," he reasoned. Thus judges, "who by training and selection are relatively good at exploring and mapping the legal landscape," could appropriately take on the business of "evolving" common law and statutes alike.[64]

Tracing his proposal back to Hart and Sacks, of whom "we are all followers," Calabresi pleaded for greater "candor." It was best to be open about motivation and method. Calabresi attributed the "reckless irritability" of students during the late sixties to their anxiety about the draft and their knowledge that their "contemporaries without academic refuge were being sent to war," and he had little use for sublimation. Though he professed to have more use for frankness and less for artifice than Bickel, he reminded his readers of the necessity of hoarding the ammunition in words that recalled his former colleague: "To deny what we are doing, to use tricks here, is to destroy by overuse a language that is easily cheapened, a language that should be reserved for the Court, in matters of high principle and not the courts in low-level tasks." His prudentialism, like Bickel's, showed his submersion in legal realism and his eagerness to give process theory an explicitly normative dimension.[65]

Thus it reflected his sense that ideals, beliefs, and attitudes had a place in law. Even as Calabresi had helped to focus the economic analysis of tort law on the concern with reducing the cost of accidents, he had always insisted on the place for questions of "justice" and "fairness." As he soon demonstrated anew, tort law took ideals, beliefs, and attitudes into account in distributing the cost of accidents, often, again, through "subterfuges." Consider the deity who offered its subjects whatever gift they wanted, as long as they paid for it with one thousand lives, he told his readers in his book *Ideals, Beliefs, Attitudes and the Law: Private Law Perspectives on a Public Law Program*. When his students spurned the present, he continued, Calabresi reminded them they had already received a far more expensive one, the automobile. All benefits carried a price, and society's values helped determine what it agreed to pay and the tradeoffs it tolerated. Ideals, beliefs, and attitudes appropriately shaped "what is expected and what seems reasonable in the most diverse sections of our law." It was best for law to face that openly, rather than vainly sneak to hide conflicts and mute divisions.[66]

By Calabresi's account, *Roe* v. *Wade* was "a disaster." The Court had gone about striking down the Texas law making it a crime to acquire an abortion for any purpose other than saving the life of the mother in the wrong way. The professor refused to cast his lot with the judicial supremacy that many believed *Roe* embodied and that Calabresi identified with the 1980s debate over original intent. Calabresi insisted that such authoritarianism made Hugo Black, the justice for whom he had clerked, Yale Law School alumnus Potter Stewart, and Alexander Bickel "spin in their graves." But Calabresi defended judicial enforcement of the right to abortion and condemned the "willful desire" of Chief Justice Rehnquist and Justice Scalia "to do anything to cast doubt on *Roe* v. *Wade*."[67]

For along with judicial intervention to protect constitutional accountability when legislatures behaved "hastily or thoughtlessly with respect to fundamental rights because of panic or crises," or simply because they were "pressed for time," Calabresi advocated judicial enforcement of the antidiscrimination principle to protect groups that had "experienced a history of discrimination" or confronted "a real danger of long-run exclusion." In constitutional theory, as elsewhere, he considered himself an egalitarian "Bickellian." What Calabresi wanted were not "*judges who are willing to impose their own values on the polity*" but those who used "jurisprudence to learn what the polity's true values are when the whole polity must bear the burden of enforcing those values." Thus for him, the key issue was how laws were written and applied. He insisted that they must "burden all of us," not just those without power in the legislative process. If a rule was important, everyone must feel its sting. That would force a rational decision as to which rules should endure. A legislature could require everyone to "abjure extramarital or oral sex," but it could not only demand that sacrifice from gays and lesbians. So, too, "*if men could become pregnant, anti-abortion laws would be clearly valid*; because men cannot, such laws must be subject to judicial scrutiny. Women count as an excluded group, or at least did at the time of *Roe* v. *Wade*, and anti-abortion laws impose a degree of control over women's lives and behavior that is not imposed on men."[68]

But Calabresi condemned the *Roe* Court for pretending that prior to viability, a fetus was not a person and therefore deserved no constitutional protection. Instead of viewing *Roe* as a conflict between those who thought life began at conception and those who said it started later, the Court should have presented the case, Calabresi contended, as showcasing the tension between women's right to sexual freedom and the sanctity of life. After elaborating both constitutional values, it should have chosen between them rather than insulting the losers by pretending that their position lacked worth. That approach would reflect the ambivalence of both court and society, bringing winners and losers closer together and representing the "honest" solution that was preferable, when possible. Thus Calabresi hopefully espoused not just honesty and ambivalence about differences, but, just as important, honesty about ambivalence as a way of fostering unity. Talk again became the remedy.[69]

Owen Fiss, who became the Alexander M. Bickel Professor of Public Law soon after he arrived at Yale, bore Bickel's imprint too. Whereas Bickel applauded *Brown* and thought the Court should reserve its prestige for the rare case like it, Fiss hoped that the Court would spend it more freely to implement the public values it articulated in *Brown*. His work reflected an abiding allegiance to the Warren Court and a hope that its resurrection as he had reshaped it would make Critical Legal Studies and Law and Economics unnecessary, enabling law professors to make reason their faith.[70]

For Fiss, who had clerked for both Thurgood Marshall and William Brennan in the 1960s, that "extraordinary period" demonstrated that "the judiciary is in the best position to discover the true meaning of our constitutional values." Fiss considered the "Second Reconstruction," a magical era "dedicated to the eradication of the social structures that had been used for almost a century to perpetuate the subjugation of blacks," the "inspiration" for much of his work. When he wrote of public morality, as Wellington and Calabresi did, he drew sustenance from the period in which the Court had seen rights as "the concrete embodiment" of public values. *Brown* was the font: "Although the Second Reconstruction depended on the activism of the Civil Rights Movement and the efforts of the Executive and Congress, the great transformation never would have come to be without *Brown* v. *Board of Education* and the judgment that segregation was unacceptable as a matter of law, not just politics."[71]

But the idyll had ended. "Although in the 1960s we undertook the Second Reconstruction and tried to build the Great Society, and we were drawn to law as public ideal, in the next decade we took refuge in the politics of selfishness." The Burger Court "sought to repudiate the legacy of the Warren Court and to block the progressive realization of the Constitution" by paying "homage to *Brown*" while undercutting it. The Burger Court rejected its predecessor's use of injunctive relief to achieve institutional change and treated adjudication as dispute settlement. Like other Americans, its members had "lost our confidence in the existence of the values that were the foundation of the litigation of the 1960s and, for that matter, in the existence of any public values" and decided, à la the realists, that "preference" was everything. In Fiss's view, that explained the rise of "the new nihilism" of both Critical Legal Studies and Law and Economics in the legal academy. Both made the normative "subjective" and the goal of public morality and values "hopeless." According to him: "We will never be able to respond fully to the negativism of critical legal studies or the crude instrumentalism of law and economics until a regenerative process takes hold."[72]

Look back to the Warren Court, he advised. To counter the danger that bureaucracy posed to contemporary constitutional values, democracy and society, he introduced a model of judging he called "structural reform." It relied, Fiss explained, on the structural injunction the Warren Court had imaginatively developed to desegregate schools, the most significant civil rights remedy and "the most distinctive contribution of the civil rights era to our remedial jurisprudence." Realizing the potential of the injunction to reorganize ongoing bureaucratic organizations, liberal federal judges had proceeded to rely on the structural injunction not just to reshape schools, but prisons, mental hospitals, housing, and the police. Fiss's model of structural reform gave federal judges the specific duty of reconstructing such bureaucracies, advo-

cated the reconstruction of the structure of the lawsuit to make it "less individualistic and more group-oriented," and directed attention to the fact that
those who participated in a lawsuit were stand-ins for larger interests and
many others. Judges' authority derived from their "independence" from politics and their devotion to a "dialogue" with the public through principled decision making.[73]

The Court's declaration that the state could not cut an individual's welfare benefits without first holding an evidentiary pre-termination hearing gave
Goldberg v. *Kelly* a special place in Fiss's pantheon. Where Mashaw maintained
that the case exposed the emptiness of purely procedural justice, Fiss extolled
it. Brennan's opinion, in his telling, showcased the need to apply the Warren
Court's procedural due process revolution to civil and criminal cases, highlighted the importance of due process for poor and rich, and had been "entirely
rational," reflecting the Court's "deliberative nature." But Brennan surprised
Fiss when he declared in a 1987 speech that the decision in *Goldberg* reflected
"passion," as well as reason, and drew on the briefs to describe the difficulty of
the lives of the named plaintiff welfare recipients. To Fiss, this was ridiculous:
"*Goldberg* v. *Kelly* was no more about particular named persons, who might
suitably be the object of our affections, than *Brown* v. *Board of Education* was
about Linda Brown. Both were about social groups and what the Constitution
promises them." Consequently, making a place for passion in the Court's decisional process was inconsistent with the norms of impartiality: reason legitimated, governed, and disciplined judicial power. The task for judges was to
enrich reason, as Fiss believed the Warren Court justices had done, not valorize
passion.[74]

This vision of law Fiss, Robert Cover, and Judith Resnik elaborated for law
students everywhere in "a realist casebook for proceduralists." The book was
notable not just for the attention it lavished on structural reform and law as an
expression of public values. It also made *Goldberg* v. *Kelly* the course centerpiece, more important even than the Federal Rules of Civil Procedure. The case
enabled them to engage in "an exploration of why we have process and why
we care about the kind of process that the law provides." Not for them a book
organized around "the linear unfolding of a lawsuit" or appellate court opinions; Fiss and his coauthors wanted to leave Langdell behind. Here was a course
that worked to bring the Warren Court's "Due Process Revolution" to the classroom, but that turned its back on immediate relevance by focusing on "the
more theoretical issues." The result was a concept of procedure more expan-
sive than that covered in the traditional first-year course, one embracing civil,
criminal, and administrative decision making. Fiss and his colleagues taught

Procedure, or, as Yale students came to call it, "metaprocedure," rather than Civil Procedure.[75]

As Fiss joined Ackerman in rejecting both Critical Legal Studies and Chicago-style Law and Economics, so he also turned to another discipline to enrich his work. Like Dworkin, Fiss made the interpretive turn in the early 1980s, drawing on literary theory to make the case that judges were constrained by their membership in interpretive communities. Hermeneutics provided hope. "When I read a case like *Brown* v. *Board of Education*, for example, what I see is not the unconstrained power of the judges to give vent to their desires and interests, but rather public officials situated within a profession, bounded at every turn by the norms and conventions that define and constitute that profession," Fiss now maintained. That permitted consensus and objectivity, despite indeterminacy and disagreement over meaning, while allowing judges and courts to give meaning to public values.[76]

Not all at Yale could keep faith alive. Fiss's colleague and casebook coauthor, Robert Cover, pointed out—and, for all his enthusiasm for legal process old and new, Wellington agreed—that legal interpretation differed from literary interpretation in an important respect. The former, Cover said, "always takes place in the shadow of coercion." Cover demonstrated that anew in *Justice Accused: Antislavery and the Judicial Process*, when he turned to the past to solve a problem of the 1960s. Bewildered by "judicial complicity in the crimes of Vietnam," he took on another "moral-formal dilemma," exploration of the "earnest, well-meaning pillars of legal respectability" who personally opposed slavery during the years before the Civil War but upheld it in their decisions on the grounds that "law" required them to do so. Though judges such as Lemuel Shaw had "really squirmed," they had "done the job," as they saw it, collaborating in injustice.[77]

In hiring Cover during the mid-1970s, Yale brought one veteran of the student movements of the late sixties who still sympathized with them to its faculty. Cover had gone south to work with the Student Nonviolent Coordinating Committee and had been jailed in Georgia. While Fiss was working for the Civil Rights Division of Lyndon Johnson's Justice Department in 1968, Cover had been a third-year law student at Columbia. During the student revolt, he and David Kairys successfully called for "the need to apply continued pressure on the university by means of a strike against classes." Then Cover went directly into law teaching. As a beginning Columbia law professor during the prosecution of the Panthers, Cover stood atop the roof of a car at one demonstration at Foley Square's Criminal Court building to urge protest. The courts' actions "are as political as, and have the same effect as, the actions of the mayor," and courts also "legitimate[d] political repression by affixing their judicial seal of approval to politically repressive prosecutions," he contended. One student evaluation summed up where Cover was as a professor during the late 1960s: "Young and radical (thank God)." Fiss acknowledged that although his and Cover's work both demonstrated a concern with equality, "there is also a difference, as important a difference as that which divided SNCC and the Department of Justice in the 1960s."[78]

There was another difference between them too. Cover's appointment had doubled the number of nonsecular Jews on the Yale law faculty. He and the Legal Service Organization's Stephen Wizner were obviously observant. In his *Harvard Law Review* Foreword, "Nomos and Narrative," Cover wrote of the power Judaism, biblical narratives, and Jewish law possessed to give meaning to the American constitutional order. Like most of his colleagues, Fiss's religion was the Constitution "as an embodiment of a public morality to be known and elaborated through the exercise of reason." Fiss thought that Cover's "view of law and, in particular, his declaration in 'Nomos and Narrative' that 'judges are people of violence' did great disservice to the federal judges who had risked so much to make *Brown* a living reality." The sixties had shaped both people.[79]

By the mid-1980s, Cover had lost the faith, if ever he had possessed it, in trusting federal courts to work for justice. Even the Warren Court, he said in a public exchange with Fiss, had not imposed public values. It was simply doing what it considered "right and justified." Further, its work in "destroying apartheid" and "reforming institutions," which Cover joined Fiss in celebrating, was but an anomaly. Given the Court's turn right, Cover especially disparaged Fiss's search for interpretive communities and disciplining rules, announcing that his colleague was trapped in the world of the Warren Court, circa 1967: "I don't see why we should legitimate the Court which is going to do what I hate, and which I'm committed against by trying to establish that what [the justices] . . . are doing is part of [a] sacred process and putting them back in the position of priests." It was time to stop treating judges as prophets. After all, Cover had said at the conclusion of *Justice Accused*, "If a man makes a good priest, we may be quite sure he will not be a great prophet."[80]

Like Cover, many claimed that Fiss, Ackerman, Ely, Dworkin, and some of their company were time-bound. They still worshiped at the shrine of the Warren Court or the shrine of judicial supremacy that the liberal federal judges and justices during the Warren era were said to embody. But to legal liberals at Yale, their work yielded a Warren Court shorn of the worst of legal realism, unsullied by the naked preference and subjectivity that process theorists had feared in *Brown* and that many more had seen at work in *Roe*. Clearly, as scholars would stress, and more than any other law school, Yale still bore "the imprint of Bickellian constitutionalism, . . . expressed in the form of desperate searches to find just the right constraining theory," one that would "make judicial decisions more objective and . . . defuse the charge that constitutional law lacked legitimacy in a democracy." The quest predated the sixties, of course, but it acquired even greater urgency in its aftermath.[81]

Indeed, much of the New Legal Process theory bore the stamp of the late sixties, though not all its proponents had been at Yale then. What guided some of the most prominent new legal process scholars, such as Fiss, was not just the remembrance of *Brown*, the lodestar of their predecessors, but the memory of the period just before the summer of 1965 when liberalism had been at the peak of its popularity and before everything had gone downhill. Critical Legal scholar Mark Tushnet had suggested that the "moralism of the oppositional politics of the Dark Ages" stood out, characterizing the mood among Yale students then as both outraged and anti-legalistic. Like Bickel and Bork after the 1960s, some New Legal Process theorists rejected moral outrage. They sought both to redefine the sixties as the early mid-1960s and to replace the hot combativeness they associated with the late 1960s with the coolness of dialogue.[82]

Though more interdisciplinary, the New Legal Process scholarship was still a species of the process theory of the 1950s and 1960s, which had always been as much a part of legal realism as part of the reaction against it. As Critical Legal scholars believed the realists themselves had done, legal liberals at Yale had backed away from realism's most destabilizing insight, sometimes by trying to transform normative visions into procedural imperatives. In the process, as Critical Legal scholars also contended the realists had done, Yale's legal liberals backed into other disciplines, helping to make interdisciplinarity the new coin of the legal academy's realm.

"LAW AND"

As dean, Wellington rebuilt the faculty, hiring some thirty professors during his decade in charge and accelerating the creation of the contemporary school. His was "as good a group of young academics as you can find anywhere in law teaching today" *and* "as good as any of their predecessors here," including "Gene's boys and girl," he said of the fifteen he hired during his first term. By the time Wellington retired from teaching at Yale in the 1990s, "he could look on a faculty more than half of whom came to the law school during his term as dean."[83]

Unlike Harvard, historically "the goal of law professors everywhere," which had to replenish its ranks largely with assistant professors during these years because "the faculty cannot agree on a candidate," Wellington extended most of his offers to tenured professors. His faculty turned to senior appointments, generally preceded by a visit, to fill the gaps created by departures, deaths, and retirements. To some extent, it had to do so. After "the slaughter of the innocents," why would a junior person take a chance on Yale, when he or she could go anywhere else with, seemingly, a better chance of promotion? Some senior Yale professors also feared that any untenured person would have to be promoted, no matter what kind of record he or she completed, to show that Yale was now singing a different tune. That did not stop the school from singing it during the mid-1970s. As Wellington told the provost, "Yale Law School is the only law school that frequently declines to promote assistant or associate professors. Indeed, our standards, within the law school world, are so stringent that we frequently lose in the competition." With but a few exceptions — Paul Gewirtz, for example, who told the press "that when he was considering whether or not to accept an [untenured] appointment at Yale, he thought about the 'bloodbath' stories [of the early 1970s] 'very, very carefully'" and reported that "others interviewing for teaching jobs at Yale routinely raise the subject" — most appointments were lateral. Invitees had been vetted elsewhere through the tenure process, as they had been at Yale during their visit. The process cut down on surprises like John Griffiths.[84]

New hires differed from their predecessors in other ways too. For all their interdisciplinary pretensions, Yale faculty members had traditionally been products of "the traditional law school mill." They possessed high grades and served as law review editors, mostly of the *Yale Law Journal*. Though most of the new professors still had attended Yale Law School and done well there, departures from the pattern proved more frequent. Recent hires also proved more likely to possess advanced degrees in other disciplines. With his enthusiasm for liberalism, Goldstein had brought in Fiss and Ackerman; with his interest in interdisciplinarity, he had brought in three with PhDs. Under Wellington, this trend accelerated: six lawyers with PhDs, in economics, history, or philosophy, or who were working toward PhDs, joined the faculty. The school now possessed a critical mass of JD/PhDs.[85]

Yale could successfully woo those with doctorates because teaching positions in the humanities and social sciences had dried up in the late 1960s. Many who might have once opted to become humanists or social scientists chose law teaching. Academic lawyers made more money than humanists and social scientists, they could publish less, they won tenure in five years, and they received secretarial assistance and research support. Further, there were more positions in law. In the 1970s, business was booming for Yale, as it was for other law schools. Everyone, so it sometimes seemed, was seeking a law degree. Of 3,682 students who applied to become members of Yale's class of 1981, 329 (11 percent) were accepted. Of the 175 registered in the first-year class, 36 percent were women, 10 percent were minorities, 22 percent held MAs, and almost 10 percent possessed PhDs. When Wellington, who routinely gave a welcoming speech to first-years, made notes about their apprehensions for his remarks, he wrote: "1. Narrowness of discipline . . . 2 Professionalization (narrowing [of student] in process) . . . 3. The law of YLS as Establishment. Training can be used equally in cause of status quo. 4. Insecurity — competition . . . 5. Really want to be an English Professor." The first four points could have appeared in a similar talk during the late sixties, but not the fifth.[86]

Yale also wanted to hire those with doctorates because increasingly, as Wellington saw, academic lawyers of the middle and late 1970s spoke in terms of "law and," valuing work that drew on economics, legal history, philosophy, and hermeneutics. As both scholarship and courses like "Metaprocedure" showed, the language of interdisciplinarity that the realists had begun speaking was taking its place alongside that of doctrinalism. Many law professors without advanced degrees, such as Ackerman and Fiss, were becoming interested in speaking it too.[87]

And so Yale wanted to lead the bandwagon. Whether they taught law or studied it, the MAs and PhDs in the student body and on the faculty found interdisciplinary scholarship attractive. Small classes meant that professors could encourage interdisciplinary scholarship without being overwhelmed by it. In theory, the school's deadlines, more flexible than those of its counterparts, also gave students time to do it properly.

From the perspective of a law school anxious to avoid conflict, which it associated with the late 1960s, *and* be on the cutting edge, interdisciplinarity must have seemed attractive. Why recruit Critical Legal scholars when you could hire humanists and social scientists grateful just to have a job? That is not to say that Yale law professors consciously viewed interdisciplinarity as a substitute for the equally trendy Critical Legal Studies. But as it turned out, interdisciplinarity enabled the school to achieve intellectual leadership without embracing "extremist" politics, since few of the interdisciplinarians it recruited, like few of the others it hired, were identified with left politics. Further, Yale had always prided itself on its interdisciplinarity. In citing "the amazingly successful 1960s 'rediscovery'" of interdisciplinarity in the legal academy, Calabresi pointed to the work on psychoanalysis and law produced by Joe Gold-stein and others. Law turned "outward," then, in part because law professors and students who might have become economists, historians, literary theo-rists, or political scientists brought the insights they had acquired from those fields to bear on law, and in Yale's case because it made sense for the school to encourage them to do so.[88]

But law professors also looked elsewhere because they hoped that other disciplines would provide them with the tools to rebuild the internal foun-dations of justice that had crumbled in *Roe* and render law as right and fair as it had seemed during the great days of the Warren Court. Thus, for ex-ample, *Taking Rights Seriously* integrated "Law and" with the New Legal Pro-cess, reaching out to philosophy to show how legal liberalism might become more principled. At other schools, as at Yale, the overwhelming majority of faculty members clung to the political and legal liberalism associated with the 1960s: of thirty-eight Harvard law professors polled in the fall of 1972, for example, thirty-four supported George McGovern. Their isolation from the Burger Court and the White House made liberal law professors both more similar and more receptive to academics in other fields, more prone to write for each other and the long term, than for judges in the here and now.[89]

As the Yale law faculty reached out to other disciplines, it paid special atten-tion to Law and Economics. The school's investment in economics had been apparent as early as 1974, when Goldstein called attention to it. By building on the foundation of Rostow and Bowman, he noted, Yale had developed "a remarkable group of faculty who are especially interested in this area: Cala-bresi, Bork, Chirelstein, Winter, Leff, Klevorick, Ackerman and others." Wel-lington claimed that "no law school in the world" was "doing more systematic work in law and economics than Yale." That was an overstatement: Chicago still did more.[90]

Yet those hired in Law and Economics in New Haven still often approached the field differently from Chicagoans. In one of Calabresi's many responses to Posner, for example, he and his student Philip Bobbitt condemned the use of the market to allocate scarce resources needed to save lives, while bringing to light other distribution mechanisms. For "we need only consider propos-als such as: Everyone can be drafted to serve in wartime but anyone can buy his way out, or cancer chemotherapy will be auctioned to the highest bidder, to see how limited is the appeal of the market in a tragic situation." So, too, at a time when Chicago-trained lawyer-economists maintained that housing code enforcement would hurt the poor it aimed to help by creating higher rents and a lower housing supply, Ackerman argued that such enforcement could, as liberals had planned during the Kennedy-Johnson years, assist the poor. "In contrast to the Chicago school, some practitioners of law and economics (originally based in New Haven) contemplate a larger role for the state and for adjudication," Fiss observed. "Through the most ingenious of arguments they are able to embrace both the market and the activist state." [91]

There was some wishful thinking here. At least one of Fiss's colleagues, who belonged to the "New Haven" school of Law and Economics, wondered aloud whether there were enough like-minded souls at Yale for the liberal reformist brand of Law and Economics to warrant the New Haven label. The law school certainly received its share of endowed chairs and other financial support from the John Olin Foundation, dedicated "to the preservation of the principles of political and economic liberty as they have been expressed in American thought, institutions and practice." [92]

Further, the Yale faculty included a number of conservative lawyer-economists. Bork, of course, had been strongly affected by Chicago. For another example, although George Priest, a Wellington hire, lacked the veneration for the common law of leading Chicagoans, such as Richard Posner and Richard Epstein, he was a devotee of Chicago purveyor Henry Manne. In "The Invention of Enterprise Liability," Priest agreed that the growth of liability reflected the movement of modern tort law from a negligence standard toward one of "enterprise liability," essentially absolute liability, as a way of preventing accidents and spreading their costs, and that enterprise liability had spread beyond products manufacturers to reach many institutional and professional providers of services. Shifting the burden away from the consumer to corporations and other service providers, Priest maintained, was wrongheaded "because, in essence, it has tied an insurance contract to product sales that is more expensive to consumers than it is worth. Products and services have been withdrawn because the addition of this insurance premium has raised prices beyond the demand of a sufficient set of consumers to make these products and services marketable." One need not be conservative to object to aspects of enterprise liability (Calabresi had questioned it earlier). But Priest, Yale's John M. Olin Professor of Law and Economics, was conservative. He had presented "The Invention of Enterprise Liability" at a conference funded in part by Aetna Insurance, and he criticized the torts casebooks of the 1960s and 1970s for their liberalism. So, too, Alan Schwartz, who would soon become Priest's colleague, said that the individual behind Rawls's veil of ignorance would choose sales contracts that included a required disclosure over strict products liability. [93]

Such individuals helped spark "tort reform," if not a counterrevolution. Tort law had seemed poised to make enterprise liability prevalent in the 1970s. But the 1980s and 1990s witnessed the "unexpected persistence of negligence" and "liability-limiting" because the negligence standard was "far less distributive and requires far less participation from governmental units, than enterprise liability alternatives." Score one for the insurance companies.[94]

Nonetheless, as Priest recognized, because of Calabresi, Yale retained its image for sixties liberalism. The long argument between Calabresi and Posner "over the importance of efficiency as a value" was perceived as "the debate between the Chicagoan and the Yalie, the conservative and the ultraliberal."[95] While perhaps only Priest, the John M. Olin professor, would have thought him "ultra" liberal, Calabresi's high profile secured Yale's continued reputation as the anti-Chicago.

The law school that was emerging, then, possessed a certain aura. The "slaughter of the innocents" apparently scared Yale off rookies. It also had helped sour Yale on sociology: the Governing Board turned its back on the discipline after letting go Griffiths, Trubek, and Abel. Though the modern Law and Society movement had once made a place for itself at Yale, by the 1980s, Stanton Wheeler was its only remaining representative. And Dark Ages memories may have helped explain Yale's lack of enthusiasm for Critical Legal Studies.

Along with larger political currents, a perception of the law school's history may also have pushed it toward an identification with a new kind of legal liberalism and, in some instances, a politically liberal brand of Law and Economics that placed it in the center-liberal mainstream of the legal academy. And unlike Chicago, Yale did not put all its eggs in the basket of Law and Economics. To a lesser extent, it demonstrated interest in history and philosophy as well. In the academic world, Yale Law School was perceived as the interdisciplinarians' premier beachhead.

Wellington celebrated that. "What we teach," he said, "is dictated primarily by the scholarly interests of the faculty. This approach to the curriculum is why Yale is what it is: the most theoretical and academically oriented law school in America."[96]

The New York Times would single out a course at Yale, "Blood Feuds," an investigation of disputes and dispute resolution, as a symbol of a trend that became evident in the mid-1970s and "a sign of changing times in American legal education." Though its teacher, William Miller, was a visiting professor from Michigan, a school that may have been even more academic and theoretical than Yale, but was less prestigious, his story pointed to Yale's importance in spreading the gospel of interdisciplinarity. A specialist in Icelandic, Miller received his PhD in English from Yale in 1975, then headed to Wesleyan. "Tenure anxieties started me looking elsewhere and law was the obvious place," he told the *Times*. He obtained his JD from Yale in 1980 and soon became "one of the most sought-after legal academics in the country." The arrival in the legal academy of individuals such as Miller, many of them trained in law at Yale, led to new course offerings. According to the *Times*: "Virtually all the leading law schools offer what detractors call 'law and a banana courses' like Ethology of Law" at Yale, "Rhetoric, Law, and Culture" at Michigan, "Anthropology of Law" at Columbia, and "Law and Economics" almost everywhere.[97]

It was Yale, however, that became the academics' law school. Since it was long known as the intellectuals' law school, its best students had always shown interest in teaching. Abe Goldstein announced in 1968 that the school had decided that "we should train a group of people who could become the interdisciplinary teachers of tomorrow." As Wellington's deanship began in 1975–76, 4.7 percent of Yale law graduates between 1948 and 1975 were engaged in full-time teaching. By contrast, 2.9 percent of Harvard's 1948–75 graduates were similarly employed; each of the other major teacher-producing law schools, under 2 percent. While Harvard's size meant that it turned out the most teachers (13.9 percent), Yale had graduated 6.8 percent. In the years that followed, Yale stepped up its production. Of those teaching in 1988–89, 13 percent held degrees from Harvard, 8.3 percent from Yale.[98]

During Wellington's deanship, then, more Yale students who had done graduate work in other fields before beginning law school or who were acquiring their JD and PhD at the same time were drawn to law teaching. At the same time, Wellington recalled, "many on the faculty became increasingly interested in teaching teachers. I attribute this to faculty members' passionate beliefs in their own ideas, their desire for power, a clear recognition of the multiplier effect and an increasing distaste for private practitioners." So closely did the school become associated with the shift toward an academic and interdisciplinary approach to law that by the late 1970s, it did not seem sufficient that Yale was "the first major law school to have joint degree programs both inside and outside of Yale." Seeking to establish a less "mechanical approach to the problem of mixing legal training with interdisciplinary competence," the faculty actually considered offering a quick doctorate itself by resuscitating a degree long dormant, the Doctorate in Civil Law. That way, its proponents said, Yale could establish a joint JD-DCL program as "a vehicle for combining professional competence and interdisciplinary training in a way that will meet the needs of students who find the other joint degree choices unattractive" and who might well require an advanced degree to find a job in law teaching. Some, however, labeled the JD-DCL proposal "dilettantish," and it was dropped.[99]

The accusations of dilettantism did not die, however. Indeed, as other law professors followed the pied piper of interdisciplinarity, the shouts grew louder. Ironically, so did the gap between elite law schools and the rest of the university. Literary theorists viewed law professors who intruded in their domain with suspicion. Philosophers parodied their philosophy. Where once historians had condemned "law office history," they now cursed law professors' "history lite." Law professors with PhDs shuddered too, joining the chorus of humanists and social scientists who jumped on law professors. The "wholly gratuitous discussions of Nietzche, Saussure, Derrida, and Foucault" that became "*de rigueur* in law review articles about section 1983, contract doctrine, poverty law, and even Uruguayan prisons," huffed one philosopher who found himself teaching in a law school, simply reflected a desperate search "for an external, non-legal source of legitimacy or authority" at just the moment that faith in law was crumbling.[100]

And a gulf opened between interdisciplinarians and their predecessors on law faculties too, some of whom worried about the transformation of "the law school . . . into a colonial outpost of the graduate school." Thus although he himself had been a cheerleader for Law and Economics, Richard Posner chose a Yale conference on the nature and purpose of legal scholarship at the beginning of Wellington's second term at which to decry "deans at leading law schools" and Wellington in particular for making the "academic lawyer who makes it his business to be learned in the law and expert in parsing cases and statutes . . . seem a paltry fellow, a Philistine who has shirked the more ambitious and challenging task of mastering political and moral philosophy, economics, history, and other social sciences and humanities so that he can discourse on large questions of policy and social justice."[101]

Such scholarship, along with scholarship about scholarship, also deepened the divide between professors, attorneys, and judges. As Yale faculty members celebrated the increasingly specialized and theoretical nature of legal scholarship, the academy came to seem more out of touch. Attorneys reported that "scholarship, not teaching, is the be-all and end-all in academia, the coin of the realm; and scholars, even traditional ones, consider law practice the province of the brain dead." The judges were citing law professors' work less too.[102]

Although many law students, even at Yale, still lined up to work at large law firms, they did not feel their professors approved, either. After he became a circuit court judge, for example, Harry Edwards reported that his clerks agreed that "law school focused much more on the intellectual . . . to the exclusion, and indeed the disdain, of the practical." From their point of view, most professors acted as if "the graduates who went into practice were those who couldn't get teaching jobs."[103]

In reality, the chasm between academics and the profession had long existed, and it may not have yawned so wide. Much theoretical work had an impact on legal practice and education. Law and Economics scholarship transformed antitrust, just as theory changed the practice and teaching of negotiation. Where 63.46 percent of law journal contents had been fully or partially devoted to doctrinal analysis in 1960, 59.05 percent were in 1985. This drop was hardly substantial. Ultimately, the "law and" electives in law school catalogues and the new interdisciplinary scholarship of the 1970s and 1980s may have aided the profession far more than the old "law and" electives that had, after all, been a staple of the elite law school catalogues for a long time.[104]

Nevertheless, and despite his pride in his faculty, the "two culture" phenomenon—the growing divide between his professors and the bar and bench—worried Wellington sometimes. "Too many very able academic lawyers who, for whatever reasons, do not venture outside the ivy-covered walls, scorn the practicing lawyer and the work (deprecate it) and look for rewards only from within the universities," he complained. And after infusing the faculty with JD-PhDs, the dean morosely told a colleague on one occasion that "everything that the younger people were critical of" in the work of one prospective appointee "could have been said about mine."[105]

"FIZZ IN THE BOTTLE"?

That was the least of Wellington's troubles. Since the 1930s, Yale had played a proud number two to Harvard, always glorying in its realist past and its reputation as the small, liberal, and quirky alternative, even when students wondered whether Yale merited it. Now everything threatened to go sour. The law school was broke. The dean needed to rebuild the faculty at a time when, although law professors' salaries were rising compared to those of humanists and social scientists, the gap between their salaries and those of practitioners was growing. The fact that the median salary for full professors at Yale Law was lower than that for their counterparts at Harvard, Stanford, Columbia, NYU, and Penn just worsened the situation. To Leon Higginbotham, the dean complained that the "problem" was that "the very best black lawyers choose not to teach," a trend he found increasingly evident among white graduates as well. "Two factors seem to contribute to this frightening phenomenon: 1) Law faculty salaries, relative to salaries in the profession. There has always been a discrepancy, but the discrepancy today is greater than it has ever been. 2) Law practice is more interesting for a longer period of time while law teaching is more difficult than it has ever been and the prospects less certain." And although Wellington proved an able fundraiser, the late 1970s was no time to solicit large sums.[106]

The problems were legion. It was not just salaries. The building was a disaster. The homeless slept in the tunnels underneath the library. Yale Law School, one of the founts of the new public interest law, had none of the loan forgiveness programs for public interest lawyers that Columbia, Harvard, and Stanford possessed. Like presidents and provosts of other universities, Yale's raided law school revenues. Indeed, the university's prolonged financial crisis that had begun under Brewster and continued under his successors, Hannah Gray and A. Bartlett Giamatti, prompted the administration to grab whatever donations to the law school it could, irritating alumni and giving them little incentive to contribute money. One committee of alumni concluded that though the "Byzantine" nature of university finance made it impossible to determine conclusively "whose ox is being gored," it seemed as if the university was "the gorer," the law school "the goree."[107]

Then there was diversity. Many thought minorities were not joining law school faculties quickly enough. As Wellington acknowledged, Yale Corporation members were putting "considerable pressure" on Woodbridge Hall with respect to affirmative action, and "it appears that the Law School looms large in their thinking." Barbara Underwood became the second woman to receive tenure at the law school. The school offered a full professorship to Harry Edwards, an African American. But Edwards turned Yale down, and Wellington's frustration was clear when he wrote one former BLSU activist that the school's appointments committee "is actively seeking to recruit minority faculty members. Thus far we have not been successful." The dean and the Appointments Committee convinced two other African Americans, Drew Days and Harlon Dalton, to become junior faculty members in 1980 and 1981. Stephen Carter would follow in 1982.[108]

Whereas in the late 1960s, at least, Yale's affirmative action program for students had been well known, now it was just one among many. And when the survival of university affirmative action in admissions programs was jeopardized anew during Wellington's first term, the law school was not out in front. Wellington recommended to Acting President Hannah Gray that Yale sign Harvard University's amicus *Bakke* brief in favor of affirmative action that Lou Pollak, by now dean of the University of Pennsylvania Law School, had helped to craft. But Yale did not. Thus the law school, like the larger university, no longer took a visible position in support of affirmative action.[109]

Surprises also abounded as Wellington entered his second term. As Abe Goldstein put it, the dean "felt the force of retirements, unexpected deaths, judicial appointments, and the two-career family." Bruce Ackerman's departure for Columbia was an especially big blow. Wellington realized that his was "a story that will play an increasingly major role in Yale's future": Ackerman had gone to Columbia because it offered his spouse, a liberal lawyer-economist, a tenured position when Yale would not. The law school lost its spark plug. Wellington rightly compared Ackerman's importance as catalyst in the school's intellectual life during the late 1970s and early 1980s to Bickel's in the 1960s. Students worried that the school was "losing some of its best faculty" and that "the quality of the Yale Law School faculty has deteriorated" since Wellington's deanship began. They warned Wellington that "this concern has reached beyond the walls of the institution to law firms and judges."[110]

The *National Law Journal* sparked a flood of letters from concerned alumni when it published a front-page article in 1981 asking whether Yale Law School had "Lost Its Fizz." In maintaining that Yale had lost "its uniqueness," Charles Reich had sparked the question. According to him, "If you get [only] people from the mainstream, you don't have any fizz in the bottle." The *Journal* harked back to the mid-1960s, when the school had effervesced with "mavericks." By its account, the late 1960s and early 1970s had undone Yale: it rehearsed the war with the students and the exodus of the junior faculty during a period, the *Journal* reported, "now commonly described simply as the 'bloodbath.'" Then Yale had followed those departures by cutting "back some of the unusual programs that made it an unusually interesting school," such as Law and Modernization. Of course, the *Journal* also recounted allegations that Yale was "intellectually inhospitable" to Critical Legal scholars.[111]

But according to the article, Yale's problems went deeper than the fact that some believed it lacked intellectual diversity and had become a "resting place for highly competent, but essentially mainstream academics." Rumors abounded of rejected offers, impending departures, and recruiting difficulties. Ralph Winter told the *Journal*, "I think there are a growing number of people in law teaching who think we don't have anymore a critical mass of good people." The "purge" had given Yale "a reputation as a risky place for young academics to start their careers." Robert Clark, who had answered the call to Harvard, weighed in from Cambridge with the opinion that Yale had "a serious—really serious—faculty recruitment problem." And Paul Gewirtz joked, "I was relieved when a colleague told me he'd heard a rumor in Washington that I'd decided to leave. . . . It's become a new status symbol here."[112]

The article stressed student anger. Some 60 percent of the third-year class had recently signed a letter to Wellington declaring that as the class graduated, "those of us who have been concerned about the quality of education at Yale Law School remain concerned about many issues, most notably (1) the failure of Yale to secure a more diverse faculty through the hiring of more women and minority faculty members; (2) the failure of Yale to take measures to facilitate students' involvement and interest in the public interest sector of the legal profession [through the hiring of a full-time employee in the placement office to help students find public interest jobs]; and (3) the failure of Yale to fully address the issues of sexism and racism in the process of selecting students for admission to Yale Law School." Students feared, rightly, that the "take-rate" for women was declining, though they realized it was not dropping much. (The only fault they did not lay at the school's door was homophobia. Though divided over this issue, the faculty had headed off this charge in 1978, when Joe Goldstein insisted the school must protect all its students. Yale had followed the example of NYU and approved adding discrimination in sexual orientation as grounds for disqualifying a prospective employer from using its facilities for recruitment. Since Yale's students registered an 8:1 preference for that result, the faculty was just keeping up with the curve.)[113]

Student signatories pledged to restrict their financial contributions to the school until the school had corrected its problems. "It was the entire spectrum of the school that signed, everybody from the radicals to the apathetic — the people who are never interested in anything at all," one told the National Law Journal. They had delivered their pledge to the dean's office while he was away, placing it "where Dean Wellington would be sure to see it — on his chair." The National Law Journal characterized the episode as "a 1960s-style protest."[114]

Actually, the incident lacked the drama of "a 1960s-style protest" at Yale Law School. In fact, Wellington was still coping with the embarrassment caused by late sixties graduates. Students of the class of 1970 used their column in the Yale Law Report to mock Goldstein, with the class secretary addressing inquiries to "Dear Abie," to "the man who led a confused rabble to the Light at the End of the Dark Ages," holding a "Dark Ages Trivia Quiz," handing out, à la Esquire, "Dark Age Dubious Achievement Awards," and promoting The Official Dark Ages Handbook. Meanwhile, 1971 graduates complained that at the alumni meal to mark the transition between Goldstein and Wellington, they had "felt somewhat like a collection of dragons assembled in honor of Saint

George. . . . Lunch on Saturday, which was devoted to three narratives—by Dean Wellington, Judge Bazelon and Abe Goldstein of the life of Abe Goldstein, made it clear that Yale Law School is much as it was, and that we are still thought to represent the dark ages."[115]

By comparison to what had gone on in the sixties, students of the seventies lacked theatricality. And indeed, it was not clear to all that members of the class of 1980 even shared the goals of their sixties predecessors. Eugene Rostow, who was en route to the Reagan administration, insisted that "the large number of signatures [by the class of 1980] represents 'displaced' student concern that the curriculum should be made more traditional"![116]

Yet their presence made the students of the late 1970s more of a nuisance than their Dark Age predecessors. For example, the administration could censor the class of 1970 column and remove the class secretary, as it did when Wellington decided "he has got to go" and that he should be thanked for his "noble service" and "tactfully" told it is time for a change. The dean had less control over those inside school walls. Increasingly, like others in some undergraduate and graduate institutions elsewhere, the young at Yale Law School would become engaged by issues of diversity, multiculturalism, and identity politics. This, too, was a quest for community, democracy, and inclusiveness—one that followed from efforts during the 1960s to increase racial and gender diversity in the student body.[117]

To the dean, student charges that the faculty and student body lacked women and minorities seemed unfair. Wellington pointed, for example, to the hiring of Days and Dalton, the tenuring of Underwood, and the invitation to visit to Lea Brilmayer (who would be hired with tenure in 1982). He told the *National Law Journal* that it was "inefficient" to hire the full-time public interest placement officer the students wanted. And from the school's perspective, as minority students' credentials had improved, they had become "the most difficult to enroll, and Yale is continually fighting financial aid offers from several law schools."[118]

Privately, Wellington made it clear that the students had angered him. Publicly, however, he denied that the students irritated him, saying that though the graduates' message had at first "surprise[d]" him, he had then asked himself, "[I]sn't this marvelous" that Yale had moved "back to a situation where students are doing what students ought to be doing? . . . I thought it amusing and on the whole a good thing." To students, that "bemused detachment" showed that "even if Harry Wellington's support for student goals is a mile wide, it is only inches deep." He might mean what he said, but his style frustrated them.

Wellington was just "going through the motions," some charged. "I'm glad I went here," one departing graduate told the *National Law Journal*, "but I think the place is falling apart." Certainly, the article suggested that. "It really is a beauty," Wellington told a friend. "Most of the material comes from people who do not get tenure at Yale. We will survive."[119]

Problems there were that made the short term rocky, but Wellington's deanship gave the school its modern shape. To explain the developments of those years, it is worth asking what role the experience of the student siege during the Dark Ages played, as opposed to the larger sixties to which the Dark Ages belonged and the reaction against the sixties. Other than Bickel, Rostow, and Bork, few faculty members wrote about how the Dark Ages had affected them. It seems likely, however, that just as memories of the law school's unrest played some role in the rise of Critical Legal Studies, those memories helped explain Yale professors' rejection of CLS. The remembrances may even have helped to account for their embrace of a revised legal process theory and interdisciplinarity. The promotion decisions of the early 1970s, which may also have been related to the Dark Ages, proved important to the school's subsequent contours. They contributed to a determination largely to hire tenured individuals from other institutions who had proven themselves, and, perhaps, their politics. They may have caused timidity. In Mark Tushnet's view, the Dark Ages, a period he interpreted to include the faculty-student conflict of the late sixties and the promotion decisions that followed, had a "long-term effect" on Yale's "intellectual atmosphere": it was the Dark Ages that explained why professors claimed "that they are boldly going where no one has gone before, all the while looking over their shoulders nervously and asking, 'Is it safe?'"[120]

Yet memories of, and reactions to, national events, such as the end of the Warren Court and the growing popularity of conservatism, probably played at least as large a role as local events in determining the intellectual directions in which Yale grew during the 1970s and Wellington's deanship. Wellington's public law professors alluded often to the impact of the sixties on their legal thought, sometimes refashioning the period, whether or not they had been at the law school during the late 1960s. And since, even more than in most other law schools, Yale's public law scholars had set its tone and created its image, that was not unimportant. As Yale's professors had sought to bolster liberalism locally and nationally against the perceived onslaughts of the left during the 1960s, so too many of those who did not turn right sought to strengthen it against the perceived onslaughts of the left and right afterward.

In the end, only two conclusions seem certain. First, just as the sixties, in one form or another, prove an indispensable backdrop for understanding the emergence of contemporary political culture, so they played some part in the emergence of the modern Yale Law School between 1975 and 1985. Second, what the law school needed by 1985 was someone who could enable Yale to leave its growing pains behind.

Chapter Ten

Epilogue

Just keeping the ship afloat would prove problematic, given Yale's financial problems. But beginning in 1985, the school's prospects brightened. Guido Calabresi, the new dean, achieved financial independence from the university administration, raised the money required to change the school's culture, tamed student dissent, and thrust himself and his school into the national spotlight, all the while creating a mood there of "affection, support and achievement, of excellence and humanity."[1]

THE CULTURE OF YES

A descendant of the Finzi-Contini, Calabresi had fled Mussolini with his family in 1939. Jewish by birth, he was Catholic by choice. Both his parents had taught at Yale, he himself had attended Yale College and Law School, and his three children were Yale College graduates. Though his wife, a Radcliffe alumna, brought diversity to the family, she had grown up in New Haven, and her ties to Yale and its law school ran deep. Calabresi's intellectual ties to Yale ran deep too: he was steeped in legal realism and liberalism. Because everyone acknowledged his brilliance, he had made the jump from Assistant Professor to Professor in just three years. He remained at Yale his entire life, despite a Harvard offer.

He loved the limelight and possessed the resilience to espouse controversial and seemingly contradictory positions. He was a vigorous advocate. As dean, he would publicly denounce the Rehnquist Court: "I despise the Supreme Court and find its aggressive, willful, statist behavior disgusting." Tellingly, however, he made this comment in the course of explaining his support for

319

Guido Calabresi. (Courtesy Yale Law School Public Affairs Office.)

Clarence Thomas's nomination as a Supreme Court justice in a *New York Times* editorial. The episode was typical. Calabresi created "a new public role" for law school deans, the dean of Columbia said. "His words are exaggerated, sometimes bordering on the ridiculous, but they set standards for his own institution and everyone else." As if to illustrate his reputation for acrobatics, when a pipe bomb exploded in an empty Yale Law classroom in 2003, injuring some faculty portraits, Calabresi's did "a 270 degree flip and landed on its back, face up, completely undamaged."[2]

There were echoes of prior Yale deans in his demeanor. Calabresi had the magnetism of Robert Maynard Hutchins, the doggedness of Charles Clark, and the ego of Eugene Rostow. But Calabresi, universally known as "Guido," was more ebullient and approachable.

Calabresi also possessed the patrician and charismatic charm of Kingman Brewster, whose legal process jurisprudence he shared, though he lacked Brewster's reticence. He considered Brewster "a terrific wartime leader," who should have left when the war ended. But Calabresi worried more about donors. "He believed in dealing with things by spending money," he said of Brewster and, as Calabresi saw it, had displayed little anxiety about acquiring it, leaving Yale's financial situation precarious. Another difference between them, Calabresi thought, was that "I wear my love of Yale on my sleeve." That he did. Among elite law school administrators who followed, only the "hyperbolic enthusiasm and salesmanship" of John Sexton at NYU, "the hugging dean," matched Calabresi's. Indeed, no one loved Mother Yale more or held higher hopes for its law school than Calabresi.[3]

In fact, the new dean declared that "Yale is the only school going where someone has the chance to be serious about legal thought, but in a way that can still influence the real world." What did Calabresi mean to say about Harvard, a friend there asked? Unembarrassed, Calabresi replied that "even individuals aren't enough — size and faculty-studio ratios matter, too — and I do think we have an advantage."[4]

He was talking through his hat. Calabresi's greatest contribution, Associate Dean Stephen Yandle has said, was to use a smoke-and-mirrors game to claim there was no problem until there was no problem. In reality, the emperor's clothes had become ratty. The law school needed money, and while the turnaround in the economy helped, Calabresi understood that it also required financial independence to attract large gifts. (His predecessors had known that too but could not win it.) Since Harvard operated on the principle of "every tub on its own bottom," its law school could accumulate a surplus for use in subsequent years. "I wanted to be able to guarantee to graduates of the school that everything they gave to Yale Law School would be used by the School and not by other parts of the University," Calabresi explained, as well as "to be sure that if the University got into even small financial problems ('sneezed'), we, as such a small part of the place, would not end up being seriously hurt ('catching pneumonia')." And so, the dean and Yandle negotiated a "treaty" with President Benno Schmidt and Yale's provost that provided for a measure of law school financial autonomy. Independence — or more accurately, semi-independence — did not enable the law school to make its own investments, which remained part of Yale's endowment, but did permit its dean to manage expenses. "As a practical matter this means that we may be able to convince them to let us spend money on our building — even though that requires considerable effort — but they will only let us invest in something like [a] . . . hotel if they are ready to do it on their own."[5] "Independence" also increased Calabresi's budgetary flexibility and reduced the percentage of gifts he had to give back to the central administration. Most of all, "independence" meant a sense of freedom.

The process of negotiating it was lengthy and contentious. "You have a choice," Calabresi told the provost's office at one crucial point. "[W]ith luck, mirrors, and an awful lot of hard work, the Law School has gotten itself in a position where it can really nail down its current preeminence. To do so it doesn't need to take new monies from the University as much as it needs independence and the ability to keep the extra monies that I have raised." But, he continued, the administration resisted, trying "to take away the bulk of the extra money I have raised in order to eliminate fictitious deficits. . . . I can't live with that."[6]

Once he got his way, donations skyrocketed, particularly since Calabresi proved a natural fundraiser. When Wellington had left the deanship, he spoke of his relief at abandoning the "utilitarian" relationships that came of asking donors for money. "That froze me because I knew I couldn't raise money if my relationships were utilitarian," Calabresi said. "That couldn't be the way I asked for money." Then, to "my joy," the new dean found that many potential donors "were just like my students, a little older and had the same idealism, and I found that I liked them." Understanding that he was unable to ask for money without explaining how he intended to use it, he began sending the school's alumni and friends a lengthy annual letter telling them what was happening at Yale and his hopes for the school. The first reaction, he recalled, came from his father-in-law, a Yale law alumnus, who said it had moved him to exceed his usual annual gift but that no one other than a father-in-law would respond that way because the letter was too long. It turned out that most recipients also opened their checkbooks. Calabresi excelled at making the touch face-to-face too. On one occasion, he finally secured access to a conservative multimillionaire who had previously refused to grant him an audience. They spoke briefly before the individual mentioned that the dean had probably come for money. Yes, he had, Calabresi answered. "I'm not going to say no to you, and I'm not going to say yes to you," came the reply. The dean thought "for what seemed like an eternity," then responded: "That's the best news I've ever heard." Puzzled, the individual asked why, adding that the answer disappointed most. "We've only known each other for fifteen minutes," Calabresi said, "and it's clear we like each other, but you don't know me, so if you give me money now you won't give me as much as I need or you can afford to." A long courtship resulted in a $20 million gift.[7]

Contributions to the school's annual fund, $8,000 in 1949–50 and under $1.5 million in 1983–84, jumped to $9.5 million a decade later during the last year of Calabresi's deanship. His friendship with Lillian Goldman, whose family had no previous ties to Yale and who was engaged in an acrimonious dispute with her children over her late husband's estate, resulted in her $20 million donation to the school. It was the third largest in Yale University's history and "probably the biggest gift in the history of American legal education" at the time. Calabresi sensed Goldman's interest in opportunities for women and, more important, her determination to reconcile with her children while retaining her right to control the fortune she and her husband had accumulated. By the time the lawsuit was settled, somewhat unusually with his help, Goldman had received ample reminder that Yale Law had accepted women long before Harvard. Her award financed the reconstruction of the law library, endowed a day care center at the law school, and funded scholarships for women. And announcement of Goldman's generosity had proven an excellent kickoff to the law school's $130 million capital campaign, nearly $80 million of which had been raised within a year of its public launch. By the time the campaign concluded, donations reached $180 million. Predictably, Yale crowed it had outdone Harvard, which had recently raised $175 million; Cambridge officials responded by announcing they had made a "conservative estimate" of the gifts received and revised their final campaign total to $181 million.[8]

Whether or not he beat Harvard, Calabresi could deal with things by spending money. His fundraising success meant that anything—from improved loan forgiveness programs, to higher salaries, to a renovated building—was possible. Now, Yale Law School could replace—or supplement?—the culture of timidity with that of "yes."

Certain most graduates "would do me in if I suggested a new building," the dean earmarked part of his proceeds for renovating the old one. Faculty offices would receive a facelift and, ultimately, be furnished with Stickley pieces and Oriental rugs. The professors sitting in them received higher salaries. Perhaps his involvement with Law and Economics helped Calabresi realize that the school had to pay anyone it wanted the salary he or she would have received had the individual stayed put and used the Yale invitation to secure an even better counteroffer. "If you get someone cheap," he explained, "you're not getting someone cheap, you're getting someone angry." And he knew that he had to assure his colleagues that if they were "as good" as those he recruited, he would bring them up to the salary levels of the new hires.[9]

Professors benefited in other ways. The dean swung at the jinx against junior faculty that had created recruitment issues for the school since the 1970s. Having helped Wellington lure five assistant professors to New Haven in 1985, Calabresi oversaw the process by which all received tenure at once, the most since 1959. The result increased diversity: only one was a white man. Calabresi also saw he had to address the problems of academic couples and gave both Bruce Ackerman and Susan Rose-Ackerman chairs so that they could return to Yale.[10]

Like the ablest administrators, Calabresi knew his professors and their work, using his understanding to develop a strategy for strengthening the institution. His colleagues marveled at his skill in judging prospective hires' intelligence by subjecting them to the "Guido test" of a brief conversation. (With characteristic Yale arrogance, Calabresi opposed seeking external referees' letters on those the school wanted to hire or promote on the grounds that scholars elsewhere often undervalued "genuinely unusual" minds.) Fit was important too. The dean insisted Yale could thrive only by building on strength. It must add to its faculty doctrinalists, "law and" humanists/social scientists, those exploring the New Legal Process, and individuals researching "law and status," the legal system's impact on historically disadvantaged groups. But, Calabresi maintained, Yale also had to build on its strength in Law and Economics, as it did.[11]

*   *   *

Notably, he did little at first to increase diversity on the left. The political makeup of Calabresi's faculty thus remained sharply different from Harvard's, whose assistant professors were beginning to come up for tenure. The homogeneity may have helped keep the peace at Yale.

That gave it an advantage, at least in the short term, over Harvard, whose civil war the media delighted in following. During Calabresi's first term, the

New Yorker announced that arguments over the promotion of Critical Legal scholars had turned Harvard into "the most unhappy place." At the same time, the *Washington Post* publicized Dean James Vorenberg's open letter to the alumni, responding to "widespread concern that a 'war-like atmosphere threatens intellectual standards at the nation's most influential law school.'" Announcing that "The Split at Harvard Law Goes Down to Its Foundations," the *New York Times* trumpeted the existence of one six-member tenure committee that had "split three ways over one candidate."[12]

The 1987 promotion decision on Clare Dalton, for example, the subject of the three-way split, was deferred, then denied when she came four votes short of the requisite two-thirds majority only recently required for tenure. Dalton blamed not just her politics, but her sex. She sued, alleging sex discrimination, and received an out-of-court settlement. David Trubek, at work on integrating empiricism with Critical Legal Studies, received the two-thirds majority necessary for the offer with tenure that he had not gotten from Yale. Nevertheless, former Harvard Law dean Derek Bok, now Harvard's president, stunned the faculty by rejecting the recommendation. The move also surprised 200 law professors around the country, who signed a petition calling on the American Association of University Professors and the Association of American Law Schools to examine whether Harvard "might now be yielding to pressure from conservative faculty and alumni to resolve the disputes at its Law School by the expedient of cashiering left-wing professors."[13]

Bok soon shocked observers even more. Like Kingman Brewster, he did not replace a liberal law dean who had unsuccessfully sought consensus with a conciliator. Rather, Bok chose Robert Clark to succeed James Vorenberg. A graduate of Harvard Law and former seminarian with a PhD in philosophy, Clark originally had to "settle . . . for Yale Law School, . . . probably because he lacked the usual credentials." There, Clark contributed to Yale's strength in Law and Economics until Harvard overlooked his failure to serve on its law review or to clerk for an appellate judge and called him home. Back in Cambridge, Clark became a Republican and aired his disdain for Critical Legal Studies, complaining that its advocates had plunged the school into "prolonged, intense, bitter conflict" by engaging "in a ritual slaying of the elders." Clark himself acknowledged many faculty members believed Bok "wouldn't have the nerve" to make him dean. But choose Clark Bok did, apparently to act as Harvard's "enforcer," much as Goldstein had served as Yale's. "I don't want to stamp out CLS people," Clark told the media. "I just want to domesticate them." That required a firm hand: where his predecessor had called faculty meetings every two weeks, Clark held two in his first four months. Where his predecessor had made himself an ex officio member of the appointments committee, Clark installed himself as chair. "He's the no bullshit dean and this is the no bullshit future," one Critical Legal scholar told the press. Conflict intensified.[14]

Calabresi's approach to hiring appeared markedly different from Clark's. Where Clark seemed determined to steer away from appointing those on the left, Calabresi's demeanor was more open. Insofar as appointments were concerned, the result might not differ all that much. The Yale faculty said its dean's mantra was "Talk left, appoint right."[15]

There was some truth to that. For one example, Calabresi brought John Langbein, a politically conservative doctrinalist and legal historian, to Yale from Chicago. Langbein's critique of the adversary system in civil and criminal procedure and his vigorous advocacy of the inquisitorial model in criminal trials might not appeal to those left of center, but his work on the comparative history of the criminal trial process, like his scholarship on trusts and succession, was at once original and important.[16]

For another, Calabresi lured housing and property specialist Robert Ellickson away from Stanford. The child of New Dealers, Ellickson had lost his faith in government as a Yale law student during the peak of Lyndon Johnson's Great Society. His book, *Order Without Law: How Neighbors Settle Disputes*, imaginatively combined Law and Society and Law and Economics scholarship. Based on fieldwork exploring how rural residents resolved disputes about wayward cattle, it demonstrated that neighbors did not bargain from legal entitlements, but frequently applied "informal norms of neighborliness to resolve disputes even when they knew that their norms were inconsistent with the law." Thus Ellickson came to appreciate "how unimportant law can be" and turned the Coase theorem on its head, while retaining Coase's faith in rationality, voluntariness, and mutuality. Where Coase contended that "the *absence* of transaction costs is what may make the law irrelevant," Ellickson argued that "the *presence* of transaction costs is what leads people to ignore law in many situations." The route differed, he concluded, but the "end reached is exactly the one that Coase predicted: coordination to mutual advantage without supervision by the state." Such findings provided grist for Ellickson's argument that it was "anachronistic for the current generation of anti-market legal scholars to be toiling to spin out armchair rationalizations for Old-Left programs," such as rent control. And neither affordable housing nor shelters would solve the problem of homelessness for those who lacked the means to buy or rent housing, Ellickson maintained. In fact, shelters *caused* homelessness by drawing in those who might otherwise stay with relatives or friends, enter an institution, or find permanent housing.[17]

Though such arguments made liberals and the left livid, Calabresi sought balance by pouring increased resources into expanding a student favorite since the late sixties, clinical education. He raised clinicians' salaries, making them commensurate with the academic faculty's. He established the William O. Douglas chair for a clinical professor, "the only name chair in the country specifically designated for a member of the Clinical faculty," which went to Stephen Wizner, director of the clinical program since the Dark Ages. He made clinicians eligible for indefinite appointments, a status akin to tenure. And he announced plans to transform the decrepit and dirty clinic into an attractive space. Most important, the dean convinced the faculty his actions assisted the entire law school community. Theoreticians profited, along with clinicians. The clinic freed theorists to teach courses such as "Metaprocedure." When the press reported that unlike Yale professors' interdisciplinary courses, their black-letter offerings proved "often uninspired, kind of half-hearted," Yale's "regular" faculty could say clinicians were teaching students how to become better lawyers in a way that some doubted doctrinal courses did. "As law school teaching and scholarship across the country have become more theoretical, and as Yale, inevitably has been the leader in this move, the importance of making available to students clinical education of the highest quality cannot be overstated," Calabresi shrewdly observed.[18]

Then, too, the clinic contributed to the school's political capital. Harold Koh, one of the five junior professors tenured from within during Calabresi's deanship and a future dean of the school himself, argued before the Supreme Court that the Bush-Clinton policy of intercepting Haitian refugees at sea and returning them to Haiti without asylum hearings was illegal, then blasted administration policy on the steps of the Court at a rally attended by Jesse Jackson. (Though the Court did not hand him a victory, Koh went on to burnish Yale's reputation for liberal public service by becoming Clinton's Assistant Secretary of State for Democracy, Human Rights and Labor.) The clinical program's many well-publicized courtroom battles and focus on homelessness, domestic abuse, immigration, and capital punishment preserved Yale's image as flagship of public interest law and "good guy" politics.[19]

The dean also used the funds he raised to establish a generous financial assistance program for graduates with heavy loan burdens who sought low-paying jobs. He threatened to resign when the Yale Corporation initially refused to approve it. The Corporation's about-face meant, as Calabresi said, that Yale became the only law school that did not place the focus on definitions of the "public interest," but on salary: "At Yale, the public interest is defined, as it should be, by each graduate for himself or herself." Thus the new Career

Options Assistance Program (COAP) would benefit "those who work for the prosecutors *or* legal aid," those who taught for pittances or started public interest firms of the left or right; "and yes, . . . those who are at the bottom of the pay scale in the Justice Department of either party." As that suggested, the New Legal Process scholar proved a New Legal Process dean, turning to the liberal solutions of neutrality and process to maintain the peace once he had raised the money that could make conflicts over scarce resources unnecessary. The same tendency marked his approach to the culture wars and the revival of activism. As both scholar and as administrator operating within the New Legal Process intellectual milieu, he worked to soften the sixties spirit.[20]

"MAKING LIBERALISM MATCH ITS CLASSIC DEFINITION"

Unlike those at Yale during the late 1960s or other law schools during the 1990s, Calabresi gloried in student discontent and disagreement about civil liberties and diversity. His deanship witnessed both. Calabresi's colleagues, who remembered the 1960s, might otherwise have dealt with them differently. "The Dark Ages have their left their impact even now," one of them said in 1992. "Issues come up and members of the faculty say, 'Well, that's like when the students invaded Lou Pollak's house in 1969.'" The cases of both Harvard and Boalt, however, indicated that shows of firmness could backfire.[21]

*   *   *

The revival of student activism was not unique to Yale. Some issues that had preoccupied sixties students had become less important to reformers. Though the style of legal education remained unpopular, it generally had become gentler, and most students apparently expected to dislike law school now. While student participation in governance, dissatisfaction with grades, and the traditional criteria for law review membership surfaced at Harvard during the early 1980s, law students elsewhere apparently demonstrated relatively little interest in participating in the work of faculty. They do not seem to have made grade reform a pressing issue, either, perhaps in part because they worried more about the job market. And most elite law schools in the late 1980s and early 1990s had seemingly embraced affirmative action in student admissions.[22]

There was, however, one overriding concern upon which law students in the 1980s and 1990s frequently focused their demands. During the Reagan-Bush years, students feared affirmative action was losing ground. Further, the diversity of student bodies made the demographic homogeneity of faculties all the more striking. There was anxiety, too, about a new wave of racism on campus. Students hoped that a more diverse faculty could change the climate, and they sought a voice, whether formal or informal, in hiring. Their campaign was part of a nationwide revival of student activism, a debate about diversity in the academy, and a movement to demand that law schools hire more women, minorities, and others with nontraditional backgrounds and perspectives. Where students of the sixties wanted more women and minorities at classroom desks, those of the 1980s and 1990s sought more behind the lectern. Even where law faculties possessed a left, professors did not take the initiative: the students led.[23]

The law school movement gathered force after students in Boalt's Coalition for a Diversified Faculty, a group first launched in the late 1970s and later revived, organized the first annual "National Strike Day" in 1989. Coalition members had at first focused their efforts on the lack of diversity at home, sitting in at Dean Jesse Choper's office in 1988. When Choper, an Earl Warren clerk, Democrat, and administrator who made Abe Goldstein look like a patsy (if the student press is to be believed), called the campus police, Boalt professor Eleanor Swift, a 1970 Yale Law School graduate, was the only faculty member to speak at a rally in support of the students charged with criminal trespass. Then, inspired by her experience on a National Lawyers Guild mission to Nicaragua, coalition member Renee Saucedo told other students they should make the effort "bigger than us." Her peers pleaded lack of resources: there was as yet no internet to link them easily to activists at other schools, and the coalition was small. Saucedo went to the Boalt Hall Library, grabbed a guide to the law schools, and began telephoning, contacting BALSA and La Raza groups across the country to ask whether they would participate in a nationwide strike. When Boalt activists learned of the enthusiastic reactions, they changed course, working with Saucedo to launch National Strike Day and make it an annual event.[24]

It was a success. At Boalt, nearly 90 percent of the students did not cross picket lines. Nationwide, more than thirty schools participated in the first National Strike Day, and schools substantially increased their hiring of professors of color, who constituted 10 percent of the full-time law professorate by 1990–91.[25]

Thus while Harvard professors continued to bicker over Critical Legal Studies and the split between left and right, their students focused on the absence of racial and gender diversity among their teachers and brought the sixties to their school. More than their professors, students seemed to understand that Critical Legal Studies had peaked, giving way to, or being replaced by, both Critical Race Theory and feminist legal theory. To some extent, both movements seemed CLS progeny, with feminists studying the interrelationship between law and gender and Critical Race Theorists concentrating on the interplay of law and race. But at Harvard, left white males on the faculty remained most interested in hiring more people like themselves. Some change had come: the number of women professors in tenured and nontenured positions increased from three to seven between 1981 and 1987, and there were now four African American male professors. But progress did not take place quickly enough for students. The faculty included no women of color, whom students assumed would become allies.[26]

The only professor wholly on their side, as they saw it, was Critical Race Theorist Derrick Bell. Where meritocrats behaved as if race, sex, and class had little impact on educational achievement, Bell contended that race, sex, and class often determined educational opportunity. Consequently, the credentials on which law school hiring committees traditionally placed such weight — grades, law review editorships, and prestigious clerkships — proved of little use as indicators of potential.[27]

Students agreed that their professors must develop a broader definition of merit. Where the battle between professors over CLS had received most attention in the 1980s, activists sensed a new war in the making in the 1990s. Clark had "sought to eliminate the label 'the Beirut of law schools,' but . . . a different sort of Beirut is forming," the *Harvard Law Record* said, one involving a "battle between the dean and the students" over diversity on the faculty.[28]

The situation did not seem to bother Clark. To detractors, he seemed intent on carrying an "intellectual glass slipper across the nation" in pursuit of a "'qualified' woman of color to join the faculty." Candidates were invited to visit for a year to see whether the shoe fit, a system derided as "rotating diversity." But to the frustration of student activists, Harvard refused to hire Cinderella. In 1990, the newly established Harvard Law School Coalition for Civil Rights, an umbrella group that brought together African Americans, Latinos, Native Americans, gays, lesbians, bisexuals, the disabled, the Harvard Chapter of the National Lawyer's Guild, and its Women's Law Association capped a day of protest with an all-night strike and sit-in outside Clark's office to protest the lack of women and minority professors. (Since it was Passover, they harkened back to the days of the Black-Jewish civil rights alliance there by singing both "We Shall Overcome" and "Dayenu.") It was the beginning of annual spring sit-ins on National Strike Day at the dean's office. "We're staying all night until the dean agrees to listen to us," students told the media. They maintained that

Clark had driven them to direct action. He showed little interest in discussion; he was once photographed shielding his face with his hands as he escaped from students and the media. This time, he had been a "no-show" at the recent diversity rally, which had drawn hundreds. When students searched for him, "they got a grunt and a door shutting them out of his inner sanctum." Here was another issue, when framed as Harvard's conflict between excellence and equality, that attracted the media and even sparked a protest led by Jesse Jackson.[29]

Like their predecessors at Yale who had pressed the faculty to admit more minorities, Harvard students had found an issue of equality about which they cared and felt disenfranchised. The chief contrast with 1960s Yale was that Harvard's young students had crafted an "organized, sophisticated, and highly mobilized" multiracial coalition. That development itself, along with the fact that the coalition's leaders were women and men, was a legacy of the 1960s.[30]

Students soon added a new twist that took them beyond the sixties. The Coalition for Civil Rights took administrators by surprise when members filed perhaps the first lawsuit ever by law students against their professors. Plaintiffs argued that Harvard damaged them by employing practices that had a disparate impact on the hiring of women and minorities and denied students access to different points of view, role models, professional and business opportunities, and a tolerant atmosphere. The coalition asked the court to enjoin the faculty from using its current hiring criteria and direct professors to establish specific goals and a timetable for increasing women and minorities. "We have negotiated. We have protested. We have taken to the streets," one activist said. "Now we use the only instrument of power Harvard Law School seems to understand."[31]

The young characterized the case as "the *Brown* v. *Board of Education* of the 1990s," preventing their teachers from "steal[ing] the show" by isolating all of them from the litigation. Told that no Harvard law professors supported them, one activist responded, "Of course not. . . . We're suing them." Unlike *Brown*, this would yield no symbolic victory: the CCR lost at trial when the court concluded coalition members lacked standing to sue. While the judge declared himself "impressed with the students' apparently sincere concern over the impact upon them of the alleged lack of diversity," and Clark maintained he was "gratified that the judge took special note to commend these students for the quality of their advocacy," students criticized the condescension. "We are trying to end discrimination at the Harvard Law School," one said. "We are not doing this as some sort of clinical." Although the Supreme Judicial Court of

Massachusetts granted direct appellate review, the coalition lost there on procedural and substantive grounds. Still, the coalition kept the suit in the courts and in the headlines for two years.[32]

Meanwhile, the pressure continued on other fronts. Despite Clark's repeated request for the cancellation of National Strike Day, the coalition organized a teach-in and boycott of classes, joined by hundreds, to protest the lack of diversity on the faculty in the spring of 1991. Only the brutal murder of Mary Jo Frug, a local law professor married to a Harvard Critical Legal scholar, halted plans to occupy Clark's office. But one week later, they were back. "For the first time in Harvard Law School's history, a group of students successfully shut down the Dean's office for an entire day."[33]

And students were inflamed anew when Clark broke the faculty deadlock over lateral appointments. The dean engineered approval of four tenured offers to a slate of professors with divergent politics. That ensured that right, center, and left would cooperate to produce the two-thirds vote necessary for each candidate, for each faction would get something. Yet although the candidates' politics varied, their race and sex did not. The same issue of the *Record* that featured news of the Coalition for Civil Rights' argument before the Supreme Judicial Court included another startling headline: "4 White Men Offered Tenure." Notably, Appointments Committee member Duncan Kennedy told students that the chosen constituted a "politically balanced slate" and represented "a package deal." The faculty still seemed disinterested in racial and gender diversity.[34]

Clearly, left faculty members did not lead or incite the rush to the barricades. "Tenured radicals" of the late 1960s, such as Kennedy, wanted students to leave the dean to them. Doubtless, when one's "caste" changes, as that of some onetime student activists had, it seems reasonable to assume one can handle the problems that caste can cause more effectively than outsiders. Thus can the paternalized become paternalists.[35]

In the words of the *New Republic*, news of the four offers "unleashed a spasm of revolt." How could the school at once embrace merit and political package deals? "It almost looks as if they did it out of spite," one activist said. Over 400 students throughout the university walked out of classes in protest. Clark fanned the fire. Explaining why students did not recognize the four offers for the "tremendous achievement" they were, the dean told the press, "The minority students need a sense of validation and encouragement, with the fundamental problem being a need for self-confidence that plays itself out as, 'Why doesn't Harvard Law School have more teachers who look like me?' In a sense we're dealing here with one of the symptoms of affirmative action."[36]

Simultaneously, Frug's murder became a civil liberties issue. Ensuring free speech was a challenge for which Clark felt ready. "My goal is to manage diversity," not bring the visions to "heel," he maintained. As dean and scholar, according to the *Boston Globe*, he hoped "to contribute another little bit of framework for the stance that until recently was called without hesitation 'liberal'; to work out the relationship between the individual and his or her community without asserting the absolute primacy of either."[37]

No luck: after bitter debate, the *Harvard Law Review* posthumously published Mary Jo Frug's last essay, "A Postmodern Feminist Legal manifesto," which was then parodied by two review members, who circulated the "He-Manifesto of Post-Mortem Legal Feminism" by "Mary Doe, Rigor-Mortis Professor of Law," complete with raunchy footnotes. Most criticized the parody, but agreement ended there. Later, the faculty would outrage First Amendment absolutists by banning "speech of a sexual nature that is unwelcome, abusive, and has the effect of educating an intimidating, demeaning, degrading, hostile, or otherwise seriously offensive educational environment."[38]

But that was not until after students had connected Clark's "inaction" on the parody to his failure of leadership on diversity and called for his resignation during their 1992 spring protest. Ignoring a pointed warning that the choice "to test the limits of appropriate behavior" this year might carry disciplinary consequences, activists donned Robert Clark masks to conceal their identities and occupied the hallway outside the dean's office for an entire day. "24 hours of excluding the Dean from his office pales in comparison to 175 years of systematic exclusion from the faculty," the students declared.[39]

Retribution followed swiftly. Declaring that the Statement of Rights and Responsibilities adopted after anti–Vietnam War demonstrations included no rules related to the parodists' behavior, the Administrative Board refused to take disciplinary action against Frug's ridiculers. At the same time, it moved against the occupiers of Clark's office, who asked for, and received, the first public Administrative Board trial in the law school's history. A two-day trial reminiscent of Eric Clay's at Yale followed, which included testimony from staff members about whether the protesters had threatened them. Like Clay's, it was open only to members of the law school "community," such as it was. The Administrative Board concluded that those who occupied the dean's office had violated the Statement by interfering with the activities of university members. And it officially reprimanded, though it did not suspend, the students who had stormed the dean's office. Many saw a double standard at work. "[W]hen I think of the Spring," one recalled bitterly, "I think of Bob Clark's refusing to take action against the . . . gang-bang upon the scholarship of Mary Jo Frug while at the same time vigorously attempting to suspend" the diversity movement's leaders.[40]

If this was going on at Harvard, Yale needed but to tread water to keep ahead. Yet Yale's success was not just a function of Harvard's setbacks. Calabresi handled dissension in general and disagreement over diversity in particular very differently. He received better press too.

*   *   *

As a university, Yale made clear its allegiance to the libertarian tradition during the last days of Brewster's presidency, when an audience shouted down William Shockley to prevent him from giving a speech contending that African Americans were genetically inferior. Historian C. Vann Woodward chaired a committee that ruled Yale must not tolerate disruption of speech, no matter how hateful. As Calabresi's deanship began, the free speech issue arose in diverse contexts.[41]

At the same time that the university administration cracked down on college and law school student opponents of apartheid who built shanties in front of Woodbridge Hall to protest Yale's refusal to divest its stock in companies doing business in South Africa, the College Executive Committee placed Wayne Dick, a conservative undergraduate, on probation for circulating unsigned fliers attacking gay members of the Yale community. Though the administration backed down on the shanties, Dick did not prevail at his first hearing because "the Committee was hopeless." There was then no right of appeal, but when the committee's membership changed, the new members suggested Dick apply for a rehearing. There, Calabresi and Woodward persuaded the committee to correct this "travesty" and to reaffirm the commitment to free speech. Dick's flier was "shameful and disgusting," the dean said, but it was protected speech, and he had been punished because his views were not considered "correct." Calabresi received great press for his role in what he called "making liberalism match its classic definition." (He also insisted on the right of Yale students to watch the pornographic "Wanda Whips Wall Street" in the law school auditorium, while delivering a speech beforehand reminding students, as he had told Dick privately after successfully defending him publicly, that words could wound.)[42]

As a liberal in the tradition of Mill as much as LBJ, Calabresi seemed to welcome every new controversy as an occasion for stressing the importance of freedom for the speech we hate. He also insisted on sharing credit. "In the law faculty, people who would be viewed as far-left, far-liberal, far-right, near-and far-everything, all joined in," Calabresi said of the Dick case. "*This* school, at least, behaved in a way that made me proud."[43]

In absolute terms, there was not then much of a "far-left": Yale still differed from Harvard in that respect. Like clinicians elsewhere, Stephen Wizner and others in the Legal Services Organization leaned left. But they were not part of the academic faculty. At the time Calabresi became dean, Harold Koh had not yet taken on the cause of Haitian refugees, and only two academics occupied the left, both scholars of what Calabresi called law and status. They were Harlon Dalton, an African American associated with Critical Race Theory in the process of establishing a reputation for himself as an expert on AIDS and the Law,[44] and Robert Cover.

During the early years of Calabresi's deanship, Cover was especially visible. Alone among the academics, Cover moved his office to the Legal Services Organization, where he could be with the clinicians and help students with cases. During the crisis that took place when administrators refused to divest Yale's holdings in companies that did business in South Africa, he "stood with us, his students," providing legal counsel when the university suspended them, leading a teach-in, and supporting them in other ways. He also represented Wayne Dick at his first hearing. But in 1987, Cover died suddenly at age forty-two before Dick's rehearing. He immediately assumed a special place in the Yale pantheon. That made sense because he embodied an important face of Yale's historic self-image. But some were cynical about "the apotheosizing of the late Robert Cover, who taught at an institution that, as suggested by its hiring practices, appears to believe that one Cover is worth ten economists (which may actually have the multiplier right). The message may be, 'Well, we may not have figured out what to do, but the fact that we revere Cover shows that we remain committed to the left of the political spectrum.'" By lauding Cover, and the faculty's behavior in the Dick case, the dean reinforced his school's image as inclusive and civil libertarian.[45]

Soon speech issues arose inside the law school. The Federalist Society had held its first conference at Yale when it was a small band of conservative law students led, among others, by Calabresi's nephew. During Calabresi's first year as dean, when the society invited Clarence Pendleton, Ronald Reagan's African American director of the Equal Employment Opportunity Commission, to speak, its posters advertising the event were defaced by graffiti labeling Pendleton a Reagan stooge. The incident alarmed the dean, who stressed, he proudly told the *Wall Street Journal*, "People who cannot engage in free speech, who remove or deface expressions of views with which they disagree, have no place in this School!" In appointing a committee of faculty and students "to consider possible responses to the poster incident," Calabresi insisted that his purpose was "not to develop 'speech rules.'" The New Legal Process school focused on consensus and public values: the dean wanted to understand how such incidents "reflect underlying problems in our community."[46]

"Speech rules" were, however, the result. The upshot was "the Wall," a portion of the building at the center of the law school dedicated to expressions of opinion by students and other members of the community, a place where "[a]nything goes, as long as it's signed." Unlike Robert Clark, Calabresi phased in the new policy in orderly fashion. Insisting anonymity was a right, some still called the Yale dean's position a retreat from the Woodward Report—which it was, as well as a retreat from Calabresi's stance in the Dick case. Yet liberalism was nothing if not flexible, and the policy was suited to the overheated environment of the small school. Further, while conceding his critics had a point, the dean also pointed to the Wall's special place as a forum for free speech. Anyone who took the time to write there should not object to "brick bats," he maintained. "*That's* what free speech is all about."[47]

Of course, in reality, exerting control was high on Calabresi's agenda. (In discussing his own scholarly attack on subterfuge, he engagingly volunteered that everyone wrote about his own weakness.) Like Clark, he hoped to manage diversity. Calabresi's liberalism was administrated, a legal process liberalism aimed at reviving public morality and achieving consensus, despite disagreement. As the dean said privately, he had tried "to control some of the excess" that "total free speech can lead to by establishing: (1) a wall, where people can say anything they wish (this tends to limit and channel the place in which this rough, turbulent, and often offensive speech takes place); and (2) a requirement that all things that go up on the wall (except for criticism of the faculty, administration, or Dean), must be signed." Requiring a signature had proven especially effective in cutting down "tastelessness." "It has meant that people have generally been controlled by peer pressure and so we have not had here the degree and pervasiveness of truly offensive displays that most other schools have had." And, lest student authors fear their former views would haunt them in future confirmation hearings, Yale's administrators thoughtfully destroyed statements on the Wall every two months.[48]

Despite its limitations, the Wall encouraged an explosion of criticism. Some of it was directed at the profession. In 1988, for example, activists encouraged everyone to wear pink triangle pins to law firm interviews and to query their interrogators about firm policies on pro bono work and the hiring of students of color, gays, and lesbians. "I think as a group at Yale, we're in a more powerful position because we're courted," one student told the *Wall Street Journal*. "In some ways that gives us a special obligation, to be as risky as we can." Students then used the Wall to share feedback on the "most often told lies" — including "A number of our people are involved in pro bono" and "I believe in values and this firm is about legal values."[49]

Calabresi portrayed this work as progress. The young in the sixties had immersed themselves in "solely social issues," he informed the *Journal*. Their successors, on the other hand, integrated social issues with their lives. That they were querying "law firms at all is interesting," he said. "Students weren't asking [such questions] . . . of law firms in the late '60s. They weren't interested in *talking* to law firms." The dean also stressed that the *Journal* had overlooked the students' questions about how the interviewers' firms treated those "deeply religious," thus reassuring irritated conservative alumni that students were open to difference. Here, Calabresi's genius for publicizing Yale and his desire to make the activists of the 1980s more constructive than their sixties predecessors made him ahistorical. Law students at a number of institutions during the late sixties had circulated questionnaires to firms about their pro bono work policies, and one such initiative had originated at Yale. Still, the dean's attitude seemed to contrast sharply with that of liberal Yale law professors who dealt with students during the Dark Ages.[50]

Calabresi welcomed criticism when students aimed it at the school too. Issues of diversity and status also preoccupied Yale's students. In 1988, the Society of American Law Teachers (SALT) ranked Yale worst for women in terms of faculty hiring. But women were noticeable not just for their physical absence. At a time when feminist legal theory was establishing a presence in the elite legal academy, Yale possessed no high-profile feminist legal scholar. It did possess an untenured teacher of feminist law, who had not yet published a great deal and who was leaving the law school without seeking tenure, publicly alleging that Calabresi had told her he did not find feminist legal theory "interesting, important or worthwhile."[51]

Yale was, in short, behind, an inauspicious situation for a dean who had avowed his interest in law and status. In denouncing Critical Legal Studies for its nihilism, Owen Fiss, one of the faculty's most prominent members, had hailed feminism as a new cause which "provoked powerful memories" of the Second Reconstruction and might regenerate belief in public values. And as he said, it was an "embarrassment" that Yale possessed more than seven professors who aligned themselves with Law and Economics and no Critical Legal scholars. Feminism might help Yale to preserve its reputation for progressivism.[52]

In fact, Calabresi wanted to hire the distinguished and controversial feminist legal theorist Catharine MacKinnon, who had revolutionized the field of sex discrimination law. But the same year that SALT revealed how few women were on the Yale law faculty, the *National Law Journal* reported that the battle within the Yale faculty over whether to offer a visiting appointment to MacKinnon had left some wondering whether the school indeed possessed "a commitment to attracting a diverse faculty—including professors who use non-traditional research methodologies (such as feminist and critical legal approaches) or who have radical liberal political beliefs." Reportedly, one of the school's tenured members had said she would find dealing with MacKinnon "obnoxious" and urged colleagues to vote against her if they would prefer to see the feminist scholar "hit by a truck and go away." Professors told the press that the debate's "political overtones" reminded them "of the very public war in recent years over Critical Legal Studies at Harvard Law School." Though that battle was moving into a new phase at Harvard, the debate reminded Yale students that their school possessed no Critical Legal scholar. Fiss conceded that the young's interest in the movement remained "strong and intense" in New Haven, "where the peculiar faculty recruitment practices of that institution have made the students feel that they are being kept from something delicious and naughty."[53]

Meanwhile the media was reporting that the Yale faculty had voted against tenuring Dalton, deciding instead to extend his contract. Students were outraged: on the "monochromatically mainstream liberal" faculty, they saw the African American "as the champion of the diverse groups who have no one else to speak for them," and as "one of the few" professors to whom gay students and those of color could "turn to for advice and support." Some were also complaining that admissions of students of color at the law school had declined, minorities felt "invisible in the curriculum and silenced in the classroom," and the curriculum was sexist and homophobic too.[54]

What followed was a strike to demand tenure for MacKinnon and Dalton, a one-day boycott of classes, and a nine-hour teach-in that drew hundreds of Yale law students to hear MacKinnon and others discuss diversity issues at the school. Ultimately, Dalton was promoted; though she won the requisite two-thirds majority for a visiting position, MacKinnon did not receive a permanent offer. (Characteristically, Calabresi, one of MacKinnon's admirers, put the best face on the school's vote against the MacKinnon offer, writing that Yale was "the only school in the land in which a $2/3$ vote in her favor has ever been obtained," and insisting that outcome was "especially remarkable since the publicity which surrounded the appointment inevitably makes people more reluctant to vote favorably." Privately, the dean labeled MacKinnon's loss of the vote for a permanent appointment "my greatest failure.") Dalton credited the students' "Tenure for Harlon" buttons and the strike with "shaking people awake" and causing his colleagues, who "had forgotten about me," to give him and his work "a second look."[55]

Other law schools witnessed similar activity, but only Yale administrators seemed to revel in it. While Clark stayed away from diversity rallies, Calabresi addressed Yale's. "There is no institution, no school in America that cannot do more," the *Harvard Law Record* reported him saying. "But I think this school has done more than most. Is that anywhere near enough? Of course not." Characterizing the strike as a "smashing success," Associate Dean Yandle said, "I can't imagine anyone not being influenced by today." Calabresi applauded "the reawakening of student activism" and "the rebirth of the teach-in" in his letter to the school's friends, while using the occasion to stress community and consensus: "Passions ran high, but when, at the senior dinner, the graduating class gave awards to those who had done most for the School, lo and behold, one of the most dedicated and fire-eating strike leaders, and one of the strongest and most thoughtful opponents of the strike, were among those chosen by their classmates (and both got universal standing applause)."[56]

Calabresi avoided defensiveness even when students targeted him. He once created a furor by characterizing a signed poster on the Wall of an erect penis, with the message, "Sexism Rears Its Unprotected Head. Men: Use Condoms or Beat it," as "exceedingly vulgar and disgusting" and branding the student who had hung the poster "self-indulgent and unnecessarily crude." Calabresi said he spoke out to protect the views of those, such as staff, but he incensed the young by singling out the student who had put up the poster, an AIDS educator, "for a personal rebuff." Unlike Clark, Yale's dean never avoided students. Now, some twenty-five of them "crowded around Calabresi for about two hours . . . in front of 'the wall' arguing with him about the poster's implications for free speech." Most loved the occasion because of its possibilities for disagreement. Calabresi, who believed that his school had so far "been able to navigate between the shoals of political correctness and the rocks of incivility," and was certain it could only do so "if Deans speak their minds," seemed to enjoy debating the students as he nursed a cup of water. And students thrived on the give-and-take. "This is why I came to Yale," one exclaimed to a reporter. The spotlight shifted from the issue to its argumentation. Process triumphed.[57]

The dean also tried to make the most of criticism students aimed at each other. When flyers were posted around the building condemning the individual(s) who had searched students' mailboxes and destroyed their invitations to the Lesbian and Gay Law Students Association annual dinner, Cala-bresi condemned "the perversion of mind that would lead someone to actions of this sort," emphasizing "that whoever did this and violated the privacy of members of this community should not be in this school." Nor, he added, in a reminder of another community's norms, did the perpetrator(s) belong in the legal profession. Straight students reacted by expressing their support for Les-bian and Gay Law Student Association members in a petition, and gays and lesbians could relax, "given the strong, widespread condemnation of an appar-ently lone prankster" — until the petition was defaced. "You could see people just come into the hall, look at the thing and get really upset," one student said. "Guido came in and stood there reading it. He was burning up. He called for a town meeting right there, and the word just spread." The dean suggested that all wear lavender armbands to show their support for LGLSA members. Donning one himself, the refugee from Fascist Italy spoke first at the meet-ing, which some 200 attended. "He was simply wonderful," one witness said of Calabresi. He was "upset and committed" and characterized the person (the dean carefully used the singular) who had committed these acts as "sick." As always, Calabresi stressed the need for charity, however, even hypothesizing that the individual "was looking for help."[58]

So, too, the dean tried to lead by example in an outbreak of bigotry after a reported sexual assault against a woman law student. Selected African Ameri-can law students received anonymous letters from "Yale Students for Racism" concluding that the crime against "one of our classmates" had been "done by two black men" and using racial slurs. Privately, Calabresi said he was not sur-prised. Though the school might be "the Garden of Eden," it belonged to a world shaped by "disgraceful" political demagoguery. Publicly, he condemned the letter as "the most vicious kind of racism." So far, so good. Yale's Black Law Students Association co-chair told the *Harvard Law Record* that though the country was becoming "more racist," Yale Law School "is generally a very accepting place." Clark had never been so lucky. But Calabresi's usually sure sense of touch then deserted him. When the incident sparked a moratorium, the dean said, "I fully share the desire of many members of the law school com-munity that we take time to show our solidarity and support for the African American students who were hurt" — but "I don't really like moratoria." If the students really wanted to show support, why not hold workshops on a week-end?[59]

It was a touchy situation for the dean, particularly since the media was pointing out that the Supreme Court had repeatedly held that "the First Amendment does protect anonymous speech," that "law school rules unambiguously guarantee the First Amendment rights of all students," and that Calabresi's statement that "he makes an exception for anonymous speech because of his belief that 'lawyers shouldn't be cowards'" was not wholly persuasive. As Benno Schmidt, the First Amendment scholar who presided over Yale, said, "Free speech protects cowards too," and historically, "the most radical, non-conforming speech has been anonymous." Unlike Woodbridge Hall, however, the dean — once again focusing on bounded disagreement — considered identifying the authors of the hate mail crucial. "We are trying very hard, both because would-be lawyers need to learn that they must take public responsibility for what they say or write," he explained, and, Calabresi added in an unusual twist, "because unless the writer is identified some students who hold unpopular views may become silent, lest they be suspected of being the racist author, thus truly chilling speech." But the authors' identities were never made public, and even the ever-optimistic dean seemed doubtful "that we can, by unambiguously bearing witness to those values we hold most dear, draw *some* good even out of such hateful occurrences." This he managed to do, however, speaking later of the moving sight of a white student who attended class during the moratorium and an African American who did not: "But to show that this would not affect their friendship, the latter accompanied the former through the picket line into the class and then left."[60]

Encouraging "love for the School on the part of the students," drawing love from hate, and using every instance that occurred to teach the need for amiable argument and small-"l" liberalism always seemed the dean's mission. The same year that African Americans received hate mail, Yale's *Journal of Law and Liberation* invited Abdul Alim Muhammad, spokesman for the Nation of Islam, to speak on the drug war in the black community. When the Black Law Students Association invited Muhammad to speak at Harvard, Clark apparently did little. Calabresi, on the other hand, joined a picket line of 200 to protest Muhammad's anti-Semitism and carried a placard reading "Racism is garbage no matter who speaks it." He also made the speech an occasion for education. He issued one letter to the community, "speaking as Dean . . . remind[ing] all of you of the rules of this School and this University that guarantee complete freedom of speech to all visitors invited by appropriate groups." He distributed another "as a *member*" of the community arguing that the invitation was "a terrible wrong."[61] But appropriately, as the author of *Ideals, Beliefs, Attitudes and the Law*, Calabresi concluded by candidly addressing his own ambivalence:

And yet what can I say of those who would invite such a . . . [person] while decrying that person's bigotry? Can I say that they cannot be members of a community with me, that they cannot be my friends? No, I would denounce what for me is their error—their lack of feeling and of sensitivity, their, admittedly unintended, support of bigotry—but still embrace them. And what can I say of those who would no longer deal with those who made such an invitation? Would I exclude them? No. Again I would attack what I view as *their* error—their concentration on their own justifiable pain, their lack of understanding of the terrible needs of others—and then embrace *them*. . . . I pray that all in this fragile but worthy place will try to understand what motivates those who hold, so deeply, views, so different, on this issue, in the hope that in time, the wounds that this event is causing on all sides may heal, and that even from these wounds we may all have learned something of value about the needs, weaknesses, and fundamental humanity of all our sisters and brothers in this School.[62]

And after Muhammad's visit had ended, the dean was on the scene to promote healing. "Consider whether clever questions or piercing rhetoric, now, do more good, than quiet talk with those who before they hurt you or were hurt by you were friends, or even just pleasant-seeming acquaintances," he advised the law school community. "Ponder whether silence, a smile, and even a hug may not be more eloquent than the analytical and forensic skills you all have in such great abundance."[63] As his words implied, his decanal style was special.

Calabresi's focus on speakers' rights, his appearance of welcoming dissent, his apparent delight at hearing criticism from students (whose notes to him, which he always answered, frequently closed by thanking him for being the sort of dean to whom they could vent), alumni, and outsiders—whether they be complaints that Yale had betrayed its past by turning its back on law and social science, or by surrendering to the forces of political correctness—fostered community. "When I get letters of complaint," Calabresi confided to one administrator, "I always telephone. I find that it takes little time and it almost always bowls them over to be called. They expect a 'form' letter and while they are only sometimes convinced of the rightness of my position, they always go away feeling flattered and happy." The dean also took on disappointments. Wellington had instituted "a formal preference" for all graduates' children that enabled those with records equivalent to non-alumni children to be admitted first when he became dean because "[w]e are indeed dependent on our alumni for our continued financial health." His successor spent hours talking with disappointed alumni *and* their children about other options and the possibility of transferring to Yale later. Just as important were the telephone calls to individuals to rejoice with them. The dean was ubiquitous. As the *New York Times* put it, "Mr. Calabresi is surely the most beloved law dean anywhere."[64]

He liked to think of Yale Law School as a "village," "a place where singers can sing and dancers can dance, a place that stands for excellence with decency and humanity, an exciting and loving place." In one welcoming address, Wellington reassuringly said that although each first-year might consider himself or herself "the mistake" made by the Admissions Committee, none was. "The mistake" immediately became part of "the class's vernacular, perhaps fanning more self-doubt than it allayed." Calabresi's famous welcoming speech was different: now that students' extraordinary achievements had brought them to New Haven, it was time to "get off the treadmill." Where better to disembark than Yale, a school that thrived on "civilized anarchy"? He made students feel that they were valuable, that they could experiment, that their individuality strengthened the school, and that despite Yale's excellence, their individuality helped make it better (a clever way of reminding them of its excellence). As part of his drive to spread "warmth and affection" through the Sterling Law Buildings, he reinstituted the Children's Holiday Party for offspring of faculty, students, and staff, with different professors taking turns as Santa, and Calabresi, clad in green tights and pointed shoes, always Santa's elf.[65]

Small wonder one student characterized Calabresi's decanal style as "somewhat touchy-feely — the 'let's hug-one-another approach' to law school," a style the dean attributed to his politics and jurisprudence: "Like most — though not all — liberals I tend to try to see the best (to be a lover) and not see the worst (to be a hater) in people," he said. And as the student acknowledged, it worked.[66]

Would it have done so during the sixties? Many of the issues that confronted Calabresi grew out of that period. It had unleashed the forces of diversity and the multiplicity of visions the dean worked to control now.

Would the classroom of the Calabresi years have satisfied students of the late sixties? Surely, the changed composition of the student body would have appealed to the women and students of color: Yale was no longer overwhelmingly white male. But public interest law, not the academy, attracted sixties activists. Though later students found COAP "fabulous," they mourned that those interested in public interest careers "just aren't in the drivers' seats as far as the power centers of the law school goes. We're the little, hyperactive kids sitting in the back." And the case method still reigned in New Haven, as elsewhere.[67]

Even so, most students of the late 1960s surely would have concluded that the next generation had it better. According to one survey, "73–79% of both males and females indicate that they enjoy the challenge of law school very much." As one student acknowledged at the end of Calabresi's deanship, many of those involved with the school, including its premature alumni, "believe that Yale is special in all sorts of other ways: the small class size and high student-to-faculty ratio allows for high quality interaction both with other students and faculty members; the lack of red tape allows for student creativity in both curricular and extracurricular choices; and the lack of a formal grading system creates a relaxed, noncompetitive environment." The requirements were few, there was COAP, and there was a lack of emphasis on black-letter law. Indeed, she confessed, she had sometimes "asked myself why anyone might care what went on at such a rarified place, and why I — or anyone else — should complain about being at what is commonly known as the 'humane law school.'"[68]

Nevertheless, she and others did. At times, such dissenters during the late 1980s and 1990s sounded so like the young Duncan Kennedy that they brought to mind "How the Yale Law School Fails." Had the next generation of students revised Kennedy's lament, it would have hit many of the same notes.

Students during the Dark Ages had yearned for democracy and community, scorned their professors' smugness and elitism, castigated the school for turning out corporate lawyers, and spoken of recapturing the lost promise of Yale's realist era. And in "How the Yale Law School Fails," Kennedy had claimed that professors terrorized and divided students, created a culture of patronage that permitted the young to advance only by kowtowing, presided over tedious classes that symbolized the failure of Yale's parochial faculty members to live up to their intellectual pedigree and pretensions, and feared students who demanded structural change. Kennedy had cast his lot with those who would make professors less hostile, students less passive.

For some, during the Calabresi years, the psychic territory of the classroom remained daunting. At Yale, as at other schools, the "terrorist version of the Socratic method" had become less prevalent beginning in the 1970s, as law teachers became "more concerned about possible real harm to students" and "also perhaps somewhat daunted by heightened concern that students will perceive them to be doing harm." Yet although the Socratic method was generally used more infrequently and kindly, Yale professors could still strike terror with the cold call.[69]

And at Yale, as elsewhere, women's experience was both different from and less positive than men's. Less comfortable in the classroom, women proved "far more" likely to say that "their confidence has somewhat diminished or diminished dramatically since they entered law school." Hear their voices, and one might be listening to a less edgy Kennedy. They described "four faces of alienation: from ourselves, from the law school community, from the classroom, and from the content of legal education." They spoke of the "generalized aggression," "[p]ervasive hostility and posturing in the classroom"; the "nervous, high-pitched, somewhat predatory laugh" of classmates at one of their number who had "said something foolish"; being "hurt by and hurting those who gave us strength, participating in the games of an institution that produced winners and losers"; seeking "community," but seeing "competition"; the difficulty of "just trying to be human in this place." Students talked of the "lack of contact and decency between students and teachers," their "distinct impression that most faculty members perceive student interaction as a waste of time, except insofar as it might be directly beneficial to the professor's research or career," and/or involve superstars they themselves had anointed. Here, the evidence indicated that women and men reacted similarly. Most professors did not even list office hours, relying on "the myth that the lack of posted office hours means that students are not restricted to any particular time," and many students maintained that setting aside office hours would be the single change that would most improve conditions of law student life. Dissidents also addressed their dissatisfaction with an education at once both overly theoretical, in its inattentiveness to the world outside, and insufficiently so, in its lack of "intellectual substance" and its "inadequate inquiry into the social, historical, political, or economic underpinnings of the cases."[70]

Some aspects of student life had nothing to do with the 1960s. Calabresi's young apparently lacked any sense of the school's history as special. They did not pointedly mourn the absence of the quality Yale "notoriously had" during the 1930s. They did not seem invested in the realists, or, even, to know of them, other than that some professors during the 1930s had made their school famous. Exactly when they stopped thinking in terms of Yale's distant history is unclear, but it seems to have happened sometime during the 1970s. By avoiding hiring the very individuals in Law and Society and Critical Legal Studies most likely to venerate the realists, the school had helped bury the sense that Yale's past should affect its present. So, too, in another development attributable to faculty hiring practices, some believed "the alienation from [classroom] content was related to the 'Law and Economics' paradigm that is so prevalent at the Yale Law School."[71]

Yet the students of the late sixties had also improved things. Their successors who found law too divorced from experience could turn to the clinic whose growth the previous generation had helped spur. Many of the most alienated "reported being able to find positive, smaller, subcommunities within the law school" that sixties activists had created—the clinic, Black Law Students Association, *Journal of Law and Feminism*.[72]

Nevertheless, and in ways that would have appalled them, the students of the Dark Ages had unintentionally made matters worse for those who followed. They had changed the grading system, but the marks of the 1980s and 1990s felt as arbitrary as ever. The young during the Calabresi years could not understand why they received Honors in some courses and Pass in others. That was, if they even knew their grades: "Many professors don't have grades submitted for work done in the Spring semester by . . . late Fall, and this compounds the spotty and vague nature of YLS transcripts." And the "screwed-up system of Honors and Passes" just forced the competition into other arenas. Yale's evaluation style could seem impenetrable, harming "those students who are not 'plugged into' the system and who tend to believe the message that YLS is a place where one can spend time learning rather than 'positioning' one's self with powerful (or any) faculty members."[73]

That had consequences. At the beginning of Calabresi's second term, a student-sponsored study revealed that although women constituted 40 percent of the school's graduating class, four had won clerkships on a federal court of appeals, compared to twenty-eight men. During the previous half-decade, one alumna and nineteen alumni had clerked on the D.C. Circuit Court of Appeals; six Yale women and twenty-seven men had clerked on the Supreme Court. The news was distressing, for clerkships had become more important. Because of Yale's reputation as the academics' law school, many of its students planned to become professors and therefore sought work with a judge. Clerkships had also become more valued rites of passage for those who planned careers in elite firms. More students in the 1980s and 1990s wanted clerkships, and thanks to the expansion of the federal courts, more existed: where 25 percent of third-year Yale students who reported their employment plans were beginning clerkships in 1971, 54 percent were doing so in 1986.[74] The women explained why they were not getting the best positions at the annual revue:

> I didn't know when I asked for my recs
> The profs didn't put out for people of my sex.
> I'm not plugged into these old boy networks
> Still, girls just want to be clerks.[75]

The gender gap was not the only problem. Between 1987 and 1991, one graduate of color from Yale clerked on the D.C. Circuit, while twenty-four whites did. Minorities "fared dramatically worse than white students—both men and women—in the clerkship process." These disparities were not unique to Yale. They reflected a larger issue: no matter whom the teacher saw in the classroom, he or she still heard largely from the white men. Outsiders still felt, and remained, outside. But the situation proved especially bad in New Haven.[76]

What was to be done about Yale's clerkship problem? "Probably a lot," the *Washington Post* editorialized. It warned, however, "the opportunity could be lost if students get hung up on laying blame and the administration gets hung up on ducking it." As was his wont, Calabresi did not duck, but got out in front. He told the women that "action should be taken, and quickly." A faculty study confirmed the gender gap, while demonstrating women less frequently applied for clerkships. Men who did not said they had not been interested. Women who did not seek clerkships explained that they did not consider their records competitive, did not believe their grades good enough, or did not know their professors well enough to ask for recommendations. But that made no sense: although there was a "lack of gender parity on *Yale Law Journal* membership," women and men received comparable grades. "The women underestimated themselves," Professor Roberta Romano hypothesized in explaining why more women did not apply for clerkships. Students proved skeptical that lack of confidence explained so much: "I don't know that many shy women here," one said. "There has to be something else going on."[77]

Of course there was. As Romano acknowledged, "the blurry grading system" was also a factor. A Yale transcript was no "help, if you're picking clerks, I'll tell you that," one D.C. Circuit Court judge grumbled. "You can't make heads or tails of it. It means you have to depend more on the personal endorsement of the professor." Because of the difficulty of "deciphering Yale transcripts and understanding the grading system," students said, "strong faculty recommendations are especially crucial for any Yale student seeking a clerkship." Men were more likely to receive them. Well under one-sixth of regular faculty members were women, and "it is easier for male students to approach men," Romano acknowledged.[78]

The students of the 1990s were not the first to say that the Dark Ages legacy of a "the blurry grading system" made the professor more important. In the 1970s, a group of students had once charged that the Honors/Pass/Low Pass/Fail grading system adopted in 1968 so served the interests of "a reactionary faculty" that their professors must have fabricated the tale of its adoption in response to the demands of activists. "Because it fails to distinguish mediocre from superior work, it has sapped incentives by leaving students in the dark about their success, by suggesting that the faculty does not care about the quality of a student's work, and by implying there is no way to make such judgments," they complained. Yale's grading system "has perverted the educational process by forcing students who hope for faculty recommendations to press themselves artificially on professors in the corridors and at social events and to cultivate professors with special relationships to prospective employers," including important judges. Thus, as a Harvard Law transfer to Yale observed, while grades did not threaten friendships, "clerkships are going to. Clerkships are key at Yale because in a sense they give an objective measure of where you stand." The lack of grades may have made students more eager to come to Yale and more cooperative in studying for exams, but more competitive in seeking recommendations from their professors for clerkships and other positions.[79]

In a place where faculty members had high opinions of their own intelligence, and gossip had some writing letters that "read to the effect: 'Although this person is not as smart as I am, etc.,'" few students stood out simply by doing good coursework. Because only two grades really existed, and just as Calabresi had warned students during the debate over grade reform during the sixties, students won professors' attention by becoming their research assistants or otherwise contriving to spend time in their offices. "It's not that if you're a woman, you're just not allowed in the door," Lea Brilmayer said. "There's something that just discourages [some] people from ever going and doing what students had to do—'brown-nose.'" Men understood that they had "to take the initiative, swallow your pride a little bit, risk rejection and manipulate. . . . And that is what gets you ahead at Yale Law School."[80]

As the students of the 1960s had hoped, grade reform had changed the atmosphere, making Yale less overtly hierarchical. The lack of anxiety about grades, in addition to its "touchy-feely" dean, helped make the school friendlier. But as their successors learned, a grading system that was essentially Honors-Pass just changed the terms of the competition. Sixties activists had not anticipated that grade reform would endow powerful professors with fiefdoms and transformed students wishing to succeed into courtiers. That it did just made the results another of many ironies and unintended consequences of the sixties.

Yale's reputation as the place future academics studied law also contributed to a culture of patronage. Graduate students who depend on professors for placement function as apprentices to masters. Wellington had spoken of the "two culture" phenomenon that separated the interdisciplinarians he hired from the bar. There were, increasingly, two parallel cultures among Yale law students as well: some wanted to become academics, others attorneys. In theory, those who hoped to teach should have related to their professors differently from those who planned to practice. But because both groups were coming to view clerkships as essential credentials and because Yale lacked a clear grading system, the race for clerkships made all those in the running for them, in effect, into graduate students.

At least with respect to clerkships, the school could make adjustments to begin leveling the playing field. As Calabresi predictably stressed, the women who had pointed to clerkship disparities soon said that there "seem to be few significant differences between hires of women and men" and thanked administration and faculty "for their efforts last year to ensure that women and men received equal treatment in the clerkship application process." By his account, the dean, delighted that women had raised the issue and had "taken the time to say thank you, . . . warned them, but most of all us, against any complacency in the future." That was the right message, for problems did remain with respect to the treatment of women and students of color at Yale. It also reflected the dean's style. He knew he could better manage confrontations by deploring and addressing the issues that gave rise to them, rather than by denying or downplaying them, and by extolling those who exposed problems. If this was subterfuge, it worked. Together, he seemed to be saying, Yale students, professors, and administrators could constructively tap the energy of the 1960s.

The dean thus domesticated the Dark Ages. The students of the sixties had craved less hierarchy; Calabresi, a Harvard transfer student marveled, introduced himself to everyone as "Guido." The dean even brought Charles Reich back each fall, hailing the return of "that extraordinary prophet and seer . . . as a visitor." "What a Long, Strange Trip It's Been," the article on Reich's reappearance announced. Would the courses Calabresi had arranged for Reich to teach lead to a permanent appointment? The dean refused comment, but the eventual answer was no. The visits, like the veneration of Robert Cover, had to suffice—and be admired. "I sometimes feel there's an attitude of 'look how wonderful Yale Law School is having such an unorthodox person here,'" one student worried. "I hope it's not true, but I think it is."[81]

It was one thing to tame the 1960s years later. Could a Calabresi have done so at the time? He and Pollak faced different situations. While unusual, Calabresi's decanal demeanor surely seemed more familiar to those who remembered the candidate of love, Jimmy Carter, than it would have in the 1960s—though it was Pollak who had originally introduced the Children's Holiday Party. Calabresi himself had been tougher in the 1960s. Years later, even the dean, who tried hard to love, still became exercised at memories of "the self-seeking, self-righteous and quite nauseating bunch that tried to get their way by threats and fires and, of course, by blocking speech they disagreed with."[82]

Nor is it clear the dean's notion of the possibilities offered by tight quarters for positive interaction would have suited the sixties. Recall that Abe Gold-stein had emphasized that community members disagreed then with "all the intensity of an overly involved family." To Calabresi, there was no such thing as overinvolvement. He compared his village to "a beehive." Typically, people became acquainted first. "Soon after, some big issue explodes in which they get to know each other's politics, but then they're arguing with people whom they already like."[83]

Thus Harvard Law, a school with far more ideological, gender, and racial diversity on its faculty during the late 1980s and early 1990s, experienced far more divisiveness around those topics than Yale. Had Harvard professors stirred up their students, we might understand why, but save for the issue of ideological diversity, it was largely students who took the initiative in Cambridge. The cynic might hypothesize that the sociology of large institutions played a role in explaining the difference and that their relative anonymity at Harvard inspired and empowered students in odd ways. Unlike Yale professors, Harvard teachers were unlikely to be able to identify the student at a sit-in and mention the student's activity in a clerkship recommendation. But Yale's smallness had intensified the conflict in the 1960s.[84]

When a "big issue" exploded then, the young were arguing with students they assumed should agree and faculty members they already disliked and mistrusted. And the young of the sixties seemed less ideologically diverse and more confident than they did later. Those on the right largely kept quiet, making the student body seem more monolithic. Meanwhile, Pollak confronted colleagues more certain they had the right answers, less mellow, and less willing to give him power.

For Calabresi exercised unusual control. Even under Rostow, the strongest twentieth-century dean before him, professors had once set the school's calendar and managed its affairs together. But Calabresi generally limited the agenda of faculty meetings to appointments and promotions. (He exercised a strong voice there too.) He handled everything from student crises to building renovation himself. He gave his colleagues independence as professors, but he expected it for himself as dean. That magnified his importance and caused the school to be identified with him. It undercut the idea that had prevailed during the 1960s of the faculty as a "collegium," united by a shared passion for law *and* governing the institution, unhappy though the collegium had been. As Calabresi acknowledged later, he did "run the faculty." Naturally, he downplayed that at the time, insisting that no one could tell Yale professors what to do, while admitting a dean could "cajole" as well as "lead by example." Cajole and lead he did, so much so that, some realized, he left little role for the faculty in governance. One professor recalled that he and his colleagues "flourished as individuals, but one of the most distinctive features of the Yale Law School— it is a community of scholars—began to disappear." Another sneered: "We are one; we are Guido."[85]

Few professors with a dean so successful and imaginative, however, would challenge the terms of the bargain. Why should they? Where his faculty was concerned, Calabresi made everything not "a problem," but "an opportunity." That included even the city of New Haven, which he liked to say, was small enough for hard work to yield discernible results. He enjoyed telling a story of Harold Koh's about his recruitment strategy. Calabresi invited Koh and his wife to New Haven for lunch. The invitees assumed they would receive an elabo- rate meal. But the dean had taken their measure. When they arrived in New Haven, Calabresi took them to Yankee Doodle for a hamburger and then to the local soup kitchen, where his wife was on duty. "All this can be yours!" the dean announced. Like Koh, most accepted Yale's call: the culture of yes made most opportunities probabilities. So, like the students, professors proved more compliant than their Dark Ages predecessors. Faculty complaints surely seemed churlish. Though the files include them, they lack the force of criticisms of Pollak—or, for that matter, of any of Calabresi's modern predecessors.[86]

By the end of his second term, the school was becoming more tranquil. Calabresi's intellectual interest in Law and Status was now paying institutional dividends. He could stress that Yale had (finally) hired two feminist legal schol- ars, Vicki Schultz, "one of the country's most interesting and powerful teach- ers and writers on issues of employment discrimination, the employment re- lationship, and women and the law," as a full professor, and feminist legal theorist Reva Siegel. William Eskridge, a scholar of gender, sexuality, and the law, would follow soon after Calabresi's term ended. And although Calabresi had once dismissed Critical Legal Studies as warmed-over realism, once it had peaked and seemed safer, he could proclaim that the school had lured to Yale with tenure Jack Balkin, someone "thoroughly steeped in the Critical Legal Studies tradition," who had already demonstrated "his capacity to engage in- llectually and charm personally every member of the faculty" (i.e., someone unlikely to spark civil warfare).[87]

The dean even professed to "glory" in the school's "flaky reputation." He believed the school must "continue to be, in the future, as it has in the past, the source of leadership in all parts of the profession as well as in the major firms"—to say nothing of media, the arts, and sports. Calabresi liked to point out that Yale's graduates included a former head of the American Ballet The- ater, numerous journalists, Commissioner of Baseball Fay Vincent, and even, he insisted, the person who "garnered the first hit ever in a major league base-ball game." The song remained the same: this was a school with a proud and tolerant history and future without limits.[88]

As Yale approached the twenty-first century, then, it seemed as if the millennium had indeed arrived. When first the *U.S. News and World Report* rankings were published in 1987, Harvard and Yale tied. But when next they appeared in 1990, Yale was ranked number one and Harvard number five. In one sense, the results did not mean much. The rankings methodology virtually guaranteed Yale first place. Its smallness and wealth enabled it to beat Harvard in expenditures per student, student/teacher ratio, and applicant/admittee ratio during the 1990s. Calabresi professed to disapprove "of such polls—they're misleading," though he admitted that "if such a ranking is done, I'm happy that Yale Law School comes out on top." But in another sense, the rankings meant a great deal. Harvard soon rebounded to number two, but Yale remained preeminent. The *Harvard Law Record* acknowledged as much—while slyly observing that the survey's showing that Yale graduates' average salary topped that of their Cambridge counterparts cast "some doubt on the much-touted claim that Harvard is a 'corporate law factory' while Yale 'serves the public interest.'"[89]

Indeed, the *Record* reserved editorial space in 1991 to proclaim that "Yale Law School *is* Number One: . . . While Harvard continues to rely, almost categorically, on the reputation established by Holmes, Langdell, and other admittedly awesome figures in the nascent development and structuring of American law, Yale moves in modern times with unrivaled stature." Though the praise was intended to prod Harvard's powerful, the conclusion stung: "If Harvard were located in a cesspool like New Haven, I doubt it would rank in the top five in student preference." Someone in Cambridge had joined the Calabresi chorus.[90]

To Yale enthusiasts, there was good reason to do so. Nineteen of the most cited legal scholars of all time taught, or had taught, at Yale. When the list was restricted to those who had received their law degrees after 1970, more than twice as many had attended Yale as any other school. The *Yale Law Journal* was the most-cited general law review of 1987–97. Boosters theorized that "New Haven may now be the capital of legal academia."[91]

But Yale also required a presence outside the legal academy. For decades, its place had preoccupied its denizens. They celebrated it (uncertainly) as the nation's best and most intellectual law school, while conceding Harvard was the best known. That had been apparent during Robert Bork's Supreme Court confirmation hearings, which had created a dilemma for Yale professors and their dean. Though Calabresi originally intended to testify for Bork, "a worthy person of great integrity and enormous ability, as well as a friend," reasoning that his defeat would result in the appointment of "someone whose views are just as bad, and who is not as able," the dean decided against doing so after he was "deluged with letters and phone calls . . . that made me realize that I simply could not be publicly attached, whatever my motives, to Mr. Reagan's choice." Like the dean, professors considered the candidate a person of integrity, but some feared his conservatism. Thus while three faculty members testified for him, three testified against Bork. No one seemed interested in the division of opinion. If anything, the hearings just solidified Yale's reputation as the "liberal" law school by focusing on Bork's ideological isolation there and producing questions for Owen Fiss from conservative senators about a report that after Reagan's landslide victory in 1984, Fiss told his class, "Not only do I not know anyone who voted for Ronald Reagan; I do not know anyone who knows anyone who voted for Ronald Reagan." The media mentioned Bork had been a Yale law professor largely as a shorthand way of showing he was smart—which no one denied. Reporter Linda Greenhouse, herself an alumna, did once refer to the Yale connections of both Bork and his antagonist on the Senate Judiciary Committee, Arlen Specter. But at the time, the media generally showed little interest in Yale's relationship to the Bork battle.[92]

In the Thomas confirmation hearings, however, as Yale Law School graduate Anita Hill confronted alumnus Clarence Thomas, the school itself became news. In part, that was because Calabresi testified for Thomas and, in one of his moments of excess, said he believed both candidates. No surprise there: they had gone to Yale. In the words of the *New York Times*, "if the four protagonists in Rashomon had also been Yalies he would undoubtedly have believed all of them as well." But the *Times* observed that "the Thomas nomination has severely tested this dean of deans," who so "ferociously—and unabashedly—loves" Yale Law School and reported that some thought "the right wing" had taken advantage of his "blind Old Blue boosterism" to legitimate Thomas. Of course the dean, who later said privately he had been "wrong" to support Thomas, wrote alumni at the time that while virtually all of the students at the school "disagreed with something I said or wrote" in the Thomas hearings "and told me so in no uncertain terms, they did it in ways that made me really proud of them."[93]

Even more important in creating fascination with the school were the images of "Yale Law's blackest and brightest" facing off in a process that involved alumni as senators (Thomas's mentor, John Danforth, and Specter), Senate staffers (James Brudney), key witnesses (not just Calabresi, for Thomas; but Drew Days, against; and John Doggett, against Anita Hill), scholars (Catharine MacKinnon), judges (Leon Higginbotham), and observers. The media took care to capture Yale law students watching the hearings, many interviewed multiple times, as well as the large banner on the Wall, "Congratulations, Justice Thomas," with its appended message, "Tough Luck, Women!" Now reporters fell over themselves to report that just as the Bork battle had featured Yale law alumni on every side, so, once again, did all roads lead to New Haven, spawning "a family tragedy" — and also "considerable institutional pride." That pride seemed peculiar, the *New York Times* observed, "given the pathos and tawdriness of the Thomas story, until one realizes how chauvinistic this community can be."[94]

Add the Clintons to the mix, and small wonder the media made Yale Law School a celebrity. "Almost every event on which national attention focused this year seems to have had a Yale Law School label," Calabresi said in 1992. He carefully managed Yale's new centrality to political culture. "The Clarence Thomas–Anita Hill hearings, the rebirth of Democratic party hopes after Harris Wofford's Senate victory in Pennsylvania, the Presidential primaries among Jerry Brown, Bill Clinton, and Paul Tsongas, Jack Danforth's role in passing the Civil Rights Act of 1992, the brave fight by Fay Vincent over the future of baseball, Pat Robertson's speech at the Republican Convention, Hillary Rodham Clinton's role in the Presidential campaign, the achievement of the North American Free Trade Agreement by Carla Hills, and the election of Bill Clinton as President of the United States, all had as key participants — good, bad or indifferent — graduates of this small School," he told alumni. Note that Republicans received their due, too, and Calabresi also carefully mentioned the two professors, hired during his deanship, who had just returned to school after service in the Bush administration.[95]

The media observed Yale's new ubiquity — in part because the school encouraged graduates to choose alternative careers and could claim so many journalists as its own. As alumni battled for the Democratic nomination in 1992, the *New York Times* was proclaiming, "Yale Alumni Take Lead Again, Even If Not In Law," while the *Boston Globe* was stressing the significance of "the Yale Connection." As the *Globe's* columnist, a law school alumnus, wrote, if so many prominent political figures "came from the same town of 1,600 people, or the same high school, reporters would be hiding in lockers trying to figure out why the place had assumed such an influence in the life of the nation." Meanwhile the *Washington Post* was reporting that "A Hot Ticket Enjoys Its Ivy Climb: As Yale Gains Prominence, View From Cambridge Can Be Crabby." When Jeff Greenfield published an article in *M: The New He-Man* entitled, "The Yale Plot to Take Over America," it seemed clear that Yale has assumed a distinctive place in popular culture.[96]

One explanation was that Yale deserved no credit for its own impact. It had simply attracted the smartest and given them a place to hobnob that was so small that they had to get to know each other well and, in the process, make useful connections. Of course, that was part of it. The legal academy's "Yale Mafia," for example, helped to explain why so many Yale graduates found teaching jobs — and at elite schools, to boot. Still, Yale graduates' prominence was not just a matter of networking. The school had painstakingly crafted an image for itself since the 1930s as a place to prepare for making policy. Calabresi was wont to boast that his law school was "the nearest thing the United States has to an Ecole Normale Superieure." The young of the late sixties who reached the pinnacles of power in the 1990s were children of the very rights revolution that legal realism, Yale, and modern American liberalism celebrated. They chose Yale at least in part because the school advertised itself as the place for them.[97]

Hillary Rodham Clinton stressed Yale's exceptionalism when she came home to the law school's Alumni Weekend a month before her husband's first presidential election. ("The tradition of the Law School is to have a controversial speaker on the Friday of Alumni Weekend," Calabresi told those displeased by the invitation. That packed the house. "In recent years we have had Lowell Weicker in the heat of the income tax issue, Bob Bork at the height of the confirmation controversy, and Arthur Liman when he was the key person in the Iran Gate investigation." In a revealing conclusion, the dean insisted that "though we thrive on controversy and even partisanship, we invite partisans from all sides.") Clinton spoke of the library fire before May Day. "Dean Pollak faced that as he faced so many situations during that year, not only with grace and dignity, but with a stated commitment to the continuing role of the rule of law, and [prodded us to consider] how we had to view even disorder in a way that led us [to] think of reasonable and legally oriented solutions." That was what Yale thought it was about — liberals committed to the rule of law. And

*The Clintons and Calabresis. (*Yale Law Report, *Fall 1993. Courtesy Yale Law School.)*

like Clinton, Calabresi had recast the late sixties as a time of hopeful activism, rather than one of siege. To the dean, in fact, what seemed important about Clinton's past was that "at the time *she* was a 'moderate,' not a totalitarian, who lacked respect for the rights of others."[98]

Of course, Calabresi's "moderate" was not everyone's. As the media was soon reporting, Bill Clinton's teacher, Robert Bork, blamed Yale Law School for the decline of western civilization and for having produced the Clintons in particular. But the school still thrived. It remained unsinged even when Clinton famously declared, "It all depends on what the meaning of the word 'is' is," a statement that helped hasten his impeachment and led one columnist to blame Yale for teaching him to talk that way. Clinton's legal travails merely brought two other students of the Dark Ages to the fore, David Kendall and Gregory Craig. Indeed, Yale made hay with controversy. Some 300 law students packed the auditorium for an event duly reported in the press at which their professors insisted that "the school doesn't teach students to parse words to twist the law."[99]

While Harvard struggled with claims it lacked diversity and produced sexist parodists, Yale boasted the president and first lady and a dean who thrived on controversy and disagreement. Now, "suddenly," Yale "occupied a prominent place on America's cultural map." Now, alumni could claim it the best *and* most recognized law school. Whatever their problems, what mattered, as Calabresi understood, was that the president and first lady had gone to Yale Law and were "very loyal" to it.[100]

Thus just as money poured in, so did students. During the 1960s, most Yale professors would have maintained their faculty was superior to Harvard's. Yet Yale law professors envied Harvard its students. While a certain kind of politicized individual might consider Yale his or her first choice, many of those Yale admitted preferred Harvard. During the late 1970s, Yale considered itself lucky if half the students it admitted decided to go there. But beginning in the early 1990s, about four out of every five accepted enrolled. Most of the remaining 20 percent did not go to law school, but pursued another career. That meant "very few students who are admitted to Yale choose to attend another law school instead." Although the school had admitted seventy fewer in 1991 than 1992, it enrolled nearly two hundred in its first-year class because everyone accepted attended. "In part this is because of the silly publicity," Calabresi said proudly, "but in part it is also because . . . the school . . . can't help but attract the best. And the best they are."[101]

By the time Calabresi departed—because Clinton had placed him on the Second Circuit bench—Yale had come to dwarf its rivals despite its smallness. It was rich. It was a celebrity in its own right. Ideologically, it was thought slightly left of center, but not too much. It was a school that mostly produced corporate lawyers, but also seemed to be a breeding ground for public servants. Further, it was a school known for its academic and interdisciplinary approach to law, one that did not just produce a disproportionate number of its own professors, but of other schools' as well. Insofar as law school could be humane and interesting, Yale seemed to be. It was both most and least competitive, attracting students because it was the most selective *and* because they knew they would pass their first-term courses, graded credit-fail, and need only worry about whether they would receive Honors or Pass afterward.

This was sweet. When Hillary Rodham Clinton came home to Yale in 2001, this time as senator, she told how she had decided to enroll there. At a Harvard cocktail party, she had met a professor "who looked as though he had stepped out of the set of the Paper Chase." A friend introduced her as a Wellesley senior who was choosing between Harvard and its "nearest competitor. And he looked down at me and he said, first of all we don't have a nearest competitor, and secondly, we don't need more women."[102] The story might have been contrived to please, but it also rung true. Clinton's implication was obvious: Yale had won.

Yale had not become Harvard. Its small size prevented that. But beginning in the late 1980s, though the Dark Ages still cast a shadow, the school had escaped another one. This was good news for an institution of legendary self-absorption.

But Harvard's shadow never entirely disappeared. By the time Robert Clark turned over the deanship to the liberal Elena Kagan two years after Clinton's Class Day speech, many agreed he had grown in the job. Problems persisted: Harvard placed 154th out of 165 schools in a 1994 National Jurist survey of "overall student satisfaction" and last in five of seven Princeton Review surveys conducted after 1993 on the quality of student life. And a 1999 study the school commissioned reported substantial student dissatisfaction with both grading system and class size, as well as frightening alienation. The climate could also seem anti-intellectual. Kagan wondered why Harvard students "were embarrassed to admit they were engrossed in the law or found it intellectually challenging." Yet, like Calabresi and his successor, Anthony Kronman, Clark had proven an outstanding fund-raiser. Further, twelve women held regular appointments at Harvard, including Lani Guinier, as did eight men of color. The student/faculty ratio had shrunk from 30:1 to 13:1. Some had pressed for slashing the number of admitted students, Clark said, but that "would mean we'd be trying to be a half-baked Yale instead of a better Harvard." Better, he insisted successfully, to hire almost forty new professors, enabling the school to swell electives and, beginning in 2001, nearly to halve the number of students in each required course, while increasing community by dividing the first-years into seven "colleges." Pointedly noting his preference for the "metropolis" over the "village," Clark celebrated Harvard's vibrant right, center, and left, its "lively and engaging and unpredictable and sometimes unwieldy intellectual environment." Harvard seemed poised for a comeback, while NYU continued to surge forward and other wealthy and prestigious private universities were about to acquire eager, young law deans.[103]

And in any event, complacency was never supposed to be the Yale way. Historically, as Calabresi recognized, its sense of insecurity (and, of course, its existence in Harvard's shadow) shaped Yale's identity. He liked to quote Grant Gilmore. Unlike other great institutions that treated the present as golden, the past as bronze, Gilmore insisted, "[t]he Golden Age of the Yale Law School is never now. It was always in the past . . . and can be again in the future if only we do a few things right. Always close, always striving, never quite there yet except in memory and hope."[104]

One reason for anxiety should have been obvious. Did students now choose Yale because of its realist aspirations, its emphasis on law as a tool of social justice, and its quirky nature, as their Dark Ages predecessors had? Or did they select it simply because it was the winner of the reputational sweepstakes? More generally, if Yale had at least for the time being eclipsed Harvard, could Yale still be Yale? As with any such questions, only time would provide the answer.

Afterword

A story about Yale Law School raises an obvious question. So what? In our rush to convince readers of the significance of a story we may have chosen for the sheer joy of telling, we sometimes claim too much for it. Yet the intellectual and political history of this law school does illuminate our understanding of legal education. Its past and products have reinforced the contours of contemporary legal education, while only partially challenging those of legal scholarship.

* * *

Even those who salute the sixties must admit that in some real ways, the period did not bring the progressive transformation so many sought. Though some of the era's activists grew up to become academics, the contemporary academy bears striking similarities to the university they challenged. While acknowledging that students of the sixties achieved a more "relevant" curriculum with the establishment of black, women's, and ethnic studies programs, for example, one historian has maintained that "these changes have been divorced from other reforms students sought, such as opening the boundaries between the community and the university, and greater student control over their education." Over time, the new programs were adapted to "traditional academic norms, making them more like the education students opposed than the one they envisaged." If "pedagogy is politics," how much have the pedagogy and politics of the contemporary academy changed?[1]

Legal education suggests the answer is not much. The career of Duncan Kennedy, class of 1970, author of "How the Yale Law School Fails," and Carter Professor of Jurisprudence at Harvard Law School, demonstrates how static legal education has remained since Langdell placed the appellate case and the professional teacher at its center. The old order did not much changeth. The object of the first year remained introducing students to the common law "in which we will argue that the basic concepts of law will be communicated to the student not through the specific principles, but through a way of thinking—

'thinking like a lawyer.' We then sort of trail off into two years of courses that have become increasingly disarticulated." By the third year, it was "no secret" that no one was paying attention.[2]

The older Kennedy fit comfortably into this system in many ways. "I think of myself as a doctrinal teacher of law," he said, one who, like Langdell, taught students to take apart appellate cases. Believing he must "teach doctrine, bar review type stuff," he sought "cases and hypo[thetical]s that will perform this function while still working well to further my second objective, which is that cases and hypos should illustrate gaps, conflicts and ambiguities in the system of black letter law." Students must "see the pervasiveness of occasions for choice by judges when they are deciding what the rules should be." Unlike Langdell and like the realists, that is, he lacked faith in the grand architecture of law. He has also worked hard—harder than the realists—at "politiciz[ing] the classroom around the students' political views" to encourage them to see themselves as representatives of constantly shifting "left or right coalitions. Who is in what coalition will vary," depending on whether the issue related to race, class, or gender. "If I succeed in splitting the students down the middle between the liberals and the conservatives, in having them duke it out and form alliances that shift over time," he explained, "I'm imposing on them that it's very difficult to escape the politics of law" and that "legal argument is indistinguishable from political argument." He thus challenged "the perspectivelessness or the apparent neutrality or the abstraction of legal studies by making the classroom into a place where students learn doctrine and legal argument in the process of defining themselves as political actors in their professional lives."[3]

Kennedy's generation of students led law professors to appease by adding new courses in poverty law and increasing the curriculum's clinical component. When their turn came to stand behind the lectern, members of that generation sometimes looked different, even if they were not women and/or minorities. Kennedy appeared at school "dressed for urban combat," sporting, say, "a black leather jacket and white T-shirt." His law professor contemporaries tended to be less fierce than many of their predecessors had seemed and less likely to teach Socratically: one recent empirical study of the decline of the Socratic method at Harvard concluded that "the turbulence of the late 1960s and early 1970s led to a dramatic restructuring of classroom dynamics," either by "forcing" or freeing teachers to become less "strict." Kennedy himself reported that "I love the dramatic aspects of large Socratic classes." But he played with the Socratic method, allowing students to pass without being penalized when he called upon them in first-year courses, and dropping it entirely in some electives. In some of his courses, as well as those of others, lectures have eclipsed Socrates altogether. "This is a lecture course, so you don't have to do the reading," Kennedy would joke the first day of his elective American legal history course. And, perhaps since more of them were engaged in active and interdisciplinary scholarly careers than their predecessors, when academic lawyers did teach cases at century's end, they were more likely to use them as vessels in which to pour their own theories of scholarship. Harvard first-years took "Kennedy," not torts, just as their Yale counterparts had long taken "Calabresi," not torts.[4]

Still, like their predecessors and successors, those at Yale during its Dark Ages kept Langdell's legal education, with its focus on the case method and doctrinal analysis, supreme. If anything, the more universal commitment to "the priority of scholarship over teaching" reduced their interest in experimenting with new methods of teaching and grading. "Langdell invented everything you love to hate about law school," Harvard Law School's official historian said in 2002. "He invented big classes, three-hour exams, the Socratic method, class rankings and the case method." Harvard Law's new dean, Elena Kagan, agreed and went further: "Law Schools are structured in the same way they were in 1870 and little has changed since. Christopher Columbus Langdell was a hell of a smart guy but what he thought in 1870 does not hold up completely today."[5]

So when critics such as Justice Clarence Thomas insisted that everything had changed, they exaggerated. "When I went to law school we were expected to take, even at Yale, a core set of subjects which all lawyers needed to know (at least in the first semester)," Thomas reminisced twenty years after his graduation in a Cumberland Law School speech. "We had giants of the field who taught us in the grand manner." When Boris Bittker interrogated students in Tax, asking "tough questions about this tax provision and that regulation, this statute and that revenue ruling," he was teaching them to get "to the core of the problem. In this way, we became schooled in the common law method which is apparently not too popular in academic circles these days, and we learned to think like lawyers." By Thomas's account, however, all was different now. "Today, some classes are more reminiscent of graduate seminars than law schools," he said, reporting that his law clerks regaled him with stories of courses "such as Cinematic Images of Lawyers and the Law, and Thinking about Thinking." The justice thought no damage would be done "if you were studying for a PhD in Comparative Literature. But for you who are to become lawyers, who are to play what Tocqueville called the leading part in the political society which is striving to be born, this sense of education produces disillusionment and disgust," in addition to providing no sense of "what awaits you in practice."[6]

In fact, though law professors have become part of the university since the 1980s, the law school has not. Had Justice Thomas looked at Cumberland's catalogue, he would have found that course offerings remain similar to those of thirty years earlier. And at elite law schools, such as Harvard and Yale, legal education had consisted of a basic cake of courses intended to prepare students for practice and a frosting of "frills" ever since Thomas Bergin claimed in the 1960s that the law professor suffered from intellectual schizophrenia. Even today, despite Yale's reputation as a place where one does not go "to learn the law," plenty is still on tap there in the classroom and the clinic.[7]

Nothing proved that more than the academy's reaction to the drumbeat of accusations by Thomas, Harry Edwards, and others in the 1990s that law schools had become refuges for JD/PhDs without experience as practitioners. The worry was unnecessary, for ironically, the addition of interdisciplinarians to the law professorate probably strengthened the hegemony of the case method, which gave the teacher who had never practiced law, but who could read and "unpack" cases well, something to do with his or her students. Professors fought off pressure from Edwards, Thomas, and the bar by insisting that those with JDs and PhDs taught courses just as the old JDs did, or that the "law student who fell asleep in 1963 and awoke in 1993 would not be astonished by his new surrounds." The fact that legal education had not been transformed, and law schools remained hiring halls to link students and employers on the basis of performance and prestige, became something to celebrate.[8]

Until pressure grows irresistible, then, the law school of the twenty-first century will most likely resemble that of the twentieth and late nineteenth. Langdell's school will remain secure. The case method is still cheap. It justifies the existence of professional law teachers who have learned to read cases well in law school and have little practical experience. And law professors themselves tend toward caution, as the realists' reaction to Jerome Frank reminds us.

Yale could use its current prestige to challenge Langdell. But Yale Law School is a boutique: it is small. It is considered special, the "best." Yet because it is special, no matter what it does, other schools might reason they could not follow suit. Few of them possess Yale's faculty-student ratio, its relative financial autonomy, its potentially liberating reputation for quirkiness. Since Yale does train a disproportionate percentage of the nation's elite law professors, however, it could exercise an enormous amount of influence by teaching people in nontraditional fashion and sending them out into the provinces as colonial servants, much as Langdell did.

Until it does, may we resort to another truism: *Plus ça change, plus c'est la même chose*? Yes and no. In part because of his classmates, Kennedy's classroom holds many more women and students of color than it did in his day, and he possesses a more diverse set of colleagues.

Yet expansion of the hierarchy's membership does not eliminate its rigidity. One need only examine the "casual conversations, the names that are dropped, the telephoned recommendations or e-mailed disavowals, the reviews of manuscripts, the formal references, let alone the teaching and mentoring relations" that are "the lifeblood of the quotidian academy" to see that whatever their politics, contemporary law schools do not simply reproduce hierarchy, as Kennedy so famously alleged. They cultivate it. Who would have imagined in the 1960s that law schools would anticipate the annual rankings so anxiously and that they would so influence the decisions of students on where to study, of professors on where to teach, and of alumni on how much to give? Who would have predicted that schools would celebrate their scholars' high ranking in citation studies? Perhaps this phenomenon is simply "the predictable expression of the commodification of distinction and the continuing expansion of market norms in to all arenas of life in the United States." Certainly it was the result of the trend toward celebrification, which helped, among other things, to create a star system in the academy. But it still seems strange that all the sound and fury about credentials in the 1960s would have paved the way for the emergence of a legal academic culture that simply employed a more quantifiable notion of meritocracy, applied not just on an individual basis, but on an institutional one as well. It is not just that legal education, as Kennedy so famously said, reproduces hierarchy, but that it has itself become more hierarchical.[9]

*   *   *

Though legal scholarship has changed more than pedagogy, those who stress the continuity with what went before score again. Between the New Deal and the end of the Warren Court, academics had seen themselves as advisers to courts and, to a lesser extent, other governmental agencies. That comfort, coinciding with law's overtures to the social sciences during the realist years, enabled professors to turn away from the example of Robert Hale. They need not pursue advanced study in one discipline or even work with a coauthor schooled in it. They could simply scavenge what they needed from other disciplines.

In contrast, the last quarter of the twentieth century was a time of change in this respect. The Warren Court was gone. Like Law and Economics, partially a Yale development, Critical Legal Studies, the offspring of Kennedy and other Dark Ages veterans and realist grandchild, created tension over appointments and academic politics. New faces did too, those of women and minorities. So did scholars from other disciplines forced to law school by the collapse of the academic job market. With Yale leading the way, Robert Hale won. Many of its new professors made legal scholarship less obviously useful to the profession and attacked colleagues without their training for abusing the humanities and social sciences. The law school became part of the university and, in terms of scholarship, more distant from the profession.

Yale's George Priest made that point when he testified in favor of the appointment to the Supreme Court of Robert Bork. Trying to reassure those who feared that Justice Robert Bork would demonstrate the extremism apparent in the writings of Professor Bork, as opposed to the relative reasonableness of the work of D.C. Circuit Judge Bork, Priest stressed "the divergence between the culture of the legal academic and judge." Contemporary legal scholarship was supposed to be "clearly extreme and often intemperate," "slashing," and "hypercritical." That was how professors had made their reputation since the 1970s, when they rushed toward the university, and Law and Economics and Critical Legal Studies appeared. Whereas in earlier times, academics received recognition "for the proposal of some well-crafted incremental change in the law which is the hallmark of the excellent judge," those days had, to Priest's relief, disappeared. "There is no stare decisis in legal scholarship. All ideas are up for grabs, and the most successful theorists are those that challenge existing ways of thinking most radically." Apparently, Duncan Kennedy's day had arrived.[10]

If Priest was right, that of John Griffiths had arrived too. The perceived intemperance of a challenge was no longer reason for exclusion from the table. But *pace* Priest, it remained unclear how different scholarship was at his and Bork's Yale, as well as at most other law schools, for that matter. At the time of the Bork battle, Yale Law School was making its mark with interdisciplinarity, liberalism, and a new legal process scholarship that was in some ways quite similar to traditional legal process work. The impact of the sixties and the "slaughter of the innocents" lingered: though the school possessed more of a right than it had when Bork was there, it still lacked a large political and

scholarly left. Were all ideas really up for grabs? Were the most successful individuals at Yale and elsewhere in the academy those who most challenged the
intellectual status quo?

Still, even at Yale, the comfortable sense of "we" that had predominated at
the Dark Ages' dawn had been shattered. In part, it was because of the students
of the late sixties; in part, because of the conservatism of the larger political
culture. The old liberal consensus could no longer be taken for granted. Perhaps that was progress.

Notes

ACKNOWLEDGMENTS

1. Lucas Cupps, "Everybody Knows Yale Law School Is Loaded: The History of the Independence Agreement," June 18, 2001 (unpublished manuscript). I am grateful to Cupps for sharing the manuscript with me.

PROLOGUE

1. "Negotiating Committee Asks Joint Student-Faculty Rule," *Yale Advocate*, February 6, 1969, at 1; "Panel: Concerns of the Yale Law Student Today," *Yale L. Report*, Special Report, September, 1969, at 4, 6.

2. Yale Law School Women's History Project, Oral History Interview with Judith Areen, 2000, by Mary Clark (unless otherwise noted, interviews were conducted by the author); Ben Stein, "Crazy Days," *Washingtonian* 50, 52 (September 1996); "Concerns of the Yale Law Student Today," at 8.

3. "Concerns of the Yale Law Student Today," at 15, 21.

4. "Students Provide Welcome for Alumni," *Yale Advocate*, May 1, 1969, at 1; "When Generations Collide," id., May 1, 1969, at 6; Robert Bork, *Slouching Toward Gomorrah: Modern Liberalism and American Decline* 49 (1996).

5. Edward Purcell, "Social Thought," 35 *Am. Qtrly.* 80, 83, 86–87 (1983); "The Port Huron Statement," reprinted in James Miller, *"Democracy Is in the Streets": From Port Huron to the Siege of Chicago* 329, 333 (1987). For discussion of community, identity politics, and the overlap between politics and culture during the 1960s, see, e.g., Wini Breines, *Community and Organization in the New Left, 1962–1968: The Great Refusal* (1989); Todd Gitlin, *The Twilight of Common Dreams: Why America Is Wracked by Culture Wars* (1995); M. J. Heale, "The Sixties as History: A Review of the Political Historiography," 33 *Reviews in Am. Hist.* 133 (2005).

6. David Farber, *The Age of Great Dreams: America in the 1960s* 105 (1994) ("understanding"); David Maraniss, *They Marched into Sunlight: War and Peace, Vietnam and America, October 1967* 136 (2003) ("worst thing").

7. Kevin Boyle, "The Times They Aren't A Changing," 29 *Reviews in American History* 304 (2001). Boyle tells one version of the story there. The narrative, as I have related it here, is drawn from my lectures over the past twenty years. In preparing them, I have gratefully drawn on sources such as William E. Leuchtenburg, *A Troubled Feast: American Society Since 1945* (1973); Allen Matusow, *The Unraveling of America: A History of Liberal-*

ism in the 1960s (1984); William Chafe, *The Unfinished Journey: America Since World War II* (5th ed., 2003); William Chafe, *Never Stop Running: Allard Lowenstein and the Struggle to Save American Liberalism* (1993); Miller, *Democracy Is in the Streets*; John Morton Blum, *Years of Discord: American Politics and Society, 1961–1974* (1991); Farber, *The Age of Great Dreams*; Terry Anderson, *The Movement and the Sixties: Protest in America from Greensboro to Wounded Knee* (1995); and James Patterson, *Grand Expectations, 1945–1974* (1996).

8. For discussions of the neglect of conservatism, see, e.g., Michael Kazin, "The Grass-Roots Right: New Histories of U.S. Conservatism in the Twentieth Century," 97 *Am. Hist. Rev.* 138 (1992); Alan Brinkley, "The Problem of American Conservatism," id., 99: 409 (1994); Leo Ribuffo, "Why Is There So Much Conservatism in the United States and Why Do Few Historians Know Anything about It?," id., 99: 438 (1994); Leonard Moore, "Good Old Fashioned New Social History and the Twentieth-Century American Right," 24 *Reviews in American History* 555 (1996); Heather Thompson, "Rescuing the Right," id., 30: 322 (2002). In the remainder of the paragraph, I have concentrated on the most relevant challenges. Thus I have not mentioned the new work on the Cold War, for example, which is at pains to suggest that those who still view the Cuban Missile Crisis as evidence Kennedy was just another Cold Warrior are mistaken. See, e.g., Aleksandr Fursenko and Timothy Naftali, *"One Hell of a Gamble": Khrushchev, Castro, and Kennedy, 1958–1964* (1997); Ernest May & Philip Zelikow, *The Kennedy Tapes: Inside the White House During the Cuban Missile Crisis* (1997). The challenge to the notion of a liberal consensus on race has come from Thomas Sugrue, *The Origins of the Urban Crisis, Race and Inequality in Postwar Detroit* (1996); Arnold Hirsch, *Making the Second Ghetto: Race and Housing in Chicago 1940–1960* (1998 ed.); Gary Gerstle, *American Crucible: Race and Nation in the Twentieth Century* (2001); Robert Self, *American Babylon: Race and the Struggle for Freedom in Postwar Oakland* (2003); and Martha Biondi, *To Stand and Fight: The Struggle for Civil Rights in New York* (2003). John Andrew discusses conservatism in the university in *The Other Side of the Sixties: The Young Americans for Freedom and the Rise of Conservative Politics* (1997), and Lisa McGirr writes on conservatism at the grass roots in *Suburban Warriors: The Origins of the New American Right* (2001). Among the most useful explorations of conservatism during the 1960s at the national level are Robert Goldberg, *Barry Goldwater* (1995); Mary Brennan, *Turning Right in the Sixties: The Conservative Capture of the GOP* (1995); Maurice Isserman and Michael Kazin, *America Divided: The Civil War of the 1960s* (2000); Jonathan Schoenwald, *A Time for Choosing: The Rise of Modern American Conservatism* (2001); Rick Perlstein, *Before the Storm: Barry Goldwater and the Unmaking of the American Consensus* (2001).

9. Robert Cohen, "The Many Meanings of the FSM: In Lieu of an Introduction," in Robert Cohen and Reginald Zelnik, eds., *The Free Speech Movement: Reflections on Berkeley in the 1960s* 1, 23 (2002).

10. Cohen points to cooperation between liberal faculty members and "radical" students, the many forms of student agitation, and the ideological diversity of the student left, in id. at 6–7, 39, and see also Robert Cohen, "Mario Savio and Berkeley's 'Little Free Speech Movement' of 1996," *Free Speech Movement*, at 449, 472, and generally, John McMillan and Paul Buhle, *The New Left Revisited* (2003). Some faculty members did identify themselves as "left-liberal" at the time. Peter Brooks, "Panthers at Yale," 37 *Partisan Rev.* 420, 423 (1970).

11. See Donatella Della Porta and Mario Diani, *Social Movements: An Introduction* 16 (1999).

12. "Worst Piece of Shit I Ever Saw," *Yale Advocate*, October 2, 1969, at 2.

13. Clyde Summers, "Louis Pollak," 127 *U. Pa. L. Rev.* 314, 314 (1978); infra, text accompanying Chapter 8, note 12 ("Dark Ages").

14. Infra.

15. John Schlegel, "The $10,000 Question," 41 *Stan. L. Rev.* 435, 459 (1989) ("differently").

16. The following are about or in large part concentrate on Yale: Frederick Hicks, *The Founders and the Founders' Collection* (1935); Hicks, *Yale Law School: From the Founders to Dutton 1845–1869* (1936); Hicks, *Yale Law School: 1895–1915, Twenty Years of Hendrie Hall* (1938); Robert Stevens, "Law School and Law Students," 59 *Va. L. Rev.* 551 (1973) (a book-length study); Laura Kalman, *Legal Realism at Yale, 1927–1960* (1986); Chris Goodrich, *Anarchy and Elegance: Confessions of a Journalist at Yale Law School* (1991); John Schlegel, *American Legal Realism and Empirical Social Science* (1995); Anthony Kronman, ed., *History of the Yale Law School: The Tercentennial Lectures* (2004).

CHAPTER ONE

1. Fitzhugh Mullan, *White Coat, Clenched Fist: The Political Education of an American Physician* (1976); Kenneth Ludmerer, *Time to Heal: American Medical Education from the Turn of the Century to the Era of Managed Care* 237–42 (1999) (changes in medical education during the 1960s); "Student Acquiescence Helps Perpetuate War," *Writ*, December 18, 1969, 8 ("future").

2. Richard Flacks, "The Liberated Generation: An Exploration of the Roots of Student Protest," 23 *J. Social Issues* 52 (1967); Flacks, "Who Protests: The Social Bases of the Student Movement," in Julian Foster and Durward Long, eds., *Protest! Student Activism in America* 134 (1970); Flacks, *Youth and Social Change* (1971); Kenneth Keniston, *Young Radicals: Notes on Committed Youth* (1968); Rebecca Klatch, *A Generation Divided: The New Left, the New Right, and the 1960s* (1999). Keniston, Flacks, and Klatch maintained that students reflected parental values. Keniston, *Young Radicals*, at 221, 239, 302; Flacks, *Youth and Social Change*, at 55; Klatch, *Generation Divided*, at 43. Louis Feuer developed the hypothesis of rebellion against parental values, popular among conservatives, in *The Conflict of Generations: The Character and Significance of Student Movements* (1969). It is possible, of course, that the young both reflected and rebelled against parental values, as Keniston suggested in *Radicals and Militants: An Annotated Bibliography of Empirical Research on Student Unrest* ix (1973), and James Wood maintained in *The Sources of Student Activism* xvi, 77 (1974). University location and ethnicity probably played an important role in whether students reflected and/or rebelled against the values of their parents. Doug Rossinow, *The Politics of Authenticity, Liberalism, Christianity, and the New Left in America* 171–72 (1998). The parents of the Jewish children who dominated the movement in the earlier years were apparently more likely than those of non-Jewish ones to support their radical children's activism. Stanley Rothman and S. Robert Lichter, *Roots of Radicalism: Jews, Christians, and the Left* 222–23, 273–74 (1996 ed.). By 1968–69, when the protest movement had become larger and attracted students from a wider variety of backgrounds, the relationship between family status and protest-proneness had become even more opaque. Milton Mankoff and Richard Flacks, "The Changing Social Base of the American Student Movement," in Robert Evans, ed., *Social Movements: A Reader and Source Book* 470, 481 (1973). The contemporary examinations of campus activists during the 1960s were published before scholars paid much attention to gender—even when, as

in the case of parietal rules applied unequally to women and men, gender would seem an obvious starting point today. Beth Bailey, "From Panty Raids to Revolution," in Joe Austin and Michael Wilard, eds., *Generations of Youth: Youth Cultures and History in Twentieth-Century America* 187, 194 (1998). Focus on the relationship between gender and student activism awaited Sara Evans's *Personal Politics: The Roots of Women's Liberation in the Civil Rights Movement and the New Left* (1979). Evans's emphasis was on white women; recent work has concentrated on the relationship between black women and activism. See, e.g., Belinda Robnet, *How Long? How Long? African American Women in the Struggle for Civil Rights* (1997); Cynthia Fleming, *Soon We Will Not Cry: The Liberation of Ruby Doris Smith* (1998); Chana Lee, *For Freedom's Sake: The Life of Fannie Lou Hamer* (1999); Barbara Ransby, *Ella Baker & the Black Freedom Movement* (2003). Black male activists received somewhat more attention than white women during the sixties, though not as much as white men. They came from poorer families than their white counterparts and were less likely to have parents with college degrees. Anthony and Amy Orum, "The Class and Status Bases of Negro Student Protest," 49 *Soc. Sci. Qtrly* 528 (1968). At eastern universities, such as Yale, as I indicate, infra, the paradigm was largely black-white. For Lipset, see, e.g., Seymour Lipset and Gerald Schaflander, *Passion and Politics: Student Activism in America* 31, xvii, 94, 224 (1971).

3. Nathan Glazer, *Remembering the Answers: Essays on the American Student Revolt* 240 (1970) ("poof"); Richard Peterson, "The Student Left in American Higher Education," in Seymour Lipset and Philip Altbach, eds., *Students in Revolt* 202, 225 (1970) ("student power"); Gerald Farber, *The Student as Nigger: Essays and Stories* (1969) (in the preface, Farber estimated that the essay had been reprinted some 500 times); Keniston, *Young Radicals*, at 180. Whatever their politics, at the time scholars generally treated the "unrest" as a function of an emergent "youth culture" available to the most privileged young people. See, e.g., Peter Manning, ed., *Youth: Divergent Perspectives* (1973); Flacks, *Youth and Social Change*, at 47; Keniston, *Young Radicals*, at 239–40, 263, 266.

4. Robert Stevens, "Law School and Law Students," 59 *Va. L. Rev.* 551, 554 (1973).

5. Robert Stevens, *Law School: Legal Education in America From the 1850s to the 1980s* 234, 235 (1983) ("growing hostility," "part of the student revolution"); Stevens, "Law School and Law Students," at 587 ("liberal or radical"), 624; Carl Hetrick and Henry Turner, "Politics and the American Law Professor," 25 *J. Legal Ed.* 342 (1973) (liberalism of law professors).

6. Stevens, "Law Schools and Law Students," at 689, 573, 690, 692, 691, 584, 579.

7. Id. at 587; Guyora Binder, "On Critical Legal Studies as Guerrilla Warfare," 76 *Geo. L. J.* 1, 24 (1987) ("summer school").

8. Official Register of Harvard University, *Harvard Law School Catalogue*, Academic Year 1970–71, September 10, 1970, at 57. John Schlegel, "Between the Harvard Founders and the American Legal Realists: The Professionalization of the American Law Professor," 35 *J. Legal Ed.* 311, 312 (1985) ("casebooks"); Stevens, *Law School*, at 35–72.

9. Christopher Columbus Langdell, *Selection of Cases on the Law of Contracts* vii (1871) ("science," "materials"); William LaPiana, *Logic and Experience: The Origin of Modern American Legal Education*, vii, 24 (1994). In addition to LaPiana, the most important revisionists include Bruce Kimball, Paul Carrington, W. Burlette Carter, and Anthony Chase. See, e.g., Anthony Chase, "The Birth of the Modern Law School," 23 *Am. J. Legal Hist.* 329 (1979); Paul Carrington, "Hail! Langdell!," 20 *Law & Soc. Inq'y.* 691 (1995); W. Burlette Carter, "Reconstructing Langdell," 32 *Ga. L. Rev.* 1 (1997); Bruce Kimball, "'Warn Students That I Entertain Heretical Opinions, Which They Are Not to Take as

Law': The Inception of Case Method Teaching in the Classrooms of the Early C. C. Langdell, 1870–1883," 17 *Law & Hist. Rev.* 57 (1999). I have done more than my share of maligning Langdell. See, e.g., Laura Kalman, "To Hell With Langdell!," 20 *Law & Soc. Inq'y.* 771 (1995).

10. Stevens, *Law School*, at 21, 23. For overviews of the history of legal education, prior to Langdell, see Stevens, *Law School*, 3–34; Steve Sheppard, "An Introductory History of Law in the Lecture Hall, 1997," in Sheppard, ed., *The History of Legal Education in the United States: Commentaries and Primary Sources* 7 (1999).

11. Paul Carrington to author, October 17, 2002 ("hard," "prove"); La Piana, *Logic and Experience*, at 7–28.

12. Langdell, *Selection of Cases on the Law of Contracts*, at vii; LaPiana, *Logic and Experience*, at 135. At least two professors before Langdell, John Pomeroy and William Hammond, used cases in their teaching. Stevens, *Law School*, at 66, n. 14; Carrington, "Hail! Langdell!," at 735–36; and see Carter, "Reconstructing Langdell," at 22, n. 85.

13. Guido Calabresi, "An Introduction to Legal Thought: Four Approaches to Law and to the Allocation of Body Parts," 55 *Stan. L. Rev.* 2113, 2115 (2003) ("consistent"); LaPiana, *Logic and Experience*, at 7–28, 55–109; Carrington, "Hail! Langdell!," at 707–712.

14. Judith Richards Hope, *Pinstripes & Pearls: The Women of the Harvard Law School Class of '64 Who Forged an Old-Girl Network and Paved the Way for Future Generations* 97 (2003) ("hazing"); Phillip Areeda, "The Socratic Method," 109 *Harv. L. Rev.* 911, 916 (1996) ("vicariously"). For a reconstruction of the dialogue in Langdell's classroom, see Kimball, "'Warn Students That I Entertain Heretical Opinions,'" at 88–122. Again, Langdell was not the first to employ the Socratic method in law teaching: Columbia's Theodore Dwight described his style as Socratic. Stevens, *Law School*, at 66, n. 18.

15. Carrington, "Hail! Langdell!," at 712 (public law courses); Duncan Kennedy, *Legal Education and the Reproduction of Hierarchy: A Polemic against the System: A Critical Edition* 31 (1983) (2004 ed.) ("art," "lawyers"). Langdell and James Bradley Thayer of Harvard threw themselves into the work of the American Social Science Association's Committee on Jurisprudence. Thomas Haskell, *The Emergence of Professional Social Science: The American Social Science Association and the Nineteenth-Century Crisis of Authority* 221 (1977). So, too, in addition to producing treatises and casebooks on private law, they wrote on the great policy issues of the day. LaPiana, *Logic and Experience*, at 123. Their work also addressed jurisprudence—famously limning, for example, the idea that the prudent judge deferred to the legislature and practiced judicial restraint. James Bradley Thayer, "The Origin and Scope of the American Doctrine of Constitutional Law," 7 *Harv. L. Rev.* 129 (1893).

16. Edward Warren, "Spartan Education," in Sheppard, *The History of Legal Education in the United States: Commentaries and Primary Sources* 712, 714, 713; Paul Carrington to author, November 14, 2002 ("stand up"); Paul Carrington, *Stewards of Democracy: Law as a Public Profession* 206 (1999).

17. Hope, *Pinstripes & Pearls*, at 83, 105, 107; Virginia Drachman, *Sisters in Law: Women Lawyers in Modern American History* 253 (1998) (practicing lawyers, 1960).

18. See <http://www.law.smu.edu/firstday/torts/> (an introduction to the use of the Socratic method in a torts class).

19. Robert Gordon, "New Developments in Legal Theory," in David Kairys, ed., *The Politics of Law: A Progressive Critique* 413, 414 (1990) ("outcomes"); David Rockwell, "The Education of the Capitalist Lawyer: The Law School," in Robert Lefcourt, ed., *Law Against the People: Essays to Demystify Law, Order, and the Courts* 90, 94 (1971).

20. Abe Fortas, "Thurman Arnold and the Theatre of Law," 79 *Yale L. J.* 988, 996 (1970) ("corporate"); Laura Kalman, *Abe Fortas: A Biography* 160 (1990) ("services").

21. Carrington, "Hail! Langdell!," at 739, 715 (resistance, exclusion); Stevens, *Law School*, at 55–63 (embrace, cheapness); Jerold Auerbach, *Unequal Justice: Lawyers and Social Change in Modern America* 94–96 (1976) (hegemony); Gerard Gawalt, "The Impact of Industrialization on the Legal Profession in Massachusetts, 1870–1900," in Gerard Gawalt, ed., *The New High Priests: Lawyers in Post–Civil War America*, 97, 108 (1984) ("science"); John Schlegel, *American Legal Realism and Empirical Social Science* 26 (1995) ("colonial service").

22. Formalism: Laura Kalman, *Legal Realism at Yale* 45–49 (1986); Neil Duxbury, *Patterns of American Jurisprudence* 2 (1995); classical legal thought: Morton Horwitz, *The Transformation of American Law, 1870–1960: The Crisis of Legal Orthodoxy* 3 (1992); classical legal science: Stephen Siegel, "John Chipman Gray and the Moral Basis of Classical Legal Thought," 88 *Ia. L. Rev.* 1513, 1518 (2001); conceptualism: Max Radin, "Legal Realism," 31 *Colum. L. Rev.* 824, 826 (1931); Thomas Grey, "Langdell's Orthodoxy," 45 *U. Pitt. L. Rev.* 1 (1983); Langdellianism: Jerome Frank, "What Constitutes a Good Legal Education?," 19 *Am. Bar Assn. J.* 723, 728 (1933). Carter notes the lack of agreement about definition in "Reconstructing Langdell," at 10. On Holmes and his lack of uniqueness, see G. Edward White, *Justice Oliver Wendell Holmes: Law and the Inner Self* 149 (1993).

23. N. E. H. Hull, *Roscoe Pound and Karl Llewellyn: Searching for an American Jurisprudence* 67 (1997) ("modern"); Duxbury, *Patterns of American Jurisprudence*, at 63 ("volteface"); Karl Llewellyn, "A Realistic Jurisprudence: The Next Step," 30 *Colum. L. Rev.* 431, 435, n. 3 (1930) ("bare"). For a discussion of Pound's lack of uniqueness see Hull, *Roscoe Pound and Karl Llewellyn*, at 78; Duxbury, *Patterns of American Jurisprudence*, at 54–58. For the story of how realism received its name, see Hull, *Roscoe Pound and Karl Llewellyn*, at 178–218.

24. Kalman, *Legal Realism at Yale*, at 70 ("broad"); and see id. at 68–75; and see Gerald Fetner, "The Law Teacher as Legal Reformer: 1900–1945," 28 *J. Legal Ed.* 508, 523 (1977); Barbara Fried, *The Progressive Assault on Laissez Faire: Robert Hale and the First Law and Economics Movement* (1998); Julius Goebel, *A History of the School of Law: Columbia University* 300–304 (1955); Brainerd Currie, "The Materials of Law Study, Part III," 8 *J. Legal Ed.* 390 (1955); William Twining, *Karl Llewellyn and the Realist Movement* 43–51, 67 (1973).

25. Jerome Frank, *Law and the Modern Mind* 10 (1930); Frank, *Courts on Trial: Myth and Reality in American Justice* 222; and see 225 (1949) ("myth"); Frank, "Why Not a Clinical Lawyer-School," 81 *U. Pa. L. Rev.* 907, 912 (1933) ("eviscerated," "breeders"); Frank, "A Plea for Lawyer-Schools," 56 *Yale L. J.* 1303, 1303 (1947) ("upper court myth," "neurotic," "seduced"); Kalman, *Legal Realism at Yale*, at 168–75; and see also id. at 138–39 for faculty's treatment of Frank.

26. Walter Wheeler Cook, Book Review, 38 *Yale L. J.* 405, 406 (1929) ("hunting").

27. Leon Keyserling, "Social Objectives in Legal Education," 33 *Colum. L. Rev.* 437, 446, n. 28 (1933) (quotations); Lawrence Friedman, *American Law in the 20th Century* 487–88 (2002).

28. *U.S. v. Butler*, 297 U.S. 1, 62 (1936). See, e.g., George Braden, "The Search for Objectivity in Constitutional Law," 57 *Yale L. J.* 571, 571–72 (1948).

29. Leon Tulin, "The Role of Penalties in Criminal Law," 37 *Yale L. J.* 1048, 1052, 1063 (1928).

30. Herman Oliphant, "A Return to Stare Decisis," 14 *A.B.A. J.* 71 (1928); Thurman

Arnold, "Criminal Attempts — The Rise and Fall of an Abstraction," 40 *Yale L. J.* 53, 57–58 (1930); and see Kalman, *Legal Realism at Yale*, at 3–44.

31. Thurman Arnold, "The Jurisprudence of Edward S. Robinson," 46 *Yale L. J.* 1282, 1282 (1937).

32. Duxbury, *Patterns of American Jurisprudence*, at 106–7 ("unimpeded"); Fried, *The Progressive Assault on Laissez-Faire*, at 13 ("notion"); Horwitz, *The Transformation of American Law*, at 207.

33. Duxbury, *Patterns of American Jurisprudence*, at 130, 330–31; Schlegel, *American Legal Realism and Empirical Social Science*, at 142–44; Hendrik Hartog, "Snakes in Ireland: A Conversation with James Willard Hurst," 12 *Law and Hist. Rev.* 370, 379 (1994); Twining, *Karl Lewellyn and the Realist Movement*, at 377; Robert Maynard Hutchins, "The Autobiography of an Ex-Law Student," 1 *U. Chi. L. Rev.* 511, 512–13 (1934).

34. Stevens, *Law School*, at 158 ("'Cases on X'"); John Johnson, *American Legal Culture, 1908–1940* 110–113 (1981); Kalman, *Legal Realism at Yale*, at 78–95; Schlegel, *American Legal Realism, and Empirical Social Science*, at 255 ("Japanese-wife").

35. Kalman, *Legal Realism at Yale*, at 26, 142, 92.

36. Robert Gordon, "Introduction: J. Willard Hurst and the Common Law Tradition in American Legal Historiography," 10 *Law and Soc'y. Rev.* 9, 38 (1975) ("tools"); Edward Purcell, *The Crisis of Democratic Theory: Scientific Naturalism & the Problem of Value* 159–78 (1973).

37. Thomas Bergin, "The Law Teacher: A Man Divided Against Himself," 54 *Va. L. Rev.* 637, 638, 646–48 (1968); and see William Twining, "Pericles and the Plumber," 83 *Law Qtrly Rev.* 396 (1967).

38. Bergin, "The Law Teacher," at 645, 646, 657; Guido Calabresi, "Joseph Goldstein: My Teacher," 110 *Yale L. J.* 903, 904 (2001).

39. See Kalman, *Legal Realism at Yale*, at 229–31; Grant Gilmore, *The Ages of American Law* 87 (1977).

40. J. T. Dillon, "*Paper Chase* and the Socratic Method of Teaching," 30 *J. Legal Ed.* 529, 531 (1979) ("both asked"); Kalman, *Legal Realism at Yale*, at 62 ("inefficient," "groping," "fifty"); Hope, *Pinstripes & Pearls*, at 94, 91, 86; Thomas Shaffer and Robert Redmount, "Legal Education: The Classroom Experience," 52 *Notre Dame Lawyer* 190, 200 (1976). See generally Kenneth Barry and Patricia Connelly, "Research on Law Students: An Annotated Bibliography," 1978 *Am. B. Found. Res. J.* 751 (1978); Ronald Pipkin, "Legal Education: The Consumers' Perspective," id. 1976: 1161 (1976).

41. Paul Carrington and James Conley, "The Alienation of Law Students," 76 *Mich. L. Rev.* 887, 894 (1978) ("rotten," "buck"); Michael Meltsner, "Feeling Like a Lawyer," 33 *J. Legal Ed.* 624, 624 (1983) ("feel," "right," "controlling"). Emphasis in the original. Areeda, a Socratic method enthusiast, provided a catalogue of the criticisms lodged against it in "The Socratic Method," at 912–20.

42. Robert Gordon, "Bargaining with the Devil," 105 *Harv. L. Rev.* 2041, 2041 (1992) ("boot camp"); John Osborne, *The Paper Chase* (1971); Thomas Shaffer and Robert Redmount, *Lawyers, Law Students and People* 8 ("monastery") (1977).

43. Michael Patton, "The Student, The Situation, and Performance during the First Year of Law School," 21 *J. Legal Ed.* 10, 49 (1968) ("depersonalization"); "Anxiety and the First Semester of Law School," 1988 *Wis. L. Rev.* 1201 (1968); Thomas Donziger, "Grades: Review of Academic Evaluations in Law Schools," 11 *Pac. L. J.* 743, 752 (1980); Phillip Kissam, "Law School Examinations," 42 *Vand. L. Rev.* 443, 439–44 (1989); and see Steve

Nickles, "Examining and Grading in American Law Schools," 30 *Ark. L. Rev.* 411 (1977); Robert Keeton, "Teaching and Testing for Competence in Law Schools," 40 *Md. L. Rev.* 203 (1981). For examples of law professor humor, see, e.g., Jerry Phillips, "Thirteen Rules for Taking Law Examinations," 24 *J. Legal Ed.* 76 (1971); Louis Schwartz, "How to Pass Law School Examinations," id., 11: 223 (1958).

44. Arthur Sutherland, *The Law at Harvard: A History of Ideas and Men, 1817–1967* 221 (1967) ("covers"); Warren, "Spartan Education," at 716; Paul Carrington to author, May 13, 2002.

45. Ben Wood, "Foreword to The Measurement of Law School Work," 24 *Colum. L. Rev.* 224, 242 (1924); John Grant, "Justice in Grading," 9 *J. Legal Ed.* 186, 187 (1956); Sutherland, *The Law at Harvard*, at 322; Hope, *Pinstripes & Pearls*, at 83.

46. Andrew Watson, "The Quest for Professional Competence: Psychological Aspects of Legal Education," 37 *U. Cin. L. Rev.* 93, 121 (1968) ("anxieties"); Joel Seligman, *The High Citadel: The Influence of Harvard Law School* 176 (1978) ("omnipresence"); Michael Swygert and Jon Bruce, "The Historical Origins, Founding, and Early Development of Student-Edited Law Reviews," 36 *Hastings L. Rev.* 739, 769–79 (1985).

47. Richard Lempert, "Law School Grading: An Experiment with Pass-Fail," 24 *J. Legal Ed.* 251, 287; and see 251–52, n. 2 (1972) ("game"); Ann Scales, "Surviving Legal De-Education: An Outsider's Guide," 15 *Vt. L. Rev.* 139, 141 (1990) (quoting partner); Seligman, *The High Citadel*, at 122 (Griswold).

48. Stevens, *Law School*, at 223, n. 47 ("exacting," quoting Harvard's David Cavers); Kalman, *Legal Realism at Yale*, at 63 (quoting Harvard students).

49. Stevens, *Law School*, at 212; Quentin Johnstone, "Student Discontent and Educational Reform in the Law Schools," 23 *J. Legal Ed.* 255, 265–67 (1971).

50. Norman Redlich, "Clinical Education: Stranger in an Elitist Club," 31 *J. Legal Ed.* 201, 202 (1981) ("did not"); Robert Borosage, "Can the Law School Succeed? A Proposal," 1 *Yale Rev. of Law & Soc. Action* 92, 93 (1970); Rockwell, "The Education of the Capitalist Lawyer," at 92.

51. Allen Redlich, "Perceptions of a Clinical Program," 44 *S. Cal. L. Rev.* 574, 576, n. 10 (1971) ("skunk farm"); Redlich, "Clinical Education" ("stranger"); Gary Bellow and Earl Johnson, "Reflections on the University of Southern California Clinical Semester," 44 *S. Cal. L. Rev.* 664, 666 (1971) (reporting on the recent rise in law schools offering clinical work); George Grossman, "Clinical Legal Education: History and Diagnosis," 26 *J. Legal Ed.* 162 (1974); Robert Condlin, "Clinical Education in the Seventies: An Appraisal of the Decade," id., 33: 60 (1983); Seligman, *The High Citadel*, at 160–64 (development of clinical education).

52. Anthony Mohr and Kathryn Rodgers, "Legal Education: Some Student Reflections," 25 *J. Legal Ed.* 403, 405 (1973).

53. Arthur Kinoy, "The Present Crisis in American Legal Education," 24 *Rutgers L. Rev.* 1, 1 (1969); Ralph Nader, "Law Schools and Law Firms," *New Republic* 20, 21 (October 11, 1969).

54. "Huge Demand For Law Grads Seen for 1969–70," *Commentator*, October 28, 1969, at 6; "Law Firm Offers $15,000," *Harvard Law Record*, February 15, 1968, at 1, 4 ("weakness"); Michael Garret and Jean Pennington, "Will They Enter Private Practice?," 57 *A.B.A. J.* 663 (July 1971); Philip Kazanjian, "Trouble in the Law: A Student's View," 58 *A.B.A. J.* 701 (July 1972) (*Harvard Law Review* editors); "Speakers Keynote Activities," *Georgetown Voice*, September 21, 1971, at 1; "Dedications Planned," *Georgetown Law Weekly*, September 15, 1971, at 1; "Dedication Clash—In Retrospect," id., September 22,

1971, at 2; John Robson, "Private Lawyers and Public Interest," 56 *A.B.A. J.* 332 (April 1970); John McGonagle, "New Lawyers and New Law Firms," id. 56:1139 (December 1970); Auerbach, *Unequal Justice*, at 278–279.

55. Paul Savoy, "Toward a New Politics of Legal Education," 79 *Yale L. J.* 444, 486, 444 (1970). Boalt students seemed surprised by the charge that the Free Speech Movement had not affected them. "Wri'Dicta," *Writ*, April, 1966, at 2. For a discussion of law students' interest in FSM, see Robert Cole, "December 1965: Some Reflections and Recollections," in Robert Cohen and Reginald Zelnik, eds., *The Free Speech Movement: Reflections on Berkeley in the 1960s* 422, 426–30 (2002); for a discussion of the constitutional issues raised by the Free Speech Movement, see Robert Post, "Constitutionally Interpreting the FSM Controversy," id. at 401.

56. See, e.g., "Art and Engineering Students in Separate Worlds," *New York Times*, May 12, 169, at A50 (exploring why engineering students at Columbia and CCNY worked so strenuously to keep classes in session during campus disorders); Ludmerer, *Time to Heal*, at 242; "Campus Events Close Law School; 'Pass-Incomplete' Grading Adopted," *Columbia Law School News*, May 13, 1968, at 1 (pass-incomplete grading was adopted for that semester only); "Siegel Trial Begins, Federal Suit Dismissed," *Writ*, November 5, 1969, at 1; "Law and Order Wins — People Free Siegel," id., November 26, 1969, at 1 (reporting acquittal of the student, Dan Siegel); "5 S.D.S. Leaders Yield to Court; Vow 'Revolution' Will Go On; Surrender After Columbia Occupation; Black Law Students Continue Study-In," *New York Times*, May 3, 1969, at A29; "BALSA Stages 'Study-In'; Black Admissions Key Issue," *Columbia Law School News*, May 13, 1969, at 1; "Dean Warren, Statement," id. at 6; "Faculty Resolution of May 9, 1969," id. at 7; "Harvard Sit-In Stirs Students," *Harvard Law Record*, April 24, 1969, at 1, 5; Seligman, *High Citadel*, at 6–7; "The Rutgers Report: The White Law School and the Black Liberation Struggle," *Law against the People*, at 232, 236, 237, 240; "Howard Students Seize Law School," *New York Times*, February 19, 1969, at A34; "Law Students Take Case to Court: Medical Protesters Return to Class," *Hilltop*, February 28, 1969, at 1; "Washington Replaces Harris as Dean of the Law School," id., February 28, 1969, at 3 (even after the U.S. Marshal had ended the one-day takeover well after midnight by presenting students in the school's Moot Courtroom with a temporary restraining order, law students at Howard boycotted classes for a month. "Boycott Enters 4th Week; Students Remain Undaunted," id., March 7, 1969, at 3); "Firebomb Hits Library Amid Wave of Blasts; No Clues Yet," *Columbia Law School News*, March 2, 1970, at 1. The fire at Yale is discussed at length in Chapter 7 in the text accompanying notes 42–53.

57. Duncan Kennedy, "How the Law School Fails: A Polemic," 1 *Yale Rev. of Law & Social Action* 72, 86, 85 (1970).

58. "May Days," 21 *Harvard Law School Bulletin*, 7, 9 (June 1970); "Strike Spurs Faculty," *Advocate*, no. 5, 1968–69, at 4; "A Day for Peace," *Res Gestae*, October 3, 1969, at 1 ("two sides"); "Student Representation on Faculty Committees 'Discussed,'" id., February 21, 1969, at 6 ("took flight").

59. See, e.g., "Yale Law School Studies Revised Grading System," *Commentator*, February 14, 1968, at 3; "Public Interest Law Firms," *Stanford Law School Journal*, November 19, 1970, at 4 (recommending a *Yale Law Journal* student note on public interest law firms in the May 1970 issue as must reading for those interested in public interest law); "Journals Veering From Grades-Only: National Trend to New Criteria," *Georgetown Law Weekly*, November 26, 1969, at 1 (an article including a subsection, "Yale Moves Away from Grades Only" in selection of Law Journal members); "Apathy Marks Student Views," *Columbia Law School News*, October 7, 1968, at 1; "Small Step Forward," id., October 28, 1968, at 4.

By Mark Green's calculations, 15 percent of Yale Law School graduates in 1969, 9 percent in 1970, and 11 percent in 1971 took public interest jobs on graduation. At Pennsylvania, the percentage was 0 percent (1969), 8 percent (1970), 10 percent (1970); at Harvard, 6 percent (1969), 6 percent (1970), 7 percent (1970); at Columbia 0 percent (1969), 5 percent (1970), 5 percent (1971); Green, "The Young Lawyers, 1972: Goodbye to Pro Bono," *New York*, February 21, 1972, 29, 33. Though a nonissue at Yale for students and something of a joke for the faculty, the question of trading in the LLB for the JD was vigorously debated elsewhere, with some claiming that since the United States taught law in a postgraduate setting, the JD was more appropriate and that it would also help students on the job market. See generally "Strong Student Support of J.D. Shows Push for Prestige Labels," *Harvard Law Record*, November 7, 1968, at 2; "Faculty Approves J.D.," id., March 13, 1969, at 1; "Tomorrow's Referendum," *Columbia Law School News*, October 13, 1967, at 4; "Overwhelming Student Vote Supports Change From LL.B.," id., November 20, 1967, at 1; "Faculty Split Over Student Degree Vote," id. at 1: "J.D. Degree," *Writ*, January 1967, at 6; Hope, *Pinstripes & Pearls*, at 155. The Yale faculty converted to a JD late, voting to replace the LLB with the JD at the end of 1970. Yale Law School Faculty Minutes, September 17 and December 17, 1970. And cf., e.g., any article in the *Yale Advocate*, infra, with the disdain for student radicalism shown in "Total Student Control," *Harvard Law Record*, November 21, 1968, at 8; "The Front Page," *Stanford Law School Journal*, December 10, 1970, at 2; "SBA Blunder No. 671," *Georgetown Law Weekly*, April 19, 1972, at 2. *The Columbia Law School News* took positions to the left of the *Record* and *Weekly*, but I would not characterize it as a "radical" paper until 1969–70, when, according to its editor, the law school administration became so upset, it tried to censor the *News*. Barry Morris, Letter to the Students, Faculty and Alumni, *Columbia Law School News*, November 11, 1969, at 8. Boalt faculty also complained when the *Writ* evinced greater radicalism beginning in 1968–69. "Constructive Criticism Please," *Writ*, November 6, 1968, at 2.

   60. Borosage, "Can the Law School Succeed?," at 94.

CHAPTER TWO

   1. Victor Navasky, "The Yales vs. The Harvards (Legal Division)," *New York Times Magazine*, September 11, 1966, at 47, 49; Mel Eflin, "The Case for Yale Law School: Students, Faculty, Ideals Take It to the Top," *Newsweek* 100, 101 (June 10, 1963).

   2. Thomas Swan, "Professor Arthur L. Corbin: Creator of the Present-Day Yale Law School," 74 *Yale L. J.* 207 (1964). See William Twining, *Karl Llewellyn and the Realist Movement* 26–40 (1973); Laura Kalman, *Legal Realism at Yale* 98–105 (1986). Jurisprudentially, Corbin was closer to the Cardozo of *The Nature of the Judicial Process* (1921), a book that greatly influenced him, than the realists. See Gant Gilmore, "The Assignee of Contract Rights and His Precarious Security," 74 *Yale L. J.* 217, 217 (1964); Friedrich Kessler, "Arthur Linton Corbin," 78 *Yale L. J.* 517, 519 (1969); Laura Kalman, *Legal Realism at Yale* 105–7, 136–41 (1986). The quotations are from John Langbein, "The Law School in a University: Yale's Distinctive Path in the Later Nineteenth Century," in Anthony Kronman, ed., *History of the Yale Law School: The Tercentennial Lectures* 53, 65 (2004).

   3. Kalman, *Legal Realism at Yale*, at 105.

   4. Thurman Arnold, *Fair Fights and Foul: A Dissenting Lawyer's Life* 35 (1965). Charles E. Clark, "Admission and Exclusion of Law Students," in Steve Sheppard, ed., *The History of Legal Education in the United States* 903, 904–5 (1999).

5. Clark, "Admission and Exclusion of Law Students," at 905.

6. "Building a University 1919–1940," <http://www.library.yale.edu/archives300/exhibits/building/part4/page1.htm>; Vicki Jackson, Louise Nemschoff, Anne Simon, *The Women's Law School Companion* 6 (1974) ("self-contained"); Kalman, *Legal Realism at Yale*, at 113–15.

7. Robert Stevens, "Law School and Law Students," 59 *Va. L. Rev.* 551, 629 (1973).

8. Robert Gordon, "Professors and Policymakers: Yale Law School Faculty in the New Deal and After," *History of the Yale Law School*, 75, 104 ("cyclone"); Gaddis Smith, "Politics and the Law School: The View from Woodbridge Hall, 1921–1963," id., 138, 144 ("West Point"); Kalman, *Legal Realism at Yale*, at 60, 56.

9. Kalman, *Legal Realism at Yale*, at 131–35; Kyle Graham, "A Moment in *The Times*: Law Professors and the Court-Packing Plan," 52 *J. Legal Ed.* 151, 156–66 (2002).

10. Unless otherwise indicated, the quotations are from id. at 117, 130–31, 174; Laura Kalman, *Abe Fortas: A Biography* 27 (1990) ("Young Hot Dogs"); *Nebbia v. New York*, 291 U.S. 502, 536–37 (1934); Barry Cushman, *Rethinking the New Deal Court: The Structure of a Constitutional Revolution* 225 (1998); Jerold Auerbach, *Unequal Justice: Lawyers and Social Change in Modern America* 177–78 (1976) (Frank on "Mr. Absolute" and "Mr. Try-It"). G. Edward White suggested that legal realism was the jurisprudential analogue of the New Deal in "From Sociological Jurisprudence to Realism: Jurisprudence and Social Change in Early Twentieth Century America," 58 *Va. L. Rev.* 999, 999 (1972). But see Neil Duxbury, *Patterns of American Jurisprudence* 153–59 (1995) (challenging that assumption). Frank overemphasized the jurisprudential originality of realism and, given the preeminence of Frankfurter and other Harvard alumni in the Roosevelt administration, he misstated the role of legal realism in explaining New Deal thought as well.

11. Michael Young, *The Rise of the Meritocracy* (1958); Harlan Phillips, *Felix Frankfurter Reminisces: Recorded in Talks with Dr. Harlan B. Phillips* 19, 26–28 (1960). See Nicholas Lemann, *The Big Test: The Secret History of the American Meritocracy* 115–122 (1999).

12. Stanley Rothman and S. Robert Lichter, *Roots of Radicalism: Jews, Christians, and the Left* 97–98 (1996 ed.).

13. Ronen Shamir, *Managing Legal Uncertainty: Elite Lawyers in the New Deal* 65 (1995) ("hard"); Kalman, *Legal Realism at Yale*, at 134.

14. Mark Tushnet, "Constitutional Scholarship: What's Next?," 5 *Con. Comm'y.* 28, 31 (1988); Philip Frickey, "Constitutional Scholarship: What's Next:," id. at 67, 68 ("practical terms").

15. Harold Lasswell and Myres McDougal, "Legal Education and Public Policy: Professional Teaching in the Public Interest," 52 *Yale L. J.* 203, 206 (1943); Duxbury, *Patterns of American Jurisprudence*, at 198 ("mission"); Kalman, *Legal Realism at Yale*, at 183–84; and see David Kennedy, "When Renewal Repeats Itself: Thinking Against the Box," 32 *N.Y.U. J. Int'l. Law and Politics* 335, 380–87 (2000).

16. Kalman, *Legal Realism at Yale*, at 150; Robert Freilich, "The Divisional Program at Yale: An Experiment for Legal Education in Depth," 21 *J. Legal Ed.* 443, 447–48 (1969) (quoting 1955 report); Eugene Rostow, *The Sovereign Prerogative, The Supreme Court and the Quest for Law* xv (1962); Navasky, "The Yales vs. the Harvards," at 49.

17. Boris Bittker, "Eugene V. Rostow," 94 *Yale L. J.* 1315, 1317 (1989) ("ideological difference"); Gordon, "Professors and Policymakers," at 122; Kalman, *Legal Realism at Yale*, 195; Ellen Schrecker, *No Ivory Tower: McCarthyism and the Universities* 251–52 (1986). The metamorphosis of liberalism is discussed in Alan Brinkley, *The End of Reform: New Deal*

Liberalism in Recession and War 6, 170, 166, 106, 226, 268–71 (1995); and see John Morton Blum, *V Was for Victory: Politics and American Culture during World War II* (1976); Mary Dudziak, *Cold War Civil Rights: Race and the Image of Democracy* (2000); Lizabeth Cohen, *A Consumers' Republic: The Politics of Mass Consumption in Postwar America* (2003).

18. Gerald Rosenberg, *The Hollow Hope: Can Courts Bring About Social Change?* 4 (1991) ("reforms") (emphasis in the original); *U.S. v. Carolene Products*, 304 U.S. 144, 152, n. 4 (1938); Barry Friedman, "The Birth of an Academic Obsession: The History of the Countermajoritarian Difficulty, Part Five," 112 *Yale L. J.* 153, 157 (2002) ("nonstop").

19. Friedman, "The Birth of an Academic Obsession," at 161 ("afoul"); William Eskridge and Philip Frickey, "An Historical and Critical Introduction to *The Legal Process*," in Eskridge and Frickey, eds., *The Legal Process: Basic Problems in the Making and Application of Law* by Henry Hart and Albert Sacks, xi, lxxviii, lxxix (1958) (1994 ed.) ("social ordering" and "interests" [quoting Henry Hart]); Robert Collins, "Growth Liberalism in the Sixties: Great Societies at Home and Grand Designs Abroad," in David Farber, ed., *The Sixties: From Memory to History* 11 (1994).

20. Laura Kalman, *The Strange Career of Legal Liberalism* 19–20 (1996). It is not my purpose to allude here to what the Court actually did in *Lochner v. New York*, (198 U.S. 45 [1905]) or with "substantive due process." Rather, I refer to how progressives perceived *Lochner* during the first half of the twentieth century and, as Gary Rowe insightfully points out, how some of us have continued to see the case, despite *Lochner* revisionism. Rowe, "The Legacy of *Lochner*: *Lochner* Revisionism Revisited," 24 *Law & Soc. Inq'y.* 221, 247, n. 27 (1999). For a discussion of the myth-making associated with substantive due process, see G. Edward White, *The Constitution and the New Deal* 241–68 (2000).

21. Hart and Sacks, *The Legal Process*, at 1148, 96; William Eskridge, *Dynamic Statutory Interpretation* 26 (1994) ("Purposivism").

22. Kalman, *Legal Realism at Yale*, at 155, 157, 203 (*Fortune*, "legalism," "sycophants"); Abraham Goldstein, "Eugene V. Rostow as Dean," 94 *Yale L. J.* 1323, 1323–24 (1985); Friedman, "The Birth of an Academic Obsession," at 231–36.

23. George Braden, "The Search for Objectivity in Constitutional Law," 57 *Yale L. J.* 571, 582 (1948).

24. *Brown v. Board of Education*, 347 U.S. 483 (1954); see Kalman, *Strange Career of Legal Liberalism*, at 26–42; Morton Horwitz, *The Transformation of American Law: The Crisis of Legal Orthodoxy* 260 (1992); Gerald Gunther, *Learned Hand: The Man and the Judge* 652–72 (1994).

25. Herbert Wechsler, "Toward Neutral Principles of Constitutional Law," 73 *Harv. L. Rev.* 1, 27 (1959).

26. *Baker v. Carr*, 369 U.S. 186, 266 (1962); Kalman, *Strange Career of Legal Liberalism*, at 51 ("air of jubilation"); "With the Editors," 83 *Harv. L. Rev.* viii (no. 4, 1970) ("Frankfurter-Hart"); Dedication, 83 *Harv. L. Rev.* 1 (1969); Owen Fiss, "A Life Lived Twice," 100 *Yale L. J.* 1117, 1129 (1991).

27. Alexander Bickel and Harry Wellington, "Legislative Purpose and the Judicial Process: The Lincoln Mills Case," 71 *Harv. L. Rev.* 1, 3 (1957); Henry Hart, "The Supreme Court," 1958 Term — Foreword: The Time Chart of the Justices," 73 *Harv. L. Rev.* 84, 100–101 (1959); Thurman Arnold, "Professor Hart's Theology," id., 1298, 1313 (1960). But see Duxbury, *Patterns of American Jurisprudence*, at 270 (contending that Wechsler added biting dimension).

28. Alexander Bickel, *The Least Dangerous Branch: The Supreme Court at the Bar of Politics* 16–17, 18–19 (1962); Friedman, "The Birth of an Academic Obsession," at 253;

Eskridge and Frickey, "An Historical and Critical Introduction to *The Legal Process*," at cxiv, n. 285; Duxbury, *Patterns of American Jurisprudence*, at 238; Robert Dahl, "Decision-Making in a Democracy: The Supreme Court as a National Policy Maker," 6 *J. Public Law* 279 (1957); Mark Graber, "The Nonmajoritarian Difficulty: Legislative Deference to the Judiciary," 7 *Studies in Am. Political Development* 35 (1993); Graber, "Constitutional Politics and Constitutional Theory: A Misunderstood and Neglected Relationship," 27 *Law & Soc. Inq'y*. 309, 312–17 (2002).

29. Bickel, *The Least Dangerous Branch*, at 128, 111, 71, 69, 64; Gary Minda, *Postmodern Legal Movements: Law and Jurisprudence at Century's End* 39 (1995); Kenneth Ward, "The Counter-Majoritarian Difficulty and Legal Realist Perspectives of Law: The Place of Law in Contemporary Constitutional Theory," 18 *J. L. & Politics* 851, 864 (2002); Gerald Gunther, "The Subtle Vices of the 'Passive Virtues' — A Comment on Principle and Expediency in Judicial Review," 64 *Colum. L. Rev.* 1, 3 (1964); Duxbury, *Patterns of American Jurisprudence*, at 289.

30. Kalman, *Legal Realism at Yale*, at 206–7; Alexander Bickel to Wallace Mendelson, November 26, 1962, Box 9, Folder 167, Alexander Bickel Papers, Yale University Archives (hereafter Bickel Papers) ("neutralists"); Alexander Bickel to Louis Jaffe, September 30, 1965, Box 9, Folder 176, id.; Bickel, *The Least Dangerous Branch*, at 244; Edward Purcell, "Alexander M. Bickel and the Post-Realist Constitution," 11 *Harv. C.R.-C.L. L. Rev.* 521, 542–43, 549 (1976).

31. Louis Pollak, "In Memoriam: Charles L. Black, Jr. and Civil Rights," 102 *Colum. L. Rev.* 876, 880 (2002) ("knighted"); Charles Black, "The Lawfulness of the Segregation Decisions," 69 *Yale L. J.* 421, 429, 427, n. 19 (1960); Black, "The Supreme Court, 1966 Term — Foreword: 'State Action,' Equal Protection, and California's Proposition 14," 81 *Harv. L. Rev.* 69, 105 (1967) ("every," "branch"); Louis Pollak, "Racial Discrimination and Judicial Integrity: A Reply to Professor Wechsler," 108 *U. Pa. L. Rev.* 1, 33 (1959); Eskridge and Frickey, "An Historical and Critical Introduction to The Legal Process," at li, cx; Eflin, "Case for Yale Law School," at 104 (describing Rostow's view).

32. Robert Cover, "The Origins of Judicial Activism in the Protection of Minorities," 91 *Yale L. J.* 1287, 1316 (1982) ("paradigmatic"); Steven Keeva, "Demanding More Justice," 80 *A.B.A. J.* 46, 48 (August 1994) ("turning point," quoting A. E. Dick Howard; emphasis in the original); *Griswold* v. *Connecticut*, 381 U.S. 479 (1965); David Garrow, *Liberty & Sexuality: The Right to Privacy and the Making of Roe v. Wade* 237–40 (1994); *In re Gault*, 387 U.S. 1 (1967).

33. Leon Higginbotham, "The Dream With Its Back Against the Wall," 46 *Yale L. Report* 23, 27 (Summer 1999); Stevens, "Law Schools and Law Students," at 630; <http://www.gwu.edu/nsarchiv/coldwar/interviews/episode-13/holmes1.html>; Judith Richards Hope, *Pinstripes & Pearls: The Women of the Harvard Law School Class of '64 Who Forged an Old-Girl Network and Paved the Way for Future Generations* 76, 159 (2003) ("understanding"). See generally Jodi Wilgoren, "Black and Blue: Yale Volunteers in the Mississippi Civil Rights Movement, 1963–1965" (Yale College senior essay, 1992).

34. John Morton Blum, *A Life with History* 156 (2004); Eflin, "Case for Yale Law School," at 101; Leon Lipson, "Eugene Rostow," 94 *Yale L. J.* 1329, 1329 (1985) ("shovel-carrying"). Rostow worked with the Lend-Lease Administration and State Department during World War II and later was assistant executive secretary to the Economic Committee for Europe. See Eugene Rostow, "The Japanese American Cases — A Disaster," 54 *Yale L. J.* 489 (1945); Rostow, *A National Policy for the Oil Industry* (1948); and Kalman, *Legal Realism at Yale*, at 200, for a discussion of Rostow's relationship with Woodbridge Hall.

35. Robert Stevens, "History of the Yale Law School: Provenance and Perspective," *History of the Yale Law School*, 1, 14–15; Brannon Denning, "The Yale Law School Divisional Studies Program, 1954–1964: An Experiment in Legal Education," 52 *J. Legal Ed.* 365 (2003); Eugene Rostow, "The Great Talent Hunt—1955–1959: Renewing the Yale Law Faculty," 7 *Yale L. Report* 7 (Winter 1961); Yale Law School Governing Board Minutes, March 7, 1959 (hereafter YLS Governing Board Minutes); Eugene Rostow to the Governing Board, March 2, 1959 (attached to id.) (explaining that he had worked out a plan with the administration by which the board could vote on ten promotions to full professor at once, but that their announcement would be staggered). On some occasions the Governing Board meetings were restricted to members of the board; on others, the "expanded" Governing Board met. The minutes of all Governing Board meetings are filed together.

36. Rostow, "The Great Talent Hunt," at 7; "Yale Law: Fork in the Road," *National Law Journal*, June 29, 1981, at 1, 26. Pollak was hired during Harry Shulman's deanship and promoted during Rostow's.

37. See Anne Standley, "Alexander Bickel, Charles Black, and the Ambiguous Legacy of Brown v. Board of Education: Competing Conceptions of Law, Justice and Democracy Within Postwar Legal Thought" 10–51 (PhD dissertation, 1993) and the tributes to Black collected in the *Yale Law Journal*, beginning at 95 *Yale L. J.* 1553 (1986), and the *Columbia Law Review*, beginning at 102 *Colum. L. Rev.* 865 (2002); Herma Hill Kay, "The Future of Women Law Professors," 77 *Iowa L. Rev.* 5, 8, 11 (1991) (Peters); Guido Calabresi to William Clinton, May 13, 1993, Box 21, Chron File, Dean's Files, Yale University Archives (hereafter Dean's Files) (describing career of Peters and her class rank).

38. Calabresi attributed the sex/religion joke to Anne Bittker (interview with Guido Calabresi, 2002); Townsend Hoopes, *The Limits of Intervention: An Inside Account of How the Johnson Policy of Escalation in Vietnam was Reversed* (1969).

39. Kalman, *Legal Realism at Yale*, at 195–99; Schrecker, *No Ivory Tower*, at 252–53.

40. Interview with Charles Reich, 2002.

41. Id.; Charles Reich, *The Sorcerer of Bolinas Reef* 132–33 (1976); James William Moore et al., *Collier on Bankruptcy* (14th ed., 1940) (1898); James William Moore et al., *Moore's Federal Practice*, 2d ed. (1948); Guido Calabresi, "Joseph Goldstein: My Teacher," 110 *Yale L. J.* 903, 903 (2001).

42. Interviews with Ronald Dworkin, 2002, and Calabresi, 2002.

43. Interview with Dworkin.

44. Bickel interview with Maggie Scarf, October 28, 1974, Box 13, Folder 8, M. Scarf tapes, Bickel Papers, Box 13, Folder 8 ("drunk," "help it"); Standley, "Alexander Bickel, Charles Black," at 168 ("displayed"), and see also 51–92; interview with Calabresi, 2002 (marriage); interview with Larry Simon, 2002 ("over again"); interview with Reich.

45. Alexander Bickel to J. Kirkpatrick Sale, May 18, 1967, Box 9, Folder 186, Bickel Papers ("most powerful"); Bickel to Harold Leventhal, January 10, 1968, Box 10, Folder 148, id. ("sick"); Statement, May 17, 1968, Box 35, Folder 4, id. (McCarthy); Bickel to William Hackett, June 18, 1968, Box 10, Folder 191, id. ("best hope"); Bickel to Anthony Lewis, July 16, 1968, id. (Brandeis); Purcell, "Alexander M. Bickel and the Post-Realist Constitution," at 548.

46. Standley, "Alexander Bickel, Charles Black," at 172 (quoting Abram Chayes).

47. Email, Tom Grey to author, June 29, 2003 (the decision was *Application of President and Directors of Georgetown College*, 331 F. 2d. 1000 [1964]); Dedication, 84 *Yale L. J.* n.p. (December 1974) ("little Earl Warrens"; "blue jeans").

48. Interview with Paul Gewirtz, 2001.

49. "Double Dactylia," *Yale Advocate*, November 22, 1968, at 2.

50. Interview with Reich.

51. Joseph Goldstein, "Psychoanalysis and Jurisprudence," 77 *Yale L. J.* 1053, 1075, 1076 (1968) ("resistance," "astronauts"); Elizabeth Goldstein, "Biography of Joseph Goldstein," 19 *Yale L. & Pol'y. Rev.* 1 (2001); "Joseph Goldstein: A Selected Bibliography," 19 *Yale L. J.* 1 (2001); Laura Holland, "Invading the Ivory Tower: The History of Clinical Education at Yale Law School," 49 *J. Legal Ed.* 504, 513, 516 (1999).

52. Anthony Kronman, "The Mystery of the 'But,'" 110 *Yale L. J.* 893, 894, 896 (2001) ("skewering," "mad," "circumvention," "deception," "loving," "impatience"); "Interview with Joseph Goldstein," 110 *Yale L. J.* 925, 926, 939 (2001) ("feelings," "curbstone").

53. Interview with Calabresi, 2002.

54. Interview with Reich.

55. Kalman, *Legal Realism at Yale*, at 206.

56. Id. at 143 ("barons"); Alexander Bickel to Clyde Summers, March 24, 1964, Box 9, Folder 171, Bickel Papers ("inches," "scars"); Grant Gilmore to Eugene Rostow, April 6, 1964, April 13, 1964, Box 129, Folder 15, Kingman Brewster Papers, Yale University Archives (hereafter Brewster Papers); Rostow to Gilmore, April 15, 1964, id.; Alexander Bickel to Harry Wellington, October 1, 1964, Box 9, Folder 177, Bickel Papers (when Goldstein became dean in 1970, he sent the message to Chicago that Gilmore's party was in power, and Gilmore, whose wife had continued to spend most of her time in the East, gratefully accepted an offer to return to New Haven. Interview with Abraham Goldstein, 2001); Bonnie Collier interview with Boris Bittker, 1996, Yale Law School Oral History Project (all Collier interviews are part of this project); Bonnie Collier interview with Harry Wellington, 2000; Bonnie Collier interview with Abraham Goldstein, 1996. Rostow assured his colleagues that while some had declined recent offers to join the faculty, there was no cause for concern in Eugene Rostow to the Governing Board, February 11, 1965, YLS Governing Board Minutes. See Eugene Rostow to R. Sargent Shriver, September 17, 1964, Box 129, Folder 15, Brewster Papers (thanking Shriver for the invitation to become Shriver's Deputy Director of the Office of Economic Opportunity and Johnson's Special Assistant and relating that he had been offered a judgeship); Alexander Bickel to Abraham Goldstein, September 14, 1964, Box 82, Folder 23, Bickel Papers (interest in third term).

57. Louis Pollak, "Ralph Brown: Farewell to a Friend," 108 *Yale L. J.* 1473, 1477 (1999).

58. "A Vigorous and Fruitful Tree: The First Annual Report of the Academic Committee to the Yale Law School Student Association," May 1967, Box 55, Student Association—Academic Committee First Annual Report, Dean's Files (the report drew on a student questionnaire [The Yale Law Survey of Student Opinion, n.d., administered March, 1967, Box 54, Folder: Student Associations, Dean's Files]; Eugene Rostow to Deans Tate and Runyon, November 13, 1957, Box 46, Chron File, October, Dean's Files ("country club," "Ranks"); Yale University Law School, A Memorandum on Admissions and Scholarships, 1962, Yale Law Library (lamenting Harvard's ability to attract abler students and reporting that it seemed to get the top Harvard College graduates and lure a large number of Yale College's best as well); Louis Pollak to Kingman Brewster, November 2, 1965, Box 36, Folder: Memoranda—Misc. (1965–70), Dean's Files ("Myths," "students and faculty").

59. Louis Pollak to Bruce Littman, April 14, 1969, Box 32, Folder L, Dean's Files ("for anything"); "Prof. Louis H. Pollak," 7 *Yale L. Report* 18 (Winter 1961) ("reacts"); Louis Pollak, "Advocating Civil Liberties: A Young Lawyer Before the Old Court," 17 *Harv. C.R.-C.L. L. Rev.* 1 (1982) (a study of Walter Pollak's professional career); Geoffrey Kabaservice interview with Louis Pollak, 1992; *Cooper* v. *Aaron*, 358 U.S. 1 (1958); interview with

Ann Hill, 2002 (Pollak's NAACP connections); "A Too Modest Proposal," *Yale Advocate*, October 24, 1968, at 2 ("eminently decent").

60. Geoffrey Kabaservice, *The Guardians: Kingman Brewster, His Circle, and the Rise of the Liberal Establishment* 216, 10, 65, 28, 80–81, 83–84, 226, 357, 413 (2004); Kabaservice, "Kingman Brewster and the Rise and Fall of the Progressive Establishment" 30, 194 (PhD dissertation, 1999) (quoting Kai Erikson on the center and Henry Hart). New Deal historian John Morton Blum, one of the faculty members close to Brewster, thought he sometimes consciously acted like FDR, though he was never an FDR Democrat. Kabaservice interview with John Blum, 1992.

61. Kabaservice, *Guardians*, at 464, 241, 301, 467–69; William Sloane Coffin, *Once to Every Man: A Memoir* 302 (1977); Alexandra Robbins, *Secrets of the Tomb: Skull and Bones, The Ivy League, and the Hidden Paths of Power* 107 (2002) (yearbook).

62. Kabaservice, *Guardians*, at 9 (quotation); Kabaservice, "Kingman Brewster and the Rise and Fall of the Progressive Establishment," at 261–85; Morton Keller and Phyllis Keller, *Making Harvard Modern: The Rise of America's University* 32–34 (2001).

63. Alexander Bickel to Abraham Goldstein, November 9, 1964, Box 82, Folder 23, Bickel Papers; Kabaservice, *Guardians*, at 154 ("straight shooting," quoting Leon Lipson); Kabaservice interviews with Myres McDougal (1991), Pollak, and Ralph Brown (1992) (reporting faculty deliberations on Brewster).

64. YLS Faculty Minutes, January 12, 1965. For discussion of opposition to Goldstein, see Myres McDougal to Kingman Brewster, October 28, 1964, Box 131, Folder 13, Brewster Papers; Alexander Bickel to Friedrich Kessler, November 10, 1964, Box 82, Folder 23, Bickel Papers.

65. Nelson Polsby to Alexander Bickel, June 13, 1969, Box 7, Folder 120, Bickel Papers. I suppose some readers will try to determine in which camp they would have fallen. Based on years of observing my own performance in faculty meetings, I think I would have been a "permissive." Inevitably, that has affected the way I have presented events.

66. Email, John Griffiths to author, February 4, 2002.

67. Alexander Bickel to Nelson Polsby, June 24, 1969, Box 10, Folder 196, Bickel Papers.

68. Robert Bork, *Slouching Toward Gomorrah: Modern Liberalism and American Decline* 36, 49 (1996); "Law School Blasts Vietnam Policy," *Yale Daily News*, February 15, 1968, at 1 (indicating that 157 Yale law students and half the faculty had signed a statement denouncing America's Vietnam policy; claiming that its war aims could not be achieved; and calling for political and military de-escalation. Faculty signatories were Alexander Bickel, Boris Bittker, Ralph Brown, Guido Calabresi, Arthur Charpentier, Marvin Chirelstein, Jan Deutsch, Thomas Emerson, Abraham Goldstein, Joseph Goldstein, John Griffiths, Robert Hudec, Jay Katz, Freidrich Kessler, Ellen Peters, Louis Pollak, Charles Reich, Egon Schwelb, John Simon, Edward Sparer, Clyde Summers, David Trubek, and Harry Wellington).

69. Collier interview with Bittker.

70. Charles Reich, "The Law of the Planned Society," 75 *Yale L. J.* 1227, 1269 (1966) ("Constitution"); Reich, "The New Property," id., 73: 733 (1965); *Goldberg* v. *Kelly*, 397 U.S. 254 (1970); Reich, "Commentary," 100 *Yale L. J.* 1465 (1991); Fred Shapiro, "The Most-Cited Articles from the *Yale Law Journal*," id., 100: 1449, 1462 (1991); Charles Reich, "Toward the Humanistic Study of Law," id., 74: 1402, 1402, 1408 (1965) ("trouble," "idealistic"); "Property Goes Intellectual," *Yale Advocate*, February 22, 1968, at 2 (Reich's reputation among students, "stifling"); "Reich and the Radical Student," id., September 26, 1968, at 2.

71. Reich, *The Sorcerer of Bolinas Reef*, at 136–54; Charles Reich, *The Greening of America*, Dedication Page, 227, 347 (1970).

72. Boris Bittker, "The Case of the Checker-Board Ordinance: An Experiment in Race Relations," 71 *Yale L. J.* 1387 (1962); Collier interview with Bittker ("relatively few"); Bittker, *The Case for Black Reparations* (1973); Mark Tushnet, "The Utopian Technician," 93 *Yale L. J.* 208 (1983).

73. Interview with Reich ("fancy"); Abraham Goldstein, "A Law School Memoir," *Yale Alumni Magazine* 38, 38 (February 1977); Collier interview with Goldstein ("radical judge," "specimen Yale"); *Durham* v. *U.S.* 214 F. 2d. 862 (1954); Abraham Goldstein to Erwin Griswold, February 24, 1964, Box 129, Folder 14, Brewster Papers ("ties"); Abraham Goldstein, *The Insanity Defense* (1967); Abraham Goldstein, "The Unfulfilled Promise of Legal Education," in Geoffrey Hazard, ed., *Law in a Changing America* 157, 162 (1968); Coffin, *Once to Every Man*, at 236, 261–78.

74. Interview with Dworkin; "Action-Oriented Dean," *New York Times*, March 10, 1970, at A49; confidential interview ("flames"). Clyde Summers agreed with that assessment. Kabaservice interview with Summers, 1992.

75. Bickel to Kessler, November 10, 1964; Kingman Brewster to Herbert Packer, January 7, 1965, Box 131, Folder 13, Brewster Papers ("maturing"). Goldstein probably remained a live candidate in Brewster's mind. At least, he warranted a telegram from the president after the matter was resolved saying that the Corporation had approved Pollak as dean. Brewster to Goldstein, March 13, 1965, id. It is unclear how serious Brewster was about the candidacy of Clark, whom he subsequently made master of one of Yale's colleges. Bonnie Collier interview with Elias Clark, 1997. When the faculty was initially asked to list people on the faculty who should receive consideration for the deanship, Bickel received but 2 votes, while Bittker won 23; Abraham Goldstein, 11; Elias Clark, 10; Harry Wellington, 10; and Louis Pollak, 6. Results of Faculty Survey, n.d. (ca. October 9, 1964), Box 131, Folder 12, id.

76. YLS Faculty Minutes, January 21, 1965.

77. "To Dream a Dream of Days Gone By," *Yale Daily News*, January 18, 1999 <http://www.yaledailynews.com/article.asp?AID=366> ("moral neutrality," "intellectual revolution"); Kabaservice, *Guardians*, at 204–5; John Lewis, "Burke," 105 *Yale L. J.* 621, 621 (1995).

78. James Patterson, *Grand Expectations: The United States 1945–1974* 477 (1996) (Kennedy federalism); Burke Marshall, *Federalism and Civil Rights* 49 (1964) ("national police force" is from the foreword, at ix, by Robert Kennedy); "Theories of Federalism and Civil Rights," 75 *Yale L. J.* 1007, 1008, 1041 (1968).

79. Gerhard Gesell to Kingman Brewster, Box 131, Folder 13, Brewster Papers (predicting Marshall's decision); Alexander Bickel to Abraham Goldstein, February 3, 1965, Box 82, Folder 23, Bickel Papers (reporting Brewster and others' prediction of Marshall's decision); Louis Pollak to Kingman Brewster, February 2, 1965, Box 131, Folder 13, Brewster Papers. Marshall reconsidered and joined the faculty in 1970, becoming Abe Goldstein's deputy dean.

80. YLS Faculty Minutes, March 11 and March 12, 1965; Kabaservice interview with Summers.

81. Interviews with Guido Calabresi, 2001, and Pollak; Harry Wellington to author, March 18, 2003; Bonnie Collier interview with Harry Wellington, July 12, 2000 ("opposition," "happy"); Alexander Bickel to Abraham Goldstein, April 26, 1965, Box 9, Folder 174, Bickel Papers, and Bickel to Harry Wellington, October 1, 1965, id., Folder 177 (both expressing satisfaction with Pollak's first days as dean). Calabresi discussed the perception

of Pollak's overreliance in our interview, apparently the source of Bickel's initial dissatisfaction with Pollak. Alexander Bickel to Guido Calabresi, January 15, 1966, Box 9, Folder 169, Bickel Papers. The 1965–66 deficit is discussed in Louis Pollak to Kingman Brewster, March 8, 1966, Box 132, Folder 4, Brewster Papers and in other documents in the folder.

CHAPTER THREE

1. Robert Bork, *Slouching Toward Gomorrah: Modern Liberalism and American Decline* 36, 37 (quotations) (1996). Standley also dates the beginning of the law school's "sixties" to Fall 1967. Anne Standley, "Alexander Bickel, Charles Black, and the Ambiguous Legacy of Brown v. Board of Education: Competing Conceptions of Law, Justice and Democracy Within Postwar Legal Thought" 137 (PhD dissertation, 1993).

2. Robert Stevens, "Law School and Law Students," 59 *Va. L. Rev.* 551, 635 (1973).

3. Interview with Charles Reich, 2002 ("settled," "indelible"); Robert Borosage, "Can the Law School Succeed? A Proposal," 1 *Yale Rev. of Law & Soc. Action* 92, 93 (1970).

4. Paul Goodman, *Growing Up Absurd: Problems of Youth in the Organized System* 14 (1956); Doug Rossinow, "Mario Savio and the Politics of Authenticity," in Robert Cohen and Reginald Zelnik, eds., *The Free Speech Movement: Reflections on Berkeley in the 1960s* 533, 539, 541 (2002) ("exploited"; SDS and "new working class"); A. S. Neill, in Albert Lamb, ed., *Summerhill School: A New View of Childhood* 5 (1992 ed.); Julie Rubin, "The Limits of Freedom: Student Activists and Educational Reform at Berkeley in the 1960s," *Free Speech Movement*, at 485, 489.

5. Beth Bailey, *Sex in the Heartland* 80–81 (1999) (*Time*); Terry Anderson, *The Movement and the Sixties: Protest in America from Greensboro to Wounded Knee* 98–101 (1995).

6. Duncan Kennedy, "The Liberal Administrative State," 41 *Syracuse L. Rev.* 801, 801 (1990) (Stevenson); interview with Duncan Kennedy, 2001 ("ruling," "taunting"); "How the Yale Law School Fails: A Polemic," Box 130, Folder 8, Brewster Papers. For the published version, "How the Law School Fails: A Polemic," see 1 *Yale Rev. Law & Social Action* 71 (1970). Where the quoted material appears in both the published and unpublished versions, I have cited the published one. The organization was the National Student Association. CIA involvement in the NSA did not become public until 1967, the year Kennedy entered law school. Prior to that, just a few NSA officers each year were told of the relationship. William Chafe, *Never Stop Running: Allard Lowenstein and the Struggle to Save American Liberalism* 105–6 (1993). It is not clear whether Kennedy, who was Overseas Representative of the NSA in Paris in 1965–66, was one of them. After leaving the NSA, he worked at Intercontinental Research Co., Inc., a management consulting firm, which may also have had CIA connections. When I spoke with Kennedy in 2001, he told me he had worked for the CIA for two years prior to beginning law school.

7. Kennedy, "How the Law School Fails," at 72, 74, 75, 89, n. 6.

8. Stevens, "Law Schools and Law Students," at 638, 641. Stevens viewed the data somewhat more positively. See id. at 638.

9. Kennedy, "How the Law School Fails," at 78; "Consideration for Kessler," *Yale Advocate*, February 9, 1970, at 4 (Kennedy remarks); Friedrich Kessler, "Arthur Linton Corbin," 78 *Yale L. J.* 517, 524 (1969) ("moral being"); John McNulty, "A Student's Tribute to Fritz Kessler," id., 104: 2133, 2135 (1995); interview with Reich (snottiness).

10. Kennedy, "How the Law School Fails," at 75, 76.

11. Stevens, "Law School and Law Students," at 645, n. 159 ("stifling") ("bang"); Ken-

nedy, "How the Law School Fails," at 77, 76, 87, 78; Duncan Kennedy, "Form and Substance in Private Law Adjudication," 89 *Harv. L. Rev.* 1685 (1976), and Kennedy, "The Structure of Blackstone's Commentaries," 28 *Buff. L. Rev.* 211 (1979).

12. Kennedy, "How the Law School Fails," at 77, 84; "How the Yale Law School Fails," at 59 ("bizarrely," "feeling").

13. Kennedy, "How the Law School Fails," at 80, 81, 84 (emphasis in the original); "How the Yale Law School Fails," at 39 ("radicals": according to Kennedy, there were about 40 radicals in 1968. Id.); Borosage, "Can the Law School Succeed?," at 100, n. 4 ("straighter"). Unlike Kennedy, Borosage believed that the faculty also admired the radicals. Id.

14. Kennedy, "How the Law School Fails," at 80, 81.

15. Id. at 80, 87–88, 83, 85.

16. Stevens, "Law School and Law Students," at 581; Jodi Wilgoren, "Black and Blue: Yale Volunteers in the Mississippi Civil Rights Movement, 1963–1965" (Yale College senior essay, 1992) 35.

17. Fred Powledge, *Model City* 90, 201, 202 (1970) (quoting Secretary of Labor Willard Wirtz on New Haven and Yale law student Richard Thornell on liberals at Yale). For discussion of the Hill Parents Association and the summer unrest, see id. at 91, 151–77; Yohuru Williams, *Black Politics/White Power: Civil Rights, Black Power, and the Black Panthers in New Haven* 75–84 (2000); Richard Balzer, *Street Time* (1972) (unpaginated).

18. Interview with David Schoenbrod, 2003 ("cloud"); Geoffrey Kabaservice, "Kingman Brewster and the Rise and Fall of the Progressive Establishment" 496 (PhD dissertation, 1999) (poll); Kabaservice, *The Guardians: Kingman Brewster, His Circle, and the Rise of the Liberal Establishment* 317, 240–41, 144 (2004) ("trouble").

19. Chafe, *Never Stop Running*, at 282, 264, 269, 253, 329.

20. William Sloane Coffin, *Once to Every Man: A Memoir* 239 (1977); interview with Douglas Rosenberg, 2003; Michael Foley, *Confronting the War Machine: Draft Resistance During the Vietnam War* 76–109 (2003).

21. Coffin, *Once to Every Man*, at 239, 243 ("prayer," "fool"); Foley, *Confronting the War Machine*, at 149, 150–59.

22. Kabaservice, *Guardians*, at 290–91, 299–300; and see John Perry Miller, *Creating Academic Settings: High Craft and Low Cunning* 147, 169–70 (1991).

23. Foley, *Confronting the War Machine* at 149, 150–59; Joseph Califano, *The Triumph and Tragedy of Lyndon Johnson: The White House Years* 201–2 (1991).

24. "Class of '70," *Columbia Law School News*, October 13, 1967, at 2. See also, e.g., "Draft Difficulties," *The Commentator*, February 14, 1968, at 4; "The Draft: What Are the Possibilities?," *Res Gestae*, October 11, 1968, at 1; "Hershey Depletes Our Ranks: Survey Shows Draft Affects Boalt," *Writ*, December 18, 1968, at 1; id., March 18, 1968 (special issue of the *Writ* on the draft); "The Law School 'Confi Guide' Grades Professors, Punctures Egos Aplenty," *Harvard Law Record*, October 3, 1968, at 4 (widespread anxiety at Harvard about draft); "Readmission for Draftees Likely: 'Half of Class May Be Drafted' — Tate," *Yale Advocate*, March 3, 1968, at 2; "2d Year Loses 35 As Draft Takes Toll," id., September 26, 1968, at 1.

25. Email, Jonathan Krown to author, March 24, 2001.

26. Borosage, "Can the Law School Succeed?," at 94.

27. Charles Black, "Some Notes on Law Schools in the Present Day," 79 *Yale L. J.* 505, 506, 507 (1970).

28. *U.S. v. O'Brien*, 391 U.S. 3367 (1968); *Street v. New York*, 394 U.S. 576 (1969); Thomas

Emerson, "Toward A General Theory of the First Amendment," 72 *Yale L. J.* 877 (1963) and Emerson, *The System of Freedom of Expression* 79–90, 88, 726 (1970).

29. Paul Savoy, "Toward A New Politics of Legal Education," 79 *Yale L. J.* 444, 450, 453 (1970).

30. Susan Braudy, *Family Circle: The Boudins and the Aristocracy of the Left* 181, 133–35 (2003).

31. Laura Kalman, *The Strange Career of Legal Liberalism* 52 (1996); Lucas Powe, *The Warren Court and American Politics* (2000).

32. Paul Campos, "Advocacy and Scholarship," 81 *Cal. L. Rev.* 817, 819, n. 4 (1993) ("interlocking"); Stanley Rothman and S. Robert Lichter, *Roots of Radicalism: Jews, Christians, and the Left* 180 (1996 ed.).

33. Black, "Some Notes on Law Schools in the Present Day," at 511, 510.

34. Id. at 506; Alan Stone, "Legal Education on the Couch," 85 *Harv. L. Rev.* 392, 398 (1971) (describing Black's mood as widespread among law professors); interview with John Simon, 2001 ("No one"); Charles Black, *Structure and Relationship in Constitutional Law* 7, 11 (1969); Akhil Amar and Vikram Amar, "Is the Presidential Succession Law Constitutional," 48 *Stan. L. Rev.* 113 (1995) (dedicated to Black); Akhil Amar, "Intratextualism," 112 *Harv. L. Rev.* 747, 790 (1999); "Black's 'Neglected Method,'" *Yale Advocate*, May 1, 1969, at 2; William Iverson, "Insanity and the Lawyers," *New Journal*, January 21, 1968, at 12, 13.

35. Emails, Richard Hughes to author, December 23 and December 28, 2001 ("we decided"); "'Yale Advocate: Law Students to Get Paper," *Yale Daily News*, November 30, 1967, at 3.

36. Hughes to author, December 28, 2001; Anderson, *The Movement and the Sixties*, at 110–111; "Tuition At YLS Highest in U.S., Pollak Believes," *Yale Advocate*, December 11, 1967, at 1; Cartoon, id. at 2 ("DYNAMIC"); "An Active Semester for LSCRRC—Elections, Research and a Project," id. at 2; "The Supreme Court?—Maybe," id. at 2; "Four New Courses Set; Seminars on Draft Law, Welfare Featured," id. at 1; "A Focus for Dissent," id. at 2. Associate Dean Brown intensely disliked the school newspaper. Ralph Brown to Kingman Brewster, February 17, 1970, Box 132, Folder 2, Kingman Brewster Papers, Yale University Archives (hereafter Brewster Papers). I imagine others shared this sentiment.

37. "Group Forms Here to Back McCarthy," *Yale Advocate*, December 11, 1967, at 1; interview with Rosenberg.

38. "Four New Courses Set," at 1. Aided by Professors Griffiths and Steven Duke, three members of the class of 1970 filed a class action against Hershey charging that he had acted improperly when he instructed local draft boards to deny I-S deferments, which allowed students who had begun the school year to complete it without being inducted, to graduate students who had held II-S student deferments since June 1967. "Sudden Blossoming: Five Draft Cases to Watch with Care," *Harvard Law Record*, February 18, 1969, at 3. They were unsuccessful. "Students Here Sue Hershey," *Yale Advocate*, November 22, 1968, at 1; "Law Students Win, Draw In Draft Cases," id., February 20, 1969, at 1. But the drive sparked law professors at the University of Michigan Law School to challenge Hershey on similar grounds. "Michigan Law Faculty Challenges Legality of Selective Service Policy," *Res Gestae Extra*, n.d. (c. late 1968–early 1969). The undated letter to the chairman of the *Yale Daily News* signed by Ralph Brown, Guido Calabresi, Marvin Chirelstein, Steven Duke, Ronald Dworkin, Abraham Goldstein, Joseph Goldstein, John Griffiths, Louis Pollak, Charles Reich, Clyde Summers, and Harry Wellington appeared as

"FBI Legal Advice," *Yale Daily News*, October 24, 1967, at 2; and see "The Right to Silence," *Columbia Law School News*, October 13, 1967, at 4 ("Somebody").

39. Interview with Paul Gewirtz, 2001.

40. W. J. Rorabaugh, *Berkeley at War: The 1960s* ix–x (1989) ("power"); Mark Rudd, "Columbia: Notes on the Spring Rebellion," in Carl Oglesby, ed., *The New Left Reader* 290, 299 (1969) (SDS slogan); "No Consensus On Grades Among First-Year Students," *Yale Advocate*, September 26, 1968, at 1, 2.

41. Their report urged a three-tiered grading system: "Distinguished" (roughly top 5 percent of the students); "Noteworthy" (roughly 20 percent); and "Qualified" (roughly 75 percent). There was no mention of failures in the law students' grading system. In sending along the report, its principal author emphasized students' moderateness. William Davis to James White, May 2, 1967, transmitting "A Vigorous and Fruitful Tree," Box 55, Folder: Student Grades, Exams, Degrees, Dean's Files, Yale University Archives (hereafter Dean's Files) ("Berkeley-style"); William Davis to Editor, June 14, 1967, id.

42. Interview with Richard Balzer, 2002; and Balzer, *Street Time.*

43. Interview with Balzer; "Grading Proposals in Limbo," *Yale Advocate*, February, 1968, at 1 ("no grades"); "What's Gone Down at the Law School: 1967–69," id., October 2, 1969, at 1, 4, 5 (the eight grades were A, B+, B, C+, C, C−, D, F); "Law Students Sign Pass-Fail Petition," *Yale Daily News*, December 12, 1967, at 1 ("antithetical").

44. "Grades: How and Why," *Yale Advocate*, February 1968, at 2. Emphasis added.

45. "Yale Law School Studying Grading," *New York Times*, January 28, 1968, at A60 (quoting a lawyer in a large Midwestern firm, who could not imagine how to judge students without grades or rankings); The Survey of Employers on Grading, Box 63, Folder 26, Alexander Bickel Papers, Yale University Archives (hereafter Bickel Papers) (a survey of thirty-seven Wall Street employers, conducted by three students, concluding that change would make it more difficult for students to obtain desirable jobs); "Pass-Fail System Appears Unlikely," *Yale Advocate*, September 26, 1968, at 1, 3 (Calabresi).

46. "Pass-Fail System Appears Unlikely," at 3 ("inside," "divert"); "Functional Grading: Teacher-Student Feedback Needed," *Yale Advocate*, February, 1968, at 2 ("meaningful"); "Faculty Action Awaited: Grading Proposals in Limbo," id., at 1, 3 ("antithetical"); "Credit/No Credit: The Case for Abolishing Grades," *Columbia Law School News*, December 8, 1969, at 3 ("exclusive").

47. Email, Tom Grey to author, June 29, 2003 ("1Ls"); "The Tiergarten," *Commentator*, May 4, 1971, at 6 (emphasis added); Nathan Glazer, *Remembering the Answers: Essays on the American Student Revolt* 245, 247 (1970).

48. Message for Pollak, December 15, 1967, Box 38, Folder: Grading, 1967–1970, Dean's Files.

49. "Grading Proposals in Limbo," at 1; Louis Pollak to Fleming James, January 18, 1968, Box 38, Folder: Grading 1967–1970, Dean's Files. Yale College had already changed its 0–100 grading scale to a four-tier system of Honors–High Pass–Pass-Fail, as had the graduate school. Kabaservice, "Kingman Brewster and the Rise and Fall of the Progressive Establishment," at 481.

50. "Grading Proposals in Limbo," at 3 ("encourage," quoting Student Association president Jim Schink). Besides Kennedy, the elected committee included another future Critical Legal scholar, Rand Rosenblatt, as well as Richard Balzer, Richard Diamond, Henry Hansmann (who is currently himself a Yale law professor), Charles Muckenfuss, and Peter Weiner. "Law Students Set Up Grade Study Committee," *Yale Daily News*, Janu-

ary 28, 1968, at 1. Peters downplayed the extent of student unhappiness. Ellen Peters to Faculty, January 26, 1968, Box 38, Folder: Grading 1967–1970, Dean's Files. The written reactions were indeed diverse. See Summary of Student Reactions to Tentative Working Draft, n.d., id.

51. "Much Discussion, But Little Progress on Grades; Tentative OK Given Plan," *Yale Advocate*, March 3, 1968, at 5 (quotations); Louis Pollak, Notice to all Students, March 7, 1968, Box 38, Folder: Grading 1967–70, Dean's Files.

52. Interview with Reich; "Ask Grading Change," *Harvard Law Record*, April 11, 1968, at 1, 6 ("almost meaningless"); "Law Faculty Quashes 4-Tier Grade Proposal," *Yale Daily News*, March 11, 1968, at 1 ("Supreme Court's"); Untitled, undated statement containing resolution passed at a meeting of the Class of 1970 on March 13, 1968, Box 38, Folder: Grading 1967–1970, Dean's Files ("total failure," "reasoned explanation").

53. Interview with Balzer.

54. Jan Deutsch, "Neutrality, Legitimacy and the Supreme Court: Some Intersections Between Law and Political Science," 20 *Stan. L. Rev.* 169 (1968).

55. Jan Deutsch, Memorandum, March 12, 1968, Box 63, Folder 26, Bickel Papers.

56. Id.

57. Kennedy, "How the Law School Fails," at 88, 85, 87 ("communication," "promising," "hopeless"); Paul Carrington, *The Romance of American Law* 1219 ("consulting") (unpublished manuscript); Borosage, "Can the Law School Succeed?," at 94 ("private time"). See also, e.g., "Absent Student Blasts Entrenched Faculty," *Columbia Law School News*, October 7, 1968, at 4 (claiming that faculty pandered to the top twenty-five students in the first-year class). NYU Law School Dean Robert McKay noted that "communication" had become the new buzzword. McKay, "'Communication' Now the Catchword of Academe," *Commentator*, December 20, 1967, at 3.

58. Kennedy, "How the Law School Fails," 87, 73, 88; Standley, "Alexander Bickel, Charles Black," at 133 (*Yale Law Journal*).

59. Borosage, "Can the Law School Succeed?," at 98 (quotations); Kennedy, "How the Law School Fails," at 88. For discussion of the change in faculty roles, see Seymour Lipset and Gerald Schaflander, *Passion and Politics: Student Activism in America* 33 (1971). More research on when universities became fixated on research as a criterion for promotion is needed.

60. "Report on the Meeting of the First Year Class," March 13, 1968, Box 63, Folder 26, Bickel Papers (indicating a majority had voted for a boycott at a meeting of March 11 and had then decided against it after hearing that Bickel believed the Peters Committee should have engaged in a more wide-ranging exploration of curriculum reform); Louis Pollak, Notice to All Students, March 11, 1968, Box 38, Folder: Grading 1967–1970, Dean's Files. Members of the Bickel Committee included Ellen Peters, Robert Bork, Jan Deutsch, John Griffiths, Robert Hudec, Friedrich Kessler, and Leon Lipson.

61. Walt Wagoner to Alexander Bickel, March 13, 1968, Box 63, Folder 26, Bickel Papers ("cowering"); Yale Law School Faculty Minutes (hereafter YLS Faculty Minutes), December 18, 1968, 9:30 A.M. ("enabled").

62. First Year Demand Committee, Memorandum to the Faculty and Students of Yale Law School, April 30, 1968, Box 63, Folder 26, Bickel Papers. The membership of the committee was unspecified.

63. Interview with Ann Hill, 2002; Ronald Fraser, ed., *1968: A Student Generation in Revolt: An International Oral History* 125 (1988). Calabresi acknowledged making this re-

mark to students on the left in the 1960s, though he did not remember saying it to Hill. Interview with Guido Calabresi, 2002.

64. "What's Gone Down at the Law School: 1967–69," at 4; Report of the Curriculum Committee on the Grading System, Tentative Draft, December 3, 1968, Richard Hughes File (I am grateful to Richard Hughes for sharing with me his materials from this period in the history of Yale Law School, hereafter referred to as Hughes File).

65. Committee for Open Meetings, Memorandum, n.d. (ca. first week in December 1968), Box 38, Folder: Grading 1967–1970, Dean's Files (the membership of the committee is unspecified); and see "Faculty Hears Grading Plan; Students Act," *Yale Advocate*, December 5, 1968, at 1.

66. Peter Broderick, "One Year Pass-Fail Experiment" (for first-year class), n.d., Box 38, Folder: Grading 1967–70 (93 percent), Dean's Files; Results of First Year Grade Referendum, n.d., id.; "Ask Liberalized Grading: Law Students Vote for Reform," December 12, 1968, *Yale Daily News*, at 1 (quoting Emerson).

67. YLS Faculty Minutes, December 18, 1968, 9:30 A.M.; Further Report of the Curriculum Committee on the Grading System, December 16, 1968, Box 38, Folder: Grading 1967–70, Dean's Files; Additional Statement of Thomas Emerson, n.d., id. Emerson's colleague, Quentin Johnstone, publicly supported pass-fail grading on an experimental basis. Quentin Johnstone, "Student Discontent and Educational Reform in the Law Schools," 23 *J. Legal Ed.* 255, 274 (1971).

68. YLS Faculty Minutes, December 18, 1968, 9:30 A.M.

69. YLS Faculty Minutes, Continuation of December 18th meeting—10:00 A.M., December 19, 1968; Louis Pollak to the Class of 1972, September 5, 1969. Dean's Files, Box 36, Folder: Memoranda—Misc. (1965–70); "Revolution at Yale: Credit/No Credit Replaces Traditional Grades," *Harvard Law Record*, January 30, 1969, at 5. The article was reprinted in *Res Gestae* under the title "Yale Adopts 'Pass-Fail' Grading System," February 28, 1969, at 5.

70. "New Grading Policy Urged," *Barrister*, May 11, 1970, at 2.

71. "Survey Discloses Questioning of Traditions: Students Ask Changes in Evaluation of Their Ability," *Harvard Law Record*, December 14, 1967, at 1 (Goldwater); "1 L's Seek Change in Grading," id., February 28, 1969, at 1, 2 ("status hierarchy"). Email, Robert Gordon to author, August 15, 2001 ("the last"); "2Ls Score Interview Queries," *Harvard Law Record*, November 6, 1969, at 1; "Group Plans New Drive for Grade Reform," id., March 11, 1971, at 3; "Student-Faculty Split," id., April 1, 1971, at 10.

72. Stanford: "The Grading Dilemma: Anyone for 3K," *Stanford Law School Journal*, December 10, 1970, at 6. Berkeley: Sandra Epstein, *Law at Berkeley: The History of Boalt Hall* 272–73 (1997); "Faculty Votes for TLM!," *Writ*, May 22, 1968, at 1. Davis: "The Faculty Meeting," *Barrister*, November 13, 1972, at 1. Columbia: "Committee Views Law School: Finds Defects in Form, Substance," *Columbia Law School News*; October 7, 1968, at 1; "Grading Re-Examined," id., November 11, 1969, at 4; "Faculty Arrogance Frustrates Students," id., January 4, 1971, at 1. NYU: "Statement By Student Co-Chairman, Committee On Grading Alternatives," *Commentator*, September 17, 1969, at 5 ("symptom"). The NYU situation became especially heated: "Disputes Flare Over Grades; SBA to Hold Open Meeting," id., at 1; "The Grading Decision," id. at 4; "Grading Poll Responses Favor Honors-Pass-Fail, Committee Recommends Acceptance by Faculty," id., May 7, 1969, at 1. At first, the Student Bar Association threatened that most first- and second-year students would refuse to turn in their exams, placing them in escrow with the association until the

faculty adopted an Honors-Pass-Fail grading system. "SBA Approves Exam Escrow Until Faculty Passes H/P/F," id., November 26, 1969, at 1. The association then backed down on the escrow plan because it feared alienating the faculty, with whom it was also engaged in negotiations about sharing governance and because its president alleged that most students opposed the plan. "SBA Rescinds Exam Escrow; Brower Expected to Resign; LSA Budget Request Refused," id., December 10, 1969, at 1. When the NYU faculty decided to return to a nine-tier letter grading system in 1971, citing the need for greater rigor and less laziness, students revived the exam escrow plan. "Faculty Opts for Tradition: Nine-Tier Grading System," id., May 4, 1971, at 1; "Students Plan Exam Escrow," id., May 4, 1971, at 1. Subsequently, the faculty adopted a five-tier grading system of Honors–Very Good–Good-Pass-Fail. "Five Tier Grading Adopted," id., September 4, 197, at 1; "New Grade Tiers, Requirements Set," id., October 12, 1971, id. at 1. Within a month, it had changed the names of the grades to Honors-Good-Satisfactory-Pass-Fail. "Grades' Names Changed," id., November 17, 1971, at 1. Michigan: Richard Lempert, "Law School Grading: An Experiment with Pass-Fail," 24 *J. Legal Ed.* 251, 281, 255–56 (1972); "'Pass-Fail' Experiment Commences," *Res Gestae*, January 23, 1970, at 2.

73. Interview with Hill; *Yale L. Reporter*, 1970, at 40. The *Yale Advocate* announced that it would suspend publication during exams in its December 5, 1968, issue, at 1.

74. "A Passing Comment," *Yale Advocate*, April 3, 1969, at 2 (complaints); "What's Gone Down at the Law School: 1967–69," at 1, 4; "Grade Reform Undermined," *Yale Advocate*, October 23, 1969, at 5 ("All").

75. Yale Law Women Association, The Student Guide to Yale Law School, 2003–04, <http://www.yale.edu/ylw/ylwstudentguide>.

CHAPTER FOUR

1. "What's Gone Down at the Law School: 1967–69," *Yale Advocate*, October 2, 1969, at 1, 4; Wini Breines, *Community and Organization in the New Left, 1962–1968: The Great Refusal* 67 (1989) ("student movement").

2. "Conflicts Erupt," *Writ*, November, 9, 1971, at 2, 4; Joseph Fashing and Steven Deutsch, *Academics in Retreat: The Politics of Educational Innovation* 266 (1971).

3. Yale Law School Faculty Minutes, September 20, 1968 (hereafter YLS Faculty Minutes). (Fred Rodell complained about the mail. Though he had long been active in school politics [Laura Kalman, *Legal Realism at Yale* 145–46, 199–200 (1986)], he had been effectively marginalized by this time); Louis Pollak to the Teaching Faculty, September 25, 1968 (reproducing Bittker's letter to Pollak of September 24, 1968), Box 36, Folder: Memoranda — Misc. 1967–1970, Dean's Files, Yale University Archives (hereafter Dean's Files); YLS Faculty Minutes, September 26, 1968; Louis Pollak to All Students, September 30, 1968, Box 36, Folder: Memoranda — Misc. 1967–1970, Dean's Files.

4. Louis Pollak to the Teaching Faculty, September 25, 1968, Box 36, Folder: Memoranda — Misc. 1967–1970, Dean's Files (Bittker); YLS Faculty Minutes, September 26, 1968 ("Strong").

5. "A Too Modest Proposal," *Yale Advocate*, October 24, 1968, at 2.

6. "Professors Speak Out on Legal Education and the Selection of Dean: Tom Emerson," *Yale Advocate*, October 23, 1969, at 3, 4; Bonnie Collier interview with Harry Wellington, July 12, 2000 (pot); Alexander Bickel to Louis Pollak, April 29, 1969, Box 10, Folder

195, Alexander Bickel Papers, Yale University Archives (hereafter Bickel Papers) (complaining about rock music in the courtyard).

7. "Ben Stein Shares His Wisdom With YPU," *Yale Daily News*, April 22, 2004, <http://www.yaledailynews.com/article.asp?AID=25898> ("kite"); Stein, "Crazy Days," at 54 ("Socratic"); Doug McAdam, *Freedom Summer* 138 (1988).

8. Louis Pollak to Macklin Fleming, June 23, 1969, Box 7, Folder: Judge Macklin Fleming, Dean's Files (the exchange between Pollak and Fleming is reprinted in "An Exchange of Letters: The Black Quota at Yale Law School: Macklin Fleming/Louis Pollak," 19 *Public Interest* 44 (Spring 1970) [hereafter cited as "An Exchange of Letters"], and these quotations are at 50–51); "Affirmative Action at Yale Law School," 37 *Yale L. Reporter* 8 (Fall 1991) ("judgment"); Yale Law School Admissions Committee, A Memorandum on Admissions and Scholarships, 1962, Yale Law Library ("fooling").

9. Ernest Gellhorn, "The Law Schools and the Negro," 1968 *Duke L. J.* 1069, 1081 (1968) (quoting the *New York Times*).

10. Pollak to Fleming, June 23, 1969, "An Exchange of Letters," at 50–51; "Affirmative Action at Yale Law School"; Robert O'Neill, "Preferential Admissions: Equalizing Access to Legal Education," 1970 *U. Tol. L. Rev.* 281, 300 (1970) (1964–65); Gellhorn, "The Law Schools and the Negro," at 1080, n. 52, 1094 (enrollment statistics; "Law teaching"). Chicanos and American Indians lagged even more behind. As late as 1970, "Spanish American" students constituted less than .005 percent of law students in the United States. Cruz Reynoso, Jose Alvarez, Albert Moreno, Mario Olmos, Anthony Quintero, William Soria, "La Raza, the Law, and the Law Schools," 1970 *U. Tol. L. Rev.* 809, 839 (1970). Of the roughly 53,000 students enrolled in American law schools in 1970, perhaps 50 were of "American Indian extraction," and historically, the attrition rate was high. Rennard Strickland, "Redeeming Centuries of Dishonor: Legal Education and the American Indian," id. 847, 865. For an early critique of credentialism from someone who would become one of its strongest opponents, see Derrick Bell, "Black Students in White Law Schools: The Ordeal and the Opportunity," id. 539, 557.

11. Infra, Chapter 9, text accompanying notes 9–10.

12. Ronald Dworkin, *Taking Rights Seriously*, at 227, 225 (1977) ("vital," "useful"); Ronald Dworkin, *A Matter of Principle* 299 (1985); interview with Ronald Dworkin, 2002. I have found no record of Dworkin's arguments on behalf of affirmative action during the late 1960s.

13. Geoffrey Kabaservice interview with Louis Pollak, 1992.

14. Sanford Rosen, "Equalizing Access to Legal Education: Special Programs for Law Students Who Are Not Eligible by Traditional Criteria," 1970 *U. Tol. L. Rev.* 330, 331, n. 25 (1970) ("data"); "Report on Special Admissions at Boalt Hall: After *Bakke*, October 5, 1976," 28 *J. Legal Ed.* 363, 364, 379 (1977).

15. Ernest Gellhorn, "The Law Schools and the Negro," 1968 *Duke L. J.* 1069, 1081, 1080 (1968). By 1967–68, the number of African American students at Case Western, Emory, Illinois, Mississippi, NYU, Pennsylvania, and UCLA had increased more than sixfold, to 122. Id. at 1080, n. 52.

16. Graham Hughes, Robert McKay, Peter Winograd, "The Disadvantaged Student and Preparation for Legal Education: The New York University Experience," 1970 *U. Tol. L. Rev.* 701, 708–10 (1970); Gellhorn, "The Law Schools and the Negro," at 1086–88; Rosen, "Equalizing Access to Legal Education," at 346–50, 357–58 (Stanford, CLEO, AALS). Under pressure from African American students, the Columbia law faculty would soon

indicate its willingness to consider the stretch-out. "Faculty Resolution of May 9, 1969," *Columbia Law School News*, May 13, 1969, at 7. Another type of outreach program was aimed at college students. Harvard brought students from historically black colleges to Cambridge in 1966 for a special summer course designed to introduce them to law study and the legal profession. Louis Toepfer, "Harvard's Special Summer Program," 18 *J. Legal Ed.* 443 (1966).

17. "The Campus Revolutions: One is Black, One White," *New York Times*, May 12, 1969, at A51; James McEvoy and Abraham Miller, "The Crisis at San Francisco State," in Howard Becker, ed., *Campus Power Struggle* 57, 70 (1970) (quoting Charles Hamilton on different goals of white and black students); Wayne Glasker, *Black Students in the Ivory Tower: African American Student Activism at the University of Pennsylvania, 1967–1990* 161 (2002); A. J. Cooper, "What's It All About? Well, Roy, Let Me Tell You," 15 *Student Lawyer J.* 16 (September 1969); <http://www.nlblsa.org./history.htm>. See also Durward Long, "Black Protest," in Julian Foster and Durward Long, eds., *Protest!: Student Activism in America* 459 (1970); Gerald de Graff, "Howard: The Evolution of a Black Student Revolt," id. at 319; Donald Downs, *Cornell '69: Liberalism and the Crisis of the American University* (1999); Karen Miller, "Negroes No More: The Emergence of Black Student Activism," in Alexander Bloom, ed., *Long Time Gone: Sixties America Then and Now* 124 (2001). Once U.S. law schools began to respond to student pressures to focus on African Americans, those in the West generally responded more quickly than their counterparts elsewhere to demands of Chicanos, Native Americans, and Asian Americans. See, e.g., "Chicanos Seek Higher Minority Admissions," *Stanford Law School Journal*, March 16, 1972, at 1; "Indians Protest: Law Lounge Drops [Laura Scudder] 'Wampum [Corn] Chips,'" *Stanford Law School Journal*, March 8, 1973, at 1; "Asians at Davis," *Barrister*, January 10, 1972, 1; "Chicano Resolutions," id. at 1; and the many articles about Chicano law students in the *Writ*, April 22, 1970 and April 19, 1971.

18. Gellhorn, "The Law School and the Negro," at 1082; Julius Lester, *Look Out, Whitey! Black Power's Gon' Get Your Mama* 114 (1968) ("taking care").

19. Richard Balzer, *Street Time* (1972). The book is not paginated.

20. Gary Gerstle, *American Crucible: Race and Nation in the Twentieth Century* 303 (2001); William Van DeBurg, *New Day in Babylon: The Black Power Movement and American Culture, 1965–1975* 65–82 (1993).

21. Geoffrey Kabaservice, *The Guardians: Kingman Brewster, His Circle, and the Rise of the Liberal Establishment* 347, 332 (2004); Fred Powledge, *Model City* 223 (1970) ("urgent and welcome").

22. "Black Students Ask School To Re-open Fall Admissions," *Yale Advocate*, May 3, 1968, at 1, 3; Geoffrey Kabaservice, Chronology, April 29, 1968 ("We cannot"); de Graaf, "Howard: The Evolution of a Black Student Revolt," at 325, 343 n. 37.

23. "Where Are They?," *Yale Advocate*, April 13, 1968, at 2; "Dean Jack Tate: A Memorial," id., 1; "Yale Law Yesterday, Yale Law Today: How Much Have Things Really Changed?" *Yale Law Docket* 5 (May 2001) (reporting that a professor called the author of the editorial, Mike Gross, into his office; accused him of attacking Tate's memory; and demanded that the *Advocate* publish a retraction); email, Mike Gross to author, September 27, 2004; "Black Students Ask School To Re-open Fall Admissions," at 3.

24. Alexander Bickel to Louis Pollak, May 13 and May 29, 1968, Box 131, Folder 1, Kingman Brewster Papers, Yale University Archives (hereafter Brewster Papers) ("I don't think"). See Richard Balzer Paper, n.d., id.

25. Bickel to Pollak, May 13, 1968.

26. "Alumni Weekend: A Lively Panel, Honored Justice," *Yale Advocate*, May 3, 1968, at 1, 4; "Tell It Like It Is," id., May 3, 1968, at 2; "Yale Law School Alumni Weekend," id., April 13, 1968, at 2; interview with Paul Gewirtz, 2001. Participating in the panel were Deans Pollak, Jefferson Fordham (University of Pennsylvania), Howard Sacks (Connecticut), and Raymond Forrester (Cornell).

27. "Tell It Like It Is," *Yale Advocate*, May 3, 1968, at 2 ("substantial disparity"; "As long as"); 1st Year Demand Committee, Memorandum to the Faculty and Students of Yale Law School, April 30, 1968, Box 63, Folder 26, Bickel Papers.

28. YLS Faculty Minutes, May 2, 1968. The suspicion with respect to recruitment went both ways: at Georgetown, for example, students charged that the faculty concentrated its minority recruitment efforts below the Mason-Dixon Line out of the belief African Americans there were less rebellious. "An Open Letter by S.B.A. Head," *Georgetown Law Weekly*, April 8, 1970, at 1, 7.

29. Among the Establishment children were the sons of William Rogers, Eisenhower's attorney general and Nixon's secretary of state, and William Colby of the CIA.

30. Interview with J. Otis Cochran, 2002. New Haven College later became the University of New Haven.

31. Interview with Cochran.

32. Id.; J. Otis Cochran, "Some Thoughts on American Law Schools, The Legal Profession, and the Role of Students," 1970 *U. Tol. L. Rev.* 623, 628, 627, 625 (1970) ("professional," "standards," "Stepin").

33. "Active BLSU Prepares Outlines for New Courses," *Yale Advocate*, March 12, 1969, at 1; supra, Chapter 1, text accompanying note 56 (reference to Columbia); "Black Awareness and Black Unity Surging Forward at Law School," *Harvard Law Record*, September 26, 1968, at 1.

34. Interview with Cochran.

35. Presentments to the Administrations of Yale University Law School, n.d. Box 131, Folder 9, Brewster Papers; Yale University Council Report of the Committee on the Law School, April 18, 1969, Box 56, Folder: Council Committee, Dean's Files.

36. Louis Pollak to J. Otis Cochran, December 16, 1968, Box 131, Folder 9, Brewster Papers; interview with Ann Hill, 2002 (black table).

37. Daniel McIntyre, "Edwin Foster Blair," *New Journal*, November 22, 1970, at 2; interview with Cochran.

38. Interview with Cochran.

39. Black Law Students Union, Statement, December 16, 1968, Box 131, Folder 9, Brewster Papers.

40. YLS Faculty Minutes, December 19, 1968, 9:30 A.M. (extension of meeting held December 18, 1968). Emphasis added.

41. Anne Standley, "Alexander Bickel, Charles Black, and the Ambiguous Legacy of Brown v. Board of Education: Competing Conceptions of Law, Justice and Democracy Within Postwar Legal Thought" 143–44 (PhD dissertation, 1993).

42. Louis Pollak to Kingman Brewster and Charles Taylor, December 18, 1968, Box 131, Folder 9, Brewster Papers.

43. YLS Faculty Minutes, December 19, 1968, 1:15 P.M. (extension of December 18th meeting regarding BLSU demands and reply thereto); "Active BLSU Prepares Outlines for New Courses," at 3 (university response to report); YLS Faculty Minutes, December 24, 1968, 10:00 A.M., December 31, 1968, 11:00 A.M. and 1:00 P.M.

44. Richard Abel to the Faculty, December 27, 1968, Box 33, Folder: Discipline Com-

mittee, 1963–69, Dean's Files ("extremist," "firm"); Louis Pollak to Kingman Brewster, June 7, 1968, Box 36, Folder: Memoranda—Misc. (1965–70), Dean's Files; YLS Faculty Minutes, December 24, 1968, 10:00 A.M.

45. YLS Faculty Minutes, December 24, 1968, 10:00 A.M. and 2:45 P.M. (emphasis added); Powledge, *Model City*, at 221 ("foreign"); Kabaservice, *Guardians*, at 265, 269 ("did not maintain," "nontraditional" [quoting Admissions Director R. Inslee Clark], Buckley).

46. YLS Faculty Minutes, December 24, 1968, 2:45 P.M.

47. The Faculty to the Black Law Students Union, December 31, 1968, Box 131, Folder 3, Brewster Papers.

48. Id.; YLS Faculty Minutes, December 31, 1968, 11:00 A.M. (quoting Bok); Rosen, "Equalizing Access to Legal Education," at 350. Yale's aid was relatively generous. Clyde Summers, "Preferential Admissions: An Unreal Solution to a Real Problem," 1970 *U. Tol. L. Rev.* 377, 399 (1970).

49. Interview with Dworkin; "An Exchange of Letters," 19 *Public Interest* 44 (September 1970).

50. Macklin Fleming to Louis Pollak, June 9, 1969, Box 7, Folder: Judge Macklin Fleming, Dean's Files, "An Exchange of Letters," at 45–46, 47, 48, 49.

51. Louis Pollak to Macklin Fleming, June 23, 1969, id. at 51.

52. Id. at 51, 52.

53. "And a Stillness Descended Upon Them," *Res Gestae*, October 17, 1969, at 10; "Support the BLSA Demands," id., October 31, 1969, at 1, 2 ("time to realize").

54. "Minority Admissions," *Stanford Law School Journal*, December 10, 1970, at 1; "Let's Change Our Name," *Barrister*, May 21, 1971, at 5; "1% Black Lawyers Revisited," id., January 24, 1972, at 3; and see Robert Stevens, "Law Schools and Law Students," 59 *Va. L. Rev.* 551, 571 (1973); "Admissions Perspective," *Georgetown Law Weekly*, October, 1, 1969, at 1, 4; Edwards, "The Black Law School Graduate," at 1424.

55. Pollak to Fleming, June 23, 1969, "An Exchange of Letters," at 51; email, Owen Fiss to author, n.d.; "Report on Special Admissions at Boalt Hall," at 381.

56. Louis Pollak to Ralph Brown, January 3, 1969, Box 56, Folder: BLSU, Dean's Files ("relatively"); Black Law Students Union to Yale Law School Faculty and Student Body, February 13, 1969, id.

57. Id.; Louis Pollak to Law School Student Body, March 14, 1969, id.

58. See Draft, Faculty Resolution on Members of Disadvantaged Groups, March 13, 1969, YLS Faculty Minutes, March 13, 1969; Louis Pollak to Law School Student Body, March 14, 1969, Box 56, Folder: BLSU, Dean's Files; Black Law Students Union to Yale Law School Faculty, April 26, 1969, id.

59. Black Law Students Union to Yale Law School Faculty, April 26, 1969.

60. Ralph Brown to Richard Cahn, September 19, 1969, Box 56, Folder: BLSU, Dean's Files.

61. Ralph Brown to Alexander Bickel, May 23, 1968, Box 10, Folder 193, Bickel Papers; Alexander Bickel, Memorandum to the Faculty, November 6, 1968, Box 60, Folder 10, Bickel Papers; Robert Borosage, "Can the Law School Succeed? A Proposal," 1 *Yale Rev. of Law & Soc. Action* 92, 95 (1970) ("sprinkling"); "Ford Foundation Grant Not 'Changing World,'" *Yale Advocate*, December 5, 1968, at 1, 3 ("rubric"); "Law School Under Attack for Ford Money Misuse," *Yale Daily News*, December 11, 1968, at 1; J. Otis Cochran to Louis Pollak, December 18, 1968, Box 131, Folder 9, Brewster Papers; Cochran to McGeorge Bundy, December 18, 1968, id. (forwarding *News* article to Ford Foundation); "Pollak Faces Reforms," February 3, 1969, *Yale Daily News*, at 4.

62. "Ford Foundation Grant Not 'Changing World,'" at 1 (Sparer course); Martha Davis, *Brutal Need: Lawyers and the Welfare Rights Movement* 22–25 (1993); David Trubek to the Faculty, November 7, 1968, Box 55, Folder: Intensive Semester Program, Dean's Files.

63. Laura Holland, "Invading the Ivory Tower: The History of Clinical Education at Yale Law School," 49 *J. Legal Ed.* 504, 514 (1999); "Legal Aid Program Plans Expansion; Stress On Urban Law," *Yale Advocate*, October 10, 1968, at 1, 4.

64. Kabaservice, *Guardians*, at 365–69; conversations with Aviam Soifer, 2002 and 2003 ("fucking") and Kabaservice interview with Aviam Soifer, 1991; Holland, "Invading the Ivory Tower," at 514–15 ("Relevancy," "barricades"). The case was *Logan v. Arafeh*, 346 F. Supp. 1265 (1972).

65. Holland, "Invading the Ivory Tower," at 518, 519–22; conversation with Soifer, 2003.

66. The Faculty to the Black Law Students Union, December 31, 1968; "Doing Their Clinical Thing: The Legal Services Program at Yale," 17 *Yale L. Report* 9, 11 (Fall 1970) ("escapism"); Conversation with Soifer, 2003 ("mandarins"); Abraham Goldstein, "Educational Planning at Yale," 20 *J. Legal Ed.* 402, 406 (1968).

67. Holland, "Invading the Ivory Tower," at 526.

68. Borosage, "Can the Law School Succeed?," at 96; "Communications," *Yale Advocate*, February 6, 1969, at 2.

69. YLS Faculty Minutes, December 19, 1968, 1:15 P.M.

70. "Law Faculty Tries to Meet Demands of Black Students," *Yale Daily News*, January 10, 1969, at 1; "Communications."

71. "Blacks Get $1,200 for Projects After Procedural Wrangling," *Yale Advocate*, February 6, 1969, at 1, 4. Emphasis in the original.

72. Interview with Cochran; "Black Student Advises White Radicals: 'We'll Do Our Thing, You Do Yours,'" *Writ*, November 27, 1968, at 1; "Communications."

73. "Bridging the Chasm," *Yale Advocate*, February 6, 1969, at 2; "Communications" ("no substitute for open, unambiguous communication").

74. "Bridging the Chasm."

75. The Council report pointed to the black students' lack of involvement in the governance issue. Yale University Council Report of the Committee on the Law School, April 18, 1969, Box 56, Folder: Council Committee, Dean's Files. The quotations in this paragraph are from Jeremy Weinberg, "Long Live the King's Yale: How Kingman Brewster's University Survived and Thrived in the 1960s" 27, 30 (Yale College senior essay, 1992).

76. Weinberg provides a full account of these developments in "Long Live the King's Yale," at 27–32; quotations are from Brewster's annual report of 1967–68 in id. at 30.

77. "Negotiating Committee Asks Joint Student-Faculty Rule," *Yale Advocate*, February 6, 1969, at 1; "Students Ask for Share in Governing Law School," *Yale Daily News*, February 10, 1969, at 1. The Student Negotiating Committee members were Peter Broderick, Barbara Brown, Michael Egger, Richard Hughes, Daniel Lewis, Jack Pomeranz, Robert Spearman, Gus Speth, William Taylor, and Walt Wagoner. At this time, there was also a new interest in the question of how much of a right to participate in matters of appointments and promotions junior faculty members should have. It is not clear who wanted junior faculty members to possess more power, though it was probably junior faculty members themselves. Nothing came of it. Bickel and J. Goldstein, Memorandum for the Governing Board, November 22, 1968, Box 130, Folder 8, Brewster Papers.

78. "Groping for Community," *Yale Advocate*, May 1, 1969, at 2; "Law, Grad Schools

Face Challenges; Tension High in Law School; 'Peaceful Revolution' At Hand," *Yale Daily News*, February 14, 1969, at 1.

79. The Yale By-Laws on Faculty were reprinted in the *Yale Advocate*, April 3, 1969, at 4; "Faculty Rejects Proposals: Resolution Bars Voting, Any Regular Representation in Faculty Meetings; Committee Members Walk Out," id. at 1, 4 (Black, Bickel, Wellington). The faculty negotiators included Pollak, Thomas Emerson, Marvin Chirelstein, Abe Goldstein, and Rostow.

80. "The First Meeting of the Committee," n.d., Richard Hughes File (hereafter Hughes File).

81. Id., emphasis in the original. The Rostow "film festival" and the reaction of students and faculty to Rostow's return is discussed in Richard Balzer, "The Law School will never be home again," *New Journal*, March 9, 1969, at 3.

82. Moore's remarks are in " 'The Great Debate,' Being a more or less exact transcription from notes of the exchange between the STUDENT NEGOTIATORS and the assembled FACULTY at a meeting BEHIND CLOSED DOORS, the thirteenth day of March, in 1969," Hughes File. The heading of the memorandum read "Confidential[,] For Eyes of Student Negotiators Only[,] Top Secret[,] Don't Let Eugene Rostow See This." On Summers, see *In re Summers*, 325 U.S. 561 (1945); Louis Pollak, " 'A Vision of the Law in Action,' " 138 *U. Pa. L. Rev.* 637, 637–38 (1990); Alan Hyde, "Clyde Summers and the Ideal of the Activist Scholar," id. at 627, 629; Julius Getman, "The Internal Scholarly Jury," 39 *J. Legal Ed.* 337, 339, n. 2 (1989) ("passion"); "Text of Summers Memorandum on Student Proposal," *Yale Advocate*, April 3, 1969, at 3; C. David Garson, "The Ideology of the New Student Left," *Protest!*, at 184, 199. See Louis Pollak to Kingman Brewster and Charles Taylor, March 13, 1968, Box 131, Folder 1, Brewster Papers, for a discussion of Summers's status at Yale.

83. "Text of Summers Memorandum," at 3.

84. A Proposal for the Governance of the Law School, n.d., Hughes File.; "Negotiating Committee Message," *Yale Advocate*, April 3, 1969, 2; "The 2d Meeting," n.d., Hughes File (Goldstein and Rostow).

85. "The Great Debate"; and see Karl Mannheim, "The Problem of Generations," in Philip Altbach and Robert Laufer, eds., *The New Pilgrims: Youth Protest in Transition* 101, 125, 126 (1972).

86. Peter Yaeger, "Heroic Struggle," *New Journal*, April 27, 1969, at 14 ("body politics"); Alexander Bickel to James Flug, April 30, 1969, Box 10, Folder 195, Bickel Papers ("balance").

87. Julie Reuben, "The Limits of Freedom: Student Activists and Educational Reform at Berkeley in the 1960s," in Robert Cohen and Reginald Zelnik, eds., *The Free Speech Movement: Reflections on Berkeley in the 1960s* 490, 492, 505 (2002).

88. Faculty Resolution adopted March 28, 1969, YLS Faculty Minutes; "The 3d Meeting," April 1, 1969, Hughes File ("insulting," "appearance"). Goldstein would have limited student participation to a nonvoting role on committees (id.), an issue Pollak wanted, and succeeded in leaving, unclear. Louis Pollak to Kingman Brewster, February 27, 1969, Box 37, Folder: President's Office 1965–70, Dean's Files. Emerson would have regularly permitted 6–10 students to attend (but not vote at) faculty meetings, regardless of whether they were on faculty committees. YLS Faculty Minutes, March 28, 1969.

89. Faculty Resolution adopted March 28, 1969.

90. SNC to Dear Faculty Member, April 2, 1969, YLS Faculty Minutes (*Yale Advocate* reprinted the letter in the April 3, 1969, issue, at 2); "Law Meetings Hit Impasse; Angry Students Walk Out," *Yale Daily News*, April 3, 1969, at 1.

91. SNC to Dear Faculty Member, April 2, 1969; Jim Laney, Jim Phelan, Robert Borosage, Robert Vizas, Patricia Wynn, "Letters to the Editor: Negotiations Lead to 'Weak Compromise,'" *Yale Advocate*, March 12, 1969, at 2 ("Christians").

92. "An End to Peace," *Yale Advocate*, April 3, 1969, at 2.

93. "Negotiations to Reopen," *Yale Daily News*, April 14, 1969, at 3 ("Tired"); Yaeger, "Heroic Struggle"; "To Boycott or Not. Or What?," *Yale Advocate*, April 17, 1969, at 1 (estimating the crowd at 300–400 students and faculty).

94. Yaeger, "Heroic Struggle" ("idea," "noticeably," "prep school"); Hughes, "The Open Meeting," April 7, 1969, Hughes File.

95. Pollak to the Class of '72, n.d., Box 36, File: Memoranda, Dean's Files ("number"); Supplement to Resolution on Student Participation, YLS Faculty Minutes, May 5, 1969; "Negotiations Reopened," April 15, 1969, Hughes File (Goldstein). Appointed representatives would take part only in those faculty meetings addressing an issue their committees had considered.

96. "Negotiations Reopened" ("blockbuster"); "4–22 Meeting," Hughes File (April 22, 1969) ("typical"); The Board of the Yale Law Student Association, Factual Statement Regarding Events of October 26, Box 131, Folder 8, Brewster Papers; YLS Faculty Minutes, April 28, 1969.

97. Memorandum from "McL" (identity unknown to this author) to Kingman Brewster, April 11, 1969, Box 131, Folder 3, Brewster Papers (reporting Pollak's views); "Reviewer's Corner: One Principle Under God," *Yale Advocate*, October 23, 1969, at 3 ("understudy"); YLS Faculty Minutes, April 28, 1969; Abraham Goldstein, "The Changing Mood: A Report from the Dean," 18 *Yale L. Report* 19, 20 (Fall–Winter 1971–72) ("simple matter," "issues"); "Professors Speak Out on Legal Education and the Selection of Dean: Abe Goldstein," *Yale Advocate*, October 23, 1969, at 3, 6 ("wish," "involved"). The minutes suggest that Black, Bickel, Bowman, and Winter formed the core of the opposition, though they sometimes received support from Abraham and Joseph Goldstein, Friedrich Kessler, Harry Wellington, Henry Poor, Arthur Leff, and Gordon Spivack, who expressed sympathy for their position by voting with them or abstaining. YLS Faculty Minutes, April 28 and May 5, 1969.

98. Members of the Student Negotiating Committee to Dear Students, May 8, 1969, Hughes File; Statement of Messrs. Hughes, Lewis, Spearman, Speth, Taylor, and Chairman Egger, id.; Pollak to the Class of '72; "Groping for Community." Three members of the student team pledged to follow the will of the majority of their classmates, but regretted that the faculty had run down the clock and continued to behave paternalistically. Statement of Miss Brown, Messrs. Pomeranz and Wagoner, Hughes File. And one student negotiator flatly recommended that students vote against its adoption, since the plan only underscored that the faculty had not changed the way it viewed students. Statement of Mr. Broderick, id.

99. Kabaservice interview with Pollak.

100. John Hersey, *Letter to the Alumni* 71 (1970) (quoting SDS statement); Kevin Mattson, *Intellectuals in Action: The Origins of the New Left and Radical Liberalism, 1945–1970* 214 (2002) ("trump," discussing views of Arnold Kaufman); "Negotiations to Reopen" (quoting unidentified Yale law professor).

101. Paul Savoy, "Toward A New Politics of Legal Education," 79 *Yale L. J.* 444, 445 (1970).

102. Louis Feuer, *The Conflict of Generations: The Character and Significance of Student Movements* 420, 8 (1969).

103. Joseph Fashing and Steven Deutsch, *Academics in Retreat: The Politics of Educational Innovation* 266–77 (1971).

104. Kenneth Keniston, *Young Radicals: Notes on Committed Youth* 306 (1968); Stevens, "*Law School and Law Students*," at 588 ("exception," "polarization").

105. Leon Sheleff, *Generations Apart: Adult Hostility To Youth* 33 (1981); Breines, *The Great Refusal*, at 2 ("tell").

106. "Lexcetera," 17 *Yale L. Report* 1, 1 (Summer 1971) (Goldstein); Bonnie Collier interview with Boris Bittker, 1996; Hersey, *Letter to the Alumni*, at 51, 116.

107. Hersey, *Letter to the Alumni*, at 105–6, 118; Roger Rosenblatt, *Coming Apart: A Memoir of the Harvard Wars of 1969* 99 (1997); Francine du Plessix Gray, "The Panthers at Yale," *New York Review of Books*, 29, 30 (June 4, 1970) ("radical types," "affection"); Kabaservice, *Guardians*, at 353–55.

108. Keniston, *Young Radicals*, at 313–14, 236, 238. Emphasis in the original.

109. "Negotiations to Reopen"; Alexander Bickel to Robert Bork, April 28, 1969, Box 10, Folder 195, Bickel Papers.

110. "Open Faculty Meetings Asked," *Harvard Law Record*, March 6, 1989, at 1; "Student Participation Committee Formed," id., September 25, 1969, at 5; "Anti-Radical Editorial Blasted By 1-Ls," id., December 5, 1968, at 9 ("participatory democracy"); "Governance to Propose Student-Faculty Council," id., May 6, 1971, at 1; "Student Decision-Making," id., September 25, 1969, at 8 ("fear"); "Faculty, Students Clash at Meeting," *Columbia Law School News*, April 17, 1970, at 1 ("fifty-fifty"); "Wednesday's Donnybrook," id. at 4 ("Bullshit").

111. Arval Morris, "Student Participation in Law School Decision Making," 22 *J. Legal Ed.* 127, 137 (1969). Morris did not identify the school.

112. Duncan Kennedy, "Boola!," 14 *Social Text* 31, 35 (No. 4, Winter 1996); interview with Pollak, 2001; Kabaservice, *Guardians*, at 398 ("rational").

113. Julian Foster, "Student Protest: Aims and Strategies," *Protest!*, 401, 417; BALSA Position Paper, April 2, 1970, Box 56, Folder: BLSU, Dean's Files ("contemptible"); "Make Room For More," *Writ*, May 11, 1972, at 3.

114. "Negotiations Lead to 'Weak Compromise.'"

CHAPTER FIVE

1. Robert Borosage, "Can the Law School Succeed? A Proposal," 1 *Yale Rev. of Law & Soc. Action* 92, 96 (1970).

2. Emails, Jonathan Krown to author, March 24, 2001, and April 11, 2001; Jonathan Krown, "The Last Day Down," *Yale Advocate*, May 1, 1969, at 2 ("rather be"); "Merry Pranksters at Yale," id., February 20, 1969, at 1 ("button-down"); "Blow Your Mind," id., February 6, 1969, at 1 (announcing mixer).

3. Tom Wolfe, *The Electric Kool-Aid Acid Test* (1968); conversation with Soifer, 2003; remaining quotations from Wavy Gravy, *The Hog Farm and Friends by Wavy Gravy: As Told to Hugh Romney and Vice Versa* 50–51, 112 (1974): "Cosmic Hog," *New Journal*, February 23, 1969, at 2. A newspaper article about the Hog Farmers' expedition to Connecticut Valley Hospital, "Ol' Wavy Gravy's Hog Hippies Do Their Thing for a Hospital," is reprinted in Wavy Gravy, *The Hog Farm and Friends*, at 190.

4. Emails, Jonathan Krown to author, March 24, 2001, and n.d.; "Merry Pranksters at

Yale," at 1; "Blow Your Mind," *Yale Advocate*, February 6, 1969, at 1; Wavy Gravy, *The Hog Farm*, at 112.

5. Borosage, "Can the Law School Succeed? A Proposal," at 95 ("legal"); Krown to author, March 24, 2001.

6. Yale Law School Women's History Project, Oral History Interview with Judith Areen, 2000, by Mary Clark.

7. See the various memoranda from Security Director John Powell to Jack Tate in Box 43, Folder: Yale University—Police, Dean's Files, Yale University Archives (hereafter Dean's Files); "Legalized Coed Living Only Needs Approval By University Officials," *Yale Advocate*, February 22, 1968, at 1; "It's Official Now—Girls Are Planning All-Year Live-In at the Law School," id., March 3, 1968, at 1; Jack Tate to John Embersits, February 14, 1968, Box 36, Folder: Memoranda—Misc. (1965–70), Dean's Files; email, Joanne Stern to author, March 8, 2002.

8. Vicky Jackson, Louise Nemschoff, and Anne Simon, *The Women's Law School Companion* 12 (1974). A 1970 survey by Janette Barnes demonstrated that while more than 70 percent of prestigious law schools indicated they recruited from men's colleges, less than 30 percent recruited from women's. James Ogloff, David Lyon, Kevin Douglas, V. Gordon Rose, "More Than 'Learning to Think Like a Lawyer': The Empirical Research on Legal Education," 34 *Creighton L. Rev.* 73, 114 (2000) (citing Barmes, "Women and Entrance to the Legal Profession," 23 *J. Legal Ed.* 276, 305 [1970]).

9. "Women Say Law Firms Discriminate," *Yale Advocate*, November 7, 1968, at 1; W. Haywood Burns, Betsy Levin, Peter Zimroth to Eugene Rostow, October 20, 1964, Box 2, Folder: Unmarked Envelope, Dean's Files; Recommendations of the Yale Law School Placement Committee, February 18, 1971, Box 131, Folder 3, Kingman Brewster Papers, Yale University Archives (hereafter Brewster Papers); Stern to author, March 12, 2002 ("apply"). See, also, e.g., future California Supreme Court Chief Justice Rose Bird's wry and poignant comment on the situation of third-year women law students at Boalt in 1965, "3d Year Girls Lament (Fondly Dedicated to Dean Hill)," *Writ*, May 1965, at 2.

10. "Women Say Law Firms Discriminate," at 1; Clark interview with Areen; "Women Need Not Apply," *Yale Advocate*, April 13, 1970, at 12 (Chicago women).

11. Donald Downs, *Cornell '69: Liberalism and the Crisis of the American University* 283 (1999) (quoting *New York Times* account); Morton Keller and Phyllis Keller, *Making Harvard Modern: The Rise of America's University* 315 (2001) ("Harvard's Vietnam," quoting James Q. Wilson); John Morton Blum, *A Life with History* 213 (2004) (role of fellows); Geoffrey Kabaservice, *The Guardians: Kingman Brewster, His Circle, and the Rise of the Liberal Establishment* 380–82 (2004).

12. Geoffrey Kabaservice interview with Stephen Cohen, 2003 (Cohen speech; "silly"); Kabaservice, *Guardians*, at 386 (providing account of Cohen speech); author interview with Cohen, 2003; Kabaservice, *Guardians*, at 386–87.

13. Herbert Hansell and Louis Hector to Yale Law Student Alumni, n.d., n.p., introducing "Panel: Concerns of the Yale Law Student Today," *Yale Law Report* (Special issue: September 1969).

14. "Concerns of the Yale Law Student Today," at 6, 9.

15. Id. at 6–9; "A Voyage to the Law Block," *Yale Advocate*, March 12, 1969, at 2 (also discusses "Dworkinian threshold").

16. "Concerns of the Yale Law Student Today," at 10–11.

17. Id. at 11–12, 15. The two professors were Charles Nesson and Curtis Berger.

18. Id. at 8.

19. Id. at 15–19.

20. Id. at 19–20, 22.

21. Id. at 22–23 (emphasis added); "A Brief Report on the Two-Year Special Appeal Launched in the Spring of 1969," n.d., Box 43, Folder: Yale Law School Fund, Dean's Files; Louis Hector to Abe Goldstein, August 5, 1970, id.

22. "Students Provide Welcome for Alumni," *Yale Advocate*, May 1, 1969, at 1 (Dennis Black and "cacophonous"); Jonathan Krown, "A Proposal for a New Approach to Gaining Student Representation," n.d., Richard Hughes File (hereafter Hughes File) ("ridiculous"); Krown to author, March 24, 2001 (Goodson, "symbolize"); email, Dennis Black to author, April 11, 2001 ("freak"); "When Generations Collide," *Yale Advocate*, May 1, 1969, at 6 ("alumni").

23. "When Generations Collide." Emphasis in the original.

24. Macklin Fleming to Louis Pollak, June 9, 1969, Box 7, Folder: Judge Macklin Fleming, Dean's Files; Interview with Cochran, 2002.

25. Hansell and Hector to Yale Law Student Alumni (emphasis added).

26. Yale University Council Report of the Committee on the Law School, April 18, 1969, Box 56, Folder: Council Committee, Dean's Files.

27. Id.

28. Id.

29. Kevin Mattson, *Intellectuals in Action: The Origins of the New Left and Radical Liberalism, 1945–1970* 18 (2002) ("need not").

30. Duncan Kennedy, "Boola!," 14 *Social Text* 31, 35, 36 (no. 4, Winter 1996); Kabaservice interview with Duncan Kennedy, 1996 ("totally machiavellian," "Mr. Tough Cop and Mr. Softie").

31. Email, Dennis Black to author, March 28, 2001.

32. Interview with Pollak; Myres McDougal to Maxwell Cohen, July 3, 1969, Box 31, Folder C, Dean's Files.

33. Kabaservice interview with Clyde Summers, 1992. See also Kabaservice interviews with Ralph Brown, 1992, and Myres McDougal, 1991; Clyde Summers, "Louis Pollak," 127 *U. Pa. L. Rev.* 314, 314 (1978).

34. Interview with Pollak; Kabaservice interview with Brown; Louis Pollak to Kingman Brewster, March 13, 1969, Box 132, Folder 3, Brewster Papers; "Two Yale Law Deans to Relinquish Posts," *New York Times*, September 13, 1969, at A55.

CHAPTER SIX

1. Robert Stevens, "Law School and Law Students," 59 *Va. L. Rev.* 551, 584, 629 (1973); interview with C. Edwin Baker, 2004.

2. Dave Nelson, "How About Those Coke Machines?," *Yale Advocate*, October 2, 1969, at 5.

3. "Conservative Comeback," id., October 2, 1969, at 2 ("imperfect balance," "functions," "herald," "THE WAR," "walls"); "Yale Law School Seeks New Dean: Students Favor Outsider," id., October 2, 1969, at 1; "What's Gone Down at the Law School: 1967–69," id. at 1: "Throw My Ticket Out the Window; Tonight I'll Be Staying Here With You," id. at 3; "Worst Piece of Shit I Ever Saw," id. at 2; "Gold Star Sweepstakes," id. at 2 ("pedestal," "haven").

4. Richard Hughes to author, December 28, 2001; see *Yale Advocate*, October 2 and 23, 1969; "The Yale Law Advocate," id., December 15, 1969, at 2 (the January 1970 issue had no specific date); "Intergalactic Communications," id., February 9, 1970, at 2; February 26, 1970; April 13, 1970. Despite the name change, the paper regularly appeared under the title the *Advocate*, often with "The Yale Law School Advocate" just below the masthead, and sometimes with the *Yale Advocate* as a header on its internal pages. I have continued to cite it as *Yale Advocate*.

5. "How About Those Coke Machines?" (quotation); Wagoner: interviews with Louis Pollak, 2001, and Richard Balzer, 2002. The latter, the instigator of the grade reform movement, viewed Wagoner to his left.

6. Robert Stevens, "Law School and Law Students," 59 *Va. L. Rev.* 551, 602 (1973); "Blacks Gain Seat on Yale Law Body," *Yale Daily News*, September 26, 1969, at 1 ("forum," "anxious"); "How About Those Coke Machines?" (the four elected were John Doggett, Philip Lee, Michael Reed, and Patricia Wynn); interview with J. Otis Cochran, 2002.

7. Stevens, "Law Schools and Law Students," at 571, placed the number of minority students in the class of 1972, at 11 percent, or 22. YLS Faculty Minutes of February 26, 1970, however, suggest that 13.5 percent of the student body was African American, and Standley, citing Cochran, places the number at 33 out of 208 (almost 14 percent). Anne Standley, "Alexander Bickel, Charles Black, and the Ambiguous Legacy of Brown v. Board of Education: Competing Conceptions of Law, Justice and Democracy Within Postwar Legal Thought" 144 (PhD dissertation, 1993). Information about students' colleges can be found in the school yearbook, the 1970 *Yale Law Reporter*, and 1997 *Yale Law School Alumni Directory*.

8. Email, Harold McDougall to author, May 29, 2002. Cochran also stressed McDougall's reluctance. Interview with Cochran. See Note: "The Case for Black Juries," 79 *Yale L. J.* 531 (1970). McDougall is identified as the author in "Case for Black Juries," *Yale Daily News*, April 29, 1970, at 2.

9. Stevens, "Law Schools and Law Students," at 571, placed the number at 35; Hillary Rodham Clinton, *Living History* 44 (2003) ("breakthrough"); *Rylands* v. *Fletcher*, L.R. 1 Ex. 265 (1866), aff'd. LR. 3 H.L. 330 (1968); email, Richard Abel to author, October 30, 2001.

10. Wavy Gravy, *The Hog Farm and Friends by Wavy Gravy: As Told to Hugh Romney and Vice Versa* 112 (1974); "Students Camp at Law School; 'Unprecedented Event Hits Yale': Abandoning University's 'Uptightness,'" *Yale Daily News*, September 22, 1969, at 1; "Yale Bubbles Up to Harvard's Hark," *Harvard Law Record*, October 23, 1969, at 1, 12 (the article was written by the *Yale Advocate*'s Richard Hughes); "Edge City on the Road," *Yale Advocate*, December 15, 1969, at 5, 6 ("uptight").

11. Jonathan Krown, "Throw My Ticket Out the Window; Tonight I'll Be Staying Here With You," *Yale Advocate*, October 2, 1969, at 3. I am unsure how long the tent city remained in existence. At the time, Borosage said students maintained it for most of fall term (Robert Borosage, "Can the Law School Succeed? A Proposal," 1 *Yale Rev. of Law & Soc. Action* 92, 95 [1970]), but according to the article in the *Harvard Law Record*, the students remained in the Yale Law School courtyard for two weeks. "Yale Bubbles Up too Harvard's Hark," at 15. Email, Jonathan Krown to author, n.d. and March 24, 2001 (discouragement of drug use, "People's Park"); Wavy Gravy, *The Hog Farm and Friends*, at 113; "Criminals Approach Boalt Hall Takeover," *Writ*, October 15, 1969, at 1 (88 percent of last year's students at Boalt had used marijuana); "Law School News Pot Survey: 491 Respond: 339 (69%) Say They Smoke Marihuana," *Columbia Law School News*, November 11, 1969, at

1; "Legalize Marihuana," *Columbia Law School News*, id. at 4; "Two-Thirds In Commentator Poll Smoke Pot; Three-Fifths of Non-Users For Legalization," *Commentator*, November 20, 1968, at 2; "Marijuana Use High," *Stanford Law School Journal*, November 2, 1972, at 1.

12. Charles Reich to Alexander Bickel, July 20, 1967, Box 7, Folder 125, Alexander Bickel Papers, Yale University Archives (hereafter Bickel Papers); interview with Charles Reich, 2002; Charles Reich, *The Greening of America* 394 (1970); Krown to author, March 24, 2001 ("embarrassment"); interview with Abraham Goldstein, 2001.

13. Interview with Louis Pollak, 2001.

14. Author interview with Stephen Cohen, 2004; William Chafe, *Never Stop Running: Allard Lowenstein and the Struggle to Save American Liberalism* 329–32 (1993).

15. Yale Law School Faculty Minutes, October 2, 1969 (hereafter YLS Faculty Minutes); Kingman Brewster, Statement of October 2, 1969, YLS Faculty Minutes; Jeremy Weinberg, "Long Live the King's Yale: How Kingman Brewster's University Survived and Thrived in the 1960s," 34 (Yale College senior essay, 1992) ("nature," "'mobilized'"); "Reviewer's Corner: One Principle Under God," *Yale Advocate*, October 23, 1969, at 3 ("blindness," "position," "stand").

16. YLS Faculty Minutes, October 2, 1969; Resolution Adopted at the Faculty Meeting on October 2, 1969, id.

17. "Canceling Classes Up to Each Prof: No Moratorium Action Taken," *Harvard Law Record*, October 9, 1969, at 1.

18. "Reviewer's Corner: One Principle Under God," at 3 ("Resigner," "cathartic"); Alexander Bickel to Ronald Dworkin, January 19, 1970, Box 10, Folder 203, Bickel Papers. Given his unhappiness, Bickel considered it still likely that he would still leave Yale, perhaps for Pennsylvania, where he had an offer of a chair that would virtually enable him to relinquish teaching. Id. The impending change in the law school administration convinced him to remain at Yale. Alexander Bickel to John Hobsetter, April 1, 1970, Box 10, Folder 206, id.

19. "Reviewer's Corner: One Principle Under God," at 3.

20. "Official Neutrality: A Veil," in Immanuel Wallerstein and Paul Starr, eds., *The University Crisis Reader: The Liberal University Under Attack* 69–70 (1971); Joseph Fashing and Steven Deutsch, *Academics in Retreat: The Politics of Educational Innovation* 281, 282 (1971) ("schizophrenia," "decried").

21. Alexander Bickel to Kingman Brewster, September 29, 1969, Box 10, Folder 199, Bickel Papers.

22. "50,000 Mass at Convocation on Green: Brewster, Lee, Udall, Denounce Viet War," *Yale Daily News*, October 16, 1969, at 1; "Brewster Responds to Harassment of Blacks," October 17, 1969, id. at 1; Geoffrey Kabaservice, *The Guardians: Kingman Brewster, His Circle, and the Rise of the Liberal Establishment* 393–94 (2004) (deChabert-Brewster arrangement, SDS); The Yale Law School Student Association to Kingman Brewster, Statement, October 15, 1969, reprinted in "Stop the Cops," *Yale Advocate*, October 23, 1969, at 1.

23. Pnina Lahav, "The Chicago Conspiracy Trial: Character and Judicial Discretion," 71 *U. Colo. L. Rev.* 1327 (2000).

24. "City Police Charge Seale in Murder," *Yale Daily News*, September 18, 1969, at 1; Yohuru Williams, *Black Politics/White Power: Civil Rights, Black Power, and the Black Panthers in New Haven* 115–119, 128–45, 163 (2000); Ward Churchill, "'To Disrupt, Discredit and Destroy': The FBI's Secret War against the Black Panther Party," in Kathleen Cleaver

and George Katsiaficas, eds., *Liberation, Imagination, and the Black Panther Party* 78, 96–98 (2001); Kenneth O'Reilly, *Racial Matters: The FBI's Secret File on Black America, 1960–1972* 296–310 (1989); Robert Self, *American Babylon: Race and the Struggle for Postwar Oakland* 214–33 (2003).

25. John Taft, *Mayday at Yale: A Case Study in Student Radicalism* 8–9 (1976) (quotations); Williams, *Black Politics/White Power*, at 135, 140–41, 162–63; "City Police Charge Seale in Murder."

26. "How Yale Screws," *Yale Advocate*, October 23, 1969, at 1; Jeff Greenfield, *No Peace, No Place: Excavations Along the Generational Fault* 217–18 (1973); "Blacks at Yale Ask Changes in Police," *New York Times*, October, 21, 1969, at A32; Gail Sheehy, *Panthermania: The Clash of Black Against Black in One American City* (1971); Tom Wolfe, *Radical Chic & Mau-Mauing the Flak Catchers* 43–53 (1970); Williams, *Black Politics/White Power*, at 145.

27. "Blacks at Yale Ask Changes in Police" ("degrading"); "BSAY Enters Woodbridge, Talks With Corporation: Discuss Harassment of Yale Blacks," *Yale Daily News*, October 13, 1969, at 1; Undated and untitled memorandum by Pollak (ca. October 29, 1969) (badges), Box 131, Folder 4, Kingman Brewster Papers, Yale University Archives (hereafter Brewster Papers); McDougall to Kalman, May 29, 2002; interview with Cochran; Standley, "Alexander Bickel, Charles Black," at 145 ("oasis," "jerked"). For a similar complaint from the founder of the Black American Law School Students Association, see A. J. Cooper, "What's It All About? Well, Roy, Let Me Tell You," *Commentator*, February 26, 1968, at 5.

28. Report of the Disciplinary Committee to the Dean and Teaching Faculty concerning Mr. Eric L. Clay '72 (hereafter Report of the Disciplinary Committee), Box 131, Folder 2, Brewster Papers.

29. "Blacks Give Reply to Grievance Plan," *Yale Daily News*, October 21, 1969, at 1.

30. Interview with Cochran; McDougall to author, May 29, 2002; "Black Students Disrupt Classes in Law School," *Yale Daily News*, October 21, 1969, at 1. The *New York Times* put the number of demonstrators at closer to sixty. "Blacks at Yale Ask Changes In Police," *New York Times*, October 21, 1969, at A32; interview with Ann Hill, 2002.

31. "Black Students Disrupt Classes in Law School"; Kate Freeland to Louis Pollak, October 31, 1969, Box 31, Folder F, Dean's Files, Yale University Archives (hereafter Dean's Files).

32. "Black Students Disrupt Classes in Law School."

33. Kingman Brewster to Glenn deChabert, October 23, 1969, Box 131, Folder 8, Brewster Papers; YLS Faculty Minutes, October 20, 1969; Louis Pollak to All Members of the Yale Law School, October 20, 1969, Box 131, Folder 2, Brewster Papers; Report of the Disciplinary Committee; Louis Pollak to the Disciplinary Policy Committee (Eugene Rostow, Elias Clark, Daniel Freed, and Joseph Goldstein) and The Disciplinary Tribunal, Box 433, Folder 13, Brewster Papers (Joseph Goldstein, Joseph Bishop, Charles Black, Ward Bowman, and Jay Katz [alternates: Robert Bork and Harry Wellington]). Apparently Black and Bishop declined to serve.

34. Louis Pollak, untitled statement to the law school community, October 29, 1969, Box 131, Folder 2, Brewster Papers; Members of the Student Negotiating Committee to Dear Students, May 8, 1969; Supplement to Resolution on Student Participation, May 5, 1969.

35. I have been unable to determine who requested the meeting in executive session. Pollak thought it might have been Bickel, Kessler, and perhaps Goldstein, but was uncertain. Interview with Pollak.

36. Id.

37. Id.

38. Kabaservice interview with Louis Pollak, 1992 ("if"); Abel to author, October 30, 2001; YLS Faculty Minutes, October 26, 1969; interview with Reich.

39. YLS Faculty Minutes, October 26, 1969; Louis Pollak to Walter Wagoner, October 27, 1969, Box 54, Folder: Student Associations, Dean's Files.

40. Interview with Cochran; "Boycott Affects Yale Law School," *New York Times*, October 29, 1969, at A52; "[Yale Law School Student Association] Factual Statement Regarding Events of October 26," Box 131, Folder 8, Brewster Papers.

41. "Factual Statement Regarding Events of October 26." Emphasis in the original.

42. Kabaservice interview with Pollak ("That's just"); "Factual Statement Regarding Events of October 26"; Louis Pollak to Walt Wagoner, October 27, 1969, Box 54, Folder: Student Associations, Dean's Files; YLS Faculty Minutes, October 26, 1969 ("students," "Why?").

43. The account and quotations are from "Factual Statement Regarding Events of October 26," with the exception of the quotation from Brown, ending "He just blew up," which is from the Kabaservice interview with Ralph Brown, 1992.

44. "Factual Statement Regarding Events of October 26"; YLS Faculty Minutes, October 26, 1969.

45. Interview with Hill.

46. YLS Faculty Minutes, October 26, 1969; interview with Cochran (dealings with Brewster).

47. Abraham Goldstein, "The Changing Mood: A Report from the Dean," 18 *Yale L. Report* 19, 19 (Fall–Winter 1971–72) ("heroes"); interview with Abraham Goldstein, 2001; YLS Faculty Minutes, October 26, 1969.

48. Robert Bork, *Slouching Toward Gomorrah: Modern Liberalism and American Decline* 40 (1996); interviews with Boris Bittker, 2001, and Reich; Alexander Bickel, Joseph Goldstein, and Leon Lipson to the Black Students Union, April 6, 1970, Box 56, Folder: BLSU, Dean's Files.

49. Interview with Pollak ("wimp," "submissive"); Bonnie Collier interview with Harry Wellington, July 12, 2000 ("total liberal"); Collier interview with Wellington, December 1, 2000 ("authoritarian").

50. David Trubek to Kingman Brewster, January 23, 1970, Box 132, Folder 3, Brewster Papers.

51. "BLSU Hits Disciplinary Proceedings," *Yale Daily News*, October 28, 1969, at 1.

52. Interview with Cochran; McDougal to Kalman, May 29, 2002.

53. "Law Students Begin Boycott of Classes," *Yale Daily News*, October 28, 1969, at 1 ("symbolizes"); "Law Students to Strike If Demands Not Met," id., October 27, 1969, at 1; untitled and undated statement of a committee of 100 law students, Box 131, Folder 8, Brewster Papers.

54. "BLSU Hits Disciplinary Proceedings," *Yale Daily News*, October 28, 1969, at 1 (quotes); and see Statement by the Black Law Students Union, October 27, 1969, Box 131, Folder 8, Brewster Papers.

55. "Law School Strike Depends Upon Radical Leaders' Appeal," *Yale Daily News*, October 28, 1969, at 1.

56. "Boycott Affects Yale Law School."

57. "Intergalactic Consciousness"; "Law School Strike Depends Upon Radical Leaders' Appeal."

58. "Law School Strike Depends Upon Radical Leaders' Appeal."

59. "Boycott Affects Yale Law School."

60. Louis Pollak to All Members of the Yale Law School Community, October 29, 1969, Box 131, Folder 4, Brewster Papers. Emphasis in the original.

61. Id.

62. Email, George Lefcoe to author, September 1, 2002.

63. Confidential interview; Testimony of J. Otis Cochran, quoted in Report of the Disciplinary Committee.

64. Lefcoe to author, September 1, 2002; Alvin Kernan, *In Plato's Cave* 162 (1999) ("Slightly veiled").

65. Paul Carrington, "Civilizing University Discipline," 69 *Mich. L. Rev.* 405, 409–19 (1971).

66. Interview with Cochran.

67. YLS Faculty Minutes, December 19, 1968 (extension of meeting held December 18, 1968).

68. Eric Clay and Melvin Watt, "Who is on Trial?," n.d., Box 251, Folder 14, Brewster Papers. For a contemporary argument by one law professor that it was prudent to allow student participation in disciplinary tribunals, see Carrington, "Civilizing University Discipline," at 401.

69. "Faculty Tribunal to Hear Student's Case," *Yale Daily News*, November 3, 1969, at 1; Standley, "Alexander Bickel, Charles Black," at 151, 147 ("equal," "overflow"); Owen Fiss, "Yale According to Joe," 110 *Yale L. J.* 113 (2001) ("posture"); interview with George Lefcoe, 2002. The desire to replicate the normal site of the hearing was the reason remembered by Sam Chauncey, then the Secretary of the University. Conversation with Chauncey, 2001. In refusing to make the trial public, Goldstein may have been aware of what had recently occurred at Columbia, when a disciplinary tribunal, which included students, tried law student Gus Reichbach for his participation in the 1968 spring revolt. A group of students, most unaffiliated with the law school, had brought the proceedings to a halt when one had jumped on the judge's table, seized the judge's gavel, and begun kicking books and papers to the floor. "Students Disrupt Hearing; Second Meeting Dec. 9th," *Columbia Law School News*, November 20, 1968, at 1.

70. *Watts* v. *United States*, 394 U.S. 705 (1969).

71. Standley, "Alexander Bickel, Charles Black," at 147, 146 ("hyperbole," "theoretical expression"); interview with Baker; Report of the Disciplinary Committee (quoting Cochran).

72. Emails, Lefcoe to Kalman, September 1 ("splendidly") and September 2, 2002; "Eric Lee Clay," <http://www.jtbf.org/article__iii__judges/clay__e.htm>. I have been unable to locate the record of the trial or to speak with Watt, Clay, or the late Joe Goldstein about it.

73. Kristine Olson, Kingsley Buhl, Bob Herbst, Kirk McKenzie, Jeff Melnick, Raphael Podolsky, Barbara Rosenberg, Russell Zuckerman to Louis Pollak, December 4, 1969, Box 33, Folder: Discipline Committee 1963–69, Dean's Files; interview with Lefcoe ("ducked"); Lefcoe to author, September 1, 2002. Some professors Lefcoe had not consulted before going to Felstiner may have considered him hypersensitive. Steven Duke recalled a student who had failed one of his courses during this period threatening to cut his throat. Duke did nothing. Neither did the student. Interview with Steven Duke, 2001.

74. Lefcoe to author, September 1, 2002 (quotations); interview with Lefcoe; David Trubek to Kalman, January 4, 2002.

75. Report of the Disciplinary Committee.

76. Standley, "Alexander Bickel, Charles Black," at 148.

77. Report of the Disciplinary Committee.

78. Emails, McDougall to author, May 29, 2002; May 31, 2002.

79. Interview with Reich.

80. I do not know whether Clay had apprised Watt of how he intended to answer such a question.

81. Report of the Disciplinary Committee.

82. Id.

83. "Without Jury [Of His] Peers," *Yale Advocate*, December 15, 1969, at 3; Olson, Buh, Herbst, McKenzie, Melnick, Podolsky, Rosenberg, Zuckerman to Dean Pollak and Members of the Law School Faculty, December 4, 1969.

84. Report of the Disciplinary Committee. Emphasis added.

85. Memorandum of L. H. Pollak on the Report of the Disciplinary Panel of November 25, 1969, relating to Eric L. Clay, '72, Box 131, Folder 2, Brewster Papers.

86. Interview with Pollak; Memorandum of L. H. Pollak on the Report of the Disciplinary Panel.

87. Standley, "Alexander Bickel, Charles Black," at 150; interview with Lefcoe.

88. Report to the Faculty of the Committee on Disciplinary Policy, April 1970, YLS Faculty Minutes; Joseph Goldstein, Partial Dissent to Disciplinary Policy Committee Report, n.d., id.; Alexander Bickel to Eugene Rostow, April 16, 1970, Box 10, Folder 206, Bickel Papers; YLS Faculty Minutes, May 6 and May 11, 1970; Alexander Bickel to Eugene Rostow, April 16, 1970, Box 10, Folder 206, Bickel Papers.

89. Olson, Buh, Herbst, McKenzie, Melnick, Podolsky, Rosenberg, Zuckerman to Dean Pollak and Members of the Law School Faculty, December 4, 1969. Olson later changed her mind and branded Pollak's solution as overly harsh in placing Clay on probation indefinitely until the faculty lifted it. "Without Jury [of His] Peers."

90. "60 Students Hold 4 Yale Officials," *New York Times*, November 4, 1969, at A35; Kabaservice, *Guardians*, at 396–99, 384; supra Chapter 5, text accompanying notes 28–29.

91. "Waitress At Yale Reinstated; 44 Protesters Are Suspended," *New York Times*, November 5, 1969, at A52; Robert Brustein, *Making Scenes: A Personal History of the Turbulent Years at Yale 1966–1979* 93–95 (1981); John Perry Miller, *Creating Academic Settings: High Craft and Low Cunning* 154–57 (1991).

92. Brustein, *Making Scenes*, at 93; Kabaservice, *Guardians*, at 398–99 (Bickel);"Executive Committee Decision on Wright Hall Occupation," *Yale Daily News*, November 12, 1969, at 2; "Suspended Yale Students Reinstated on Probation," *New York Times*, November 12, 1969, at A96; John Morton Blum, *A Life With History* 207–10 (2004).

93. Interviews with Pollak and Cochran.

94. "Without Jury [of His] Peers"; interview with Pollak ("mighty").

95. *Shaw* v. *Reno*, 509 U.S. 630 (1993); *Shaw* v. *Hunt*, 517 U.S. 899 (1996); *Hunt* v. *Cromartie*, 526 U.S. 521 (1999); *Easley* v. *Cromartie*, 532 U.S. 234 (2001); "Who We Are: Lewis and Munday, A Professional Corporation," <http://www.lewismunday.com/who1.htm>; Confirmation Hearings on Federal Appointments, Hearings Before the Committee on the Judiciary, United States Senate, One Hundred Fifth Congress, First Session, Confirmation of Appointees to the Federal Judiciary, March 18; May 7; June 25, July 22, 1997, Part I, Serial No. J-105-4, May 7, 1997, 260, 264 ("dozens," "life"); "Clay Sworn In as 6th Circuit Judge," *Michigan Lawyers Weekly*, November 10, 1997; and see Deborah Moss "Activist Past, Mainstream Future," 74 *Am. Bar Assn. J.* 50 (February 1, 1988) (profile of Lewis, White, and Clay).

96. *Simmons-Harris* v. *Zellman*, 234 F. 3d 945 (2000); reversed, 122 S.Ct. 2460 (2002); *Byrd* v. *Collins*, 227 F. 3d. 756 (2000); *In re John W. Byrd, Jr.*, 269 F. 3d. 585 (2001); "U.S. Appeals Court Hears Debate on Race-Based Admissions," *New York Times*, December 7, 2001, at A27 (oral argument query); *Grutter* v. *Bollinger*, 288 F. 3d. 732, 758, 763, 764, 765 (2002); Lefcoe to author, September 2, 2002.

97. Louis Pollak to Joseph Goldstein, December 2, 1969, Box 132, Folder 5, Brewster Papers; Abel to author, April 30, 2002; Standley, "Alexander Bickel, Charles Black," at 156; Friedrich Kessler, Alexander Bickel, Guido Calabresi, Ralph Winter, Memorandum to the Faculty, n.d. [November-December 1969], Box 60, Folder 10, Bickel Papers.

98. Standley, "Alexander Bickel, Charles Black," at 151 (quoting Watt).

99. Stevens, "Law School and Law Students," at 682.

CHAPTER SEVEN

1. "One Final Word," *Res Gestae*, April 24, 1970, at 10.

2. Ruth Rosen, *The World Split Open: How the Modern Women's Movement Changed America* 196–201 (2000); Alice Echols, *Daring to Be Bad: Radical Feminism in America, 1967–75* 11 (1990).

3. "Subtle Discrimination: Women in Law—Oppressed Minority," *Writ*, December 18, 1968, at 1, 5. Sixties feminists did not invent the concept of the personal as political. Barbara Ransby, *Ella Baker & the Black Freedom Movement* 369 (2003). For that matter, they did not invent modern feminism, either. See, e.g., Daniel Horowitz, *Betty Friedan and the Making of The Feminine Mystique: The American Left, The Cold War, and Modern Feminism* (1998).

4. "Panel Considers Uses of Law," *Stanford Law School Journal*, September 23, 1971, at 1, 3; "Greenhalgh Remarks Denounced As Sexist: Woman Professor's Cancellation Sparks 'Responsibility' Lecture," *Georgetown Law Weekly*, September 7, 1972, at 1; "The Writ Proudly Presents Vikki," *Writ*, February, 1966, at 5; "'He' Belies Sexism, Where Are the Sisters?," *Writ*, December 8, 1972, at 1.

5. Vicki Jackson, Louise Nemschoff, and Anne Simon, *The Women's Law School Companion* 1 (1974); Laura Kalman, *Abe Fortas* 328–58 (1990); "Creatures Flame, Pornography Flops In 'Repulsive' Fortas Film Festival," *Yale Advocate*, November 7, 1968, at 2; "Mixer!," *Yale Advocate*, September 26, 1968, at 3.

6. Sara Evans, *Personal Politics: The Roots of Women's Liberation in the Civil Rights Movement and the New Left* 235 (1979).

7. Email, Ann Freedman to author, October 26, 2002.

8. Jane Lazarre, *The Mother Knot* 32, 33, 43–44 (1997); *Women's Law School Companion*, at 14.

9. Email, Alexandra Denman to author, March 28, 2002; Ann Hill, "If Men Were Taught Cooking," *Yale Advocate*, February 26, 1970, at 1, 3, 4 ("human," "people," "painful," "real," "if we").

10. Freedman to author, October 26, 2002 (Barbara Babcock taught the course); Barbara Brown, Thomas Emerson, Gail Falk, and Ann Freedman, "The Equal Rights Amendment: A Constitutional Basis for Equal Rights for Women," 80 *Yale L. J.* 871 (1971) (unusually, Emerson insisted the women be listed as coauthors, instead of crediting them with assisting him in a footnote; Freedman to author, October 26, 2002); *Abele* v. *Markle*, 452 F. 2d 1121 2d Cir. (1971); Abbe Smith and William Montross, "The Calling of Criminal De-

fense," 50 *Mercer L. Rev.* 443, n. 399 (1971) (Roraback); *Women's Law School Companion*, at 6, 14; interview with Ann Hill, 2001.

11. Denman to author, March 28, 2002; "Mory's 'Poor Little Sheep' Face Dry Future Over Sex Bias Charge," *New York Times*, February 1, 1972, at A33.

12. "Women of the Law School Unite!," *Yale Advocate*, December 15, 1969, at 3; *Women's Law School Companion*, at 14, 4; "free our sisters free ourselves," *Yale Advocate*, December 15, 1969, at 2 (reprinting Yale Law Women Association letter to Ellis MacDougall, Connecticut Commissioner of Corrections); "Secretaries Can't Get No Satisfaction," id. at 2. It is unclear how many minority women law students were involved in Yale's women's movement.

13. Friedan's speech is described in "Unsexing the Law," *Yale Advocate*, February 26, 1970, at 2; Millet's visit is announced in id.; Rita Mae Brown, *A Plain Brown Rapper* 37 (1976).

14. Email, Ann Hill to author, April 30, 2004; "If Men Were Taught Cooking," *Yale Advocate*, February 26, 1970, at 1, 2.

15. *Women's Law School Companion*, at 13; interview with Hill.

16. Class Notes, '70, 24 *Yale Law Report* 33 (Spring 1978); "If Men Were Taught Cooking," at 1, 2 (emphasis in the original); interview with Hill.

17. "If Men Were Taught Cooking," at 2; interview with Hill.

18. Yale Law School Faculty Minutes, March 4, 1970 (hereafter YLS Faculty Minutes); and see id. at March 7, 1970. (James William Moore was specifically accused of using a double standard. Moore denied that he did, while arguing that the school needed African American students and they deserved more than one semester to become used to law study. Id., March 4. Both the March 4 and March 7 meetings were held in executive session; Yale Law School Women's History Project, Oral History Interview with Judith Areen, 2000, by Mary Clark.) One student was permitted to remain and ultimately graduated on schedule. It is unclear whether the other was also permitted to stay and did not do sufficiently well to graduate or whether he was forced to withdraw immediately.

19. YLS Faculty Minutes, February 26, 1970; Yale University Council Report of the Committee on the Law School, December 3, 1970, Box 43, File: University Council, Dean's Files, Yale University Archives (hereafter Dean's Files) ("significant"). The higher CP reflected an increase in the average LSAT score from 517 for accepted minority students entering in 1969 to 573 for minority students entering in 1970. In the end, over 14.5 percent of the class enrolled in 1970 was black. But whereas the law school had accepted 28–40 percent of its minority applicants in 1968 and 26 percent in 1969, it accepted 16 percent of black applicants in 1970. T. Bingham to Lloyd Cutler, October 30, 1970, ["Data requested on the Yale Law School" for the University Council Report], Box 43: Folder: University Council, Dean's Files.

20. Geoffrey Kabaservice interviews with Louis Pollak, 1992, and Ralph Brown, 1992; interview with Charles Reich, 2002.

21. Judith Richards Hope, *Pinstripes & Pearls: The Women of the Harvard Law School Class of '64 Who Forged an Old-Girl Network and Paved the Way for Future Generations* 35 (2003); interview with Hill.

22. Lani Guinier, Michelle Fine, and Jane Balin, *Becoming Gentlemen: Women, Law School, and Institutional Change* 86–87 (1997); Lani Guinier, *The Tyranny of the Majority: Fundamental Fairness in Representative Democracy* (1994); Guinier, *Lift Every Voice: Turning a Civil Rights Setback into a New Vision of Social Justice* (1998); Guinier and Gerald Tores, *The Miner's Canary: Enlisting Race, Resisting Power, Transforming Democ-*

racy (2002); Andrew Thomas, *Clarence Thomas: A Biography* 142 (2001) ("prove," "Every time"); Jane Mayer and Jill Abramson, *Strange Justice: The Selling of Clarence Thomas* 58–59 (1994) ("offended," "they let"); *Adarand v. Pena*, 515 U.S, 200, 240, 241 (1995); quotations from *Grutter v. Bollinger*, 539 U.S. 306 (2003); and see Daryl Scott, *Contempt and Pity: Social Policy and the Image of the Damaged Black Psyche, 1880–1996* 188–89 (1996).

23. Clyde Summers, "Preferential Admissions: An Unreal Solution to a Real Problem," 1970 *U. Tol. L. Rev.* 377, 384, 395, 396 (1970).

24. Derrick Bell, "Black Students in White Law Schools: The Ordeal and the Opportunity," 1970 *U. Tol. L. Rev.* 539, 552 (1970) ("one major"); Ernest Gellhorn, "The Law Schools and the Negro," 1968 *Duke L. J.* 1069, 1091 (1968); conversation with Summers, 2004. For a rebuttal to Summers, see Harry Edwards, "A New Role for the Black Law Graduate — A Reality or an Illusion," 69 *Mich. L. Rev.* 1407, 1419–22 (1971).

25. BLSU Steering Committee to Faculty, February 13, 1970, Box 56, Folder: BLSU, Dean's Files.

26. BLSU to the Faculty, April 3, 1970, id. ("sacrosanct"); Geoffrey Kabaservice, *The Guardians: Kingman Brewster, His Circle, and the Rise of the Liberal Establishment* 401–2 (2004) ("'get Yale,'" quoting Flora Lewis); "Chronology" (a chronology of events at Yale from April 19 to May 3, 1970, Box 37, Folder: President's Office 1965–70 [hereafter May Day Chronology], Dean's Files); Yohuru Williams, *Black Politics/White Power: Civil Rights, Black Power, and the Black Panthers in New Haven* 153, 157 (2000).

27. Kabaservice, *Guardians*, at 405 ("radicals," "bring together," quoting Brewster); Peter Brooks, "Panthers at Yale," 37 *Partisan Rev.* 420, 438, 428, 426 (quotations); and see Brooks, Comment, id. at 547, 547 (1970).

28. Kabaservice, *Guardians*, at 404 (reporting rumors that between 50,000 and half a million protesters were coming); May Day Chronology.

29. Brooks, "Panthers at Yale," at 431; John Taft, *Mayday at Yale: A Case Study in Student Radicalism* 79–80 (1976) ("God knows"), and see id. at 96, 84–97, 113–14 (1976); Alvin Kernan, *In Plato's Cave* 171, 170 (1999) (1789, "played its cards").

30. Kabaservice, *Guardians*, at 409; Kernan, *In Plato's Cave*, at 175 ("risk") (Kernan had suggested the possibility of closure to Brewster, id.); email, Peter Brooks to author, December 1, 2003 ("completely silent," "scared").

31. Williams, *Black Politics/White Power*, at 154 ("pragmatic"; quoting Brewster assistant Sam Chauncey); Kabaservice, *Guardians*, at 9 ("test"); May Day Chronology.

32. Kabaservice, *Guardians*, at 407, 417 ("In spite," Cochran); Francine du Plessix Gray, "The Panthers at Yale," *New York Review of Books*, 29, 31 (June 4, 1970).

33. Kernan, *In Plato's Cave*, at 169 ("deadly"); Taft, *Mayday at Yale*, at 128 ("Fear"); May Day Chronology.

34. "Hopes and Fears at Yale," *Washington Post*, May 1, 1970, in May Day Chronology.

35. Taft, *Mayday at Yale*, at 22 ("die like a Panther, die like a man") (the language of the left was often aggressively macho [Doug Rossinow, *The Politics of Authenticity, Liberalism, Christianity, and the New Left in America* 299 (1998)]); undated, untitled BLSU brochure, Box 56, Folder: BLSU, Dean's Files (Doggett); Pollak, Statement, April 29, 1970, Box 37, Folder: President's Office 1965–70, Dean's Files; Kabaservice interview with Pollak ("civil rights business").

36. Alexander Bickel to C. Vann Woodward, March 1, 1971, Box 10, Folder 215, Alexander Bickel Papers, Yale University Archives (hereafter Bickel Papers) ("repression," "political trial," "Goebbels"); Alexander Bickel, Joseph W. Bishop, Charles Black, J. H.

Hexter, Martin Shubik, C. Vann Woodward to Kingman Brewster, April 25, 1970, id., Folder 206; Taft, *Mayday at Yale*, at 30 ("official welcome").

37. Alexander Bickel, "The Tolerance of Violence on Campus," *New Republic*, 15, 16 (June 13, 1970) (emphasis in the original); *Rights in Conflict: The Violent Confrontation of Demonstrators and Police in the Parks and Streets of Chicago During the Week of the Democratic National Convention of 1968: A Report Submitted by Daniel Walker, Director of the Chicago Study Team, to the National Commission on the Causes and Prevention of Violence* 5 (1968).

38. May Day Chronology.

39. Conversation with Ann Freedman and Harriet Katz, 2001 (research for defense counsel); Trial Report Committee to Members of the Yale Community, Box 60, Folder 11, Bickel Papers; Kalman interview with Cohen, 2004 ("On that basis"); Jeff Greenfield, *No Peace, No Place: Excavations Along the Generational Fault* 223 (1973) ("trusted"; emphasis in the original).

40. Kalman interview with Cohen; Greenfield, *No Peace, No Place*, at 224 ("revolutionary violence"); Brooks, "Panthers at Yale," at 425.

41. Brooks, "Panthers at Yale," at 425, 427; Kabaservice interview with William Farley, 1991 ("And the feeling").

42. James McNulty to Louis Pollak, April 27, 1970, Box 43, Folder: Yale University—Police, Dean's Files; and see May Day Chronology. Pollak put the number of students who helped at over 100. Pollak to Joseph McCrindle, May 12, 1970, Box 32, Folder Mac/Mc, Dean's Files.

43. Class Notes '71, 20 *Yale L. Report* 47, 48 (Spring 1974).

44. Kalman interview with Cohen; "Law School Vote Rejects Shutdown," *Yale Daily News*, April 28, 1970, at 1; Louis Pollak to the Faculty, April 27, 1990, Box 260, Folder 814, Reuben Holden Papers, Yale University Archives (warning of rumors that undergraduates would disrupt classes the following day because they were annoyed more law students had not joined strike).

45. "Students Reject Yale Law Strike—But Many Voice 'Sympathy' for Panther Protest—Books are Burned," *New York Times*, April 28, 1970, at A1, 44; "Law School Vote Rejects Shutdown."

46. "Law School Vote Rejects Shutdown."

47. Id.; Kabaservice, *Guardians*, at 9 ("considered"); "Students Reject Yale Law Strike"; interview with Baker. Peter Brooks spoke of Tom Hayden's speech comparing Brewster to Cambodia's Prince Sihanouk. But as Brooks pointed out, the Nixon administration's antipathy toward Sihanouk was one reason for the invasion of Cambodia on April 30. The right might topple Brewster too, he thought. Brooks, "Panthers at Yale," at 438.

48. Kabaservice interview with Clyde Summers, 1992; interview with Pollak; Pollak to McCrindle, May 12, 1970 ("one gratifying"); Pollak to S. Burns Weston, June 24, 1970, Box 37, Folder: President's Office, 1965–70, Dean's Files.

49. Bonnie Collier interview with Abraham Goldstein, 1996.

50. Louis Pollak, Louis Hector, Herbert Hansell to Fellow Alumnus, April 24, 1970, Box 37, Folder: President's Office 1965–70, Dean's Files; Robert Bork, *Slouching Toward Gomorrah: Modern Liberalism and American Decline* 42 (1996) (Winter, fire extinguishers); Harry Wellington to Carl Dreyfus, April 11, 1968, Box 1, Folder D, Dean's Files (riot damage); "Riot Insurance," 77 *Yale L. J.* 541 (1968) (riot insurance); Anne Standley, "Alexander Bickel, Charles Black, and the Ambiguous Legacy of Brown v. Board of Education: Competing Conceptions of Law, Justice and Democracy Within Postwar Legal Thought"

156 (PhD dissertation, 1993); Lazarre, *Mother Knot*, at 36, 37; interview with George Lefcoe, 2002. Alumni Weekend was moved to the fall and has remained there ever since.

51. Pollak to McCrindle, May 12, 1970; "Students Reject Yale Law Strike," *New York Times*, April 28, 1970, at A1, 44; Bork, *Slouching Toward Gomorrah*, at 1; and see Law School Vote Rejects "Showdown," *Yale Daily News*, April 28, 1970, at 1; John Hersey, *Letter to the Alumni* 95 (1970) (mercury and riot guns).

52. McNulty to Pollak, April 27, 1970 ("undetermined"); Pollak to Weston, June 24, 1970 (awaiting verdict); interview with Pollak; Louis Pollak, "Ralph Brown: Farewell to a Friend," 108 *Yale L. J.* 1473, 1476 (1999) (accident); Pollak to Jacques Schlenger, June 25, 1970, Box 37, Folder: President's Office 1965–70, Dean's Files.

53. Remarks of Senator Hillary Rodham Clinton, Class Day, Yale University, May 20, 2001, <http://clinton.senate.gov/clinton/speeches/001420.html>; Bork, *Slouching Toward Gomorrah*, at 1, 37, 46–47; Bickel, "Tolerance of Violence on Campus," at 17.

54. Interview with Calabresi, 2002; Anthony Kronman, "My Senior Partner," 104 *Yale L. J.* 2129, 2131 (1995) ("politicization"); Friedrich Kessler, "The Future of the Law School," 16 *Yale L. Report* 4, 6 (Spring 1970).

55. Standley, "Alexander Bickel, Charles Black," at 171; Alexander Bickel, Campus Unrest, Notes for Remarks, Peninsula Harvard Club, California 1970, November 4, Box 28, Folder 37, Bickel Papers ("fascist romance"); Bickel, "Tolerance of Violence on Campus," at 17; Alexander Bickel, *The Morality of Consent* 136 (1975) ("the sort").

56. "1939? The Hitler Analogy," *Yale Daily News*, May 1, 1970, at 2; Bickel, *The Morality of Consent*, at 139 ("liberals"); Duncan Kennedy, "Boola!," 14 *Social Text* 31, 35 (No. 4, Winter 1996). Robert Brustein also compared student demonstrators to Nazis who protested Weimar. Brustein, *Making Scenes: A Personal History of the Turbulent Years at Yale 1966–1979* 85 (1981).

57. Yuen Foong Khong, *Analogies at War: Korea, Munich, Dien Bien Phu, and the Vietnam Decisions of 1965* 129, 134 (1992). It may be that as a group, American academic lawyers proved more hostile to student demonstrators than their Arts and Science colleagues. It was Cornell law professors, for example, who administered the coup de grace to the presidency of James Perkins. They sent him an open letter disputing his claims that he had widespread support on campus; articulating their anxiety about academic freedom; and conveying their fear about the spread of anarchy on the campus. Donald Downs, *Cornell '69: Liberalism and the Crisis of the American University* 293–94 (1999).

58. Joseph Bishop, *Obiter Dicta: Opinions, Judicious and Otherwise, on Lawyers and the Law* 131, 160 (1971).

59. Brooks, "Panthers at Yale," at 423; Hersey, *Letter to the Alumni*, at 33; Kabaservice, *Guardians*, at 357 ("force of nature"); Williams, *Black Politics/White Power*, at 155 ("extensive").

60. Greenfield, *No Peace, No Place*, at 236; Taft, *Mayday at Yale*, at 149, 120, 155 ("symbolically"); Greenfield, *No Peace, No Place*, at 237; Bickel, "The Tolerance of Violence on Campus," at 151; Louis Pollak to Alumni and Other Friends of Yale Law School, June 1, 1970, Box 32, Dean's Files, Folder: Letter from Dean Pollak to Alumni and Friends of the Law School and Miscellaneous correspondence Relating to the Letter" ("enormously proud"); Pollak to Weston, June 24, 1970. The alumni and lawyers on the Committee on the Law School, which periodically reviewed the law school for the Yale Corporation, were certain law students had served as voices of moderation in the trial. Yale University Council Report of the Committee on the Law School, December 3, 1970, Box 43, Folder: University Council, Dean's Files.

61. Brustein, *Making Scenes*, at 115 ("surfeit"); Kabaservice, *Guardians*, at 412.

62. Hillary Clinton, *Living History* 46 (2003) ("told," "chilled"); "The Education of Hillary Rodham Clinton: Candidate's Wife Learned to Love 'the System' at Yale Law School," *Legal Times*, October 19, 1992, at 2.

63. "Endorse Strike: Law Students Hit War," *Yale Daily News*, May 5, 1970, at 1 (quotations); Pollak to Alumni and Other Friends of the Law School (reporting strike vote of 239–12, with 9 abstentions); Bill Brockett, Statement, n.d., Box 34, Folder: Alumni Weekend October 1970, Dean's Files (negative vote of two students); Clinton, *Living History*, at 46 ("seriously," "citizens"); Hillary Rodham Clinton, "What I Learned in Law School," 39 *Yale L. Report* 1, 4 (Fall 1992) ("difficult and turbulent"); "Education of Hillary Rodham Clinton." The many different motions introduced at the meeting can be found in an undated document in Box 258, Folder 796, Kingman Brewster Papers, Yale University Archives (hereafter Brewster Papers).

64. Walt Wagoner, WYNBC Commentary, WYNBC News, May 6, 1970, 12 noon, Box 34, Folder: Alumni Weekend October 1970, Dean's Files.

65. Brockett, Statement.

66. YLS Faculty Minutes, May 5, 1970.

67. Id.

68. Kabaservice, *Guardians*, at 420 ("students"; "how to stop"); Kernan, *In Plato's Cave*, at 175–76, 177.

69. Robert Schaus and James Arnone, *University at Buffalo 1887–1987* 87 (1992).

70. Collier interview with Goldstein.

71. Wagoner, WYNBC News Commentary.

72. Alexander Bickel to Phil Neal, October 5, 1971, Box 10, Folder 219, Bickel Papers; Mary McGrory, "Law Students' Peace Lobby: Senate Doors Open for Yale," May 18, 1970, Box 2, Folder 125, id.

73. Pollak to Alumni and Other Friends of the Law School, June 1, 1970.

74. Report of the Dean of the Law School, 1965–1970, Record Unit 12, Box 19, Brewster Papers.

75. Mark Green, "The Young Lawyers, 1972: Goodbye to Pro Bono," *New York*, February 21, 1972, 29, 33. Ronald Dworkin was highly amused when, on a trip to Paris, he ran into Erich Segal, the Yale classicist who had made as much of a splash with *Love Story* (1970) as Reich had with *Greening*, and was introduced to Segal's hosts as Reich's colleague. Ronald Dworkin to Harry Wellington, January 8, 1971, Box 1, Folder D, Dean's files.

76. Email, Ben Stein to author, February 12, 2002; "YLS 'Crusaders' Try To Fill Power Vacuum," *Yale Advocate*, April 17, 1969, at 1. The student who founded Yale Law School Legislative Services was William Drayton.

77. Tom Hilbink interview with Sanford Jaffe, November 11, 1999 ("not necessarily," "five fellows"); "Ex-Environment Activist Will Take Helm at Edison Utility: John Bryson Co-Founded National Resources Defense Council in 1970," *Los Angeles Times*, October 1, 1990, at A1 ("sued," "shadow"); interview with David Schoenbrod, 2003; "A Message from NRDC's President and Executive Director," <http://www.savebiogems/org/about/execs.asp>; "E-law: What Started It All?," <http://www.nrdc.org/legislation/helaw.asp>. See generally, Austin Sarat and Stuart Scheingold, eds., *Cause Lawyering: Professional Commitments and Social Responsibilities* (1998).

78. "Placement—Class of 1970," 17 *Yale L. Report* 40 (Fall 1970); Green, "The Young Lawyers, 1972," at 33 (Rutgers, "largest"); "Ex-Environmental Activist," at A1 ("pollut-

ers"); David Schoenbrod, "Confessions of an Ex-Elitist," *Commentary* 36, 38 (November 1999).

79. "No Room in the Corporate Inn," *Yale Advocate*, October 23, 1969, at 7 (emphasis in the original); "Placement Crisis: Growing Unrest With Law Firms," id. at 1 (questionnaires); "Law Firm Queries Advocated," *Harvard Law Record*, September 18, 1969, at 1 (discussing origins of questionnaire circulated by Harvard Law Student Mark Green, after he spent the summer working with Ralph Nader); "Only 10% Answer Questionnaire: Law Firm Survey Response Small," *Harvard Law Record*, October 30, 1969, at 1; "Nader Petition Circulated; Will Be Sent to Law Firms," *Columbia Law School News*, October 27, 1969, at 3.

80. Supra, Chapter 3, text accompanying notes 6–15.

81. "Journal Considers Reform," *Yale Advocate*, December 15, 1969, at 7; Paul Savoy, "Toward a New Politics of Legal Education," 79 *Yale L. J.* 444 (1970); "Journal Adopts Jeffress Plan," *Yale Advocate*, February 9, 1970, at 6; "Legal Theory and Legal Education," 79 *Yale L. J.* 1153, 1153 (1970) (the note was written by Rand Rosenblatt); "Twenty Years With the Editors," id. at 1198, 1204.

82. "Professors Speak Out on Legal Education and the Selection of Dean: Tom Emerson," *Yale Advocate*, October 23, 1969, at 3, 4; Comment, "The New Public Interest Lawyers," 79 *Yale L. J.* 1069, 1107, 1139 (1970); Stephen Wexler, "Practicing Law for Poor People," id. at 1049; Edgar and Jean Camper Cahn, "Power to the People or the Profession?—The Public Interest in Public Interest Law," id. at 1005; Eugene Rostow, "Thurman Arnold," id. at 983; Abe Fortas, "Thurman Arnold and the Theatre of the Law," id. at 988; "Introduction to the Issue," id. at 979, 981.

83. Russell Pearce, "Lawyers as America's Governing Class," 8 *Univ. Chicago Roundtable* 381, 419, 420 (2001).

84. Supra, text accompanying Chapter 4, note 91.

CHAPTER EIGHT

1. Yale Law School Governing Board Minutes (enlarged), February 24, February 27, 1970 (hereafter YLS Governing Board Minutes); David Trubek to Kingman Brewster, January 23, 1970, Box 132, Folder 3, Kingman Brewster Papers, Yale University Archives (hereafter Brewster Papers) ("erosion," "trouble"); John Simon to Brewster, December 20, 1969, id., ("difficult"); Charles Reich to Brewster, November 16, 1969, id. ("unhappy"); Ralph Brown to Brewster, February 17, 1970, id., Folder 2, id. (Rostow). See, e.g., Alexander Bickel to Brewster, December 22, 1969, id. Folder 3, (Manning); Simon to Brewster, December 20, 1969 (Wellington); Robert Stevens to Brewster, December 24, 1969, id., Folder 3 (Goldstein).

2. W. A. Brockett to Brewster, October 22, 1969, Box 132, Folder 3, Brewster Papers ("hard-liner"); J. Otis Cochran to Alexander Bickel, March 30, 1970, Box 2, Folder 36, Alexander Bickel Papers, Yale University Archives (hereafter Bickel Papers) ("cordial"); confidential interview. (Ralph Brown likewise recalled that several professors believed that Goldstein's behavior at Pollak's house disqualified him from becoming dean. Geoffrey Kabaservice interview with Ralph Brown, 1992.)

3. Michael Tigar, "New Frontiers," 78 *Yale L. J.* 892, 900, 901 (1969); Statement of the Elected Student Representatives of the Yale Law School to the Yale Corporation, n.d., Box 131, Folder 4, Brewster Papers (signed by William Brockett, J. William Heckman, John

Rupp, Pattrick Murray, an illegible name, and Benjamin Stein); Richard Balzer, Ann Hill, Walt Wagoner to Kingman Brewster, November 18, 1969, Box 132, Folder 2, id. ("push," "hard put"). There are a number of student letters to Brewster in id., Folders 2–4.

4. YLS Governing Board Minutes, March 7, 1970.

5. "Immigrant's Son to Head Yale Law," *New York Times*, March 10, 1970, at A1, 49; "Action-Oriented Dean," id. at A49.

6. Robert Brustein, *Making Scenes: A Personal History of the Turbulent Years at Yale 1966–1979* 119 (1981); "Lexcetera," 17 *Yale L. Report* 1 (Summer 1971) (Brewster); Yale University Council Report of the Committee on the Law School, December 3, 1970, Box 43, Folder: University Council, Dean's Files, Yale University Archives (hereafter Dean's Files); and see T. Bingham to Lloyd Cutler, ["Data requested on the Yale Law School" for the University Council Report], October 30, 1970, id.

7. Geoffrey Kabaservice, *The Guardians: Kingman Brewster, His Circle, and the Rise of the Liberal Establishment* 421 (2004); interview with Stephen Cohen, 2004; John Hart Ely, *War and Responsibility: Constitutional Lessons of Vietnam and Its Aftermath* 33 (1993) (Cooper-Church was enacted in modified form; McGovern-Hatfield defeated); David Maraniss, *First in His Class: The Biography of Bill Clinton* 234 (1995) ("Clinton rarely attending"); Statement released by Student Association, April 20, 1972, Box 43, Folder: Student Organizations, Dean's Files; interview with Ann Hill, 2002.

8. Bingham to Cutler, October 30, 1970 ("relative success"). (The number of Chicano and Puerto Rican students at the school remained low, as it probably did in most elite eastern law schools. As late as 1972–73, about 1.5 percent of the student body was Chicano and Puerto Rican. Albert Sanchez to James Thomas, March 20, 1973, Box 43, Folder: Student Organizations, Dean's Files); Vicki Jackson, Louise Nemschoff, Anne Simon, *The Women's Law School Companion* 13, 10, 2, 4, 6 (1974); interview with Ann Hill, 2002; Statement released by Student Association, April 20, 1972.

9. Class Notes '70, 18 *Yale L. Report* 27 (Spring 1972); Class Notes '71, 23 *Yale L. Report* 38 (Fall 1976); and see Class Notes '72, 24 *Yale L. Report* 36–37 (Fall 1977).

10. Interview with C. Edwin Baker, 2004; Mark Green, "The Young Lawyers, 1972: Goodbye to Pro Bono," *New York*, February 21, 1972, 29, 33 (Reich). See, e.g., "The Application Explosion," *Stanford Law School Journal*, February 11, 1971, at 1.

11. Harry Wellington to Friedrich and Eva Kessler, January 27, 1971, Box 1, Folder K, Dean's Files; Wellington to Ronald Dworkin, December 7, 1970, Box 1, Folder D, Dean's Files (making same point); Yale University Council Report of the Committee on the Law School, December 3, 1970, and Yale University Council Report of the Committee on the Law School, April 18, 1969, Box 56, Folder: Council Committee, Dean's Files; Robert Bork to Alexander Bickel, October 18, 1970, Box 82, Folder 23, Bickel Papers.

12. Abraham Goldstein, "The Changing Mood: A Report from the Dean," 18 *Yale L. Report* 19, 20 (Fall–Winter 1971–72) ("psychodrama"). I have not been able to locate reference in print by Goldstein to "the dark ages." Goldstein most likely would have made the remark at an Alumni Weekend (Abraham Goldstein to author, April 24, 2003), perhaps as an off-the-cuff comment when he spoke to alumni of "The Changing Mood." Some reports have Goldstein alluding to "the dark years." Class Notes '70, 19 *Yale L. Report* 39 (Spring 1973).

13. "Lexcetera," 17 *Yale L. Report* 1 (Summer 1971). Emphasis in the original.

14. Wini Breines, *Community and Organization in the New Left, 1962–1968: The Great Refusal* 18, 32, 95 (1989).

15. I cannot even say this with complete certainty, however, since I found letters about

Griffiths's teaching in the Brewster Papers, infra n. 49, an odd location for evaluations of an assistant professor.

16. Kabaservice, *Guardians*, at 429–30; Jeremy Weinberg, "Long Live the King's Yale: How Kingman Brewster's University Survived and Thrived in the 1960s" 49, 19–20 (Yale College senior essay, 1992); Richard Merelman, *Pluralism at Yale: The Culture of Political Science in America* 74–101 (2003); and see John Morton Blum, *A Life with History* 184–85 (2004); Arthur Charpentier to Richard N. Cooper, November 1, 1972, Box 53, Folder: Budget-Related Correspondence, Dean's Files; Unmarked, undated statement, id., Folder: '72–73 Budget, id. Goldstein's successor, Harry Wellington, felt similarly. Wellington to Howard Friedman, October 13, 1977, Box 16, Chron File, id.

17. Kabaservice, *Guardians*, at 199 ("complex"); Alvin Kernan, *In Plato's Cave* 132–34 (1999); John Perry Miller, *Creating Academic Settings: High Craft and Low Cunning* 103–5 (1991).

18. Bruce Ackerman, "The Marketplace of Ideas," 90 *Yale L. J.* 1131, 1134–35 (1981). Emphasis in the original. On evaluations, see email, Lee Albert to author, n.d.; Richard Abel to author, October 30, 2001; Richard Abel, "Evaluating Evaluations: How Should Law Schools Judge Teaching," 40 *J. Legal Ed.* 407 (1990).

19. YLS Governing Board Minutes, December 10, 1970, and November 14, 1972; Arthur Leff, "Injury, Ignorance and Spite—The Dynamics of Coercive Collection," 80 *Yale L. J.* 1 (1970); "Contract As a Thing," 19 *Am. U. L. Rev.* 131 (1970); "Medical Devices and Paramedical Personnel: A Preliminary Context for Emergency Problems," 1967 *Wash. U. L. Q.* 332 (1967); "Unconscionability and the Code—The Emperor's New Clause," 115 *U. Pa. L. Rev.* 485 (1965); John Hart Ely, "Legislative and Administrative Motivation in Constitutional Law," 79 *Yale L. J.* 1205 (1970); Fred Shapiro, "The Most-Cited Articles from The Yale Law Journal," id., 100: 1449, 1462 (1991); Robert Bork to Alexander Bickel, October 18 1970, Box 82, Folder 23, Bickel Papers; Meeting on Appointments with Elected Students 1971–72, Box 34, Folder: Appointments Committee 1970–74, Dean's Files. Reisman's curriculum vitae in Box 131, Folder 4, Brewster Papers, included two books in press, *Nullity and Revision: The Review and Enforcement of International Judgments and Awards* (1970) and *The Art of the Possible: Diplomatic Alternatives in the Middle East* (1970), and a number of articles, including Myres McDougal and Reisman, "Rhodesia and the United Nations: The Lawfulness of International Concern," 62 *Am. J. Int'l. Law* 721 (1969); Reisman, "The Enforcement of International Judgments and Awards," id., 63: 1 (1968); Reisman, "The Multifaceted Phenomenon of International Arbitration," 24 *Arb. J.* 69 (1969); Reisman, Book Review, 20 *Syracuse L. Rev.* 166 (1968); Reisman, "International Non-Liquet: Recrudescence and Transformation," 3 *Int'l. Lawyer* 770 (1969); McDougal, Harold Lasswell and Reisman, "Theories about International Law: Prologue to A Configurative Jurisprudence," 8 *Va. J. Int'l. Law* 189 (1969); Lung-Chu Chen and Reisman, "Who Owns Taiwan: A Search for International Title," 85 *Yale L. J.* 599 (1972).

20. Laura Kalman, *Legal Realism at Yale* 195–99 (1986) (the faculty also denied a promotion to John Frank during the 1950s, but its decision was based on its evaluation of his work as superficial. Id. at 195); YLS Governing Board Minutes, March 7, 1959.

21. Bonnie Collier interview with Abraham Goldstein, 1996 (at least one of those fired, however, was unaware of any efforts by the dean to help him find a job elsewhere. Interview with Lee Albert, 2001); Eugene Rostow to Tonia Ouellette, December 3, 1992, Box 25, Folder O, Dean's Files; Rostow to Tonia Ouellette, February 11, 1993, id. ("promotion controversy").

22. Interview with Guido Calabresi, 2001; Kalman, *Legal Realism at Yale*, 195–99.

23. Mark Tushnet, "Critical Legal Studies: A Political History," 100 *Yale L. J.* 1515, 1530, n. 60 (1991); Louis Pollak to Victor Stone, March 13, 1968, Box 32, Folder R, Dean's Files; interview with Ronald Dworkin, 2002.

24. Abraham Goldstein, "A Law School Memoir," *Yale Alumni Magazine* 38, 38 (February 1977).

25. Louis Pollak to Truman Hobbs, July 12, 1966, Box 31, Folder H, Dean's Files.

26. Interview with Harry Wellington, 2001.

27. Report of the Inspection Team on the Yale Law School, May, 1975, Box 33, Folder: Expanded Governing Board, Dean's Files.

28. "Yale Law: Fork in the Road," *National Law Journal*, June 29, 1981, at 1, 27, ("purge"); John Schlegel, "Notes Toward an Intimate, Opinionated, and Affectionate History of the Conference on Critical Legal Studies," 36 *Stan. L. Rev.* 391, 392 (1984) ("'left'"); and see Calvin Trillin, "A Reporter at Large: Harvard Law," *New Yorker*, 53, 64, (April 13, 1992); (Yale's left "purged"); Bonnie Collier interview with Abraham Goldstein, 1996 ("don't," "unmistakably"); interview with Goldstein, 2001; John Griffiths to Tonia Ouellette, February 11, 1993 ("structural firing"). I am grateful to John Griffiths for giving me a copy of this letter.

29. Interview with Charles Reich, 2002; and see Tonia Ouellette, "The History of Academic Freedom and Tenure: A Study of the Departures from Yale Law School in the Late 1960s and Early 1970s," December 18, 1992, hereafter cited as "A Study of the Departures." I am grateful to Ouellette for sharing a copy of her paper with me.

30. Abraham Goldstein, Book Review, 82 *Yale L. J.* 1092, 1092, 1093 (1973) (reviewing *New Directions in Legal Education: A Report Prepared for the Carnegie Commission on Higher Education* [1972] [quoting Packer and Ehrlich on "academic wasteland"]; Robert Stevens, *Law School: Legal Education in America from the 1850s to the 1980s* 242 (1983). See Preble Stolz, "The Two-Year Law School: The Day The Music Died," 25 *J. Legal Ed.* 37 (1973).

31. Abraham Goldstein, "Redirecting Legal Education," 17 *Yale L. Report* 3, 4, 5 (Fall 1970).

32. Harry Kalven and Hans Zeisel, *The American Jury* (1966); Neil Duxbury, *Patterns of American Jurisprudence* 330–63 (1995).

33. Richard Posner, *Overcoming Law* 85 (1995) ("adoption"); Daniel Farber, "Of Coase and the Canons; Reflections on Law and Economics," in J. M. Balkin and Sanford Levinson, eds., *Legal Canons* 184, 187 (2000) ("don't matter"); Ronald Coase, "The Problem of Social Cost," 3 *J. L & Econ.* 1 (1960); Duxbury, *Patterns of American Jurisprudence*, at 395 ("bomb"); Richard Posner, "The Economic Approach to Law," 53 *Tex. L. Rev.* 757, 775 (1975) (legislation designed); Richard Posner, *The Economics of Justice* 128, 133, 138–39 (1981).

34. Duxbury, *Patterns of American Jurisprudence*, at 310–11 (and suggesting it was bad intellectual history).

35. Robert Bork and Ward Bowman, "The Crisis in Antitrust," 65 *Colum. L. Rev.* 363 (1965); Bork, *The Antitrust Paradox: A Policy at War With Itself* (1978); Duxbury, *Patterns of American Jurisprudence*, at 363 ("only"); Ralph Winter, "Improving the Economic Status of Negroes Through Laws Against Discrimination: A Reply to Professor Sovern," 34 *U. Chi. L. Rev.* 917 (1967); Harry Wellington and Ralph Winter, "The Limits of Collective Bargaining in Public Employment," 78 *Yale L. J.* 1107 (1969); Harry Wellington and Ralph Winter, *The Unions and the Cities* (1971); Robert Ellickson, "Symposium on Post-

Chicago Law and Economics: Bringing Culture and Human Frailty to Rational Actors: A Critique of Classical Law and Economics," 65 *Chi.-Kent L. Rev.* 23, 28 (1989).

36. Guido Calabresi, "Some Thoughts on Risk Distribution and the Law of Torts," 70 *Yale L. J.* 499 (1961); Richard Posner, "Economic Approach to Law," 53 *Tex. L. Rev.* 757, 759–61 (1975); Guido Calabresi, "An Introduction to Legal Thought: Four Approaches to Law and to the Allocation of Body Parts," 55 *Stan. L. Rev.* 2113, 2138 (2003) ("Yale"); Guido Calabresi, *The Cost of Accidents* 26 (1970).

37. Bryant Garth and Joyce Sterling, "From Legal Realism to Law and Society: Re-shaping Law for the Last Stages of the Social Activist State," 32 *Law & Soc'y. Rev.* 409 (1998); David Trubek, "Back to the Future: The Short, Happy Life of the Law & Society Movement," 18 *Fla. St. U. L. Rev.* 4, 48, 39 (1990) ("objectivist"); Robert Kidder, "From the Editor," 22 *Law & Soc'y. Rev.* 625, 625 (1988) ("defeated"); David Trubek, Austin Sarat, William Felstiner, Herbert Kritzer, and Joel Grossman, "The Costs of Ordinary Litiga-tion," 31 *UCLA L. Rev.* 72 (1983) ("defeated"); Marc Galanter, "Reading the Landscapes of Disputes: What We Know and Don't Know (and Think We Know) about our Allegedly Contentious and Litigious Society," id. at 4; Reid Hastie et al., *Inside the Jury* (1983); Malcolm Feeley, *The Process Is the Punishment: Handling Cases in a Lower Criminal Court* (1979); Stewart Macaulay, "Non-Contractual Relations in Business: A Preliminary Study," 28 *Am. Soc. Rev.* 55 (1963); John Heinz and Edward Laumann, *Chicago Lawyers: The Social Structure of the Bar* (1982).

38. See Bryant Garth, "James Willard Hurst as Entrepreneur for the Field of Law and Social Science," 18 *Law & Hist. Rev.* 37, 42 (2000).

39. Daniel Ernst, "Willard Hurst and the Administrative State: From Williams to Wis-consin," id. at 1, 22, 23 ("gossip"); William Eskridge and Philip Frickey, "An Historical and Critical Introduction to the Legal Process," in Eskridge and Frickey, eds., Henry Hart and Albert Sacks, *The Legal Process: Basic Problems in the Making and Application of Law* lxx–lxxiv (1958) (1994 ed.) (casebook); Stewart Macaulay, "Willard's Law School," 1997 *Wisc. L. Rev.* 1163 (1997); William Novak, "Law, Capitalism, and the Liberal State: The Historical Sociology of James Willard Hurst," 18 *Law & Hist. Rev.* 97, 98 (2000) ("big"); Garth, "J. Willard Hurst as Entrepreneur," at 41 ("progeny"). See, e.g., Willard Hurst, *Law and the Conditions of Freedom in the Nineteenth-Century United States* (1956) and *Law and Economic Growth: The Legal History of the Lumber Industry in Wisconsin, 1836–1915* (1964).

40. Garth and Sterling, "From Legal Realism to Law and Society," at 431. See, e.g., Alexander Bickel, *The Unpublished Opinions of Mr. Justice Brandeis: The Supreme Court at Work* (1957); Bickel, "Mr. Taft Rehabilitates the Court," 79 *Yale L. J.* 1 (1969); Bickel and Benno Schmidt, *History of the Supreme Court of the United States: The Judiciary and Responsible Government, 1910–21* (1985); Robert Stevens and B. S. Yaney, *The Restrictive Practices Court: A Study of the Judicial Processes and Economic Policy* (1965); Brian Abel-Smith and Robert Stevens, with the assistance of Rosalind Brooke, *Lawyers and the Courts: A Sociological Study of the English Legal System, 1750–1965* (1967); Robert Stevens, "Two Cheers for 1870: The American Law School," 5 *Perspectives in Am. Hist.* 405 (1971).

41. Lester Mazor, "The Materials of Law Study: 1971," in Herbert Packer and Thomas Ehrlich, eds., *New Directions in Legal Education* 319 (1972); Carl Auerbach, "Perspective: Division of Labor in the Law Schools and Education of Law Teachers," 23 *J. Legal Ed.* 251, 253 (1970); Garth and Sterling, "From Legal Realism to Law and Society," at 426; Jefferson Fordham, "Eight Years of Challenge and Development in the Life of the Association of American Law Schools," 24 *J. Legal Ed.* 94, 105 (1971).

42. YLS Governing Board Minutes, April 24, 1970; Louis Pollak to the Faculty Appointments Committee, February 10, 1970, Box 34, Folder: Appointments Committee 1970–74, Dean's Files.

43. John Griffiths, "Charity versus Social Insurance in Unemployment Compensation Laws," 73 *Yale L. J.* 357 (1963); "Extradition Habeas Corpus," 74 *Yale L. J.* 78 (1964); Charles Reich, "The Law of the Planned Society," 75 *Yale L. J.* 1227, 1235 (1966) (final examination); email, John Griffiths to author, February 5, 2002. Wellington explicitly proposed this change in rules after the Griffiths vote. Harry Wellington to Appointments Committee, September 24, 1970, Box 34, Folder: Appointments Committee 1970–74, Dean's Files.

44. *In re Griffiths*, 413 U.S. 717 (1973); Griffiths to author, February 5, 2002 ("close"); John Griffiths to Thomas Emerson, cc: The Faculty, April 25, 1969, Box 38, Grading 1967–1970, Dean's Files ("hypocrisy"); John Griffiths to the Teaching Faculty, February 21, 1968, Box 63, Folder 26, Bickel Papers ("hostile").

45. Quotations from Griffiths to author, February 5, 2002; John Griffiths and Cathryn Grey, *The Draft Law and Antiwar Protests* (1968); John Griffiths, *The Draft Law: A 'College Outline' for the Selective Service Act and Regulations* (1968); "University Releases Draft Law Pamphlet," *Yale Daily News*, December 2, 1968, at 1.

46. Griffiths to author, February 5, 2002; John Griffiths and J. William Heckman, *The Draft Law* vii–viii (3d ed., 1970) (discussing history of pamphlets).

47. Griffiths to author, February 5, 2002; "Interrogations in New Haven: The Impact of Miranda," 76 *Yale L. J.* 1519, 1613 (1967); John Griffiths and Richard Ayres, "A Postscript to the Miranda Project: Interrogation of Draft Protestors," 77 *Yale L. J.* 300 (1967).

48. Ouellette, "A Study of the Departures" (prosecution of Rostow); email, Griffiths to author, February 7, 2002; Eugene Rostow to Abraham Goldstein, May 16, 1971, May 6, 1971, in Box 53, Folder: Faculty Correspondence and Misc., Dean's Files.

49. John Ely and John Griffiths to the Faculty, September 22, 1969, Box 36, Folder: Memoranda—Misc. (1965–70), Dean's Files; Griffiths to author, February 5, 2002 ("reservations"); email, William Felstiner to author, April 18, 2001. I saw no negative letters and found two quite positive ones. Alex Capron to Louis Pollak, April 20, 1970, Box 131, Folder 4, Brewster Papers; Malcolm Pfunder to Louis Pollak, April 19, 1970, id., though Capron's did mention that some students had been dissatisfied with Griffiths's classes in 1968–69.

50. Griffiths to author, February 5, 2002. Griffiths emphasized that he remembered Pollak's words clearly. Id.

51. The professor, Arthur Rosett, received tenure anyway. Conversation with Rosett, 2004.

52. Herbert Packer, "Two Models of the Criminal Process," 113 *U. Pa. L. Rev.* 1, 13, 61, 66–67 (1964) ("crime control," "assembly line," "due process," "obstacle course," "probably"); Packer, *The Limits of the Criminal Sanction* 342–44 (1968).

53. John Griffiths, "Ideology in Criminal Procedure or A Third 'Model' of the Criminal Process," 79 *Yale L. J.* 359, 362–64, 367 (1970); *In re Gault*, 387 U.S. 1, 20 (1967); Griffiths to author, February 5, 2002; Laura Kalman, *Abe Fortas* 250–55 (1990).

54. Griffiths, "Ideology in Criminal Procedure," at 371, 391, 412, 372, 373, 417.

55. Daniel Bell, *The End of Ideology: On the Exhaustion of Political Ideas in the Fifties* 350, 400 (1988 ed.).

56. Griffiths to author, February 5, 2002; Griffiths to Ouellette, February 11, 1993 (Bickel and Bork).

57. Packer, *The Limits of the Criminal Sanction*, at 5. For a contemporary reconsidera-

tion of Packer that provides an overview of criticisms of his work, see Kent Roach, "Four Models of the Criminal Process," 89 J. Crim. Law & Criminology 671 (1999). For a discussion of legal scholarship during the 1970s, see Ronald Dworkin, "Legal Research," 102 Daedalus 53 (Spring 1973).

58. YLS Governing Board Minutes, November 5, 1965 ("trail," "variance," "essential"); Abraham Goldstein, "Reflections on Two Models: Inquisitorial Themes in American Criminal Procedure," 26 Stan. L. Rev. 1009, 1012 (1974).

59. Charles Reich to Alexander Bickel, April 17, 1970, Box 7, Folder 125, Bickel Papers; Charles Reich to Harry Wellington, April 16, 1970, Box 1, Folder G, Dean's Files ("What kind of work," "future"); Griffiths to author, February 5, 2002.

60. John Griffiths, "The Limits of Criminal Law Scholarship," 79 Yale L. J. 1388, 1471, 1470, 1391 (1970); Griffiths to author, February 5, 2002. This was not the only slash-and-burn book review Griffiths wrote at the time. See Griffiths, Book Review, 77 Yale L. J. 827 (1968) (reviewing Ann Fagan Ginger, The New Draft Law: A Manual for Lawyers and Counselors).

61. YLS Governing Board Minutes, November 5, 1965; interview with Reich; Herbert Packer to Alexander Bickel, March 15, 1970, Box 6, Folder 16, Bickel Papers ("shambles"); Herbert Packer to Kingman Brewster, December 3, 1969, Box 132, Folder 1, Brewster Papers.

62. Alexander Bickel to Frederick Wiener, April 3, 1968, Box 10, Folder 190, Bickel Papers; Griffiths to author, February 5, 2002; Alexander Bickel to Herbert Packer, April 9, 1970, Box 10, Folder 206, Bickel Papers.

63. Herbert Packer to Leon Lipson, March 17, 1970, Box 6, Folder 16, Bickel Papers (Packer sent copies of the letter to Bickel, Goldstein and Wellington); Packer to Benjamin Heineman, October 19, 1970, Box 37: Folder Yale Law Journal, Dean's Files ("major portion"; "belligerently"). Heineman was the editor-in-chief of the Journal); "Prof. Herbert Packer Gives Views On Politics, Criminal Law, and Wine," Stanford Law School Journal, May 11, 1972, at 4, 6 (stroke and students); George Packer, Blood of the Liberals 246–51, 268–71 (2000); interview with Wellington.

64. Louis Pollak to Steven Duke, April 20, 1970, Box 131, Folder 4, Brewster Papers ("petulant") (I have not been able to find Duke's letter); Abraham Goldstein to the Governing Board, April 21, 1970, Box 132, Folder 11, Brewster Papers; conversation with Clyde Summers, 2004. I have been unable to locate the Appointments Committee memorandum.

65. Interview with Reich.

66. Exhibit 1, May 5, 1970, YLS Governing Board Minutes, April 24, 1970. The faculty voted to extend his term as assistant professor by a vote of 32–1.

67. See, e.g., John Griffiths, "The Requirement of a 'Voluntary Act' in the Ghanian Law of Criminal Responsibility," 10 U. Ghana L. J. 149 (1973); "The Distribution of Legal Services in the Netherlands," 4 British J. Law and Soc'y. 260 (1977); "Legal Reasoning from the External and the Internal Perspectives," 53 N.Y.U. L. Rev. 1124 (1978); "Is Law Important?," 54 N.Y.U. L. Rev. 339 (1978); "The General Theory of Litigation—A First Step," 5 Zeitschrift fur Rechtssoziologie 145 (1983); "The Division of Labor in Social Control," in Donald Black, ed., Toward a General Theory of Social Control, 2 vols., 1:37 (1984); "Heeft de Rechtssociologie een Toegevoegde Waarde? Reflecties Naar Aanleiding van een Oratie van Kees Schuyt," 59 Mens en Maatschappij 82 (1984); "Village Justice in the Netherlands," 23 J. Legal Pluralism 17 (1984); "Recent Anthropology of Law in the Netherlands and Its Historical Background," in K. Von Benda Beckmann and F. Strijbosch, eds., Anthropology of

Law in the Netherlands: Essays on Legal Pluralism 11 (1986); "What Is Legal Pluralism?," 24 *J. Legal Pluralism* 1 (1986); "De Rechtspsychologie Benadering van Rechterlijk Beslissings-gedrag: Enkele Kanntekenigen Bij Recent Nederlands OnderZoek," 61 *Mens en Maatschappij* 199 (1986); "What Do Dutch Lawyers Actually Do in Divorce Cases?," 20 *Law and Society Rev.* 135 (1986); "Een Toeschouwers Perspectief op de Euthanasie Disscusie," 62 *Nederlands Juristenblad* 691 (1987); "De Sociale Werking van Rechtsregels en het Emancipatoire Potentieel van Wetgeving," in T. Havinga and B. Sloot, eds., *Recht: Bondgenoot of Barriere Bij Emancipatie* 27 (1990); "Rechtssociologische Reflecties op het Idee van Dading in Plaats van Strafrecht," in P. G. Wiewel, ed., *Dading in Plaats van Strafrecht* 135 (1993); "Euthanasie als Controle-Probleem," 68 *Nederlands Juristenblad* 121 (1993); "Dworkin Over Euthanasie," 68 *Nederlands Juristenblad* 1313 (1993); "The Regulation of Euthanasia and Related Medical Procedures that Shorten Life in the Netherlands," 1 *Medical L. Int'l.* 137 (1994); "Recent Developments in the Netherlands Concerning Euthanasia and Other Medical Behavior that Shortens Life," 1 *Medical L. Int'l.* 347 (1994); "Assisted Suicide in the Netherlands: The *Chabot* Case," 58 *Modern L. Rev.* 232 (1995); "Assisted Suicide in the Netherlands: Postscript to *Chabot*," id. at 895 (1995); "De Jury als Spiegel voor Neder-lands," 70 *Nederlands Juristenblad* 1359 (1995) (trans. "Dutch Political Culture Reflected in the Mirror of the Jury," 1997 *Maastricht J.* 153 [no. 4] [1997]); "Normative and Rational Choice Accounts of Human Social Behavior," 2 *European J. Law and Econ.* 285 (1996); *De Sociale Werking van Recht: Een Kennismaking met de Rechtssociologie en Recht* (ed.) (1996); "Euthanasie: Legalisering of Decriminalisering?," 72 *Nederlands Juristenblad* 619 (1997); "De Interdisciplinaire Studie van de Rechtspolitek," 1998 *Recht der Werkelijkheid* 3 (no. 1) (1998); "Legal Knowledge and the Social Working of Law: The Case of Euthanasia," in H. van Schooten, ed., *Semiotics and Legislation, Jurisprudential, Institutional and Sociological Perspectives* 81 (1999); "Wat Is de Medische Exceptie?," 54 *Medisch Contact* 656 (1999); "Self-Regulation by the Dutch Medical Profession of Medical Behavior that Potentially Shortens Life," in H. Karabbendam and H. M. ten Napel, eds., *Regulating Morality: A Comparison of the Role of the State in Mastering the Mores in the Netherlands and the United States* (2000); "Some questions to Hans Crombag About Dutch Psychology of Law," in P. van Koppen and N. Roos, eds., *Rationality, Information and Progress in Law and Psychology, Liber Amiocorum Hans Crombag* 11 (2000); "Legal Pluralism," in N. J. Smelser and P. B. Bates, eds., *International Encyclopedia of the Social and Behavioral Sciences* xx (2001); "Is the Dutch Case Unique," in A. J. Klijn, ed., *Regulating Physician-Negotiated Death* xx (2002). Though I do not read Dutch, I have cited a number, but by no means all, of Griffiths's publications lest readers of American law reviews conclude he had written little after he left Yale.

68. John Hart Ely to Abraham Goldstein, February 12, 1971, Box 63, Folder: John Hart Ely; email, Lee Albert to author, September 4, 2001; interview with Reich; Griffiths to Ouellette, February 11, 1993.

69. Interviews with Albert and Larry Simon, 2002; Abel to author, April 30, 2002.

70. The file of Governing Board Minutes for 1970–75 is incomplete. The meeting on Hudec occurred in mid-February 1972. Guido Calabresi to W. Michael Reisman, September 12, 1989, Box 27, Chron File, Dean's Files (describing the confusion in the files and saying he had checked Hudec's file). The crucial meeting on Trubek apparently occurred in December 1972. Id.; David Trubek to Abraham Goldstein, December 18, 1972, Box 44, Blue Notebook, Dean's Files (resigning as chair of the Program in Law and Modernization, in part because of the Governing Board's recent action). Because of the absence of Governing Board minutes, I cannot tell whether the Trubek and Hudec cases actually

came to a vote, or what the vote was. The Governing Board minutes for the Albert meeting have not survived either.

71. Interviews with Albert and Louis Pollak, 2001 (preemption, pedestrian); Ouellette, "A Study of the Departures" ("tenure decision"); Yale Law School Faculty Minutes, December 19, 1968, 10:00 A.M., Extension of the December 18th Meeting; Report of the Curriculum Committee on the Grading System, Tentative Draft, Richard Hughes File; Report of the Disciplinary Committee to the Dean and Teaching Faculty concerning Mr. Eric L. Clay '72, Box 131, Folder 2, Brewster Papers. Hudec's book reviews were in 5 *J. World Trade Law* 365 (1971); 12 *Va. J. Int. Law* 152 (1971). For the articles see, "The GATT Legal System: A Diplomat's Jurisprudence," 4 *J. World Trade Law* 615 (1970); "Gatt or GABB? The Future Design of the General Agreement on Tariffs and Trade," 80 *Yale L. J.* 1299 (1971). The GATT book appeared later: Hudec, *The GATT Legal System and World Trade Diplomacy* (1975); "Bibliography of works by Robert E. Hudec (as of December 31, 2000)," *The Political Economy of International Trade Law: Essays in Honor of Robert Hudec*, ed. Daniel Kennedy and James Southwick 667 (2002); and see Joel Trachtman, "Robert E. Hudec 1934–2003," 97 *Am. J. Int'l. Law* 311 (2003).

72. Emails, Richard Abel to author, October 30, 2001 (quotations); and April 30, 2002.

73. Harry Wellington to Norman Dorsen, January 15, 1969, Box 1, Folder D, Dean's Files ("absolutely first-rate" and reporting judgment of some colleagues); Harry Wellington and Lee Albert, "Statutory Interpretation and the Political Process: A Comment on *Sinclair* v. *Atkinson*," 72 *Yale L. J.* 1547 (1963); Martha Davis, *Brutal Need: Lawyers and the Welfare Rights Movement* 74 (1993) ("superior"); Albert to author, September 4, 2001 ("frightful"); "Conference [with students]," n.d. (ca. November 1972), Box 82, Folder 18, Bickel Papers.

74. Lee Albert, "Standing to Challenge Administrative Action: An Inadequate Surrogate for Claims for Relief," 83 *Yale L. J.* 425 (1974); Lee Albert and Larry Simon, "Enforcing Subpoenas Against the President: The Question of Mr. Jaworski's Authority," 74 *Colum. L. Rev.* 545 (1974); Guido Calabresi to Herman Schwartz, January 3, 1975 (discussing Bickel's reactions) (letter given me by Calabresi); Albert to author, September 4, 2001 (quotations); interview with Albert ("nuances").

75. Calabresi to Schwartz, January 3, 1975.

76. John Simon to Earl Warren, October 24, 1966, letter given to me by Larry Simon (praising Simon as student [Larry Simon and John Simon were not related to each other]); Larry Simon, "Twice in Jeopardy," 75 *Yale L. J.* 262 (1965).

77. Interview with Larry Simon, 2002.

78. Id.; Simon to Warren, October 24, 1966 ("lively"); interview with Calabresi, 2002; Meeting on Appointments with Elected Students, 1971/72; Meeting with Elected Student Representatives; "Conference [with students]," n.d. [November, 1972], Box 82, Folder 18, Bickel Papers; "Law in High School Is Course Objective," *Yale Advocate*, April 3, 1969, 1.

79. Larry Simon, "The School Finance Decisions: Collective Bargaining and Future Finance Systems," 82 *Yale L. J.* 409 (1973). Larry Simon, "*Serrano* Symposium: The Death Knell to Ad Valorem School Financing: Part III," 5 *Urban Lawyer* 104 (1973); interviews with Steven Duke, 2001, and Guido Calabresi, 2001 (doubt about Simon's scholarly intentions); Albert ("complained"); Simon ("drawer," "stupid"); Larry Simon to Art Leff, October 22, 1973, Box 34, Folder: Appointments Committee 1970–73, Dean's Files (planned shift in focus).

80. Addenda, November 20, 1973, YLS Governing Board Minutes; John Simon to Larry Simon, December 11, 1973, letter given me by Larry Simon.

81. Interview with Larry Simon; Abraham Goldstein to Governing Board, Box 291, Folder 5, Brewster Papers.

82. Charles Clark and David Trubek, "The Creative Role of the Judge: Restraint and Freedom in the Common Law Tradition," 71 *Yale L. J.* 255, 268 (1961); David Trubek, "Back to the Future: The Short, Happy Life of the Law and Society Movement," 18 *Fla. St. Univ. L. Rev.* 4, 23, 24 (1990).

83. Interview with Calabresi, 2001 (desire for work); Ouellette, "A Study of the Departures" ("fancy," resentment); interview with Louis Pollak, 2001.

84. Trubek, "Back to the Future," at 6 ("amenable"); Trubek to Goldstein, December 18, 1972. Among others, Wheeler's program drew Donald Black, who taught at Yale during the early 1970s and would become University Professor of the Social Sciences at Virginia.

85. Email, David Trubek to author, January 3, 2002 ("initially"); Trubek, "Back to the Future," at 6, 31.

86. Trubek, "Back to the Future," at 30–31 ("need," "Dean"); James Gardner to William D. Carmichael, May 22, 1972, Box 44, Blue Notebook, Dean's Files (quoting Trubek and agreeing with him); Trubek to author, January 3, 2002 ("both").

87. David Trubek, "Max Weber on Law and the Rise of Capitalism," 1972 *Wisc. L. Rev.* 720, 752 (1972) ("contemporary"); Trubek, "Toward a Social Theory of Law: An Essay on the Study of Law and Development," 82 *Yale L. J.* 1, 11 (1972) ("Western"); Eric Branfman, Benjamin Cohen, and David Trubek, "Measuring the Invisible Wall: Land Use Controls and the Residential Patterns of the Poor," 82 *Yale L. J.* 483 (1973); David Trubek, J. Gouvea Viera, and Paulo Fernandes de Sa, *O Mercado de Capitais e Os Incentivos Fisiais* (1971) (for a condensed version of Trubek's contribution in English, see Trubek, "Law, Planning, and the Development of the Brazilian Capital Market," Yale Law School Studies in Law and Modernization No. 3 [1971]).

88. Trubek, "Toward a Social Theory of Law," at 1, n. 2 ("liberal legalism"). David Trubek and Marc Galanter, "Scholars in Self-Estrangement: Some Reflections on the Crisis in Law and Development Studies in the United States," 1974 *Wisc. L. Rev.* 1062 (1974).

89. Tushnet, "Critical Legal Studies: A Political History," at 1533, 1531; Schlegel, "Notes Toward an Intimate, Opinionated, and Affectionate History of the Conference on Critical Legal Studies" at 393; "State Street Study Made By Students," *Yale Advocate*, April 13, 1968, at 1.

90. Email, Trubek to author, January 4, 2002.

91. Ouellette, "A Study of the Departures" ("all"); interview with Goldstein (I have not seen the evaluations); interviews with Calabresi (2001), Albert, and Pollak.

92. Infra, Chapter 10, text accompanying n. 13.

93. Interview with David Trubek, 2001; quotations from Ouellette, "A Study of the Departures."

94. Email, Richard Abel to author, October 30, 2001; Bonnie Collier interview with Robert Stevens, 1999.

95. Statement, n.d., prepared by Abel for the Appointments Committee (I am grateful to Abel for providing me with a copy of his self-assessment); Louis Pollak to Kingman Brewster and Charles Taylor, August 14, 1967, Box 130, Folder 7, Brewster Papers.

96. Abel, Statement, n.d.; interviews with Calabresi, 2001, and Harry Wellington, 2001; Guido Calabresi to Margo Melli, February 5, 1974 (letter given me by Calabresi); Student Conference, n.d., Box 832, Folder 18, Bickel Papers.

97. Abraham Goldstein to Governing Board, November 30, 1973, Box 291, Folder 5, Brewster Papers; Richard Abel, "A Bibliography of the Customary Laws of Kenya (with special reference to the Laws of Wrongs)," 2 *African Law Studies* 1 (1969) (expanded version in id. at 6: 78 [1970]); Abel, "Case Method Research in the Customary Law of Wrongs in Kenya — Part I: Individual Case Analysis," 5 *E. African L. J.* 247 (1969), and "Part II: Statistical Analysis," id. at 6: 20 (1970) (the two articles are abridged in Abel, "Customary Laws of Wrongs in Kenya: An Essay in Research Method," 17 *Am. J. Comp. Law* 573 [1973]); Abel, "A Comparative Theory of Dispute Institutions in Society," 8 *Law and Soc'y. Rev.* 217 (1974); Abel, "Law Books and Books About Law," 26 *Stan. L. Rev.* 175, 184, 228 (1973).

98. Abel to author, October 30, 2001; confidential interview.

99. Abel to author, October 30, 2001; confidential interviews.

100. Guido Calabresi to Michael Reisman, September 12, 1989, Box 27, Chron File, Dean's Files.

101. Abel to author, October 30, 2001 ("snub"); Ouellette, "A Study of the Departures" ("left quietly"); "Yale Law: Fork in the Road," at 27 ("appease").

102. Interviews with Calabresi, 2002, and Duncan Kennedy, 2001; Email, Richard Abel to author, April 30, 2002.

103. "Yale Law: Fork in the Road," at 27 (Albert); interview with Larry Simon.

104. Interviews with Calabresi, 2002, and Reich.

105. Email, Tom Grey to author, June 29, 2003 (seminar); interview with Dworkin; Dean's Report, 1971–72; Abraham Goldstein to Appointments Committee, Sept 23, 1970, Folder: Appointments Committee: 1970–74, Dean's Files; Abraham Goldstein to the Expanded Governing Board, February 3, 1972 (reporting terms of offer voted in October 1971, with quotations) and February 15, 1972, Box 291, Folder 5, Brewster Papers (reporting Dworkin had cabled his acceptance of the terms of the offer).

106. Dean's Report, 1971–72; interviews with Ronald Dworkin, 2002, and Reich; confidential interviews; YLS Governing Board Minutes, May 31, 1973 ("developments," "voted").

107. Charles Reich, *The Sorcerer of Bolinas Reef* 171 and see 226–27 (1976); Charles Reich to Abraham Goldstein, May 1, 1974, Box 291, Folder 5, Brewster Papers ("practical-minded"; "do not look"); interview with Reich.

108. Harry Wellington to A. Bartlett Giamatti, December 12, 1978, Box 16, Chron File, Dean's Files; and see Wellington to Robert Lane, December 6, 1978, id.; John Hart Ely, "Commentary," 100 *Yale L. J.* 1473, 1474 ("siege") (1991); Wellington interview with Collier, July 12, 2000.

109. Bernard Wolfman made this comment about general awareness of Yale's troubles at a Harvard Law School workshop where I presented a version of this manuscript; interview with Pollak.

110. The retirees were Fleming James, Friedrich Kessler, Harold Lasswell, Myres McDougal, James William Moore, and Fred Rodell.

111. Baker left Yale for Indiana, though he still had two years remaining as an associate professor. The faculty never voted on his promotion. Harry Wellington to Ulrich Haynes, November 15, 1978, Box 16, Chron File, Dean's Files.

112. Abraham Goldstein to Kingman Brewster, August 6, 1973, Box 291, Folder 2, Brewster Papers.

113. Report of the Inspection Team on the Yale Law School to the American Bar Association and the Association of American Law Schools, May 1975; Dean's Report 1978–79. The minimum goal of the campaign had been $10 million. Id.

114. Goldstein, "A Law School Memoir," at 39 ("moving"); email, Michael Churgin to author, March 3, 2003 ("saving," "words"); Dean's Report, 1974–75.

115. "Law School Splits on Dean Selection," *Yale Daily News*, October 22, 1974, Box 291, Folder: Law School Deanship Selection Committee 1974–75, Brewster Papers; Trudy Bialic to *Yale Daily News*, October 25, 1974, id.

116. Carl Boggs, "Rethinking the Sixties Legacy: From New Left to New Social Movements," in Staughton Lyman, ed., *Social Movements: Critiques, Concepts, Case-Studies* 331 (1995) (rejecting the thesis that protest disappeared after the 1960s and emphasizing the continuity between 1960s radicalism and what followed); Jo Freeman and Victoria Johnson, eds., *Waves of Protest: Social Movements Since the Sixties* x (1999) (maintaining there was more protest over wider range of issues in the 1970s than the 1960s). But some say that protest movements were not active on campus in the middle and late 1970s. See, e.g., Robert Rhoads, *Freedom's Web: Student Activism in an Age of Cultural Diversity* 5 (1998); Mark Boren, *Student Resistance: A History of the Unruly Subject* 189 (2001).

117. "Law School Splits on Dean Selection"; Note to Kingman Brewster, typed on Boris Bittker to Deanship Committee, October 10, 1974, Box 291, Folder 4, Brewster Papers ("mild," "Viva Guido"). The signature of the note's author is illegible.

118. Michael Darnall, Remarks to President Kingman Brewster on Selection of New Dean for Yale Law School, December 10, 1974, Box 6, Folder: Deanship, Dean's Files. The declining number of black matriculates was also addressed in Black Law Students Union to Administration, Faculty and Student Organizations Chairpersons of Yale Law School, n.d., Box 53, Folder: BLSU, Dean's Files (lamenting that there were only one-third as many black students in the class of 1977 as there had been in the class of 1972).

119. Boris Bittker to Expanded Governing Board, November 19, 1974, Box 291, Folder 4, Brewster Papers ("significant"); Law School Student Representatives to Kingman Brewster, Student Criteria For Selection of the Next Dean, n.d., id. (the signatories were Marilyn Garcia, Beverly Hodgson, Don Sloan, Mallory Duncan, Jane Kaplan, and Paul Sugarman); YLS Governing Board Minutes (expanded), December 18, 1974 (reporting that Wellington had received seventeen first-place votes and eight second-place votes; Calabresi, seven first-place and thirteen second-place votes).

120. Interview with Guido Calabresi, 2003.

121. Harry Wellington to author, March 18, 2003.

CHAPTER NINE

1. Leon Lipson, "Eugene Rostow," 94 *Yale L. J.* 1329, 1334 (1985); Eugene Rostow, *Is Law Dead?* 10, 45 (1971); Rostow, *The Ideal in Law* 83, 91 (1978).

2. Alexander Bickel to Robert Bork, April 28, 1969, Box 10, Folder 195, Bickel Papers ("blew up"); Anthony Lewis, "The Heavenly City of Professor Bickel," *New York Times*, October 10, 1969, Box 14, Folder 34, Alexander Bickel Papers, Yale University Archives (hereafter Bickel Papers) (quotes); Isidore Silver, "The Warren Court Critics: Where Are They Now That We Need Them?," 3 *Hastings Const. L. Q.* 373, 418 (1976).

3. Alexander Bickel, *The Supreme Court and the Idea of Progress* 45, 99, 100 (1970). For further discussion of Bickel's Holmes Lectures and the reaction to them, see Maurice Holland, "American Liberals and Judicial Activism: Alexander Bickel's Appeal from the New to the Old," 51 *Ind. L. J.* 1025 (1976); Leon Friedman, "Judicial Activism," *Commen-*

tary, May 1970, 94; William Wiecek, Book Review, *Saturday Review*, April 4, 1970, 37; Joseph Alsop, "Warren Court Attacked Again, This Time by the U.S. Left," *Washington Post*, December 3, 1969, all in Box 14, Folder 40, Bickel Papers; J. Skelly Wright, "Professor Bickel, the Scholarly Tradition, and the Supreme Court," 54 *Harv. L. Rev.* 769 (1971); Edward Purcell, "Alexander M. Bickel and the Post-Realist Constitution," 11 *Harv. C.R.-C.L. Law Rev.* 521, 555–56 (1976).

4. David Rudenstine, *The Day The Presses Stopped: A History of the Pentagon Papers Case* 111 (1996); John Dean, *The Rehnquist Choice: The Untold Story of the Nixon Appointment That Redefined the Supreme Court* 57 (2001) ("Frankfurter-type"); interview with Calabresi, 2002 (message); Daniel Polsby to Alexander Bickel, August 13, 1971, Box 7, Folder 120, Bickel Papers ("Last year").

5. Alexander Bickel, *The Morality of Consent* 3, 25, 4, 8, 112, 60, 123 (1975); Purcell, "Alexander M. Bickel and the Post-Realist Constitution," at 559–63.

6. Bickel, *The Morality of Consent*, at 27, 112, 92, 121; Alexander Bickel, "Watergate and the Legal Order," *Commentary*, January, 1974, pp. 24–25.

7. Bickel, *The Morality of Consent*, at 92–93, 119, 72, 138–39, 73, 76, 77.

8. Id. at 138, 128.

9. Id. at 132–33 ("pressures," "ox"); Alexander Bickel and Philip Kurland, Brief of Anti-Defamation League of B'nai B'rith as Amicus Curiae in Support of Jurisdictional Statement or in the Alternative Petition for Certiorari, Supreme Court of the United States, Number 73-225, October Term, 1973, at 22–24. Bickel insisted that Kurland had done most of the work on the brief. Alexander Bickel to Josef Diamond, March 5, 1974, Box 11, Folder 240, Bickel Papers. But given the similarity between the language about affirmative action in the brief and in Bickel's last book, *The Morality of Consent*, that must have been an overstatement. Privately, Bickel proved even more passionate in his opposition to affirmative action and support of *De Funis*. Alexander Bickel to Peter Steinfels, March 26, 1974, id., Folder 241. The Court dodged the issue of the constitutionality of affirmative action by declaring the case moot. *De Funis* v. *Odegaard*, 416 U.S. 312 (1974).

10. John Ehrman, *The Rise of Neoconservatism: Intellectuals and Foreign Affairs 1945–1994* 34 (1995) ("former"); Norman Podhoretz, *Breaking Ranks: A Political Memoir*, 302 (1980); Nathan Glazer, *Affirmative Discrimination: Ethnic Inequality and Public Policy*; Terry Anderson, *The Pursuit of Fairness: A History of Affirmative Action* 143 (2004). The group included Sidney Hook, Gertrude Himmelfarb, Daniel Boorstin, Nathan Glazer, and Seymour Lipset.

11. Joseph Bishop, *Obiter Dicta: Opinions, Judicious and Otherwise, on Lawyers and the Law* 131 (1976); and see, e.g., id. at 130, 149, 160. Both Rostow and Bishop signed the CANI Steering Sub-Committee Brief of Amici Curiae for the Committee on Academic Nondiscrimination and Integrity and the Mid-America Legal Foundation, *The Regents of the University of California* v. *Allan Bakke*, In the Supreme Court of the United States, October Term, 1977, No. 76-811, 2.

12. Ethan Bronner, *Battle for Justice: How the Bork Nomination Shook America* 72–73 (1989) (quoting from Bork's essay).

13. Robert Bork, "Neutral Principles and Some First Amendment Problems," 47 *Ind. L. J.* 1, 10, 7, 20 (1971) (quotes); Bork, "The Supreme Court Needs a New Philosophy," 78 *Fortune* 138, 170, 174 (December 1968); Bronner, *Battle for Justice*, at 72.

14. Cass Sunstein, Tanner Lectures on Human Values (a portion of which were published under the title "Incompletely Theorized Agreements," 145 *Harv. L. Rev.* 1733 (1995)

("spell"); Laura Kalman, *The Strange Career of Legal Liberalism* 42–57 (1996); *Roe* v. *Wade*, 410 U.S. 113 (1973); *Reed* v. *Reed*, 404 U.S. 71 (1971); *Frontiero* v. *Richardson*, 411 U.S. 677 (1973); *Furman* v. *Georgia*, 408 U.S. 238 (1972).

15. Gary Leedes, "The Supreme Court Mess," 59 *Tex. L. Rev.* 1361, 1437 (1979) ("classic"); Bickel, *The Morality of Consent*, at 28.

16. But see David Garrow, *Liberty & Sexuality: The Right to Privacy and the Making of Roe v. Wade* 599 (1994) (*Roe* was not a radical decision for its time).

17. John Hart Ely, "The Wages of Crying Wolf: A Comment on Roe v. Wade," 82 *Yale L. J.* 920, 926 (1973).

18. *San Antonio Independent School District* v. *Rodriguez*, 411 U.S. 1 (1973); *Milliken* v. *Bradley*, 418 U.S. 717 (1974); *Rizzo* v. *Goode*, 423 U.S. 362 (1976); *Washington* v. *Davis*, 426 U.S. 229 (1976); Owen Fiss, "The Supreme Court, 1978 Term — Foreword: The Forms of Justice," 93 *Harv. L. Rev.* 1, 4, 20–23 (1979); *National League of Cities* v. *Usery*, 426 U.S. 833 (1976); *overruled*, *Garcia* v. *San Antonio Metro Transit Authority*, 469 U.S. 528 (1985). But some legal liberals tried to snatch victory from the jaws of defeat. See Frank Michelman, "States Rights and States' Roles: Permutations of 'Sovereignty' in *National Leagues of Cities* v. *Usery*," 86 *Yale L. J.* 1165 (1977); Lawrence Tribe, "Unraveling *National League of Cities*: The New Federalism and Affirmative Rights to Essential Government Services," 90 *Harv. L. Rev.* 1065 (1977); Dedication, n.p., 86 *Yale L. J.* (May 1977).

19. Owen Fiss, "Thurgood Marshall," 125 *Harv. L. Rev.* 49, 51 (1991); David Broder, *Changing of the Guard: Power and Leadership in America* 235 (1980) (quoting Burger on young people); Warren Burger, "The Special Skills of Advocacy: Are Specialized Training and Certification of Advocates Essential to Our System of Justice," 42 *Fordham L. Rev.* 227 (1973); William Rehnquist, "Observation: The Notion of a Living Constitution," 54 *Tex. L. Rev.* 693, 706 (1976); Kalman, *Strange Career of Legal Liberalism*, at 129–30 (describing the event at which Cover spoke and quoting him); James Simon, *In His Own Image: The Supreme Court in Richard Nixon's America* (1973).

20. William Eskridge and Philip Frickey, "The Making of the Legal Process," 107 *Harv. L. Rev.* 2031, 2051 ("our legal culture," "baselines," "cynical, conflictual"); William Eskridge and Philip Frickey, "An Historical and Critical Introduction to The Legal Process," in Eskridge and Frickey, eds., *The Legal Process: Basic Problems in the Making and Application of Law* by Henry Hart and Albert Sacks, li, cxxii, cxix (1958) (1994 ed.) ("reasoned," quoting Griffiths).

21. Erwin Griswold, "Preface," in Eskridge and Frickey, eds., *The Legal Process* vii, viii; "Faculty Divisions Spark Pointed Political Debate," *Harvard Law Record*, March 2, 1984, 1, 6 (Kennedy).

22. "A Discussion on Critical Legal Studies at the Harvard Law School," presented by The Harvard Society and The Federalist Society, The Harvard Club, New York City, May 13, 1985, 8–9 ("rag-tag").

23. "A Discussion on Critical Legal Studies," at 9. This is not to say that Kennedy and others rooted CLS only in legal realism. But Critical Legal scholars tended to characterize legal realism as one of their wellsprings or, at least, to say they continued some part of the realist project. See, e.g., Gary Peller, "The Metaphysics of American Law," 73 *Cal. L. Rev.* 1151, 1152, 1219–1259 (1985).

24. Joseph Singer, "The Player and the Cards: Nihilism and Legal Theory," 94 *Yale L. J.* 1, 5 (1984) ("law varies"); James Boyle, *Critical Legal Studies* xix (1992) ("manipulable"); Mark Kelman, *A Guide to Critical Legal Studies* 13, 303, n. 27 (1987) ("settled").

25. Karl Klare, "Law Making as Praxis," 40 *Telos* 123, 132 n. 29 (1979).

26. Joan Williams, "Critical Legal Studies: The Death of Transcendence and the Rise of the New Langdells," 62 *N.Y.U. L. Rev.* 429, 487 (1987); "Professor Frug Urges Critical Look at Law," *Harvard Law Record*, December 3, 1982, at 9 ("Helms").

27. "We Get 7 Supreme Court Clerks," *Yale Advocate*, February 6, 1969, at 3; Joan Roelofs, "The Warren Court and Corporate Capitalism," 39 *Telos* 94, 94 (1979).

28. Richard Delgado, "The Ethereal Scholar: Does Critical Legal Studies Have What Minorities Want?," 22 *Harv. C.R.-C.L. L. Rev.* 301, 305 (1987) ("isolated"); William Fisher, "The Development of Modern American Legal Theory and the Judicial Interpretation of the Bill of Rights," in Michael Lacey and Knud Haakonssen, eds., *A Culture of Rights: The Bill of Rights in Philosophy, Politics, and Law—1791 and 1991*, ed. 266, 294 (1991) ("rights"); Roberto Unger, "The Critical Legal Studies Movement," 96 *Harv. L. Rev.* 563, 575 (1983); and see Unger, *Knowledge and Politics* (1975) and *Law in Modern Society: Toward a Criticism of Social Theory* (1976).

29. Duncan Kennedy, "Form and Substance in Private Law Adjudication," 89 *Harv. L. Rev.* 1685, 1685, 1713, 1723, 1762, 1724 (1976). For Kennedy's questioning of process theory as a student in Harry Wellington's Legal Process course, see Eskridge and Frickey, "An Historical and Critical Introduction to *The Legal Process*," at cxx.

30. Kennedy, "Form and Substance in Private Law Adjudication," at 1685, 1751, 1688, 1774–76.

31. Duncan Kennedy, "The Structure of Blackstone's Commentaries," 28 *Buff. L. Rev.* 205, 213 (1979); Unger, *Law in Modern Society*, at 128, 129.

32. Mark Tushnet, "Critical Legal Studies: A Political History," 100 *Yale L. J.* 1515, 1526 (1991) ("all the way"); Morton Horwitz, *The Transformation of American Law 1780–1860* 34, 259, 254 (1977); Robert Gordon, "Critical Legal Histories," 36 *Stan. L. Rev.* 57, 98 (1984) ("charges"). By the 1970s, though, some were beginning to challenge the realists' depiction of late nineteenth-century judges as the personification of greed and evil. See, e.g., Charles McCurdy, "Justice Field and the Jurisprudence of Government-Business Relations: Some Parameters of Laissez-Faire Constitutionalism, 1863–1897," 61 *J. Am. Hist.* 970 (1975).

33. Daniel Ernst, "The Critical Tradition in the Writing of American Legal History," 102 *Yale L. J.* 1019, 1024–27 (1993); Morton Horwitz, "The Rule of Law: An Unqualified Human Good?," 86 *Yale L. J.* 561, 566 (1977) (quotations) (emphasis in the original).

34. Robert Gordon, "New Developments in Legal Theory," in David Kairys, ed., *The Politics of Law: A Progressive Critique* 413, 417 (1990).

35. Fisher, "The Development of Modern American Legal Theory," at 292. On the popular press, see, e.g., Calvin Trillin, "A Reporter at Large: Harvard Law," *New Yorker*, 53, 56 (March 26, 1984); "War Between Professors Pervades Harvard Law," *Washington Post*, December 21, 1985, at A5. But Robert Clark contended that Critical Legal scholars were trying to make their movement less frightening by comparing Critical Legal Studies to legal realism, which had become something somehow to be admired even as its content was forgotten. "A Discussion on Critical Legal Studies at the Harvard Law School," at 33.

36. Duncan Kennedy, *Legal Education and the Reproduction of Hierarchy: A Polemic against the System: A Critical Edition* 31 (1983) (2004 ed.) (the 1983 pamphlet received national attention from the right after Brian Timmons, a second-year Harvard law student, discussed its author's proposals in "That's No Okie, That's My Torts Professor," *Wall Street Journal*, April 3, 1990, at A20; and see "Timmons Attracts National Attention For CLS-Bashing," *Harvard Law Record*, May 4, 1990, at 3; Kelman, *A Guide to Critical Legal Studies*, at 299, n. 12 ["no one"]).

37. "Battle at Harvard Law Over Tenure; So-Called Crits v. Traditionalists," *National Law Journal*, June 22, 1987, at 3; "The Split at Harvard Law Goes Down to Its Foundations," *New York Times*, October 6, 1985, Section 4, at 7.

38. Trillin, "A Reporter at Large: Harvard Law," at 73, 59, 76 ("freeze," "returned," "Rome" [quoting Duncan Kennedy]); "A Discussion on Critical Legal Studies at Harvard Law School," at 11 ("generational"); Vicki Quase, "Are Lawyers Really Necessary?: Barrister Interview with Duncan Kennedy," 14 *Barrister* 10, 36 (Fall 1987) ("Beirut" [quoting David Trubek]).

39. Yale Law School Governing Board Minutes (expanded), March 30, 1977 (Kelman) (hereafter YLS Governing Board Minutes); Harry Wellington to Ellen Peters, April 1, 1977, Box 16, Chron File, Dean's Files, Yale University Archives (hereafter Dean's Files) (Kelman); Harry Wellington to Duncan Kennedy, April 4, 1977, id. (indicating the faculty had spent a great deal of time on Kelman); confidential communication ("How far"). See, e.g., Trillin, "A Reporter at Large: Harvard Law," at 53, 64; Tushnet, "Critical Legal Studies: A Political History," at 1544, n. 107.

40. YLS Governing Board Minutes, Exhibit: Memorandum of Poll, Governing Board, December 15, 1970 (reporting vote of 21–7); Alexander Bickel to Abraham Goldstein, January 5, 1971, Box 10, Folder 214, Bickel Papers; interview with Kennedy. Wellington was a very strong supporter of Kennedy's, whom he compared to the later Perry Miller and considered one of his best students ever. Harry Wellington to Albert Sacks, December 2, 1975, Box 16, Chron File, Dean's Files; Wellington to Kennedy, January 9, 1976, id.; Wellington to Charles Lister, September 30, 1969, Box 1, Folder L, Dean's Files. Interestingly, though, Wellington did apparently send Kennedy's polemic to a psychologist for evaluation. William Kessen to Wellington, October 22, 1969, Box 1, Folder K, Dean's Files.

41. Abraham Goldstein to the Expanded Governing Board, April 3, 1972, Box 291, Folder 5, Kingman Brewster Papers, Yale University Archives (hereafter Brewster Papers) (Unger); Harry Wellington to Expanded Governing Board, November 9, 1979, Box 12, HHW Masters 1975–76, Dean's Files (Minow); Gary Minda, *Postmodern Legal Movements: Law and Jurisprudence at Century's End* 108 (1995); email, Martha Minow to author, August 12, 2001 (liberalism); Guido Calabresi to A. Dan Tarlock, August 3, 1990, Box 58, Chron File, Dean's Files ("superb," "associated"); YLS Governing Board Minutes, December 21, 1982 (Expanded) (Brest); YLS Governing Board Minutes, November 11, 1981 (Expanded) (Gordon). The person most sympathetic to Critical Legal Studies who actually accepted an offer during this period (the 1970s through the early 1990s) was Lucinda Finley, who later left Yale without tenure for reasons I believe were unassociated with the movement.

42. John Schlegel, "Notes Toward an Intimate, Opinionated, and Affectionate History of the Conference on Critical Legal Studies," 36 *Stan. L. Rev.* 391, 399–400 (1984).

43. Trillin, "A Reporter at Large: Harvard Law," at 56. Even if one advocates a broad enough definition of realism so that it encompasses the jurisprudence of Holmes, Pound, and Frankfurter (see William Fisher, Morton Horwitz, and Thomas Reed, *American Legal Realism* xiii–xv, 3–4, 9, 26 [1993]; Kalman, *Strange Career of Legal Liberalism*, at 250, n. 1), it still seems clear legal realism had little impact on legal education at Harvard during the 1920s and 1930s. Laura Kalman, *Legal Realism at Yale* 45–66 (1986).

44. Singer, "The Player and the Cards," at 6 ("criteria"); Guido Calabresi to David Trubek, November 24, 1986, Box 57, Chron File, Dean's Files ("surprised"); Kalman, *Legal Realism at Yale*, at 139; Guido Calabresi to Paul Carrington, 35 *J. Legal Ed.* 23, 23–24 (1985) (Calabresi also included Arthur Leff in the group of nihilists); Guido Calabresi to Richard

Fischl, September 4, 1987, Box 27, Chron File, Dean's Files ("wrong," "those"). Richard Fischl rebuts the charge of nihilism in "The Question That Killed Critical Legal Studies," 17 *Law & Soc. Inq'y.* 779 (1992).

45. Guido Calabresi to Richard Fischl, September 28, 1987, Box 27, Chron File, Dean's Files. For the defenses, see Calabresi to Carrington, supra; Owen Fiss to Paul Carrington, 35 *J. Legal Ed.* 24 (1985).

46. Gordon, "New Developments in Legal Theory," at 417; interviews with Boris Bittker, Paul Gewirtz, and Owen Fiss, 2001; Mark Kelman, "Trashing," 36 *Stan. L. Rev.* 292, 292 (1984) ("specific") (emphasis in the original); Quase, "Interview: Are Lawyers Necessary?" ("infected," quoting Kennedy). Earlier, feminists had used "trashing" to attack elitism and hierarchy. Roth Rosen, *The World Split Open: How the Modern Women's Movement Changed America* 227–29 (2000). On Stanford, see Trillin, "A Reporter at Large: Harvard Law," at 76.

47. Arthur Leff, "Economic Analysis of Law: Some Realism about Nominalism," 60 *Va. L. Rev.* 451, 459, 454 (1974).

48. Unger, *Knowledge and Politics*, at 295; Arthur Leff, "Memorandum," 29 *Stan. L. Rev.* 879, 887–88, 889 (1977).

49. Arthur Leff, "Unspeakable Ethics, Unnatural Law," 1979 *Duke L. J.* 1229, 1229–30, 1249 (1979).

50. Kalman, *Legal Realism at Yale*, at 197–98; Harry Wellington, *Interpreting the Constitution: The Supreme Court and the Process of Adjudication* 158, 84, 88, 109–12 (1990).

51. William Eskridge and Gary Peller, "The New Public Law Movement: Moderation as a Postmodern Cultural Form," 89 *Mich. L. Rev.* 707, 789 (1991); Harold McDougall, "Social Movements, Law, and Implementation: A Clinical Dimension for the New Legal Process," 75 *Cornell L. Rev.* 83, 98 (1989) ("attempt"). Robert Weisberg gave "The New Legal Process" its name and identified Yale as its headquarters in "The Calabresian Judicial Artist: Statutes and the New Legal Process," 35 *Stan. L. Rev.* 213, 239 (1983). Calabresi, of course, agreed with this assessment. Guido Calabresi, "An Introduction to Legal Thought: Four Approaches to Law and to the Allocation of Body Parts," 55 *Stan. L. Rev.* 2113, 2123 (2003).

52. Calabresi, "An Introduction to Legal Thought," at 2124–26; Eskridge and Frickey, "An Historical and Critical Introduction to The Legal Process," at cxxviii; Jerry Mashaw, *Greed, Chaos, and Governance: Using Public Choice to Improve Public Law* 31 (1997). (For development of the contention that process theory always possessed a normative and substantive element, see Kalman, *Strange Career of Legal Liberalism*, at 22–42, 91–92, 295, n. 73.)

53. Robert Burt, *The Constitution in Conflict* 359–62 (1993); Robert Burt, "Alex Bickel's Law School and Ours," 104 *Yale L. J.* 1854 (1995). Burt, however, claimed that the legal reasoning persuasive to Bickel's generation had become less persuasive to the generations that followed. "Alex Bickel's Law School and Ours," at 1856, 1858, 1865–66.

54. Robert Nozick, *Anarchy, State and Utopia* (1974); John Rawls, *A Theory of Justice* 251–57, 136–37, 14–15 (1971). For discussion of Rawls's attraction for political liberals, see Mark Tushnet, "Truth, Justice, and the American Way," 57 *Tex. L. Rev.* 1307, 1316–17 (1979).

55. Ronald Dworkin, *Taking Rights Seriously* 149 (1977); Eskridge and Frickey, "An Historical and Critical Introduction to The Legal Process," at cxvii; Vincent Wellman, "Dworkin and the Legal Process Tradition: The Legacy of Hart and Sacks," 29 *Az. L. Rev.* 413 (1987); Wellman, "Legal History: Positivism, Emergent and Triumphant," 97 *Mich. L. Rev.* 1722, 1728 (1999).

56. John Hart Ely, *Democracy and Distrust: A Theory of Judicial Review* 58–59, 74, 75, 72 (1980) (emphasis in the original). For reaction at Yale, see, e.g., Wellington, *Interpreting the Constitution*, at 67–69.

57. Bruce Ackerman, *Private Property and the Constitution* (1977); Ackerman, *Reconstructing American Law* 20 (1984) ("danger"); Ackerman, "Court Should Be Focused on Justice, Not Politics," *Milwaukee Journal Sentinel*, January 13, 2003, at 11A.

58. Bruce Ackerman, *Social Justice in the Liberal State* 378, 239, 252, 8 (1981), 100; Ackerman, *Reconstructing American Law*, at 110, 100 ("shallow," "affirmation"); Ackerman, "Rooted Cosmopolitanism," 104 *Ethics* 516, 518 (1994) ("liberal dialogue").

59. Bruce Ackerman, *We the People: Foundations*, at 10–11, 6–7, 22, 34–57 (1990). Ackerman first announced the theory of "We the People" in "The Storrs Lectures: Discovering the Constitution," 93 *Yale L. J.* 1013 (1984). Another early hint as to the direction in which he was headed appeared in Ackerman, "Beyond *Carolene* Products," 98 *Harv. L. Rev.* 713 (1985).

60. Ackerman, "Rooted Cosmopolitanism," at 527 ("civil rights movement," "successful"); Ackerman, *We the People: Foundations*, at 141, 305.

61. Kalman, *Strange Career of Legal Liberalism*, at 147–63, 212–17; Bruce Ackerman, *We the People 2: Transformations* 407 (1998) ("distinguished"); Laura Kalman, "Law, Politics, and the New Deal(s)," 108 *Yale L. J.* 2165, 2213 (1999).

62. Anthony Kronman, "My Senior Partner," 104 *Yale L. J.* 2129, 2131 (1995) ("political," "ideal"); Anthony Kronman, *The Lost Lawyer: Failing Ideals of the Legal Profession* 225, 168 (1993) ("marginal," "contempt"); Kronman, "Alexander Bickel's Philosophy of Prudence," 94 *Yale L. J.* 1567, 1568, 1607 (1985). Whereas Burt thought prudentialism had dwindled, supra, Kronman believed that prudentialism still had a strong impact on the classroom. Kronman, *Lost Lawyer*, at 268.

63. Guido Calabresi, *A Common Law for the Age of Statutes* 1 (1982) ("orgy," quoting Grant Gilmore); Philip Bobbitt, *Constitutional Fate: Theory of the Constitution* 73 (1982).

64. Calabresi, *A Common Law for the Age of Statutes*, at 81, 82, 96–97. For a discussion of the desirability of avoiding subterfuges, see, e.g., Guido Calabresi and Philip Bobbitt, *Tragic Choices* 26 (1978).

65. Calabresi, *A Common Law for the Age of Statutes*, at 87, 177, 180; Calabresi and Bobbitt, *Tragic Choices*, at 164 ("reckless," "contemporaries").

66. Guido Calabresi, *Ideals, Beliefs, Attitudes and the Law: Private Law Perspectives on a Public Law Problem* 89, 1, 115 (1985).

67. Id. at 97 ("disaster"); Guido Calabresi, "The Supreme Court, 1990 Term: Foreword: Antidiscrimination and Constitutional Accountability: What the Bork-Brennan Debate Ignores," 105 *Harv. L. Rev.* 80, 109, 110, 142 (1991).

68. Calabresi, "Antidiscrimination and Constitutional Accountability," at 103–4, 91, 103, 148, 93, 92. Emphasis in the original.

69. Calabresi, *Ideals, Beliefs, Attitudes, and the Law*, at 92–93, 99, 116–17. So, too, Robert Burt condemned *Roe* for cutting off the possibility of dialogue between abortion's proponents and opponents. Burt, *The Constitution in Conflict*, at 348–49.

70. Owen Fiss, *Law as It Could Be* xiii, 14, 15 (2003) (*Law as It Could Be* is a collection of Fiss's essays dating back to the 1970s). Unlike Bickel and some other sixties liberals, Fiss was focused more on group than individual rights, urging the rethinking of equal protection analysis for Fourteenth Amendment purposes in terms of harm to subordinated and disadvantaged groups, whose members possessed limited political power. Owen Fiss, "Groups and the Equal Protection Clause," 5 *Philosophy and Public Affairs* 106,

157 (1976); Owen Fiss, *Liberalism Divided: Freedom of Speech and the Many Uses of State Power* 4 (1996).

71. Fiss, *Law as It Could Be*, at 47, 244, 58, 149.

72. Id. at 204, ix, 205.

73. Id. at xi, 106, xii, 210, 202; Owen Fiss, *The Civil Rights Injunction* (1978). Historically, courts had used the equitable remedy of the injunction only to prevent irreparable injury or to remedy a specific past wrong. After conservative judges in the late nineteenth and early twentieth century had transformed the injunction, relying on it to block social change, Frankfurter and other progressives exhorted the court to subordinate the injunction to legal remedies, such as monetary damages. In creating the structural injunction, Fiss believed the Warren Court had engaged in an act of redemption.

74. Fiss, *Law as It Could Be*, at 205, 206, 213, 216; *Goldberg v. Kelly*, 397 U.S. 254 (1970) Jerry Mashaw, "Administrative Due Process: The Quest for a Dignitary Theory," 61 *B.U. L. Rev.* 885, 888 (1981); Mashaw, "The Supreme Court's Due Process Calculus for Administrative Adjudication in *Mathews v. Eldridge*: Three Factors in Search of a Theory of Value," 44 *U. Chi. L. Rev.* 28, 58 (1976); Mashaw, *Due Process in the Administrative State* 26 (1985).

75. Linda Mullenix, "Legal Scholarship: God, Metaprocedure, and Metarealism at Yale," 87 *Mich. L. Rev.* 1139, 1141 (1988) ("realist casebook"); Robert Cover, Owen Fiss, Judith Resnik, *Procedure* vii, xi (1988 ed.) ("exploration," "linear"); Robert Cover and Owen Fiss, *The Structure of Procedure* iii–iv (1979) ("Revolution," "more theoretical"); William Eskridge, "Metaprocedure," 98 *Yale L. J.* 945, 946 (1989).

76. Owen Fiss, *Law as It Could Be*, at 201, 149–171; Ronald Dworkin, *A Matter of Principle* 119–177 (1985); Ronald Dworkin, *Law's Empire* (1986). See Kalman, *Strange Career of Legal Liberalism*, at 112–21; Eskridge and Frickey, "An Historical and Critical Introduction to *The Legal Process*," at cxxviii–cxxx.

77. Harry Wellington, "Challenges to Legal Education: The 'Two Cultures' Phenomenon," 37 *J. Legal Ed.* 327, 329 (1987); Robert Cover, "The Supreme Court, 1982 Term — Foreword, Nomos and Narrative," 97 *Harv. L. Rev.* 4, 40 (1983); Robert Cover, *Justice Accused: Antislavery and the Judicial Process* xi, 5, 6, 7 (1975).

78. "Campus Events Close Law School; 'Pass-Incomplete' Grading Adopted," *Columbia Law School News*, May 13, 1968, at 1; "Law Rally at Foley Square Seeks Reform of Court System," id., May 13, 1969, at 3; Stephen Wizner, "Tribute," 96 *Yale L. J.* 1707, 1710 (1987); "A Consumer's Guide to Columbia Law School," *Columbia Law School News*, April 17, 1970, at 4; Owen Fiss, "Tribute," 96 *Yale L. J.* 1717, 1720–21 (1987).

79. Fiss, *Law as It Could Be*, at 91, 210; Sanford Levinson, *Constitutional Faith* (1988); Wizner, "Tribute," at 1710.

80. Kalman, *Strange Career of Legal Liberalism*, at 129–31; Cover, Fiss, Resnik, *Procedure*, at 729–30; Cover, *Justice Accused*, at 259.

81. Daniel Farber and Suzanna Sherry, *Desperately Seeking Certainty: The Misguided Quest for Constitutional Foundations* 145, 140 (2002); Kalman, *Strange Career of Legal Liberalism*, at 67, 91–92, 129; and see the following reviews of Calabresi, *A Common Law for the Age of Statutes*: Archibald Cox, 70 *Cal. L. Rev.* 1463, 1470–73 (1982); Abner Mikva, "The Shifting Sands of Legal Topography: A Common Law for the Age of Statutes," 96 *Harv. L. Rev.* 534, 541–42 (1982); Steve MacIssac, 81 *Mich. L. Rev.* 754, 764–65, 773 (1982); Mark Tushnet, "Metaprocedure?," 63 *S. Cal. L. Rev.* 161, 164–67 (1989); Christopher Wolfe, "The Result-Oriented Adjudicator's Guide to Constitutional Law," 70 *Tex. L. Rev.* 1325, 1325 (1992) (Wellington). For discussion of CLS and realism, see Morton Horwitz, *The Transformation of American Law, 1870–1960: The Crisis of Legal Orthodoxy* 209–10 (1992).

I have never thought that the realists backed into the social sciences as a way of backing away from the implications of their own work about judging. Perhaps Critical Legal scholars were projecting the developments they saw in their own era back onto the 1930s.

82. Tushnet, "Critical Legal Studies: A Political History," at 1533.

83. Dean's Report, 1980–81 ("anywhere"); Harry Wellington to Jasper Cummings, August 6, 1981, Box 4, Folder: Yale University Council Committee on Yale Law School, Dean's Files ("predecessors"); Goldstein, "On Harry Wellington at Yale," at 14 ("look on"). The list of Wellington's hires included Barbara Black, Lea Brilmayer, Robert Burt, Stephen Carter, Morris Cohen, Harlon Dalton, Mirjan Damaska, Perry Dane, Drew Days, Donald Elliot, Lucinda Finley, Jack Getman, Paul Gewirtz, Michael Graetz, Henry Hansmann, Reinier Kraakman, Anthony Kronman, Jerry Mashaw, Jay Pottenger, George Priest, Roberta Romano, Peter Schuck, and Oliver Williamson.

84. "Split at Harvard Law Goes Down to Its Foundations," *New York Times*, October 6, 1985, Section 4, at 7; Faculty Appointments Process, n.d., ca. early 1980s, Box 13, Folder: Appointments Committee, 1981/82 Dean's Files; confidential interviews; Harry Wellington to William Brainard, April 27, 1983, Box 17, Chron File, Dean's Files; "Yale Law: Fork in the Road," *National Law Journal*, June 29, 1981, at 1, 27 (quoting Gewirtz and discussing case of William E. Nelson, who was not promoted).

85. Joel Seligman, *The High Citadel: The Influence of Harvard Law School* 123 (1978) ("traditional"). The Goldstein hires with PhDs were Alvin Klevorick, Robert Clark, and William Nelson. I do not include Grant Gilmore, who rejoined the faculty under Goldstein and whose doctorate was in French literature, in this group. The Wellington hires with PhDs were Jerry Mashaw, Anthony Kronman, Barbara Black, Reinier Kraakman, Henry Hansmann, and Oliver Williamson.

86. Kalman, *Strange Career of Legal Liberalism*, at 60–61; Harry Wellington, Orientation Meeting, September 3, 1980, Box 15, unmarked and unnumbered file, Dean's Files. The statistics on the class of 1981 are in YLS Faculty Minutes, October 24, 1978.

87. Arthur Leff, "Law And," 87 *Yale L. J.* 989 (1978); Kalman, *Strange Career of Legal Liberalism*, at 115–117, 127–31.

88. Martha Minow, "Law Turning Outward," 73 *Telos* 79, 91 (1987); Calabresi, "An Introduction to Legal Thought," at 2121.

89. "McGovern Sweeps Poll with 83%," *Harvard Law Record*, October 20, 1972, 1, 4; Carl Hetrick and Henry Turner, "Politics and the American Law Professor," 25 *J. Legal Ed.* 342 (1973); Kalman, *Strange Career of Legal Liberalism*, at 77.

90. Dean's Report, 1973–74, at 6; Harry Wellington to Michael Horowitz, June 16, 1976, Box 16, Chron File, Dean's Files.

91. Calabresi and Bobbitt, *Tragic Choices*, at 31; Neil Komesar, "Return to Slumville: A Critique of the Ackerman Analysis of Housing Code Enforcement and the Poor," 82 *Yale L. J.* 1175 (1973); Bruce Ackerman, "Regulating Slum Markets on Behalf of the Poor: Of Housing Codes, Housing Subsidies and Income Redistribution Policy," id., 80: 1093 (1971); Fiss, *Law as It Could Be*, at 198.

92. Gary Minda, "The Jurisprudential Movements of the 1980s," 50 *Ohio St. L. J.* 599, 606, n. 28 (quoting Susan Rose-Ackerman) (1989). See, e.g., Michael Rustad and Thomas Koenig, "Taming the Tort Monster: The American Civil Justice System as a Battleground of Social Theory," 68 *Brooklyn L. Rev.* 1, 76, n. 463 (2002) (Yale Law School second to University of Chicago Law School in Olin Foundation Law School Funding for 1999); <http://www./jmof.org/history__purposes/html>.

93. George Priest, "The Emergence of Law & Economics as an Academic Discipline:

Henry Manne and the Market Measure of Intellectual Influence," 50 *Case W. Res. L. Rev.* 325 (1999); Priest, "The Invention of Enterprise Liability: A Critical History of the Intellectual Foundations of Modern Tort Law," 14 *J. Legal Stud.* 461, 466–85 (1985); George Priest, "Can Absolute Manufacturer Liability Be Defended?," 9 *Yale J. of Reg.* 237, 240 (1992) ("in essence"); Priest, "The Current Insurance Crisis and Modern Tort Law," 96 *Yale L. J.* 1521, 1525 (1987); Guido Calabresi and Jon Hirschoff, "Toward a Test for Strict Liability in Torts," id., 81: 1055, 1055, 1081 (1972); Gregory Keating, "The Idea of Fairness in the Law of Enterprise Liability," 95 *Mich. L. Rev.* 1266, 1361, n. 220 (1997) (Aetna); Rustad and Koenig, "Taming the Tort Monster: The American Civil Justice System as a Battleground of Social Theory," at 82 (casebooks); Alan Schwartz, "The Case Against Strict Liability," 60 *Fordham L. Rev.* 819 (1992); Schwartz, "Proposals for Products Liability Reform: A Theoretical Synthesis," 97 *Yale L. J.* 353 (1988).

94. G. Edward White, "The Unexpected Persistence of Negligence, 1980–2000," 54 *Vand. L. Rev.* 1337, 1344, 1346, 1365 (2001); George Priest, "The Culture of Modern Tort Law," 34 *Val. U. L. Rev.* 573 (2000).

95. Priest, "The Emergence of Law & Economics as an Academic Discipline," at 328.

96. Harry Wellington to A. Bartlett Giamatti, April 17, 1984, Box 17, Chron File, Dean's Files.

97. "What Do Law Schools Teach? Almost Anything," *New York Times*, December 23, 1988, at B8.

98. Abraham Goldstein, "Educational Planning at Yale," 20 *J. Legal Ed.* 402, 405 (1968); Donna Fossum, "Law Professors: A Profile of the Teaching Branch of the Legal Profession," 1980 *Am. Bar Fdn. Res. J.* 501, 507–8 (1980); Robert Borthwick and Jordan Schau, "Gatekeepers of the Profession: An Empirical Profile of the Nation's Law Professors," 25 *U. Mich. J. Law Reform* 191, 226–30 (1991).

99. Email, Harry Wellington to author, September 3, 2002 ("many"); Guido Calabresi to Peter Baugher, December 5, 1985, Box 57, Chron Files, Dean's Files ("first"); Harry Wellington to Faculty and Student Representatives, April 25, 1979, appending Report of the Dean's Planning Group on Graduate Education, Yale Law School Faculty Minutes (hereafter YLS Faculty Minutes); confidential communication ("dilettantish").

100. Charles Collier, "The Use and Abuse of Humanistic Theory in Law: Reexamining the Assumptions of Interdisciplinary Scholarship," 41 *Duke L. J.* 191, 205 (1991) ("gratuitous"). See also, e.g., Kalman, *Strange Career of Legal Liberalism*, at 113–19, 171–80; Brian Leiter, "Intellectual Voyeurship in Legal Scholarship," 4 *Yale J. Law and Humanities* 79 (1992); Martha Nussbaum, "The Use and Abuse of Philosophy in Legal Education," 45 *Stan. L. Rev.* 1627 (1993); Martin Flaherty, "History 'Lite' in Modern American Constitutionalism," 95 *Colum. L. Rev.* 523 (1995).

101. Francis Allen, "The Dolphin and the Peasant: Ill-Tempered, but Brief, Comments on Legal Scholarship," *Property Law and Legal Education: Essays in Honor of John E. Cribbett*, ed. Peter Hay and Michael Hoeflich 183, 195 (1989) ("outpost"); Richard Posner, "The Present Situation in Legal Scholarship," 90 *Yale L. J.* 1113, 1129, 1119 (1981) ("academic lawyer").

102. George Priest, "Social Science Theory and Legal Education: The Law School as University," 33 *J. Legal Ed.* 437 (1983); J. Cunyon Gordon, "A Response from the Visitor from Another Planet," 91 *Mich. L. Rev.* 1953, 1960 (1993) ("be-all"); Louis Sirico and Jeffrey Margulies, "The Citing of Law Reviews by the Supreme Court: An Empirical Study," 34 *UCLA L. Rev.* 131, 134 (1986).

103. Harry Edwards, "The Growing Disjunction between Legal Education and the

Profession," 91 *Mich. L. Rev.* 34, 61 (1992); and see Donald Ayer, "Stewardship," 91 *Mich. L. Rev.* 2150 (1993).

104. Laura Kalman, "Professing Law: Elite Law School Professors in the Twentieth Century," in Austin Sarat, Robert Kagan and Bryant Garth, *Looking Back at Law's Century* 337 (2002); Richard Posner, "The Deprofessionalization of Legal Teaching and Scholarship," 91 *Mich. L. Rev.* 1921, 1925 (1993) (antitrust); Bryant Garth and Joanne Martin, "Law Schools and the Construction of Competence," 43 *J. Legal Ed.* 469, 505; Michael Saks, Howard Larsen, and Carol Hodne, "Is There a Growing Gap among Law, Law Practice, and Legal Scholarship? A Systematic Comparison of Law Review Articles One Generation Apart," 30 *Suffolk Univ. L. Rev.* 353, 366 (1996).

105. Wellington, "Challenges to Legal Education: The 'Two Cultures' Phenomenon," at 327; Jack Getman, *In the Company of Scholars* 268 (1992).

106. Harry Wellington, Letter to Partners of Major Law Firms, January 1981, Box 17, Chron File, Dean's Files; Wellington to John Subak, November 14, 1980, Box 17, Chron File, Dean's Files, Appendix A, Box 4, Folder: Yale University Council Committee on Yale Law School; Harry Wellington to Leon Higginbotham, January 9, 1979, Box 16, Chron File, id.

107. Report to the President of the Yale University Council on the Law School, December 19, 1990, Box 4, Folder: Yale University Council Committee on the Law School, Dean's Files (quotations). For complaints about the building, see, e.g., Louis Pollak to Kingman Brewster, November 29, 1967, Box 130, Folder 7, Brewster Papers; Guido Calabresi to Adam Walinsky, November 24, 1986, Box 57, Chron File, Dean's Files; Calabresi to Daphna Mitchell, July 16, 1986, Box 22, Folder M, Dean's Files; Calabresi to Ronald Maclean, November 8, 1987, id. Stephen Yandle told me about the homeless in a 2001 conversation.

108. Harry Wellington to Ellen Peters, September 16, 1974 (the letter may well have been misdated and written in 1975), Box 16, Chron File, Dean's Files; Harry Wellington to Harry Edwards, December 19, 1975, id.; YLS Governing Board Minutes, December 16, 1975 (expanded); Harry Wellington to John Doggett, March 19, 1979, Box 16, Chron Files, Dean's Files. See generally Donna Fossum, "Law Professors: A Profile of the Teaching Branch of the Legal Profession," 1980 *Am. Bar Fdn. Res. J.* 501 (1980); Fossum, "Women Law Professors," id. at 903; Richard Chused, "The Hiring and Retention of Minorities and Women on American Law School Faculties," 137 *U. Pa. L. Rev.* 537 (1988); Richard Delgado, "Minority Law Professors' Lives," 24 *Harv. C.L.-C.R. L. Rev.* 349 (1989).

109. *Regents of the University of California* v. *Bakke*, 438 U.S. 265 (1978); Harry Wellington to Louis Pollak, May 27, 1977, Box 16, Chron File, Dean's Files; Wellington to Hanna Gray, May 27, 1977, Box 16, Chron File, Dean's Files; John Morton Blum, *A Life with History* 248 (2004).

110. Abraham Goldstein, "On Harry Wellington at Yale," 45 *N.Y.L. Sch. L. Rev.* 13, 14 (2002); Harry Wellington to Hanna Gray and Kingman Brewster, February 23, 1976, Box 16, Chron File, Dean's Files ("increasingly") (Wellington was writing there about Leon Lipson, whom he worried would be lost to Yale if the University of Pennsylvania created a job for his spouse); Wellington to James Tobin, January 10, 1975, id. (Ackerman's place in school); Harry Wellington to Student Representatives, April 2, 1976, Box 12, HHW Masters 1975–76, Dean's Files (characterizing student concerns: "losing," "walls," "quality").

111. "Yale Law: Fork in the Road," at 26–27.

112. Id. at 26, 27, 28.

113. Id. at 27; "Admissions Information" (1976–1979), appended to James Thomas, Re-

port to the Faculty, Admissions: Class of 1979, September 13, 1976, YLS Faculty Minutes and see YLS Faculty Minutes, September 21, 1976; Calabresi, "Joseph Goldstein," at 905; YLS Faculty Minutes, May 4, 1978; Derek Dorn, "Sexual Orientation and the Legal Academy: The Experience at Yale" (unpublished manuscript). I am grateful to Dorn for sharing it with me.

114. "Yale Law: Fork in the Road," at 1, 27, 28.

115. Class Notes '70, 22 *Yale L. Report* 60 (Winter 1975–76) ("Dear Abie," "rabble"); id. 23: 34 (Spring 1977) (quiz); id. 24: 33 (Spring 1978) (Dubious Achievements); 28: 84 (Winter 1981) (Handbook); Class Notes '71, id. 23: 57 (Winter 1976–77).

116. "Yale Law: Fork in the Road," at 28.

117. Id. at 28; 25 *Yale L. Report* 27 (Fall 1978) (complaining that Wellington had censored his column); Harry Wellington to James Zirkle and Ellen Tweed, October 29, 1982, Box 15, Dean's Files, File: Alumni Weekend, Dean's Files ("got," "noble," "tactfully"); id. 29: 85 (Fall 1982–83). See Rhoads, *Freedom's Web*, at 22–23, 78–79, 233–34 for a vigorous rebuttal of the charge that the quest for multiculturalism created a preoccupation with difference and fragmented the left.

118. YLS Governing Board Minutes (expanded), March 31, 1982; Harry Wellington to Expanded Governing Board, April 1, 1982, id. (reporting Brilmayer had accepted); "Yale Law: Fork in the Road," at 28; YLS Faculty Minutes, September 21, 1976 ("continually fighting").

119. Harry Wellington to Robert Keeler, November 11, 1981, Box 17, Chron File, Dean's Files (anger); "Fork in the Road," at 28, 26. Wellington to William Warren, June 24, 1981, Box 17, Chron File, Dean's Files ("beauty").

120. Tushnet, "Critical Legal Studies: A Political History," at 1533, n. 75.

CHAPTER TEN

1. Guido Calabresi to Friends and Graduates of the Yale Law School, December 7, 1993. I am grateful to Georganne Rogers for sharing with me her file of annual decanal letters to friends and alumni, hereafter cited as Calabresi to Friends and Graduates.

2. Guido Calabresi, "What Clarence Thomas Knows," *New York Times*, July 28, 1991, Section 4, at 15 ("despise"); and see Guido Calabresi, "The Supreme Court, 1990 Term: Foreword: Antidiscrimination and Constitutional Accountability: What the Bork-Brennan Debate Ignores," 105 *Harv. L. Rev.* 80 (1991); "At the Bar: Wouldn't Anyone Want to be a Law School Dean? Not Really, As Some Current Searches Confirm," *New York Times*, March 11, 1994, at B18 (quoting Columbia Law School Dean Lance Liebman); Jack Balkin Blog, May 22, 2203, <http://balkin/blogspot.com/>, "Balkinization" (Calabresi's portrait).

3. Interview with Calabresi, 2003; James Traub, "John Sexton Pleads (and Pleads and Pleads) His Case," *New York Times Magazine*, May 25, 1997, Section 6, at 27, 27 ("hyperbolic"); Mark Levine, "Ivy Envy," id., June 8, 2003, Section 6, at 72, 74 ("hugging dean").

4. "'Citizen of Yale' Is Named New Dean of the Law School," *New York Times*, January 31, 1985, at B1; David Shapiro to Guido Calabresi, February 4, 1985, Box 23, Folder S, Dean's Files, Yale University Archives (hereafter Dean's Files); Calabresi to Shapiro, February 7, 1985, Box 23, Folder S, Dean's Files. Yale is often characterized as mother, Harvard as father.

5. Conversation with Stephen Yandle, 2001; Laura Kalman, *Legal Realism at Yale, 1927–*

1960 127 (1986); Guido Calabresi to Julian Cornell, June 8, 1992, Box 21, Chron File, Dean's Files ("I wanted"); Guido Calabresi to Joel Schiavone, May 4, 1993, Box 25, Chron File, id. ("practical matter"). Lucas Cupps provides an excellent discussion of the negotiation of the independence agreement, especially given the number of documents that remain restricted and of individuals who remain unwilling to talk about it, in "Everybody Knows Yale Law School Is Loaded: The History of the Independence Agreement," June 18, 2001 (unpublished manuscript). The characterization of semi-independence was Yandle's. "Law, Med Schools May Avoid Financial Squeeze," *Yale Daily News*, February 13, 1991, at 1. See, e.g., Guido Calabresi to William Brainard and Chip Long, December 1, 1987, Box 57, Chron File, Dean's Files.

6. Guido Calabresi to William Brainard and Chip Long, December 1, 1987, Box 27, Chron File, Dean's Files; Cupps, "Everybody Knows Yale Law School Is Loaded."

7. Interviews with Guido Calabresi, 2003 (quotations) and 2001.

8. Interview with Calabresi, 2003; <http://www.law.yale.edu/outside/html/Alumni-Affairs/alum-give.htm> ($8000); Calabresi to Friends and Graduates, December 7, 1993; interview with Carroll Stevens, 2004 (I am grateful to Stevens and his office for supplying me with annual campaign figures); "For Woman Behind Throne, A Share of an Empire," *New York Times*, July 21, 1991, at A25; "$20 Million to Yale Law School," *New York Times*, September 22, 1992, at B6; "Yale Law Nets Record Gift," *Yale Daily News*, September 22, 1992, at 1 ("biggest gift"); "Lillian Goldman, 80, Yale Law School Donor and Advocate for Women's Education," *New York Times*, August 21, 2002, at C17; "Yale's Entry In Dispute of Goldman's Will Prompts A Debate on Law School's Role," *Wall Street Journal*, March 31, 1989, Section 2, at 5; "Harvard and Yale Both Claim Their Schools Are Top Fund Raisers," *Chronicle of Higher Education*, November 21, 1997, at A35.

9. Guido Calabresi to Tery Segal, May 7, 1990, Box 58, Chron File, Dean's Files; interview with Calabresi, 2001.

10. Interview with Calabresi, 2001. The five were Akhil Amar, Harlon Dalton, Paul Kahn, Harold Koh, and Kate Stith. For a discussion of Amar's work, see Laura Kalman, *The Strange Career of Legal Liberalism* 222–26 (1996).

11. Interview with Calabresi, 2001, and Jack Balkin, 2001.

12. Calvin Trillin, "A Reporter at Large: Harvard Law," *New Yorker*, March 26, 1984, 53, 73; "War Between Professors Pervades Harvard Law: Letter to Alumni Denies Threat to Standards," *Washington Post*, December 21, 1985, at A5; "The Split at Harvard Law Goes Down to Its Foundations," *New York Times*, October 6, 1985, at E7.

13. "Letter Calls for Harvard Probe; Academic Freedom in Peril?," *National Law Journal*, August 10, 1987, at 3; "Ideologies Collide at Harvard Law; 2 Left-Wing Scholars Are Denied Tenure," *Washington Post*, June 12, 1987, at A4; "Appointments Committee Balks at Dalton Tenure," *Harvard Law Record*, April 19, 1985, at 1; Clare Dalton, "'The Political Is Personal' In Tenure Decisions," *Harvard Law Record*, April 22, 1986, at 7; "The Law Professor Who Sued Harvard Tells Why the Deck is Stacked Against Women," *Boston Globe*, October 25, 1993, at Living:36. David Trubek, "Where the Action Is: Critical Legal Studies and Empiricism," 36 *Stan. L. Rev.* 575 (1984). Even the law school's recent decision to require a two-thirds majority, as opposed to a simple majority, must have seemed politically motivated. "Letter Calls for Harvard Probe; Academic Freedom in Peril?"

14. "An Unconventional Traditionalist As the New Dean in the Contentious Environment of Harvard Law School, Robert Clark is Learning the Perils of Challenging the Status Quo," *Boston Globe Sunday Magazine*, March 4, 1990, at 12. For the universally negative reactions of Critical Legal scholars on Harvard's faculty to the announcement of Clark's

selection, see "Conservative to Head Harvard Law," *Boston Globe*, February 18, 1989, at Metro:1; "A Discussion on Critical Legal Studies at Harvard Law School," at 7, 21 ("ritual"); "At Harvard Law, a New Era Dawns," *National Law Journal*, August 7, 1989, at 1 ("no bull-shit").

15. Interview with Balkin. Calabresi's hires included Bruce Ackerman, Ian Ayres, Jack Balkin, Jules Coleman, Robert Ellickson, Daniel Esty, John Langbein, Roberta Romano, Carol Rose, Jed Rubenfeld, Susan Rose-Ackerman, Vicki Schultz, Alan Schwartz, Reva Siegel, Robert Solomon, and James Whitman.

16. John Langbein, *Comparative Criminal Procedure: Germany* (1977), 32; Langbein, "The German Advantage in Civil Procedure," 52 *U. Chi. L. Rev.* 823 (1985); Langbein, "Money Talks, Clients Walk," *Newsweek*, April 17, 1995, 32; Langbein and Lloyd Weinreb, "Continental Criminal Procedure: 'Myth' and Reality," 87 *Yale L. J.* 1549 (1977); Langbein, *Prosecuting Crime in the Renaissance: England, Germany, France* (1974); Langbein, "The Criminal Trial Before the Lawyers," 45 *U. Chicago L. Rev.* 263 (1978); Langbein, "Shaping the Eighteenth-Century Criminal Trial: A View From the Ryder Sources," 50 *U. Chicago L. Rev.* 1 (1983); Langbein, "Substantial Compliance with the Wills Act," 88 *Harv. L. Rev.* 489 (1975); Langbein, "The Nonprobate Revolution and the Future of the Law of Succession," 97 *Harv. L. Rev.* 1108 (1984); Langbein, "The Contractarian Basis of the Law of Trusts," 105 *Yale L. J.* 625 (1995); Langbein, "The Secret Life of the Trust: The Trust as an Instrument of Commerce," 107 *Yale L. J.* 165 (1997).

17. Robert Ellickson, "Taming the Leviathan: Will the Centralizing Tide of the Twentieth Century Continue into the Twenty-First?," 74 *S. Cal. L. Rev.* 101, 103 (2000) (emphasis in the original); Ellickson, *Order without Law: How Neighbors Settle Disputes* viii, vii, 280, 4, 286 (1991); Ellickson, "Rent Control: A Comment on Olsen," 67 *Chi.-Kent L. Rev.* 947, 953–54 (1991) ("anachronistic"); Ellickson, "Controlling Chronic Misconduct in City Spaces: Of Panhandlers, Skid Rows, and Public-Space Zoning," 105 *Yale L. J.* 1165 (1996); Ellickson, "The Homelessness Muddle," 99 *Pub. Int.* 45, 50–51 (Spring 1990).

18. See, e.g., Stephen Munzer, "Ellickson on 'Chronic Misconduct' in Urban Spaces: Of Panhandlers, Bench Squatters, and Day Laborers," 32 *Harv. C.R.-C.L. L. Rev.* 1 (1997); Stephen Wizner, "Homelessness: Advocacy and Social Policy," 45 *U. Miami L. Rev.* 377 (1991); Calabresi to Friends and Graduates, November 15, 1991 ("only name"); Laura Holland "Invading the Ivory Tower: The History of Clinical Education at Yale Law School," 49 *J. Legal Ed.* 504, 529–33 (1999); Hirsch, "Yale Law," *Connecticut* 103, 104–105 (November 1994) (quoting Jeffrey Rosen, a Yale Law School graduate and the legal affairs editor of the *New Republic*); interview with Calabresi, 2001; Calabresi to Friends and Graduates, October 20, 1989.

19. "The Supreme Court: High Court Backs Policy of Halting Haitian Refugees," *New York Times*, June 22, 1993, at A1; "In Front of High Court, Koh Blasts Clinton's Haiti Policy," *Yale Daily News*, March 3, 1993, at 1; "Law Students Nationwide Protest U.S. Haitian Policy," id., March 31, 1993, at 6; Laura Consiglio, "Students: Fledging Lawyers Get a Taste of What It's Like to Help," 50 *Yale Alumni Magazine* 36 (February 1987) (work of clinical program); "2 Yale Law Students Put Lessons to Work in Lead-Poison Case: Result Is a $1 Million Victory," *Connecticut Law Tribune*, October 23, 1989, at 1 (victory of two students in Yale's clinical program in holding landlords liable when son of tenant ate lead paint); "Homeless Helped By Yale Students," *New York Times*, April 25, 1987, Section 11, at 4 (work by students in clinical program to help homeless with their legal problems); "City's Homeless Granted Right to State Shelter," *Yale Daily News*, September 21, 1989, at 1 (suggesting national implications of clinical law students' victory in convincing

a New Haven Superior Court judge that the eviction of more than 100 families from state housing was unconstitutional). The case, *Savage v. Aronson*, 214 Conn. 256 (1990), was reversed in the Connecticut Supreme Court; Yale student Graham Boyd argued it there. It is discussed in Wizner, "Homelessness: Advocacy and Social Policy," at 387–389, 399–400.

20. Calabresi to Friends and Graduates, November 19, 1992. See "Law School to Cancel Some Loans," *New York Times*, April 2, 1989, Section 12 CN, at 9. Wellington and Calabresi had together worked with the provost to develop the Public Interest Career Assistance Program (PICA), a loan deferral and forgiveness program for those who chose careers in public interest law. Harry Wellington and Guido Calabresi to William Brainard, May 31, 1985, Box 57, Chron File, Dean's Files; Calabresi made its approval a condition of his acceptance of the deanship. For his threat of resignation and the Corporation's about-face, see Calabresi to William Brainard, September 5, 1985, Box 57, Chron File, id.; interview with Calabresi, 2001; Calabresi to Margaret Marr, November 18, 1986, Box 57, Chron File, Dean's Files. For a full description of COAP's provisions, see "Lexcetera: Career Options Assistance Program," 35 *Yale L. Report* 22 (Spring 1989).

21. Geoffrey Kabaservice interview with Burke Marshall, 1992.

22. "Committee Recommends 'No-Sanction' Pass," *Harvard Law Record*, April 15, 1983, at 1; "1Ls Urge Grade-Blind Law Review," id., February 10, 1984, at 1; "Student Protest Disrupts Closed Faculty Meetings," id., May 4, 1984, at 1; "Student Input on Appointments Proposed," id., March 9, 1984, 1; "Faculty Says No to Council," id., April 20, 1984, at 1; "Student Protest Disrupts Closed Faculty Meetings," id., May 4, 1984, at 1.

23. Andrea Guerrero, *Silence at Boalt Hall: The Dismantling of Affirmative Action* 37–47 (2002); see also Sumi Cho and Robert Westley, "Historicizing Critical Race Theory's Cutting Edge: Key Movements That Performed the Theory," in Francisco Valdes, Jerome Culp, and Angela Harris, eds., *Crossroads, Directions, and a New Critical Race Theory* 32, 40–48, 57–59 (2002); Donald Downs, *Restoring Free Speech and Liberty on Campus* 135–53 (2005).

24. Guerrero, *Silence at Boalt Hall*, at 34–35, 49–55; "Boalt Students Call for Boycott of Law Classes," *Daily Californian*, March 22, 1988, at 1; "Boalt 'Steeped in Racism,'" id., March 22, 1988, at 4; "Rubin to be Associate Dean," *Boalt Hall Cross-Examiner*, November 1989, at 1, 4; "Point Counter Point: Dean Choper and Renee Saucedo: Politics of Protest," id., September 1989, at 5; "Law School: Just for Research? Choper Discusses Clinics, Teaching, Public Service," id., March 1990, at 1; "Rapping With the Dean," id., October 8, 1990, at 1, 4; "Second Town Meeting on Faculty Diversity Sparks Debate," id., December, 1990, at 8; "Students Arrested at Boalt Hall: University Police Arrest 28 After Daylong Sit-In at Dean's Office," *Daily Californian*, March 23, 1988, at 1; "Protesters Face Criminal Charges," *Boalt Hall Cross-Examiner*, September 1989, at 4; "Boalt 10 Trial Delayed," id., November 1989, at 1; interview with Renee Saucedo, 2002 ("bigger"); email, Paul Burke to author, July 18, 2002 (Burke was another member of the CDF); see also Paul Carrington, "Accreditation and the AALS: The Boalt Affair," 41 *J. Legal Ed.* 363 (1991).

25. Guerrero, *Silence at Boalt Hall*, at 53.

26. See generally Neil Duxbury, *Patterns of American Jurisprudence* 503–9 (1995), and Gary Minda, *Postmodern Legal Movements: Law and Jurisprudence at Century's End* 140–41, 173–75 (1995) (discussing the complex relationship of feminist legal theory and Critical Race Theory to CLS); Kimberle Crenshaw, "The First Decade: Critical Reflections, or 'A Foot in the Closing Door,'" *Crossroads, Directions, and a New Critical Race Theory*, 9, 16, n. 12 (suggesting that the major figures in CLS reacted even more hostilely to Critical Race Theory than they did to feminist legal theory). Two of the professors, Charles Ogletree

and Derrick Bell, were then visitors, but would soon join—or in Bell's case, rejoin—the faculty.

27. Derrick Bell, *Confronting Authority: Reflections of an Ardent Protester* (1995)

28. "Of Diversity and Respect," *Harvard Law Record*, May 4, 1990, at 4.

29. Emma Jordan, "Images of Black Women in the Legal Academy: An Introduction," 6 *Berkeley Women's Law J.* 1, 5 (1990–91) ("slipper," "'qualified'"); Bell, *Confronting Authority*, at 63 ("rotating"); "Protesters Camp Out at Law Dean's Office," *Boston Globe*, April 7, 1990, at Metro:27; "Students Protest Dean on Diversity," *Harvard Law Record*, April 11, 1990, at 1 (singing); "Years of Faculty Neglect Necessitate Sit-In," id. at 5 ("no-show," "sanctum"); "Flexibility, Determination at Harvard Law," *Boston Globe*, October 30, 1990, at Metro:21; "Jesse Jackson Exhorts Harvard to Diversify Law Faculty," id., March 12, 1992, Metro:40. The photograph appeared on the front page of the April 11, 1990, issue of the *Harvard Law Record*.

30. Elaine Kerlow, *Poisoned Ivy: How Egos, Ideology and Power Politics Almost Ruined Harvard Law School* 100–101 (1994).

31. "Students Sue HLS Over Faculty Hiring: School Seeks More Time to File Reply," *Harvard Law Record*, November 30, 1990, at 1; Kerlow, *Poisoned Ivy*, at 105; "Students Take Diversity Fight Against Harvard to State Court," *National Law Journal*, March 4, 1991, at 4 ("We have").

32. "CCR Holds Public Meeting," *Harvard Law Record*, February 28, 1992, at 1 ("*Brown*"); Kerlow, *Poisoned Ivy*, at 105, 109 ("steal," "Of course"); "Discrimination Suit Dismissed: CCR Says It Will Appeal," *Harvard Law Record*, March 1, 1991, at 1, 8 ("impressed," "gratified," "trying," "clinical"); "SJC Affirms Ruling Dismissing Harvard Law Students' Bias Suit," *Boston Globe*, July 11, 1992, at Metro:26. The suit was not popular with all students, who were more obviously ideologically diverse than those of the sixties. See, e.g., "Students Intervene in CCR Suit," *Harvard Law Record*, February 8, 1991, at 1; "The Radical Fringe Must Be Stopped," id., February 15, 1991, at 4.

33. "Students Strike for Diversity: Rally Roils Campus; CCR Vows Further Action," *Harvard Law Record*, April 12, 1991, at 1; "Cambridge Police Have a Knife, No Motive in Professor's Murder," *Boston Globe*, April 6, 1991, at Metro:1; "An Accomplished Life, A Brutal Death," id., April 14, 1991, Metro:1; "Students Storm Dean Clark's Office," *Harvard Law Record*, April 12, 1991, at 2 ("first time").

34. Kerlow, *Poisoned Ivy*, at 124; "4 White Men Offered Tenure," *Harvard Law Record*, March 6, 1992, at 1 (the four were Robert Mnookin, Joseph Weiler, Henry Hansmann, and Joseph Singer; only Hansmann did not accept the offer); "Students Say Announcement Violates Policy," id., March 6, 1992, at 1; "Spring of Shame and Pain," id., September 18, 1992, at 6 ("politically," "package"); Bell, *Confronting Authority*, at 83–86.

35. Indeed, Roger Kimball's *Tenured Radicals: How Politics Has Corrupted Our Higher Education* (1990, 1998) focused on the scholarship, more than workplace politics, of sixties radicals now occupying senior positions in the academy. Professors who had come to maturity in the 1960s and who had once considered themselves radical refused to throw themselves into new battles led by a younger generation of students elsewhere too. See, e.g., Robert Johnston, "Where Have All the Tenured Radicals Gone?," <http://lists.village.virginia.edu/lists__archive/sixties-l/1472.html>.

36. Ruth Shalit, "Hate Story: Racial Strife at Law School; Harvard Law School Hiring of Charles Ogletree," *New Republic*, 8 (June 7, 1993) ("spasm"); "Students Say Announcement Violates Policy" ("almost"); "The Road From False Promises to True Diversity," *Harvard Law Record*, March 6, 1992, at 9; Kerlow, *Poisoned Ivy*, at 164–67; "Clark, Students

Discuss Diversity on 'Zero Day,'" *Harvard Law Record*, March 20, 1992, at 1; "Harvard Law School Finds Its Counterrevolutionary," *Wall Street Journal*, March 25, 1992, at A13 ("tremendous," "minority").

37. "Flexibility, Determination at Harvard Law," *Boston Globe*, October 30, 1990, at Metro:21; "Rebuilding Beirut: A Liberal Vision for Harvard Law," id., February 11, 1990, Business:A1 ("contribute"). See Christopher Newfield, "What Was Political Correctness? Race, the Right and Managerial Democracy in the Humanities," 19 *Critical Inquiry* 308 (1993).

38. Mary Jo Frug, "A Postmodern Feminist Legal Manifesto (An Unfinished Draft)," 116 *Harv. L. Rev.* 1045 (1992); "Sexist Cruelty Strikes at Harvard Law," *Legal Times*, April 27, 1992, at 28; "The Revue in the Center of Controversy," *Harvard Law Record*, April 17, 1992, at 11; "The-Not-So-Civil War at Harvard Law School; Revue Parody Lays Bare Deeper Divisions," *Boston Globe*, April 26, 1992, at 74. For an account of the debate, see Kerlow, *Poisoned Ivy*, at 57–71, 253–60, 291.

39. "Griswold 9 Take Over Dean's Office," *Harvard Law Record*, April 10, 1992, at 1 (quotation); "Student Groups Call for Dean Clark's Resignation," id., April 17, 1992, at 19.

40. "The Griswold Nine: From Start to Finish," id., September 18, 1992, at 6 ("When"); Kerlow, *Poisoned Ivy*, at 277–91.

41. Harry Wellington, "Free Speech at Yale," 22 *Yale L. Report* 3, 3 (Fall 1975).

42. "War of the Words: Four Years in Yale's New Battle for Freedom of Expression," *Yale Daily News*, Commencement, 1989, 12; Guido Calabresi to Leo Graybill, July 15, 1986, Box 27, Chron File, Dean's Files; Calabresi to Maurice Nessen, January 4, 1988, id. On Wayne Dick, see Guido Calabresi to Robert Keeler, September 26, 1986, Box 57, Chron File, id. ("travesty"); Guido Calabresi to Peggy and Skok Little, September 19, 1986, id. ("hopeless") (and see Nat Hentoff, *Free Speech for Me but Not for Thee: How the American Left and Right Relentlessly Censor Each Other* 127–29 [1992]); Guido Calabresi to Gerald Conway, January 10, 1989, Box 27, Chron File, Dean's Files ("making liberalism"). For Calabresi's actions with respect to "Wanda Whips Wall Street," I have relied on an interview with Calabresi in 2002 and a letter from Michael Manley to Guido Calabresi, May 28, 1988, Box 62, Folder M, id. (discussing Calabresi's speech to the crowd before the film began).

43. Guido Calabresi to Samuel Neal, July 1, 1986, Box 57, Chron File, Dean's Files.

44. Harlon Dalton, Scott Burris, and the Yale AIDS Law Project, eds., *Aids and the Law: A Guide for the Public* (1987); Harlon Dalton, *Racial Healing* (1995).

45. Tanina Rostain, "Tribute," 96 *Yale L. J.* 1713, 1716 (1987) ("us"); Fiss, "Tribute," at 1722; SALT: Robert Cover Biography, <http://www.saltlaw.org/publicinterestcover. htm>; Tushnet, "Critical Legal Studies," at 1540, n. 96 ("pantheon," "apotheosizing"); and see "Students and Professors at Yale Try to Carry Activist's Torch," *National Law Journal*, February 5, 1990, at 4.

46. Guido Calabresi to Michael Weinberger, March 26, 1987, Box 23, Folder W, Dean's Files (Calabresi's nephew); Guido Calabresi to The Editor, *Wall Street Journal*, February 25, 1987, Box 58, Chron File, id. Calabresi was responding to an editorial entitled "Freedom 101 (Ltd. Enrollment)," February 25, 1987, Section 1, at 28.

47. Guido Calabresi to Victor Johnson, March 1, 1993, Box 24, Folder J, Dean's Files (reporting Cover's view); "Yale Law: Inside the School That Cast the Thomas/Hill Drama," *Chicago Tribune*, October 28, 1991, Section 5, at 1 ("[a]nything," and see Lawrence Lessig, *Code and Other Laws of Cyberspace* 79–80 [1999]); Guido Calabresi to Michael Socarras, October 9, 1986, Box 57, Chron Files, Dean's Files; Calabresi to Victor Johnson,

March 1, 1993, Box 24, Folder J, id. (critics); Calabresi to Robin Kelsey, December 14, 1992, Box 21, Chron File, id. ("brick bats," "That's" [emphasis in the original]). In 1997, Harvard Law School's Society for Law, Life & Religion, a Christian students' group, placed posters around the school denouncing homosexuality. Soon afterward, anonymous members of the "HLS Society for Law, Loathing and Hate" put up their own parodies of the poster. Clark first issued a memorandum railing against the second poster as uncivilized, then circulated another acknowledging that offensive parodies were permissible, but that law school policy did not permit anonymous posters. "At Harvard, Debate Flies Over 'Ex-Gay' Ministry; Dueling Posters Prompt Free-Speech Discussion," *Boston Globe*, October 11, 1997, at B1.

48. Interview with Calabresi, 2002; Calabresi to Mrs. Gerald Sirkin, December 10, 1992, Box 21, Chron File, Dean's Files ("tastelessness"); Guido Calabresi to John Murtha, December 10, 1992, id. (remaining quotations); conversation with Mike Thompson, Associate Dean, 2001 (confirmation hearings).

49. "Student Scribblers," *National Law Journal*, November 28, 1988, at 4; "Yale Law Students Turn the Tables on Job Interviewers," *Wall Street Journal*, October 19, 1988, at 68 ("as a group"); "On the Wall: Yale Students Rate Firms: Good, Bad, and a Bit Ugly," *Connecticut Law Tribune*, November 25, 1988, at 1, 4; and see "Students Grill Potential Bosses: What Is Life Really Like There," June 19, 1989, *National Law Journal*, June 19, 1989, at 4 ("lies"); Steven Brill, "Boycott Cleary, Gottlieb!," *American Lawyer* 3, 4 (September 1989) (contending that because of law firms' need for large groups of associates, students had more leverage to press them to adopt desired policies than they did to prod law schools to increase minority faculty appointments).

50. "Yale Law Students Turn the Tables on Job Interviewers" (emphasis in the original); Calabresi to Friends and Graduates, October 20, 1989 ("deeply religious"); interview with Calabresi, 2002.

51. Deborah Moss, "Women in Law," 74 *Am. Bar Assn. J.* 49, 53 (June 1988); "A Battle for Yale Law School's Soul? Offer to a Feminist Draws Fury," *National Law Journal*, February 15, 1988, at 3 (quoting Lucinda Finley).

52. Fiss, *Law As It Could Be* 205, 193 (2003).

53. "A Battle for Yale Law School's Soul?," at 3 (reporting alleged comments of Lea Brilmayer, "overtones," "war"); Owen Fiss, "The Law Regained," 74 *Cornell L. Rev.* 245, 246 (1989). Brilmayer's comments may not have been correctly reported; Calabresi characterized the article as inaccurate. Guido Calabresi to Benno Schmidt and William Nordhaus, February 9, 1988, Box 27, Chron File, Dean's File.

54. "Yale Law Promotes Five, Increases Faculty Diversity," *Connecticut Law Tribune*, February 5, 1990, at 3 ("monochromatically"); "Law Students Stage Boycott," *Yale Daily News*, April 7, 1989, at 1, 7 ("champion," "few"); "Striking a Blow for Law School Diversity," id., April 6, 1989, at 2.

55. "Striking a Blow for Law School Diversity"; Guido Calabresi to Michele Baker, May 25, 1990, Box 58, Chron File, Dean's Files; Calabresi to David Yaasky, June 4, 1990, id. (both characterizing MacKinnon as one of his best students and speaking of how much he had learned from her); Guido Calabresi to Kate Tilson, February 1, 1988, Box 27, id. ("only school," "remarkable"); interview with Calabresi, 2002 ("failure"); "Yale Law Promotes Five, Increases Faculty Diversity" (Dalton).

56. "Years of Faculty Neglect Necessitate Sit-In"; "Law Students Stage Boycott," at 7 (Yandle); Guido Calabresi to Friends and Graduates, October 20, 1989.

57. Guido Calabresi to the Law School Community, December 1, 1992, Box 21, Chron

File, Dean's Files ("exceedingly," "self-indulgent"); "Dean Rebukes Law Student," *Yale Daily News*, December 2, 1992, at 1, 7 ("personal," "crowded"); "Law Faculty Criticize Dean for Poster Memo," id., December 3, 1992, at 1, 5; Guido Calabresi to Morgan Ames, December 14, 1992, Box 21, Chron File, Dean's Files ("navigate," "deans"); "AIDS Poster Causes Furor at Yale Law," *New Haven Register*, December 3, 1992, at 3, 5 ("This").

58. "Law School Outraged at Gay Harassment," *New Haven Independent*, May 21, 1987, at 1, 4.

59. Guido Calabresi to Lawrence Levine, October 19, 1990, Box 58, Chron File, Dean's Files; "Racist Letters Spark Uproar at Law School," *Yale Daily News*, September 21, 1990, at 1 ("classmates," "two black," "most vicious"); "To Show Minority Solidarity, Yale Students Stage Moratorium," *National Law Journal*, October 22, 1990, at 4 ("fully," "like"); "Racist Hate Mail Stuns Yale Law School," *Harvard Law Record*, October 5, 1990, at 2; "Law Students Strike Against Racism," *Yale Daily News*, October 11, 1990, at 1, 3 ("easy"). Sometime after the 1960s, the Black Law Students Union had become the Black Law Student Association.

60. Jeff Rosen, "Hate Mail," *New Republic*, 19, 21–22 (February 18, 1991) (criticizing Calabresi and quoting Schmidt); Guido Calabresi to Friends and Graduates, November 5, 1990 ("trying," "unambiguously"; emphasis in the original); and November 15, 1991 ("to show").

61. Guido Calabresi to Marnia Robinson, May 5, 1993, Box 21, Chron File, Dean's Files; "Many Black Faces, Many Black Views," *Harvard Law Record*, October 25, 1991, at 8; "200 Protest Speech by Nation of Islam Leader," *Yale Daily News Review*, March 2, 1990, at 1 (sign); Guido Calabresi to the Law School Community, February 8, 1990. That reminder may not have been necessary since Jewish law students acknowledged Muhammad's right to speak at Yale, stressing that what hurt them was the invitation. "Nation of Islam Spokesman Brings Controversy to Yale." *Yale Daily News*, February 9, 1990, at 1.

62. Calabresi to the Law School Community, February 8, 1990. Emphasis in the original.

63. Guido Calabresi to Faculty, Staff, and Students, February 16, 1990, Box 58, Chron File, Dean's Files.

64. "At the Bar; For President Clinton, Old-School Ties Take Precedence Over Senators' Wishes in a Search for a Judge," *New York Times*, October 29, 1993, at B9. When Calabresi received an eloquent and bitter letter from William Felstiner lodging the complaint Yale had turned its back on law and social science, he passed it along to the Appointments Committee. Felstiner to Calabresi, November 27, 1991, Box 24, Folder F, Dean's Files. Calabresi commented to me that he wished he had received more such complaints. He seemed sincere. Interview with Calabresi, 2001. The complaint Yale had surrendered to the forces of political correctness was a frequent theme of letters from alumni whenever a negative article about the school in the *Wall Street Journal* appeared. The dean explained how he responded to a complaint in Guido Calabresi to Dorothy Robinson, September 22, 1992, Box 21, Chron File, Dean's Files. Wellington spoke of the alumni preference in Harry Wellington to Mark Zimmerman, November 10, 1981, Box 17, id.; Calabresi described how it operated in a letter to Victor Johnson, January 18, 1993, Box 20, id. For an example of Calabresi's approach to rejections, see Guido Calabresi to Leonard Marks, April 19, 1988, Box 62, Folder M, id. For an example of the call to rejoice, see Catherine Weiss to Guido Calabresi, May 3, 1993, Box 25, Folder W, id. (expressing her shock and gratitude that Calabresi had found the time to telephone). (Having reviewed much of Calabresi's cor-

respondence, I share Weiss's wonder. Indeed, I defy anyone to read it without exclaiming of Calabresi at some point, even if in exasperation: "Damn, he's good!")

65. Norman Boucher, "Yale Law Review: Is the Law School of Bill Clinton, Jerry Brown, Clarence Thomas, and Anita Hill Still Producing Public Servants, or Has the Ivy League's Conscience Gone Corporate?," *Boston Globe Magazine*, April 26, 1992, at 15, 39 ("village"); Hirsch, "Yale Law," at 103 ("place"); Catherine Weiss and Louise Melling, "The Legal Education of Twenty Women," 40 *Stan. L. Rev.* 1299, 1326, n. 90 (1988) ("mistake"); Paula Gabler, "'Just Trying to Be Human in This Place': The Legal Education of Twenty Women," 10 *Yale J. Law and Feminism* 165, 178 n. 69 (1998) ("treadmill"); David Bollier and Tracy Thompson, "Dean Guido Calabresi," 32 *Yale L. Report* 23, 27 (1985) ("civilized"); Guido Calabresi to Friends and Graduates, November 2, 1987 ("warmth and affection"); interview with Calabresi, 2002.

66. Guido Calabresi to Louise Frankel, November 1, 1991, Box 60, Chron File, Dean's Files ("Like"); Owen Jones to Calabresi, February 15, 1988, January 30, 1988, Box 61, Folder J, id. ("somewhat").

67. Gabler, "Just Trying to Be Human in This Place," at 247, 246.

68. "Student Law School Experience Survey," in information and data gathered by the Dean's Ad Hoc Committee on the status of Women at Yale Law School 8 (1996), reporting on experience of students in 1996, 1997, and 1998, Yale Law Library; Gabler, "Just Trying to Be Human in This Place," at 173. Gabler's article focuses on those who entered Yale in 1994, just as Calabresi's deanship concluded.

69. Paul Brest, "Plus ça Change," 91 *Mich. L. Rev.* 1945, 1948 (1993) ("terrorist"); Paul Carrington, "Hail! Langdell!," 20 *L. & Soc. Inq'y.* 691, 748 (1995) ("concerned"). I have drawn from Weiss and Melling, "Legal Education of Twenty Women" (reporting the experience of twenty women from the class of 1987); "Information and Data gathered by the Dean's Ad Hoc Committee on the Status of Women"; and "Summary of Selected Comments by Survey Respondents," Yale Law Library; "The Clerkship Surveys," reporting on data from clerkship surveys distributed to all second- and third-year students in 1991 and 1996, id.; "Student Law School Experience Survey," reporting on experience of students in classes of 1996, 1997, and 1998, id.; and Gabler, "Just Trying to Be Human in This Place" (reporting on experience of twenty women in the class of 1997).

70. Gabler, "Just Trying to Be Human in This Place," at 166, n. 4, 184, 207 (providing citations to the large body of empirical literature on women's experience in law school, "just," "distinct"); "Student Law School Experience Survey," at 5 (less comfortable) (see also, e.g., Sarah Berger, Angela Burton, Peggy Davis, Elizabeth Ehrenfest Steinglass, and Robert Levy, "'Hey! There's Ladies Here!!,'" 73 *N.Y.U. L. Rev.* 1022 (1998) [reviewing Guinier, Fine, and Balin, *Becoming Gentlemen*; Linda Wrightman, *Women in Legal Education: A Comparison of the Law School Performance and Law School Experience of Women and Men* (1996)]; Elizabeth Mertz with Wamucil Njogu and Susan Gooding, "What Difference Does Difference Make? The Challenge for Legal Education," 48 *J. Legal Educ.* 1 (1998); and Louise Harmon and Deborah Post, *Cultivating Intelligence: Power, Law, and the Politics of Teaching*); Weiss and Melling, "Legal Education of Twenty Women," at 1299, 1335, 1305, 1338, n. 110, 1321, 1326, 1358, 1346–47 ("four faces," "generalized," "nervous," "hurt by," "community," "competition," "'lack of contact,'" "real world," "intellectual substance," "inadequate inquiry"); Jane Park to Ad Hoc Committee on the Status of Women, May 6, 1996, Re: Student Responses, 5, "Student Law School Experience Survey" ("myth"); and see Gabler, "Just Trying to Be Human in This Place," at 214, 255, for similar

complaints about the lack of posted office hours. For a more recent discussion of gender at Yale, see Yale Law Women, "Yale Law School Faculty and Students Speak About Gender: A Report on Faculty Student Relations at Yale Law School," <http://www.yale.edu/ylw>.

71. Gabler, "Just Trying to Be Human in This Place," at 196.

72. Weiss and Melling, "Legal Education of Twenty Women," at 1348; Gabler, "Just Trying to Be Human in This Place," at 237 ("reported").

73. "Summary of Selected Comments by Survey Respondents," at 10 ("[m]any professors," "plugged"); Gabler, "Just Trying to Be Human in This Place," at 189 ("screwed-up").

74. "At Yale Law, a Gender Gap in Who Gets Clerkships Sparks Debate," *Washington Post*, May 13, 1991, at F5. Women did much better at the district court level. "Few Top Clerkships for Yale Women," *Connecticut Law Tribune*, July 1, 1991, at 1. The comparative data between 1971 and 1986 are from the Report from the Placement Policy Committee Chair in the Yale Law School Faculty Minutes, April 13, 1988 (hereafter YLS Faculty Minutes).

75. "At Yale Law, a Gender Gap." They set their song to Cyndi Lauper's tune in "Girls Just Want to Have Fun."

76. Id. ("fared"); Gabler, "Just Trying to Be Human in This Place," at 249 (dominance of white men in classroom). At Harvard, twenty-two men and twelve women had obtained the most competitive appellate clerkships in 1991, as compared to seventeen Yale men and two Yale women. "Few Top Clerkships for Yale Women."

77. "At Yale Law, a Gender Gap" ("a lot," "opportunity," "action"); Gabler, "Just Trying To Be Human in This Place," at 177, n. 68 ("lack"); "Gender Gap," *Connecticut Law Tribune*, November 11, 1991, at 17 (Romano, "shy women"). Gender was the focus because Yale's placement office had not segregated data by color, but by sex. "Few Top Clerkships for Yale Women."

78. "Gender Gap" ("blurry," Romano); "Few Top Clerkships for Yale Women" ("no help," "can't," "deciphering").

79. The students' complaint was in an undated memorandum, which Bittker thought dated from around 1972 and which he gave to Pollak. Box 38, Folder: Grading 1967–1970, Dean's Files. But at a 1972 Yale Law School faculty meeting, student representatives did not seem to favor adoption of a high pass grade. YLS Faculty Minutes, May 12, 1972. Surely some faculty members were even more annoyed by Yale's grading system than students. At one point, Calabresi strongly favored numerical grades. Guido Calabresi to Harry Wellington, February 15, 1972, Box 1, Folder C, Dean's Files. Nonetheless, the law school clung to the grading system it had adopted in the 1960s, though Wellington said he tried to force his colleagues to reexamine it. Harry Wellington to James Oakes, May 7, 1982, Box 17, Chron File, Dean's Files. The observation that clerkships could threaten friendships is from "Portrait of an HLSer turned Yalie," *Harvard Law Record*, March 17, 2000, at 3. The Student Guide to Yale Law School, 2003–04, also discusses competition around clerkships. <http://www.yale.edu/ylw/ylwstudentguide>. For the suggestion that Yale's grading system may account for its success in recruiting students, see Tom Smith, "The Mystery of Yale Law School," <http://Leiterreports/typepad.com/blog/2004/04/the__mystery__of__html>.

80. "Yale Law Spreads Its Vision of Law by Educating Professors," *Yale Daily News*, March 4, 1999, at 1, 4 ("Although"); "Few Top Clerkships for Yale Women," at 12 ("It's Not," "initiative"); "At Yale Law, A Gender Gap in Who Gets Clerkships Sparks Debate" ("brown-nose").

81. "Portrait of an HLSer turned Yalie," at 4; Calabresi to Friends and Graduates,

November 19, 1992; Laurel Leff, "What a Long, Strange Trip It's Been," *Connecticut Law Tribune*, April 20, 1992, at 1.

82. Supra, text accompanying Chapter 3, note 63, and Chapter 6, note 67; Guido Calabresi to Victor Johnson, April 19, 1993, Box 21, Chron File, Dean's Files.

83. Supra; "Yale Law: Inside the School That Cast the Thomas/Hill Drama," at 4.

84. Calabresi to Friends and Graduates, November 19, 1992.

85. Interview with Calabresi, 2002; Bollier and Thompson, "Dean Guido Calabresi," at 27 ("cajole," "lead"); confidential interviews.

86. Calabresi to Friends and Graduates, November 19, 1992 ("opportunity," "problem"); interview with Calabresi, 2002. I have not read the correspondence of deans prior to Thomas Swan, but I doubt professors were as contented under Swan's predecessors as they were under Calabresi, either.

87. Calabresi to Friends and Graduates, December 7, 1993 (Schultz and Balkin).

88. Hirsch, "Yale Law," at 105, 106; "Yale Law Alumni Focus on Reunion, or Tries To," *New York Times*, October 13, 1991, at A34 ("continue," "first hit").

89. "Brains For The Bar," *U.S. News & World Report*, November 2, 1987, 72, 73; "Law," id., March 19, 1990, 59; "America's Top-Ranked Law School," id. at 61; Brian Leiter, "Measuring the Academic Distinction of Law Faculties," 29 *J. Legal Stud.* 451, 452, n. 1 (2000); Kerlow, *Poisoned Ivy*, at 164; "U.S. News Ranks Yale Law Highest in National Survey," *Yale Daily News*, March 28, 1990, at 3 (quoting Calabresi); "Top 25 Law Schools," *U.S. News & World Report*, April 29, 1991, 74; "Yale #1 Again!!," *Harvard Law Record*, March 20, 1992, at 1, 4; and see "Academics Continue to Debate the Relative Virtues of Ranking," *National Law Journal*, June 25, 1990, at 4.

90. "Yale Law School *is* Number One," *Harvard Law Record*, November 1, 1991, at 4. Emphasis in the original. The *Record*'s editor-in-chief that year had nursed a grudge against his law school since his first year, when he had sent a letter to the *Record* denouncing Harvard and saying that perhaps he should have gone to Yale. Robert Arnold, Letter to the Editor, id., September 21, 1990, at 4.

91. Fred Shapiro, "The Most-Cited Legal Scholars," 29 *J. Legal Stud.* 409, 420, 423 (2000); Shapiro, "The Most-Cited Law Reviews," id. at 389, 394.

92. Guido Calabresi to Michael Socarras, August 12, 1987, Box 27, Chron File, Dean's Files ("worthy"); Calabresi to Louise and James Frankel, September 16, 1987, id. ("whose views"); Calabresi to Stephen Reinhardt, September 16, 1987, id., ("deluged"). Yale law school professors who been Bork's colleagues or students sent Senator Danforth a statement saying that although they had divided over the nomination, they all admired Bork as an individual. "Statement To Be Sent to Senator Danforth," n.d., id. Burke Marshall, Paul Gewirtz, and Owen Fiss testified against Bork's confirmation; John Simon, George Priest, and Eugene Rostow testified in favor. Nomination of Robert H. Bork to Be Associate Justice of the Supreme Court of the U.S., Committee on the Judiciary, Senate, September 21, 1987, Part I (Marshall, 1087); Part II, September 25, 1987 (Fiss, 2491; Gewirtz, 2555; Priest, 2435; and Simon, 2445); Part III, September 29, 1987 (Rostow, 3279). On Yale as shorthand for Bork's intelligence, see, e.g., Editorial, "Robert Bork Is More Than Just A Resume," *Business Week*, July 20, 1987, 190.

93. "For President Clinton, Old-School Ties Take Precedence" ("Rashomon"); "At the Bar: In a Confirmation Hearing Filled with Yalies, the Law School's Dean Is Caught in the Crossfire," *New York Times*, October 11, 1991, at B7 ("dean of deans," "ferociously," "blind"); Calabresi to Reginald Alleyne, October 21, 1993, Box 20, Chron File, Dean's Files ("wrong"); Calabresi to Friends and Graduates, November 15, 1991 ("disagreed," "told").

94. Michael Thelwell, "False, Fleeting, Perjured Clarence: Yale's Blackest and Brightest Go to Washington," in Toni Morrison, ed., *Race-Ing Justice, En-Gendering Power: Essays on Anita Hill, Clarence Thomas, and the Construction of Social Reality*, 86, 89 (1992); "Yale Law School Focuses on Reunion, or Tries To" ("tawdriness"); "Yale Law: Inside the School That Cast the Thomas/Hill Drama," at 1 (banner).

95. Calabresi to Friends and Graduates, November 19, 1992. The Bush administration veterans were Donald Elliott and Michael Graetz.

96. "Yale Alumni Take Lead Again, Even If Not In Law," *New York Times*, March 20, 1992, at B16; Steve Stark, "The Yale Connection," *Boston Globe*, ca. March 1992, courtesy Yale Law School Public Affairs Office; "A Hot Ticket Enjoys Its Ivy Climb: As Yale Gains Prominence, View From Cambridge Can Be Crabby," *Washington Post*, January 19, 1993, at A8; Jeff Greenfield, "The Yale Plot To Take Over America," *M: The New He-Man* 76 (May 1992).

97. "Yale Law Spreads Its Vision of the Law By Educating Professors," *Yale Daily News*, March 4, 1999, at 1, 4; Guido Calabresi to Friends and Graduates, September 27, 1985 ("Ecole"). Yale has retained its special success in placing its graduates on the faculties of elite law schools. To cite but one example, more than twice as many members of the University of Virginia law faculty in 2004 held Yale law degrees compared to those who possess Harvard JDs. "Yale Law School in the Sixties Marked by Student Radicalism, Schism in the Left," November 20, 2003, <http://www.law.virginia.edu/home2002/html/news/2003__fall/yale.htm>. And see Lawrence Solum, "Hiring Trends at 18 'Top' American Law Schools," <http://lsolum.blogspot.com/archives/2004__07__01__lsolum__archive.html#108912594144211701>.

98. Hillary Rodham Clinton, "What I Learned in Law School," 39 *Yale L. Report* 1, 4 (Fall 1992); "The Education of Hillary Rodham Clinton: Candidate's Wife Learned to Love 'the System' at Yale Law School," *Legal Times*, October 19, 1992, at 2; Guido Calabresi to Victor Johnson, April 19, 1993, Box 21, Chron File, Dean's Files.

99. "Bork Blames Yale For Decline of Western Civilization," December 8, 1996, *Chicago Tribune*, Section: Perspective, 2; and see Robert Bork, *Slouching Toward Gomorrah: Modern Liberalism and American Decline* (1996); "Legal Hair-Splitters Can't Ask Us To Take Their Words at Face Value," *Connecticut Post*, September 16, 1998, courtesy Yale Law School Public Affairs Office; "Yale Law: Don't Blame Us For President," *Newsday*, September 26, 1998, at A12.

100. Hirsch, "Yale Law," at 104 ("suddenly," "occupied"); Guido Calabresi to Ian Stock, November 23, 1992, Box 25, Folder S, Dean's Files ("very loyal"). Both Clintons spoke at Alumni Weekend, 1993, the occasion of Bill Clinton's twentieth reunion. Hillary Clinton introduced the president. For his speech, see the weekly compilation of Presidential Documents, 2047–2054, Presidential Documents On Line Via GPO Access, October 9, 1993, Volume 29, No. 41: 2047.

101. The 1970s data are in James Thomas, "Admissions: Class of 1979," September 13, 1976, YLS Faculty Minutes; interview with Calabresi, 2002. Henry Hansmann, "Higher Education As An Associative Good," Paper prepared for the 1998 Symposium of the Forum for the Future of Higher Education, Aspen, September 28 and 29, 1998; Calabresi to Friends and Graduates, November 19, 1992.

102. Remarks of Senator Hillary Rodham Clinton, Class Day, Yale University, May 20, 2001, <http://clinton.senate.gov/clinton/speeches/001420.html>.

103. Seth Stern, "Harvard Law Changes the Pace of Its Paper Chase," *Christian Science Monitor*, October 24, 200, at 13 (National Jurist survey, Princeton review, and 1999 study);

"Kagan Holds Town Hall," *Record*, April 24, 2003, <http://www.hlrecord.org/news/42695 .html> ("embarrassed") (formerly *Harvard Law Record*); "Looking Back: 14 Years of Robert Clark," id., April 24, 2003, <http://www.hlrecord.org/news/424577.html> ("half-baked"); Lewis Rice, "The Man of the Moment," *Harvard Law Bulletin*, Summer 2003, <http:/www.Harvard.edu/alumni.bulletin/>. The wealthy and prestigious law schools about to acquire new deans included Columbia (David Schizer) and Stanford (Larry Kramer).

104. Calabresi to Friends and Graduates, November 19, 1992 (quotation; emphasis in the original); Guido Calabresi, "In Memory of Grant Gilmore: Grant Gilmore and the Golden Age," 91 *Yale L. J.* 1, 1 (1982).

AFTERWORD

1. Julie Reuben, "Reforming the University: Student Protests and the Demand for a 'Relevant' Curriculum," in Gerald DeGroot, ed., *Student Protest: The Sixties and After* 153, 168 (1998); Maria-Regina Kecht, "The Challenge of Responsibility," in Knecht, ed., *Pedagogy Is Politics: Literary Theory and Critical Teaching* 5 (1992).

2. "Rubin to be Assoc. Dean," *The Boalt Hall Cross-Examiner*, November 1989, at 1, 4.

3. "A Discussion on Critical Legal Studies at the Harvard Law School," presented by The Harvard Society and The Federalist Society, The Harvard Club, New York City, May 13, 1985, 31 ("think"); Duncan Kennedy, "Politicizing the Classroom," 4 *S. Cal. Rev. L. & Women's Stud.* 81, 81–82, 84, 87–88 (1994).

4. Peter Goodrich, "The Personal and the Political: Duncan Kennedy as I Imagine Him: The Man, The Work, His Scholarship, and the Polity," 22 *Cardozo L. Rev.* 971, 974, 973 (2001) ("dressed," "black"); Orin Kerr, "The Decline of the Socratic Method at Harvard," 78 *Neb. L. Rev.* 113, 131 (1999); "Duncan Kennedy," 48 *Harvard Law Bulletin* 24 (Fall 1996) ("love"); Marc Granetz, "Duncan the Doughnut," *New Republic*, March 17, 1986, at 22; Jeffrey Kahlenberg, *Broken Contract: A Memoir of Harvard Law School* at 160 ("This is") (1972).

5. Philip C. Kissam, "The Ideology of the Case Method/Final Examination Law School," 70 *U. Cin. L. Rev.* 137, 169 (2001) ("priority"); "Professor Hopes to Write History of HLS," *Record*, November 21, 2002, <http://www.hlrecord.org/news/329240.html> (quoting Daniel Coquillette); "Kagan Holds Town Hall," *Record*, April 24, 2003, <http:// www.hlrecord.org./news/42695.html>.

6. Clarence Thomas, "Speech: Cordell Hull Speakers Forum," 25 *Cumb. L. Rev.* 611, 613, 614 (1994).

7. Brian Leiter, "Measuring the Academic Distinction of Law Faculties," 29 *J. Legal Stud.* 451, 454, n. 7 ("place") (2000).

8. James White, "Letter to Judge Harry Edwards," 91 *Mich. L. Rev.* 2177, 2179–80 (1993); Paul Brest, "Plus ça Change," 91 *Mich. L. Rev.* 1945, 1950 (1993) ("asleep").

9. Peter Goodrich, "The Personal and the Political," at 977–78 ("casual," "stuff"); Leiter, "Measuring the Academic Distinction of Law Faculties," at 452 ("predictable").

10. Nomination of Robert H. Bork to Be Associate Justice of the Supreme Court of the U.S., Committee on the Judiciary, Senate, September 25, 1987, Part II, 2435, 2437. Priest, however, described it as a post–World War II development. Id. at 2435.

Index

ABA Code of Professional Responsibility, 226
Abel, Richard: and faculty-student relationship, 63, 166, 265, 266; and Vietnam War, 165, 166; and Pollak's executive session faculty meeting, 172; and failed promotion, 234, 239, 263–66, 309; and Law and Society, 245, 260, 264, 265; and Griffiths, 255, 265; and interdisciplinarity, 256, 265; and legal realism, 262, 267; publications of, 264–65; and Critical Legal Studies, 282
Abele v. Markle (1971), 197
Academic lawyers: and liberalism, 12; professionalization of, 18; and social sciences, 18–19, 23, 245; and law practice, 20; and publication, 23, 235; and legal realism, 23–24; and law review membership, 26; and students' aspirations, 26–27; and judicial review, 41–46; Jewish academic lawyers, 49; salaries of, 50, 305, 312–13; and idealistic students, 63; and minorities, 101; and affirmative action, 118; positions for, 306; and interdisciplinarity, 306, 310, 311, 312, 362; and diversity, 328–31; former radicals as, 332, 439 (n. 35); Yale graduates as, 355, 357, 363–64, 446 (n. 97); and case and Socratic methods, 363; and legal scholarship, 365; and student demonstrators, 411 (n. 57). *See also* Harvard law faculty; Yale law faculty
Acheson, Dean, 16
Ackerman, Bruce: and Abraham Goldstein, 241, 269, 305; and Bickel, 294, 295, 296; and Calabresi, 294, 324; and liberalism, 294–95, 305; and Warren Court, 295, 303; and judicial review, 295–96; Kronman compared to, 297; and interdisciplinarity,

306; and Law and Economics, 307, 308; departure for Columbia, 314
ACLU, 223
Affirmative action: and Bickel, 101, 102, 113, 277, 425 (n. 9); and Yale law faculty, 101–2, 113, 116, 122, 138, 189, 202–3; and Pollak, 102, 116, 313–14; and meritocracy, 102, 202, 330; and informal preference for alumni children, 103; and Cochran, 115–16; and Yale Law School, 118, 119, 313–14; and Griffiths, 246; and neoconservatives, 277–78; and Rostow, 278, 425 (n. 11); and revival of student activism, 328–29; and Harvard law faculty, 332
African American law students: and Columbia Law School, 29, 111; and University of Wisconsin, 30–31; and Yale law faculty-student relationship, 98, 104, 105–9, 111–19, 121, 122–24, 138, 139, 140, 149, 172, 175–76, 200, 201, 202; and admission requirements, 100–101, 102; and Yale Law School's enrollment, 104, 230, 315; and police harassment, 111, 169–70, 189; and Yale Law Student Association, 161; and campus police, 169, 170; demonstration of, 170, 178, 191; and Clay, 180, 191; enrollment concerns, 200–201, 230, 424 (n. 118); and academic success, 202–3; and racism, 340–41; and clerkships, 346. *See also* Black Law Students Union
African American students, 103–5, 138, 169, 170–71, 175
Agnew, Spiro, 207, 208, 220
Ahern, James, 168
Albert, Lee, 234, 239, 255–57, 258, 266, 267, 421 (n. 70)

449